Perspectives in
MEDICAL
SOCIOLOGY

Third Edition

Perspectives in
MEDICAL
SOCIOLOGY

Third Edition

Phil Brown
Brown University

WAVELAND

PRESS, INC.

Prospect Heights, Illinois

For information about this book, write or call:
Waveland Press, Inc.
P.O. Box 400
Prospect Heights, Illinois 60070
(847) 634-0081
www.waveland.com

Printed in the United States of America

7 6 5 4 3 2

Contents

Preface to the Third Edition

This new edition contains 25 selections from the last edition, along with 12 new ones. The topics are pretty much the same as in the second edition, though some parts and sections have been reorganized. The overall framework, as presented in the Introduction to the book, is still the same.

Perspectives in Medical Sociology is centered around the theme that health and illness cannot be understood simply by looking at biological phenomena and medical knowledge. Rather, it is necessary to situate health and illness in the framework of larger political, economic, and cultural forces. This approach to medical sociology is a modern and critical one, which offers a more structural perspective than do traditional analyses of health and illness. This new viewpoint arises from the dramatic intellectual growth and expanded breadth of medical sociology in recent years, and from the need to situate the American health care system's deepening problems in a fresh perspective.

Perspectives in Medical Sociology contains much recent scholarship, a good deal of it written in the last few years. Yet it also includes a sufficient number of "classic" works. Further, the book encompasses all the areas of medical sociology that an instructor expects to find in order to introduce students to the field.

This collection employs a macro-level approach that views medical sociology as influenced by political economy, institutional structures, and professionalism. The book also presents a micro-level approach that focuses on interaction between patients and providers. In addition, I place much emphasis on integrating the macro- and micro-levels. There is one other theme—the role of social movements in health care—a development that is increasingly visible and important. This theme is not only presented in an entire section of the book, it is also developed throughout the introductions and selections in other parts. The effects of race, class, and gender on health and illness play a major role in this collection. This volume also presents the student with articles that utilize a broad range of research methods, and the introductory material points these out.

Part 1, "The Social Context of Health and Illness," contains sections on Social Inequality, Health, and Illness; Theories and Perspectives on Health and Illness; and Environmental and Occupational Health. Part 2, "Being Ill and Getting Care," contains sections on Experiencing Illness and Seeking Care; Interaction and Negotiation Between Patients and Providers; Alternatives to Formal Medicine; and Technology, Experimentation, and Social Control. Part 3, "The Health Care System," contains sections on The Health Care Industry; Institutional Settings; Health Care Providers; and Social Movements, Social Change, and Health.

Perspectives in Medical Sociology offers a compilation of articles which is as inclusive as possible, enabling the instructor to use this collection as a basic text for medical sociology courses. Although the book is intended to be used in the order in which it is presented, it can be used selectively or in another sequence. This book is intended for both undergraduate and graduate students. Students are guided through the material by a comprehensive General Introduction, by introductory essays for each of the three parts, and by introductions to the sections within each part. Graduate students and advanced undergraduates are aided by research aids in two appendices: "Sources of Data" points the student to locations of basic data on health and illness; and an "Annotated Bibliography of Journals in Medical Sociology and Related Fields" directs students to sources for material for research papers, class presentations, and general interest.

Most selections in this volume are written by sociologists, but a number are the product of other fields, such as public health, medicine, epidemiology, psychology, political science, and history. This reflects the diversity of material employed by medical sociologists, and it also makes the book accessible for courses in other health-related disciplines. Some selections are complete articles or book chapters, while others are edited; edited selections contain no ellipses, in order to prevent the reader from getting distracted. Introductory material does not contain references; this serves to entice students into reading the introductions, and in many cases these references would simply be repeating references made in the selections.

Medical sociology is a tremendously exciting field. My intent throughout is to make it interesting, accessible, and challenging to the student, as well as to the instructor who teaches the material. I will be pleased to hear instructors' and students' comments on their use of the book.

Acknowledgments

Susan Bell, Chloe Bird, Ann Dill, and Donald Light spent time in helping me think about the selections. Their input has been a great support in shaping this third edition. Students in my courses in medical sociology have given much useful feedback to the topics and selections in the book. I offer my appreciation to the authors of the selections, particularly those with whom I had contact in the process of revising and editing articles. Neil Rowe and Gayle Zawilla at Waveland Press have been a pleasure to work with. Berit Kosterlitz and Geoff Surrette were very helpful in handling reprint permissions. Kenya Lucas helped out as a research assistant. The Department of Sociology at Brown University facilitated my work with a grant, and I offer my sincere appreciation.

Introduction to the Book

A new killer epidemic—AIDS—strikes the world and alters patterns of disease and death, affects sexual practices, threatens legal rights, and overwhelms health care institutions. Toxic wastes create illness, death, and fear in workplace and community. Tens of millions of Americans find themselves without medical insurance in a society where medical care is a valuable but sometimes scarce commodity. Public hospitals close their doors, while private profit-making ones expand without apparent limits. Medical technology offers unheard-of hope in the form of organ transplants and surgery, yet proliferates in a context of unclear expectations about ethical issues and the allocation of resources. Traditional patterns of doctors' status and practices are altered by government regulation, insurance companies, managed care, and public challenges. Health policy and universal health insurance become central points of political debate, and health issues take on the character of social movements.

These and many other health issues affect each of us every day of our lives. Many less dramatic features of health and illness also play a role in our daily existence: our complaints about illness, our interactions with doctors, how illness affects our work.

Why study medical sociology? In a way, it's all quite simple: we are conceived, we are born, we live in sickness and in health, and we die. These are fundamental elements of human existence, and we seek to understand them better and, increasingly, to better control them. Typically, we grasp only some of the issues involved in health and illness and are unable to understand the whole picture. Thus we need a perspective that can link together many components: biomedical data, professional practice, institutional structures, economics and financing, demographics of disease and death, and the individual experience of health, illness, and medical care. Medical sociology offers a way to make the linkages, to compose and focus the whole picture, to make social sense of the varied manifestations of health and illness.

In earlier periods, religious leaders might have been consulted on matters of health and illness. In modern societies, doctors are the more likely source. Increasingly, other authorities have entered the contest for expert knowledge on health affairs: philosophers, economists, bioethicists, psychologists, political scientists. But in neither traditional nor modern civilizations do any of these sources typically provide a strong link between health and illness on the one hand, and social structure on the other. Social structure includes a society's forms of political organization, economic structure; hierarchies of status, power, and wealth; family and kinship networks, value systems, forms of social interaction, and formal and informal institutions of education, health, welfare, and punishment.

Indeed, those who often speak with the authority of their society on medical matters are those with some sort of self-interest that makes it hard for them to go beyond their particular view of the world. That is where sociology—and more specifically, where medical sociology—steps in. As a discipline, sociology seeks to provide an understanding of social structures, ranging from the smallest interactions (such as interpersonal communication) to national-level issues (such as income inequality and social policy) to the largest world-size affairs (such as international relations and war). Further, sociology attempts to provide theoretical linkages between levels of social structure, so that individual entities are not studied in isolation from their surroundings. For example, the particular set of attitudes to health held by members of a racial or ethnic group are related to the ways that members seek medical care and interact with providers. At the same time, the racial or ethnic group as a whole must be seen in light of its history, public and professional attitudes toward the group, and the group's standing in the hierarchies of status, power, and wealth.

As a specialty area of sociology, medical sociology seeks to make connections and linkages as mentioned above, with particular attention to the domains of health and illness. Medical sociology is concerned with the distribution of disease and how that differs on the basis of class, race, sex, ethnicity, education, and other social factors. It is concerned with the different ways that people conceptualize disease and illness, with reference to the above categories. Medical sociology is also interested in conceptual differences based on conflicts between lay and professional beliefs. Medical sociology looks at the sources of morbidity (disease) and mortality (death) as stemming from political, economic, cultural, and professional forces, as well as from biomedical factors. Medical sociology is also interested in how people experience illness and how they make their way to various providers and institutions to seek care. It is likewise interested in the interaction between help seekers and help providers. As a further interest, medical sociology examines the backgrounds, structures, and functions of health care providers and institutions. From this, it is a logical next step to examine issues of health policy, and to investigate how basic social structures relate to illness, treatment, and health policy. Since the societal determinants of health and illness are paramount, medical sociology increasingly emphasizes the interactions between health and social change.

The health of the people might be a result of their wealth, or so we might think. Since the United States is such a wealthy and powerful nation, we might expect its citizens to have a health status consistent with that position. When we hear of a heroic new surgical or drug treatment with astounding results, we might be tempted to say, "Yes, our health system is the finest." But in much of the routine day-to-day life of most Americans, health status and access to health care are not so perfect. A country's wealth *should* relate to the public's health, but the United States falls behind many industrialized nations that spend less money on health care. Key measures of a nation's health, such as life expectancy, infant mortality, and maternal mortality, show the United States to rank fairly low among major industrialized countries. A major task of medical sociology is to examine how such an expensive and seemingly advanced health care system can be at variance with the overall health of the population.

This nutshell view of the scope of medical sociology sets the stage for what we study in this subdiscipline. Medical sociology is a vital and growing field—in fact, it is the second largest section (around 1,000 members) in the American Sociological Association—which is undergoing many significant debates, alterations, and reformulations of its scope, theory, methods, and audience. It is useful for the reader to know that these changes are occurring, and that this book represents the broader and more modern perspective emerging in the field of medical sociology.

Central Themes

Perhaps the most overarching theme of *Perspectives in Medical Sociology* is that health and illness cannot be understood with reference to biological phenomena and medical knowledge alone. Rather, it is necessary to bring to bear a variety of political, economic, and cultural forces. This focus on large-scale social structural factors is often termed a *macro-level approach*. We can consider medical sociology to be influenced by three major categories of social structure. First, political economy deals with the class, race, and sex differentials so central to the social order. Political economy also includes the overall economic order and political system. Second, professionalism concerns the development of the medical profession, its present value systems and practices, and the conflicts between lay and professional perspectives. Third, institutional structures includes health institutions, health regulatory bodies, and related institutions and agencies. Some social structural factors—such as class, sex, and race—play major roles in health status, in how people and caregivers view health, how and when they seek help for illness, and how they interact with health institutions and providers. Help seeking and interaction, in turn, are affected by the structure of the health care system and its major professional grouping, doctors.

The exploration of *lay illness experience and the interaction between people and their health providers*, or a *micro-level approach*, is the second theme. A belief in the social nature of health and illness does not imply a monolithic view of the health care system. For example, despite what an emphasis on professionalism tells us about the extraordinary social power of physicians, patients' expectations of physicians' behavior are a complementary part of medical interaction. Individuals bring to medical encounters their own backgrounds and agendas, and these are involved in an interplay with professional and institutional frames. Even if one party (the doctor) is dominant, the impact of the weaker party (the patient) is nevertheless significant. As with other parts of society, *social interaction* in medical settings is a fundamental part of the social fabric that is necessary for understanding health and illness.

A third theme, which ties together the first two, is that medical sociology should *link both micro- and macro-levels of analysis*. Some scholars focus on only one level and lose much understanding. For example, if we want to understand what goes on in the interaction between client and health provider, we cannot simply analyze the language, information exchange, and power relationships in that encounter. After all, the encounter is influenced by the larger context—including issues of professional, institutional, sociocultural, political, and economic factors. Likewise, suppose we want to examine the effects of managed care by health maintenance organizations (HMOs) and other insurers, resulting in discharging women one day after childbirth. We cannot only look at aggregate data on hospital length of stay. We must also explore the policy's impacts on particular interchanges between providers and consumers, such as doctor-patient discourse concerning potentially premature hospital discharge. As well, we look at how citizens organized politically to get many state governments to outlaw such early discharge.

The *role of social movements* in health care is a fourth central theme of this book. Social movements include formal and informal organizations, as well as more general social trends, which seek to change some element of the social structure. While the focus on social movements is clearly indicated by the material in the final section, "Social Movements, Social Change, and Health," the theme crops up throughout the book. Nearly all changes in the social structure result from social movements that are characterized by varying degrees of cohesiveness and formal organization. The democratic freedoms we may take for granted today, for example, are all products of social movements. Products of such struggles include the abolition of slavery and the outlawing of segregation, women's suffrage and equal rights for women, Social Security, the right to organize labor unions, and workers' compensation. Of course, not all of these rights are firm and complete, and this fact engenders continuing social movement efforts.

Since health and illness are pivotal elements of society, it is not surprising that social movements play major roles in the health care system. Witness, for example, the history of efforts at food and drug regulation, occupational safety and health organizing, environment activism, the women's health movement, the enactment of Medicare and Medicaid, consumer efforts to eradicate disease, self-help movements, endeavors to expand access to care, struggles to keep public hospitals open, campaigns to expand informed consent, drives to correct substandard conditions in mental hospitals and other institutions, and efforts to curtail unlimited expansion of profit-making hospital chains. These social movements have not only aimed to achieve specific goals, but in the process they have often altered our perspectives on the very definitions of health and illness, and the proper ways to create and sustain a healthy society.

The four themes mentioned above recur throughout the book, not only in sections that are specifically dedicated to them. Keeping these themes in mind will allow you to make better use of the book's selections. More importantly, focusing on these themes will give you a better sense of what the field of medical sociology as a whole is all about.

Format and Special Features of the Book

My intent is to provide a selection of articles which is as inclusive as possible. This is important because I view this collection as a basic text for medical sociology courses. The material has been tested and refined in actual medical sociology courses, and it works well in the order in which it is presented, although it can be used in a different order.

Although the majority of the selections are by sociologists, you will find many articles by others in the fields of public health, medicine, epidemiology, political science, history, and anthropology. This is because medical sociology has been successful at integrating much material from those other disciplines. Students reading this book for courses in other fields (e.g., public health, health education, health and public policy) will find therefore that they are not totally surrounded by a discipline "different" from their own.

I also have worked to provide the reader with a sample of many different *methods of research* and *sources of data*. It is important to understand how researchers obtain their information and how they analyze it. Each section of the book will include varied data sources and methodologies, and introductory essays will note this. Even if this is the student's only medical sociology course, such knowledge will be useful in observing how scholars locate and use data and in seeing the bases upon which conclusions and inferences are drawn. For the student who will go on to further study, and for the graduate student, this may be even more significant, for the information can be applied to the student's own research in the field.

I have provided further *research aids* in two appendices. First, "Sources of Data" by Steven Jonas is a valuable compilation of information on where to get basic data on health and illness. Even if students do not consult these sources, they may find it quite informative to read over the appendix just to get a sense of where researchers obtain data. Second, I have constructed an "Annotated Bibliography of Journals in Medical Sociology and Related Fields" that offers assistance in figuring out where to look for material for research papers, class presentations, and general interest. Students may find it very informative to spend some time in the library simply leafing through the last year or two of various journals, in order to see what topics and areas have sparked recent scholarly interest.

With these preliminary remarks in place, let's move on to explore the exciting field of medical sociology.

PART I

The Social Context of Health and Illness

A core conception of this book is that *health and illness must be understood in a social context*. In the creation of disease and death, biomedical factors are often eclipsed by social factors. For instance, modern sanitation and improved living conditions are widely acknowledged to have been more important than medical advances in the modern decrease in the death rate. Even when we look at the effects of biomedical causes, social factors—such as race, class, and access to care—often result in differential rates of disease and death. Nor does medical knowledge alone provide sufficient understanding of the underlying causes of morbidity (disease) and mortality (death). For example, medical practitioners and researchers often fail to take into account environmental variables such as workplace and community toxic wastes. Nor do practitioners and researchers tend, for example, to focus on such phenomena as the correlation between mortality and a society's overall social inequities. Even social concepts which have arisen in part from within medicine—e.g., the role of stress in illness—are generally underutilized by medical professionals in explaining health status.

Part 1 includes three sections. In "Social Inequality, Health, and Illness," we examine health and social inequality: how the distribution of disease and death varies by race, class, and gender. The section on "Theories and Perspectives in Health and Illness" includes a range of modern viewpoints that are widely used to understand health and illness. In the next section, "Environmental and Occupational Health," we take a look at how community and workplace hazards play major roles in health. These areas have long been overlooked but are increasingly coming under closer scrutiny.

1

Section 1

Social Inequality, Health, and Illness

We start with *social inequality* because it is useful to understand the key social variables that affect health status. The readings in this first section familiarize us with both overall statistics and with a framework for situating them in a social context. It is not enough to know that rates of disease and death are different; sociologists want to know why they are different and what this means for health care and for other social institutions.

As a field, epidemiology has not always been as politically conscious as medical sociology. As we will see later in the topic on environmental and occupational issues, epidemiology often falls short because its demand for statistically significant levels of proof are different from those needed for social policy applications, and because it does not generally conceive of health and illness with reference to political, economic, and institutional structures. Thus medical sociologists have applied their insights to epidemiological questions, not in the interests of furthering epidemiology per se, but as a means of improving sociological analysis.

A social epidemiological background allows us to examine some central forces in health and illness. I generally see class, race, and gender as the key social variables in any sociological area. Social class (people's position in the hierarchy of economic wealth and political power) is fundamentally related to basic political and economic structures of the society, especially in terms of the unequal distribution of wealth and power. Likewise, race is tied up with unequal relations and a brutal history of slavery and segregation. In addition, race plays a major role in the relations between the developed and underdeveloped countries. Gender involves a core disparity in social power between two halves of the human species. The readings in this first section aim to introduce you to the key social factors, and you will continue to encounter these social factors throughout the rest of the readings.

Michael McCally and his colleagues, in "Poverty and Ill Health:

Physicians Can, and Should, Make a Difference," show us that large-scale societal factors are the major determinants of health. All over the world, at many different times, there has been a strong relationship between class and health, with poorer people faring worse on nearly all outcomes. The wider the disparity in socioeconomic status (SES), the wider the range of health disparity; hence, increasing class stratification in the United States since the 1970s has led to an increase in health status differentials. McCally et al. go further than just analysis; they urge their medical colleagues to reduce the social causes of sickness through economic social interventions, reduction of environmental toxics exposures, expansion of health service access, and teaching physicians to be aware of socioeconomic issues affecting their patients.

David R. Williams' contribution, "Race, Socioeconomic Status, and Health: Patterns and Explanation," provides us with a summary of essential information on the health ramifications of race. While much of the race differences are attributable to class differences—far more blacks than whites are poor—we still find race differences within any given SES level. Williams notes that different conceptualizations of race lead to different data on race differences in health. We need to be attuned to how these, or any other, definitions shape what we take to be actual facts.

In "Women Get Sicker, But Men Die Quicker: Gender and Health," Judith Lorber shows how gender affects health status, attitudes toward illness, and use of health services. Women generally have more acute illness and more of many types of chronic illness than men, though they have lower mortality rates. They make greater use of health services yet also do more self-care, are more likely to be hospitalized, and tend to have a regular source of care. Lorber adds an interesting component, through examining gender differences at different stages of the life course. Lorber points to the methodological problems of separating out social causes, which often combine as multiple factors to affect health. In addition, she shows how gender interacts with race and class, making it difficult to always know what is the specific contribution of gender.

1
Poverty and Ill Health: Physicians Can, and Should, Make a Difference

Michael McCally, Andrew Haines, Oliver Fein, Whitney Addington, Robert S. Lawrence, and Christine K. Cassel

A growing body of research confirms the existence of a powerful connection between socioeconomic status and health. This research has implications for both clinical practice and public policy and deserves to be more widely understood by physicians. Absolute poverty, which implies a lack of resources deemed necessary for survival, is self-evidently associated with poor health, particularly in less developed countries. Over the past two decades, economic decline or stagnation has reduced the incomes of 1.6 billion people. Strong evidence now indicates that relative poverty, which is defined in relation to the average resources available in a society, is also a major determinant of health in industrialized countries. For example, persons in U.S. states with income distributions that are more equitable have longer life expectancies than persons in less egalitarian states.

There are numerous possible approaches to improving the health of poor populations. The most essential task is to ensure the satisfaction of basic human needs: shelter, clean air, safe drinking water, and adequate nutrition. Other approaches include reducing barriers to the adoption of healthier modes of living and improving access to appropriate and effective health and social services. Physicians as clinicians, educators, research scientists, and advocates for policy change can contribute to all of these approaches. Physicians and other health professionals should understand poverty and its effects on health and should endeavor to influence policymakers nationally and internationally to reduce the burden of ill health that is a consequence of poverty.

Poverty and social inequalities may be the most important determinants of poor health worldwide. Socioeconomic differences in health status exist even in industrialized countries where access to modern health care is widespread.[1] In this chapter, we make a formal argument for physician concern and action about poverty based on the fol-

Reprinted with permission from *Annals of Internal Medicine*, Vol. 129 (91), November 1998, pp. 726–733.

lowing assertions. Physicians have a professional and a moral responsibility to care for the sick and to prevent suffering. Poverty is a significant threat to the health of both individual persons and populations; thus, physicians have a social responsibility to take action against poverty and its consequences for health. Physicians can help improve population health by addressing poverty in their roles as clinicians, educators, research scientists, and participants in policymaking.

Concepts of Poverty and Health

Poverty is a multidimensional phenomenon that can be defined in both economic and social terms. An economic measure of poverty identifies an income sufficient to provide a minimum level of consumption of goods and services. A sociologic measure of poverty is concerned not with consumption but with social participation.[2] Poverty leads to a person's exclusion from the mainstream way of life and activities in a society.[3] There is a difference between absolute poverty, which implies a lack of resources deemed necessary for survival in a given society, and relative poverty, which is defined in relation to the average resources available in a society. Economic measures are easy to obtain, but social measures may provide a better understanding of the causes and consequences of poverty. Steps have been taken toward the development of indices of deprivation, which have promising uses in health services and public health research.[4]

In 1978, the World Health Organization (WHO), in the Alma-Ata Declaration, spelled out the dependence of human health (defined broadly) on social and economic development and noted that adequate living conditions are necessary for health.[5] Despite their knowledge of this, governments and major development organizations have largely continued to view health narrowly as a responsibility of the medical sector, outside the scope of economic development efforts. Consequently, governments have encouraged many large-scale but narrowly focused economic development efforts, ignoring the connection between poverty and health.[6] In developed countries, governments promote various practices, such as heavy pesticide applications, that are designed to increase economic development and competitiveness but that are environmentally unsound and personally unhealthy.

Poverty Causes Death and Illness on a Massive Scale

During the second half of the 1980s, the number of persons in the world who were living in extreme poverty increased. Currently, extreme poverty afflicts more than 20% of the world's population. A recent report from WHO points out that up to 43% of children in the developing world—230 million children—have low height for their age and that about 50 million children have low weight for their height.[7] Micronutrient malnutrition (deficiencies of vitamin A, iodine, and iron) affects about 2 billion persons worldwide.

It has been estimated that if developing countries enjoyed the same health and social conditions as the most developed nations, the current annual toll of more than 12 million deaths in children younger than 5 years of age could be reduced to less than 400,000. An average person in one of the least developed countries has a life expectancy of 43 years; the life expectancy of an average person in one of the most developed countries is 78 years.[7] This is not to deny that real gains in health have occurred in recent decades. For example, since 1950, life expectancy at birth in several developing countries has increased from 40 to more than 60 years. Similarly, worldwide, mortality rates for children younger than 5 years of age decreased from 280 to 106 per 1000, on average. Some countries show much sharper declines,[7] but indices of health in these countries still fall far short of those in wealthier nations.

Poverty and Sustainable Development

The relation between poverty and health is complex, and we believe that it is best understood in the framework of a new notion of "ecosystem health," which places poverty and health in the nexus of environment, development, and population growth.[8] Ecosystems provide the fundamental underpinning for public health in both developed and less developed countries, not only through food production, for example, but also through their roles in economic development. For instance, they supply forest resources and biomass fuels and serve as habitats for the vectors of disease.[9] Sustainability is produced by using resources in ways that meet the needs of current populations without compromising the ability of future generations to meet their own needs[10] and is predicated on the need to ensure a more equitable sharing of today's resources. Meeting the needs of the world's poor implies limitation of the current use of resources by industrialized nations.

Barriers to the benefits of development include rapid population growth, environmental degradation, and the unequal distribution of resources. At one extreme, traditional, preindustrial societies are characterized by relatively high birth rates coupled with high death rates attributable to acute infectious diseases and the hazards of childbearing; this leads to slow population growth. At the other extreme, in the most developed countries, population stability has occurred. In the intermediate situation, in less developed countries, population stability has not been reached, and the global population thus continues to increase. In some less developed countries, a "demographic trap" exists in which the development of resources cannot keep pace with the requirements of the growing population and poverty is worsened.[11] The most developed countries escape the trap by buying additional essential resources in the global marketplace to make up the difference.

Environmental degradation exaggerates the imbalance between population and resources, increases the costs of development, and increases the extent and severity of poverty. For example, the need for fuel wood, timber for export, and farmland results in deforestation, which increases soil erosion, flooding, and mud slides and reduces agricultural productivity. As a result, biological diversity is lost, production becomes increasingly reliant on pesticides and fertilizers, and use of expensive fossil fuels increases. Water is a critical resource. In Punjab, the breadbasket of India, the major aquifer is decreasing at a rate of 20 cm per year, threatening health by reducing agricultural productivity and the supply of clean water.[12] Economic development without regard to long-term environmental and social consequences also threatens sustainability by damaging the systems that sustain healthy communities.

Inequalities in Health Are Socially Determined

The strong and pervasive relation between an individual person's place in the structure of a society and his or her health status has been clearly shown in research conducted over the past 30 years.[13–16] In 1973, Kitagawa and Hauser[17] published convincing evidence of an increase in the differential mortality rates according to socioeconomic level in the United States between 1930 and 1960. They found that rates of death from most major causes was higher for persons in lower social classes. In Britain, research into health inequalities was summarized in 1980 in The Black Report,[18] which was updated in 1992[19] and is currently under review by an official working group. The report was prepared by a labor government-appointed research working group chaired by Sir Douglas Black, formerly Chief Scientist at the Department of Health and, at the time, President of the Royal College of Physicians. The Black Report concluded that "there are

marked inequalities in health between the social classes in Britain"
(Figure 1). Marmot and colleagues, in the well-known Whitehall studies of British civil servants begun in 1967, showed that mortality rates
are three times greater for the lowest employment grades (porters)
than for the highest grades (administrators) and that no improvement
occurred between 1968 and 1988.[20-22]

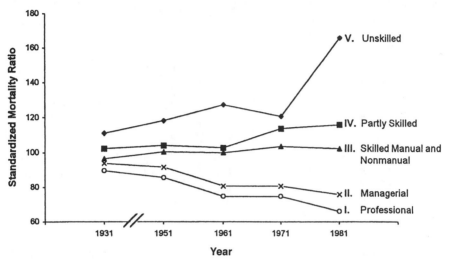

**Figure 1. Comparison of standardized mortality ratios for men 15 to 64 years of age by
social class over five decades in England and Wales.** Figures have been adjusted to the
classification of occupations used in 1951. Information on men 20 to 64 years of age in
Great Britain was obtained from Black and colleagues (18).

Such findings could, in theory, be due to differences in age, smoking, nutrition, types of employment, accident rates, or living conditions, but the Whitehall study participants were from a relatively
homogeneous population of office-based civil servants in London.
They had largely stable, sedentary jobs and access to comprehensive
health care. A second observation of the Whitehall investigations,
confirmed by the Multiple Risk Factor Intervention Trial (MRFIT)
studies in the United States, is that conventional risk factors (smoking, obesity, low levels of physical activity, high blood pressure, and
high plasma cholesterol levels) explain only about 25% to 35% of the
differences in mortality rates among persons of different incomes
(Figure 2).[23, 24]

An equally striking finding is Wilkinson's observations of the relation between income distribution and mortality.[25, 26] Wilkinson
assembled two sets of observations. First, he found no clear relation

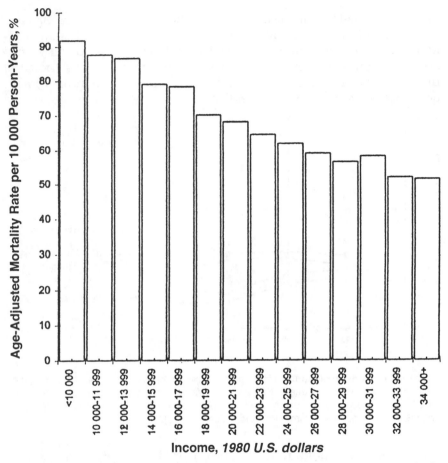

Figure 2. Income and age-adjusted mortality rate among 300,000 white men in the United States. Data obtained from Smith and colleagues (23).

between income or wealth and health when comparisons were drawn between countries (for example, there is no relation between per capita gross domestic product and life expectancy at birth in comparisons between developed countries at similar levels of industrialization). But Wilkinson also showed a strong relation between income inequality and mortality within countries, a relation that has been confirmed more recently.[27, 28] The countries with the longest life expectancy are not necessarily the wealthiest but rather are those with the smallest spread of incomes and the smallest proportion of the population living in relative poverty. These countries (such as Sweden) generally have a longer life expectancy at a given level of economic development than less equitable nations (such as the United States).

Recent analysis of U.S. data supports earlier observations that the distribution of wealth within societies is associated with all-cause mortality and suggests that the relative socioeconomic position of the individual in U.S. society may be associated with health. Populations in U.S. states with income distributions that are more equitable have longer life expectancies than do those in less egalitarian states, even when average per capita income is taken into account.[27, 28] Authors of the studies that revealed these findings recently introduced the notion of "social capital," which is defined as civic engagement and levels of mutual trust among community members, as an important variable intervening between income inequality and health status.[29] Evans and associates[15] suggest that one's control of the work environment is an important connection between social and occupational class and mortality.

The Robin Hood index, also known as the Pietra ratio, is used to estimate the percentage of total income that would have to be transferred from groups above the mean to groups below the mean to equalize income distribution. A higher Robin Hood index value represents greater disparity in incomes. The strong correlation between income distribution and mortality rates shows that income disparity, in addition to absolute income level, is a powerful indicator of overall mortality (Figure 3).[27]

Inequalities in Income and Health Are Worsening

Many of the improvements in life expectancy and infant mortality rates that have occurred around the world are overshadowed by the countervailing influence of increasing disparities between rich and poor. Since 1980, economic decline or stagnation has affected 100 countries, reducing the incomes of 1.6 billion persons.[19] Between 1990 and 1993, the average income decreased by 20% or more in 21 countries, particularly countries in eastern Europe and the countries of the former Soviet Union.[30] The net worth of the world's 358 richest persons is equal to the combined income of the poorest 45% of the world's population: 2.3 billion persons. Between 1960 and 1991, the ratio of the global income of the richest 20% of the world's population relative to the poorest 20% increased from 30:1 to 61:1.[30, 31]

Many recent improvements in population health have been threatened and, in some cases, reversed at the same time that income differentials have widened. For example, the proportion of underweight

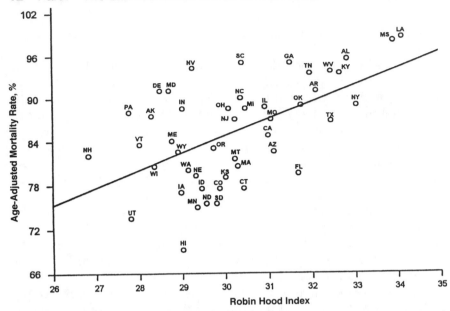

Figure 3. Age-adjusted mortality in the United States in 1990 and the Robin Hood index of income inequality. Circles represent the states of the Unitee States. Data were not available for New Mexico, Rhode Island, and Virginia. Adapted from Kennedy and colleagues [27] with permission.

children in Africa may decrease from 26% in 1990 to 25% in 2005, but the total number of underweight children is projected to increase from 31.6 million to 39.2 million because of population growth.

In the United States and the United Kingdom, income distribution has become more unequal. According to the United Nations Development Programme, income distributions within each of these countries are now among the most unequal distributions in the world's industrialized countries.[31, 32] For example, in the United Kingdom, the proportion of persons with an income less than half of the national average increased from less than 10% in 1982 to more than 20% in 1993, and unskilled men in Scotland now have a mortality rate three times that of professional men.[33] This represents a widening from a twofold differential in the early 1970s. In the United Kingdom, the difference in mortality rates between rich and poor has increased because mortality rates have decreased faster among the rich than among the poor,[34] and the proportion of children below the official poverty line has tripled in the past 10 years.[35, 36] In the United States, inequality in income increased in all states except Alaska between 1980 and 1990.[37]

Effective Interventions Reduce III Health Due to Poverty

Some evidence suggests that improving the income of the poorest persons improves health in both developed and less developed countries. International data have been used to show that the doubling of per capita income (adjusted for purchasing power parity) from $1000, using 1990 figures, corresponds to an increase of 11 years in life expectancy. The relation flattens off above an average per capita income of approximately $5000 (Figure 4).[30] The distribution of income within households also influences health. It has been suggested, for example, that it takes 10 times more spending to achieve a given improvement in child nutrition in Guatemala when income is earned by the father than when it is earned by the mother because the mother is more likely to spend the money on essentials for the family.[30]

An important, possibly unique, randomized trial in Gary, Indiana, suggests that increasing the income of poor expectant mothers receiving welfare increased the birthweight of their babies.[38] Education, particularly for mothers, has dramatically affected health. In Peru, for instance, the children of mothers with 7 or more years of education have a reduction in child mortality of nearly 75% compared with the children of mothers with no schooling. Studies in several countries have shown that mothers who have completed secondary or higher education are much more likely to treat childhood diarrhea appropriately with oral rehydration therapy. Families are also likely to be smaller when women are more educated.[30]

A recent systematic review of the effectiveness of health service interventions, predominantly in industrialized countries, to reduce poverty-related inequalities in health suggests several characteristics of interventions that may be successful, although they do not directly affect income.[39] These include programs that target high-risk groups; outreach programs that include home visits; and programs that overcome barriers to the use of services by providing transportation or convenient access and by using prompts and reminders. Large-scale multidisciplinary interventions involving a range of agencies and programs may be cost-effective. The Special Supplemental Food Program for Women, Infants and Children (WIC) was initiated in 1972 in the United States and provides healthy food, education about nutrition, and health services to low-income women and their children. Data analysis suggests substantial reductions in the number of babies with low and very low birth weights as a result.[40] The project paid for itself through equivalent savings in medical care. Project Head Start provides preschool children and their families with edu-

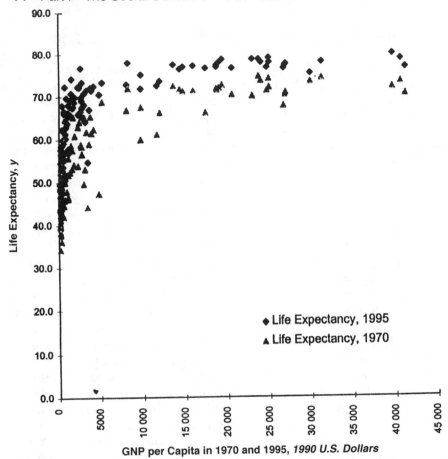

Figure 4. Life expectancy at birth and gross national product (*GNP*) in 1970 and 1995 in rich and poor countries in 1990 U.S. dollars. Triangles represent life expectancy in 1970; diamonds represent life expectancy in 1995. Data obtained from World Development Indicators, World Bank, 1995.

cation, health care, and social services. Short- and long-term benefits have been shown in health, developmental, and social outcomes.[41]

Economic analysis confirms that primary care interventions, including measures designed to reduce childhood malnutrition, improve immunization against childhood diseases, provide chemotherapy against tuberculosis, provide condoms and education to combat the spread of HIV, and reduce smoking (including consumer taxes on tobacco) are cost-effective.[42]

Physicians Have Special Responsibilities

It is widely accepted that physicians have a special and central professional responsibility to treat disease and reduce mortality rates, a responsibility that arises from their knowledge of medicine and medical practice.[43] The physician-patient relationship is a fiduciary one, based on the inherent responsibility of physicians to deserve the trust of patients. Professionalism also extends this relationship to society, which confers on the profession respect and certain kinds of autonomy and authority. In the context of the physician-society relationship, the physician's fiduciary responsibility takes the form of concern for the public health. Most major traditions of medical ethics suggest that physicians have a special responsibility for the care of poor persons, defined as those who cannot afford to pay for treatment.[44]

In addition, physician responsibilities in patient care extend to the social context of health and disease. Physicians regularly attempt to influence both patients' lifestyles and their environments to help prevent illness. They do so because illness is often precipitated by behavioral and social factors. Physicians in practice have an obligation to act on behalf of the general public welfare (for example, by reporting infectious diseases to the proper authorities). Recently, it has become widely accepted that physicians should work to promote smoking cessation, encourage use of seatbelts, and prevent firearm injury. Health hazards should not be ruled out as medical concerns because their remedy requires social or political action. Although the proper form and extent of political involvement for physicians may at times be controversial, concern for the health of the public has been an important responsibility of the medical profession at least since the Industrial Revolution.[45]

It may be argued that although physicians have a responsibility to care for persons who are ill even though they are poor and cannot pay, medicine has no particular responsibility with respect to the general condition of poverty. Physicians' efforts to mitigate poverty may be seen as going beyond the bounds of the patient-physician relationship. However, efforts against poverty may have parallels in widely accepted attempts by physicians to prevent child abuse or health hazards in the workplace. Although patients may not ask to be protected from toxins or abuse, physicians have agreed that they have a responsibility to assist patients who may be in danger and, when possible, to prevent harm. If poverty is connected to ill health in a direct and powerful way, it can be argued that physicians have some degree of responsibility for addressing poverty itself to the best of their ability.

Physicians Can Help Mitigate the Health Inequalities Caused by Poverty

A panel convened by the King's Fund of London recently proposed four types of interventions to correct health inequalities related to poverty: addressing social and economic factors; reducing barriers to the adoption of healthier ways of living; improving the physical environment; and improving access to appropriate, effective health and social services.[46] Physicians have clear roles to play in each of these efforts.

Physicians can address social and economic factors both on the level of the individual patient and on the level of the community. By being aware of socioeconomic factors, such as insurance status, educational background, occupational history, housing conditions, and social isolation, physicians can make more comprehensive diagnoses and tailor therapies to patients' needs. Unfortunately, in residency training, the social history (if it is taken at all) is often labeled "noncontributory." Raik and colleagues[47] examined the content of resident case presentations on inpatient rounds and found remarkably low rates of mention of socioeconomic factors. Physicians as teachers can address these factors on rounds and in describing their own patients to trainees and colleagues.

On the community level, physicians can advocate for public policies to improve the health of the disadvantaged. Jarman[48] showed that physicians know that it is more complicated and takes more time to care for poor patients than for patients who are not poor. With this evidence, he was able to persuade the National Health Service in the United Kingdom to take patient economic status into account in rewarding general practitioners who work in deprived areas. Given the growth of managed care in the United States, physicians should be at the forefront of those calling for poverty-based risk adjustments to capitated payments.

As research scientists, physicians can advance the understanding of the mechanisms by which deprivation leads to ill health and the development of more effective interventions to reduce inequality in health.[49] Similarly, physicians who are aware of the adverse effects of international debt on health can urge debt relief for the poorest countries.[50]

Physicians may also be able to assist in removing barriers to healthy lifestyles—for example, campaigning against the promotion of tobacco, which is increasingly being targeted to adolescents in less developed countries and in minority communities in the United States.[51]

Physicians can affect environmental factors associated with poverty by advocating for legislation to maintain and improve the quality of air, drinking water, and food. Physician-led public health efforts in the United States have been instrumental in reducing the incidence of lead poisoning, which is strongly associated with poverty. Internationally, physicians are participating in local initiatives surrounding Agenda 21, developed at the 1992 Earth Summit in Rio de Janeiro, Brazil. More than 1300 local communities in 31 countries have developed their own action plans, many of which feature health issues. Through the WHO Healthy Cities Project, cities have addressed such issues as smoking, sanitation, air pollution, and socioeconomic differences in health.[52]

Approaches to improving access to effective health and social services in the United States and elsewhere have been extensively reviewed.[39, 53] However, more than 800 million persons lack access to health services worldwide, and the increasing imposition of user fees (copayments and deductibles) in many countries has exacerbated inequities in care.[54] Physicians and their associations should lead the movement for universal access to health care.[55]

An international meeting on health and poverty hosted by WHO and Action in International Medicine (which has approximately 100 affiliated organizations in more than 30 countries) urged associations of health professionals to engage in activities to reduce health inequalities due to poverty.[56] Dr. Gro Harlem Brundtland, the newly appointed Director General of WHO, has indicated that she intends to make the reduction of ill health due to poverty a priority for her term of office.[57] The United Nations Declaration of Human Rights includes access to the basic necessities of life, such as food and water, as well as health care. However, 50 years after the Declaration was written, we are still far from providing this access to everyone. Physicians have an important role to play in helping to transform the rhetoric of the Declaration into reality.

References

[1] Graubard S. R., ed. Health and wealth. Daedalus. 1994;123:1–216.
[2] Rainwater L. What Money Buys: Inequality and the Social Meaning of Income. New York: Basic Books; 1974.
[3] Ringen S. The Possibility of Politics: A Study in the Political Economy of the Welfare State. New York: Oxford Univ Pr; 1987.

[4] Townsend P. The International Analysis of Poverty, London: Harvester-Wheatsheaf; 1993.

[5] Primary Health Care: Report of the International Conference on Primary Health Care, Alma-Ata, USSR, 6–12 September 1978. Geneva: World Health Organization; 1978.

[6] Cooper Weil D. E., Alicbusan A. P., Wilson J. F., Reich M. R., Bradley D. J. The Impact of Development Policies on Health: A Review of the Literature, Geneva: World Health Organization; 1990.

[7] The World Health Report 1995: Bridging the Gaps. Report of the Director-General. Geneva: World Health Organization; 1995.

[8] Shahi G. S., Levy B. S., Louis G. E., Binger A., Kjellstrom T., Lawrence R. S. The environment-development-health interface. In: Shahi G. S., Levy B. S., Binger A., Kellstrom T., Lawrence I. R. S., eds. International Perspectives on Environment, Development, and Health: Toward a Sustainable World. A Collaborative Initiative of the World Health Organization, the United Nations Development Programme, and the Rockefeller Foundation. New York: Springer; 1997.

[9] Ewert A. W., Kessler W. B. Human health and natural ecosystems: impacts and linkages. Ecosystem Health. 1996;2:271–8.

[10] Brundtland G. H. Our Common Future: The World Commission on Environment and Development. New York: Oxford Univ Pr; 1987.

[11] McCally M. Human health and population growth. In: Chivian E., McCally M., Haines A., Hu H., eds. Critical Condition: Human Health and the Environment. Cambridge, MA: MIT Pr; 1995.

[12] Brown L. R. Dividing the Waters. State of the World 1996. New York: WW Norton; 1996.

[13] Frank J. W., Mustard J. F. The determinants of health from a historical perspective. Daedalus. 1994;123:1–19.

[14] Feinstein J. S. The relationship between socioeconomic status and health: a review of the literature. Milbank Q. 1993;71:279–322.

[15] Evans R. G., Barer M. L., Marmor T. R. Why Are Some People Healthy and Others Not? The Determinants of Health of Populations. New York: Aldine de Gruyter; 1994.

[16] Fein O. The influence of social class on health status: American and British research on health inequalities. J Gen Intern Med. 1995;10:577–86.

[17] Kitagawa E. M., Hauser P. M. Differential Mortality in the United States: A Study in Socioeconomic Epidemiology. Cambridge, MA: Harvard Univ Pr; 1973.

[18] Black D., Morris J. N., Smith C., Townsend P. Inequalities in Health Care: The Black Report. New York: Penguin; 1982.

[19] Townsend P., Davidson N., Whitehead M. Inequalities in Health. London: Penguin; 1992.

[20] Marmot M. G. Social differentials in health within and between populations. Daedalus 1994;123:197–216.

[21] Marmot M. G., Shipley M. J., Rose G., Inequalities in death-specific explanations of a general pattern? Lancet, 1984;1:1003–6.

[22] Marmot M. G., Smith G. D., Stansfeld S., Patel C., North F., Head J., et al. Health inequalities among British civil servants: the Whitehall II study. Lancet. 1991;337:1387–93.

[23] Smith G. D., Wentworth D., Neaton J. D., Starriler R., Stamler J. Socioeconomic differentials in mortality risk among men screened for the Multiple Risk Factor Intervention Trial: I: White men. Am J Public Health. 1996;86:486–96.

[24] Smith G. D., Wentworth D., Neaton J. D., Stamler R., Stamler J. Socioeconomic differentials in mortality risk among men screened for the Multiple Risk Factor Intervention Trial: II: Black men. Am J Public Health. 1996;86:497–504.

[25] Wilkinson R. G. National mortality rates: the impact of inequality? Am J Public Health. 1992;82:1082–8.

[26] Wilkinson R. G. Divided we fall [Editorial]. BMJ. 1994;308:1113–4.

[27] Kennedy B. P., Kawachi I., Prothrow-Stith D. Income distribution and mortality: cross sectional ecological study of the Robin Hood index in the United States. BMJ. 1996;312:1004–7.

[28] Kaplan G. A., Pamuk E. R., Lynch J. W., Cohen R. D., Balfour J. L. inequality in income and mortality in the United States: analysis of mortality and potential pathways. BMJ. 1996;312:999–1003.

[29] Kawachi I., Kennedy B. P., Lochner K., Prothrow-Stith D. Social capital, income inequality, and mortality. Am J Public Health. 1997;87:1491–8.

[30] World Bank. World Development Report 1993: Investing in Health. New York: Oxford Univ Pr; 1993.

[31] United Nations Development Programme. Human Development Report 1996. New York: Oxford Univ Pr; 1996.

[32] United Nations Development Programme. Human Development Report 1994. New York: Oxford Univ Pr; 1994.

[33] Smith T. The changing pattern of mortality in young adults aged 15 to 34 in Scotland between 1972 and 1992. Scott Med J. 1994;39:144–5.

[34] Watt G. C. All together now: why social deprivation matters to everyone. BMJ. 1996;312:1026–9.

[35] McKee M. Poor children in rich countries [Editorial]. BMJ. 1993;307:1575–6.

[36] Judge K, Benzeval M. Health inequalities: new concerns about the children of single mothers. BMJ. 1993;306:677–80.

[37] Income and Poverty. Washington, DC: US Bureau of the Census; 1993.

[38] Kehrer B. H., Wolin C. M. Impact of income maintenance on low birth weight: evidence from the Gary Experiment. J Hum Resour. 1979;14:434–62.

[39] Arblaster L., Lambert M., Entwistle V., Forster M., Fullerton D., Sheldon T., et al. A systematic review of the effectiveness of health service interventions aimed at reducing inequalities in health. J Health Serv Res Policy. 1996;193–103.

[40] Rush D., Horvitz D. G., Seaver W. B., Alvir J. M., Garbowski G. C., Leighton J., et al. The National WIC Evaluation: evaluation of the Special Supplemental Food Program for Women, Infants, and Children. I. Background and introduction. Am J Clin Nutr. 1988;48:389–93.

[41] Schorr E. B., Schorr D. Within Our Reach: Breaking the Cycle of Disadvantage. New York: Anchor Books; 1988.

[42] Jamison D. T., Mosely W. N., Meashom A. R., Bobadilla J., eds. Disease Control Priorities in Developing Countries: A Summary. Washington, DC: World Bank; 1993.

[43] Jonsen A. R., Jameton A. J. Social and political responsibilities of physicians. J Med Philos. 1977;2:376–400.

[44] Amundsen D. W. History of medical ethics. In: Encyclopedia of Bioethics. New York: MacMillan; 1995;1522–36.

[45] Rosen G. From Medical Police to Social Medicine: Essays on the History of Health Care. New York: Science History Publications; 1974.

[46] Benzeval M., Judge K., Whitehead M., eds. Tackling Inequalities in Health: An Agenda for Action. London: King's Fund; 1995.

[47] Raik B., Fein O., Wachspress S. Measuring the use of population perspective on internal medicine attending rounds. Acad Med. 1995;70:1047–9.

[48] Jarman B. Identification of underprivileged areas. Br Med J (Clin Res Ed). 1983;286:1705–9.

[49] Townsend P., Phillimore P., Seattle A. Health and Deprivation: Inequality and the North. London: Croom Helm; 1988.

[50] Logie D. E., Benatar S. R. Africa in the 21st century: can despair be turned to hope? BMJ. 1997;315:1444–6.

[51] Aguirre-Molina M., Gorman D. M. Community-based approaches for the prevention of alcohol, tobacco, and other drug use. Annu Rev Public Health. 1996;17:337–58.

[52] von Schirnding Y. Intersectoral Action for Health: Addressing Health and Environmental Concerns in Sustainable Development. Geneva: World Health Organization; 1997.

[53] Gepkens A., Gunning-Schlepers U. Interventions to reduce socioeconomic health differences: a review of the international literature. European Journal of Public Health. 1996;6:218–26.

[54] Creese A. User fees [Editorial]. BMJ. 1997;315:202–3.

[55] American College of Physicians. Universal Coverage: Renewing the Call to Action. Philadelphia: American Coll Physicians; 1996.

[56] Haines A., Smith R. Working together to reduce poverty's damage [Editorial]. BMJ. 1997;314:529–30.

[57] Brundtland G. H. Interview. BMJ. 1998;316:13.

2
Race, SES, and Health: The Added Effects of Racism and Discrimination

David R. Williams

This chapter provides an overview of the ways in which race and socioeconomic status (SES) combine to affect health status. It first considers patterns of racial differences in health and the role that SES plays in accounting for these disparities. It then describes the nature of racism the ways in which policies linked to the historic legacy and the persistence of racism have created adverse living conditions that are pathogenic for minority populations. Residential segregation has restricted African Americans' access to desirable educational and employment opportunities. In combination with other racist mechanisms it has created the concentrated disadvantage characteristic of many minority communities. The stability of these societal processes has led to remarkable stability in racial economic inequality and in the nonequivalence of SES indicators across race. Finally, the paper considers the ways in which economic discrimination, discrimination in medicine, perceptions of racial bias and the stigma of inferiority can have pathogenic consequences.

Race, SES and Health

In the United States, race and ethnicity predict variations in health. Table 1 illustrates these associations by comparing the mortality rates for all of the major racial/ethnic minority groups to those of the white population.[1] National mortality data reveal that the overall death rate for American Indians is similar to that of whites. However, compared to whites, American Indians have lower death rates for cardiovascular disease and cancer but higher rates of death from injuries, the flu and pneumonia, diabetes, suicide, and cirrhosis of the liver. It should be noted that mortality rates for American Indians who live on or near reservations are higher than the national rates for their group.[2] The overall mortality rates for the Hispanic population is lower than that of the white population but Hispanics have

From the *Annals of the New York Academy of Science* (1999) 896, pp. 173–188. Reprinted with permission of the New York Academy of Science.

higher death rates for diabetes, cirrhosis of the liver, and HIV/AIDS than whites. For all of the leading causes of death in the United States, the Asian Pacific Islander population has mortality rates that are considerably lower than those of whites.

Table 1 Age Adjusted Death Rates (per 100,000 Population) for Whites and Minority/White Ratios for the 10 Leading Causes of Death United States, 1996[a]

Causes	White (W) (Rate)	Black/W Ratio	AmI[b]/W Ratio	API[b]/W Ratio	Hispanic/W Ratio
All causes	466.8	1.58	0.98	0.59	0.78
1. Heart disease	129.8	1.47	0.78	0.55	0.68
2. Cancer	125.2	1.34	0.68	0.61	0.62
3. Stroke	24.5	1.80	0.86	0.98	0.80
4. Pulmonary disease	21.5	0.83	0.59	0.40	0.41
5. Unintentional injuries	29.9	1.23	1.93	0.54	0.97
6. Flu and pneumonia	12.2	1.45	1.15	0.81	0.80
7. Diabetes	12.0	2.40	2.32	0.73	1.57
8. HIV/AIDS	7.2	5.75	0.58	0.31	2.26
9. Suicide	11.6	0.57	1.12	0.52	0.58
10. Liver cirrhosis	7.3	1.27	2.84	0.36	1.73

[a]Taken from the National Center for Health Statistics.[1]
[b]AmI, American Indian; API, Asian-Pacific Islander.

Several factors must be considered to put these data into perspective. First, a nontrivial proportion of non-black minorities are misclassified as white on the death certificate. This numerator problem leads to an underestimate of the death rates for American Indians, Asian and Pacific Islanders and Hispanics.[3–4] Second, there is considerable heterogeneity within each of the major racial/ethnic populations that importantly predicts variation in health status within each group. Third, a relatively high proportion of the Hispanic, and especially the Asian American population, is foreign-born and their health profile reflects in part, the impact of immigration. Immigrants tend to enjoy better health status than the native born population, even when those immigrants are lower in SES.[5–6] However, with increasing length of stay in the U.S. and adaptation to mainstream behavior, the health status of immigrants deteriorates.

African Americans (or blacks) have an overall death rate that is 1.6 times higher than that of the white population. Elevated mortality rates for the black compared to the white population exists for eight of the ten leading causes of death. These racial disparities have been documented for a long time and have been widening in recent years for multiple indicators of health status. Table 2 presents the mortality rates for blacks and the black/white mortality ratios for 1950 and 1995.[1] Although the overall mortality rate for African Americans has declined over time, for several causes of death (cancer, diabetes, suicide, cirrhosis of the liver, and homicide) the mortality rate is higher in 1995 than in 1950. Moreover, the black/white ratio for all-cause mortality in 1995 is virtually identical to that of 1950. Black/white mortality ratios over this 45-year period are virtually unchanged for some causes of death, such as stroke and unintentional injury, and smaller for two causes of death (the flu and pneumonia and homicide). However, the black/white mortality ratios in 1995 are larger than those in 1950 for heart disease, cancer, diabetes, and cirrhosis of the liver.

Table 2 Mortality Rates for Blacks and Black/White Ratios (Age-Adjusted Death Rates per 100,000 for the Leading Causes of Death in 1995)[a]

Causes of Death	1950		1995	
	Black Rate	B/W Ratio	Black Rate	B/W Ratio
All causes	1236.7	1.55	765.7	1.58
1. Heart disease	379.6	1.26	198.8	1.49
2. Cancer	129.1	1.04	171.6	1.35
3. Cerebrovascular disease	150.9	1.81	45.0	1.82
4. Pulmonary disease	—	—	17.6	0.83
5. Unintentional injury	70.9	1.27	37.4	1.25
6. Flu and pneumonia	57.0	2.49	17.8	1.44
7. Diabetes	17.2	1.24	28.5	2.44
8. HIV/AIDS	—	—	51.8	4.67
9. Suicide	4.2	0.36	6.9	0.58
10. Cirrhosis	7.2	0.84	9.9	1.34
11. Homicide	30.5	11.73	33.4	6.07

[a]Taken from the National Center for Health Statistics.[1]

Socioeconomic status (SES) predicts variation in health within minority and white populations and accounts for much of the racial differences in health. Table 3 illustrates these data for life expectancy. At age 45, white males have a life expectancy that is almost five years more than their black counterparts.[7] Similarly, white females have a life expectancy at age 45 that is 3.7 years longer than that of have a life expectancy at age 45 that is 3.7 years longer than that of their black peers. However, there is considerable variation in life expectancy within both racial groups.[1] Black men in the highest income group live 7.4 years longer than those in the lowest income group. The comparable numbers for whites was 6.6 years. Thus, the SES difference within each racial group is larger than the racial difference across groups. A similar pattern is evident for women, although the SES differences are smaller. At age 45, black women in the highest income group have a life expectancy that is 3.8 years longer than those in the lowest income group. Among whites, the SES difference is 2.7 years. Also evident in the life expectancy data is an independent effect of race even when SES is controlled. At every level of income, for both men and women, African Americans have lower levels of life expectancy than their similarly situated white counterparts. This pattern has been observed across multiple health outcomes and for some indicators of health status, such as infant mortality, the racial gap becomes larger as SES increases.[1]

Table 3 United States Life Expectancy, at Age 45, by Family Income (1980 Dollars)[a]

Family Income	Females			Males		
	White	Black	Difference	White	Black	Difference
All[b]	36.3	32.6	3.7	31.1	26.2	4.9
1. Less than $10,000	35.8	32.7	3.1	27.3	25.2	2.1
2. $10,000–$14,999	37.4	33.5	3.9	30.3	28.1	2.2
3. $15,000–$24,999	37.8	36.3	1.5	32.4	31.3	1.1
4. $25,000 or more	38.5	36.5	2.0	33.9	–32.6	1.3

[a]1979–1989; Taken from the National Center for Health Statistics.[1]
[b]1989–1991; Taken from the National Center for Health Statistics.[7]

Race and Racism in the U.S.

How do we understand these differences? What is race, and what contribution does racism make to these persisting patterns of racial differences in health? Our current racial categories were created prior to the development of valid scientific theories of genetics and do not capture biological distinctiveness.[8–10] The American Association of Physical Anthropology[11] recently stated that "Pure races in the sense of genetically homogenous populations do not exist in the human species today, nor is there any evidence that they have ever existed in the past." There is considerable biological variation in human populations but our racial categories fail to capture it. There is more genetic variation within our existing racial groups than between them. Moreover, genetics is not static but changes over time as human populations interact with their natural and social environment. In the United States, our racial groups importantly capture differences in power, status and resources. Three of the five official racial/ethnic categories were used in the inaugural census in 1790 and these groups were not regarded as equal. In compliance with the First Article of the United States Constitution, that census enumerated whites, blacks as three-fifths of a person, and civilized Indians (that is, Indians who paid taxes). The Thirteenth Amendment abandoned the three-fifths rule and over time new racial categories were developed to keep track of new immigrants.[12]

Historically, racial categorization has been rooted in racism and racial classification schemes have had an implicit or explicit relative ranking of various racial groups. Within the U.S. context, whites have always been at the top, blacks at the bottom, and other groups in-between. The construct of racism can enhance our understanding of racial inequalities in health. By racism, I mean an ideology of inferiority that is used to justify unequal treatment (discrimination), of members of groups defined as inferior, by both individuals and societal institutions. This ideology of inferiority may lead to the development of negative attitudes and beliefs towards racial outgroups (prejudice), but racism primarily lies within organized institutional structures and not in individual attitudes or behaviors.[13]

First, is the endorsement of an ideology of inferiority a relic of a bygone era? On the one hand, there have been dramatic improvements in the racial climate in the United States in the last 50 years.[14] For example, national data reveal that in 1942 only 32% of whites with school age children believed that white and black children should go to the same schools. Ninety-six percent of white parents supported that view in 1995. Similarly, in 1958 only 37% of whites stated that they would vote for a qualified black man for President of the United States. In 1997, 95% of whites indicated that they would vote for a black person for president. At the same time, other data indicate that racial attitudes are complex. Overwhelming support for the principle of equality coexists with a reluctance to support policies that would reduce racial inequalities.[14] Moreover, data on stereotypes reveal the persistence of negative images of minority racial/ethnic populations in the United States. National data reveal that most blacks are prone to violence, 29% that most blacks are unintelligent, and 56% that most blacks prefer to live off welfare.[15] These data also reveal a reluctance to endorse positive stereotypes of African Americans. Only 17% of whites indicated that most blacks are hard-working, 15% that most blacks are not prone to violence, 21% that most blacks are intelligent, and 12% that most blacks prefer to be self-supporting. These data are even more striking when compared with whites' perceptions of themselves and other groups. In general, whites view all minority racial groups more negatively than themselves, with blacks being viewed more negatively than any other group. Hispanics tend to be viewed twice as negatively as Asians. Jews tend to be viewed more positively, and southern whites more negatively, than whites in general.

Racism and SES

How does racism affect health? First, and most importantly, racism has restricted socioeconomic attainment for members of minority groups. By determining access to educational and employment opportunities segregation has been a key mechanism by which racial inequality has been created and reinforced.[16] It is generally recognized that there are large racial differences in SES, and health researchers routinely adjust for SES when examining the race-health association. However, SES is not just a confounder of racial differences in health but part of the causal pathway by which race affects health. Race is an antecedent and determinant of SES, and racial differences in SES reflect, in part, the successful implementation of discriminatory policies premised on the inferiority of certain racial groups.

Arguably, the single most important policy of this type that continues to have pervasive adverse effects on the socioeconomic circumstances and the health of African Americans is residential segregation. Beliefs about black inferiority and an explicit desire to avoid social contact with this out-group led to the development of policies in the early twentieth century that aimed at ensuring the physical separation of blacks from whites in residential areas.[17] This physical separation was possible through cooperative efforts of major societal institutions.[18] Between 1900 and the 1940s, federal housing policies, the lending practices of banks, restrictive covenants, and discrimination by the real estate industry, individuals and vigilant neighborhood organizations ensured that housing options for blacks were restricted to the least desirable residential areas. Audit studies reveal that explicit discrimination in housing per-

Audit studies reveal that explicit discrimination in housing persists,[19] but most of the institutional discrimination that created segregation is now illegal. However, the structure of segregation and its consequences have remained relatively intact over time.

Table 4 shows the average levels of segregation in the thirty metropolitan areas with the largest black populations between 1970 and 1990.[20] Data are provided for two of the most commonly used measures of segregation. The index of dissimilarity, a measure of unevenness, captures the percent of blacks who would have to change neighborhood residence to achieve complete integration. The isolation index indicates the percent of blacks in the census tract where the average black person resides. Segregation is slightly higher in the North than in the South but in both regions the levels of segregation are very high. In 1990, for example, 78% of blacks in northern metropolitan areas would have to move in order to achieve a random distribution of blacks and whites. In the South, 67% of blacks would have to move. Similarly, in 1990 the average African American living in the North resided in a census tract that was 69% black. In the South, the average black lived in a neighborhood that was 65% black. There has been little change in these levels of segregation in the last 20 years. While other groups have experienced residential segregation in the United States, no immigrant population has ever lived under the high levels of segregation that currently characterize the living circumstances of African Americans.[16] Moreover, the high level of segregation of the black population is not self-imposed because blacks reflect the highest support for residence in integrated neighborhoods.[21]

Table 4 Average Segregation in 30 Metropolitan Areas with Largest Black Populations[a]

Area[b]	1970	1980	1990
Non-South			
1. Unevenness	84.5	80.1	77.8
2. Isolation	68.7	66.1	68.9
South			
1. Unevenness	75.3	68.3	66.5
2. Isolation	69.3	63.5	64.9

[a]Taken from Massey.[20]
[b]Unevenness, percent of blacks who would have to change residence to achieve even spatial distribution; isolation, percent of blacks in the census tract where the average black person resides.

Residential segregation has led to racial differences in the quality of elementary and high school education. Because the funding of education is at the local level, community resources importantly determine the quality of the neighborhood school. Residential segregation had led to the concentration of poverty in residential areas and thus the concentration of poverty in the classroom. Notwithstanding a unanimous Supreme Court ruling in *Board vs. Board of Education*, elementary and high school public education in the United States today is still highly segregated and decidedly unequal.[22] Moreover, even in integrated schools, black students are disproportionately allocated or tracked into low ability and non-college preparatory classes that are characterized by a less demanding curriculum and lower teacher expectations.[18]

Two-thirds of African American students and three-fourths of Hispanic students attend schools where more than half the students are black or Latino.[23] The proportion of black and especially Hispanic students in predominantly minority schools has been increasing in recent years. There is nothing inherently negative with having most of one's fellow classmates being members of minority groups. The problem is the very strong relationship between racial composition of schools and concentrated poverty. In the United States a student in an intensely segregated African American and/or Latino school is 14 times more likely to be in a high-poverty school than a student in a school where less than 10% of the students are black and Latino.[22] Nationally, the correlation between minority percentage and poverty is .66.[23] In metropolitan Chicago this percentage is .90 for elementary schools.[22] There are millions of poor whites in the United States, but most poor white families do not live in areas of concentrated poverty and thus have access to better options in terms of educational opportunities. In 96% of predominantly white schools in the United States the majority of the students come from middle-class backgrounds.

Residential segregation also adversely affects SES by having a profound negative impact on employment. Several mechanisms appear to be at work. William Julius Wilson[24–25] has documented that the selective out-migration of whites and some middle class blacks from the core areas of cities (where most blacks reside) to the suburbs over the last several decades has been accompanied by the movement of high-pay, low-skill jobs to the suburbs. This movement of jobs is related to larger processes of urbanization and industrialization, but some evidence suggests that considerations of race have explicitly played a role. African Americans have had significantly higher rates of industrial job losses than whites in recent decades, and research reveals that both U.S.-based and foreign companies explicitly use the racial composition of areas in their decision-making process regarding where to locate new plants.[26] This is true both for the placement of new plants and for the relocation of other plants to more rural and suburban areas. Consistent with this evidence, a *Wall Street Journal* analysis of over 35,000 U.S. companies that report to the Equal Employment Opportunity Commission found that blacks were the only racial group that experienced a net job loss during the 1990–1991 economic downturn.[27] African Americans had a net job loss of 59,000 jobs, compared with net gains of 71,100 for whites, 55,100 for Asians, and 60,000 for Latinos. These job losses did not reflect individual discrimination but rather were the result of restructuring, relocation, and downsizing. In many cases, they reflected the movement of employment facilities to suburban, rural, and southern areas where the proportion of blacks in the labor force was low.

Discrimination at the individual level also plays a role in reducing employment opportunities for minority group members. Studies of white employers reveal that they consciously and deliberately use negative racial stereotypes to deny employment opportunities to black applicants.[28–29] Some of the best evidence of the persistence of discrimination in employment comes from audit studies conducted by the Urban Institute. In these studies, white applicants were favored over black applicants with identical qualifications 20% of the time.[19] Thus, negative racial stereotypes of African Americans appear to play a role both when individual employers evaluate potential applicants, as well as when corporate decision makers deliberate about the location of employment facilities.

Impoverished segregated areas have multiple adversities that may combine in additive and interactive ways to adversely affect SES. Lack of access to jobs produces high rates of male unemployment. There is a strong relationship, for both blacks and whites, between rates of marriage and rates of male unemployment and average male earnings. Thus, the concentration of economic disadvantage in impoverished segregated areas is a major force underlying high rates of out of wedlock births and female-headed households and the consequent feminization of poverty that occurs in many urban areas.[30–31] The resulting concentration of poverty isolates youth in segregated communities from both role models of stable employment and social networks that can provide linkages to employment opportunities.[24] Long-term exposure to these conditions can undermine a strong work ethic and devalue academic success.

Racism can also affect SES attainment through the impact of negative racial stereotypes on educational outcomes. Steele[32] has reviewed the evidence which suggests that the negative cultural images of blacks may adversely affect academic performance. He indicates that there is little racial difference between blacks and whites on standardized tests in the first grade. However, a racial gap widens with each year in school and is two full grade levels by the sixth grade. This pattern is not explained by either SES or group differences in skills. Moreover, achievement gaps between blacks as well as non-Asian minorities are evident at all levels of SES and sometimes widen with increasing SES. Further, at every skill level, non-Asian minorities receive lower grades than whites. A similar pattern exists for women relative to men, but only in those areas of academic performance where women are stereotypically viewed as deficient (such as in the physical sciences and in advanced math courses). Research from the U.K., Israel, Japan, India and other countries reveals that groups viewed as lower in social status consistently have lower academic achievement.[33] Steele[32] suggests that among lower-SES blacks the internalization of negative societal stereotypes may become a self-fulfilling prophecy leading to low performance. In contrast, among high-SES, self-confident blacks, the threat of poor performance in a stereotype-relevant domain may lead to anxieties that adversely affect academic performance.

Stability of Racial Inequality

Institutional policies have played a major role in creating large racial differences in SES. Because of the persistence of the institutional mechanisms underlying racial inequality there has been remarkable stability in the racial gap in SES over time. The President's Council of Economic Advisors recent review of trends in racial economic inequalities documented that the expansion of the black middle class, and the convergence toward equality between blacks and whites, was greatest in the 1960s.[34] In spite of current efforts to dismantle affirmative action policies, the data clearly show that the economic progress of blacks relative to whites stalled in the mid-1970s and there have been 20 years of stagnation since then. Moreover, income inequality has increased since 1970 overall and within both racial groups.

Table 5 shows that in 1978, the median family income of blacks ($25,288) was 59 cents for every dollar earned by whites in median family income ($42,695). In 1996, the black/white ratio of median family income was identical to that of 1978, and there had been little change during the intervening 23 years. Similarly, the poverty levels for both blacks and whites have been relatively stable over time.[34] The poverty rate of blacks (30.6%) was 3.5 times higher than that of whites (8.7%) in 1978. The black poverty rate declined to 28.4 in

Table 5 Median Income and Poverty Rates for Whites and Blacks, United States 1978–1996[a]

Year	Median Income			Poverty Rate		
	Whites	Blacks	B/W Ratio	Whites	Blacks	B/W Ratio
1978	42,695	25,288	0.59	8.7	30.6	3.52
1980	41,759	24,162	0.58	10.2	32.5	3.19
1982	40,379	22,317	0.55	12.0	35.6	2.97
1984	41,809	23,302	0.56	11.5	33.8	2.94
1986	44,105	25,201	0.57	11.0	31.1	2.83
1988	44,981	25,636	0.57	10.1	31.3	3.10
1990	44,315	25,717	0.58	10.7	31.9	2.98
1992	43,245	23,600	0.55	11.9	33,4	2.81
1994	43,284	26,148	0.60	11.7	30.6	2.62
1996	44,756	26,522	0.59	11.2	28.4	2.54

[a]Taken from the Economic Report of the President[34]

1996 and the poverty rate of whites increased somewhat to 11.2 in 1996. Thus, the black/white ratio fell slightly, with blacks being 2.5 times more likely to live in poverty in 1996, compared to whites. Longer trend data tell the same story. Table 6 presents the unemployment rates for blacks and whites from 1950 to 1995.[34] Since 1950, African Americans have had unemployment rates that have been about twice as high as that of whites. Over time, the unemployment of both blacks and whites has moved up and down with the business cycle, but the changes for African Americans have been at about twice the rate for whites. There have been modest gains in unemployment in the last few years but in 1995, blacks still had an unemployment rate that was twice that of whites. These data provide striking evidence of persistent racial inequality in the United States.

Table 6 Unemployment Rates for Blacks and Whites, 1950–1995[a]

Year	Black	White	B/W Ratio
1950	9.0	4.9	1.84
1955	8.7	3.9	2.23
1960	10.2	5.0	2.04
1965	8.1	4.1	1.98
1970	8.2	4.5	1.82
1975	14.8	7.8	1.90
1980	14.3	6.3	2.27
1985	13.7	6.2	2.21
1990	11.4	4.8	2.38
1995	9.6	4.9	1.96

[a]Taken from the Economic Report of the President[34]

Because of the operation of these large-scale societal processes, indicators of SES are not equivalent across racial groups. That is true at the level of the community, the household, and the individual. Because of residential segregation, black and white neighborhoods differ dramatically in the availability of jobs, family structure, opportunities for marriage, educational quality, and exposure to conventional role models. They also differ in the quality of life and access to resources and amenities that sustain health. For example, Sampson and Wilson[35] found that in the 171 largest cities in the United States, there is not even one city where whites live in ecological equality to blacks in terms of poverty rates and rates of single parent households. In fact, Sampson and Wilson concluded that, "The worst urban context in which whites reside is considerably better than the average context of black communities." [35]

Table 7 presents racial differences in the income return from education for blacks, whites and Hispanics in 1996.[36] These national data reveal that at every level of education blacks and Hispanics have lower levels of income than whites. Although part of this difference may be due to differences in educational performance and quality, some evidence suggests that other factors are at work. For example, a recent study documented that even after taking racial differences in test scores into account, young black males earned 7.5% less than their white counterparts.[37] Other data reveal that blacks have higher costs for goods and services than whites due to higher prices on average for a broad range of services such as housing, food, and insurance in the central city areas where blacks live than in suburban areas where most whites reside.[38]

Moreover, racial differences in income understate the true magnitude of the racial differences in economic resources. National data reveal that at every level of income there are large racial differences

Table 7 Median Income by Educational Attainment for Whites, Blacks, and Hispanics Aged 18 Years and Older, United States 1996[a]

Education Level	White	Black	Hispanic
Not a high school graduate	$9,762	$7,365	$9,486
High school graduate	$16,331	$13,294	$13,408
Some college or associate degree	$23,480	$20,249	$20,225
Bachelor's degree or more	$30,121	$26,160	$25,302
Professional degree	$56,436	$42,237	—

[a]Taken from the U.S. Bureau of the Census.[36]

in wealth. For example, white households have a median net worth that is 10 times that of African American households.[39] Whites in the lowest quintile of income have a median net worth of $10,257 compared to $1 for comparable blacks. Since much of the wealth of most American families exists in the form of home equity, a substantial part of this racial difference is linked to housing policies and institutional discrimination experienced in the past.[40] These racial differences in economic circumstances are consequential to the day-to-day struggle for survival for minority group members. In the early 1990s, the Census Bureau's Survey of Income and Program Participation collected data on the economic hardship experienced by American households. These data reveal that after adjustment for SES (income, education, transfer payments, home ownership, employment status, disability, and health insurance) and demographic factors (age, gender, marital status, the presence of children, and residential mobility), African Americans were more likely than whites to experience six of nine hardships examined: unable to meet essential expenses, unable to pay for rent or mortgage, unable to pay full utility bill, had utilities shut off, had telephone service shut off, and evicted from apartment or home.[41] There were no racial differences on lacking visits to a doctor and not having enough food. Blacks were less likely than whites to have no visit to a dentist.

Racism and Health: Direct Effects

A growing body of research also suggests that in addition to its effects on health indirectly through socioeconomic position, exposure to racism and discrimination can also more directly adversely affect health. First, residential segregation can create pathogenic housing and living conditions. Segregation is often a key determinant of quality of life in neighborhoods. Residents of highly segregated neighborhoods have less access to a broad range of services provided by municipal authorities.[42] Reductions in spending and the delivery of services leads to the neglect and deterioration of the physical environment in poor neighborhoods. The redlining by banks can result in the disproportionate representation of undesirable land uses, such as deserted factories, warehouses, and landfills in segregated areas. Persons who reside in segregated neighborhoods may also be disproportionately exposed to environmental toxins and poor quality housing. The largest black-white difference in mortality noted earlier was for homicide. Research reveals that the combination of concentrated poverty, male joblessness, and residential instability leads to high rates of single parent households and these factors together account for variation in the levels of violent crime.[35] Importantly, the association between these factors and violent crime for whites was virtually identical in magnitude with the association for African Americans.

Several studies have found a positive association between both adult and infant mortality and residence in segregated areas. One recent study has documented elevated mortality rates for both blacks and whites in cities high on two indices of segregation compared to cities with lower levels of segregation.[43] This pattern suggests that beyond some threshold of segregation, the adverse conditions linked to highly segregated cities may negatively affect the health of all persons who reside there.

Another mechanism by which discrimination can affect health status is through access to medical care. The stigma of racial inferiority appears to affect the way that minority group members are treated in the health care system. A large body of evidence indicates that even after adjustment for SES, health insurance, and clinical status whites are more likely than blacks to receive a broad range of specific medical procedures.[44] Especially striking is data from the Veterans Administration Hospital System[45] and from analyses of the receipt of diagnostic and treatment procedures among black and white inpatients covered by Medicare.[46] Among Medicare inpatients, blacks were less likely than whites to receive all of the 16 most common procedures. Further examination revealed that there were only four procedures that blacks were more likely to receive than whites. Blacks were more likely than whites to have the amputation of a lower limb, the removal of both testes, the removal of tissue related to decubitus ulcers and the implantation of shunts for renal dialysis.[47] These procedures all reflected delayed diagnosis or initial treatment, poor or infrequent medical care and the failure in the management of chronic disease.

A recent study by Hannan et al.[47] demonstrated that African Americans were less likely than whites to receive bypass surgery when rigorous criteria demonstrated that the procedure was appropriate, as well as when rigorous criteria indicated that it was necessary. Similarly, a study by Peterson et al.[48] documented that blacks were less likely than whites with comparable disease to receive bypass surgery even among those patients with the most severe disease and with the greatest predictive benefit of survival. Moreover, this study found that the five-year survival rate was significantly lower for blacks. Other recent research indicates that patient preferences and patient refusals play little role in racial differences in the receipt of medical procedures.[47] Taken together, these studies suggest that consciously or unconsciously, a nontrivial proportion of the health care workforce discriminates against African Americans.

Some research also suggests that the subjective experience of discrimination may be an important type of stress that can adversely affect health. A review of these studies reveals that exposure to stress in a laboratory setting can lead to cardiovascular and psychological reactivity among blacks, as well as for a broad range of other groups.[49] In addition, population-based epidemiologic studies also reveal that experiences of discrimination are adversely related to both physical and mental health. One recent study of a major metropolitan area characterized exposure to a broad range of unfair treatment experiences.[50] This study documented that compared to whites, African Americans experienced higher levels of both chronic and acute measures of discrimination and markedly higher levels of discrimination based on race or ethnicity. Importantly, analyses of these data documented that most of the racial difference in physical health was accounted for by SES. However, the consideration of experiences of discrimination made an incremental contribution in accounting for racial differences in self-reported measures of physical health. Studies of the health consequences of experiences of discrimination are still in their infancy and there is an urgent need for prospective studies that would identify the temporal ordering of the relationship between discrimination and health.

What does it mean for a child to grow up in a society where he or she is viewed as being inferior and where those messages are routinely communicated in multiple ways? A small body of research suggests that the prevalence of negative stereotypes and cultural images of stigmatized groups can adversely affect health status. Researchers have long identified that one response of minority populations would be to accept the dominant society's ideology of their inferiority as accurate. Several studies have operationalized the extent to which African Americans internalize or endorse these negative cultural images. These studies have found that internalized racism is positively related to psychological distress, depressive symptoms, substance use and chronic physical health problems.[51–53]

Conclusion

Striking racial differences in health and their persistence over time are not acts of God. Neither can they be understood as simply reflecting racial differences in individual behavior or biology. Instead, considerable evidence suggests that they reflect, in large part, the successful implementation of specific policies. Racism has been responsible for the development of an organized system of policies and practices designed to create racial inequality. Research is needed that would identify how large societal forces shape individual beliefs and behavior and combine with pre-existing resources and vulnerabilities to affect health status. Social factors ultimately affect health through specific physiological mechanisms and processes. The concept of allostatic load provides a useful framework for tracing the pathways from environmental exposure to adverse changes in health status via explicit physiological processes.[54] Racial differences in health importantly reflect the impact of the social environment and the cumulation of adversity across multiple domains. Efforts to improve the health of racial minority group members and reduce racial disparities in health may have to be equally comprehensive in the implementation of strategies that address the fundamental underlying causes of these disparities.

Acknowledgments

Preparation of this paper was supported by grant 1 RO1 MH59575 from NIMH and the John D. And Catherine T. MacArthur Foundation Research Network on Socioeconomic Status and Health. I wish to thank Scott Wyatt and Colwick Wilson for research assistance and Car Nosel for preparing the manuscript.

Notes

[1] National Center for Health Statistics. 1998. Health, United States, 1998 with Socioeconomic Status and Health Chartbook. USDHHS. Hyattsville, MD.

[2] Department of Health and Human Services-Indian Health Service. 1997. Regional Differences in Indian Health. DHHS. Rockville, MD.

[3] Sorlie, P. D., E. Rogot, and N. J. Johnson. 1992. Validity of demographic characteristics on the death certificate. *Epidemiology* 3:181–84.

[4] Hahn, J. A. 1992. The state of federal health statistics on racial and ethnic groups. *JAMA* 267:268–71.

[5] Singh, G. K., & S. M. Yu. 1996. Adverse pregnancy outcomes: Differences betwen U.S.- and foreign-born women in major U.S. racial and ethnic groups. *American J. of Public Health* 86:837–43.

[6] Hummer, R. A., R. G. Rogers, C. B. Nam, & F. B. LeClere. 1999. Race/ethnicity, nativity, and U.S. adult mortality. *Social Science Quarterly* 80:136–53.

[7] National Center for Health Statistics. 1997. U.S. Decennial Life Tables for 1989–91. *United States Life Tables* 1(1):12–29. Hyattsville, MD.

[8] Mongatu, A. 1964. *The Concept of Race*. Glencoe: New York Press.

[9] Gould, S. J. 1977. Why We Should Not Name Human Races: A Biological View. In *Ever Since Darwin*, S. J. Gould (Ed.), pp. 231–36. New York: W. W. Norton.

[10] Lewontin, R.C. 1972. The Apportionment of Human Diversity. In *Evolutionary Biology*, vol 6. T. Dobzhansky, M. K. Hecht, & W. C. Steere (Eds.), pp. 381–86. New York: Appleton-Century-Crofts.

[11] American Association of Physical Anthropology. 1996. AAPA statement on biological aspects of race. *American Journal of Physical Anthropology* 101:569–70.

[12] Anderson, M., & S. E. Feinberg. 1995. Black, white, and shades of gray (and brown and yellow). *Chance* 8:15–18.

[13] Bonilla-Silva, E. 1996. Rethinking racism: toward a structural interpretation. *American Sociological Review* 62:465–80.

[14] Schuman, H., C. Steeh, L. Bobo, & M. Krysan. 1997. *Racial Attitudes in America: Trends and Interpretations*, Rev. Ed. Cambridge, MA: Harvard University Press.

[15] Davis, J. A., & T. W. Smith. 1990. *General Social Surveys, 1972–1990*, NORC ed. Chicago: National Opinion Research Center

[16] Massey, D. S., & N. A. Denton. 1993. *American Apartheid: Segregation and the Making of the Underclass*. Cambridge, MA: Harvard University Press.

[17] Cell, J. 1982. *The Highest Stage of White Supremacy: The Origin of Segregation in South Africa and the American South*. New York: Cambridge University Press

[18] Jaynes, G. D., & R. M. Williams. 1987. *A Common Destiny: Blacks and American Society*. Washington, DC: National Academy Press.

[19] Fix, M., & R. J. Struyk. 1993. *Clear and Convincing Evidence: Measurement of Discrimination in America*. Washington, DC: Urban Institute Press.

[20] Massey, D. Residential Segregation and Neighborhood Conditions in U.S. Metropolitan Areas. In Neil Smelser, Wiliam Julius Wilson, and Faith Mitchell (Eds.), *America Becoming: Racial Trends and Their Consequences*. National Research Council.

[21] Bobo, L., & C. L. Zubrinsky. 1996. Attitudes on residential integration: Perceived status differences, mere in-group preference, or racial prejudice? *Social Forces* 74:883–909.

[22] Orfield, G., & S. E. Eaton. 1996. *Dismantling Desegregation: The Quiet Reversal of* Brown v. Board of Education. New York: The New Press.

[23] Orfield, Gary. 1993. The growth of segregation in American schools: Changing patterns of separation and poverty since 1968. A report of the Harvard Project on School Desegregation to the National School Boards Association.

[24] Wilson, W. J. 1987. *The Truly Disadvantaged*. Chicago: University of Chicago Press.

[25] Wilson, W. J. 1996. *When Work Disappears: The World of the New Urban Poor*. New York: Alfred A. Knopf.

[26] Cole, R. E., & D. R. Deskins, Jr. 1988. Racial factors in site location and employment patterns of Japanese auto firms in America. *California Management Review* 31:9–22.

[27] Sharpe, R. 1993. In latest recession, only blacks suffered net employment loss. *Wall Street Journal* LXXIV, no. 233.

[28] Kirschenman, J., & K. M. Neckerman. 1991. "We'd Love to Hire them, But . . .": The Meaning of Race for Employers. In *The Urban Underclass*, C. Jencks & P. E. Peterson (Eds.), pp. 203–32. Washington, DC: The Brookings Institution.

[29] Neckerman, K. M., & J. Kirschenman. 1991. Hiring strategies, racial bias, and inner-city workers. *Social Problems* 38:433–47.

[30] Testa, M., N. M. Astone, M. Krogh, & K. M. Neckerman. 1993. Employment and marriage among inner-city fathers. In *The Ghetto Underclass*, W. J. Wilson (Ed.), pp. 96–108. Newberry Park, CA: Sage.

[31] Wilson, W., & K. M. Neckerman. 1986. Poverty and Family Structure: The Widening Gap between Evidence and Public Policy Issues. In *Fighting Poverty*, S. H. Danziger and D. H. Weinberg (Eds.), pp. 232–59. Cambridge, MA: Harvard University Press.

[32] Steele, C. M. 1997. A threat in the air: how stereotypes shape intellectual identity and performance. *American Psychologist* 52:613–29.

[33] Fischer, C. S., M. Hout, M. S. Jankowski, S. R. Lucas, A. Swidler, & K. Voss. 1996. Race, ethnicity and intelligence. In *Inequality by Design: Cracking the Bell Curve Myth*, Fischer, Hout, Jankowski, Lucas, Swidler & Voss (Eds.). Princeton, NJ: Princeton University Press.

[34] Economic Report of the President. 1998. Washington, DC: U.S. Government Printing Office.

[35] Sampson, R. J., & W. J. Wilson. 1995. Toward a Theory of Race, Crime, and Urban Inequality. In *Crime and Inequality*,. J. Hagan & R. D. Peterson (Eds.), pp. 37–54. Stanford, CA: Stanford University Press.

[36] U.S. Bureau of the Census. 1997. Income by educational attainment for persons 18 years old and over, by age, sex, race, and Hispanic origin: March 1996. *Current Population Report*. Washington, DC: U.S. Government Printing Office.

[37] Neal, D. A., & W. R. Johnson. 1996. The role of premarket factors in black-white wage differences. *Journal of Political Economy* 104:869–95.

[38] Williams, D. R., & C. Collins. 1995. U.S. socioeconomic and racial differences in health. *Annual Review of Sociology* 21:349–86.

[39] Eller, T. J. 1994. Household Wealth and Asset Ownership: 1991. U.S. Bureau of the Census, Current Population Reports, P70-34. Washington, DC: U.S. Government Printing Office.

[40] Oliver, M. L., & T. M. Shapiro. 1997. *Black Wealth/White Wealth: A New Perspective on Racial Inequality*. New York: Routledge.

[41] Bauman, K. 1998. Direct Measures of Poverty as Indicators of Economic Need: Evidence from the Survey of Income and Program Participation. U.S. Census Bureau Population Division Technical Working Paper No. 30.

[42] Alba, R. D., & J. R. Logan. 1993. Minority proximity to whites in suburbs: An individual-level analysis of segregation. *American Journal of Sociology* 98:1388–1427.

[43] Collins, C., & D. R. Williams. Segregation and mortality: the deadly effects of racism? *Sociological Forum*. 14(3):493–521.

[44] Council on Ethical and Judicial Affairs. 1990. Black-white disparities in health care. *JAMA* 263:2344–46.

[45] Whittle, J., J. Conigliaro, C. B. Good, and R. P. Lofgren. 1993. Racial differences in the use of invasive cardiovasular procedures in the Department of Veterans Affairs. *New England Journal of Medicine* 329:621–26.

[46] McBean, A. M., & M. Gornick. 1994. Differences by race in the rates of procedures performed in hospitals for Medicare beneficiaries. *Health Care Financing Review* 15:77–90.

[47] Hannan, E. L., M. van Ryne, J. Burke, D. Stone, D. Kumar, D. Arani, W. Pierce, S. Rafii, T. A. Sanborn, S. Sharma, J. Slater, & B. A. DeBuono. 1999. Access to coronary artery bypass surgery by race/ethnicity and gender among patients who are appropriate for surgery. *Medical Care* 37:68–77.

[48] Peterson, E. D., L. K. Shaw, E. R. DeLong, D. B. Pryor, R. M. Califf, & D. B. Mark. 1997. Racial variation in the use of coronary-revascularization procedures—Are the differences real? Do they matter? *New England Journal of Medicine* 337(7):480–86.

[49] Williams, D. R., M. Spencer, & J. S. Jackson. Race-Related Stress and Physical Health: Is Group Identity a Vulnerability Factor or a Resource? In *Self, Social Identity, and Physical Health: Interdisciplinary Explorations*, R. J. Contrada & R. D. Ashmore (Eds.), pp.71–100. New York: Oxford University Press. In Press.

[50] Williams, D. R., Y. Yu, J. Jackson, & N. Anderson. 1997. Racial differences in physical and mental health: Socioeconomic status, stress, and discrimination. *Journal of Health Psychology* 2:335–51.

[51] Taylor, J., & B. Jackson. 1990. Factors affecting alcohol consumption in black women, part II. *International Journal of Addictions* 25:1415–27.

[52] Williams, D. R., & A-M. Chung. Racism and Health. In *Health in Black America*, R. Gibson & J. S. Jackson (Eds.). Thousand Oaks, CA: Sage Publications. In Press.

[53] Taylor, J., D. Henderson, & B. B. Jackson. 1991. A holistic model for understanding and predicting depression in African American women. *Journal of Community Psychology* 19:306–20.

[54] McEwen, B. S., and T. Seeman. 1999. Protective and damaging effects of mediators of stress: elaborating and testing the concepts of allostasis and allostatic load. *Ann. N.Y. Acad. Sc.* 896.

3
Women Get Sicker but Men Die Quicker: Gender and Health

Judith Lorber

> In any gender-dichotomized society, the fact that we are born bio-
> logically female or male means that our environments will be dif-
> ferent: we will live different lives. Because our biology and how
> we live are dialectically related and build on one another, we can-
> not vary gender and hold the environment constant. (Hubbard
> 1990, p.128)

There is a saying in epidemiology—"women get sicker, but men die
quicker." It is a succinct way of summing up the illness and death
rates of women and men in modern industrialized societies. In
industrialized countries, in the early years of the twentieth century,
women outlived men only by two to three years; today, women live
almost seven years longer (Stillion 1995). Racial differences increase
these gender differences. In the United States, although life expectancy for a white infant born in the early 1990s is almost seven years
longer for a girl than for a boy, for Black infants, the difference is
nine years (Kranczer 1995). The combined racial and sex difference
between the longest life expectancy (white girls) and the shortest
(Black boys) is almost fifteen years. (See Table 1.) Black women and
men not only die earlier but are prone to more illnesses and physical
traumas throughout their lives than white women and men. Paradoxically, although white women have the longest life expectancy, they
have more illnesses throughout their adult lives than white men (Verbrugge 1985, 1989a, 1989b). Although women as well as men are
subject to heart diseases, cancers, and other life-threatening physical problems, on the whole, women live longer than men in industrialized countries because men get the killer diseases earlier
(Verbrugge 1990).

In societies where women's social status is very low, their life
expectancy is lower than in industrialized countries because of a
combination of social factors: eating last and eating less, complications of frequent childbearing and sexually transmitted diseases

Table 1 1993 Life Expectancy at Birth in the United States, by Sex and Race

Sex	Female	Male	Sex Difference
All	78.9	72.1	6.8
White	79.5	73	6.5
Black	73.7	64.7	9
Racial Difference	5.8	8.3	14.8

Source: Kranczer 1995, Table 2, based on data from the National Center for Health Statistics.

because they have no power to demand abstinence or condom use, infections and hemorrhages following genital mutilation, neglect of symptoms of illness until severe, and restricted access to modern health care (Santow 1995; see Table 2). The relationship between women's health and their social status is starkly demonstrated by how care is allocated within the family in many traditional societies:

> A lower-status individual, such as a young female, was likely to be treated only with home remedies; when assistance was sought outside the household it was more likely to be from a traditional than a modern therapist. A higher-status individual, such as a male of almost any age or an adult mother of sons, was likely to be taken directly to a private medical practitioner. (Santow 1995, p. 154)

Table 2 Male-Female Life Expectancy Rates for Developed and Developing Countries, 1990–1995

Region	Male Life Expectancy	Female Life Expectancy	Female-Male Ratio
World	62.7	66.7	106.4
Developed	71.0	78.0	109.9
Developing	61.1	63.9	104.6
Africa	51.4	54.6	106.2
North America	72.7	79.4	109.2
Latin America[a]	65.2	70.9	108.2
Asia[b]	63.6	66.1	103.9
Europe	71.9	78.5	109.2
Former U.S.S.R.	65.7	74.7	113.7
Oceania[c]	69.9	75.6	108.2

[a]Includes Mexico   [b]Excludes Japan   [c]Excludes Australia and New Zealand
Source: World Health Organization 1995, p. 60.

Illness and death rates are not linear or uniformly progressive. Because of a combination of social and environmental factors, life expectancy rates for Russian men have declined from 65.5 years in 1991 to 57.3 years in 1995 (Specter 1995). When a woman moves to another country, her risk of dying of breast cancer gradually changes, for the better or worse, to match the risk in her new place of residence (Kliewer and Smith 1995; Ziegler 1993).

The social epidemiologist's task is to explain these variances in *morbidity* (rates of illness) and *mortality* (rates of death) and to tease out the fundamental causes that produce persistent group differences. Some of these are genetic and physiological and some are social. For example, sickle cell anemia and breast cancer cluster in different racial ethnic groups but access to knowledge, healthy environments, and up-to-date treatment cluster by social class:

> The reason is that resources like knowledge, money, power, prestige, and social connectedness are transportable from one situation to another, and as health-related situations change, those who command the most resources are best able to avoid risks, diseases, and consequences of disease. (Link and Phelan 1995, p. 87)

Morbidity and mortality rates are useful for policy recommendations only when accompanied by data on social factors, such as economic resources, access to health services, community supports, and cultural values. What Nancy Krieger calls "ecosocial theory"

> asks how we literally incorporate, biologically, social relations (such as those of social class, race/ethnicity, and gender) into our bodies, thereby focusing on who and what drives population patterns of health, disease, and well being. (1996, p. 135)

The rates of illness and death that are used to assess the health of groups of people are themselves influenced by social factors. For example, reports of sudden infant death syndrome (SIDS) are more common where mothers are poor, have little education, and are from disadvantaged racial/ethnic groups. Biological or medical models predict a random distribution over social classes. The high rates for children of lower socioeconomic status can be interpreted two ways—either social factors, such as poverty, are more important than biological causes, or deaths of poor infants are attributed to SIDS more often than with children from more affluent families (Nam, Eberstein, and Deeb 1989). In either case, social factors are significant, but their effects are quite different. SIDS may be more prevalent among the lower socioeconomic classes because of social factors, or it may be just as prevalent among the middle and upper classes but is more often reported as a cause of death for a child in a poor family because no one investigates further for other causes.

Another measurement problem in social epidemiology influenced by social factors is how morbidity (illness) is assessed: Is it by days off from work, visits to health care professionals, hospital days, medication use, or self-assessment? Women are likely to take more days off, see physicians and other health care workers more often, use more medication, and assess themselves as sicker. That is, women are more likely to attend to minor symptoms than men are, for a variety of reasons, among them familiarity with the health care system through reproductive needs. Men are encouraged from childhood to be stoical, and so are not likely to see a doctor for non-serious health problems. When they do get sick, they are likely to have more and longer hospital visits. Thus, by epidemiological measures, women are sicker than men most of their adult lives, but the health behavior that produces their high illness rates probably increases their longevity. According to Lois Verbrugge, "Women's greater health care in early years diminishes the severity of their problems compared to same-age men, and it ultimately helps extend their lives" (1985, p. 173). Women are not more fragile physically than men, just more self-protective of their health.

Still another social epidemiological issue is immediate and proximate cause of death. The most immediate cause for an 85-year-old woman may be pneumonia, a frequent cause of death in the elderly, but long-term causes may be just as significant. These might be poor nutrition, poor housing, and no support services. Or the causes of death might be multiple. Drinking and smoking combined with high blood pressure, which are frequently reactions to poverty and lack of opportunities for advancement, can precipitate a fatal stroke or heart attack. According to Robert Staples,

> Black men suffer a disproportionate burden of illness. The drug and alcoholism rate for blacks, for example, is about four times higher than whites. Whereas black men suffer higher rates of diabetes, strokes and a variety of chronic illnesses, they are also at the mercy of public hospitals, and, therefore, are the first victims of government cutbacks. When they do go to a hospital, they are more likely to receive inadequate treatment. (1995, p. 123)

So what did a particular Black man die from?

Social factors are not easily teased apart for any group.[1] Women tend to have more non-life-threatening illnesses because of the stresses of routinized jobs, child care, and care of elderly parents, and the "double day" of work and housework (Bird and Fremont 1991; Muller 1990; Ross and Bird 1994; Verbrugge 1986). Men are more prone to chronic and life-threatening diseases, such as heart attacks, because of their lifestyle, and, to a lesser extent, their occupations (Helgeson 1995, Waldron 1995). They are also more at risk for traumas, accidents, and homicide, because they are more likely to get into dangerous situations (Stillion 1995; Veevers and Gee 1986). Women are more likely to attempt suicide, but men are more likely to be successful because they use deadlier methods (Canetto 1992; World Health Organization 1995). Married men tend to be healthier mentally and physically than married women, but they have a worse time physically and mentally for about six months after a divorce, separation, or being widowed (Farberow et al. 1992; Gove 1984), or until they find another woman to look after their physical and emotional needs.

The statistical patterns of morbidity and mortality—who gets sick with what and who dies when from what—are outcomes of individual behavior shaped by cultural and social factors, such as availability of clean water and good food, access to medical knowledge and technology, and protection from environmental pollution, occupational traumas, and social hazards like war, violent crime, rape, battering, and genital mutilation. For the individual, health is as much affected by combined social statuses (gender, race, ethnic group, social class, occupation, and place of residence) as by personal choices (Calnan 1986; Staples 1995; Stillion 1995; Waldron 1995). Indeed, individual behavior is heavily circumscribed by social statuses—not everyone chooses health risks; for some people, health risks are built into their daily lives.[2] On a broader social system level, rates of illness and death are significantly affected by the behavior of health care providers, the policies of health care institutions and agencies, and the financial support of state and national governments for research and treatment (McKinlay 1996).

Because social factors are so intertwined, gender cannot be separated out from class, race and ethnicity, or age group. To give you an idea of some of the gendered patterns of morbidity and mortality that are the combined result of risky and protective behavior, environments, social expectations, and economic and other resources, I will organize them by life cycle—birth, adolescence and young adulthood, health behaviors in adulthood, work and family, old age, and death.

Birthing and Getting Born: Have Money or Be a Boy

For mothers, economic resources can spell the difference between life and death. For their infants, in poor countries that favor men, all the advantages go to boys. The physical hazards that produce infertility are evenly incurred by men and women, but the social effects and treatments are much harder on women.

Childbirth and Infancy

One of important contributors to women's longer life expectancy in the twentieth century is the reduction of illness and death in childbirth.[3] The use of antibiotics for puerperal infections ("childbed fevers") and surgical interventions to prevent heavy blood loss has made dying in childbirth a rare occurrence in many countries. However, because of uneven access to prenatal care and safe abortions and inadequate treatment of childbirth complications, women in the child-bearing years still suffer from high mortality and morbidity rates in many parts of the world, including the United States (Dixon-Mueller 1994; Sundari 1994). The health of the mother directly affects the health of the infant. In industrialized countries,

> the condition that enables us to predict with the greatest accuracy whether or not a baby will be stillborn, sick, malformed, premature, or will die in the first year of life, is the mother's socioeconomic status. If she belongs to a disadvantaged social class this means, among other things, low income, poor health, hard domestic and extra-domestic work, low educational level, and bad housing. (Romito and Hovelaque 1987, p. 254)[4]

The more economic resources a country has, the better the health care and the lower the death rate of women in childbirth and their newborns in their first year.[5] Physiologically, girl babies are stronger at birth, and the female hormones generated at puberty are protective until menopause. However, women's longer life expectancy in developed countries, compared to men, reflects the effects of a healthier environment, better health care, and good nutrition, which are indicative of enough economic resources to feed women and girls as well as men and boys and to give pregnant women good health care. (See Table 3.) Another related set of statistics is whether or not girls and women are taught to read and write and the number of children they have. Educated women are good earners and too valuable to keep at home having children; hence, they have fewer and more widely spaced children and their maternal mortality rates drop.

In countries that put a high premium on having sons, neglect and infanticide of baby girls and deliberate abortions of female fetuses after prenatal sex testing has resulted in an imbalanced sex ratio (proportion of boys to girls or men to women) (Renteln 1992). Africa,

Table 3 Health Care and Maternal and Infant Mortality Rates for Developed and Developing Countries

Region	Prenatal Care-1990[a]	Attended by Trained Personnel[a]	Maternal Mortality 1988[b]	Infant Mortality 1990–95[b]
World	64	60	370	68
Developed	98	99	26	12
Developing	59	55	420	69
Africa	59	42	630	95
North America	95	99	12	8
Latin America[c]	72	76	200	47
Asia[d]	57	56	380	62
Europe	99	99	23	10
Former U.S.S.R.	100	100	45	20
Oceania[e]	70	50	600	22

[a]Percent of births   [b]Deaths per 100,000 live births   [c]Includes Mexico
[d]Excludes Japan   [e]Excludes Australia and New Zealand
Source: World Health Organization 1995, p. 60.

Europe, and North America have a sex ratio of 95 girls to 100 boys, considered balanced because more boys than girls are born to compensate for the higher natural death rate of male children. In China, India, Bangladesh, and West Asia, the sex ratio is 94 girls to 100 boys, and in Pakistan it is 90 girls to 100 boys. Given the number of men, there should have been about 30 million more women in India today, and 38 million more women in China (Sen 1990).

These numbers do not necessarily reflect a complete devaluation of girls but rather a preference for boys if family size has to be limited. In China, for example, peasants feel that the ideal family is a son and a daughter; a daughter is an emotional and financial backup in case the son proves unfilial in the parents' old age (Greenhalgh and Li 1995). State policy, however, has forcefully discouraged a second child if the first is a son and forbidden a third child in almost all cases. Thus, many families have one or two sons and no daughters. Sex selection using amniocentesis occurs in the United States as well, but the practice is not well-documented, and the effects have not significantly changed the ratio of girls to boys (Burke 1992).

Infertility

Although much of the research on fertility and birth centers on women, this focus reflects the assumption that procreation is the concern of women because men can't get pregnant.[6] But men's fertility is just as vulnerable to environmental and occupational hazards as women's; toxic chemicals and other occupational hazards are equally likely to affect sperm production as viability of ova and fetal development (Bertin 1989; Hatch 1984; Vogel 1990).[7] Even with the knowledge of risk, there is little protection for workers in jobs where the workforce is predominantly women, such as nurses and anesthetists, who are exposed to radiation and powerful anesthetics, and assemblers in electronics factories who work with potentially harmful solvents (Draper 1993). In 1991, the U.S. Supreme Court decided that employers could not use protection of the fetus as a rationale for barring fertile women from hazardous jobs. The decision to take a job that might cause infertility is now up to workers themselves (including men at risk of sperm deformity), but the government could insist that employers reduce *all* workers' exposure to occupational hazards, or equip them with protective devices.[8]

In addition to job-related hazards, sexually transmitted diseases, malnutrition, and inadequate health care have contributed to higher rates of infertility among African Americans, and they are less likely to have access to expensive procreative technologies (Nsiah-Jefferson and Hall 1989). Recent data, however, indicate that their rates of both voluntary and involuntary childlessness are becoming similar to those of white Americans (Boyd 1989).

Infertility is more detrimental physiologically and socially for women than for men, even though male infertility has been very difficult to treat.[9] Women have more at stake but less bargaining power in the decisions over what to do about not being able to conceive. Whether the woman or the man is infertile, the woman is the one who usually seeks help. If she is determined to try to have a biological child with her partner, she has to assure his willingness to undergo whatever procedures physicians deem appropriate to their medical situation. She will also need his sympathy and emotional support throughout the days, months, and often years of repeated attempts to get pregnant. An infertile man might want to forget about having children entirely because he might feel that the examinations, tests, and intercourse and masturbation on demand sully his masculinity. Given his stress over his infertility, he might be unwilling or unable to provide much emotional support (Lorber and Bandlamudi 1993; Lorber and Greenfeld 1990; Nachtigall, Becker, and Wozny 1992).

The newest procreative technology, in vitro fertilization (IVF), or out-of-the-body conception, has been used in cases of both female and male infertility. This method involves giving a woman hormones to make her produce more than one ovum a month, removing the ova, fertilizing them with sperm in a Petri dish, and incubating the gametes for a day or two until the resultant cell division produces an embryo that can be implanted in the woman's womb (Fredericks, Paulson and DeCherney 1987). In male infertility, IVF provides a technological means for a man who has low sperm count, poor sperm motility, or badly shaped sperm to impregnate and for his fertile partner to have *his* child (Spark 1988). In theory, IVF works in male infertility because a very small amount of good sperm is needed to get one to fertilize an egg in a Petri dish. In the newest techniques, sperm is taken directly from the testicles, and just one is injected into an ovum (Palermo, Cohen, and Rosenwaks 1996).

All the rest of the procedures, which involve not only administering hormones and surgery but many blood tests and sonograms, have to be undergone by the woman, who may be able to conceive with a much simpler procedure, donor insemination. If motherhood and not pregnancy is her goal, she may prefer to adopt. But if she refuses to undergo fertility treatments, her infertile male partner's opportunity to have a biological child in this relationship is lost. He has everything to gain and less to undergo. This imbalance in the demands of treatment sets up the dynamics of gender bargaining in male infertility (Lorber 1987, 1989; Lorber and Bandlamudi 1993). Some women also have procreative problems; others see the problem as theirs in any case. They are willing to undergo IVF when their male partner is infertile because they feel they have no other options to have a biological child. Some women who have no fertility problems do it for altruistic reasons, but some simply succumb to psychological pressure from their male partner.

Willingness to undergo repeated trials of IVF, even if they are unsuccessful, may be a rational decision for women, since families, the media, and the medical system all favor undergoing treatment.[10] Going through IVF proves to themselves, their mates, and family members that they have done everything they could to have a biological child together (Lorber and Greenfeld 1990). These latent gains are what make IVF so popular throughout the world, despite its low success rate of about 15–25 percent in female infertility and zero to 10 percent in male infertility. Doing IVF is often an obligatory rite of passage, not only to try to have a child, but also to try "to reach a secondary objective as a necessary substitute, that is, protection against social stigmatization and a means to obtain social recognition as an involuntary childless woman" (Koch 1990, pp. 240–41). Involuntary infertility is a form of sick role, because the individual is not held responsible for her or his condition; to refuse treatment implies that the condition is voluntary and therefore not a true "illness" deserving sympathy and emotional support. Procreative pathology has its meaning within the social expectation that heterosexual adults have "their own"—biological—children if at all possible. Not being able to conceive does not harm physically, but socially and psychologically; the treatment, however, can be physically as well as emotionally and financially costly, especially for women.

Adolescence and Young Adulthood: Good and Bad Social Pressures

Poor teenage girls in the United States are like women in poor countries—if they get good prenatal care and have social support after the birth, they and their children thrive. But if they are stigmatized and therefore put off getting prenatal care, they are likely to have premature births and low birth weight babies, with accompanying health hazards. Even without childbirth, the lives of poor young men of color are the most endangered of all groups in the United States, exposing them to a host of physical and emotional traumas. Young women in college are prone to eating disorders, but in general, their health behaviors tend to be more protective than those of young men in college. The situation for young girls in non-Western countries, particularly in Africa, is starkly different. Genital mutilation is a gender-specific health issue in many countries of the world.[11]

Teenage Pregnancy

Teenage childbearing is a social problem that can be viewed from a health perspective (the effect on the body of a growing girl of having a baby in the teen years and the health of the infant) and from a social perspective (why teenage boys and girls want to have babies and what happens to those girls who do get pregnant). The data from recent research shows that social conditions are more crucial than age or racial ethnic identity in predicting whether young, unmarried girls will have a pregnancy and what the physical and emotional outcome will be for the mother and the child (Luker 1996).

According to the providers in 200 randomly selected reproductive health and other service programs in New York City, girls of Puerto Rican and Dominican background got pregnant in their teen years because they lacked information about sexual relationships, procreation, and birth control (Fennelly 1993). But the reason they couldn't acquire this knowledge were the contradictory attitudes of the Hispanic culture, attitudes that condemned sexuality outside of marriage but valued pregnancy and having children no matter when it occurred. The positive attitudes towards fatherhood among young men in many cultures, and their intentions to play a significant role in the lives of their children and their children's mothers, also make it difficult for teenage girls to practice birth control or have an abortion (Anderson 1989; Marsiglio 1988; Redmond 1985).

Once sexual activity begins, Black teenage girls from high-risk social environments are 8.3 times more likely to become pregnant than Black girls from low-risk social environments (Hogan and Kitagawa 1985). The data were based on a random sample of over 1,000 Black girls aged 13–19 who lived in Chicago in 1979. High risks in this study were being poor, living in an impoverished neighborhood with a non-nuclear family and many siblings, and having a sister who had also been a teenage mother. Another study, of 268 Canadian teenagers who were interviewed during pregnancy and four weeks after delivery, found that those who had strong support from their families were less likely to have low-birth-weight babies or postpartum depression (Turner, Grindstaff and Phillips 1990).

Pregnancy soon after menarche is considered the norm in all but highly industrialized societies, and in most cultures, having a child, not marriage, is the mark of adulthood. In industrialized countries, the incidence of teenage pregnancy is low where sex education is part of the school curriculum and contraceptives and early abortions are widely available (Jones and Forrest 1985). Teenage pregnancy and childbirth may result in frequent premature births, which seems to be a more serious problem than low birth weight (Fraser 1995; Wilcox, Skjaerven, and Buekens 1995). Among Black women, premature births are high when there is a combination of related factors: teenage, single, no high school graduation, and welfare support (Lieberman et al. 1987). The major *social* (not physiological) problem for the teenage mother is the risk of ending up in poverty if she is not already poor or staying poor if she is (Chilman 1989; Forsyth and Palmer 1990; Luker 1996).

Endangered Species

Even with childbearing, young women are less vulnerable to early death than the young men of their racial/ethnic groups. Because of multiple risk factors, young Black men living in disadvantaged environments are the most likely to die before they reach adulthood. Young Black men have been called an endangered species because of their early death rates, with homicides, suicides, and accidents the leading causes of death of those between 15 and 24 years old (Gibbs 1988, Staples 1995). For Black and white men between 15 and 19 years old, the annual homicide rate rose 154 percent from 1985 to 1991, with almost all of the increase due to the use of guns (Butterfield 1994). HIV infection and AIDS also have a high incidence in young Black and Hispanic men, especially when they are intravenous drug users. However, the consequent illnesses and deaths occur later on, between the ages of 29 and 41 (Kranczer 1995).

Young men's "taste for risk" has been attributed to sociobiological factors (Wilson and Daly 1985), but more plausible explanations are the seductiveness of danger, displays of masculinity, and, for Black men, despair over the future (Staples 1995). Another social factor is the recruitment into often violent sports (Messner 1992). Although a path to upward mobility for poor and working-class boys, few become successful professional athletes. Those who break into professional teams have only a few years to make it, and they cannot afford to be sidelined by injuries. "Playing hurt" and repeated orthopedic surgeries have a high physical toll. Injuries, alcoholism, drug abuse, obesity, and heart disease take about fifteen years off the life expectancy of professional football players in the United States (Messner 1992, p. 71)

Responses to Social Pressures

Health-threatening behavior, such as smoking, drinking, and illegal drug use, is influenced by a variety of social factors, but peer-group pressure is among the most significant for young men and women of all racial/ethnic groups (Coombs, Paulson and Richardson 1991; Johnson and Marcos 1988; Johnson 1988; van Roosmalen and McDaniel 1992). Drinking in college is declining among men and women, but college men still drink more often and more heavily than college women and are much more likely to get into fights, hurt others, drive while drunk, and damage property (Perkins 1992). Women as well as men who drink heavily are likely to hurt themselves physically and others emotionally and to do poorly in school.

Young women tend to adopt a somewhat healthier lifestyle than young men on such measures as using seat belts, getting adequate amounts of sleep and exercise, eating a healthy diet, taking care of their teeth, and managing stress (Donovan, Jessor and Costa 1993; Oleckno and Blacconiere 1990). However, young middle-class women are vulnerable to eating disorders, especially in the college years (Hesse-Biber 1989).

Anorexia (self-starvation) and bulimia (binge eating and induced vomiting) are extreme ways to lose weight in order to meet today's Western cultural standards of beauty and to maintain control over one's body (Bordo 1993; Brumberg 1988). The importance of society's views of femininity in eating disorders is highlighted by research comparing heterosexual women, who are subject to pressure from the media and the significant men in their lives to stay thin to be sexually attractive, and lesbians, whose views of beauty are not influenced by men's opinions. Lesbians are heavier than comparable heterosexual women, more satisfied with their bodies, and less likely to have eating disorders (Herzog et al. 1992). Men also have an idealized body image, which may encourage anorexia and bulimia, especially among those with sexual conflicts or who identify as homosexual (Herzog, Bradburn, and Newman 1990; Herzog et al. 1984; Kearney-Cooke and Steichen-Asch 1990).

A different rationale for eating problems was found in intensive interviews with 18 women who were heterogenous in race, class, and sexual orientation (Thompson 1992). For these African-American, Latina, and white women, binge eating and purging were ways of coping with the traumas of their lives—sexual abuse, poverty, racism, and prejudice against lesbians. Eating offered the same comfort as drinking, but was cheaper and more controllable. Rather than a response to the culture of thinness, for these women, anorexia and bulimia were "serious responses to injustices" (p. 558).

College athletes are prone to anorexia and bulimia when they have to diet to stay in a weight class (Andersen 1990; Black 1991). A study of 695 athletes in 15 college sports found that 1.6 percent of the men and 4.2 percent of the women met the American Psychiatric Association's criteria for anorexia, and 14.2 percent of the men and 39.2 percent of the women met the criteria for bulimia (Burckes-Miller and Black 1991). The researchers argue that the reasons for strict weight control are not standards of beauty but the pressures of competition, to meet weight category requirements, to increase speed and height, and to be able to be lifted and carried easily in performances. Eating disorders here are an occupational risk taken not only by young athletes but by dancers, models, jockeys, and fitness instructors, as well as professional gymnasts, figure skaters, runners, swimmers, and wrestlers.

Genital Mutilation

For some young girls, being able to control the shape of your body by what you eat might look like paradise—not just to those who don't have enough to eat, but to those girls aged three to eighteen whose families insist on having their genitals amputated so that they can be properly married. Hanny Lightfoot-Klein estimated that the number of women living in Africa in the 1980s who had their clitorises and vaginal lips cut off was 94 million (1989, p. 31). The estimates for Egypt are that 80 to 97 percent of girls have mutilated genitals (MacFarquhar 1996). In the Sudan, these procedures are done on 90 percent of young girls, and in Mali on 93 percent (Dugger 1996b). In 1996, the United States passed a law making all of these procedures illegal, and other countries with large immigrant populations have also done so (Dugger 1996c).

For more than two thousand years, in a broad belt across the middle of Africa, clitoridectomies and infibulation (scarring of the labia to create adhesions that keep most of the vaginal opening closed until marriage) have been used to ensure women's virginity until marriage and to inhibit wives' appetites for sexual relations after marriage. Ironically, these mutilating practices do neither, but result in the infliction of pain as part of normal sexuality. Childbirth is more dangerous because of tearing and bleeding, and the risks of infection throughout life are high.

The procedures range from mild sunna (removing the prepuce of the clitoris) to modified sunna (partial or total clitoridectomy) to infibulation or pharaonic circumcision, which involves clitoridectomy and excision of the labia minora and the inner layers of the labia majora, and suturing the raw edges together to form a bridge of scar tissue over the vaginal opening, leaving so small an opening that normal bladder emptying takes fifteen minutes and menstrual blood backs up (see descriptions in Lightfoot-Klein, pp. 32–36). Many women have reinfibulation after childbirth and go through the process over and over again. It is called *adlat el rujal* (men's circumcision) because it is designed to create greater sexual pleasure for men, not unlike the rationale for episiotomy and tight suturing in Western obstetrical practice (Rothman 1982, pp. 58–59).

In Lightfoot-Klein's interviews with women throughout the Sudan who had clitoridectomies and infibulation, 90 percent described experiencing full orgasms during intercourse once the period of excruciatingly painful opening through penile penetration was over (pp. 80–102). However, Asma El Dareer's survey of 2,375 women, almost all of whom had had full infibulation, found that only 25 percent experienced sexual pleasure all or some of the time (1982, p. 48). One of the Sudanese men Lightfoot-Klein interviewed said that his wife's evident suffering was preferable to no reaction at all (1989, p. 8).

Circumcision of boys is much more common, and occurs in societies throughout the world, where it is done for both religious and health reasons. Although there is some debate over whether sensitivity is reduced or enhanced, male circumcision does not seem to diminish either the man's or the woman's pleasure (Gregersen 1983, pp. 100–10). Removal of the prepuce lowers the risk of HIV infection in circumcised men and cervical cancer in their women sexual partners. Another practice, subincision, where the penis is cut through and flattened and urination is subsequently done squatting, occurs in only a few places in the world.

Adulthood: Health by Choice or by Circumstances?

Many of the risky health behaviors in adulthood, such as drinking and smoking cigarettes, seem to be a matter of individual choice. But a closer look reveals that social factors linked to gender, race and ethnicity, and economic class produce the situational circumstances that influence health-related behaviors.

A comparison of 654 African-American and 474 white women aged 19 to over 70 living in upstate New York found that poorer, older, religious African-American women were most likely to abstain from alcohol (Darrow et al. 1992). A study of 4,099 white women and men and 888 Black women and men living in New York State also found that Black women were most likely to abstain from drinking (Barr et al. 1993). Black men in this study were more likely than white men to abstain, but also most likely, of all four groups, to be heavy drinkers when they did drink. A study of gendered styles of drinking showed that women of all racial ethnic groups who drank were less likely than men to become visibly intoxicated and to abandon control, behavior that would be considered unfeminine (Robbins and Martin 1993).

When economic status was added to the analysis, it was found that the poorest and least educated Black men had significantly higher rates of alcohol and illicit drug consumption and alcohol-related problems, such as accidents and run-ins with the police, boss, fellow workers, and family members. They are, as result, more likely to suffer from high blood pressure and die early of coronary artery disease, especially if they also smoke (Staples 1995; Waldron 1995). The New York State study found that the more education a Black man had, the fewer alcohol-related problems he experienced, but that Black men with college degrees experienced such problems on an average of one a month, while their white counterparts averaged only 3.4 alcohol-related problems per year. Educated Black men are likely to be under increased stress because the stakes for success are so high.

Both legal and illegal drugs are commonly used by professional athletes (Messner 1992, pp. 76–81). Team doctors routinely inject painkillers and cortisone so injured players can "play hurt" and supply amphetamines to enhance performance and anabolic steroids to increase muscle mass. Steroid use among women and men body builders who enter competitions is endemic, despite their virilizing effects in women and feminizing effects in men (Fussell 1993, Mansfield and McGinn 1993).

Among laypeople, women are more twice as likely as men to be prescribed psychotropic drugs for anxiety (tranquilizers and sleeping pills), but men often obtain such medications from women—their wives, sisters, or friends—when they are under stress because of their jobs or lack of a job (Ettorre, Klaukka, and Riska 1994). Both women and men physicians prescribe these medications to women more than they do to men with similar difficulties, but men physicians are significantly more likely to do so (Taggart et al. 1993). Elizabeth Ettorre and Elianne Riska (1995) argue that both the gendered use patterns and the prescribing patterns reflect powerlessness: Prescribing tranquilizers for women stressed out by their triple duties as wives, mothers, and paid workers treats the symptoms, not the causes, which women physicians are more likely to recognize. When men in difficult social situations ask sympathetic women they know rather than their men physicians for tranquilizers, the same gender dynamics of status and powerlessness seem to be at issue.

Homicide rates are greater for disadvantaged men but paradoxically higher for educated women in the labor force (Gartner 1990). A cross-national, longitudinal comparison of 18 industrialized countries found that as women's lives between 1950 and 1985 moved away from traditional roles, they were more likely to be murdered (Gartner, Baker, and Pampel 1990). The authors argue that although women confined to the home are subject to violence from husbands and other men relatives, women who work for pay, especially in nontraditional occupations, and single women living on their own are also vulnerable to being killed by acquaintances and strangers.

The one place women maintain their life expectancy advantage despite risk behavior is with smoking—they outlive men even if they smoke heavily, leading to the conclusion that other factors provide protective health benefits for women (Rogers and Powell-Griner 1991).

Work and Family: Protection and Danger

Jobs and families are complex variables with good and bad effects on the physical and mental health of women and men. Both are are-

nas for social support, which is beneficial to health; both are sometimes hazardous environments with detrimental physical effects;
and both produce stresses.[12]

Work-Family Demands and Rewards

Although having a paid job outside the home usually enhances
women's physical and mental health, jobs can be physically hazardous to women as well as men. Many of women's jobs are as physically dangerous as some men's jobs (Chavkin 1994; Fox 1991).
Nursing, for example, can be highly stressful emotionally; hospitals
also expose the nurse to infections, radiation, and dangerous chemicals (Coleman and Dickinson 1984; Kemp and Jenkins 1992). Full-
time housewives are not so protected, either: the home is a similarly
stressful and dangerous work environment, full of toxic chemicals
and potential allergens (Rosenberg 1984).

The job and the home can also produce high levels of psychological stress for women and men, and workplace and family stresses
can spill over into each other (Eckenrode and Gore 1990). For
women especially, the boundaries between work and family are permeable because even when they have full-time jobs, they usually have
the main responsibility for childcare, household maintenance, and
providing help to kin outside the household (Gerstel and Gallagher
1994; Lai 1995; Lennon and Rosenfeld 1992). In dual career marriages, women often resent having a "double shift"—paid work plus
housework—and men in turn feel that demands are made on them
in the home that husbands in traditional marriages don't have (Glass
and Fujimoto 1994). However, marriage extends men's and women's
life spans, but through different means (Lillard and Waite 1995):

> "His" marriage seems to consist of a settled life, improved per-
> haps by the household management skills and labors of his
> wife. . . . "Her" marriage seems to offer primarily the benefits of
> improved financial well-being. . . . (p. 1154)

The effects of workplace and family stress, role conflict, depression, and negative feelings on vulnerability to illness are hard to document. The connection between stress and heart attacks, for example,
is not proven (Waldron 1995). Moreover, some "hardy personalities"
thrive under stress, according to a study of men executives (Maddi
and Kobasa 1984; also see Ouellette 1993). A study of the effects of
combined roles (work, marriage, and motherhood) in a sample of
1,473 Black and 1,301 white women found that work was signifi-

cantly associated with lower blood pressure only for educated Black women (Orden et al. 1995). Being married was correlated with raised blood pressure for white women, but motherhood with lower blood pressure, even for single mothers. As an example of work's beneficial physical effects, separate studies found that older Black women and men had better health if they were employed (Coleman et al. 1987; Rushing, Ritter, and Burton 1992). This finding is not surprising, since employment usually means a higher income, which in turn means better nutrition and greater access to health care. In addition, people with health problems are not as able to hold down jobs.

The gender differences related to paid jobs and family demands are minimized when women and men live and work in similar unpressured environments. A comparison of the health status of 230 women and men on two Israeli kibbutzes, where work and family life are communal and health care is free, found that they were alike in their health status and illness behavior and that the men had life expectancies as long as those of the women (Anson, Levenson, and Bonneh 1990).

Battering

The home is not only a place of potential environmental hazards and stress, it can also be the site of physical violence. The average yearly number of recorded acts of violence against women in the United States from 1979 to 1987 was 56,900 by husbands, 216,100 by divorced or separated husbands, and 198,800 by boyfriends (Harlow 1991, p. 1).

Men whose masculinity is tied to norms of dominance but who do not have the economic status to back up a dominant stance are likely to be abusive to the women they love, either psychologically or physically, and often both (Walker 1984, Yllö 1984). James Ptacek's interviews with 18 men in a counseling program for husbands who battered found that they felt they had a right to beat their wives: "There is a pattern of finding fault with the woman for not being good at cooking, for not being sexually responsive, for not being deferential enough . . . for not knowing when she is 'supposed' to be silent, and for not being faithful. In short, for not being a 'good wife'" (1988, p. 147).

Wife beating was once approved in most communities and is still condoned today where there is an ideology of men's authority over their wives. Marital rape has only recently been accorded recognition as a genuine sexual assault (Finkelhor and Yllö 1985). The response of doctors, nurses, and the police to battering reflects these mores. In general, neither the medical system nor the law has given battered women much attention or protection (Blackman 1989, Kurz 1987, Warshaw 1989).

Women who stay in such relationships are likely to have been well socialized into the emotionally supportive feminine role but to be socially or economically superior to the men who batter them (Walker 1984). Beth Richie (1996) found that the 26 African-American battered women she interviewed had had girlhoods of relative privilege and thought they could be ideal wives and mothers. They felt they could not admit to their families that they had failed to live up to their early promise as "good girls." They could not go to the police because their batterers had embroiled them in illegal activities. Julie Blackman's interviews with 172 battered women found that they did not have a sense of injustice over what was happening to them because they could not see any alternatives outside of the situation (1989, pp. 67–82). Even women who had acted on alternatives, such as calling the police or going to shelters for battered women, did not feel that they had severed the relationship (pp. 153–66).

Old Age: Women Live Longer But Not Better

Although the physiological aspects of old age seem to override social factors, in that women of every racial/ethnic group in industrial societies outlive the men of their group, the quality of their lives in old age can suffer because of poverty and few social supports.

The later years of life present women and men with sex-specific health risks. The older men get, the more likely they are to develop prostate cancer, especially among Blacks (Weitz 1996, pp. 53–55). It can be cured by surgery, but the operation often has side effects, such as impotence and urinary incontinence. After menopause, women are faced with the question of whether to use estrogen replacement therapy, which carries the risk of breast cancer (Bush 1992). Without it, they may suffer from bone fragility and increased risk of heart disease (Bilezikian and Silverberg 1992; Jonas and Manolio 1996; Nachtigall and Nachtigall 1995).

In addition to these sex-specific physiological risks, social factors make getting older and dying different experiences for women and men. With longer life expectancy, many women in industrialized countries can expect to outlive their husbands or long-term male companions (Verbrugge 1989b). Most patients in places with Western medical systems go to a hospital for acute illnesses, surgery, and medical crises in chronic conditions, but hospitals in the United States now routinely send even very sick patients home within a week. Many more surgical procedures are done on an out-patient or one-night basis. With the shift of care from hospitals to home, some-one needs to give medications and injections and change wound dressings (Glazer 1990). Even if home health care givers are hired, someone needs to supervise and fill in; this "someone" is usually a wife or other woman relative.

Shopping, cleaning, laundry, bedmaking, and paying bills are additional chores that women relatives do for sick and frail elderly people living at home (Graham 1985). The question is, who takes care of elderly widows and those who have never married? Women 85 years and older are more likely to be poor and living with rela-tives or in nursing homes than men of that age are (Longino 1988). Thus, for many women, the advantage of long life may not look like such a dividend after all.

Dying: Gendered Death Dips

One area in which social factors and physiological outcomes inter-twine dramatically are "death dips." These are statistical drops in the expected rate of death in the weeks or days before a socially mean-ingful event, followed by a statistical rise a week or two later. Since social meanings are gendered, we would expect that death dips would be, too. And so they are.

In his 1970 Ph.D. Princeton University dissertation, "Dying as a Form of Social Behavior," David P. Phillips documented an intriguing epidemiological statistic—famous people were less likely to die in the month preceding their birthday than in the month after. He argued that they had postponed their deaths in order to participate in their public birthday celebrations. He also found, examining official tables of dates of death, that ordinary people also postponed dying until after important social occasions, such as presidential elections in the United States, and among Jews, the holiest day of the year, the Day of Atonement (Yom Kippur), and Passover, the popular celebration of liberation from Egyptian slavery (Phillips and Feldman 1973; Phil-lips and King 1988).

This and subsequent research has revealed that the death-dip phenomenon around major religious holidays is quite gendered, because of the different meanings of these events to women and men (Idler and Kasl 1992; Phillips and King 1988; Phillips and Smith 1990; Reunanen 1993). The Passover death-dip, for example, occurs only among men. There was a 25.8 percent rise in deaths in the week after Passover among white men with unambiguously Jewish names who died in California between 1966 and 1984; for women there was no such difference in deaths immediately before and after Passover (Phillips and King 1988). Statistical analysis of the death rates in a different population found the same gender pattern for all the major Jewish holidays (Idler and Kasl 1992). These researchers' explanation is that Jewish men's involvement in religious observances is more central to their lives than to Jewish women. Jewish women's death patterns are similar to all non-observant Jews—they are more likely to die in the month preceding a major holiday than in the month after, while Jewish men and all observant Jews are more likely to die in the month after (Idler and Kasl 1992, Table 4).[13]

The opposite pattern is true for Black and white Catholics and Protestants—women and men, observant and non-observant, postpone death until after Christmas and Easter (Idler and Kasl 1992, Table 3). In fact, women are more likely to postpone dying until after these events, which tend to be family-oriented rather than purely religious celebrations. A Finnish analysis of 60,000 deaths for the 1966– 1986 period found that only women postponed dying until after Christmas, a family-centered holiday where the senior woman cooks the celebratory meal (Reunanen 1993).[14] A similar gendered phenomenon occurs around the Harvest Moon Festival among Chinese women aged 75 and older; their mortality rate is lower in the week before the holiday than in any other six-month period studied (Phillips and Smith 1990). Older women play the central part in the Harvest Moon Festival; the senior woman of the household supervises daughters and daughters-in-law in the preparation of an elaborate meal. The shift in dying does not occur among elderly Chinese men.

The dip in expected deaths the week before a major religious festival and the concomitant rise the week after has been documented for Chinese women with cerebrovascular and cardiac diseases and for Jewish men with these diseases and also with malignant tumors (Phillips and Smith 1990). Such psychosomatic and gendered effects of social beliefs are even starker among Chinese-Americans born in a year considered ill-fated in Chinese astrology who have a disease considered particularly detrimental for that birth year (Phillips, Ruth and Wagner 1993). Their average age of death occurs almost two years earlier than among non-Chinese and those born in more advantageous years who have the same illnesses. Women with the ill-fated combination of birth year and disease lose more years of life than men. The gender pattern, the authors speculate, is due to greater traditionalism among Chinese-American women. However, the researchers argue that the crucial factors are behavior as well as beliefs:

> Patients with ill-fated combinations of birth year and disease may refuse to change unhealthy habits because they believe their deaths are inevitable and thereby reduce their longevity. For example, earth patients with cancer may be less likely to quit smoking and fire patients with heart disease may be less likely to change their diets or exercise habits. (p. 1144)

How should a social epidemiologist classify these early deaths? Is the cause individual behavior, cultural beliefs, community practices, gender, race, social class? Or all of the above?

Summary

Basic epidemiological statistics, such as life expectancy, cause of death, and illnesses throughout life, reflect the economic resources of a society and the social status of women and men and girls and boys.

Women's longer life expectancy in modern industrialized societies depends in great part on access to medical care in pregnancy and childbirth. The effects of childbearing in adolescence, which often results in premature births and low birth-weight infants who may be physically underdeveloped, are outcomes of poverty, lack of prenatal care, and few social supports. When friends and family provide care and concern during pregnancies, the outcome is likely to be physically and psychologically favorable for both infants and mothers.

Hazardous work environments affect fetal development and sperm production and may result in infertility in men as well as women. In social stigma and extensiveness of treatment, however, the burden of infertility is much greater for women than for men.

From available data, we know that Black and Hispanic adolescents of both genders are more vulnerable to poor health and early death because they live in dangerous social environments, but girls and young women are less likely to engage in health-endangering behavior than boys and young men. Because of the combination of social factors in their disadvantaged neighborhoods and in their compensatory risk-defying actions, young Black and Hispanic men in United States inner cities have high rates of death from homicide, suicide, and accidents before they reach adulthood and from AIDS later on. A social practice with severely detrimental physical effects is mutilation of the genitals of young girls to keep them chaste and marriageable. This practice is very widespread in Egypt and throughout Africa.

In adulthood, economic factors affect the health risks of women and men of various racial/ethnic groups differently—poor men from disadvantaged racial/ethnic groups are more vulnerable to occupational traumas and homicide; poor women from these groups to having and raising children in poverty. For all adults, smoking, drinking, taking drugs, lack of exercise, and poor diets are health-related behaviors somewhat under individual control, although having the time to exercise and the money to buy nutritional food may be large situational obstacles to a healthy lifestyle. In addition, peer-group and family supports—social, psychological, and economic—influence individual health behaviors. These supports can be detrimental as well as protective, and their effects are gendered. Peer-groups encourage alcohol consumption among college men and extreme forms of dieting among college women, for instance. But eating and drinking problems can also be responses to poverty and prejudice.

Juggling work and family responsibility may be more stressful for women than for men, but employment is beneficial to the physical and mental health of both women and men, providing not only income but a social circle. Having little control over one's work situation produces a high level of stress, so that people in low-level jobs and middle management may suffer more depression and psychosomatic illnesses than people in high positions. Men from disadvantaged racial/ethnic groups and all women are most likely to have jobs with little mobility and autonomy. However, stress may not always be detrimental to health; some people have been found to thrive on it.

The home can also be the site of violence: most women who are battered suffer at the hands of their husbands and lovers. A few fight back, and when they do, the violence escalates, often ending in homicide (Walker 1989).

Old age and dying, like being born, is a gendered social phenomenon. Life expectancy and timing of death are influenced as much by social as physiological factors. Religion, family, income, and access to medical care are significant in the longevity and quality of life of elderly women and men.

The "death dip" phenomenon, in which people with chronic or terminal illnesses postpone dying until after a meaningful event, such as a birthday, national election, or religious holiday, demonstrates the power of the social and psychological over physiology. The influence of gender is evident in the variable meaning of these events to different groups of women and men.

In sum, from the beginning to the end, and throughout life, the human experiences of birth and death, disability and illness are embedded in social contexts. Because gender is such an important part of social life, women's and men's experiences, as we have seen, are different in sickness and in health, when rich and when poor, and in death, their lives are quite far apart.

Notes

[1] On the problems of constructing categories of race and ethnicity, see Jones, Snider and Warren 1996.

[2] A substantial proportion of some morbidity rates are not explained by well-known risk factors. In breast cancer, for instance, only half of the cases in the United States are related to early menarche, having a family history of breast cancer or a personal history of benign breast disease, having a baby after the age of 19 or not having children, and being in the upper two-thirds in income (Madigan et al. 1995). Note that these factors are both physiological and social and that the social factors are circumstances over which a woman may have little control.

[3] For the detrimental effects of extensive technology in childbirth, see Rothman 1982, 1986, 1989.

[4] In her editorial preface to the September/October 1995 issue of the *Journal of the American Medical Women's Association*, which is devoted to prenatal care and women's health, Wendy Chavkin notes that "the common thread woven throughout these articles is that improvements in pregnancy outcome require care for women before and after pregnancy" (p. 143). See also Lazarus (1988a) and Lieberman et al. (1987).

[5] For a detailed and harrowing account of how mothers in the poorest area of Brazil choose which of their infants to feed and which to let die, see Scheper-Hughes 1992.

[6] Theoretically, it is physiologically possible for a man to gestate a fetus (Teresi 1994).

[7] According to a review of studies of dropping sperm counts and sperm quality in Western countries, men's fertility may be on the endangered list (Wright 1996).

[8] For discussions of the political and policy issues, see Merrick and Blank (1993).

[9] Abbey, Andrews and Halman 1991; Andrews, Abbey and Halman 1991; Greil 1991; Lasker and Borg 1995; Miall 1986; Pfeffer 1987; Sandclowski 1993; Spark 1988.

[10] Callan et al. 1988, Crowe 1985, Franklin 1990, Koch 1990, Williams 1988.

[11] Immigration and asylum seekers have brought genital mutilation to the attention of Western countries (see Crossette 1995; Dugger 1996a, 1996b, 1996c; MacFarquhar 1996; Rosenthal 1996; Walker 1992).

[12] For reviews and research, see Bird and Fremont 1991, Farrell and Markides 1985, Gove 1984, Lennon 1994, Loscosso and Spitze 1990, Muller 1990, Pugliesi 1995, Roxburgh 1996, Sorensen and Verbrugge 1987, Waldron 1995.

[13] Idler and Kasl did not break down their observant vs. non-observant data by gender.

[14] I am indebted to Elianne Riska for bringing this paper to my attention and for supplying me with an English summary and a description of Finnish Christmas customs.

Bibliography

Andersen, Arnold E. (ed.). 1990. *Males with Eating Disorders*. New York: Brunner/Mazel.

Anderson, Elijah. 1989. "Sex Codes and Family Life among Poor Inner-City Youths." *Annals of the American Academy of Political and Social Science* 501:59–78.

Anson, Ofra, Arieh Levenson, and Dan Y. Bonneh. 1990. "Gender and Health on the Kibbutz." *Sex Roles* 22:213–35.

Barr, Kellie E.M., Michael P. Farrell, Grace M. Barnes, and John W. Welte. 1993. "Race, Class, and Gender Differences in Substance Abuse: Evidence of Middle-Class/Underclass Polarization among Black Males." *Social Problems* 40:314–27.

Bertin, Joan E. 1989. "Women's Health and Women's Rights: Reproductive Hazards in the Workplace." Pp. 289–303 in Kathryn Strother Ratcliff (ed.), *Healing Technology: Feminist Perspectives*. Ann Arbor: University of Michigan Press.

Bilezikian, John P. and Shonni J. Silverberg. 1992. "Osteoporosis: A Practical Approach to the Perimenopausal Woman." *Journal of Women's Health* 1:21–27.

Bird, Chloe E. and Allen M. Fremont. 1991. "Gender, Time Use, and Health." *Journal of Health and Social Behavior* 32:114–29.

Black, David R. (ed.). 1991. *Eating Disorders among Athletes*. Reston, VA: American Alliance for Health, Physical Education, Recreation and Dance.

Blackman, Julie. 1989. *Intimate Violence: A Study of Injustice*. New York: Columbia University Press.

Bordo, Susan R. 1993. *Unbearable Weight: Feminism, Western Culture, and the Body*. Berkeley: University of California Press.

Boyd, Robert L. 1989. "Racial Differences in Childlessness: A Centennial Review." *Sociological Perspectives* 2:183–99.

Brumberg, Joan Jacobs. 1988. *Fasting Girls: The Emergence of Anorexia Nervosa as a Modern Disease*. Cambridge, MA: Harvard University Press.

Burckes-Miller, Mardie E. and David R. Black. 1991. "College Athletes and Eating Disorders: A Theoretical Context." Pp. 11–26 in David R. Black (ed.), *Eating Disorders among Athletes*. Reston, VA: American Alliance for Health, Physical Education, Recreation and Dance.

Burke, B. Meridith. 1992. "Genetic Counselor Attitudes towards Fetal Sex Identification and Selective Abortion." *Social Science and Medicine* 34:1263–69.

Bush, Trudy L. 1992. "Feminine Forever Revisited: Menopausal Hormone Therapy in the 1990s." *Journal of Women's Health* 1:1–4.

Butterfield, Fox. 1994. "Teen-Age Homicide Rate Has Soared." *The New York Times*, 14 October.

Calnan, Michael. 1986. "Maintaining Health and Preventing Illness: A Comparison of the Perceptions of Women from Different Social Classes." *Health Promotion* 1:167–77.

Canetto, Silvia Sara. 1992. "Gender and Suicide in the Elderly." *Suicide and Life Threatening Behavior* 22:80–97.

Chavkin, Wendy (ed.). 1994. *Double Exposure: Women's Health Hazards on the Job and at Home*. New York: Monthly Review Press.

Chilman, Catherine S. 1989. "Some Major Issues Regarding Adolescent Sexuality and Childbearing in the United States." *Journal of Social Work and Human Sexuality* 8:3–25.

Coleman, Lerita M., Toni C. Antonucci, Pamela K. Adelmann, and Crohan, Susan E. 1987. "Social Roles in the Lives of Middle-Aged and Older Black Women." *Journal of Marriage and the Family* 49:761–71.

Coleman, Linda and Cindy Dickinson. 1984. "The Risks of Healing: The Hazards of the Nursing Profession." Pp. 37–56 in Wendy Chavkin (ed.), *Double Exposure: Women's Health Hazards on the Job and at Home*. New York: Monthly Review Press.

Coombs, Robert H., Morris J. Paulson, and Mark A. Richardson. 1991. "Peer vs. Parental Influence in Substance Use among Hispanic and Anglo Children and Adolescents." *Journal of Youth and Adolescence* 20:73–88.

Darrow, Sherri L., Marcia Russell, M. Lynne Cooper, Pamela Mudar, and Michael R. Frone. 1992. "Sociodemographic Correlates of Alcohol Consumption among African-American and White Women." *Women and Health* 18:35–51.

Dixon-Mueller, Ruth. 1994. "Abortion Policy and Women's Health in Developing Countries." Pp. 191–210 in Elizabeth Fee and Nancy Krieger (eds.), *Women's Health, Politics, and Power*. Amityville, NY: Baywood.

Donovan, John E., Richard Jessor and Frances M. Costa. 1993. "Structure of Health-Enhancing Behavior in Adolescence: A Latent-Variable Approach." *Journal of Health and Social Behavior* 34:346–62.

Draper, Elaine. 1993. "Fetal Exclusion Policies and Gendered Constructions of Suitable Work." *Social Problems* 40:90–107.

Dugger, Celia W. 1996a. "A Refugee's Body Is Intact but Her Family Is Torn." *The New York Times*, Oct. 12, Saturday News Section, pp. 1, 28.

Dugger, Celia W. 1996b. "Genital Ritual Is Unyielding in Africa." *The New York Times*, October 5, Saturday News Section, pp. 1, 6.

Dugger, Celia W. 1996c. "New Law Bans Genital Cutting in the United States." *The New York Times*, October 12, Saturday News Section, pp. 1, 28.

Eckenrode, John and Susan Gore (eds.). 1990. *Stress Between Work and Family*. New York: Plenum.

El Dareer, Asma. 1982. *Woman, Why Do You Weep? Circumcision and Its Consequences*. London: Zed Books.

Ettore, Elizabeth and Elianne Riska. 1995. *Gendered Moods: Psychotropics and Society*. New York: Routledge.

Ettorre, Elizabeth, Timo Klaukka, and Elianne Riska. 1994. "Psychotropic Drugs: Long-Term Use, Dependency and the Gender Factor." *Social Science and Medicine*. 12:1667–73.

Farberow, Norman L., Dolores Gallagher-Thompson, Michael Gilewski, and Larry Thompson. 1992. "The Role of Social Supports in the Bereavement Process of Surviving Spouses of Suicide and Natural Deaths." *Suicide and Life-Threatening Behavior* 22:107–24.

Fennelly, Katherine. 1993. "Barriers to Birth Control Use among Hispanic Teenagers: Providers' Perspectives." Pp. 300–311 in Barbara Blair and Susan E. Cayleff (eds.), *Wings of Gauze: Women of Color and the Experience of Health and Illness*. Detroit: Wayne State University Press.

Finkelhor, David and Kersti Yllö. 1985. *License to Rape: Sexual Abuse of Wives*. New York: Holt, Rinehart & Winston.

Forsyth, Craig J., and Eddie C. Palmer. 1990. "Teenage Pregnancy: Health, Moral and Economic Issues." *International Journal of Sociology of the Family* 20:79–95.

Fox, Steve. 1991. *Toxic Work: Women Workers at GTE Lenkurt*. Philadelphia: Temple University Press.

Fraser, Alison M. 1995. "Association of Young Maternal Age with Adverse Reproductive Outcomes." *New England Journal of Medicine* 332:1113–17.

Fredericks, Christopher M., John D. Paulson and Alan H. DeCherney (eds.). 1987. *Foundations of In Vitro Fertilization*. Washington, DC: Hemisphere.

Fussell, Sam. 1993. "Body Builder Americanus." *Michigan Quarterly Review* 32:577–96.

Gartner, Rosemary. 1990. "The Victims of Homicide: A Temporal and Cross-National Comparison." *American Sociological Review* 55:92–106.

Gartner, Rosemary, Kathryn Baker, and Fred C. Pampel. 1990. "Gender Stratification and the Gender Gap in Homicide Victimization." *Social Problems* 37:593–612.

Gerstel, Naomi and Sally Gallagher. 1994. "Caring for Kith and Kin: Gender, Employment, and the Privatization of Care." *Social Problems* 41:519–39.

Gibbs, Jewelle Taylor (ed.). 1988. *Young, Black and Male in America: An Endangered Species*. Dover, MA: Auburn House.

Glass, Jennifer and Tetsushi Fujimoto. 1994. "Housework, Paid Work, and Depression among Husbands and Wives." *Journal of Health and Social Behavior* 35:179–91.

Glazer, Nona. 1990. "The Home as Workshop: Women as Amateur Nurses and Medical Care Providers." *Gender & Society* 4:479–99.

Gove, Walter R. 1984. "Gender Differences in Mental and Physical Illness: The Effects of Fixed Roles and Nurturant Roles." *Social Science and Medicine* 19:77–91.

Graham, Hilary. 1985. "Providers, Negotiators, and Mediators: Women as the Hidden Carers." Pp. 25–52 in Ellen Lewin and Virginia Oleson (eds.), *Women, Health, and Healing*. New York: Tavistock.

Greenhalgh, Susan and Jiali Li. 1995. "Engendering Reproductive Policy and Practice in Peasant China: For a Feminist Demography of Reproduction." *Signs: Journal of Women in Culture and Society* 20:601–41.

Gregerson, Edgar. 1983. *Sexual Practices: The Story of Human Sexuality*. New York: Franklin Watts.

Harlow, Caroline Wolf. 1991. *Female Victims of Violent Crime*. Washington, DC: U.S. Department of Justice, Bureau of Justice Statistics.

Hatch, Maureen. 1984. "Mother, Father, Worker: Men and Women and the Reproductive Risks of Work." Pp. 161–79 in Wendy Chavkin (ed.), *Double Exposure: Women's Health Hazards on the Job and at Home*. New York: Monthly Review Press.

Helgeson, Vickie. 1995. "Masculinity, Men's Roles, and Coronary Heart Disease." Pp. 68–104 in Don Sabo and David Frederick Gordon (eds.), *Men's Health and Illness: Gender, Power and the Body*. Newbury Park, CA: Sage.

Herzog, David B., Isabel Bradburn, and Kerry Newman. 1990. "Sexuality in Males with Eating Disorders." Pp. 40–53 in Arnold E. Andersen (ed.), *Males with Eating Disorders*. New York: Brunner/Mazel.

Herzog, David B., Kerry L. Newman, C.J. Yeh, and Meredith Warshaw. 1992. "Body Image Satisfaction in Homosexual and Heterosexual Women." *International Journal of Eating Disorders* 11:391–96.

Herzog, David B., Dennis K. Norman, Christopher Gordon, and Maura Pepose. 1984. "Sexual Conflict and Eating Disorders in 27 Males." *American Journal of Psychiatry* 141:989–90.

Hesse-Biber, Sharlene J. 1989. "Eating Patterns and Disorders in a College Population: Are College Women's Eating Problems a New Phenomenon?" *Sex Roles* 20:71–89.

Hogan, Dennis P. and Evelyn M. Kitagawa. 1985. "The Impact of Social Status, Family Structure, and Neighborhood on the Fertility of Black Adolescents." *American Journal of Sociology* 90:825–855.

Hubbard, Ruth. 1990. *The Politics of Women's Biology*. New Brunswick, NJ: Rutgers University Press.

Idler, Ellen L. and Stanislav V. Kasl. 1992. "Religion, Disability, Depression, and the Timing of Death." *American Journal of Sociology* 97:1052–1079.

Johnson, Richard E. and Anastasios C. Marcos. 1988. "Correlates of Adolescent Drug Use by Gender and Geographic Location." *American Journal of Drug and Alcohol Abuse* 14:51–63.

Johnson, Valerie. 1988. "Adolescent Alcohol and Marijuana Use: A Longitudinal Assessment of a Social Learning Perspective." *American Journal of Drug and Alcohol Abuse* 14:419–39.

Jonas, Helen A. and Teri A. Manolio. 1996. "Hormone Replacement and Cardiovascular Disease in Older Women." *Journal of Women's Health* 5:351–61.

Jones, Elise and Jacqueline Darroch Forrest. 1985. "Teenage Pregnancy in Developed Countries: Determinants and Policy Implications." *Family Planning Perspectives* 17:53–63.

Kearney-Cooke, Ann and Paule Steichen-Asch. 1990. "Men, Body Image, and Eating Disorders." Pp. 54–74 in Arnold E. Andersen (ed.), *Males with Eating Disorders*. New York: Brunner/Mazel.

Kemp, Alice Abel and Pamela Jenkins. 1992. "Gender and Technological Hazards: Women at Risk in Hospital Settings." *Industrial Crisis Quarterly* 6:137–52.

Kliewer, Erich V. and Ken R. Smith. 1995. "Breast Cancer Mortality among Immigrants in Australia and Canada." *Journal of the National Cancer Institute* 87:1154–1161.

Koch, Lene. 1990. "IVF—An Irrational Choice?" *Issues in Reproductive and Genetic Engineering* 3:235–42.

Kranczer, Stanly. 1995. "U.S. Longevity Unchanged." *Statistical Bulletin* 76(3):12–20.

Krieger, Nancy. 1996. "U.S. Inequality, Diversity, and Health: Thoughts on 'Race/Ethnicity' and 'Gender.'" *Journal of the American Medical Women's Association* 51:133–36.

Kurz, Demie. 1987. "Emergency Department Response to Battered Women: A Case of Resistance." *Social Problems* 34:501–13.

Lai, Gina. 1995. "Work and Family Roles and Psychological Well-Being in Urban China." *Journal of Health and Social Behavior* 36:11–37.

Lennon, Mary Clare and Sara Rosenfeld. 1992. "Women and Mental Health: The Interaction of Job and Family Conditions." *Journal of Health and Social Behavior* 33:31–27.

Lieberman, Ellice, Kenneth J. Ryan, Richard R. Monson, and Stephen C. Schoenbaum. 1987. "Risk Factors Accounting for Racial Differences in the Rate of Premature Birth." *New England Journal of Medicine* 317:743–48.

Lightfoot-Klein, Hanny. 1989. *Prisoners of Ritual: An Odyssey into Female Circumcision in Africa*. New York: Harrington Park Press.

Lillard, Lee A. and Linda J. Waite. 1995. "'Til Death Do Us Part: Marital Disruption and Mortality." *American Journal of Sociology* 100:1131–56.

Link, Bruce G. and Jo Phelan. 1995. "Social Conditions as Fundamental Causes of Disease." *Journal of Health and Social Behavior* (Extra Issue):80–94.

Longino, Charles F., Jr. 1988. "A Population Profile of Very Old Men and Women in the United States." *Sociological Quarterly* 29:559–64.

Lorber, Judith and Dorothy Greenfeld. 1990. "Couples' Experiences with *In Vitro* Fertilization: A Phenomenological Approach. Pp. 965–71 in S. Mashiach et al. (eds.), *Advances in Assisted Reproductive Technologies*. New York: Plenum.

Lorber, Judith and Lakshmi Bandlamudi. 1993. "Dynamics of Marital Bargaining in Male Infertility." *Gender & Society* 7:32–49.

Lorber, Judith. 1987. "*In Vitro* Fertilization and Gender Politics." *Women & Health* 13:117–33.

Lorber, Judith. 1989. "Choice, Gift, or Patriarchal Bargain? Women's Consent to *In Vitro* Fertilization in Male Infertility." *Hypatia* 4:23–36.

Luker, Kristin. 1996. *Dubious Conceptions: The Politics of Teen Pregnancy*. Cambridge, MA: Harvard University Press.

MacFarqhar, Neil. 1996. "Mutilation of Egyptian Girls: Despite Ban, It Goes On." *The New York Times*, August 8, p. A3.

Maddi, Salvatore R. and Suzanne C. Kobasa. 1984. *The Hardy Executive: Health under Stress*. Homewood, IL: Dow Jones-Irwin.

Mansfield, Alan, and Barbara McGinn. 1993. "Pumping Irony: The Muscular and the Feminine." Pp. 49–68 in Sue Scott and David Morgan (eds.), *Body Matters: Essays on the Sociology of the Body*. London: Falmer Press.

Marsiglio, William. 1988. "Commitment to Social Fatherhood: Predicting Adolescent Males' Intentions to Live with Their Child and Partner." *Journal of Marriage and the Family* 50:427–41.

McKinlay, John B. 1996. "Some Contributions from the Social System to Gender Inequalities in Heart Disease." *Journal of Health and Social Behavior* 37:1–26.

Messner, Michael. 1992. *Power at Play: Sports and the Problem of Masculinity*. Boston: Beacon Press.

Muller, Charlotte. 1990. *Health Care and Gender*. New York: Russell Sage.

Nachtigall, Lila E. and Lisa B. Nachtigall. 1995. "Estrogen Issues in Relation to Cardiovascular Disease." *Journal of the American Medical Women's Association* 50:7–10.

Nachtigall, Robert D., Gay Becker, and Mark Wozny. 1992. "The Effects of Gender-specific Diagnosis on Men's and Women's Responses to Infertility." *Fertility and Sterility* 57:113–21.

Nam, Charles B., Isaac W. Eberstein, and Larry C. Deeb. 1989. "Sudden Infant Death Syndrome as a Socially Determined Cause of Death." *Social Biology* 36:1–8.

Nsiah-Jefferson, Laurie and Elaine J. Hall. 1989. "Reproductive Technology: Perspectives and Implications for Low-income Women and Women of Color." Pp. 93–117 in Kathryn Strother Ratcliff (ed.), *Healing Technology: Feminist Perspectives*. Ann Arbor: University of Michigan Press.

Oleckno, William A. and Michael J. Blacconiere. 1990. "Wellness of College Students and Differences by Gender, Race, and Class Standing." *College Student Journal* 24:421–29.

Orden, Susan R., Kiang Liu, Karen J. Ruth, David R. Jacobs, Jr., Diane E. Bild, and Joyce Serwitz. 1995. "Multiple Social Roles and Blood Pressure of Black and White Women: The CARDIA Study." *Journal of Women's Health* 4:281–91.

Ouellette, Suzanne K. 1993. "Inquiries into Hardiness." Pp. 77–100 in L. Goldberger and S. Breznitz (eds.), *Handbook of Stress: Theoretical and Clinical Aspects*, 2nd ed. New York: Free Press.

Palermo, G. D., J. Cohen, and Z. Rosenwaks. 1996. "Intracytoplasmic Sperm Injection a Powerful Tool to Overcome Fertilization Failure." *Fertility and Sterility* 65:899–908.

Perkins, H. Wesley. 1992. "Gender Patterns in Consequences of Collegiate Alcohol Abuse: A 10-Year Study of Trends in an Undergraduate Population." *Journal of Studies on Alcohol* 53:458–62.

Phillips, David P. and Kenneth A. Feldman. 1973. "A Dip in Deaths Before Ceremonial Occasions: Some New Relationships Between Social Integration and Mortality." *American Sociological Review* 38:678–96.

Phillips, David P. and Elliot W. King. 1988. "Death Takes a Holiday: Mortality Surrounding Major Social Occasions." *Lancet* 337:728–32.

Phillips, David P., Todd E. Ruth, and Lisa M. Wagner. 1993. "Psychology and Survival." *Lancet* 342:1142–45.

Phillips, David P. and Daniel G. Smith. 1990. "Postponement of Death Until Symbolically Meaningful Occasions." *Journal of the American Medical Association* 263:1947–51.

Ptacek, James. 1988. "Why Do Men Batter Their Wives?" Pp. 133–57 in Kersti Yllö and Michele Bograd (eds.), *Feminist Perspectives on Wife Abuse*. Newbury Park, CA: Sage.

Redmond, Marcia A. 1985. "Attitudes of Adolescent Males toward Adolescent Pregnancy and Fatherhood." *Family Relations* 34:337–42.

Renteln, Alison Dundes. 1992. "Sex Selection and Reproductive Freedom." *Women's Studies International Forum* 15:405–26.

Reunanen, Antti. 1993. "Juhlan Aika Ja Tuonen Hetki" ("The Time of Celebration and the Time of Death"). *Duodecim* 109:2098–103.

Richie, Beth E. 1996. *Compelled to Crime: The Gender Entrapment of Battered Black Women*. New York: Routledge.

Robbins, Cynthia A. and Steven S. Martin. 1993. "Gender, Styles of Deviance, and Drinking Problems." *Journal of Health and Social Behavior* 34:302–21.

Rogers, Richard G. and Eve Powell-Griner. 1991. "Life Expectancies of Cigarette Smokers and Nonsmokers in the United States." *Social Science and Medicine* 32:1151–59.

Romito, Patrizia and Françoise Hovelaque. 1987. "Changing Approaches in Women's Health: New Insights and New Pitfalls in Prenatal Preventive Care." *International Journal of Health Services* 17:241–58.

Rosenberg, Harriet G. 1984. "The Home is the Workplace: Hazards, Stress, and Pollutants in the Household." Pp. 219–45 in Wendy Chavkin (ed.), *Double Exposure: Women's Health Hazards on the Job and at Home*. New York: Monthly Press.

Ross, Catherine E. and Chloe E. Bird. 1994. "Sex Stratification and Health Lifestyle: Consequences for Men's and Women's Perceived Health." *Journal of Health and Social Behavior* 35:161–78.

Rothman, Barbara Katz. 1982. *In Labor: Women and Power in the Birthplace*. New York: Norton.

Rushing, Beth, Christian Ritter, and Russell P. D. Burton. 1992. "Race Differences in the Effects of Multiple Roles on Health: Longitudinal Evidence from a National Sample of Older Men" *Journal of Health and Social Behavior* 33:126–39.

Santow, Gigi. 1995. "Social Roles and Physical Health: The Case of Female Disadvantage in Poor Countries." *Social Science and Medicine* 40:147–61.

Sen, Amartya K. 1990. "Gender and Cooperative Conflicts." Pp. xx–xx in Irene Tinker (ed.), *Persistent Inequalities: Women and World Development*. New York: Oxford University Press.

Spark, Richard F. 1988. *The Infertile Male: The Clinician's Guide to Diagnosis and Treatment*. New York: Plenum.

Specter, Michael. 1995. "Plunging Life Expectancy Puzzles Russians." *The New York Times*, 2 August.

Staples, Robert. 1995. "Health among Afro-American Males." Pp. 121–8 in Don Sabo and David Frederick Gordon (eds.), *Men's Health and Illness: Gender, Power and the Body*. Newbury Park, CA: Sage.

Stillion, Judith. 1995. "Premature Death among Males: Extending the Bottom Line of Men's Health." Pp. 46–7 in Don Sabo and David Frederick Gordon (eds.), *Men's Health and Illness: Gender, Power and the Body*. Newbury Park, CA: Sage.

Sundari, T. K. 1994. "The Untold Story: How the Health Care systems in Developing Countries Contribute to Maternal Mortality." Pp. 173–90 in Elizabeth Fee and Nancy Krieger (eds.), *Women's Health, Politics, and Power.* Amityville, NY: Baywood.

Taggart, Lee Ann, Susan L. McCammon, Linda J. Allred, Ronnie D. Horner, Harold J. May. 1993. "Effect of Patient and Physician Gender on Prescriptions for Psychotropic Drugs." *Journal of Women's Health* 2:353–57.

Thompson, Becky Wansgaard. 1992. " 'A Way Outa No Way': Eating Problems among African-American, Latina, and White Women." *Gender & Society* 6:546:61.

Turner, R. Jay, Carl F. Grindstaff and Norma Phillips. 1990. "Social Support and Outcome in Teenage Pregnancy." *Journal of Health and Social Behavior* 31:43–57.

Van Roosmalen, Erica H. and Susan A. McDaniel. 1992. "Adolescent Smoking Intentions: Gender Differences in Peer Context." *Adolescence* 27:87–105.

Veevers, Jean E. and Ellen M. Gee 1986. "Playing It Safe: Accident Mortality and Gender Roles." *Sociological Focus* 19:349–60.

Verbrugge, Lois M. 1985. "Gender and Health: An Update on Hypotheses and Evidence." *Journal of Health and Social Behavior* 26:156–82.

Verbrugge, Lois M. 1986. "Role Burdens and Physical Health of Women and Men." *Women & Health* 11:47–77.

Verbrugge, Lois M. 1989a. "The Twain Meet: Empirical Explanations of Sex Differences in Health and Mortality." *Journal of Health and Social Behavior* 30:282–304.

Verbrugge, Lois M. 1989b. "Gender, Aging, and Health." Pp. 23–78 in Kyriakos S. Markides (ed.), *Aging and Health: Perspectives on Gender, Race, Ethnicity, and Class.* Newbury Park, CA: Sage.

Verbrugge, Lois M. 1990. "Pathways of Health and Death." Pp. 41–49 in Rima D. Apple (ed.), *Women, Health and Medicine in America.* New York: Garland.

Vogel, Lise. 1990. "Debating Difference: Feminism, Pregnancy, and the Workplace." *Feminist Studies* 16:9–32.

Waldron, Ingrid. 1995. "Contributions of Changing Gender Differences in Behavior and Social Roles to Changing Gender Differences in Mortality." Pp. 22–45 in Don Sabo and David Frederick Gordon (eds.), *Men's Health and Illness: Gender, Power and the Body.* Newbury Park, CA: Sage.

Walker, Lenore E. 1984. *The Battered Woman Syndrome.* New York: Springer.

Warshaw, Carole. 1989. "Limitations of the Medical Model in the Case of Battered Women." *Gender & Society* 3:506–17.

Weitz, Rose. 1996. *The Sociology of Health, Illness, and Health Care: A Critical Approach.* Belmont, CA: Wadsworth.

Wilcox, Allen, Rolv Skjaerven, and Pierre Buekens. 1995. "Birth Weight and Perinatal Mortality: A Comparison of the United States and Norway." *Journal of the American Medical Association* 273:709–11.

Wilson, Margo and Martin Daly. 1985. "Competitiveness, Risk Taking, and Violence: The Young Male Syndrome." *Ethology and Sociobiology* 6:59–73.

World Health Organization. 1995. *Women's Health: Improve our Health, Improve the World.* Position paper, Fourth World Conference on Women, Beijing, China.

Yllö, Kersti. 1984. "The Status of Women, Marital Equality, and Violence against Wives." *Journal of Family Issues* 5:307–20.

Ziegler, R.G. 1993. "Migration Patterns and Breast Cancer Risk in Asian-American Women." *Journal of the National Cancer Institute* 85:1819–27.

Section II

Theories and Perspectives on Health and Illness

As with any discipline, there are various ways to approach data and issues. In this section, we examine some of the more modern approaches that are commonly employed in medical sociology. Although medical sociologists do not always adhere to strictly defined perspectives as illustrated here, they often enough define themselves and others as belonging to particular schools of thought. These selections may also help you to identify your own point of view and to critically assess works you will read in this field in light of it.

At the core of *Perspectives in Medical Sociology* is the notion that biomedical knowledge alone is insufficient to explain health and illness and to understand the ways in which people and institutions deal with health and illness. This core belief is central to newer approaches to medical sociology that criticize the narrow *medical model* for its reliance on solely biological levels of explanations.

The critique of the medical model has led many sociologists to develop a *social construction of illness* perspective which posits that health matters are like other social problems in that they may exist for a long time before they are perceived as problems. For example, incest, child abuse, and spouse abuse have long been present in family life. Yet only with the growth of modern social movements, especially the women's movement, have these problems been brought to public attention. The definition of something as a problem involves the social conflict between those who would gain and those who would lose from such a perception. In some cases, the gains and losses involve people or groups of people, such as professional groupings (e.g., psychiatrists, alcoholism counselors). At other times, they involve overarching social institutions. For instance, in the case of family violence and incest, the losses accrue to the conservative and traditional patriarchal family structure that has produced and condoned such actions.

To cite another example, we now regard lead poisoning as an important health hazard, yet it required action from radical health professionals and black and Puerto Rican community activists in the 1960s and 1970s to bring this problem to public attention. In this case, the "losers" included large landlords faced with the cost of lead paint removal and paint manufacturers faced with revisions of their production process. This phenomenon of social movements bringing attention to health hazards will return in the next section on Environmental and Occupational Health, and an article specifically on lead poisoning appears in the last section on Social Movements, Social Change, and Health.

Phil Brown's "Naming and Framing: The Social Construction Of Diagnosis and Illness" develops this social constructionist approach, seeing it as a synthesis of symbolic interactionism and structural/political economic approaches. This perspective looks at how a social or medical problem was identified and acted upon, taking into account the underlying social stratification system, and the roles of professionals, institutions, government, pharmaceutical companies, patients, and their families. Using this approach, we ask why did a condition get identified at a certain point in time, why was action taken or not, who benefits by identification of the issue, and how do divergent perspectives on the problem conflict with each other?

A number of modern sociologists have adopted a *medicalization* viewpoint, which is very much akin to the constructionist perspective discussed above. Writers in this tradition believe that a large number of social problems which are not primarily or solely medical, have come under the medical gaze. In particular, many life processes which are ordinary and routine have been defined and treated as deviations from a norm of health. Usually this means taking away the social context of the problem, and focusing primarily on the labeled individual. In "Medicalization and Social Control," Peter Conrad, a key formulator of the concept of medicalization, updates this important concept. He notes that some areas of life are being *demedicalized*, taken (in whole or part) out of the realm of medical definitions. Conrad also points out that some forms of medicalization do not take away a social context for suffering but actually add that context. An example is viewing post-traumatic stress disorder as the result of a wartime or sexual trauma, rather than simply an individual problem. This puts the blame on social structures rather than individual people.

Susan Bell's "Experiences of Illness and Narrative Understandings" takes up an approach that has recently offered interesting new ways to look at the experience of illness—the narrative approach. She shows how attention to people's narratives of illness and clinical encounters can situate those experiences in the appropriate social context, a context far more complex than just the biomedical definition of disease. Bell takes up issues of the sociology of knowledge— how do we come to know certain facts and relationships? She also addresses the growing awareness of reflexivity in research—how does the researcher's presence affect the reality of the observed person's experience?

In recent years, we have come to understand that *stress* is a significant factor in producing ill health. We have also learned that people's *social supports* and the ways in which people *cope* with stress are important influences on how stress affects their health and help seeking. The growing importance attached to stress is manifested in current approaches toward health education, corporate wellness programs, and stress reduction courses. Leonard Pearlin and Carol Aneshensel's article, "Stress, Coping, and Social Supports," points to four major ways in which coping and social supports affect stress: preventing the stressful condition, altering the stressful condition, changing the meaning of the situation, and managing stress symptoms.

4

Naming and Framing: The Social Construction of Diagnosis and Illness

Phil Brown

The social construction of diagnosis and illness is a central organizing theme in medical sociology. By studying how illness is socially constructed, we examine how social forces shape our understanding of and actions toward health, illness, and healing. We explore the effects of class, race, gender, language, technology, culture, the political economy, and institutional and professional structures and norms in shaping the knowledge base that produces our assumptions about the prevalence, incidence, treatment, and meaning of disease.

Despite the fact that the notion of social construction is such a common organizing theme, it is rarely defined in a systematic fashion and has many meanings that are often divergent. This chapter seeks to refine our understanding of the social construction of diagnosis and illness. It begins by examining the multiplicity of competing versions of social constructionism and by pointing out the problems of relativism in the traditional approaches. I then put forth a new version of social constructionism, which synthesizes elements of symbolic interactionist and structural/political economic approaches. Next I discuss the major role of diagnosis in social construction, leading to the need for a sociology of diagnosis. I emphasize controversial and conflictual diagnoses as a first step toward a more general sociology of diagnosis. Following that I put forth a typology of social construction of diagnosis, involving four combinations based on whether a condition is generally accepted and whether a biomedical definition is applied. Next I detail a series of stages in the social construction of a condition. In that process, I turn attention both to the initial social discovery (essentially a matter of diagnosis) and to illness experience. This is followed by stages of treatment and outcome, which recursively affect social construction. I conclude by noting the health policy implications of the social constructionist perspective.

Reprinted with permission of the American Sociological Association from the *Journal of Health and Social Behavior*, Vol. 33, pp. 267–81, copyright © 1995.

Definitions and Disputes—Versions of Social Construction

There are three main versions of social constructionism that apply to medical sociology. The first, and most prominent, draws on the work of Spector and Kitsuse (1977, p. 75) and argues that social problems are the "activities of individuals or groups making assertions of grievances and claims with respect to some putative conditions." The Spector and Kitsuse perspective is not concerned with whether there is a real condition; the focus of interest is the social definition. The early social constructionists were concerned with formulating a break with a positivist worldview that saw social facts, including social problems, as given and measurable entities. Using ethnomethodology, symbolic interactionism, and related approaches and theories, social problems scholars sought to uncover the hidden world of everyday interaction and definition making. This includes approaches based on the "micropolitics of trouble," interest group competition for public resources, claimsmaking by the media, and workplace constructions of meanings.

Much debate on social constructionism centers on the degree of "reality" in phenomena—are social problems objectively real, or are they created by purposive action of social labelers and problem finders? Best (1989) makes a distinction between "contextual constructionism" and "strict constructionism." Contextual constructionism gives credence to the actual condition, though it does not put primary emphasis on the condition. Strict constructionism deals only with the claims made by social actors, not the putative condition itself. For the strict approach, even statistics purporting to provide prevalence of the condition are suspect, since such statistics are also a form of construction and ought receive no more credence than other claims. Woolgar and Pawluch (1985) argue that social constructionists actually do have a "realist" position, since they choose certain issues for their attention. These issues apparently have a constant reality but only become important when the scholar chooses to analyze them. Hence, Woolgar and Pawluch tell us, there is a selective realism in constructionism.

Strict constructionists believe that constructionism challenges sociological realism and centers itself on the "assumption that social realities are accomplished through interactional and interpretive practices." They somehow make the leap that such constructionism "cannot be subsumed within more general, realist theories of society" (Miller and Holstein 1993b). I cannot see why a solid sociological framework cannot argue for the centrality of structural/political-economic factors, while also posing an interpretive, reflexive approach.

This first version of social constructionism is the one most commonly employed by medical sociologists. Social constructionism, as traditionally defined, can contribute to an understanding of how health and illness are rife with biased definitions and forms of social control; it can help us learn about experience of illness and clinical interaction. But traditional constructionism is limited, since it refuses to accept any elements of a structural perspective, in particular the notion that fundamental social structures of the society play key roles in health and illness. These include the core stratification elements of race, class, and gender, as well as professional and institutional factors.

For example, much medical sociology in the social constructionist vein focuses on talk. This makes sense, given that symbolic interactionism emphasizes the human agency in people's exchanges of meanings. Yet to focus on talk is a simplification of the larger meaning of interaction. In creating meanings and interpretations, people's interaction also includes how they play out their social roles, and how they relate to professional and institutional structures where the interaction takes place. Put otherwise, there must be a context for talk. Interestingly, a number of scholars who support a strong conversational analysis or discourse analysis perspective actually do provide a contextualization, even if they still view the discourse as central (cf. Mishler 1984).

A second version of constructionism, based more on European postmodern theory, originates as early as Foucault's (1961) *Madness and Civilization*. The postmodern approach shares with the more American constructionism a critique of positivism. But postmodern approaches would be dissatisfied with other constructionist emphasis on given sets of social actors, groups, and institutions. Instead, postmodernist approaches would say that to even center on those sets of institutions and actors is a false reliance on existing structures. The postmodern alternative is to deconstruct language and symbols in order to show the creation of knowledge, and to explore the ever changing, indeterminate "realities" of the situation. Interestingly, this departs from the original approach of Foucault, who, despite his emphasis on language and definition making, based his analysis of asylum creation on the transition from feudalism to capitalism, migration, and the development of the psychiatric profession. Actually, some scholarship based on Foucault does take such a social approach. Armstrong (1983) looks at the social production of knowledge as a result of changes in social perceptions of space and time, including the proper location (home or institution) of medical care.

Turner's (1992:151–174) development of a sociology of the body also stems from Foucault. It is concerned with symbolism, in that most of the symbols and rituals in social structures are focused on actions regarding the body. Turner is mainly concerned with the embodied person as an active agent of social action. This postmodern constructionism views the legacy of medical social control as specifically targeted at the body; control may be in terms of physical and emotional health, as well as by the moral cultures of self-beautification and self-maintenance.

There is a third constructionist approach more related to the sociology of science. This viewpoint, most associated with Latour (1987), argues that the production of scientific facts is the result of mutually conceived actions by scientists in the workaday life of the laboratory, combined with scientists' efforts to promote their work in public and official venues. This "science in action" perspective is worth noting, since a number of medical sociologists utilize elements of the sociology of science. This approach is useful for medical sociology in examining the work of professionals' discovery of disease and the development of medical technology, though it is less valuable when considering elements of lay discovery and of interaction between people/patients and the world of medicine.

So we have seen that there are many different opinions about what social constructionism means. Medical sociologists have frequently used this term in a very broad-stroke fashion. For example, Bury (1986) conceives of social constructionism as a broad umbrella, containing often contradictory elements that range from those who believe in a perfectly relativist standpoint to those using political-economic analyses. Bury's broad umbrella even includes some perspectives that ignore cultural features, something quite against the grain of any social constructionism. The wide variety of definitions of social constructionism belies any claim that there is a unitary social constructionist theory or perspective.

A New Version of Social Construction

I view social constructionism as a synthesis of symbolic interactionism and structural/political economic approaches. Depending on the subject matter, one or the other of these two may predominate, though ultimately we should be moving toward a greater synthesis of these two approaches. The symbolic interactionist/structural synthesis I propose is, in truth, hardly a new theoretical statement. In practice, this synthesis is widely found in much of medical sociology. Freidson's (1970) pathbreaking *Profession of Medicine* is the best example, with a whole section of five chapters called "The Social Construction of Illness." Other leading medical sociologists have made similar linkages (Waitzkin 1989; Zola 1972), and much published work in the field does so, too, even without specifically stating it. Even some of the postmodernist medical sociologists, who criticize conflict-oriented social structural approaches, wind up referring to the pervasive power of social institutions and structures. Turner's (1992) sociology of the body, for example, sees the importance of commodity production and advertising in the creation of socially constructed notions of proper bodies.

It is important from the outset to note that the *social construction of medical knowledge* is distinct from the *social construction of illness*; traditional constructionist writing generally has not taken this into account. The social construction of medical knowledge deals mainly with the origins of professional beliefs, and with diagnosis. It deals with the ways of knowing that are based on the dominant biomedical framework, contemporary moral and ethical views, the socialization of medical providers (especially physicians), the professional and institutional practices of the health-care system, and the larger social structures of the society. Here, we are more concerned with diagnosis and the structural approach predominates. Scholarship on the construction of medical knowledge includes social factors such as: professional advancement (Freidson 1970; Wright and Treacher 1982), patriarchal attitudes (Scully 1980), and corporate and imperialist labor market needs (Walsh 1987; E. Brown 1979).

The social construction of illness deals mainly with the illness experience. It has to do with a more interactionist approach of experience at personal, dyadic, and group levels. Here we are concerned with the lay experience of illness, and the symbolic interactionist approach predominates (this is discussed more extensively in a later section). Of course the constructions of medical knowledge and illness are connected, in that people deal with their own and others' illnesses largely in accordance with the dominant social elements of medical knowledge.

Using the framework I have laid out, we may consider the social construction of a phenomenon to involve a multiplicity of social forces that combine to create and modify the phenomenon. Rather than a given biomedical fact, we have a set of understandings, relationships, and actions that are shaped by diverse kinds of knowledge, experience, and power relations and that are constantly in flux.

This social constructionist perspective looks at how the phenomenon was identified and acted upon. This involves the impact of the underlying social stratification system, and the roles of professionals, institutions, governments, media, pharmaceutical companies, patients, and people with illness and disabilities as well as their families. This social constructionism requires us to ask questions such as: Why did a condition get identified at a certain point in time? Why was action taken or not taken? Who benefits, or at least avoids trouble, by identification and action? How did the divergent perspectives on the phenomenon merge or clash? How does the person's experience of the illness affect the course of the disease, as well as the social outcome of the illness?

With this social constructionist perspective, medical sociology can link together and make social sense of health and illness across three levels: the micro-level (such as self-awareness, individual action, and interpersonal communication), meso-level (such as hospitals, medical education), and macro-level (such as the nation's health status, the structure and political-economy of the health care system, and national health policy). By analyzing these three levels of knowledge and action, we are better able to understand the consequences of health policy.

My approach asks that we take a critical look at the world of medicine, but we do not view that world as an epiphenomenon. It is quite possible to believe that biomedical components are important, while still emphasizing both social forces and people's interactive definition making (Lock 1988). We are, after all, talking about phenomena that occur in people's bodies. If we do not take this reality seriously, our search for socially constructed definitions will be very short-sighted. I cannot see that an appreciation of actual conditions must automatically prevent us from grasping the social construction of the definition and treatment.

My scope is not to synthesize the voluminous literature on social construction.[1] Rather, I intend to develop theoretical and analytic tools for understanding and furthering this perspective.

One of my differences with much traditional social constructionism is that it fails to deal with aspects of social causation. Because traditional constructionism holds that there are no constituted, objective problems, it obviously believes that social causation is irrelevant. My viewpoint on this is that medical sociology loses its explanatory power if it denies social causation. The next section locates causation centrally within the bounds of social construction.

Social Causation and Social Construction

The *social causation* of health status is actually a prerequisite, or at least a concurrent requirement for the perspective put forth here. One of the cardinal principles of the sociology of health and illness is that social factors are integral to health status. Causation encompasses three categories: (1) *Underlying social causes*, such as social structural elements of the society (e.g., class, race, sex, or military spending); (2) *proximate social causes*, such as neighborhood structure, migration, environmental and workplace hazards; and (3) *mediating social causes*, such as social supports, social networks, marital and family status.

There is no room to go into even the briefest of summaries of the literature on social causation, but the reader is referred to the first section of this reader on Social Inequality, Health and Illness. But it is worth noting that some scholars might accept a wide variety of explanations of social causation of health and illness yet not accept a social constructionist approach to understanding the person's experience of illness, the professional role in defining problems, and issues of service delivery. For example, they might readily agree that class, gender, and race affect the epidemiologic distribution of psychosis or cardiovascular disease but might not consider relevant to a causal model that social actors and institutions affect the labeling, discovery, and treatment of those conditions. Because of this possibility, we need both social causation and social constructionist explanations to produce a complete view.

Social construction begins with social discovery, the ways in which people, organizations, and institutions determine that there is a disease or condition. Other components of social constructions follow: the experience of illness, decisions regarding treatment, and social understandings of what constitutes outcomes. Later, I will present an outline of these stages of social construction, since my intent is to propose a general model. Within this, my primary focus will be on diagnosis, with a secondary focus on illness experience. These two areas are the most fertile locations for observing social construction. Illness experience has been more widely studied and hence is a secondary focus here. Since diagnosis has been less developed, I now proceed with a general discussion of the logic of a sociology of diagnosis.

The Logic of a Sociology of Diagnosis

Diagnosis is integral to the theory and practice of medicine. For social scientists the process of making the diagnosis is central to subsequent constructions of illness. Diagnosis represents the time and location where medical professionals and other parties determine the existence and legitimacy of a condition. Diagnosis is a matter of the "politics of definitions" (Conrad and Schneider 1992, p. 22), whereby illness designations are created from social conflict. Diagnostic discovery is frequently laden with disputes, which provides a lens for viewing many of the social conflicts that revolve around issues of medicine and health.

Yet despite the frequent discussion of diagnostic concerns in medical sociological research on illness, scholars have not elaborated the common threads of diagnostic processes. We see many examinations of the social construction of a particular disease entity, with some attention paid to diagnostic issues. Indeed, a considerable body of work in medical sociology is concerned with lay-professional differences in disease and illness conception and experience, and with the social construction of disease (cf. Freidson 1970; Schneider and Conrad 1981). That research directly touches on diagnostic issues, although they are not usually considered specifically as such. Most specific studies of diagnosis are in studies of psychiatry. While this can help us in developing a general view of diagnosis, it is not sufficient, largely since there are specifics about psychiatric diagnosis which are not completely generalizable. In particular, there is more room in psychiatry for a high degree of interpretation and direct bias, which we see far less in medicine. For example, competing schools within psychiatry (e.g., psychoanalytic and biopsychiatric) hold tremendously divergent beliefs on the very existence of certain conditions.

One reason for emphasizing diagnosis is found in a core assumption of medical sociology—the distinction between disease and illness (Schneider and Conrad 1981). *Disease* is a more biomedical phenomenon, though strongly affected by social forces. The distribution of disease and death differs on the basis of class, race, sex, ethnicity, education, and other social factors. The key issue here is how social position or social factors affect the production of disease. *Illness* reflects a more subjective phenomenon. The same social forces that affect the distribution of disease also lead to varying perceptions, conceptions and experiences of health status. This explains why people differ in making their way to various providers and institutions to seek care. In particular, some people with the same symptoms or conditions as others choose widely disparate ways of dealing with those symptoms or conditions. These structurally different perceptions then cloud the treatment encounter.

For sociology, Blaxter (1978) tells us, diagnosis has two meanings—*process* and *category*. Process is the set of interactions which leads to the definition of the category and to its imposition in particular cases. This is the core of my discussion of social discovery. Category is the nosological location in medical knowledge where the diagnosis resides. This involves the often-reified definitions of disease into which professionals and others fit their observations. In both of Blaxter's types—process meaning and category meaning—diagnosis has various functions. For patients, diagnosis can provide personal, emotional control by knowing what is wrong. For medical professionals, diagnosis also provides control by mastering the knowledge of the problem at the individual care level. As well, diagnosis frequently determines the course of treatment, though treatment also is determined by many other factors. For both patient and professional, diagnosis can lead to a prognosis. Physicians also employ diagnosis as a vehicle for building the whole body of medical knowledge.

Diagnosis is central to the work of all medical professionals. Differential diagnosis is probably the most rewarded skill for medical students and doctors in training. As Balint (1957) discusses, physicians are confronted with what is often an "unorganized illness," an agglomeration of complaints and symptoms which may be unclear, unconnected, and mysterious. Their job is to understand and interpret that material in order to arrive at an "organized illness." In other cases, patients may present more clear-cut material that requires less organizing work. Certainly much medical work consists of routine diagnoses of problems, many of which are not conflicted or political. I am less concerned with the routine, nonconflictual diagnoses of daily medical work. My focus primarily concerns the conflicted diagnoses because they offer a window into some of the most pressing issues of power in medical experience.

For socially powerful groups and institutions, diagnosis can be a tool for social control, such as the medical labeling of homosexuality as mental illness. Our conception of medicalization (Conrad 1992) involves social control at very routine levels of socialization, labeling of behavior, and prescriptions for medical intervention. Diagnosis is central to such social control, since *giving the name* has often been the starting point for social labelers. Diagnosis is a *language of medicine*, a crucial component of what Elliot Mishler (1984) calls the "voice of medicine," in contrast to the "voice of the life-world." Diagnosis locates the parameters of normality and abnormality, demarcates the professional and institutional boundaries of the social control and treatment system, and authorizes medicine to label and deal with people on behalf of the society at large. This labeling is often enough the legal basis for provision of health services, welfare benefits, unemployment certification, worker's compensation claims, and legal testimony (Zola 1972; Brown 1990).

Diagnostic categories are often fought out as turf battles between medicalizers and their opponents, as in alcoholism, drug abuse, and child abuse. For social groups that have been in subservient roles, diagnosis can give credence to conditions that may legitimate their suffering as well as legitimize themselves. It offers them a tool for engaging in politically charged definitional settings. Black lung, environmental disease, and posttraumatic stress disorder (PTSD) are good examples. Victims of violence and sexual abuse can benefit from a diagnosis, in this case PTSD, because it removes the blame from the victim, takes a social view of the problem, and opens the door for access to care and insurance coverage (Scott 1990).

Last, for sociologists and other scholars, diagnosis serves as a pathway into the history of medical knowledge and practice. We can also understand the relationship between medical knowledge and other forms of social knowledge and action. After all, Blaxter (1978) tells us, diagnosis is "a museum of past and present concepts of the nature of disease." Taking that one step further than just concepts, I believe we can view diagnosis also as the *sociomedical archives* wherein we find the history of action by all levels of the health care system. These archival elements of diagnosis are found, for example, in succeeding revisions of the American Psychiatric Association's Diagnostic and Statistical Manual (DSM) or the International Classification of Diseases (ICD). They are also found in the textbooks of medicine. These archives also include the records of legislation, regulation, and litigation that have given names and meaning to conditions. Mass media and public beliefs also are found in these sociomedical archives, for those historically changing public understandings are important components of social action concerning diagnoses.

Theoretical and Analytical Models

I present here two ways to theoretically and analytically understand social construction processes. The first is a more theoretical approach that deals with diagnosis. It is a typology of conditions and definitions that locates commonalities across four categories of social construction. This model is useful for a "rough cut" that provides a broad category of social construction of disease. This allows us to better refine our concepts of social constructionism. With this in hand we then must trace the development of the construction. For this, the second, a more analytical and procedural approach, follows from the first. It is a stages model, which is more useful in examining the chronology of social construction, beginning with social discovery. It helps us to identify the range of social actors involved in disease discovery and illness experience and provides a framework for future case studies.

A Typology of Conditions and Definitions

Social construction involves a real or putative *condition* and a *biomedical definition*. The condition is the disease, disability, or physical state. It is either generally *accepted* or *not accepted* as a biomedical entity. The biomedical definition is the presence or absence of a specific identification of the condition on the part of medical science. The biomedical definition is either *applied* or *not applied*. The *definitional setting* is the way that these two elements interact, and the social construction of a condition is shaped. The following typology illustrates this.[2]

Figure 1
Typology of Conditions and Definitions

	Condition generally accepted	Condition not generally accepted, or condition is questionable
Biomedical definition applied	1 Routinely Defined Conditions (infectious diseases, chronic diseases, injuries)	2 Medicalized Definitions (late luteal phase dysphoric disorder, chronic fatigue syndrome, chronic pain syndrome)
Biomedical definition not applied, or there is conflict on making a definition	3 Contested Definitions (occupational diseases, environmentally induced diseases, multiple chemical sensitivity)	4 Potentially Medicalized Definitions (genetic predispositions to diseases)

In cell 1, we have *routinely defined conditions* which are usually *accepted*, and for which biomedical definitions are *applied*. These constitute probably the vast majority of situations. Diagnoses here are typically less conflictual than others and are not the main focus of this analysis. Nevertheless, there may be significant bargaining between patient and provider over the giving of a diagnosis. Recalling Balint's (1957) notion of the "unorganized illness" being "organized" by the doctor, we can picture situations where a person may on the one hand desire, or on the other hand fear or resist, a diagnosis that may have a large impact on them. When a cold is redefined as a flu, or sniffles as allergy, there may be social benefits for the patient, such as exemption from social responsibilities. When what begins as an acute injury is defined as a more serious and long-term disability, the person may face activity limitation, job loss, and stigma.

Since these cell-1 types are the vast majority of conditions, and since they tend to be the least conflictual, the social construction is more centered on the illness experience than on the diagnosis. Hence, despite the clarity of the biomedical definition and diagnosis, much of people's experience of these conditions involves adjustments and adaptations in nonmedical realms. The social construction of treatment is also relevant: choices are made about caregiving on the basis of local medical cultures, race, class, gender, insurance status, and other social variables (illness experience and treatment issues are discussed in more detail in the later section on stages of social construction).

In cell 2, there are *medicalized definitions*, cases where the condition is generally *not accepted* and/or is widely considered to be nonmedical, yet a biomedical definition is *applied*. Often, the labeling processes by which these diagnoses are made represent forms of social control. Sometimes these medicalized definitions are mainly a feature of professional expansionism, as with late luteal phase dysphoric disorder (LLPDD, the psychiatrized definition of premenstrual syndrome), and chemical dependency. In the cases of LLPDD, psychiatry enforces gender norms by pathologizing normal functioning. With chemical dependency, medicine replaces or collaborates with the criminal justice system.

In other cases, labeling is not a form of social control but is sought by people as a way to legitimate their condition. For instance, a diagnosis of chronic fatigue syndrome may be helpful in excusing absence from, or poor performance in, work or school. Chronic pain also may require similar legitimation. Here, there is a congruence with professional and institutional expansion; pain clinics have grown rapidly, treating what professionals often believe to be somaticized manifestations of psychological problems. Legitimation does not necessarily require secondary gain; it may be important for self-esteem for people to legitimate their complaints in their own and others' eyes.

Cell 3 includes *contested definitions*, situations where there are generally *accepted* conditions but no widely *applied* medical definition. Diseases caused by environmental and occupational exposures are a prime example of this. For example, many people complain of cancers, rashes, respiratory problems, immune-system dysfunction, and cardiac problems that they believe may be caused by a local contamination source. Medical and governmental authorities, however, are often unable and/or unwilling to recognize these conditions as syndromes or diseases attributable to contamination. This has occurred in numerous community and workplace toxic exposures, leading to a large social movement of toxic waste activists and to considerable epidemiological research confirming these environmental health effects. It has also occurred in military settings such as the Persian Gulf War, where early complaints of rashes, muscle and joint pain, headaches, and respiratory problems were initially disparaged; following considerable veterans' organizing and public discussion, Congress held hearings to push the military to study the phenomenon. Official and scientific opposition to these toxic effects is based on opposition to lay involvement in science and medicine, resistance to new etiological pathways, rigid criteria concerning sample sizes, a preference for false negatives over false positives, and fear of the political and economic consequences of recognizing the source (typically corporate and military) of contamination (Brown 1992).

Cell 4 contains *potentially medicalized definitions*, what we might consider a "latent" class of phenomena which are not *accepted* medical conditions and to which medical definitions *not been applied* yet might be in the future. Because there are so many bodily differences, there are endless possibilities for potential medicalization. The best current example is genetic screening, which increasingly locates characteristics that are not necessarily pathological but are "predispositions" to future conditions. These include predisposition to diseases based on known or estimated genetic ratios, including Huntington's Disease, various cancers, and hemophilia. When we talk about potential medicalization, we are talking here about the genes, not the actual diseases that might develop. Sometimes these are calculated on family genotypes, but often these are determined only on population-based estimates of predispositions, such as genetic markers for increased risk of cancer. Hence, data that may appear statistically sound in terms of large populations are used to clinically label individuals. These screening approaches wind up defining as pathology the genetic makeup, rather than the disease that may arise. For some professionals, predispositions are not *yet* conditions, while for others, predispositions will *never* become conditions. Genetic *differences* exist, but only certain parties decide that these are in fact *defects*, and therefore that they should be treated in certain ways, such as excluding people from particular jobs and from insurance coverage (Nelkin and Tancredi 1989; Draper 1991). Such insurance exclusion has indeed become well known as national discussions of health reform bring more such cases to light. Workplace exclusion policies are often carried out as "blaming-the-victim" responses that target individuals rather than workplace hazards.

Even non-genetic predispositions can fit into this potentially medicalized category. In the case of a predisposition to clinical hypertension, there is an arbitrary cutoff point of a certain blood pressure. For many people this pressure might never become clinical hyptertension. By locating blood tests to show a worker's higher susceptibility to lead poisoning, the company excludes the person rather than cleaning up the workplace environment. Whether the initial impetus is workplace or insurance exclusion, the person then has a medical record establishing them as having a certain medical condition.

Not all diagnoses will fit neatly into a single cell. Indeed, the ongoing social construction of diagnosis and illness means that there will be complexity and change. Sometimes the history of a condition and definition moves it from one cell to another. For instance, asbestos causes mesothelioma, but early attempts to make this case were challenged by many medical professionals and institutions. Hence, the particular relationship between asbestos and mesothelioma was denied, even though deniers might believe in other etiologies for the disease. It was originally a contested definition in cell 3. But a definitional shift occurred, mainly due to social activism, and finally this particular relationship was widely accepted, making it a cell-1 type of routinely defined condition.[3] Homosexuality was a cell-2 medicalized type for psychiatry until activist pressure convinced the American Psychiatric Association to delete homosexuality as a mental disorder.

Similarly, there are diagnoses which at a single point in time will fall into one cell for one group, and another cell for another. For example, late luteal phase dysphoric disorder (LLPDD) is a medicalized type (cell 2) for psychiatry, since a nonpsychiatric condition is labeled psychiatric. For gynecology and for many women's health organizations, however, there is no LLPDD entity but only a normal gynecological event, making it a routine type (cell 1) (see Figert 1993).

The above points on the changing nature of constructions informs us that the typology alone is insufficient, since it locates the type of the construction without necessarily tracing its development. Whether a construction remains as one type, or changes, we need to study the developmental components of that construction. That is the intent of the following scheme.

Stages of Social Construction of Disease

Finding the common elements in the process of the social discovery of disease can help identify the relative importance of various social forces across different disease discovery processes. Another advantage is that this stages model helps others to conduct new investigations. These stages typically occur chronologically, although not all cases will follow the precise order, nor will they necessarily go through all the stages.

There are some similarities between my model and Conrad and Schneider's (1992:266–271) "sequential model" of the medicalization of deviance. Conrad and Schneider argue that labelers first make a definition of behavior as deviance, prior to the existence of a medical definition. Second, medical professionals go "prospecting," wherein they float the medical definition for debate. In the third stage of claimsmaking, both medical and nonmedical parties engage in further delineating the problem as medical. Fourth comes legitimacy, usually through an appeal to state authority in legislatures and courtrooms. Finally, an institutionalization stage occurs when the definition is firmly within the official world. This sequential model is useful, but it specifically applies to medicalized definitions, for which it offers a rich framework. It would not, however, be applicable to contested definitions, such as toxic waste-induced diseases.

I place most of my emphasis on the first stage, "Identification and Diagnosis—The Social Discovery of Disease" and the second stage, "Illness Experience." The subsequent stages of "Treatment" and "Outcome" are certainly important, and indeed may recursively influence the social discovery and illness experience stages, but are not the main focus for now.

Identification and Diagnosis—Social Discovery of Disease

Lay initiation Stemming from a critique of the biomedical model, medical sociology understands that laypeople are often central to the discovery of diseases and conditions. People are often more aware, via direct experience, of problems which might not routinely come to medical attention.

The social construction of "conflictual" diseases involves lay (and usually a subsequent social movement) initiation of the discovery process. Conflictual diseases are those, such as toxic waste-induced diseases and iatrogenic effects of contraceptive technology, in which lay discovery conflicts with biomedical and other societal authority. Not all conflictual diagnoses are lay initiated. For instance, pediatricians and other physicians introduced hyperactivity as a condition, leading to considerable conflict both within and outside of medicine (Conrad 1975). But lay-initiated definitions are extremely likely to be conflictual by virtue of the lay source of discovery.

The social construction of disease also involves the ways in which "non-conflictual" diseases are discovered and/or defined. Very occasionally, lay discovery is central to non-conflictual diseases, as with Lyme Disease. This neurological disorder with potentially severe outcomes is transmitted via deer ticks. Residents of Southern New England pioneered in detection, and their efforts led to more specific diagnostic categorization, public health warnings, and research in epidemiology and treatment.

But usually, non-conflictual conditions are those where people are not trying to convince the world of medicine and the relevant social institutions. For such diseases and conditions (typically cell-1 types, according to the earlier typology), there is no dispute over the discovery of the disease because both laypeople and professionals already accept it as a medical condition; the social construction is a construction of the illness experience. For example, Schneider and Conrad (1981) contrast sociological typologies of epilepsy (e.g., pragmatic, secret, and unadjusted adaptation) with biomedical ones (e.g., grand mal, petit mal). These divergent typologies reflect different social positions of doctors and patients, as well as the fact that the patient is experiencing personal and social effects on his or her life, while the physician is dealing with a concrete biomedical entity.

On their own, lay discoveries may not succeed. Even if lay efforts are the initiators, sympathetic professionals (doctors, epidemiologists) and institutions (medical societies and philanthropies) are usually needed for successful claimsmaking. Frequently social movements are needed to propel such professional and institutional action.

Social movements   Social movements are central to many discovery processes. Lay discovery typically predates a social movement, though once a sufficient number of individuals recognize and act on a disease, they may form activist organizations to press their claims. These movements mainly have been in women's health, environmental health, occupational safety and health, civil rights, and disability rights/independent living. Some movements seek government and medical recognition of unrecognized or under-recognized diseases, such as black lung, sickle-cell anemia, and post-traumatic stress disorder. The disability rights movement has had a great impact on the conceptualization of many chronic diseases and conditions. Other movements seek to affirm the knowledge of yet-unknown etiological factors in already recognized diseases, such as the relationship between DES and vaginal cancer (Bell 1986). Some movements work to overturn medicalized definitions, e.g., homosexuality and LLPDD as mental illnesses (Kirk and Kutchins 1992; Figert 1993). Others act to affirm knowledge of yet unrecognized effects and side effects of medications and technologies, as with organizing around silicon breast implants (Zimmerman 1995). In some cases, prior formation of social movements makes it easier for newly discovered diseases to be identified and pursued. For instance, once a women's health movement exists, it is more likely to rapidly deal with new problems, such as breast implants.

Professional factors   Professional factors can include discovery, as well as resistance to discovery. Medical science makes routine and extraordinary discoveries, as with pediatric radiology and child abuse (Pfohl 1977), although these discoveries do not always come to broad public light or become standard practice. Frequently, media or social movement action is needed to catalyze what might otherwise be lost or less widely disseminated skills. We also know that general social conditions can delay routine discovery. A current example is the way that anti-choice movements and federal policy have suppressed valuable research and treatment uses of fetal tissue and of the drug RU486.

Professional expansionism and moral entrepreneurship are more often the subject matter of medical sociology than is routine professional discovery. Obstetricians have used prenatal diagnosis to increase the detection of conditions that are then labeled dangerous and hence lead to obstetrical interventions (Rothman 1989). Psychiatry enlarged its sphere to include gynecological conditions via LLPDD (Figert 1993). Children's diagnoses especially are on the rise, including the amorphous category of learning disabilities. In an era of deinstitutionalization, children's admissions to psychiatric facilities are rapidly increasing.

There is also an intraprofessional variant of moral entrepreneurship; e.g., expansionist changes in DSM diagnoses have been due to the triumph of biopsychiatry over psychoanalysis and community psychiatry (Brown 1990; Kirk and Kutchins 1992). More broadly, the saturation of the biomedical model leaves physicians and their allies in government less able to perceive health and illness through the lay lens (Freidson 1970). They are therefore more likely to view routine social and bodily phenomena as pathological entities. This tendency to medicalize most likely increases with the level of specialization.

Resistance to discovery is also common, especially with regard to syndromes and diseases which are iatrogenic effects. Psychiatry was extremely reluctant to recognize tardive dyskinesia, a movement disorder stemming from neuroleptic drugs. Despite clear and early warnings in the psychiatric literature, practitioners and their professional association found it hard to recognize a disease which called into question their most effective treatment (Brown and Funk 1986).

Organizational and institutional factors   Organizational and institutional factors also determine the type and amount of conditions discovered. We see self-perpetuation and institutional moral entrepreneurship, as when alcohol treatment facilities locate more cases of alcoholism, or when an expanding mental health system locates more mentally ill people. Sometimes this is merely expanding the pool of people who already have the condition; other times it involves new, less severe conditions that are viewed as needing treatment. There are also boundary disputes, such as arguments about the homeless mentally ill, between mental health and social welfare sectors. Here, mental health professionals are diminishing the extent of mental illness in order to reduce their responsibility, while the social service sector assumes a greater amount of mental illness in order to get the mental health sector to take more responsibility (Snow et al. 1986).

There is, as with professional resistance to discovery, organizational and institutional resistance to discovery. AIDS is perhaps the best known example, where the scientific discovery of the disease and its etiology were held up due both to professionals and to institutions and organizations, largely because of stigma, stereotypes, and judgmental attitudes toward gay men. The professional's social location has much to do with the construction of disease. Occupational physicians working for unions will be likely to diagnose diseases as caused by occupational hazards, while corporate physicians will be more likely either to not recognize the disease or to attribute it to personal habits (Walsh 1987). Thus, coal company physicians claimed that black lung (silicosis) was really asthma and emphysema brought on by tobacco smoking (Smith 1987).

Experience of Illness

Once there has been some form of discovery, the continuing forms in which people experience illness contribute to an ever-changing construction. Medical sociology counters a singular biomedical worldview with a social view that sees the interaction of biological and social factors. People may have the same disease yet experience it quite differently. For example, the existence of a cardiac condition might lead one person to severely restrict physical activity, even if that was not necessary. Another person, however, might actively reorient dietary habits and figure out a healthy physical exercise regimen.

These differences might arise from individual personality. For example, Kleinman (1988) found that for chronic pain sufferers, pain is a symbol and a metaphor for their life situation, as with one person for whom "The stiff neck is a kind of symbol, an icon of what I need to become: tough, stiff-necked."

Differences in perception of health problems often stem from race, class, sex, ethnic, and national differences, as noted in the now classic report by Zola (1973) on patient help-seeking in three clinics. He found differences not based on physiology among Italian, Irish Catholic, and Anglo-Saxon Protestants in the experience of illness and the ways that complaints were presented to doctors.

More generally, differences in illness experience stem from broader social perceptions and interactions, such as interpersonal crises, perceived interference with social or personal relations, social support from family and friends, sanctioning on the part of another family member, perceived interference with work or physical activity, and temporalizing (time-bound perceptions of symptoms) (Zola 1966). People feel and act on symptoms in many "non-medical" ways. For instance, what may seem an illogical form of noncompliance with doctor's orders may be a well thought-out plan to avoid medical and social "side effects" which might impair personal or work life (Conrad 1985). This perspective may be especially useful for chronic diseases which have become our predominant health problems, and for which medical knowledge often lacks successful interventions.

People bring entirely different worldviews to their illness, especially in the ways they frame an etiology. In looking at rheumatoid arthritis sufferers Williams (1984) found that one imputed a political and economic causality; another located etiology in a nest of social relationships and psychological makeup; another used a spiritual explanation. Each of these people produced a coherent self-analysis for their own narrative, thus providing a way to repair the rupture which chronic disease caused in their relationship with the world.

This is very similar to Kleinman's (1988) amplification of the distinction between disease and illness. He adds other forms of social experience. One is *sickness*, by which he means "the understanding of a disorder in its generic sense across a population in relation to macrosocial forces," meaning economic, political, and institutional. Kleinman also adds *explanation and emotion*, which is "the struggle of sick persons, their families, and practitioners to fashion serviceable explanations of the various aspects of illness and treatment."

In light of the above, it is understandable that people do not always experience disease as illness. Conversely, not all experienced illness as the result of a particular disease. Some people manage to avoid active symptoms, or to attribute them to other sources, or to accommodate to them. At the other side of the equation, certain people experience symptoms that are not traceable to a known cause, and some spend much time fearing they will catch any number of diseases. A large number of visits to doctors are for very minor symptoms. Varying estimates tell us that between 20 percent and 30 percent of visits to primary doctors are for psychological attention. Not surprisingly, primary care doctors, rather than psychiatrists, account for the bulk of psychiatric drug prescriptions.

Chronic illness forces people to come to new terms with the experience of time, a change in relation to past, present and future (Freund and McGuire 1991:155). When experienced as overwhelming, unpredictable, and uncontrollable, chronic illness often causes damage to the self since sufferers cannot plan their lives. This damage to the self causes a redefinition of illness experience (Charmaz 1991). Sufferers lose much, if not all, of their independence. They are often undermined in their reciprocity in relations, putting them under further strain (Freund and McGuire 1991:156). These core concerns force people to formulate an understanding of their personal biography and to make a "narrative reconstruction" (Williams 1984).

For people with stigmatizing illness, much of the illness experience is wrapped up in avoiding public awareness. This is often the case with disfiguring and sexually transmitted diseases, which bear a high degree of moral judgement. Epilepsy is one such case, where sufferers attempt to avoid seizures that may give away what for many is a secret (Schneider and Conrad 1981). People with AIDS spend much time hiding their illness, its symptoms, and the medications, though after a certain course of the disease it becomes impossible to continue hiding it (Weitz 1991).

Studies of the lay experience of illness stem from a "bottoms-up" approach in sociology, which places people in the center stage as active knowers. For many, this is based on Blumer's (1969) three basic premises: (1) People act on the basis of meanings that things have for them; (2) Meanings derive from social interaction; and (3) Meanings are modified by their interpretations in practice. Yet even this core symbolic interactionism is dependent on social structures, since the social interaction that provides the fabric for the generation of meanings is an interaction defined largely by the dominant structures of the society. In the case of health, these include professionalism and medical institutional structure, in addition to class, race, gender, and family structure.

The lay experience of illness cannot be completely separated from elements of clinical interaction, even though there is no space to take up this larger concern. Briefly, we know that people's understandings of illness are shaped in large part by health providers, and that the dynamic interaction between patient and provider leads to conflicted and/or negotiated diagnosis and treatment. Professionalism, gender roles, and class and race differences are the chief forces that shape such interaction.

For one example, an increasingly biological trend in psychiatry has convinced more people that mental illness is a purely biological phenomenon without social etiology or social exacerbation. This has led many self-help groups and family-and-friends associations to renounce previous critical stances by patients' rights organizations and innovative professionals in favor of purely biological explanations. This leads many people to accept a more mechanistic and positivist approach in which they rely solely on drug treatment and eschew collective responses (Kovel 1988; Mirowsky and Ross 1989). This is a situation where a larger social construction alters the personal experience of illness for some people.

The experience of illness is often inextricably tied up with structural issues. For example, we may look at obstetrical reforms (presence of fathers at birth, birthing suites, midwives, vaginal birth after cesarean) as stemming from women's experience of illness as a lay experiential phenomenon rather than a medical one. Ultimately, these lay experiences led to changes in health-care delivery due to the women's health movement. In a sense, we can view the women's health movement as a *sociopolitical form of illness experience*.

Rather than being merely individual experiences of illness, or even collections of individual experiences, they are collective social constructions and productions of reality.

Another example of sociopolitical forms of illness experience can be seen in community response to toxic waste contamination. Here we have the situation where disease exists for a long time before it is recognized. Laypeople recognize symptoms that they attribute to toxic contamination, and they notice disease clusters which they push health providers and public health officials to investigate (Brown 1992).

Treatment

At first glance, it may seem hard to place treatment in the context of social construction of disease, since treatment appears to be a subsequent phase. Yet treatment is a logical sequel. In constructing their definition of an illness, people also construct what they consider appropriate ways to treat it. In the previous section on illness experience, we saw that people's choices for care are based not solely on medical criteria, but on other criteria such as family responsibilities, perceived stigma, and interference with work. Indeed, social constructionist approaches to what medicine terms "compliance" have given us a firm basis for viewing choice of care as an integral part of illness experience (Conrad 1985).

Our growing awareness of the importance of self-care is further evidence for this connection. People interpret and respond to conditions based on their social and economic circumstances, personal biographies, health beliefs, self-concepts, and through reinterpreting present, past, and expected future symptoms and illness (Haug, Wykle, and Namazi 1989). In choosing self-care, either alone or in combination with professional care, people define and structure the future of their illness experience (Dill et al. 1994). That illness experience is further shaped by the informal caregivers and social networks that play roles in self-care.

On a more political level, there are many occasions where a condition is diagnosed, yet there is discretion about whether it is treated. That discretion is often a matter of how the condition is socially constructed. The infamous Tuskegee syphilis experiment is perhaps the most overt example—black people were viewed as inferior and as material for human experimentation, hence it was possible for physicians, the Public Health Service, and major foundations to intentionally withhold life-saving treatment (Jones 1981).

If unethical treatment seems a matter of the past, it is noteworthy that medical researchers today still condone their past actions. In 1993, the Department of Energy, along with some involved hospitals and state health and mental health departments, made public that for decades radioactive experimentation had been conducted on unwilling and incompetent populations such as prisoners and retarded patients. Quite shockingly, several leading experimenters affirmed in 1993 and 1994 that they found nothing wrong with such practices because those practices conformed to acceptable science of the era, and that the work contributed to human knowledge (Allen 1993). The social construction here, however, must include the cold war attitude that radiation was a powerful weapon for all purposes, and the attitude of technological imperative supported unproven research even if there were expected side effects.

Even if such egregious actions no longer occur, political decisions are still made on other levels, where people and institutions make choices about allocating services to those in need. For instance, despite enormous knowledge of the prevalence of lead poisoning, poor and minority children most at risk are very underserved (Berney 1993). This produces both a greater epidemic of lead poisoning and a more politicized construction of lead hazards.

Indeed, there is frequently politicization of disease as a result of social allocation of treatment, research, and prevention. Recent increases in breast cancer, for instance, have led many to view the increase as a result of environmental toxins and also to fault government agencies and the health care system for failing to take the epidemic seriously enough (Arditi 1993). Public and social-movement perspectives on the social nature of disease, and on acceptable treatment, may determine actual treatment. AIDS activism, for instance, has led to greater reliance on community-based treatment and to lay constructions of acceptable drug trials.

The availability of treatment can further the professional framing of a normal process as medicalized. For instance, the presence of synthetic estrogens helped push physicians to medicalize menopause as an estrogen deficiency disease (McCrea 1983). Medical technology in the form of fetal monitoring has led to increased "discovery" of fetal distress, leading to dramatic increases in cesarean sections.

Outcome

Organizational factors often determine belief in success, and hence in allocation of services. Roth's (1963) study of TB patients is a good example of how staff construct a view whereby certain patients wind up eligible for accelerated treatment and then release. In part, patients had to urge staff to see that they were ready to move on to the next stage, despite an absence of clear, standardized clinical criteria.

Social factors influence outcome in many ways. The WHO schizophrenia study found better recovery from schizophrenia in less developed countries. Richard Warner (1985) found that there is better recovery from schizophrenia in times of labor shortage. And the Vermont Longitudinal Study learned that there was better recovery from schizophrenia when psychosocial preparation was used before release (Harding et al. 1987). These findings all indicate a high degree of social action in the determination of outcome. For the WHO study and from Warner's research, we can understand macro-structural factors as central. From the Vermont study, we know that professional and institutional expectations are important. In the absence of positive expectations, though, the socially constructed belief about schizophrenia is that it is far more unremitting than it is in fact. A more positive belief concerning outcome would alter the way in which both organized psychiatry and the general public view schizophrenia. As well, when clinicians and administrators become aware of these outcome studies and use them to formulate policy, they contribute to a revised (and more optimistic) social construction of schizophrenia.

Even the personal experience of illness can affect outcome. One example is the growing literature which shows that elderly people's self-assessment of health predicts mortality, after controlling for presence of health problems, disability, and biological risk factors (Idler and Kasl 1991). I believe we can view this phenomenon of health self-assessment as a form of illness experience, in which people hold more positive views of their selves.

There is a more aggregate experience of illness as well. Community integration can occur in occupational and environmental health, where activists reframe a situation, turn it into a social problem, and strengthen community ties. Such community integration can also aid victims of toxic-waste sites by allowing them to see their problem as more broadly social and shared (Brown and Mikkelsen 1990). This is generally the case with social movements in health care—social movements provide an avenue for reinterpreting personal problems into social ones, thus redefining the very conceptualization of the illnesses at stake.

Social Policy Implications

There are many ways that understanding the social construction of illness has contributed, and will continue to contribute, to health policy. Medical sociology has long shown the importance of lay understanding and action. At the clinical level, sociological study of illness experience has uncovered a vast array of fears, expectations, folk beliefs, self-care concepts, and relational issues. Many forward-looking clinicians have used this knowledge to provide more patient-centered care through understanding the interpersonal significance of the clinical interaction (Balint 1957) and by eliciting a "patient explanatory model" of illness (Kleinman 1988). The wealth of past contributions by social science researchers as well as clinical applications developed by joint medical/social science teams should be used to increase support for sociological participation in medical settings, as well as for research grant support.

Such sociological participation can play a useful role in medical education, through using social science approaches to illness experience in courses and clerkships. It would be best to integrate these concerns in regular courses and clerkships, rather than segregating this material in electives that may be less central in medical training. Postgraduate education should also include training in social science approaches specifically tailored to the specialty training. Medical professionals can employ these social science perspectives to elicit a more comprehensive picture of their patients' history, including their lay belief systems and self-care practices. Physicians might be encouraged to engage in research projects in collaboration with social scientists at their hospital or at the affiliated university, in which they might actually test the efficacy of more patient-centered approaches.

At broader social levels, lay constructions at the group level have shaped changes in the health-care system. For example, women health activists have long found considerable research and advocacy support from sociologists in their efforts to break down patriarchal attitudes and practices, and to institute woman-centered alternatives (Ruzek 1978). When we look at occupational illnesses and toxic waste-induced diseases, we see the importance of relying on lay detection through "popular epidemiology" (Brown 1992). In these and related areas, sociologists contribute both their analytic capacities and their skills at speaking with laypeople in health settings and communities. These abilities should be more widely tapped for health policy and planning. We should encourage federal health agencies and private health foundations to solicit requests for proposals from social scientists and from social scientist/clinician teams to investigate the contributions of such lay awareness.

Sociologists have been in the forefront of those who show that health and illness are often more affected by political, economic, and cultural factors than by biomedical ones. With AIDS, we know that bias against homosexuals played an important role in delaying recognition. Stemming from this knowledge, the implications for prevention and treatment are that we need social action to combat stigma and bias, that the work of gay health activists is an essential element in the campaign to eradicate AIDS, and that scientists and physicians need be more aware of the social medicine components of this disease. Sociologists need to find more ways to connect to such social medicine approaches, both to foster them and to provide useful evaluation.

Sociologists need to emphasize the importance of social movements in the health-care system. Movements and activists in the areas of AIDS, women's health, occupational health, and environmental health have been integral in several ways: (1) They have shown how to obtain more resources for the prevention and treatment of already recognized diseases (e.g., sickle cell anemia, AIDS); (2) They have pioneered in developing education and prevention efforts used by both laypeople and the medical sector; and (3) They have been major players in getting legislation for disease recognition, prevention, and treatment. Here, too, sociologists need to find ways to demonstrate to the medical and health policy communities the importance of social movements, including in evaluation studies.

Because the sociological approach to the social construction of health and illness examines how socioeconomic factors cause and exacerbate disease, we can use our scholarship to design research to demonstrate that improvements in non-medical sectors, such as housing, income supports, and education improve health status.

Medical sociology has pioneered in studying how chronic conditions and disabilities have become viewed as part of daily life rather than as abnormalities. This has contributed to the disability rights movement and to the growing public acceptance of that movement's goals (Zola 1982; Fine and Asch 1988). Sociological study of disability has sharpened our focus on the normality of symptoms, adjustments to a condition, chronicity, impact of the built/social environment on living with a condition, social/cultural changes as major impediments and/or gains, and the centrality of the body (Zola 1982). By emphasizing the significance of social movements, sociologists can show how collective action shapes social definitions of disease and disability and how social movements in health are often at the cutting edge of new approaches which later become more acceptable to the mainstream health-care system. This can help policymakers appreciate such movements rather than seeing them as neces-sarily threatening. The social construction perspective has developed extensively in recent years. It offers much promise for building a firmer theoretical foundation, for conducting better research, and for influencing health policy. We owe it to ourselves to make good on this potential.

Notes

1 For those interested in more details on the literature of social construction, see Freidson (1970), Lock and Gordon (1988), and Freund and McGuire (1991).
2 Peter Conrad was particularly helpful in thinking through this typology.
3 Interestingly enough, despite the voluminous evidence of this link, the eminent epidemiologist Richard Doll (1992) has recently tried to minimize the connection between asbestos and mesothelioma.

Acknowledgments

I am grateful to Ellen Annandale, Adele Clarke, Peter Conrad, Ann Dill, Mary Fennell, Bernice Pescosolido, and the reviewers for comments on earlier drafts.

References

Allen, Scott. 1993. "Radiation Used on Retarded." *Boston Globe*, December 26.
Arditti, Rita. 1993. Presentation at Environmental Health Network conference, Bethesda, MD, September 18, 1993.
Armstrong, David. 1983. *Political Anatomy of the Body: Medical Knowledge in Britain in the Twentieth Century*. Cambridge: Cambridge University Press.
Balint, Michael. 1957. *The Doctor, His Patient, and the Illness*. New York: International Universities Press.
Bell, Susan. 1986. "A New Model of Medical Technology Development: A Case Study of DES." *Research in the Sociology of Health Care* 4:1–32.
Berney, Barbara. 1993. "Round and Round It Goes: The Epidemiology of Childhood Lead Poisoning, 1950–1990." *The Milbank Quarterly* 71:3–39.
Best, Joel. 1989. "Afterword." Pp. 243–252 in Joel Best, ed., *Images of Issues: Typifying Contemporary Social Problems*. New York: Aldine.
Blaxter, Mildred. 1978. "Diagnosis as Category and Process: The Case of Alcoholism." *Social Science and Medicine* 12:9–17.
Blumer, Herbert. 1969. *Symbolic Interactionism: Perspective and Method*. Englewood Cliffs, NJ: Prentice-Hall.

Brown, E. Richard. 1979. *Rockefeller Medicine Men: Medicine and Capitalism in America*. Berkeley: University of California Press.

Brown, Phil. 1990. "The Name Game: Toward a Sociology of Diagnosis." *Journal of Mind and Behavior* 11:2–3.

———. 1992. "Toxic Waste Contamination and Popular Epidemiology: Lay and Professional Ways of Knowing." *Journal of Health and Social Behavior* 33:267–281.

Brown, Phil and Steven C. Funk. 1986. "Tardive Dyskinesia: Barriers to the Professional Recognition of an Iatrogenic Disease." *Journal of Health and Social Behavior* 29:116–132.

Brown, Phil and Edwin J. Mikkelsen. 1990. *No Safe Place: Toxic Waste, Leukemia, and Community Action*. Berkeley: University of California Press.

Bury, Michael. 1986. "Social Constructionism and the Development of Medical Sociology." *Sociology of Health and Illness* 8:37–169.

Charmaz, Kathy. 1991. *Good Days, Bad Days: The Self in Chronic Illness*. New Brunswick, NJ: Rutgers University Press.

Conrad, Peter. 1975. "The Discovery of Hyperkinesis: Notes on the Medicalization of Deviant Behavior." *Social Problems* 23:12–21.

Conrad, Peter. 1985. "The Meaning of Medications: Another Look at Compliance." *Social Science and Medicine* 20:29–37.

Conrad, Peter. 1992. "Medicalization and Social Control." *Annual Review of Sociology* 18:209–232.

Conrad, Peter and Joseph W. Schneider. 1992. *Deviance and Medicalization: From Badness to Sickness*. Philadelphia: Temple.

Dill, Ann, Phil Brown, Desiree A. Ciambrone, and William Rakowski. 1994. "The Meaning and Practice of Self-Care by Older Adults: A Qualitative Assessment." Forthcoming, *Research on Aging*.

Doll, Richard. 1992. "Environmental Disease." *American Journal of Public Health*. 82:936–940.

Draper, Elaine. 1991. *Risky Business: Genetic Testing and Exclusionary Practices in the Hazardous Workplace*. Cambridge, England: Cambridge University Press.

Figert, Anne E. 1993. "Diagnosis as Professional Battlegrounds: The Case of LLPDD and the DSM-III-R." Paper presented at the Annual Meeting of the American Sociological Association, Miami Beach, August 15.

Fine, Michelle and Adrienne Asch. 1988. "Disability Beyond Stigma: Social Intervention, Discrimination, and Activism." *Journal of Social Issues* 44:3–21.

Freidson, Eliot. 1970. *Profession of Medicine: A Study of the Sociology of Applied Knowledge*. Chicago: University of Chicago Press.

Freund, Peter E. S. and Meredith B. McGuire. 1991. *Health, Illness, and the Social Body: A Critical Sociology*. Englewood Cliffs, NJ: Prentice-Hall.

Harding, Courtenay M., George W. Brooks, Takamura Ashikaga, John S. Strauss, and Alan Breier, 1987. "The Vermont Longitudinal Study of Persons with Severe Mental Illness, I: Methodology, Study Sample, and Overall Status 32 Years Later." *American Journal of Psychiatry* 144:718–726.

Haug, Marie, May J. Wykle, and Kevan H. Namazi. 1989. "Self-Care Among Older Adults." *Social Science and Medicine* 29:171–183.

Idler, Ellen L. and Stanislav Kasl. 1991. "Health Perceptions and Survival: Do Global Evaluations of Health Status Really Predict Mortality?" *Journal of Gerontology: Social Sciences* 46:S55–S65.

Jones, James. 1981. *Bad Blood: The Tuskegee Syphilis Experiment*. New York: Free Press.

Kirk, Stuart A. and Herb Kutchins. 1992. *The Selling of DSM: The Rhetoric of Science in Psychiatry.* New York: Aldine de Gruyter.

Kleinman, Arthur, 1988. *The Illness Narratives: Suffering Healing and the Human Condition.* New York: Basic.

Kovel, Joel. "A Critique of DSM-III." 1988. *Research in Law, Deviance, and Social Control* 9:127–146.

Latour, Bruno. 1987. *Science in Action: How to Follow Scientists and Engineers Through Society.* Cambridge: Harvard University Press.

Lock, Margaret. 1988. "Introduction." Pp. 3–10 in Margaret Lock and Deborah Gordon, eds., *Biomedicine Examined.* Boston: Kluwer.

Lock, Margaret and Deborah Gordon, eds., 1988. *Biomedicine Examined.* Boston: Kluwer.

McCrea, Frances B. 1983. "The Politics of Menopause: the 'Discovery' of a Deficiency Disease." *Social Problems* 31:111–123.

Miller, Gale and James A. Holstein. 1993a. "Reconsidering Social Constructionism" Pp. 5–24 in Gale Miller and James A. Holstein, eds., *Reconsidering Social Constructionism.* Hawthorne, NY: Aldine De Gruyter.

Miller, Gale and James A. Holstein. 1993b. "Social Constructionism and its Critics: Assessing Recent Challenges." Pp. 535–547 in Gale Miller and James A. Holstein, eds., *Reconsidering Social Constructionism.* Hawthorne, NY: Aldine De Gruyter.

Mirowsky, John and Catherine E. Ross. 1989. "Psychiatric Diagnosis as Reified Measurement." *Journal of Health and Social Behavior* 30:11–25.

Mishler, Elliot. 1984. *The Discourse of Medicine.* Norwood, NJ: Ablex.

Nelkin, Dorothy and Laurence Tancredi. 1989. *Dangerous Diagnostics: The Social Power of Biological Information.* New York: Basic.

Pfohl, Stephen J. 1977. "The 'Discovery' of Child Abuse." *Social Problems* 24:310–323.

Roth, Julius. 1963. *Timetables: Structuring the Passage of Time in Hospital Treatment.* Indianapolis: Bobbs-Merrill.

Rothman, Barbara Katz. 1989. *Recreating Motherhood: Ideology and Technology in a Patriarchal Society.* New York: Norton.

Ruzek, Cheryl. 1978. *The Women's Health Movement: Feminist Alternatives to Medical Control.* New York: Praeger.

Schneider, Joseph. 1985. "Social Problems Theory: The Constructionist View." *Annual Review of Sociology* 11:209–229.

Schneider, Joseph and Peter Conrad. 1981. "Medical and Sociological Typologies: The Case of Epilepsy." *Social Science and Medicine* 15A:211–219.

Scott, Wilbur. 1990. "PTSD in DSM-III. A Case of the Politics of Diagnosis and Disease." *Social Problems* 37:294–310.

Scully, Diana. 1980. *Men Who Control Women's Health: The Miseducation of Obstetrician-Gynecologists.* Boston: Houghton-Mifflin.

Smith, Barbara Ellen. 1987. *Digging Our Own Graves: Coal Miners and the Struggle Over Black Lung Disease.* Chicago: University of Chicago Press.

Snow, David, A. S. Baker, and L. Anderson. 1986. "The Myth of Pervasive Mental Illness among the Homeless." *Social Problems* 33:407–423.

Spector, Malcolm and John Kitsuse. 1977. *Constructing Social Problems.* Menlo Park, CA: Cummings.

Turner, Bryan S. 1992. *Regulating Bodies: Essays in Medical Sociology.* London: Routledge.

Waitzkin, Howard. 1989. "A Critical Theory of Medical Discourse: Ideology, Social Control, and the Processing of Social Context in Medical Encounters." *Journal of Health and Social Behavior* 30:220–239.

Walsh, Diana Chapman. 1987. *Corporate Physicians: Between Medicine and Management*. New Haven: Yale University Press.

Warner, Richard. 1985. *Recovery from Schizophrenia: Psychiatry and Political Economy*. Boston: Routledge.

Weitz, Rose. 1991. *Life with AIDS*. New Brunswick, NJ: Rutgers University Press.

White, Kevin. 1991, "The Sociology of Health and Illness." *Current Sociology* 39(2):1–115.

Williams, Gareth. 1984. "The Genesis of Chronic Illness: Narrative Re-Construction." *Sociology of Health and Illness* 6:176–200.

Woolgar, Steven and Dorothy Pawluch. 1985. "Ontological Gerrymandering: The Anatomy of Social Problems Explanations." *Social Problems* 32:214–227.

Wright, Peter and Andrew Treacher. 1982. *The Problem of Medical Knowledge: Examining the Social Construction of Medicine*. Edinburgh: University of Edinburgh Press.

Zimmerman, Susan. 1995. "Medical Management of Femininity: Women's Experiences with Silicon Breast Implants." Presentation at American Sociological Association Annual Meeting, Washington, DC, August 21, 1995.

Zola, Irving K. 1966. "Culture and Symptoms: An Analysis of Patients' Presenting Complaints." *American Sociological Review* 31:615–630.

———. 1972. "Medicine as an Institution of Social Control." *Sociological Review* 20:487–504.

———. 1973. "Pathways to the Doctor—From Person to Patient." *Social Science and Medicine* 7:677–689.

Zola, Irving K. 1982. *Missing Pieces: A Chronicle of Living with a Disability*. Philadelphia: Temple University Press.

5
Medicalization and Social Control

Peter Conrad

Introduction

Medicalization describes a process by which nonmedical problems become defined and treated as medical problems, usually in terms of illnesses or disorders. This article reviews the work of sociologists, anthropologists historians, physicians, and others who have written about medicalization. While I briefly discuss some of the seminal writings on the topic, the emphasis here is on work published after 1980, because a compilation of earlier writings is available elsewhere (see Conrad & Schneider 1980a).

The Emergence of Medicalization

During the 1970s the term medicalization crept into the social scientific literature. While it literally means "to make medical," it has come to have wider and more subtle meanings. The term has been used more often in the context of a critique of medicalization (or overmedicalization) than as a neutral term simply describing that something has become medical.

Critics of the widening realm of psychiatry were the first to call attention to medicalization, although they did not call it that (e.g. Szasz 1963). Pitts (1968), Freidson (1970) and Zola (1972) presented the initial examinations of medicalization and medical social control. They took their inspiration from sources as different as Parsons (1951) and labeling theory. Parsons was probably the first to conceptualize medicine as an institution of social control, especially the way in which the "sick role" could conditionally legitimate that deviance termed illness. Freidson and Zola based their conceptions, in part, on the emergent social constructionism embedded in the then current labeling or societal reaction perspective.

A number of "case studies" of the medicalization of deviance were published in the 1970s: Conrad (1975) on hyperactivity in children, Scull (1975) on mental illness, Pfohl (1977) on child abuse, and Schneider (1978) on alcoholism as a disease. Other studies analyzed changes from nonmedical to medical definitions and treatments, although they did not necessarily use a medicalization framework (e.g. Foucault 1965, Gusfield 1967, Wertz & Wertz 1989). Illich (1976) used the conception "the medicalization of life" in his influential critique of medicine. Thus, by the time Conrad & Schneider (1980a) wrote *Deviance and Medicalization: From Badness to Sickness*, there was already a substantial literature to build upon.

Medicalization and Definitions

Although much has been written about medicalization, the definition has not always been clearly articulated. Most agree that medicalization pertains to the process and outcome of human problems entering the jurisdiction of the medical profession, but there are differences in the way they see the process. One of the most straightforward definitions is presented by Zola (1983:295): Medicalization is a "process whereby more and more of everyday life has come under medical dominion, influence and supervision." In an early statement, Conrad (1975:12) sees it as "defining behavior as a medical problem or type of treatment for it." While these definitions are serviceable they both make the assumption that the problem must move into the jurisdiction of the medical profession; in certain instances, however, the medical profession is only marginally involved or even uninvolved (e.g. alcoholism). This has led to some confusion about what constitutes demedicalization.

The key to medicalization is the definitional issue. Medicalization consists of defining a problem in medical terms, using medical language to describe a problem, adopting a medical framework to understand a problem, or using a medical intervention to "treat" it. This is a sociocultural process that may or may not involve the medical profession, lead to medical social control or medical treatment, or be the result of intentional expansion by the medical profession. Medicalization occurs when a medical frame or definition has been applied to understand or manage a problem; this is as true for epilepsy as for "gender dysphoria" (transexualism). The interest in medicalization has predominantly focused on previously nonmedical problems that have been medicalized (and, often, thought to be inappropriately medicalized), but actually medicalization must include all problems that come to be defined in medical terms.

While the definitional issue remains central, a broader conceptual frame helps clarify the meaning of medicalization (Conrad & Schneider 1980b). Medicalization can occur on at least three distinct levels: the conceptual, the institutional, and the interactional levels. On the conceptual level a medical vocabulary (or model) is used to "order" or define the problem at hand; few medical professionals need be involved, and medical treatments are not necessarily applied. On the institutional level, organizations may adopt a medical approach to treating a particular problem in which the organization specializes. Physicians may function as gatekeepers for benefits that are only legitimate in organizations that adopt a medical definition and approach to a problem, but where the everyday routine work is accomplished by nonmedical personnel. On the interactional level, physicians are most directly involved. Medicalization occurs here as part of doctor-patient interaction, when a physician defines a problem as medical (i.e. gives a medical diagnosis) or treats a "social" problem with a medical form of treatment (e.g. prescribing tranquilizer drugs for an unhappy family life). Thus it becomes clearer that medicalization is a broad definitional process, which may or may not directly include physicians and their treatments (although it often does). Subcultures, groups, or individuals may vary in their readiness to apply, accept, or reject medicalized definitions (Cornwell 1984).

There have been general and specific critiques of medicalization. The general critiques argue that the medicalization case has been overstated and that there are considerable constraints to medicalization (Fox 1977, Strong 1979). The specific critiques focus more directly on the conceptual validity of the case studies (Woolgar & Pawluch 1985, Bury 1986). The theoretical frame underlying these cases of medicalization is a type of social constructionism (cf. Spector & Kitsuse 1977, Schneider 1985), although this is not explicitly noted in all the writings. Put simply, this perspective presents reality and knowledge as "socially constructed," shaped by its human constructors, and brackets the assumption that there is any a priori reality "out there" to be discovered. These medicalization studies document the historical "discovery" of a medical problem, with attention to who said what, when, and with what consequences. This requires examining the professional literature, events, and claims-making activities (cf. Spector & Kitsuse 1977).

Bury's (1986) critique is the most relevant to medicalization studies. He contends that since social constructionism assumes the relativity of all knowledge, constructionism itself is affected by the same forces as scientific knowledge. It is not an independent "judge" (as analysts seem to assume); so on what basis can we differentiate a "discovery" from an "invention"? Bury further contends this has led analysts to exaggerate the extent of medicalization in contemporary society. In a response, Nicholson & McLaughlin (1987:118) make the important point that displaying the social and contextual nature of knowledge—e.g. how medical categories emerge—does not necessarily mean the knowledge is false.

Occasionally medicalization analyses are criticized for positing a social model to replace the medical model (Whalen & Henker 1977). This is a spurious criticism; it is the critics who focus on the issue of causation. Nearly all medicalization analyses bracket the question of causation of the particular behavior or condition and focus instead on how the problem came to be designated as a medical one. Medicalization researchers are much more interested in the etiology of definitions than the etiology of the behavior or condition (Conrad 1977). Indeed, this may reflect a weakness in medicalization research; analysts have offered or examined few viable alternatives to medicalized approaches to problems like alcoholism (Roman 1980b).

Medicalization has occurred for both deviant behavior and "natural life processes." Examples of medicalized deviance include: madness, alcoholism, homosexuality, opiate addiction, hyperactivity and learning disabilities in children, eating problems from overeating (obesity) to undereating (anorexia), child abuse, compulsive gambling, infertility, and transexualism, among others. Natural life processes that have become medicalized include sexuality, childbirth, child development, menstrual discomfort (PMS), menopause, aging, and death. While the specific origins and consequences of each of these arenas of medicalization may differ, many of the issues are similar.

Contexts of Medicalization

Analysts have long pointed to social factors that have encouraged or abetted medicalization: the diminution of religion, an abiding faith in science, rationality, and progress, the increased prestige and power of the medical profession, the American penchant for individual and technological solutions to problems, and a general humanitarian trend in Western societies. While factors like these do not explain increasing medicalization over the past century, they have provided the context. Sociologists have examined two important contextual aspects affecting medicalization: secularization and the changing status of the medical profession.

Secularization

Numerous writers have suggested that medicine has "nudged aside" (Zola 1972) or "replaced" (Turner 1984, 1987) religion as the dominant moral ideology and social control institution in modern societies. Many conditions have become transformed from sin to crime to sickness. In Weberian terms, this is of a piece with the rationalization of society (Turner 1984). The argument is that secularization leads to medicalization.

There is some recent evidence to support this, largely in the writings of social historians (see also Clarke 1984). Brumberg (1988:7) sees anorexia as a type of secularized salvation:

> From the vantage point of the historian, anorexia nervosa appears to be a secular addiction to a new kind of perfectionism, one that links personal salvation to the achievement of an external body configuration rather than an internal spiritual state.

Although physicians had little to do with it, social responses to suicide were secularized in the eighteenth century due to a general loss in confidence in diabolical powers; according to MacDonald (1989), suicide was more or less medicalized by default. Homosexuality was medicalized in part in response to harsh religious and criminal sanctions; if it was hereditary, then the deviant behavior was not a voluntary act (Conrad & Schneider 1980a:181–85, but also see Greenberg 1988:406–11). Infertility used to be in the realm of the gods, as evidenced by fertility votives found the world over, but now it is firmly within the jurisdiction of medicine (Rothman 1989, Greil 1991).

It is often assumed that religious groups by definition resist secularization and medicalization, since these may erode theological turf. In a recent article, Bull (1990) questions this line of reasoning. He uses the case of Seventh Day Adventists, who have developed a rather substantial medical presence. He argues that this group "promotes secularization through their implacable opposition to the public role of religion" (p. 255) and that it also "operates a dynamic and effective instrument for extending and defending medical regulation of society" (p. 256) through their health regulations and doctrines. Thus Adventists encourage both secularization and medicalization, rather than being affected by it.

In fact, medicalization may have a rather ambivalent relation to marginal religious groups. On the one hand, medicalization has been used to oppose and neutralize cults, particularly in the name of treating "brainwashed" members (Robbins & Anthony 1982). On the other hand, some healing cults among the poor and marginal classes have embraced the medical view. The symbols of some traditional Latin American healing cults fuse the power of religious healing and modern medicine by basing their beliefs and worship on the imagery of particular doctors as medical saints (Low 1988).

While it is true that medicine is in important ways nudging aside religion as our moral touchstone, the interface of medicine and religion is more complex than a simple secularization thesis would suggest.

The Medical Profession, Pediatrics and Medicalization

Although "medical imperialism" cannot be deemed the central explanation for medicalization (Zola 1972, Conrad & Schneider, 1980b), the organization and structure of the medical profession has an important impact. Professional dominance and monopolization have certainly had a significant role in giving medicine the jurisdiction over virtually anything to which the label "health" or "illness" could be attached (Freidson 1970:251). As we note later, the impact of the enormous changes in the organization of medicine in the last two decades on medicalization is an area in need of study, as well as is the reciprocal effects of medicalization on the profession (Schneider & Conrad 1980).

While it is difficult to predict future changes, a well researched historical example can provide insight.

In a provocative paper, Pawluch (1983) shows how in a changing social environment pediatricians were able to adapt their orientations to maintain their practices. In the context of an improved standard of living, public health measures, and preventive vaccinations, there were fewer sick children for pediatricians to treat. Pawluch argues that pediatricians weathered this professional crisis by changing the focus of their practices, first by becoming "baby feeders," and recently by including children's troublesome behavior in their domain. The new "behavioral pediatrics" enabled pediatricians to maintain and enhance their medical dominance by expanding their medical territory. This led to the medicalization of a variety of psychosocial problems of children.

Halpern (1990), in an important article, contests some of Pawluch's interpretation. She argues that routinization of work, rather than market decline, preceded behavioral pediatrics. To the recently trained academic specialists, general outpatient care seemed "unappealingly routine" (Halpern 1990:30). The "new pediatrics" was a vehicle for academic generalists to secure a place in medical schools dominated by subspecialists and to make their own training and

routine clinical work more stimulating. She argues that understimu-
lated specialists in search of professional standing rather than un-
derused clinical practitioners took the lead in medicalization. While
the data cannot be conclusive, based on a review of studies, Halpern
suggests that pediatricians do not seem to have increased their treatment of psychosocial disorders in recent decades. She further suggests
that physicians need not treat the medicalized disorders themselves,
but can become the managers of medical care, while auxiliaries and
extenders provide treatments in a medical frame. Put another way,
Halpern suggests that medicalization in pediatrics occurred more on
the conceptual and institutional levels than on the interactional level
of patient treatment (cf. Conrad & Schneider 1980b).

Whether Halpern's "routinization hypothesis" or Pawluch's "market
hypothesis" is more nearly correct, or some combination of both as
Halpern (1990:35) seems to indicate, it is clear that medicalization is
in part a by-product of intraprofessional issues that underlie the
growth of behavioral pediatrics. The cases of hyperactivity (Conrad
1975, 1976) and learning disabilities (Carrier 1983, Erchak & Rosenfeld 1989) are examples of the increased medicalization of childhood
behavioral problems.

Medical Social Control

Social control is a central and important concept in sociology. Most
societies develop therapeutic styles of social control (Horwitz 1991),
especially when individualism is highly valued. Durkheim (1893/1933)
differentiated between repressive and restitutive controls, seeing the
latter as more characteristic of complex societies. The social control
aspect of medicine was conceptualized initially by Parsons (1951),
when he depicted illness as deviance and medicine and the "sick role"
as the appropriate mechanism of social control. Early analysts (Pitts
1968, Zola 1972) indicated that medical social control would likely
replace other forms of control; while this has not occurred, it can be
argued that medical social control has continued to expand (see below,
The Range of Medicalization). While numerous definitions of medical
social control have been offered (Pitts 1968, Zola 1972, Conrad 1979,
O'Neill 1986), in terms of medicalization "the greatest social control
power comes from having the authority to define certain behaviors,
persons and things" (Conrad & Schneider 1980a:8). Thus, in general,
the key issue remains definitional—the power to have a particular set
of (medical) definitions realized in both spirit and practice.

This is not to say that medical social control is not implemented by the medical profession (it generally is), or that it is not abetted by powerful forms of medical technology (it often is). It is to say that without medicalization in a definitional sense, medical social control loses its legitimacy and is more difficult to accomplish. The development of a technique of medical social control (e.g. a pharmaceutical intervention) may precede the medicalization of a problem, but for implementation some type of medical definition is necessary (e.g. Conrad 1975). More typically, however, medicalization precedes medical social control.

In the context of medicalizing deviance, Conrad (1979) distinguished three types of medical social control: medical ideology, collaboration, and technology. Simply stated, medical ideology imposes a medical model primarily because of accrued social and ideological benefits; in medical collaboration doctors assist (usually in an organizational context) as information providers, gatekeepers, institutional agents, and technicians; medical technology suggests the use for social control of medical technological means, especially drugs, surgery, and genetic or other types of screening. While these are overlapping categories, they do allow us to characterize types of medical social control. Perhaps the most common form is still "medical excusing" (Halleck 1971), ranging from doctor's notes for missing school to disability benefits, to eligibility to the insanity defense.

To these categories we can add a fourth—medical surveillance. Based on the work of Foucault (1973, 1977), this form of medical social control suggests that certain conditions or behaviors become perceived through a "medical gaze" and that physicians may legitimately lay claim to all activities concerning the condition. Perhaps the classic example of this is childbirth, which, despite all the birthing innovations of the last two decades (Wertz & Wertz 1989), remains firmly under medical surveillance. Indeed, the medical surveillance of obstetrics has now expanded to include prenatal lifestyles, infertility, and postnatal interaction with babies (Arney 1982).

Some significant developments have occurred in medical social control over the past decade. In terms of ideological control, PMS (premenstrual syndrome) has emerged as an explanation of a variety of types of female deviance (Riessman 1983). In terms of collaboration, many work organizations have implemented Employee Assistance Programs (EAPs) (Roman 1980a, Sonnenstuhl 1986) and worksite screenings for drugs (Walsh et al. 1992) and AIDS, both strategies for medical detection (identification), and in the case of EAPs, medical intervention. Forms of medical technological control which have been recently examined by social scientists include penile implants for male sexual dysfunction (Teifer 1986), hormonal and surgical treatments for transsexualism (Billings & Urban 1992), genetic screening (Hubbard & Henifin 1985), and chemical executions in implementing the death penalty (Haines 1989). Beyond the childbirth example, analysts have examined the extension of medical surveillance to the body (Armstrong 1983, Turner 1984), mental illness and homelessness (Snow et al. 1986), and to a certain extent, lifestyle (Conrad & Walsh 1992; but see discussion in The Range of Medicalization section).

Medical collaboration and technology can have deadly outcomes. The most disturbing (and horrifying) case of medical control is the German physicians' genocidal collaborations with the Nazis, including formulating and carrying out the eradication of the "genetically defective" (Lifton 1986, Proctor 1988). These also included the medical technological interventions in concentration camp killings which were couched as medical operations (Lifton, 1986). Fortunately, most forms of medical social control are not so diabolical or lethal, but the case of the Nazi doctor exemplifies the extreme, destructive use of medical social control.

In a very different context, Bosk (1985) examines the profession's social control of itself—in terms of self-regulation and control of deviance—and finds the profession to be tolerant and forgiving of its own, as opposed to its less tolerant treatment of lay population deviance. This has been manifested recently by the emergence of the notion of "impaired physicians" as a medicalized explanation for physician deviance (Stimson 1985, T. Johnson 1988). The impaired physician concept is largely based upon the extant medicalization of substance abuse, and it allows the medical profession to "take charge of a significant amount of physician deviance, and to keep it away from the control of licensing and disciplinary bodies" (Stimson 1986:161). Thus the profession uses medicalized social control to reinforce its claims for self-regulation.

One needs to be cautious in making claims about the actual functioning of medicalized social control. While EAPs certainly appear to be a strategy for controlling deviant work performance, studies suggest that most employees using EAPs are self-referrals rather than supervisor referrals (Sonnenstuhl 1982, 1986), raising the question of whether these can be classified as a means of corporate social control.

Social control is rarely an either/or situation. As several researchers have pointed out, changes in social control may be cyclical and are subject to change (Conrad & Schneider, 1980a). Peyrot (1984) aptly reminds us that new clinical perspectives cannot be expected to fully supplement earlier modes of social control; for example, drug addiction remains within the purview of the criminal justice system despite medicalization (see also Johnson & Waletzko 1991). Thus it is not surprising that we find medical-legal hybrids in areas like addiction, drinking-driving, and gambling.

The Process of Medicalization

Conrad & Schneider (1980a:261–77) presented a five-stage sequential model of the medicalization of deviance based on the comparison of several historical cases. While analysts have used this model to examine compulsive gambling (Rosencrance 1985), premenstrual syndrome (Bell 1987a), and learning disabilities (Erchak & Rosenfeld 1989), there has been little evaluation or development of this conceptual model. Peyrot's (1984) reframing of the stages and cycles of drug abuse is one of the few published critiques. Perhaps the model is inappropriate for other cases or is too general to be useful; still, it is unclear why the model has been ignored rather than criticized or modified. This is not to say that analysts have ignored the process of medicalization. If there is a theme to the issues raised in the discussion, it centers on the degree to which physicians and the medical profession are active in the medicalization process. Physicians were involved as claims-makers with hyperactivity (Conrad 1975), child abuse (Pfohl 1977), aging (Estes & Binney 1989), menopause (McCrea 1983, Bell 1987b, 1990), PMS (Riessman 1983, Bell 1987a), and the emergence of behavioral pediatrics (Pawluch 1983, Halpern 1990). Medical claims-making usually takes the form of writing in professional journals, official professional reports, activities in speciality organizations, and developing special clinics or services.

There are also cases where generally physicians are uninvolved or their initial involvement is minimal; the most obvious cases are in substance abuse—alcoholism (Schneider 1978), opiate addiction (Conrad & Schneider 1980a) and EAPs (Roman 1980a, Sonnenstuhl, 1986). At least two reported cases exist of active medical resistance to medicalization. Haines (1989) suggests the medical profession resists medical involvement in lethal injections for criminal executions, a process perceived as a threat to their professional interests. Kurz (1987) reports that there is resistance among medical emergency department (ED) personnel to the medicalization of woman battering. Some resistance to medicalization on the interactional or doctor-patient level is not surprising in situations like the ED or in busy practices where only limited medical resources are available (cf. Strong 1979).

Organized lay interests frequently play a significant role in medicalization (Conrad & Schneider 1980a). Scott (1990), for example, suggests in the case of post traumatic stress disorder (PTSD) that a small group of Vietnam veterans consciously and deliberately worked along with psychiatrists to create such a diagnosis and to have it institutionalized in DSM-III. Sexual addiction, which received considerable mass media publicity, while having advocates, has never been legitimated in DSM-III or in any other "official" source (Levine & Troiden 1988). Similar lay claims-making can be seen in the cases of alcoholism (Schneider 1978) and EAPs (Trice & Bayer 1984), as well as in various challenges to medicalization described below (see section on Demedicalization).

Patients sometimes are actively involved in medicalization. There is evidence for this from historical studies of childbirth (Wertz & Wertz 1989), homosexuality (Greenberg 1988, Hansen 1989), and more recently for PMS (Riessman 1983). It is clear that patients are not necessarily passive and can be active participants in the process of medicalization (cf. Gabe & Calnan 1989).

Taken together these studies support the contention that medicalization is an interactive process and not simply the result of "medical imperialism" as well as that the medical profession can take a variety of roles and positions in the process (cf. Strong 1979, Conrad & Schneider 1980b).

Degrees of Medicalization

In most cases medicalization is not complete; some instances of a condition may not be medicalized, competing definitions may exist, or remnants of previous definition cloud the picture. Therefore rather than seeing medicalization as an either/or situation, it makes sense to view it in terms of degrees. Some conditions are almost fully medicalized (e.g. death, childbirth), others are partly medicalized (e.g. opiate addiction, menopause), and still others are minimally medicalized (e.g. sexual addiction, spouse abuse).

We do not yet have a good understanding of which factors affect the degrees of medicalization. Certainly the support of the medical profession, availability of interventions or treatments, existence of competing definitions, coverage by medical insurance, and the presence of groups challenging the medical definition, are all likely to be significant factors.

Two examples can highlight some of the issues. While the claim has been made that battering or spouse abuse is a medical problem

(Goodstein & Page 1981), evidence suggests that it is only minimally medicalized (Kurz 1987). This is particularly interesting because child abuse has been more completely medicalized (Pfohl 1977). In this case, issues of competing definitions, "ownership" (Gusfield 1981) and lack of medical support seem to be factors. The dominant definition of spouse abuse is not medical but feminist; the feminist movement championed the problem and its "treatment" (battered women's shelters) and thus can be said to "own" the problem (see Tierney 1982, Wharton 1987). As a second example, general agreement exists that menopause has been medicalized on a conceptual level (MacPherson 1981, Bell 1990). Data from a cross-sectional patient survey in Canada suggest, however, that it has not been medicalized to any great extent, and the use of hormone treatments for "symptoms" is relatively low (Kaufert & Gilbert 1986). Thus medicalization may be uneven; on the doctor-patient (interactional) level, menopause does not seem highly medicalized, while on a conceptual level it certainly is.

There is another dimension to the degree of medicalization: how expansive is the medical category? While some categories are narrow and circumscribed, others can expand and incorporate a variety of other problems. Hyperactivity initially applied only to overactive, impulsive, and distractible children (especially boys); however, now as attentional deficit disorder (ADD) it has become more inclusive. The diagnosis has expanded to include more teenagers, adults, and hypoactive girls (Wender 1987). Despite, or perhaps because of, evidence that ADD is an inadequately specified category (Rubinstein & Brown 1984), labeling and treatment seem to be increasing. One study found a consistent doubling of the rate of treatment for ADD children every four to seven years, so that 6% of all public elementary school students were receiving stimulant medications in 1987 (Safer & Krager, 1988). The rates rose faster in secondary than elementary schools.

Another interesting case is Alzheimer's Disease (AD). Although some analysts don't use a medicalization frame (Gubrium 1986, Fox 1989), that which was historically termed senility is now a broader and more inclusive category (Halpert 1983). AD was once an obscure disorder; it is now considered among the top five causes of death in the United States. Fox (1989) suggests that the key issue in the change in conceptualization of AD was the removal of "age" as a criterion, thus ending the distinction between AD and senile dementia. This dramatically increased the potential cases of AD, by including cases of senile dementia above 60 years old. Cognitive decline now became defined as a result of a specific disease rather than an inevitable aspect of aging.

Some have suggested that expanding the definition of AD has shrunk the range of what is deemed to constitute normal aging (Robertson 1990), as well as resulted in a failure to recognize the extent to which cognitive decline can be socially produced (Lyman 1989).

A final example of category expansion is alcoholism. In recent years family members of alcoholics have been partly medicalized as enablers, codependents, and "adult children of alcoholics" (Lichtenstein 1988). Worksite programs have also expanded from "industrial alcoholism programs" to Employee Assistance Programs, and EAPs now are broadened into emotional health programs that include substance abuse, smoking, family problems and work dilemmas in their purview (Sonnenstuhl 1986, Conrad & Walsh 1992). In part this may result from a "murkiness" in the disease concept (Roman & Blum 1991), which allows for a certain malleability and expansiveness.

The Range of Medicalization

Publications in the 1980s enumerated the medicalization of numerous forms of deviance and natural life processes. Studies in the past decade have particularly examined the breadth of the medicalization of women's lives: battering, gender deviance, obesity, anorexia and bulimia, and a host of reproductive issues including childbirth, birth control, infertility, abortion, menopause and PMS. As Riessman (1983) notes, for a variety of complex reasons, women may be more vulnerable to medicalization than men. In any case, it is abundantly clear that women's natural life processes (especially concerning reproduction) are much more likely to be medicalized than men's, and that gender is an important factor in understanding medicalization.

In addition to studies of the medicalization of women's lives, considerable research on the medicalization of aging and alcoholism has been published. Estes & Binney (1989) have examined both the conceptual and policy (practice) aspects of the medicalization of aging. They note how more and more aspects of aging have come into medical jurisdiction and how the medical frame has become dominant in aging research, funding, and studies, especially as related to the National Institute of Aging. Estes & Binney point to the important role of Medicare in medicalizing problems of the elderly; because physicians are the only ones authorized to certify the need for care, increased services are seen in a medical frame. This point is illustrated by the medical shaping of Home Health Agencies (Binney et al. 1990). Several authors (Binney et al. 1990, Azzarto 1986) take the medicalization of elderly services as a measure of the medicalization of aging. When we include the previously discussed studies of menopause and Alzheimer's Disease, our knowledge base on the medicalization of aging broadens and deepens. Zola (1991) has recently argued that the issues of aging and disability are converging; as most people age they will develop disabilities, and barring death, most people with disabilities will age. Given the changing American demographic patterns into the twenty-first century, and the continuing insurance coverage only for "medical" problems, it seems likely that the medicalization of aging will persist and expand. And since a majority of the elderly are women, it is likely aging and gender issues will continue to converge.

The medicalization of deviant drinking and alcohol use has long been a topic of sociological interest (Gusfield 1967, Schneider 1978, Levine 1978). The emphasis of those studies has been on the impact of prohibition and repeal, the emergence of Alcoholics Anonymous, and the development of the disease concept. Work has continued along these lines (e.g. Denzin 1987), especially questioning the scientific validity of the disease concept (Fingarette 1988). But much of the medicalization-oriented writing in the last decade has focused on specific issues like EAPs and to a lesser extent, the expansion of the concept of alcoholism (Peele 1989). Some new areas may be on the horizon. Roman & Blum (1991:780) suggest that the "health warning labels" on alcohol products "increase perceived risk associated with alcohol consumption." They may affect public conceptions of alcoholism by making the drinker more responsible for his or her health problems. This may reinvigorate the moral elements of the moral-medical balance in the definition of alcoholism. It is likely, however, that the disease concept will continue to dominate thinking about alcoholism, with the success of Alcoholics Anonymous and the continued organizational supports for the disease concept, especially in terms of third party reimbursement for treatment of alcoholism, workplace EAPs, and encouragement from the alcohol beverage industry (Roman 1988, Peele 1989).

A key aspect of medicalization refers to the emergence of medical definitions for previously nonmedical problems. Thus when social or behavioral activities are deemed medical risks for well-established biomedical conditions, as is becoming common, we cannot say that it is a case of medicalization. There is some confusion around this, especially in terms of the recent concerns with health and fitness (e.g. Crawford 1980). In the 1980s "health promotion" and "wellness" activities were touted as increasing individual health and reducing risk of disease. For example, not smoking, low cholesterol diets, and exercising regularly could reduce the risk of heart disease. Although health promotion may create a "new health morality" (Becker 1986), based on individual responsibility for health (and lifestyle change), it does not constitute a new medicalization of exercise or diet. While the process is similar to medicalization in that it fuses behavioral and medical concerns, it may be better conceptualized as "healthicization." With medicalization, medical definitions and treatments are offered for previous social problems or natural events; with healthicization, behavioral and social definitions are advanced for previously biomedically defined events (e.g. heart disease). Medicalization proposes biomedical causes and interventions; healthicization proposes lifestyle and behavioral causes and interventions. One turns the moral into the medical, the other turns health into the moral (Conrad 1987).

Consequences of Medicalization

Although medical interventions typically are judged by how efficacious they are, the social consequences of medicalization occur regardless of medical efficacy. They are independent from the validity of medical definitions or diagnoses or the effectiveness of medical regimens.

Numerous analysts have described consequences of medicalization. Conrad & Schneider (1980a:245–52) separate the consequences into the "brighter" and "darker" sides. Like most sociologists, they emphasize the darker side: assumption of medical moral neutrality, domination by experts, individualization of social problems, depoliticization of behavior, dislocation of responsibility, using powerful medical technologies, and "the exclusion of evil." The criticism of medicalization fundamentally rests on the sociological concern with how the medical model decontextualizes social problems, and collaterally, puts them under medical control. This process individualizes what might be otherwise seen as collective social problems.

These issues have been reflected and developed in subsequent writings. For example, Carrier (1983:952) argues how learning disability theory "misrecognizes and thus masks the effects of social practices and hierarchy." This has been noted for other problems as well (Lyman 1989, Riessman 1983). Medicalized conceptions of battering can lead to therapy and distract from a focus on patriarchal values and social inequality (Tierney 1982). Medical control may also affect public opinion and social policy. Rosenberg (1988, p. 26) suggests that policymakers have a penchant for medical solutions because they are "less elusive than the economic and political measures which are its natural counterparts." In a highly stratified society, medicalization may have implications for social justice (Gallagher & Ferrante 1987, Light 1989).

A few cases of medicalization bring up different issues. Post traumatic stress disorder is an instance where the cause of the disorder was shifted from the particularities of an individual's background to the nature of war itself; it is "normal" to be traumatized by the horrors of war (Scott 1990). Also of interest is the example of medical organizing against nuclear war. By depicting the devastation from nuclear war as "the last epidemic," Physicians for Social Responsibility and later the American Medical Association turned a political issue into a medical one. This was a very successful strategy for claims-making and organizing, and allowed physicians to make political statements in the name of health. To a degree both of these examples decontextualized the issue (war), but with different consequences than those in medicalizing deviance. One of the main differences here was that the issue turned on the effects of war, more than on war itself. In general, sociologists remain skeptical about medicalization, although ambivalent in the recognition of certain gains and losses (Riessman 1983).

Demedicalization

Medicalization is a two-way process. Demedicalization refers to a problem that no longer retains its medical definition. In the late nineteenth century, masturbation was considered a disease and was the object of many medical interventions (Engelhardt 1974). By the twentieth century it was no longer defined as a medical problem nor was it the subject of medical treatment. Some analysts have suggested that the use of medical auxiliaries (e.g. midwives or physician assistants) instead of doctors represents demedicalization (Fox 1977, Strong 1979). This, however, confuses demedicalization with deprofessionalization. Demedicalization does not occur until a problem is no longer defined in medical terms and medical treatments are no longer deemed to be appropriate solutions. Demedicalization could be said to have taken place, for example, if childbirth were defined as a family event with lay attendants, if chronic drunkenness were reconstituted as an educational problem, or if menopause reverted to a natural life event, inappropriate for any medical intervention.

Childbirth in the United States has been medicalized for more than a century. The medical monopoly of childbirth is more recent (Wertz & Wertz 1989). In the last 15 years, the childbirth, feminist, and consumer movements have challenged medicine's monopoly of birthing. This has given rise to "natural childbirth," birthing rooms, nurse-midwives, and a host of other reforms, but it has not resulted in the demedicalization of childbirth. Childbirth is still defined as a medical event, and medical personnel still attend it. In the context of American society, even lay midwifery may not mean complete demedicalization. In Arizona licensed lay midwives have been pressured toward a more medical model of childbirth, especially through licensing and legal accountability in a medically dominated environment (Weitz & Sullivan 1985).

The classic example of demedicalization in American society is homosexuality. In response to the protest and picketing of the gay liberation movement (with some sympathetic psychiatric allies), in 1973 the American Psychiatric Association officially voted to no longer define (i.e. include in DSM-III) homosexuality as an illness. This represented at least a symbolic demedicalization (Conrad & Schneider 1980a, Bayer 1981). Here politicization of medicalization created an overt conflict which resulted in the demedicalization. Although some argue that lesbianism has yet to be demedicalized (Stevens & Hall 1991), it seems evident that today homosexuality is at least as often considered a lifestyle as an illness. As several observers note (e.g. Murray & Payne 1985), the onset of the AIDS epidemic has led to a partial remedicalization of homosexuality, albeit in a different form.

There are two other examples of demedicalization worth noting. The Independent Living Movement asserts that, in the lives of people with disabilities, "much of [the] medical presence is both unnecessary and counter-productive . . . [and] management of stabilized disabilities is primarily a personal matter and only secondarily a medical matter" (DeJong 1983, p. 15). They actively work to demedicalize disability, including reshaping its definition, and work to create environments and situations where people with disabilities can live independently and with minimal contact with medical care.

A most interesting example has emerged almost serendipitously. Winkler & Winkler (1991) suggest that single women who practice artificial insemination (AI) with "turkey basters" or other such materials, present a fundamental challenge to medicalization. This subterranean practice has been well-known in the women's health movement for some time and apparently has proved quite successful. Because this practice requires no medical intervention, it raises important questions about the necessity of medical expertise and control even for infertile couples. The authors contend that demedicalization is already underway and argue for the demedicalization of AI for those women without reproductive maladies of their own.

Given the stature and power of medicine, demedicalization is usually only achieved after some type of organized movement that challenges medical definitions and control. Other factors can affect demedicalization. Some types of technology can lead to a degree of demedicalization: turkey basters and take-home pregnancy tests are but two examples. And the recent upsurge in self-care erodes medical control. Changes in public policy or in insurance reimbursement eligibility can also affect demedicalization.

Cross-Cultural Research

Most studies of medicalization have been in the American context. It is not clear whether medicalization is simply more advanced in American society or whether other societies have yet to be adequately studied.

Few cross-cultural or comparative studies have explicitly focused on medicalization. A significant exception are Lock's reports that in Japan menopause is less medicalized than in North America (Lock 1986) but that aging itself is increasingly medicalized (Lock 1984, see also Lock 1987). From a different perspective, Kleinman (1988) describes how in China patients suffering from difficulties with sleep, low energy, joylessness, and sadness are diagnosed having neurasthenia; he suggests that most could be rediagnosed as having a major depressive disorder (1988:13). In China the patients receive a physiological diagnosis, in North America a psychiatric one. While diagnosis and treatment differ, it can be argued that chronic demoralization is medicalized in both societies.

Given the dominance of Western biomedicine in the world, it would not be surprising to see the diffusion of biomedical categories to non-Western societies. Some unsystematic evidence suggests that this may be occurring for certain problems; for example, the medicalization of childbirth is increasing in societies that make medical childbirth a priority or that can afford the necessary medical resources (e.g. Colfer & Gallagher 1992). The extent to which deviant behavior is medicalized is still unclear, however. For example, when I asked neurologists and psychiatrists in Indonesia whether they saw or treated patients with anorexia, the overwhelming response was that such a disorder did not exist in Indonesia and doctors did not treat it; Earls (1981) reports the same situation in China. Nearly two decades ago Maccoby (1974) reported finding no hyperactive children in the schoolrooms of the People's Republic of China; more recent reports suggest that it has become the most common child psychiatric disorder, and large numbers of Chinese children are being treated with stimulant medications for hyperactivity or attentional deficit disorder (Earls 1981). This raises questions about whether Western medicalized concepts are exported to non-Western societies, about the degree to which and under what conditions they are adopted, and about the impact and meaning they have in other cultures. In another context, it is clear that infant-formula manufacturers were active in promoting the medicalization of infant feeding in the Third World (Van Esterik 1989). We do not yet have much knowledge about the role of drug manufacturers and medical entrepreneurs in promoting and exporting medical definitions and treatments.

More cross-cultural studies would expand our understanding of medicalization in new directions. For example, how are anorexia, hyperactivity, obesity, and PMS defined and treated in other cultures? What does it mean whether or not a non-Western society medicalizes a particular problem? How does a problem's definition relate to the culture and medical belief system? When certain phenomenon are found or identified in only a few cultures, anthropologists typically conceptualize these as Western "culture-bound syndromes" (Ritenbaugh 1982, Littlewood & Lipsedge 1987, T. Johnson 1987). How does medicalization interplay with culture-boundedness? What types of cultural and structural factors in societies encourage or discourage the medicalization of life's problems?

Issues in the Future of Medicalization

Throughout this essay I have touched on a number of issues in medicalization research. Here I want to point to several that are critical for expanding our understanding of medicalization and demedicalization.

Medicine in the United States is changing. Medical authority is declining (Starr 1982); increasingly physicians are now employees (McKinlay & Stoeckle 1988). Corporate structures have increased power in terms of third parties and the "buyers" of health services, to name only the most major changes. These are fundamental changes in the organization of medicine. What impacts are they having on medicalization? Similarly, what is the impact of the dismantling of the welfare state (and subsequent cutbacks)? Will this engender a redefinition to "badness" rather than sickness?

What is the relationship between the economic infrastructure of health care—primarily insurance reimbursement—and medicalization? What is the effect of continuing rising health costs and subsequent policy concerns with cost containment? Does this fuel or constrain medicalization and how? What impact could universal health insurance have on medicalization? Comparative studies of other industrialized health systems would be useful here.

Few authors have yet examined the influence of the AIDS epidemic on medicalization. While it clearly has an impact on the definition and treatment of homosexuality, and probably on drug addiction as well, we know little about the impact. And since AIDS is affecting medicine and our society in many ways, how else is it affecting medicalization? For example, what does HIV testing mean for extending medical surveillance?

While cases like obesity and "chronic fatigue syndrome" are still only partly investigated, in general, I believe we need to go beyond the accumulation of cases to investigate more carefully the causes of medicalization. This includes unearthing previously undetected dimensions of medicalization and contributing to a more integrated theory.

References

Armstrong, D. 1983. *Political Anatomy of the Body*. New York: Cambridge. 176 pp.
Arney, W. R. 1982. *Power and the Profession of Obstetrics*. Chicago: Univ. Chicago. 290 pp.
Azzarto, J. 1986. Medicalization of problems of the elderly. *Health Soc. Work* 11:189–95.
Bayer, R. 1981. *Homosexuality and American Psychiatry: The Politics of Diagnosis*. New York: Basic.
Becker, M. 1986. The tyranny of health promotion. *Public Health Rev.* 14:15–25.
Bell, S. E. 1987a. Premenstrual syndrome and the medicalization of menopause: a sociological perspective. In *Premenstrual Syndrome: Ethical and Legal Implications in a Biomedical Perspective*, ed. B. E. Ginsburg, B. F. Carter, pp. 151–71. New York: Plenum.
———. 1987b. Changing ideas: the medicalization of menopause. *Soc. Sci. Med.* 24:535–42.
———. 1990. Sociological perspectives on the medicalization of menopause. *Ann. New York* 592:173–8.

Billings, B. B., Urban, T. 1982. The socio-medical construction of transexualism: an interpretation and critique. *Soc. Probl. 29*:266–82.

Binney, E. A., Estes, C. L., Ingman, S. R. 1990. Medicalization, public policy and the elderly: social services in jeopardy? *Soc. Sci. Med. 30*:761–71.

Bosk, C. L. 1985. Social control and physicians: the oscillation of cynicism and idealism in sociological theory. In *Social Controls and the Medical Profession*, ed. J. P. Swazey, S. R. Scher, pp. 31–48. Boston: Oelgeschlager, Gunn. 268 pp.

Brumberg, J. J., 1988. *Fasting Girls: The Emergence of Anorexia Nervosa as a Modern Disease*. Cambridge: Harvard Univ. Press. 366 pp.

Bull, M. 1990. Secularization and medicalization. *Br. J. Sociol. 41*:245–61.

Bury, M. R. 1986. Social constructionism and the development of medical sociology. *Sociol. Health Illness 8*:137–69.

Carrier, J. G. 1983. Masking the social in educational knowledge: the case of learning disability theory. *Am. J. Sociol. 88*:948–74.

Clarke, J. N. 1984. Medicalization and secularization in selected English Canadian fiction. *Soc. Sci. Med. 18*:205–10.

Colfer, C. J., Gallagher, E. B. 1992. Home and hospital birthing in Oman: an observational study with recommendations for hospital practice. In *Health and Health Care in Developing Countries*, ed. P. Conrad, E. B. Gallagher. Philadelphia, PA: Temple Univ. Press. Forthcoming.

Conrad, P. 1975. The discovery of hyperkinesis: notes on the medicalization of deviant behavior. *Soc. Probl. 23*:12–21.

_____. 1976. *Identifying Hyperactive Children: The Medicalization of Deviant Behavior*. Lexington, MA: D. C. Heath. 122 pp.

_____. 1977. Medicalization, etiology and hyperactivity: a reply to Whalen and Henker. *Soc. Prob. 24*:596–98.

_____. 1979. Types of medical social control. *Sociol. Health Illness 1*:1–11.

_____. 1987. Wellness in the workplace: potentials and pitfalls of worksite health promotion. *Milbank Q. 65*:255–75.

Conrad, P., Schneider, J. 1980a. *Deviance and Medicalization: From Badness to Sickness*. St. Louis: Mosby. 311 pp.

_____. 1980b. Looking at levels of medicalization: a comment of Strong's critique of the thesis of medical imperialism. *Soc. Sci. Med. 14A*:75–79.

Conrad, P., Walsh, D. C. 1992. The new corporate health ethic: lifestyle and the social control of work. *Int. J. Health Serv. 22*:89–111.

Cornwell, J. 1984. *Hard-Earned Lives: Accounts of Health and Illness in East London*. New York: Tavistock. 250 pp.

Crawford, R. 1980. Healthism and the medicalization of everyday life. *Int. J. Health Serv. 10*:365–88.

DeJong, G. 1983. Defining and implementing the Independent Living concept. In *Living for Physically Disabled People*, ed. N. M. Crewe, I. K. Zola, pp. 4–27. San Francisco: Jossey-Bass. 429 pp.

Denzin, N. K. 1987. *The Recovering Alcoholic*. Newbury Park, CA: Sage. 246 pp.

Dull, D., West C. 1991. Accounting for cosmetic surgery: the accomplishment of gender. *Soc. Probl. 38*:54–70.

Durkheim, E. 1933. *The Division of Labor in Society*. New York: Free Press (Originally published, 1893). 350 pp.

Earls, F. 1981. *Child psychiatry in China: summary of a three month visit*. Unpublished paper, Dep. Psychiatry, Harvard Medical School. 8 pp.

Engelhardt, H. T. 1974. The disease of masturbation: values and the concept of disease. *Bull. Hist. Med. 48*:234–48.

Erchak, G. M., Rosenfeld, R. 1989. Learning disabilities, dyslexia, and the medicalization of the classroom. In *Images of Issues*, ed. J. Best, pp. 79–97. New York: Aldine de Gruyter. 257 pp.

Estes, C. L., Binney, E. A. 1989. The biomedicalization of aging: dangers and dilemmas. *The Gerontol. 29*:587-96.

Fingarette, H. 1988. *Heavy Drinking: The Myth of Alcoholism as a Disease*. Berkeley: Univ. California. 195 pp.

Foucault, M. 1965. *Madness and Civilization*. New York: Random. 239 pp.

_____. 1973. *The Birth of the Clinic*. New York: Vintage. 215 pp.

_____. 1977. *Discipline and Punish*. New York: Random. 333 pp.

Fox, P. 1989. From senility to Alzheimer's Disease: the rise of the Alzheimer's Disease movement. *Milbank Q. 67*:58–101.

Fox, R. C. 1977. The medicalization and demedicalization of American society. *Daedalus 106*:9–22.

Freidson, E. 1970. *Profession of Medicine*. New York: Dodd, Mead.

Gabe, J., Calnan, M. 1989. The limits of medicine: women's perception of medical technology. *Soc. Sci. Med. 28*:223–32.

Gallagher, E. B., Ferrante, B. 1987. Medicalization and social justice. *Soc. Justice Res. 1*:377-92.

Galliher, J. F., Tyree, C. 1985. Edwin Southerland's research on the origins of sexual psychopath laws: an early case study of the medicalization of deviance. *Soc. Probl. 33*:100–13.

Goodstein, R. K., Page, A. W. 1981. Battered wife syndrome: overview of dynamics and treatment. *Am. J. Psychiatry 138*:1036–44.

Greenberg, D. F. 1988. *The Construction of Homosexuality*. Chicago: Univ. Chicago Press. 635 pp.

Greil, A. L. 1991. *Not Yet Pregnant: Infertile Couples in Contemporary America*. New Brunswick, NJ: Rutgers Univ. Press. 243 pp.

Gubrium, J. F. 1986. *Oldtimers and Alzheimers*. Greenwich, CT: JAI. 222 pp.

Gusfield, J. R. 1967. Moral passage: the symbolic process in the public designations of deviance. *Soc. Probl. 15*:175–88.

_____. 1981. *The Culture of Public Problems: Drinking-Driving and the Symbolic Order*. Chicago: Univ. Chicago Press. 248 pp.

Haines, H. 1989. Primum non nocere: chemical execution and the limits of medical social control. *Soc. Probl. 36*:442–54.

Halleck. S. L. 1971. *The Politics of Therapy*. New York: Science House. 283 pp.

Halpern, S. A. 1990. Medicalization as a professional process: postwar trends in pediatrics. *J. Health Soc. Behav. 31*:28–42.

Halpert, B. P. 1983. Development of the term "senility" as a medical diagnosis. *Minn. Med. 66*:421–24.

Hansen, B. 1989. American physicians' earliest writings about homosexuals, 1880–1900. *Milbank Q. 67*, Suppl 1:92-108.

Horwitz, A. V. 1991. *The Logic of Social Control*. New York: Plenum. 290 pp.

Hubbard R., Henifin, M. S. 1985. Genetic screening of perspective parents and workers: scientific and social issues. *Int. J. Health Serv. 15*:231–44.

Illich, I. 1976. *Medical Nemesis*. New York: Pantheon. 294 pp.

Johnson, J. M., Waletzko, L. 1991. Drugs and crime: a study in the medicalization of crime control. *Perspect. Soc. Probl. 3*:197–220.

Johnson, T. M. 1987. Premenstrual syndrome as a Western culture-specific disorder. *Cult. Med. Psychiatry 11*:337–56.

_____. 1988. Physician impairment: social origins of a medical concern. *Med. Anthro. Q. 2*:17–33.

Kaufert, P. A., Gilbert, P. 1986. Women, menopause, and medicalization. *Cult. Med. Psychiatry 10*:7–21.

King, D. 1987. Social constructionism and medical knowledge: the case of transexualism. *Sociol. Health Illness 9*:352–77.

Kleinman, A. 1988. *Rethinking Psychiatry: From Cultural Category to Personal Experience*. New York: Free Press. 237 pp.

Kurz, D. 1987. Emergency department responses to battered women: resistance to medicalization. *Soc. Probl. 34*:69–81.

Levine, H. G. 1978. The discovery of addiction: changing conceptions of habitual drunkenness in *America. J. Stud. Alcohol 39*:143–74.

Levine, M. P., Troiden, R. R. 1988. The myth of sexy compulsivity. *J. Sex. Res. 25*:347–63.

Lichtenstein, M. 1988. *Co-dependency: the construction of a new disease*. Pres. Annu. Meet. East. Sociol. Soc., Philadelphia, PA.

Lifton, R. J. 1986. *Nazi Doctors: Medical Killing and Psychology of Genocide*. New York: Basic. 561 pp.

Light, D. W. 1989. Social control and the American health care system. In *Handbook of Medical Sociology*, ed. H. E. Freeman, S. Levine, pp. 456–74. 548 pp.

Littlewood, R., Lipsedge, M. 1987. The butterfly and the serpent: culture, psychopathology and biomedicine. *Cult. Med. Psychiatry 11*:289–335.

Lock, M. 1984. Licorice in leviathan: the medicalization of the care of the Japanese elderly. *Cult. Med. Psychiatry 8*:121–39.

_____. 1986b. Ambiguities of aging: Japanese experience and acceptance of menopause. *Cult. Med. Psychiatry 10*:23–46.

_____. 1987. Protests of a good wife and wise mother: the medicalization of distress in Japan. In *Health, Illness and Medical Care in Japan*, ed. E. Norbeck, M. Lock, pp. 130–57. Honolulu: Univ. Hawaii Press. 202 pp.

Low, S. M. 1988. The medicalization of healing cults in Latin America. *Am. Ethnol. 15*:136–54.

Lyman, K. A. 1989. Bringing the social back in: a critique of the medicalization of dementia. *The Gerontol. 29*:597–605.

Maccaby, E. E. 1974. Impressions of China. *Soc. Res. Child Dev. Newslett.* (Fall): 5.

MacPherson, K. I. 1981. Menopause as a disease: the social construction of a metaphor. *Adv. Nurs. Sci. 3*:95–113.

McCrea, F. B. 1983. The politics of menopause: the "discovery" of a deficiency disease. *Soc. Probl. 31*:111–23.

McDonald, M. 1989. The medicalization of suicide in England: laymen, physicians, and cultural change, 1500–1870. *Milbank Q. 67* (Suppl.) 1:69–91.

McKinlay, J. B., Stoeckle, J. 1988. Corporatization and the social transformation of doctoring. *Int. J. Health Serv. 18*:191–205.

Murray, S. O., Payne, K. W. 1985. *The Remedicalization of homophobia: scientific evidence and the San Francisco bath decision*. Pres. Annu. Meet. Soc. Study Soc. Probl. Washington, DC.

Nicholson, M., McLaughlin, C. 1987. Social constructionism and medical sociology: a reply of M. R. Bury. *Sociol. Health Illness 9*:107–26.

O'Neill, J. 1986. The medicalization of social control. *Can. Rev. Sociol. Anthropol.* 23:350–64.

Parsons, T. 1951. *The Social System.* New York: Free Press. 575 pp.

Pawluch, D. 1983. Transitions in pediatrics: a segmental analysis. *Soc. Probl.* 30:449–65.

Peele, S. 1989. *Diseasing of America: Addiction Treatment Out of Control.* Boston: Houghton Mifflin. 321 pp.

Peyrot, M. 1984. Cycles of social problem development. *Sociol. Q.* 25:83–96.

Pfohl, S. J. 1977. The "discovery" of child abuse. *Soc. Probl.* 24:310–23.

Pitts, J. 1968. Social control: the concept. In *International Encyclopedia of Social Sciences* (Vol. 14) ed. D. Sills. New York: Macmillan.

Proctor, R. 1988. *Racial Hygiene: Medicine Under the Nazis.* Cambridge: Harvard Univ. Press. 313 pp.

Riessman, C. K. 1983. Women and medicalization: a new perspective. *Soc. Policy* 14(Summer):3–18.

Ritenbaugh, C. 1982. Obesity as a culture-bound syndrome. *Cult. Med. Psychiat.* 6:347–61.

Robbins, T., Anthony D. 1982. Deprogramming, brainwashing and the medicalization of deviant religious groups. *Soc. Probl.* 29:266–82.

Robertson, A. 1990. The politics of Alzheimer's Disease: a case study in apocalyptic demography. *Int. J. Health Serv.* 20:429–42.

Roman, P. 1980a. Medicalization and social control in the workplace: prospects for the 1980s. *J. Appl. Behav. Sci.* 16:407–23.

_____. 1980b. Alternatives to the medicalization of deviant behavior. *Psychiatry* 43:168–74.

_____. 1988. The disease concept of alcoholism: sociocultural and organizational bases of support. *Drugs & Society* 2:5–32.

Roman, P., Blum T. 1991. The medicalized conception of alcohol related problems: some social sources and some social consequences of murkiness and confusion. In *Society, Culture and Drinking Patterns Reexamined*, ed. D. Pittman, H. White, pp. 753–74. New Brunswick, NJ: Rutgers Univ. Press.

Rosenberg, C. E. 1988. Disease and social order in America: perceptions and expectations. In *AIDS: The Burdens of History*, ed. E. Fee, D. M. Fox, pp. 12–32. Berkeley: Univ. California Press. 362 pp.

Rosencrance, J. 1985. Compulsive gambling and the medicalization of deviance. *Soc. Probl.* 3:275–85.

Rothman, B. K. 1989. *Recreating Motherhood: Ideology and Technology in a Patriarchal Society.* New York: Norton. 284 pp.

Rubinstein, R. A., Brown, R. T. 1984. An evaluation of the validity of the diagnostic category of Attention Deficit Disorder. *Am. J. Orthopsychiat.* 54:398–414.

Safer, D. J., Krager, J. M. 1988. A survey of medication treatments for hyperactive/inattentive students. *J. Am. Med. Assoc.* 260:2256–59.

Schneider, J. W. 1978. Deviant drinking as a disease: deviant drinking as a social accomplishment. *Soc. Probl.* 25:361–72.

_____. 1985. Social problems theory: the constructionist view. *Annu. Rev. Sociol.* 11:209–29.

Schneider, J. W., Conrad, P. 1980. The medical control of deviance: contests and consequences. In *Research in the Sociology of Health Care*, (Vol. 1), ed. I. A. Roth, pp. 1–53. Greenwich, CT: JAI.

Scott, W. J. 1990. PTSD in DSM-III: a case of the politics diagnosis and disease. *Soc. Probl.* 37:294–310.

Scull, A. T. 1975. From madness to mental illness: medical men as moral entrepreneurs. *Eur. J. Sociol.* 16:218–61.

Snow, D. A., Baker, S. G., Anderson, L. et al. 1986. The myth of pervasive mental illness among the homeless. *Soc. Probl.* 33: 407–23.

Sonnenstuhl, W. J. 1982. A comment on medicalization in the workplace. *J. Appl. Behav. Sci.* 18:123–25.

_____. 1986. *Inside an Emotional Health Program.* Ithaca, NY: ILR Press. 196 pp.

Spector, M., Kitsuse, J. I. 1977. *Constructing Social Problems.* Menlo Park, CA: Cummings. 184 pp.

Starr, P. 1982. *The Social Transformation of American Medicine.* New York: Basic, 514 pp.

Stevens, P. E., Hall, J. M. 1991. A critical historical analysis of the medical construction of lesbianism. *Int. J. Health Serv.* 21:291–308.

Stimson, G. V. 1985. Recent developments in professional control: the impaired physician movement in the USA. *Sociol. Health Illness* 7:141–66.

Strong, P. M. 1979. Sociological imperialism and the profession of medicine: a critical examination of the thesis of medical imperialism. *Soc. Sci. Med.* 13A:199–215.

Szasz, T. 1963. *Law, Liberty and Psychiatry.* New York: Macmillan. 281 pp.

Tierney, K. J. 1982. The battered women movement and the creation of the wife abuse problem. *Soc. Probl.* 29:207–20.

Teifer, L. 1986. In pursuit of the perfect penis: the medicalization of male sexuality. *Am. Behav. Sci.* 29:579–99.

Trice, H. M., Beyer, I. M. 1984. Employee assistance programs: blending performance-oriented and humanitarian ideologies to assist emotionally disturbed employees. *Res. Commun. Mental Health* 4:245–97.

Turner, B. S. 1984. *The Body and Society.* Oxford: Basil Blackwell. 280 pp.

Turner, B. S. 1987. *Medical Power and Social Knowledge.* Newbury Park, CA: Sage. 254 pp.

Van Esterik, P. 1989. *Beyond the Breast-Bottle Controversy.* New Brunswick, NJ: Rutgers Univ. Press. 242 pp.

Waitzkin, H. 1991. *The Politics of Medical Encounters: How Patients and Doctors Deal with Social Problems.* New Haven: Yale Univ. Press. 311 pp.

Walsh, D. C., Elinson, L., Gostin, L. 1992. Worksite drug testing. *Annu. Rev. Publ. Health 13:* In press.

Weitz, R., Sullivan, D. 1985. Licensed lay midwifery and the medical model of childbirth. *Sociol. Health Illness* 7:36–55.

Wender, P. 1987. *The Hyperactive Child, Adolescent and Adult.* New York: Oxford. 320 pp.

Wertz, R., Wertz D. 1989. *Lying In: A History of Childbirth in America.* (Expanded edition.) New Haven: Yale Univ. Press. 323 pp. (Originally published, 1977).

Whalen, C. K., Henker, B. 1977. The pitfalls of politicization: a response to Conrad's "The discovery of hyperkinesis: notes on the medicalization of deviant behavior." *Soc. Probl.* 24:583–95.

Wharton, C. S. 1987. Establishing shelters for battered women: local manifestations of a social movement. *Qual. Sociol.* 10:146–63.

Winkler, D., Winkler, N. J. 1991. Turkey-baster babies: the demedicalization of artificial insemination. *Milbank Q.* 69:5–40.

Woolgar, S., Pawluch, D. 1985. Ontological gerrymandering: the anatomy of social problems explanations. *Soc. Probl. 32*:214–27.

Zola, I. K. 1972. Medicine as an institution of social control. *Sociol. Rev. 20*:487–504.

_____. 1983. *Socio-Medical Inquiries*. Philadelphia: Temple Univ. Press. 349 pp.

_____. 1991. The medicalization of aging and disability. In *Advances in Medical Sociology*, pp. 299–315. Greenwich, CT: JAI.

6
Experiences of Illness and Narrative Understandings

Susan E. Bell

Introduction

This chapter reviews the literature about the experience of illness and narrative. It connects the emergence and growth of the field of illness studies and the "narrative turn" in it to transformations in social and academic life. Throughout, it links this discussion to familiar problems in contemporary sociology about the meaning of knowledge, the possibility of producing accurate knowledge about social life, and about the constitution of a "self" (Seidman 1992; Smith 1987). In other words, it asks how we can know about the experience of illness if all knowers and all knowledge are situated; and how we can understand the lives and selves of people with illnesses if identity is no longer conceived of as unitary, autonomous, and stable.

Sociological Context

In the first serious attempt to establish a field of studies and define a sociology of illness experience, Peter Conrad (1987:4–5) wrote that it "must consider people's everyday lives living with and in spite of illness. Such a perspective necessarily focuses on the meaning of illness, the social organization of the sufferer's world, and the strategies used in adaptation." This definition intentionally draws scholarly attention away from medical settings and medical perspectives on disease and towards the non-medical settings and non-medical perspectives of everyday life. Similarly, in its most general sense, "the narrative approach begins and ends with everyday life: the experiences, speech, purposes, and expectations of agents as they express them in their [written or spoken] stories about themselves" (Hinchman and Hinchman 1997:xvi). A widely used definition of nar-

Written especially for *Perspectives in Medical Sociology*, 3/E.

rative—a term used interchangeably with story in this chapter—is a discourse that consists of a sequence of temporally related events connected in a meaningful way for a particular audience in order to make sense of the world and/or people's experiences in it (Hinchman and Hinchman 1997:xvi). This definition of narrative includes everyday life and also draws attention to ways in which all knowledge—including scientific and nonscientific knowledge, medical and non-medical knowledge—is produced, communicated, and sustained. Its intention is to counter traditional models of knowledge by stressing that there are multiple truths, constructed by knowers who are socially and historically located, about a world that is neither fixed nor independent of knowers. Narratives are produced in every imaginable setting, ranging from the dinner table to the doctor's office, from the playground or lecture hall to the research interview and journal article. People produce them for many reasons; these include remembering, engaging, entertaining, convincing, and even fooling their audiences (Bamberg and McCabe 1998:iii).

Approaches to the study of narrative and the experience of illness reflect and address general problems in sociology. The first problem concerns knowledge. According to modern social science, knowledge results from applying methods of science to the social world. Because they rest on the solid ground of facts and the scientific method, the social science knowledge is a real, true mirror of the social world. This perspective assumes that social life is patterned and purposeful and, conversely, that the standards of social science—like those of the natural sciences—are objective and value-free (Seidman 1994). Over the past twenty years, an increasing number and range of scholars have questioned the assumptions upon which modern social science is based. They argue that sociologists may want to tell the truth, but there is no *real*, fixed world existing independently of any knower embodied in *facts* that can be *truthfully* (universally) known (Davis and Fisher 1993). In medical sociology, early ethnographers simultaneously provided the basis both for questioning the authority of medical knowledge about illness and for questioning the possibility of knowing the truth about the experience at all, when they turned away from physician-centered knowledge of the experience of illness (Charmaz and Olesen 1997; Conrad and Bury 1997). These possibilities remained only implicit in their work, for, as Alan Radley (1993:7) puts it, they made the assumption that "there are subjective experiences, in this context a 'patient's view', that needs to be accommodated." Although they questioned the adequacy of a biomedical model of disease on its own, early ethnographers did not question the existence or the adequacy of an opposite, subjectivist view. They assumed that a lifeworld exists, and that sociologists can know it if they turn their attention away from the medical world of doctors and towards the lifeworld of "sufferers."[1]

Recent studies of the experience of illness have begun to challenge this oppositional way of thinking. It is not enough to turn away from a one-dimensional biomedical perspective to use a one-dimensional sociological model, such as one that emphasizes "isolation, stigma, or the 'master status' of illness and disability labels" (Bury 1991:463). To do so simply replaces one inadequate, unidimensional perspective with another. As Michael Kelly and David Field (1996:241) write, "Illness, like life itself, is a multi-phenomenal experience and therefore a multi-layered object of analysis." To understand the multi-layered experience of illness, sociologists have begun to look at sick persons and their families and care givers outside of medical care; their experiences with care givers inside of medical care; their experiences beyond illness; and the experiences of medical care givers themselves (Weitz 1991; Fine and Asch 1988a).

Disenchantment with the "dominant 'Cartesian' paradigm of rationality" at the core of modern social science has led some scholars to narrative because narrative emphasizes the plurality of truths that cultures and subcultures claim about themselves instead of assuming that there is one set of indisputable truths that can be known and told (Hinchman and Hinchman 1997:xiv). According to narrative theory, narratives are not merely representations or explanations of events that take place, or of feelings that these events evoke in people going through them. Narratives, like the events they portray, take place in specific historical contexts and in shifting relations of power. Narratives "are constructed, creatively authored, rhetorical, replete with assumptions, and interpretive" (Riessman 1993:4–5). At any point in time there is a plurality of truthful narratives that differently positioned members of a culture can reasonably claim. Because narratives are constructed at particular moments in time and directed to particular audiences, they are about pasts of the moments in which they are told; a truthful narrative might be substantially different if told in other moments or to other audiences (Williams 1984:198).

Another problem for sociology concerns knowing. According to modernist sociology, the particular identity of the researcher and his or her relationship with a particular subject is unproblematic. As long as the researcher adheres to the ethics and scientific standards of research, the work will be unbiased and generalizable, and the rights of the subject will be protected through informed consent.

However, in recent years, these assumptions have been questioned and the identity of the researcher as well as the relationship between researcher and subject have become matters of scholarly concern (Mishler 1986; Smith 1987; Reinharz 1992).

An increasing number of scholars claim that there is no objective, disembodied, value-free position from which the social scientist (knower) can know truth (Riessman 1993). Both the knower and the world(s) she studies are "historically and culturally variable . . . firmly situated within and helping to construct the context of inquiry itself" (Davis and Fisher 1993:6–7). Together, the problems of knowledge and knowing suggest that knowledge of the social world is partial, not universal, constructed by knowers who are themselves socially and historically positioned.

There are different ways researchers have brought themselves into the domain of study in the field of illness experience. The first is a recognition that, as in all human research, who the researcher is and the framework of understanding she brings to the research are significant parts of the research process and have an effect on the production of knowledge. This has led some sociologists to argue in favor of making the researcher a visible part of the analysis (Smith 1987; Paget 1993; DeVault 1996). The second is that understanding the experience of illness involves more than "simply" the experiences of others; it also involves the experiences of sociologists attempting to understand the experiences of others (Weitz 1991). Finally, the researcher has entered the domain of study by turning his or her sociological "eye" toward his or her own experiences, reflecting on these experiences sociologically. This is exemplified in autobiographical accounts by sociologists and anthropologists about their experiences of having illnesses (Zola 1982; Murphy 1987; Frank 1991; Butler and Rosenblum 1991; Paget 1993) or caring for family members who are ill (Butler and Rosenblum 1991; Todd 1994; Ellis 1995).

One of the common denominators in narrative studies is researchers' "awareness of subjectivity and reflectivity in their means of knowing" (Lieblich 1994:xi). Narrative approaches to studying social life bring researchers into the investigative process. Catherine Kohler Riessman (1993:1) puts the argument simply: "story telling . . . is what we do with our research materials and what informants do with us. The story metaphor emphasizes that we create order, construct texts in particular contexts." Story telling is a twofold process. At first, informants and researchers are co-authors during an interview, and then they are co-authors after an interview when a researcher re-presents and transforms the interview texts and discourses. Yet, these co-authors are not equal participants in the process. Instead, they are social actors whose production of a story is embedded in social relations of gender, class, race, sexuality, professional status, and so forth (Langellier 1989; forthcoming). This approach encourages scholars to reflect on how "research strategies, data samples, transcription procedures, specifications of narrative units and structures, and interpretive perspectives" produce social science narratives (Mishler 1995:117). It also encourages them to consider not only the epistemological but also the social and political consequences for scholars and their respondents of the narratives that are produced (Estroff 1995; Langellier forthcoming).

A third problem for sociology concerns notions of self and identity. According to modern social science, one of the distinguishing features of modern society is the differentiation of individuals from one another and the rise of autonomous "selves" (Seidman 1994:60). The predominant (reigning) conception of the modern self defines it as individualistic, unitary, rational, and active. This view of the (adult) self maximizes characteristics associated with masculinity and minimizes characteristics associated with femininity (i.e. interpersonal commitments, including friendship, love, and caregiving relationships). It downplays the difficulty of resolving conflicts that arise between these commitments and personal aims (Meyers 1997:2). In addition, this view of the self assumes that the individual is a "stabilized entity," one that "is generally imbued with a structure of self-descriptions (concepts, schemata, prototypes) that remains stabilized until subjected to external influences from the social surroundings" (Gergen and Gergen 1997:162). This view of a stable self "ignores the multiple, sometimes fractious sources of social identity constituted by one's gender, race, class, ethnicity, sexual orientation, and so forth" (Meyers 1997:2) as well as the capacity of individuals to shape the configuration of this structure (Gergen and Gergen 1997:162).

Even the earliest studies of the experience of illness adopted an alternative view of the self, building on the ideas of George Herbert Mead and William James. According to this symbolic interactionist view of the self, a "self" is both product and process. It is product because it is a "relatively stable, coherent, organization of characteristics, attributes, attitudes, and sentiments that a person holds about himself or herself" (Charmaz 1991:279, note 2). In this respect, a self is an organized entity, with boundaries, parts, and elements that are integrated through memory and habit (Charmaz 1999:73). A self is also a process, a reflexive phenomenon that changes in response to emergent events. These events include interactions with others, feelings of cultural constraints and imperatives, and evaluations of self in relation to experiences, situations, others, and society generally (Charmaz 1991:279, note 2). A self develops from, but is not determined by, past discourses of meaning, present social identifications, and future motivations and goals (Charmaz 1987; 1995).

Disenchantment with modern views of the self has led some scholars to narrative, because it emphasizes the active, self-shaping quality of human thought and the power of stories to create and refashion personal identity (Hinchman and Hinchman 1997:xiv). Through narratives, people construct identities by locating themselves or being located within what Margaret Somers and Gloria Gibson call "a repertoire of emplotted stories" (1994:38–39) and Catherine Kohler Riessman calls "a community of life stories" or "'deep structures' about the nature of life itself" (1993:2). People are especially likely to construct narratives in order to make meaning of unanticipated or apparently unrelated events. Through narratives, people create order, coherence, and connection between events that are not obviously connected to one another and thereby create "important reference points in the interface between self and society" (Williams 1984:198).

Experiencing Illness

There are multiple interrelated reasons why the field of experience of illness studies took off in the 1970s. The first concerns the distribution of disease. Although chronic illness began to replace infectious diseases as "the dominant health care challenge" by the 1920s, not until the 1970s was it recognized as the predominant type of medical "problem." When the first National Health Survey was conducted in 1935, 22 percent of the U.S. population had a chronic disease, orthopedic impairment, or a deficit in vision or hearing. By 1987, the proportion had more than doubled, to over 45 percent of the U.S. population (Hoffman, Rice, and Sung 1996:1473).

A second reason for the emergence of this field of study stems from changes in medical practice that directed attention to the "whole person" as opposed to "the part," signaled by physician Leon Eisenberg (1977:10–11), in his now classic if admittedly "somewhat overstated contrast" that "patients suffer 'illnesses'; physicians diagnose and treat 'diseases.'" Disease is an abnormality "in the structure and function of body organs and systems," whereas illness is an experience of "disvalued changes in states of being and in social function" (Eisenberg 1977:11). That is, "illness refers to how the sick person and the members of the family or wider social network perceive, live with, and respond to symptoms and disability" (Kleinman 1988:3). Making a distinction between disease and illness made it possible to turn the focus of analysis from the perspective of the physician to that of the patient, and to explore the ways in which physicians reconfigured patient's and family's problems into "narrow technical issues." This shift of focus also created the possibility of exploring the consequences of this reconfiguration: "Treatment assessed solely through the rhetoric of improvement in disease processes may confound the patient's (and family's) assessments of care in the rhetoric of illness problems," leading to conflict between people who are sick and people who are medical practitioners (Kleinman 1988:6). These problems can arise in all episodes of disease and illness, but they are exacerbated when the diseases never entirely disappear: "chronic illness persists over time; it does not go away. It is, therefore, not simply a discrete episode in the course of a life narrative but rather a permanent feature of that narrative" (Toombs, Barnard, and Carson 1995: xi. See also Radley 1993).

Simultaneous with these calls in the 1970s within medicine for more patient-centered care were calls outside of it for empowering patients in medical encounters and in the institution of medicine more generally (Boston Women's Health Book Collective 1971). According to women's health movement activists who were subsequently joined by disability rights activists (Fine and Asch 1988b), medicine's focus on disease not only systematically silences patients' viewpoints but also reproduces unequal relations of power.

A third reason for the emergence of this field is medical sociologists' turn from a study of sociology *in* medicine to sociology *of* medicine, primarily in the tradition of symbolic interaction (Conrad 1987: 3–4). Whereas in a sociology *in* medicine the institution of medicine defines sociologists' research problems, a sociology *of* medicine takes "the institution of medicine itself as a problematic focus of inquiry" (Charmaz and Olesen 1997:457). In the late 1950s, a few University of Chicago trained sociologists began to examine illness from the patient's perspective even though at the time the field was dominated by sociology in medicine. This early ethnographic work about illness contributed to the development of a sociology of medicine (Charmaz and Olesen 1997:457).

From its inception, study of the experience of illness has for all practical purposes meant study of the experience of chronic illness. This reflects the rise in the sheer numbers of people living with chronic illnesses, as well as differences in expectations and experiences of those diagnosed with chronic, as opposed to acute, illness. As Kleinman notes, some acute illnesses "are brief, minimally disruptive of our life activities," while others "are more distressing; they take longer to run their course." But chronic illnesses, by definition, never entirely disappear (Kleinman 1988:7). Beyond this, however, they are more likely than acute illnesses to disturb seriously a person's "essential relationships and very sense of self" (Freund and McGuire 1991:168). However, even with acute critical illnesses the body may be restored to health, but life "does not go back to where it was before" (Frank 1991:57).

At first, the field turned to subjective ("insider") accounts, in opposition to the objective ("outsider") accounts of illness. It looked to the "sufferers" of illness and gave them "voice" but left the medical caregiver and the sociologist out of the picture. Early work on identity produced the concepts of "stigma" (Goffman 1963), "biographical disruption" (Bury 1982), and "identity levels" (Charmaz 1987). Subsequent work in the field has developed and critically assessed these concepts, while simultaneously enlarging our understanding of the relationship between illness and identity (Bell 2000).

To date, studies of the experience of illness have been dominated by British and U.S. sociologists whose focus of attention has primarily been on Western culture. The effect of this Western bias on the development of concepts and theories (for example, stigma) has been explored in recent studies of epilepsy in China (Kleinman, Wang, Li, Cheng, Dai, Li, and Kleinman 1995) and infertility in India (Riessman forthcoming). There has been consistent attention to ways in which class differences have affected people's experiences of illness, notably in their access to and use of material resources and their construction of meanings (Bury 1982; Williams 1984; Corbin and Strauss 1988; Blair 1993; Blaxter 1993). Recently, more attention has been given to ways that racial/ethnic and gender identities and locations in the social structure have shaped illness experiences (Anderson, Blue, and Lau 1991; Charmaz 1994; Hill 1994; Castro 1995; Dyk 1995; Bell and Apfel 1995; Langellier forthcoming).

Narrative

In the social sciences generally, there is an outpouring of narrative research today. The analysis of written and spoken narrative discourse has become a central topic for scholars. Indeed, the word "narrative" has become ubiquitous throughout the academic community, crossing disciplines, theoretical frameworks, methodological perspectives, and national borders (Josselson 1993; Mishler 1995). Interest in narratives and narrative analysis reflects attempts in medical sociology to extend the theoretical and methodological frameworks linking illness with self-identity, critical features of the life course, social interaction, and elements of the social structure (Bury 1997:136).

Narrative approaches are also a response to criticisms of biomedicine's traditional focus on disease as opposed to illness (see above). According to the biomedical model (Mishler 1981), health and disease are universal to the human species. Diseases have specific etiologies and can be diagnosed in individuals on the basis of objective signs and symptoms. References to individual life experiences that do not specify objective indications of disease are superfluous to a biomedical understanding of disease. Critics of the biomedical way of knowing argue that it strips away the social context of health and disease and ignores patients' experiences and self-understandings of their problems (Mishler 1984; 1986). By contrast, narrative gives people "triumph over the alienation created by the institutional appropriation of the body through an official, medical discourse that interpolates that body in an exquisite physiological detail but denies the voice of the person who is the lived body" (Frank 1996:62).

At first, as with the field of illness studies more generally, narrative studies of illness dichotomized the distinction between everyday and medical ways of knowing and telling. They equated everyday understandings of illness with sick persons' narratives, and biomedical "truths" about disease with physicians' non-narrative discourse. Almost immediately this dichotomization gave way to a more complex understanding of illness narratives, when scholars began to recognize that narratives are also central aspects of medical culture, especially in (late) modern medical clinics (Mishler 1986, 1995; Atkinson 1997; Hyden 1997). At times, "in the modern clinic the patient is but a pretext for a round of orations, narratives, and disputations" (Atkinson 1997:328).

In addition to exploring the ways narrative creates and sustains the cultural authority of medicine, scholars have also explored intersections between medical and lay narratives of illness (Williams 1984; Atkinson 1997). Although narrative studies, like the sociology of health and illness more generally, are dominated by investigations about physicians and medical culture, a few scholars have explored the construction of illness narratives by and about other health care providers (Gray 1993; Mattingly 1998).

Narrative accounts enable researchers to understand the experiences of sick people that simply cannot be "captured" by other qualitative or quantitative methods (Conrad 1990). According to Arthur Kleinman (1988:30, 29), suffering "remains central to the experience of illness" and narrative methods (including ethnography, biography, history, psychotherapy) are ways of creating knowledge about suffering, of grasping "the complex inner language of hurt, desperation, and moral pain (and also triumph) of living an illness." This is a form of knowledge that is foreign to modern medicine as well as to clinical and behavioral science research. The institution of medicine arranges "for therapeutic manipulation of disease problems in place of meaningful moral or spiritual response to illness problems" (Kleinman 1988:28). Similarly, clinical and behavioral science research typically uses symptom scales and survey questionnaires and behavioral checklists to quantify functional impairment and disability, but this is a "thinned-out image of patients and families [and] has statistical, not epistemological, significance; it is a dangerous distortion" (Kleinman 1988:28). For Kleinman, thus, there are medical and social scientific reasons to study/listen for illness narratives because this form of knowing provides knowledge of the experience of illness that ordinarily is missed by the clinical and behavioral sciences.

Narrative formats are among the cultural resources available for understanding "life in time" (Mattingly and Garro 1994:771). When a person's life is interrupted by an illness, narrative offers "an opportunity to knit together the split ends of time, to construct a new context" and to fit the disruption caused by illness "into a temporal framework" (Hyden 1997:53).[2]

Beyond accounting for the connection between events in time, narratives also have the "capacity to describe a world through the evocation of sensory images, to interweave even contradictory pictures and symbols and thus offer contradictory explanations in the very same story" (Mattingly and Garro 1994:771). Narratives of illness draw upon culturally shared images and conventions to present and interpret experience and to draw connections between individual and society (Hyden 1997; Mattingly and Garro 1994). In this way, they have the potential of connecting the personal experiences of individuals to public issues of social structure (Williams 1984; Carricaburu and Pierret 1995; Bell, 1988, 1999).

Narratives of illness, like narratives more generally, are not simply reports of experiences. Instead, they "formulate reality and an attitude toward it. They shape experience and organize behavior . . ." (Good and Good 1994:841). According to Arthur Frank (1996:56), when people are ill, their bodies are affected by exterior inscriptions (diagnoses, surgery, social attitudes and so forth), as well as by interior "reality," such as "the pain of tumors creating pressure on organs." Narrative gives a person critical distance and thereby allows him/her the capacity to reflect on pain, "fragmented griefs and unresolved angers" about a disease and its treatment (Frank 1996:57). In this process, "illness becomes experience, which [is] the perpetually shifting synthesis of this perpetually spiraling dialectic of flesh, inscription and intention" (Frank 1996:58). Narrative is constantly engaged in the work of interrogating inscriptions, and that interrogation can become resistant and responsible, just as it has the capacity to become docile and appropriated.

Finally, joining together narrative and the experience of illness has enabled some scholars to explore the ways in which narratives connect selves to one another (Ellis 1995). Narratives about illness are collaboratively performed events (Langellier 1989; forthcoming). They emerge in the relationship between a teller and audience when a person represents his or her experience of illness to others who are present during the telling and present in the teller's imagination (Riessman forthcoming). In addition, they are created within clinical interactions, during "existential negotiations between clinicians and patients, ones that concern the meaning of illness, the place of therapy within an unfolding illness story, and the meaning of a life which must be remade in the face of serious illness" (Mattingly 1994:821). Written narratives of illness, like all written narratives, also connect narrators with readers, who can even imaginatively rewrite them (Riessman forthcoming).

To date, narrative analysts have focused their attention on establishing the credibility and possibilities of narrative approaches as a whole. As the number and range of narrative projects has grown, so has a more nuanced awareness of potential weaknesses and limitations of these approaches to studying the experiences of illness. Even though narrative analysts have consistently examined the ways in which location in the social structure affects experiences and narratives, they have given less attention to ways that narratives vary for people of different ages, for those with different diseases, or for those located within different cultures (Hyden 1997; Bury 1997). Related to this is the question of which dimensions of illness experience are likely to evoke narratives, and which are better understood through other, non-narrative, forms of knowing (Atkinson 1997). From the beginnings of this approach, some analysts have also explored the ways in which "a" narrative is "evidence for or against the proposition that [the] image of the past would have been substantially different in other presents" (Williams 1984:198). That is, some narrative analysts are concerned about the possibility of falling into what Paul Atkinson (1997:335) calls "the trap of Romanticism:" depicting "a" story told by a person about her illness experiences to another person as "the" story of her illness.

Conclusion

Studies of living with illness address questions mirroring those of major importance within sociology as a whole and within the academy more generally concerning knowledge, knowers, and selves. In this chapter, I have explored how scholarship in two fields of work— experience of illness and narrative—has emerged, how it has developed understandings of illness, and how in the course of developing this understanding it has contributed to discussions about epistemological questions in sociology. Along with unresolved tensions and undeveloped areas within each field are promising lines of new research that are increasingly nuanced, attentive to differences, and self-reflexive.

Acknowledgements

Thanks are due to Carlo Rabaza for research assistance, to Sara Dickey, Elliot Mishler, and Peter Conrad for their thoughtful readings of and responses to an earlier version of this article, and to Phil Brown. Support from a Kenan Fellowship for Faculty Development, Bowdoin College, is also gratefully acknowledged.

Notes

[1] The term "suffering" is widely used in studies of the experience of illness. In his classic discussion of recent and new directions in the experience of illness, Conrad (1987:5) suggests that "we self-consciously reconceptualize our respondents as *sufferers* or 'people with . . .' rather than patients." Although replacing "patient" with "sufferer" functions to distinguish experiences in the world of medicine from those in everyday life, it is not without problems. According to the dictionary definition of the word, a person who suffers is one who receives chiefly negative experiences. Thus, changing from "patient" to "sufferer" does not change the association of "illness" with "passivity," even though this is a change in meaning sought by most scholars in the field. In addition, the word "suffer" equates "illness" with loss, pain, and damage. Although these are accompaniments with illness, they are qualities that do not encapsulate the experience of illness. See Fine and Asch (1988a) for an extended critique of the use of the metaphor of "suffering victim" to describe people with disabilities generally.

2 This approach assumes that "life itself has an implicit narrative structure" (Hinchman and Hinchman 1997:xx). However, there is another current of thought about the relationship between what might be called "brute data" and narrative: that these data "are not inherently sequential, developmental, or meaningful" (Hinchman and Hinchman 1997:xx). Accordingly, narrative imposes order and meaning on chaotic, recalcitrant material. It is beyond the scope of this chapter to explore in detail the potential consequences of these opposing assumptions for narrative analysis of illness experiences. For more on this topic generally, see Riessman (1993), Mishler (1995), Hinchman and Hinchman (1997) and Mattingly (1998).

References

Anderson, Joan M., Connie Blue, and Annie Lau. 1991. "Women's Perspectives on Chronic Illness: Ethnicity, Ideology and Restructuring of Life." *Social Science and Medicine* 33(2):101–113.

Atkinson, Paul. 1997. "Narrative Turn or Blind Alley?" *Qualitative Health Research* 7(3): 325–344.

Bamberg, Michael and Allyssa McCabe. 1998. "Editorial." *Narrative Inquiry* 8(1):iii–v.

Bell, Susan E. 1988. Becoming a Political Woman: The Reconstruction and Interpretation of Experience Through Stories. Pp. 97–123 in *Gender and Discourse: The Power of Talk*, ed. A. D. Todd and S. Fisher. Norwood, NJ: Ablex.

———. 1999. "Narratives and Lives: Women's Health Politics and the Diagnosis of Cancer for DES Daughters." *Narrative Inquiry* 9(2):1–43.

———. 2000. "Experiencing Illness in/and Narrative." In *Handbook of Medical Sociology*, 5th ed., ed. C. Bird, P. Conrad, and A. Fremont. New York: Prentice-Hall.

Bell, Susan E. and Roberta J. Apfel. 1995. "Looking at Bodies: Insights and Inquiries about DES-Related Cancer." *Qualitative Sociology* 18(1):3–19.

Blair, Alan. 1993. "Social Class and the Contextualization of Illness Experience." Pp. 27–48 in *Worlds of Illness*, ed. A. Radley. New York and London: Routledge.

Blaxter, Mildred. 1993. "Why Do the Victims Blame Themselves?" Pp. 124–142 in *Worlds of Illness*, ed. A. Radley. New York and London: Routledge.

Boston Women's Health Book Collective (eds.). 1971. *Our Bodies, Ourselves*. Boston: Free Press.

Bury, Michael. 1982. "Chronic Illness as Biographical Disruption." *Sociology of Health & Illness* 4(2):167–182.

———. 1991. "The Sociology of Chronic Illness: A Review of Research and Prospects." *Sociology of Health & Illness* 13(4):451–468.

———. 1997. *Health and Illness in a Changing Society*. London and New York: Routledge.

Butler, Sandra and Barbara Rosenblum. 1991. *Cancer in Two Voices*. San Francisco: Spinsters Book Company.

Carricaburu, Daniele and Janine Pierret. 1995. "From Biographical Disruption to Biographical Reinforcement: The Case of HIV-positive Men." *Sociology of Health & Illness* 17(1):65–88.

Castro, Roberto. 1995. "The Subjective Experience of Health and Illness in Ocuituco: A Case Study." *Social Science and Medicine* 41(7):1005–1021.

Charmaz, Kathy. 1987. "Struggling for a Self: Identity Levels of the Chronically Ill." *Research in the Sociology of Health Care* 6:283–321.

————. 1991. *Good Days, Bad Days: The Self in Chronic Illness and Time*. New Brunswick, NJ: Rutgers.

————. 1994. "Identity Dilemmas of Chronically Ill Men." *The Sociological Quarterly* 35(2):269–288.

————.1995. "Between Positivism and Postmodernism: Implications for Methods." *Studies in Symbolic Interaction* 17:43–72.

————.1999. "'Discoveries' of Self in Illness." Pp. 72–82 in *Health, Illness, and Healing: Society, Social Context, and Self*, ed. K. Charmaz and D. A Paterniti. Los Angeles: Roxbury.

Charmaz, Kathy and Virginia Olesen. 1997. "Ethnographic Research in Medical Sociology: Its Foci and Distinctive Contributions." *Sociological Methods & Research* 25(4):452–494.

Conrad, Peter. 1987. "The Experience of Illness: Recent and New Directions." *Research in the Sociology of Health Care* 6:1–31.

————. 1990. "Qualitative Research on Chronic Illness: A Commentary on Method and Conceptual Development." *Social Science and Medicine* 30(11):1257–1263.

Conrad, Peter and Mike Bury. 1997. "Anselm Strauss and the Sociological Study of Chronic Illness: A Reflection and Appreciation." *Sociology of Health & Illness* 19(3):373–376.

Corbin, Juliet M. and Anselm Strauss. 1988. *Unending Work and Care: Managing Chronic Illness at Home*. San Francisco and London: Jossey-Bass.

Davis, Kathy and Sue Fisher. 1993. "Power and the Female Subject." Pp. 3–20 in *Negotiating and the Margins: The Gendered Discourses of Power and Resistance*, ed. S. Fisher and K. Davis. New Brunswick, NJ: Rutgers.

DeVault, Marjorie L. 1996. "Talking Back to Sociology: Distinctive Contributions of Feminist Methodology." *Annual Review of Sociology* 22:29–50.

Dyk, Isabel. 1995. "Hidden Geographies: The Changing Lifeworlds of Women with Multiple Sclerosis." *Social Science and Medicine* 40(3):307–320.

Eisenberg, Leon. 1977. "Disease and Illness: Distinctions Between Professional and Popular Ideas of Sickness." *Culture, Medicine and Psychiatry* 1:9–23.

Ellis, Carolyn. 1995. *Final Negotiations: A Story of Love, Loss, and Chronic Illness*. Philadelphia: Temple.

Estroff, Sue E. 1995. "Whose Story Is It Anyway? Authority, Voice, and Responsibility in Narratives of Chronic Illness." Pp. 77–102 in *Chronic Illness: From Experience to Policy*, ed. S. K. Toombs, D. Barnard, and R. A. Carson. Bloomington and Indianapolis: Indiana University Press.

Fine, Michelle and Adrienne Asch. 1988a. "Disability Beyond Stigma: Social Interaction, Discrimination, and Activism." *Journal of Social Issues* 44(1):3–21.

————. 1988b. *Women with Disabilities: Essays in Psychology, Culture, and Politics*. Philadelphia: Temple.

Frank, Arthur W. 1991. *At the Will of the Body: Reflections on Illness*. Boston: Houghton Mifflin.

————. 1996. "Reconciliatory Alchemy: Bodies, Narratives and Power." *Body & Society* 2(3):53–71.

Freund, Peter E.S. and Meredith B. McGuire. 1991. *Health, Illness, and the Social Body: A Critical Sociology*. Englewood Cliffs, NJ: Prentice Hall.

Gergen, Kenneth J. and Mary M. Gergen. [1983] 1997. "Narratives of the Self." Pp. 161–184 in *Memory, Identity, Community*, ed. L. P. Hinchman and S. K. Hinchman. Albany: State University of New York Press.

Goffman, Erving. 1963. *Stigma: Notes on the Management of Spoiled Identity.* Englewood Cliffs, NJ: Prentice-Hall.

Good, Byron J. and Mary-Jo DelVecchio Good. 1994. "In the Subjunctive Mode: Epilepsy Narratives in Turkey." In collaboration with Isenbike Togan, Zafer Ilbars, A. Guvener, and Ilker Gelisen. *Social Science and Medicine* 38(6):835–842.

Gray, David E. 1993. "Negotiating Autism: Relations between Parents and Treatment Staff." *Social Science and Medicine* 36(8):1037–1046.

Hill, Shirley A. 1994. *Managing Sickle Cell Disease in Low-Income Families.* Philadelphia: Temple.

Hinchman, Lewis P. and Sandra K. Hinchman. 1997. "Introduction." Pp. vii–xxxii in *Memory Identity Community: The Idea of Narrative in the Human Sciences*, ed. L. P. Hinchman and S. K. Hinchman. Albany: State University of New York Press.

Hoffman, Catherine, Dorothy Rice, and Hai-Yen Sung. 1996. "Persons with Chronic Conditions: Their Prevalence and Costs." *Journal of the American Medical Association* 276(18):1473–1479.

Hyden, Lars-Christer. 1997. "Illness and Narrative." *Sociology of Health & Illness* 19(1):48–69.

Josselson, Ruthellen. 1993. "A Narrative Introduction." Pp. ix–xv in *The Narrative Study of Lives*, vol. 1, ed. R. Josselson and A. Lieblich. Newbury Park, CA: Sage.

Kelly, Michael P. and David Field. 1996. "Medical Sociology, Chronic Illness, and the Body." *Sociology of Health & Illness* 18(2):241–257.

Kleinman, Arthur. 1988. *The Illness Narratives: Suffering, Healing & The Human Condition.* New York: Basic.

Kleinman, Arthur, Wen-Zhi Wang, Shi-Chuo Li, Xue-Ming Cheng, Xiu-Ying Dai, Kun-Tun Li, and Joan Kleinman. 1995. "The Social Course of Epilepsy: Chronic Illness as Social Experience in Interior China." *Social Science and Medicine* 40(10):1319–1330.

Langellier, Kristin M. 1989. "Personal Narratives: Perspectives on Theory and Research." *Text and Performance Quarterly* 9:243–276.

———. Forthcoming. "'You're Marked': Breast Cancer, Tattoo and the Narrative Performance of Identity." In *Narrative and Identity*, ed. D. Carlbaugh and J. Brockmeier.

Lieblich, Amia. 1994. "Introduction." Pp. ix–xiv in *The Narrative Study of Lives*, vol. 2, ed. A. Lieblich and R. Josselson. Newbury Park, CA: Sage.

Mattingly, Cheryl. 1994. "The Concept of Therapeutic 'Emplotment.'" *Social Science and Medicine* 38(6):811–822.

———. 1998. *Healing Dramas and Clinical Plots: The Narrative Structure of Experience.* New York: Cambridge.

Mattingly, Cheryl and Linda C. Garro. 1994. "Introduction." *Social Science and Medicine* 38(6):771–774.

Meyers, Diana Tietjens. 1997. "Introduction." Pp. 1–11 in *Feminists Rethink the Self*, ed. D. T. Meyers. Boulder, CO: Westview Press.

Mishler, Elliot G. 1981. "Viewpoint: Critical Perspectives on the Biomedical Model." In *Social Contexts of Health, Illness, and Patient Care*, ed. E. G. Mishler, L. R. Amara-Singham, S. T. Hauser, R. Liem, S. D. Osherson, and N. E. Waxler. New York: Cambridge.

———. 1984. *The Discourse of Medicine: Dialectics of Medical Interviews.* Norwood, NJ: Ablex.

———. 1986. *Research Interviewing: Context and Narrative.* Cambridge, MA: Harvard.

———. 1995. "Models of Narrative Analysis: A Typology." *Journal of Narrative and Life History* 5(2):87–123.

Murphy, Robert F. 1987. *The Body Silent*. New York: H. Holt.

Paget, Marianne A. 1993. *A Complex Sorrow: Reflections on Cancer and an Abbreviated Life*, ed. Marjorie L. DeVault. Philadelphia: Temple.

Radley, Alan. 1993. "Introduction." Pp. 1–8 in *Worlds of Illness: Biographical and Cultural Perspectives on Health and Disease*, ed. A. Radley. London and New York: Routledge.

Reinharz, Shulamit. 1992. *Feminist Methods in Social Research*. New York: Oxford.

Riessman, Catherine Kohler. 1993. *Narrative Analysis*. Newbury Park, CA: Sage.

———. Forthcoming. "'Even If We Don't Have Children [We] Can Live': Stigma and Infertility in South India." In *Narrative and Cultural Construction of Illness and Healing*, ed. C. Mattingly and L. C. Garro. Berkeley: University of California.

Seidman, Steven. 1992. "Postmodern Social Theory as Narrative with a Moral Intent." Pp. 47–81 in *Postmodernism and Social Theory*, ed. S. Seidman and D. Wagner. Oxford, U.K. and Cambridge, MA: Blackwell.

———. 1994. *Contested Knowledge: Social Theory in the Postmodern Era*. Oxford, U.K. and Cambridge, MA: Blackwell.

Smith, Dorothy E. 1987. *The Everyday World as Problematic: A Feminist Sociology*. Boston: Northeastern.

Somers, Margaret R. and Gloria D. Gibson. 1994. "Reclaiming the Epistemological 'Other': Narrative and the Social Constitution of Identity." Pp. 36–99 in *Social Theory and the Politics of Identity*, ed. C. Calhoun. Cambridge, MA: Blackwell.

Todd, Alexandra Dundas. 1994. *Double Vision: An East-West Collaboration for Coping with Cancer*. Hanover: Wesleyan University Press (published by University Press of New England).

Toombs, S. Kay, David Barnard, and Ronald A. Carson. 1995. "Preface." Pp. ix–xiv in *Chronic Illness: From Experience to Policy*, ed. S. K. Toombs, D. Barnard, and R. A. Carson. Bloomington: Indiana University Press.

Weitz, Rose. 1991. *Life with AIDS*. New Brunswick, NJ: Rutgers.

Williams, Gareth. 1984. "The Genesis of Chronic Illness: Narrative Re-Construction." *Sociology of Health & Illness* 6(2):175–200.

Zola, Irving Kenneth. 1982. *Missing Pieces: A Chronicle of Living with a Disability*. Philadelphia: Temple.

7
Stress, Coping, and Social Supports

Leonard I. Pearlin and Carol S. Aneshensel

Investigations into the harmful health consequences of stress have generally followed the basic paradigm illustrated in Figure 1. The problematic life circumstances that give rise to stress and tax the individual's ability to respond are of two general types: events, usually of an undesirable and relatively abrupt nature, that result in discontinuity or change requiring readjustment; and persistent or continuing problems that occur within ongoing social roles. Although typically considered discretely, these two sources of stress are interrelated. Thus, life event change may lead to stress by altering the meaning of existing role strain, intensifying strain, or creating new strains within social roles (Pearlin et al. 1981). Role strains often present themselves insidiously and become relatively fixed and ongoing in daily experiences as chronic, low-key frustrations and hardships (Pearlin and Lieberman 1979).

Included in the broad spectrum of health outcomes that have been studied as consequences of these "naturalistic" stressors are emotional distress, physical morbidity, and mortality. Stressful experience has been regarded as contributing to specific health conditions such as heart disease (e.g., Jenkins 1976) or cancer (e.g., Schmale and Iker 1971), as well as to nonspecific morbidity, including common, relatively minor physical ailments such as colds, flu, or chronic pain (e.g., Aneshensel and Huba 1984) and psychological disorder. As emphasized in several recent overviews (Kasl 1984; Kessler, Price, and Wortman 1985; Thoits 1983), methodological problems plague this body of research and inhibit confidence in assertions about the etiological role of stress. These uncertainties notwithstanding, the weight of evidence indicates that stressful circumstances exert an influence on health and well-being (Bunney et al. 1982). The magnitude of the harmful impact of stress, however, has consistently been shown to be modest in size. This has served to direct attention to those factors that exacerbate, ameliorate, or otherwise mediate the impact of stress on health and well-being, specifically to the role of coping and social supports.

Figure 1 **The Basic Stress Paradigm**

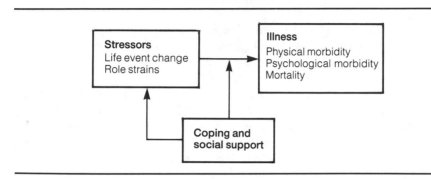

There is something beguilingly presumptive in the labels *coping* and *social supports*. The very terms imply a built-in positive consequence. They suggest that when people behave in a manner we designate as coping, or that when people have social relationships we refer to as supportive, certain desirable effects are taking place. However, this is not necessarily the case. In their study of people who had lost a spouse or child, for example, Wortman and Lehman (in press) find that would-be supporters were commonly judged by the bereaved individuals to be unhelpful. The authors speculate that would-be supporters are occasionally ineffective because the victims' loss can lead to feelings of threat, vulnerability, and helplessness on the part of the supporters. There may be, additionally, some uncertainty and anxiety over appropriate behavior, which in turn impedes empathic responses.

These findings are but a modest illustration of the broad array of mechanisms, forms, and limiting conditions that are involved in the study of coping and social supports. To immerse ourselves in these issues would quickly take us beyond the scope of this chapter. Therefore, we shall confine ourselves to an examination of the consequences or, as we refer to them, the functions of coping and social supports. Following in part from earlier conceptualizations (Pearlin and Schooler 1978), four types of functions can be distinguished: (1) *prevention* of the stressful situation; (2) *alteration* of the stressful situation; (3) *changing the meaning* of the situation; and (4) *manage-*

ment of the symptoms of stress. Within the context of the stress paradigm shown in Figure 1, the functions of coping and social supports can be seen in relation to both the stressor and its effect on health. We shall describe each of these functions in turn.

Preventive Functions

Virtually nothing is known of how coping and supports protect health by preventing stressful problems from surfacing in people's lives. Yet all of us have had occasion to wonder if certain friends and acquaintances are not "snakebitten"—living under a cloud, hounded by relentless misfortune—while others appear to sail through life untouched by serious difficulties. Such difference, of course, may very well be explained by differences in the basic circumstances and life chances of people, their emotional resources, and their involuntary random exposure to hardship. But can such differences also be explained by differences in coping repertoires and access to and use of supports? Perhaps, but we cannot be sure at this time. The reasons we cannot be certain involve the methods used to study coping and supports within the framework of the stress paradigm. Simply put, researchers typically begin to examine people's coping behavior and social supports *after* a health-threatening problem emerges. As a result, more is known of how people deal with problems than of how they avoid them.

Although we lack concrete information, it is possible to speculate about the preventive functions of coping and social supports. With regard to coping, we must recognize that there is a large class of potential health-threatening stressors whose occurrence can be forecasted far in advance of their actual appearance. We refer particularly to life-cycle transitions that can entail rather profound life change. Getting married, having children, launching them onto their own uncharted seas, entering grandparenthood, and retiring from work are such changes. These sorts of changes are remarkably free of lasting deleterious health consequences (Pearlin 1980). One explanation is their predictability: because these life-cycle changes are foreseeable, they permit long periods of anticipatory or preparatory coping. We cannot be sure, of course, whether anticipatory preparation actually prevents problems from arising or simply helps us deal with them once they do arise. We suspect that the avoidance of problems and the readiness to deal appropriately with them are both learned beforehand.

Successfully confronting a problem at one point can help prevent the recurrence of the same problem at a later point. Menaghan's (1982) longitudinal analysis of marital problems, which are closely associated with psychological depression, provides a good example. She found that people who coped effectively with marital problems were more likely to be free of such problems four years later than those coping with the same type of problems with less effective means. Thus, efficacious coping can have a double function. Not only does it reduce stress in the short run but it actually provides a preventive barricade against the future emergence of problems in that role area. Concomitantly, of course, the less successful people are in coping with existing problems, the more likely these problems will endure into or reappear in the future.

Social supports also have preventive functions. Indeed, supports may be more important to the prevention of health-related problems than coping. The most obvious way in which such functions would be accomplished is through the "wisdom" the group imparts to its members: the ability both to anticipate problems and, once recognized, to adopt appropriate avoidance strategies. Clearly, people acquire such abilities from others. Among the norms that we absorb from our membership and reference groups are those that define what is undesirable and should be avoided, what is acceptable but should be approached warily, and what should be actively sought after. Without being aware of it, we learn a litany of dos and don'ts that will presumably shield us from risk. On the other hand, the very supports that shield may also function to increase the exposure to stress and health risks. The more extensive one's social network, for example, the more likely one is to be touched by stressors occurring to others, such as, the death of a close friend. Similarly, to the extent that a person's reference groups engage in certain patterns of behavior, such as smoking or heavy drinking, pressures to conform to group standards can have harmful health effects.

The Alteration of the Problematic Situation

If stressors cannot be prevented or avoided, the next most desirable function of coping and social supports would seem to be modification of the situation (or one's behavior within it) in a way that eliminates or reduces its stress-producing properties. For example, if one is having problems at work, changing the problematic aspects of the work situation would be highly desirable. It is reasonable to suppose that this is a function that people would seek to maximize. With regard to coping, it is surprising that behavior serving this function does not appear particularly prominent in people's repertoires (Pearlin and Schooler 1978). One possible reason is that some problematic situations are recognized by people as intractable, as not meriting efforts to change them. Second, the source of one's stress may not always be apparent. We are capable of experiencing health-damaging stress without being certain of its origins; or, more likely, we attribute the stress to one situation while in reality it comes from another. Thus, coping may be misdirected. Third, one may decide not to act directedly upon the situation because the action might trigger consequences one does not wish to face. A worker might ask his boss to eliminate dangerous job conditions but risk the possibility of being fired. Coping actions intended to alter certain aspects of a situation are also quite capable of producing unintended and unwanted alterations, thus inhibiting efforts directed at change.

Social supports, perhaps more than coping, can actively function to change situations. They do so, we believe, largely through the exercise of what is usually referred to as instrumental (in contrast to expressive) support. Instrumental supports are those that broadly involve the giving of material help, assistance, or information (House 1981). One's network, of course, serves as a nexus for such support and can be used to change certain kinds of problematic situations. If someone is unemployed, for example, relatives, friends, or neighbors, functioning as a referral system for the person, may alert him to job opportunities. Or, short of helping him find a new job, they might ease the burden by providing loans, gifts of food, or other material goods. Of course, some stressful situations can no more be changed successfully by a support group than by the individual caught up in it. Nevertheless, the resources of support groups are potentially powerful instruments in altering the stressful properties of situations.

The Alteration of Meaning

Because many situations that eventually damage psychological and physical health are resistant to change, people engage instead in actions that change the meaning of the situation. The situation remains intact, but perceptions, beliefs, and knowledge are modified in a way that reduces its threatening or harmful qualities.

A number of cognitive and perceptual devices that neutralize the meaning of potentially stressful situations have been identified (Pearlin and Schooler 1978). For example, people often trivialize problematic situations, defining them as too unimportant to be painful or threatening. Since the importance that we assign to a situation influences the threat we feel when things go wrong, diminishing a situation's importance minimizes its threat. Another perceptual process entails the relegation of difficult situations to the commonplace and normal. If we can regard a marital problem, for example, as similar to the problems that our best friends also experience, we can explain our difficulties as a normative, to-be-expected set of experiences. Misery does not simply love company; misery is in active search of company and is often assuaged by it. Many other perceptual devices that people employ vary in form but perform the same function: they endow a situation with a meaning that reduces its stress-arousing qualities.

Along with coping, social supports also contribute importantly to the perceptual management of the threatening properties of stressful circumstances. A natural product of interaction in groups is the acquisition of norms, that is, shared ways of defining situations—appraising them as good or bad, desirable or undesirable—and of prescribing or approving modes of action and reaction. Thus, although an individual's experiences might be unique, the ways the individual assesses and acts upon them may be a consequence of internalized group standards. The norms of membership and reference groups can legitimize and reinforce the perception of a situation as threatening, or they can help define the same situation as ordinary, trivial, fatalistically inexorable, or undeserving of concern, worthy only of being ignored. The objective properties of a situation often do not by themselves determine its threatening quality. Instead, people's normative aspirations, values, and ideologies shape perceptions and combine with the objective situation in giving rise to threat.

Evidence shows that support groups also mediate the stress process by helping the individual maintain a positive self-concept in the face of hardship (Pearlin et al. 1981). Here the group does not influence the perception of the situation as much as it influences the perception of the self in the situation. The support group, in effect, helps the individual maintain self-esteem and a sense of mastery by interpreting the stressful situation as one that does not reflect negatively on these prized elements of self. The maintenance of the self in difficult life situations is a crucial defense against stress.

Control of Stress Symptoms

A final function of coping and supports is seen in behaviors that control symptoms, particularly states such as anxiety and depression, keeping them within manageable bounds so that they do not overwhelm the individual. Folkman and Lazarus (1980) refer to this process as emotion-focused coping, in contrast to that which is problem focused. Much of the popular understanding of coping relates to this function, as does the "stress management" industry that has evolved in recent years. One can turn to biofeedback or bird-watching, to meditation or massage, running or rebirth, drinking or daydreaming—indeed to virtually any activity that provides some relief either from awareness of problematic circumstances or from the tensions and other symptoms associated with them. Dealing effectively with symptoms of distress enables individuals to direct their attention to the important demands of their lives (Mechanic 1962). Based on current knowledge, it is not possible to identify techniques that are superior to others in providing relief. However, some that effectively control symptoms in the short run might very well have deleterious consequences in the long run. To take but one example, alcohol use may provide some immediate relief from symptoms of distress, but too much over too long a period can have a devastating impact on health (Aneshensel and Huba 1983; Pearlin and Radabaugh 1976).

How do social supports function for the control of symptoms? One way is by validating the individual's response to the stressor. Those confronting major life crises or persistent strains are often perplexed and frightened by their emotional and physiological arousal; open discussion of the problem and legitimization of these fears by others can be a critical factor in enabling the individual to manage distress and avoid being overwhelmed by it (Wortman and Lehman, in press). Much of what is called expressive support is provided through these kinds of exchanges. In addition, of course, social life itself is diversionary. The things that individuals do to relieve tensions are often done in groups; some stress management behaviors, in fact, require other people. Once more, then, we find that coping and social supports have striking parallel functions within the stress paradigm.

References

Aneshensel, C. S., and G. J. Huba. 1983. Depression, alcohol use, and smoking over one year: A four-wave longitudinal causal model. *Journal of Abnormal Psychology* 92(2):134–150.

Bunney, W., Jr., A. Shapiro, R. Adler, J. Davis, A. Herd, I. Kopin, D. Krieger, S. Matthyse, A. Stunkard, and M. Weissman. 1982. Panel report on stress and illness. In *Stress and human health*, ed. G. R. Elliott and C. Eisdorfer, pp. 255–321. New York: Springer Publishing.
Folkman, S., and R. S. Lazarus. 1980. An analysis of coping in a middle-aged community sample. *Journal of Health and Social Behavior* 21:219–239.
House, J. S 1981. *Work stress and social support*. Reading, MA: Addison-Wesley.
Jenkins, C. S. 1976. Recent evidence supporting psychologic and social risk factors for coronary disease. *New England Journal of Medicine* 294:987–994, 1033–1038.
Kasl, S. V. 1984. Stress and health. *Annual Review of Public Health* 5:319–341.
Kessler, R. C., R. H. Price, and C. B. Wortman. 1985. Social factors in psychopathology: Stress, social support and coping processes. *Annual Review of Psychology* 36:531–572.
Mechanic, D. 1962. *Students under stress: A study in the social psychology of adaptation*. New York: Free Press.
Menaghan, E. 1982. Measuring coping effectiveness: A panel analysis of marital problems and coping efforts. *Journal of Health and Social Behavior* 23(3):220–234.
Pearlin, L. I. 1980. The life cycle and life strains. In *Sociological theory and research*, ed. H. M. Blalock, pp. 349–360. New York: Free Press.
Pearlin, L. I., and M. A. Lieberman. 1979. Social sources of emotional distress. In *Research in community and mental health*, ed. R. Simmons, 1:217–248. Greenwich, CT: JAI Press.
Pearlin, L. I., M. A. Lieberman, E. G. Menaghan, and J. T. Mullan. 1981. The stress process. *Journal of Health and Social Behavior* 22:337–356.
Pearlin, L. I., and C. W. Radabaugh. 1976. Economic strains and the coping function of alcohol. *American Journal of Sociology* 82:652–663.
Pearlin, L. I., and C. Schooler. 1978. The structure of coping. *Journal of Health and Social Behavior* 19:2–21.
Schmale, A. H., and H. P. Iker. 1971. Hopelessness as a predictor of cervical cancer. *Social Science and Medicine* 5:95–100.
Thoits, P. A. 1983. Dimensions of life events that influence psychological distress: An evaluation and synthesis of the literature. In *Psychosocial stress: Trends in theory and research*, ed. H. B. Kaplan, pp. 33–103. New York: Academic Press.
Wortman, C. B., and D. R. Lehman. In press. Reactions to victims of life crises: Support attempts that fail. In *Social support: Theory, research, and application*, ed. I. B. Sarason and B. R. Sarason. The Hague: Martinus Niihof.

Section III

Environmental and Occupational Health

It is astonishing that environmental and occupational health concerns have only recently been thrust into the public spotlight. To be sure, miners, factory workers, and railway workers have long been struggling with occupational safety and health issues. Preservation-oriented environmentalists, too, have always fought for their cause. Yet these activists' efforts have only fairly recently become part of a growing national environmentalist concern, which is in part reflected in the creation of the federal Environmental Protection Administration (EPA) in 1969 and the Occupational Safety and Health Administration (OSHA) in 1970.

What is striking in terms of the late development of public interest and public policy in this area is that the stakes are so high. Each year over 115,000 workers die from work-related hazards, and 2 million suffer accidents or illness serious enough to make them miss work. Each year, 22 billion pounds of toxic chemicals are released in the United States, much of it winding up in public drinking water or in airborne particles, where it causes cancers and other diseases. The same corporate mentality that callously uses people's labor without regard for their health also produces a disregard for public safety in terms of production and dumping of hazardous waste materials. Corporate profit motives are aided by government failure to enforce existing regulations. The Reagan and Bush administrations in the 1980s, with a strong anti-regulation ideology, moved to diminish the authority of EPA, OSHA, and other regulatory agencies. Popular resistance curbed much of that effort concerning environmental regulation (though they succeeded in occupational health deregulation), but the Republican-dominated Congress elected in 1994 embarked on a program to further reduce environmental protection, including health-related regulations.

Environmental activism has been a major social movement in the last decade or so, and much of its effects have been directed toward environmental health issues. Phil Brown's article on environment

155

---

health activism, "Toxic Waste Contamination and Popular Epidemiology: Lay and Professional Ways of Knowing," shows how people in Woburn, Massachusetts worked out their own methods of getting scientific knowledge and political power in order to deal with an epidemic of childood leukemia which they traced to corporate dumping of toxic wastes. This citizens' effort at *popular epidemiology* is akin to a wide range of other lay health-related action, such as womenSs efforts to secure reproductive rights. As well, the lay/professional disputes over identification of health problems is very applicable to a wide range of health issues where such conflict occurs.

David Kotelchuck, in "Worker Health and Safety at the Beginning of a New Century," shows how occupational health regulation and enforcement were curtailed in the 1980s, despite ample evidence that injury and death on the job were large problems. He tells us that some states even tried to prosecute factory owners who knowingly put their workers at grave risk, only to have the federal government attack those efforts. Kotelchuck also informs us of a range of new issue and on-the-job illnesses that will be major concerns in the coming period. We should remember that union membership dropped precipitously in the last two decades, and that individual unions suffered sharp defeats by government and industry; this diminished their power to fight for occupational safety and health policy. That is a lesson about the importance of larger social forces and social movements in the search for a healthier life.

8
Popular Epidemiology and Toxic Waste Contamination: Lay and Professional Ways of Knowing

Phil Brown

Medical sociology has long been concerned with differences between lay and professional ways of knowing (Fisher 1986; Roth 1963; Stimson and Webb 1975; Waitzkin 1989). Because of their different social backgrounds and roles in the medical encounter, clients and providers have divergent perspectives on problem definitions and solutions (Freidson 1970). Professionals generally concern themselves with disease processes, while laypeople focus on the personal experience of illness. For professionals, classes of disorders are central, while those who suffer the disorders dwell on the individual level (Zola 1973). From the professional perspective, symptoms and diseases universally affect all people, yet lay perceptions and experience exhibit great cultural variation. Similarly, lay explanatory approaches often utilize various causal models that run counter to scientific notions of etiology (Fisher 1986; Freidson 1970; Kleinman 1980). Medical professionals' work consists of multiple goals, among which patient care is only one; patients are centrally concerned with getting care (Strauss et al. 1964).

Recently, lay perceptions on environmental health have manifested themselves in a burgeoning community activism. Following the landmark Love Canal case (Levine 1982), the childhood leukemia cluster in Woburn, Massachusetts has drawn attention to the lay-professional gap. Beginning in 1972, Woburn residents were startled to learn that their children were contracting leukemia at exceedingly high rates. By their own efforts the affected families and community activists attempted to confirm the existence of a leukemia cluster and to link it to industrial toxins that leached into their water supply. They pursued a long course of action that led to a major community health study, a civil suit against W. R. Grace Chemical Corporation and Beatrice Foods, and extensive national attention.

Reprinted by permission of the American Sociological Association from the *Journal of Health and Social Behavior*, Vol. 33, pp. 267–281, copyright © 1992.

Building on a detailed study of the Woburn case, and utilizing data from other toxic waste sites, this chapter discusses conflicts between lay and professional ways of knowing about environmental health risks. This discussion centers on the phenomenon of *popular epidemiology*, in which laypeople detect and act on environmental hazards and diseases. Popular epidemiology is but one variant of public participation in the pursuit of scientific knowledge, advocacy for health care, and public policy, as witnessed in such diverse cases as AIDS treatment, nuclear power development, and pollution control. The emphasis on ways of knowing makes sense because knowledge is often what is debated in struggles to win ownership of a social problem (Gusfield 1981, pp. 36–45).

In their popular epidemiological efforts, community activists repeatedly differ with scientists and government officials on matters of problem definition, study design, interpretation of findings, and policy applications. In examining the stages through which citizens become toxic waste activists, this paper emphasizes lay-professional differences concerning quality of data, methods of analysis, traditionally accepted levels of measurement and statistical significance, and relations between scientific method and public policy.

Study Background

There were two sets of interviews with the Woburn litigants. The first (eight families) comprised open-ended questions on individual experiences with the toxic waste crisis, including personal and family problems, coping styles, and mental health effects. These were conducted in 1985 by a psychiatrist and re-analyzed in 1988 for an earlier phase of this research (Brown 1990). This reanalysis involved both the researcher and the psychiatrist rereading the interview material several times, and then discussing what themes were most prominent. This process defined themes for discussion of the original, largely psychosocial, interviews. As well, it directed the creation of the interview schedule for the reinterview. For example, respondents in the original interviews expressed considerable anger at the corporations accused of contaminating the wells, and at the government officials who were investigating the disease cluster. This provided initial information on these important concerns and directly yielded more specific reinterview questions. The second set of interviews in 1988 (except for one family that did not wish to participate) comprised twenty open-ended questions on residents' perceptions of community activism, the litigation, government and corporate responsibility for toxics, and the relationship between lay and scientific approaches.

Fourteen community activists, apart from the litigants, were also interviewed in 1990. In addition to basic personal data, respondents were asked nineteen open-ended questions concerning toxic waste activism, knowledge about toxic wastes and their detection and remediation, attitudes toward corporate and governmental actors, and attitudes and participation in other environmental and political concerns. Other data were obtained from interviews with, formal presentations by, and official documents provided by the families' lawyer, state public health officials, federal environmental officials, and public health researchers. Additional data came from legal documents, public meetings, archival sources, and research on other similar sites.

Material from all interviews, documents, meetings, and other sources was coded in two ways. First, codes were devised from prior knowledge gained from the first litigant interviews, from the themes which the litigant reinterview questions and other interview questions were expected to tap, and from existing literature on toxic waste sites. Second, additional codes were identified in the process of reading through the transcripts. In this second case a number of codes were quickly apparent, such as the pride which citizens had in their nascent scientific abilities. The coding process therefore identified the beliefs and experiences of involved parties, enabling me to make interpretations of those beliefs and experiences. In many instances, there was considerable congruence with other scholars' findings in case studies of toxic waste sites; this provided a degree of reliability.

In addition to this coding process, all data was examined in terms of its place in the historical/chronological development of the toxic waste crisis. While a clear line of unfolding events was previously apparent, the data culled from the detailed research allowed me to fill in fine-grained detail. This approach enabled me to create the stages model of popular epidemiology described in the next section. Here, too, other toxic waste studies offered support for the development of such a schema.

Lay Ways of Knowing

Popular Epidemiology

Traditional epidemiology studies the distribution of a disease or condition, and the factors that influence this distribution. These data are used to explain the etiology of the condition and to provide preventive, public health, and clinical practices to deal with the condition (Lillienfeld 1980, p. 4). A broader approach, seen in the risk-detection and solution-seeking activities of Woburn and other "contaminated communities" (Edelstein 1988), may be conceptualized as *popular epidemiology.*

Popular epidemiology is the process by which lay persons gather scientific data and other information, and also direct and marshal the knowledge and resources of experts in order to understand the epidemiology of disease. In some of its actions, popular epidemiology parallels scientific epidemiology, such as when laypeople conduct community health surveys. Yet popular epidemiology is more than public participation in traditional epidemiology, since it emphasizes social structural factors as part of the causal disease chain. Further, it involves social movements, utilizes political and judicial approaches to remedies, and challenges basic assumptions of traditional epidemiology, risk assessment, and public health regulation. In some cases, traditional epidemiology may reach similar conclusions as popular epidemiology. Yet scientists generally do not become political activists in order to implement their findings, despite exceptions such as Irving Selikoff's work on asbestos diseases.

Popular epidemiology is similar to other lay advocacy for health care, in that lay perspectives counter professional ones and a social movement guides this alternative perspective. Some lay health advocacy acts to obtain more resources for the prevention and treatment of already recognized diseases (e.g., sickle cell anemia, AIDS), while others seek to win government and medical recognition of unrecognized or under-recognized diseases (e.g., black lung, post-traumatic stress disorder). Still others seek to affirm the knowledge of yet-unknown etiological factors in already recognized diseases (e.g., DES and cervical cancer, asbestos and mesothelioma). Popular epidemiology is most similar to the latter approach, since original research is necessary both to document the prevalence of the disease and the putative causation.

From studying Woburn and other toxic cases (e.g., Levine 1982; Nash and Kirsch 1986; Couto 1986; Krauss 1989; Edelstein 1988), we observe a set of stages of citizen involvement. Participants do not necessarily complete a stage before beginning the next, but one stage usually occurs before the next begins:

1) A group of people in a contaminated community notice separately both health effects and pollutants.

2) These residents hypothesize something out of the ordinary, typically a connection between health effects and pollutants.

3) Community residents share information, creating a common perspective.

4) Community residents, now a more cohesive group, read about, ask around, and talk to government officials and scientific experts about the health effects and the putative contaminants.

5) Residents organize groups to pursue their investigation.

6) Government agencies conduct official studies in response to community groups' pressure. These studies usually find no association between contaminants and health effects.

7) Community groups bring in their own experts to conduct a health study and to investigate pollutant sources and pathways.

8) Community groups engage in litigation and confrontation.

9) Community groups press for corroboration of their findings by official experts and agencies.

10) Community groups keep continued vigilance, lest their gains be washed away by government action.

1) *Lay Observations of Health Effects and Pollutants.* Many people who live at risk of toxic hazards have access to data otherwise inaccessible to scientists. Their experiential knowledge usually precedes official and scientific awareness, largely because it is so tangible. Knowledge of toxic hazards in communities and workplaces in the last two decades has often stemmed from lay observation (Edelstein 1988; Freudenberg 1984a).

Although the first official action—closing Woburn's polluted wells—occurred in 1979, there was a long history of problems in the Woburn water. Residents had for decades complained about dishwasher discoloration, foul odor, and bad taste. Private and public laboratory assays had indicated the presence of organic compounds. The first lay detection efforts were begun earlier by Anne Anderson, whose son, Jimmy, had been diagnosed with acute lymphocytic leukemia in 1972.

2) *Hypothesizing Connections.* Anderson put together information during 1973–74 about other cases by meetings with other Woburn victims in town and at the hospital where Jimmy spent much time. Anderson hypothesized that the alarming leukemia incidence was caused by a water-borne agent. In 1975 she asked state officials to test the water but was told that testing could not be done at an individual's initiative (DiPerna 1985, pp. 75–82). Anderson's hypothesis mirrored that of other communities, where people hypothesize that a higher than expected incidence of disease is due to toxics.

3) *Creating a Common Perspective.* Anderson sought to convince the family minister, Bruce Young, that the water was somehow responsible, although he at first supported her husband's wish to

dissuade her. The creation of a common perspective was aided by a couple of significant events. In 1979 builders found 184 55-gallon drums in a vacant lot; they called the police, who in turn summoned the state Department of Environmental Quality Engineering (DEQE). When water samples were then taken from a number of municipal wells, wells G and H showed high concentrations of organic compounds known to be animal carcinogens, especially trichloroethylene (TCE) and tetrachloroethylene (PCE). EPA recommends that the TCE be zero parts per billion and sets a maximum of five parts per billion; Well G had forty times that concentration. As a result the state closed both wells (Clapp 1987; DiPerna 1985, pp. 106–108).

In June 1979, just weeks after the state closed the wells, a DEQE engineer driving past the nearby Industriplex construction site thought he saw violations of the Wetlands Act. A resultant EPA study found dangerous levels of lead, arsenic, and chromium, yet EPA told neither the town officials nor the public. The public only learned of this months later, from the local newspaper. Reverend Young, initially distrustful of Anderson's theory, came to similar conclusions once the newspaper broke the story. Working with a few leukemia victims he placed an ad in the Woburn paper, asking people who knew of childhood leukemia cases to respond. Working with John Truman, Jimmy Anderson's doctor, Young and Anderson prepared a questionnaire and plotted the cases on a map. Six of the 12 cases were closely grouped in East Woburn.

4) *Looking for Answers from Government and Science.* The data convinced Dr. Truman, who called the Centers for Disease Control (CDC). The citizens persuaded the City Council in December 1979 to formally ask the CDC to investigate. Five days later, the Massachusetts DPH reported on *adult* leukemia mortality for a five-year period, finding a significant elevation only for females. This report was cited to contradict the residents' belief that there was a childhood leukemia cluster.

5) *Organizing a Community Group.* In January 1980 Young, Anderson, and twenty others (both litigants and non-litigants) formed For a Cleaner Environment (FACE) to solidify and expand their efforts (DiPerna 1985, pp. 111–125). FACE pursued all subsequent negotiations with local, state, and federal agencies. It campaigned to attract media attention, and made connections with other toxic waste groups.

Community groups in contaminated communities provide many important functions. They galvanize community support, deal with government, work with professionals, engage in health studies, and provide social and emotional support. They are the primary information source for people in contaminated communities, and often the most—even the only—accurate source (Gibbs 1982; Edelstein 1988, p. 144). Through their organization, Woburn activists report pride in learning science, in protecting and serving their community, in guaranteeing democratic processes, and in personal empowerment.

6) *Official Studies Are Conducted by Experts.* In May 1980 the CDC and the National Institute for Occupational Safety and Health sent Dr. John Cutler to collaborate with the DPH on further study. By then, the Woburn case had national visibility due to national newspaper and network television coverage. In June 1980 Senator Edward Kennedy asked Anderson and Young to testify at hearings on the Superfund, providing further important public exposure. Five days after Jimmy Anderson died, the CDC/DPH study was released in January 1981, stating that there were 12 cases of childhood leukemia in East Woburn, when 5.3 were expected. Yet the DPH argued that the case-control method (12 cases, 24 controls) failed to find characteristics (e.g., medical histories, parental occupation, environmental exposures) that differentiated victims from non-victims, and that lacking environmental data prior to 1979, no linkage could be made to the water supply (Parker and Rosen 1981). That report helped bolster community claims of a high leukemia rate, although the DPH argued that the data could not implicate the wells. Cutler and his colleagues argued that in addition to the absence of case-control differences and the lack of environmental water exposure data, the organic compounds in the wells were known as animal, but not human, carcinogens (Cutler et al. 1986; Condon 1991; Knorr 1991).

The government agencies and their scientific experts worked to maintain their "ownership" of the problem by denying the link with toxics, and by maintaining control of problem solution (Gusfield 1981, pp. 10–15). Activists struggled to solidify their claim to ownership of the problem, to redefine causal responsibility, and to take on political responsibility. While epidemiologists admit to the uncertainties of their work, their usual solution is to err on the side of rejecting environmental causation, whereas community residents make the opposite choice.

7) *Activists Bring In Their Own Experts.* The activists had no "court of appeals" for the scientific evidence necessary to make their case. It became FACE's mission to obtain the information themselves. The conjuncture of Jimmy Anderson's death and the DPH's

failure to implicate the wells led the residents to question the nature of official studies. They received help when Anderson and Young presented the Woburn case to a seminar at the Harvard School of Public Health (HSPH). Marvin Zelen and Steven Lagakos of the Department of Biostatistics became interested; working with FACE members, they designed a health study, focusing on birth defects and reproductive disorders, widely considered to be environmentally related. The biostatisticians and activists teamed up in a prototypical collaboration between citizens and scientists (Lagakos 1987; Zelen 1987). The FACE/HSPH study was more than a "court of appeals," since it transformed the activists' search for credibility. No longer did they have to seek scientific expertise from outside; now they were largely in control of scientific inquiry.

Sources of data for the Woburn health study included information on twenty cases of childhood leukemia (ages 19 and under) which were diagnosed between 1964 and 1983, the DEQE water model of wells G and H, and the health survey. The survey collected data on adverse pregnancy outcomes and childhood disorders from 5,010 interviews, covering 57 percent of Woburn residences with telephones. The researchers trained 235 volunteers to conduct the survey, taking precautions to avoid bias[1] (Lagakos et al. 1984).

8) *Litigation and Confrontation.* During this period, the DEQE's hydrogeological investigations found that the bedrock in the affected area was shaped like a bowl, with wells G and H in the deepest part. DEQE's March 1982 report thus determined that the contamination source was not the Industriplex site as had been believed, but rather facilities of W. R. Grace and Beatrice Foods. This led eight families of leukemia victims to file a $400 million suit in May 1982 against those corporations for waste disposal practices which led to water contamination and disease. A smaller company, Unifirst, was also sued but quickly settled before trial (Schlictmann 1987). In July 1986 a federal district court jury found that Grace had negligently dumped chemicals; Beatrice Foods was absolved. An $8 million out-of-court settlement with Grace was reached in September 1986. The families filed an appeal against Beatrice, based on suppression of evidence, but the Appeals Court rejected the appeal in July 1990, and in October 1990 the United States Supreme Court declined to hear the case (Brown 1987; 1990; Neuffer, 1988).

The trial was a separate but contiguous struggle over facts and science. Through consultant physicians, immunologists, epidemiologists, and hydrogeologists, the families accumulated further evidence of adverse health effects. The data were not used in the trial, which never got to the point of assessing the causal chain of pollution and illness. Nevertheless, the process made the residents more scientifically informed.

9) *Pressing for Official Corroboration.* In February 1984 the FACE/Harvard School of Public Health data were made public. Childhood leukemia was found to be significantly associated with exposure to water from wells G and H. Children with leukemia received an average of 21.2 percent of their yearly water supply from the wells, compared to 9.5 percent for children without leukemia. Controlling for risk factors in pregnancy, the investigators found that access to contaminated water was associated with perinatal deaths since 1970, eye/ear anomalies, and CNS/chromosomal/oral cleft anomalies. With regard to childhood disorders, water exposure was associated with kidney/urinary tract and lung/respiratory diseases (Lagakos et al. 1984). If only the children that were *in utero* at the time of exposure are studied, the positive associations are even stronger (Lagakos 1987).

Due to lack of resources, this study would not have been possible without community involvement. Yet precisely this lay involvement led professional and governmental groups—the DPH, the Centers for Disease Control, the American Cancer Society, the EPA, and even the Harvard School of Public Health Department of Epidemiology—to charge that the study was biased. The researchers conducted extensive analyses to demonstrate that the data were not biased, especially with regard to the use of community volunteers as interviewers (see note 1). Still, officials argued that interviewers and respondents knew the research question, respondents had potential recall bias, and the water model measured only household supply rather than individual consumption (Condon 1991; Knorr 1991). Thus, although activists expected the results to bring scientific support, they saw only criticism.

10) *Continued Vigilance.* Whether or not activists have been successful in making their case, they find the need to be continually involved in cleanups, additional official surveillance, media attention, and overall coordination of efforts. Woburn activists had to keep defending their data. They were looking for confirmation from a DPH reanalysis of reproductive health effects.

The DPH reanalysis (WEBS—Woburn Environment & Birth Study) was conducted, but then kept under wraps for several years. Then in 1994, the DPH reported only on reproductive disorders and birth defects, and said they were still working on the leukemia reanalysis. The officials claimed they found no excess of reproductive disorders and birth defects for Woburn. However, the FACE activists, Harvard biostatisticians, and various scholars in the natural, life, and social sciences examined the DPH report. Most striking was that the most intensive study period for the DPH was a prospective study for 1989–1991, long after the wells were closed. As a result, the citizens and their supporters believe the state continues to deny the health effects of Woburn's past contamination.

In May 1996 the DPH released their report, "Woburn Childhood Leukemia Follow Study," that detailed their reanalysis of the leukemia data. They concurred with the Woburn activists that there was a significant dose-response relationship ($p < .05$) between leukemia and mothers drinking contaminated water (from wells G and H) during pregnancy. Some family members wept on hearing the results, and the families were pleased and vindicated by this finding.

Wells G and H are being cleaned up with an air stripper that creates droplets that volatilize the water and remove the volatile organic compounds (VOCs), a process that is expected to produce drinkable water from those wells in fifty years. It is not clear, though, why this is a useful thing to do, even though EPA procedures call for a cleanup; the wells have been offline for a long time and suitable water is provided from other sources. At the Industriplex site, originally thought to be the contamination source, the contaminated area has been capped, in order to develop the area as a commercial property. The EPA touts Industriplex as a model for its "brownfields" development program. Woburn activists are not pleased with that, since they don't believe it can be sufficiently cleaned up to be useful. In particular, the site continues to leach arsenic and chromium into the Aberjona River, from where it is distributed downstream to the Mystic Lakes. Activists are also upset that the upcoming Superfund reauthorization bill may remove third-party liability at cleanups, making it impossible to hold the polluting firms responsible.

Only two new case of childhood leukemia were diagnosed in Woburn from 1985 to the 1990s; this is a little less than what would be expected by chance (that is, slightly less than the background rate), and far less than the number of cases previously recorded when Wells G and H were operating. This provides evidence that the closure of the contaminated wells removed the cause of the leukemia cluster.

This last stage shows the importance of continued vigilance, even in situations where activists appear to have already made their case.

Having laid out the stages of popular epidemiological involvement, I now elaborate on the main lay-professional disputes: lay participation, standards of proof, constraints on professional practice, quality of official studies, and professional autonomy.

Professional Ways of Knowing

Traditional science contains a narrowly circumscribed set of assumptions about causality, the political and public role of scientists, and corporate and governmental social responsibility (Ozonoff and Boden 1987). Political-economic approaches argue that scientific inquiry is tied to corporate, political, and foundation connections that direct research and interpretation toward support for the status quo (Dickson 1984; Aronowitz 1988). It is useful to draw on both the political-economic perspective, which provides a social context for science, and the ethnomethodological/constructivist perspective, which shows us the internal workings of the scientific community (e.g., Latour 1987). There is a dynamic relationship between these two approaches—social movement actions provide the impetus for new scientific paradigms, and those new paradigms in turn spawn further social movement action.

The critics of the Woburn health survey did not represent *all science*, since residents received help from scientists who support community involvement and who believe that contaminated communities fail to receive fair treatment. Often such scientists have worked without compensation. Some began as critics of mainstream approaches, while others became critical only during the investigation. Some believed in a different causal paradigm, and some were critical of prevailing canons of significance levels. Others simply believed they could conduct better studies than official agencies.

Lay pressure for a different scientific approach is not directed at "pure" science. In environmental health, we are dealing with *combined* government/professional units, e.g., DPH, EPA, CDC. The end goal for activists is mainly acceptance by *government agencies*, since they have the power to act. At the same time, activists seek to become "popular scientists" who can win the support of scientific experts for the sake of knowledge.

Popular Participation and the Critique of Value-Neutrality

Activists disagree that epidemiology is a value-neutral scientific enterprise conducted in a sociopolitical vacuum. Critics of the

Woburn health study argued that the study was biased by the use of volunteer interviewers and by prior political goals. Those critics upheld the notion of a value-free science in which knowledge, theories, techniques, and applications are devoid of self-interest or bias. Such claims are disputed by the sociology of science, which maintains that scientific knowledge is not absolute, but rather the subject of debate among scientists (Latour 1987). Scientific knowledge is shaped by social forces such as media influence, economic interest, political pressure, and social movement activism (Aronowitz 1988; Dickson 1984). On a practical level, scientific endeavors are limited by financial and personnel resources (Goggin 1986; Nelkin 1985); lay involvement often supplies the labor power needed to document health hazards. Science is also limited in how it identifies problems worthy of study. As an academic and official enterprise, science does not take its direction from the lay public.

Toxic activists see themselves as correcting problems not addressed by the established scientific community. The centrality of popular involvement is evident in the women's health and occupational health movements that have been major forces in pointing to often unidentified problems and working to abolish their causes. Among the hazards and diseases thus uncovered are DES, Agent Orange, asbestos, pesticides, unnecessary hysterectomies, sterilization abuse, and black lung (Berman 1977; Rodriguez-Trias 1984; Scott 1988; Smith 1981). In these examples and in Woburn, lay activists are not merely research assistants to sympathetic scientists, but often take the initiative in detecting disease, generating hypotheses, pressing for state action, and conceiving and overseeing scientific studies.

Standards of Proof

Many scientists and public health officials emphasize various problems in standards of proof, ranging from initial detection and investigation to final interpretation of data. Assessment of public health risks of toxic substances involves four steps. Hazard identification locates the existence and extent of toxics. Dose-response analysis determines the quantitative effects of the substance. Exposure assessment examines human exposure to the substances. Risk characterization integrates the first three steps in order to estimate the numbers of people who will be affected and the seriousness of the effects. From the scientific point of view, there is considerable uncertainty about each of these steps (Upton et al. 1989).

Scientists and officials focus on problems such as inadequate history of the site, the unclarity of the route of contaminants, determining appropriate water sampling locations, small numbers of cases, bias in self-reporting of symptoms, getting appropriate control groups, lack of knowledge about characteristics and effects of certain chemicals, and unknown latency periods for carcinogens (Condon 1991; Knorr 1991). Epidemiologists are usually not choosing the research questions they think are amenable to study, based on clear hypotheses, firmer toxicological data, and adequate sample size. Rather, they are responding to a crisis situation, engaging in "reactive epidemiology" (Anderson 1985). Traditional approaches also tend to look askance at innovative perspectives favored by activists, such as the importance of genetic mutations, immune disregulation markers, and non-fatal and non-serious health effects (e.g., rashes, persistent respiratory problems) (Ozonoff and Boden 1987; Gute 1991).

For public health officials, disputes over toxic studies arise from shortcomings in knowledge about toxic waste-induced disease. A DPH official involved in Woburn for over a decade reflected on the vast changes in knowledge, personnel, and attitudes over that period. At first, public health researchers knew little about how to investigate clusters, environmental epidemiology was a new field, the state had few qualified scientists, and officials did not know how to involve the public. The DPH was trying out new approaches as they proceeded, without clear established protocols (Condon 1991).

Activists view scientists as too concerned with having each element of scientific study as perfect as possible. Residents believe that there have been visible health effects, clear evidence of contamination, and strong indications that these two are related. From their point of view, the officials and scientists are hindering a proper study, or are hiding incriminating knowledge. Residents observe corporations denying that they have dumped toxic waste, or that substances have no health effects. When public health agencies find no adverse health effects, many people view them as supporting corporate polluters. While residents agree with officials that cluster studies and environmental health assessment are new areas, they believe the agencies should spend more effort on what residents consider crucial matters.

The level of statistical significance required for intervention is a frequent source of contention. Many communities that wish to document hazards and disease are stymied by insufficient numbers of cases to achieve statistical significance. Some professionals who work with community groups adhere to accepted significance levels

(Lagakos et al. 1984), while others argue that such levels are as inappropriate to environmental risk as to other issues of public health, such as bomb threats and epidemics (Paigen 1982). Ozonoff and Boden (1987) distinguish statistical significance from public health significance, since an increased disease rate may be of great public health significance even if statistical probabilities are not met. They believe that epidemiology should mirror clinical medicine more than laboratory science, by erring on the safe side of false positives.

Hill (1987) argues that even without statistical significance we may find a clear association based on strength of association; consistency across persons, places, circumstances, and time; specificity of the exposure site and population; temporality of the exposure and effect; biological plausibility of the effect; coherence with known facts of the agent and disease; and analogy to past experience with related substances. Pointing to the above, as well as to more "provable" experimental models and dose-response curves, Hill argues that there are no hard and fast rules for establishing causality. Given the potential dangers of many classes of materials, he believes it often wise to restrict a substance to avoid potential danger.

Epidemiologists prefer false negatives to false positives—i.e., they would prefer to falsely claim no association between variables when there is one than to claim an association when there is none. This burden of proof usually exceeds the level required to argue for intervention. As Couto (1986) observes:

> The degree of risk to human health does not need to be at statistically significant levels to require political action. The degree of risk does have to be such that a reasonable person would avoid it. Consequently, the important political test is not the findings of epidemiologists on the probability of nonrandomness of an incidence of illness but the likelihood that a reasonable person, including members of the community of calculation [epidemiologists], would take up residence with the community at risk and drink from and bathe in water from the Yellow Creek area or buy a house along Love Canal.

Indeed, these questions are presented to public health officials, wherever there is dispute between the citizen and official perceptions. Beverly Paigen (1982), who worked with laypeople in Love Canal, makes clear that standards of evidence are value-laden:

> Before Love Canal, I also needed a 95 percent certainty before I was convinced of a result. But seeing this rigorously applied in a situation where the consequences of an error meant that pregnancies were resulting in miscarriages, stillbirths, and children

with medical problems, I realized I was making a value judgment
. . . whether to make errors on the side of protecting human
health or on the side of conserving state resources.

This dispute suggests the need for a more interactive approach to
the *process* of scientific knowledge making. Applying Latour's (1987)
"science in action" framework, the real meaning of epidemiological
"fact" cannot be seen until the epidemiologist experiences the citi-
zenry and the problem being studied. Conversely, the public has no
clear sense of what epidemiology can or cannot do for them until
they or their neighbors are part of a study sample. In addition, both
parties' perceptions and actions are jointly produced by their connections with other components, such as media, civic groups, and
politicians. Latour's method tells us to ask of epidemiological
research: for *whose* standards, and by what version of *proof*, is a
"standard of proof" determined and employed?

Institutional Constraints on Professional Knowledge and Action

Professional knowledge formation is affected by various institutional constraints. Professionals rarely view public initiatives as worthy of their attention. Laypeople have fewer scientific and financial
resources than government and corporations (Paigen 1982). Without
an ongoing relationship with the community, professionals enter
only as consultants at a single point, and are unlikely to understand
the larger framework of lay claimsmaking.

University-based scientists, a potential source of aid, frequently
consider applied community research to be outside the regular academic reward structure (Couto 1986). Further, universities' increasing dependency on corporate and governmental support has made
scholars less willing to challenge established authority (Goggin
1986). Grant support from federal agencies and private foundations
is less likely to fund scholars who urge community participation and
who challenge scientific canons and government policy.

Scientists ally themselves with citizen efforts often because they see
flaws in official responses. For challenging state authority, they are
sometimes punished as whistleblowers. When Beverly Paigen, a biologist at the New York State Department of Health (DOH), aided Love
Canal residents' health studies, she was harassed by her superiors.
The DOH withdrew a grant application she had written, without even
telling her, and refused to process an already funded grant. She was
told that due to the "sensitive nature" of her work, all grants had to go
through a special review process. Her professional mail was opened

and taped shut, and her office was entered and searched at night. Paigen's state tax was audited, and she saw in her file a clipping about her Love Canal work. Later, the state tax commissioner wrote her and apologized. Two officials in the regional office of the Department of Environmental Conservation were demoted or transferred for raising questions about the state's investigation (Paigen 1982). Similar cases have been documented elsewhere (Freudenberg 1984a, p. 57).

Quality and Accessibility of Official Data

Massive complaints in Massachusetts about the state's response to lay concerns over excess cancer rates in twenty Massachusetts communities (including Woburn) led to state senate (Commonwealth of Massachusetts 1987) and university (Levy et al. 1986) investigations which found that the DPH studies were poorly conceived and methodologically weak. Most lacked a clear hypothesis, failed to mention potential exposure routes, and as a result rarely defined the geographic or temporal limits of the population at risk. Methods were presented erratically and inconsistently, case definitions were weak, environmental data were rarely presented, and statistical tests were inappropriately used (Levy et al. 1986). Frequently, exposed groups were diluted with unexposed individuals, and comparison groups were likely to include exposed individuals (Ozonoff and Boden 1987). This situation is striking, since the damaging effects of the poor studies and nonresponsiveness to the community led to the resignation of the public health commissioner, Bailus Walker, then head of the American Public Health Association (Clapp 1987).

State agencies are often unhelpful. A survey of all fifty states' responses to lay cancer cluster reports found that there were an estimated 1,300–1,650 such reports in 1988, clearly a large number for agencies already short-staffed. Many state health departments discouraged informants, in some cases requesting extensive data before they would go further. Rather than deal specifically with the complaint, many health departments gave a routine response emphasizing the lifestyle causes of cancer, the fact that one of three Americans will develop some form of cancer, and that clusters occur at random (Greenberg and Wartenberg 1991).

Officials may withhold information on the basis that it will alarm the public (Levine 1982), that the public does not understand risks, or that it will harm the business climate (Ozonoff and Boden 1987). Many scientists oppose public disclosure on the grounds that laypersons are unable to make rational decisions (Krimsky 1984). Often enough toxic activists are called "anti-scientific," when in fact they may simply work at science in a nontraditional manner. Indeed, toxic activists express support for scientists as important sources of knowledge (Freudenberg 1984b). FACE activists report that they have become highly informed about scientific matters, and are proud of it.

A cardinal assumption of science is that its truth and validity are affirmed by widespread recognition of the findings through open access to data among members of the scientific community. Yet the Massachusetts cases were not even shared with all appropriate scientists. Local health officials typically heard of elevated cancer rates through the media, rather than from state health officials. The EPA began a secret investigation of the Woburn data, leaving out researchers and Woburn residents who had already been involved in many investigations. Formed in 1984, the study group's existence was only discovered in 1988 (Kennedy 1988). In the EPA's view, there was no intent at secrecy, merely an internal "tell us what you think of this thing." (Newman 1991).

Professionalism, Controversy, and Information Control

It is particularly ironic that epidemiology excludes the public, since the original "shoe-leather" work that founded the field is quite similar to popular epidemiology. Woburn residents' efforts are very reminiscent of John Snow's classic study of cholera in London in 1854, where that doctor closed the Broad Street pump to cut off contaminated water. Yet modern epidemiology has come far from its original shoe-leather origins, turning into a laboratory science with no room for lay input.

The combination of epidemiologic uncertainty and the political aspects of toxic waste contamination leads to scientific controversy. According to Latour (1987, p. 132), rather than a "diffusion" of ready-made science, we must study how "translations" by many parties of undecided controversies lead to a consensual reality. From the point of view of traditional epidemiologists, citizens' translations get in the way of consensual production of science. Yet in fact, the scientific community is itself disunified on most issues of environmental epidemiology, and laypeople are partaking in the related consensual production.

In this struggle, citizens use controversy to demystify expertise and to transfer problems from the technical to the political arena (Nelkin 1985). This redefinition of the situation involves a lay approach to "cultural rationality" as opposed to the scientific establishment's "technical rationality" (Krimsky and Plough 1988). This is the form of struggle described earlier when residents ask officials whether they would live in and drink water from the contaminated community. We may also view gender differences as representative of differing rationalities. Women are the most frequent organizers of lay detection, partly because they are the chief health arrangers for their families, and partly because they are more concerned than men with local environmental issues (Levine 1982; Blocker and Eckberg 1989). From this perspective, women's cultural rationality is concerned with who would be willing to drink local water, and how their families experience daily life.

Bad Science, Good Science, Popular Science

One way to look at official support for lay involvement is to view it as simply "good politics," whereby the government provides a formal mechanism for citizen participation in such areas as Environmental Impact Statements and Recombinant DNA Advisory Panels. However, public participation was limited in these cases to minor roles on panels that already had an official agenda (Jasanoff 1986; Krimsky 1984).

But as we observe in popular epidemiology, lay involvement is not merely "good politics." It is also "good science," since it changes the nature of scientific inquiry. This involves four elements that have been addressed throughout:

1. Lay involvement identifies the many cases of "bad science," e.g., poor studies, secret investigations, failure to inform local health officials.

2. Lay involvement points out that "normal science" has drawbacks, e.g., opposing lay participation in health surveys, demanding standards of proof that may be unobtainable or inappropriate, being slow to accept new concepts of toxic causality.

3. The combination of the above two points leads to a general public distrust of official science, thus pushing laypeople to seek alternate routes of information and analysis.

4. Popular epidemiology yields valuable data that often would be unavailable to scientists. If scientists and government fail to solicit such data, and especially if they consciously oppose and devalue it, then such data may be lost.

We see these four elements in many contaminated communities, but in Woburn the lay contribution to scientific endeavor has been exceptional. The Woburn case was the major impetus for the establishment of the state cancer registry (Clapp 1987). Activism has also contributed to increasing research on Woburn: the DPH and CDC are conducting a major five-year reproductive outcome study of the city, utilizing both prospective and retrospective data, and citizens have a large role in this process. The DPH is conducting a case-control study of leukemia, and an MIT study will study genetic mutations caused by trichloroethylene (TCE), to investigate their role in causing leukemia (Latowsky 1988).

Popular epidemiology can sway government opinion over time, especially when activists doggedly stick to their own work while constantly participating with official bodies. The since-retired DPH Commissioner who took office in 1988, Deborah Prothrow-Stith, asked for a more official relationship with FACE. Upon visiting Woburn, the commissioner said she was "struck with how epidemiology is dependent on the role the public plays in bringing these things to light" (Mades 1988). A DPH official in 1990, going over the chronology of events, noted that the FACE/Harvard School of Public Health study found positive associations between well water and adverse reproductive outcomes, a position the DPH avoided for the preceding six years since the study was published (Kruger 1990). Other officials now view the study as an important source of research questions and methods, which informs the ongoing official studies, as well as a prompt to government action. Indeed, they expect that the new studies may show evidence of adverse health effects (Condon 1991; Knorr 1991).

Popular epidemiologists also provide continuity in the scientific process. As a leading activist stated, "We have been the institutional memory of studies in Woburn. We have seen agency heads come and go. We have seen project directors come and go. Our role has been to bring those efforts together and to help the researchers investigate what was going on all throughout the area" (Latowsky 1990). To understand the significance of that position, we may observe that as late as 1990 an EPA Remedial Project Manager for the Woburn site could hear a question, "Is the leukemia cluster a cause for urgency of cleanup?" and respond that "Our investigation is not concerned with the cluster of leukemia. It's really irrelevant. We're on a schedule based on our regulations" (Newman 1990).

Ozonoff (1988) sums up the Woburn impact:

> In hazardous waste, three names come up—Love Canal, Times Beach, and Woburn. Woburn stands far and above them all in the amount of scientific knowledge produced. All over the country, Woburn has put its stamp on the science of hazardous waste studies.

Of particular value is the discovery of a TCE syndrome involving three major body systems—immune, cardiovascular, and neurological—which is increasingly showing up in other TCE sites.

How Do We Know If Lay Investigations Provide Correct Knowledge?

It is obviously necessary to evaluate the correctness of findings which result from popular epidemiology. Such knowledge is not "folk" knowledge with an antiscientific basis. In most cases, popular epidemiology findings are the result of scientific studies involving trained professionals, even if they begin as "lay mapping" of disease clusters without attention to base rates or controls. Indeed, lay-involved surveys are sometimes well-crafted researches with defendable data. Laypeople may initiate action, and even direct the formulation of hypotheses, but they work *with* scientists, not in place of them. Thus, the end results can be judged by the same criteria as any study. But since all scientific judgments involve social factors, there are no simple algorithms for ascertaining truth. Scientific inquiry is always full of controversy; what is different here is that laypeople are entering that controversy.

Public health officials worry that some communities might exaggerate the risks of a hazard, or might be wrong about the effects of a substance. Yet if this occurs, it must be seen in the context whereby community fears have too often been brushed aside and where data has been withheld. Given the increasing cases (or at least recognition of those cases) of technological disasters, drug side effects, and scientific fraud, public sentiment has become more critical of science. In response, lay claims may be erroneous. But this is the price paid for past failures and problems, and is a countervailing force in democratic participation (Piller 1991). Exaggerated fears may be understood as signs of the need to expand public health protection, rather than justifications to oppose lay involvement. Even if a community makes incorrect conclusions, their database may still remain useful for different analyses. As mentioned before, the DPH disagrees with the Harvard/FACE conclusions, yet they are now testing those same relationships in their own study.

Conclusion—Causes and Implications of Popular Epidemiology

Popular epidemiology stems from the legacy of health activism, growing public recognition of problems in science and technology, and the democratic upsurge regarding science policy. This paper has pointed to the difficulties that communities face due to differing conceptions of risk, lack of resources, poor access to information, and unresponsive government. In popular epidemiology, as in other health-related movements, activism by those affected is necessary to make progress in health care and health policy. In this process there is a powerful reciprocal relationship between the social movement and new views of science. The striking awareness of new scientific knowledge, coupled with government and professional resistance to that knowledge, leads people to form social movement organizations to pursue their claimsmaking. In turn, the further development of social movement organizations leads to further challenges to scientific canons. The socially constructed approach of popular epidemiology is thus a result of both a social movement and a new scientific paradigm, with both continually reinforcing the other.

Dramatically increasing attention to environmental degradation may make it easier for many to accept causal linkages previously considered too novel. Further, this expanding attention and its related social movements lead to the identification of more disease clusters. This may lead to the reevaluation of problems of low base rates in light of how other sciences (e.g., physics, paleontology) conduct research on low base-rate phenomena. As well, growing numbers of similar cases containing small sample sizes and/or low base-rate phenomena may allow for more generalizability. These increasing cases also produce more anomalies, allowing for a paradigm shift.

Causal explanations from outside of science also play a role. Legal definitions of causality, developed in an expanding toxic tort repertoire, are initially determined by judicial interpretation of scientific testimony. Once constructed, they can take on a life of their own, directing public health agencies and scientists to adhere to scientific/ legal definitions which may or may not completely accord with basic science. At the least, they set standards by which scientific investigations will be applied to social life, (e.g., court-ordered guidelines on claims for disease caused by asbestos, nuclear testing, DES).

Lay and professional approaches to knowledge and action on environmental health risks are structurally divergent, much as Freidson (1970) conceives of the inherent differences and conflicts between patient and physician. Yet, just as modern efforts from the side of both medicine and its clientele seek an alternate model, so too does popular epidemiology offer a new path. Popular epidemiology offers a bridge between the two perspectives, a bridge largely engineered and constructed by lay activists, yet one which potentially brings citizens and scientists together.

Note

[1] The researchers conducted extensive analyses to demonstrate that the data were not biased. They found no differences when they compared baseline rates of adverse health effects for West Woburn (never exposed to wells G and H water) and East Woburn (at a period prior to the opening of the wells). They examined transiency rates to test whether they were related to exposure and found them to be alike in both sectors. Other tests ruled out various biases potentially attributable to the volunteer interviewers (Lagakos et al. 1984).

Acknowledgements

The research for this paper was supported in part by funding from the Wayland Collegium of Brown University, the Brown University Small Grants Program, and by Biomedical Research Support Grant #5-27178 from the National Institutes of Health. Robert Gay, Martha Lang, and Beth Parkhurst were very helpful as research assistants. Elizabeth Cooksey and Carol Walker assisted by transcribing audiotapes. Peter Conrad, Stephen R. Couch, Ann Dill, Sheldon Krimsky, Donald Light, Alonzo Plough, and Irving K. Zola read earlier drafts and contributed valuable comments and ideas. Richard Clapp and Gretchen Latowsky helped with material that updated this article after its original publication.

References

Anderson, Henry A. 1985. "Evolution of Environmental Epidemiologic Risk Assessment." *Environmental Health Perspectives* 62:389–392.

Aronowitz, Stanley. 1988. *Science as Power: Discourse and Ideology in Modern Society.* Minneapolis: University of Minnesota Press.

Brown, Phil. 1987. "Popular Epidemiology: Community Response to Toxic Waste-Induced Disease in Woburn, Massachusetts." *Science, Technology, and Human Values* 12:78–85.

Brown, Phil and Edwin J. Mikkelsen. 1990. *No Safe Place: Toxic Waste, Leukemia, and Community Action.* Berkeley: University of California Press.

Berman, Daniel. 1977. "Why Work Kills: A Brief History of Occupational Health and Safety in the United States." *International Journal of Health Services* 7:63–87.

Blocker, T. Jean and Douglas Lee Eckberg. 1989. "Environmental Issues as Women's Issues: General Concerns and Local Hazards." *Social Science Quarterly* 70:586–593.

Clapp, Richard. Interview, March 14, 1987.

Commonwealth of Massachusetts. 1987. "Cancer Case Reporting and Surveillance in Massachusetts." Senate Committee on Post Audit and Oversight. Boston, Massachusetts, September 1987.

Condon, Susanne. 1991. Interview, August 7, 1991.

Couto, Richard A. 1985. "Failing Health and New Prescriptions: Community-Based Approaches to Environmental Risks." Pp. 53–70 in Carole E. Hill, ed., *Current Health Policy Issues and Alternatives: An Applied Social Science Perspective.* Athens: University of Georgia Press.

Cutler, John J., Gerald S. Parker, Sharon Rosen, Brad Prenney, Richard Healy, and Glyn G. Caldwell. 1986. "Childhood Leukemia in Woburn, Massachusetts." *Public Health Reports* 101:201–205.

Dickson, David. 1984. *The New Politics of Science.* New York: Pantheon.

DiPerna, Paula. 1985. *Cluster Mystery: Epidemic and the Children of Woburn, Mass.* St. Louis: Mosby.

Edelstein, Michael. 1988. *Contaminated Communities: The Social and Psychological Impacts of Residential Toxic Exposure.* Boulder: Westview.

Epstein, Samuel S., Lester O, Brown, and Carl Pope. 1982. *Hazardous Waste in America.* San Francisco: Sierra Club Books.

Fisher, Sue. 1986. *In the Patient's Best Interests.* New Brunswick, NJ: Rutgers University Press.

Freidson, Elliot. 1970. *Profession of Medicine.* New York: Dodd, Mead.

Freudenberg, Nicholas. 1984a. *Not in Our Backyards: Community Action for Health and the Environment.* New York: Monthly Review.

———. 1984b. "Citizen Action for Environmental Health: Report on a Survey of Community Organizations." *American Journal of Public Health* 74:444–448.

Gibbs, Lois Marie. 1982. "Community Response to an Emergency Situation: Psychological Destruction and the Love Canal." Paper presented at the American Psychological Association, August 24, 1982.

Goggin, Malcolm L. 1986. "Introduction. Governing Science and Technology Democratically: A Conceptual Framework." Pp.3–31 in Malcolm L. Goggin, ed., *Governing Science and Technology in a Democracy.* Knoxville: University of Tenessee Press.

Greenberg, Michael and Daniel Wartenberg. 1991. "Communicating to an Alarmed Community About Cancer Clusters: A Fifty-State Study." *Journal of Community Health* 16:71–82.

Gusfield, Joseph R. 1981. *The Culture of Public Problems.* Chicago: University of Chicago Press.

Gute, David. 1991. Interview, August 14, 1991.

Hill, Austin Bradford. 1987. "The Environment and Disease: Association or Causation." Pp. 15–20 in Kenneth Rothman, ed., *Evolution of Epidmiologic Ideas.* Chestnut Hill, MA: Epidemiology Resources.

Jasanoff, Sheila. 1986. "The Misrule of Law at OSHA." Pp. 155–178 in Dorothy Nelkin, ed., *The Language of Risk: Conflicting Perspectives on Occupational Health.* Beverly Hills: Sage.

Kennedy, Dan. 1988. "EPA to Say Pollutants Caused Leukemia." *Woburn Daily Times,* May 9, 1988.

Kleinman, Arthur. 1980. *Patients and Healers in the Context of Culture.* Berkeley: University of California.

Knorr, Robert. 1991. Interview, August 7, 1991.

Krauss, Celene. 1989. "Community Struggles and the Shaping of Democratic Consciousness." *Sociological Forum* 4:227–239.

Krimsky, Sheldon. 1984. "Beyond Technocracy: New Routes for Citizen Involvement in Social Risk Assessment." Pp.43–61 in James C. Peterson, ed., *Citizen Participation in Science Policy.* Amherst: University of Massachusetts Press.

Krimsky, Sheldon and Alonzo Plough. 1988. *Environmental Hazards: Communicating Risks as a Social Process.* Boston: Auburn House.

Kruger, Elaine. 1990. "Environmental Exposure Assessment and Occurrence of Adverse Reproductive Outcomes in Woburn, Mass." Presentation at conference, Investigations in the Aberjona River Watershed. Woburn, Massachusetts. May 18, 1990.

Lagakos, Steven. Interview, April 6, 1987.

Lagakos, Steven W., Barbara J. Wessen, and Marvin Zelen. 1984. "An Analysis of Contaminated Well Water and Health Effects in Woburn, Massachusetts." *Journal of the American Statistical Association* 81:583–596.

Latour, Bruno. 1987. *Science in Action: How to Follow Scientists and Engineers Through Society.* Cambridge: Harvard University Press.

Latowsky, Gretchen. 1988. Interview May 26, 1988.

———. 1990. "FACE's Role in the Community." Presentation at conference, Investigations in the Aberjona River Watershed. Woburn, Massachusetts. May 18, 1990.

Levine, Adeline Gordon. 1982. *Love Canal: Science, Politics, and People.* Lexington, MA: Heath.

Levy, Barry S., David Kriebel, Peter Gann, Jay Himmelstein, and Glenn Pransky. 1986. "Improving the Conduct of Environmental Epidemiology Studies." Worcester, MA: University of Massachusetts Medical School, Department of Family and Community Medicine, Occupational Health Program.

Lilienfeld, Abraham. 1980. *Foundations of Epidemiology,* 2nd ed. New York: Oxford.

Mades, Nancy. 1988. "Commissioner Wants FACE-DPH Pact," *Woburn Daily Times,* April 7, 1988.

Nash, June and Max Kirsch. 1986. "Polychlorinated Biphenyls in the Electrical Machinery Industry: An Ethnological Study of Community Action and Corporate Responsibility." *Social Science and Medicine* 23:131–138.

Nelkin, Dorothy, ed. 1985. *The Language of Risk: Conflicting Perspectives in Occupational Health.* Beverly Hills: Sage.

Neuffer, Elizabeth. 1988. "Court Orders New Hearings in Woburn Pollution Case." *Boston Globe,* December 8, 1988.

Newman, Barbara. 1990. "Investigations and Remediation at the Wells G and H Site." Presentation at conference, Investigations in the Aberjona River Watershed. Woburn, Massachusetts. May 18, 1990.

Newman, Barbara. 1991. Interview September 6, 1991.

Ozonoff, David. 1988. Presentation at conference, "Examining Woburn's Health." April 24. Trinity Episcopal Church, Woburn, Massachusetts.

Ozonoff, David and Leslie I. Boden. 1987. "Truth and Consequences: Health Agency Responses to Environmental Health Problems." *Science, Technology, and Human Values* 12:70–77.

Paigen, Beverly. 1982. "Controversy at Love Canal." *Hastings Center Report* 12(3):29–37.

Parker, Gerald and Sharon Rosen. 1981. "Woburn: Cancer Incidence and Environmental Hazards." Massachusetts Department of Public Health, January 23, 1981.

Piller, Charles. 1991. *The Fail-Safe Society: Community Defiance and the End of American Technological Optimism.* New York: Basic.

Rodriguez-Trias, Helen. 1984. "The Women's Health Movement: Women Take Power." Pp. 107–126 in Victor Sidel and Ruth Sidel, eds., *Reforming Medicine: Lessons of the Last Quarter Century.* New York: Pantheon.

Roth, Julius. 1963. *Timetables.* Indianapolis: Bobbs-Merrill.

Rubin, James H. 1987. "Justices Limit Right of Citizens to Sue on Water Pollution Violations." *New York Times*, December 2, 1987.

Schlictmann, Jan. Interview, May 12, 1987.

Scott, Wilbur J. 1988. "Competing Paradigms in the Assessment of Latent Disorders: The Case of Agent Orange." *Social Problems* 35:145–161.

Smith, Barbara Ellen. 1981. "Black Lung: The Social Production of Disease." *International Journal of Health Services* 11:343–359.

Stimson, Gerry V. and Barbara Webb. 1975. *Going to See the Doctor*. London: Routledge.

Strauss, Anselm, Leonard Schatzman, Rue Bucher, Danuta Ehrlich, and Melvin Sabshin. 1964. *Psychiatric Ideologies and Institutions*. New York: Free Press.

Upton, Arthur C., Theodore Kneip, and Paolo Toniolo. 1989. "Public Health Aspects of Toxic Chemical Disposal Sites." *Annual Review of Public Health* 10:1–25.

Waitzkin, Howard. 1983. *The Second Sickness: Contradictions of Capitalist Health Care*. New York: Macmillan.

———. 1989. "A Critique of Medical Discourse: Ideology, Social Control, and the Processing of Social Context in Medical Encounters." *Journal of Health and Social Behavior* 30:220–239.

Zelen, Marvin. Interview, July 1, 1987.

Zola, Irving K. 1973. "Pathways to the Doctor—From Person to Patient." *Social Science and Medicine* 7:677–689.

9
Worker Health and Safety at the Beginning of a New Century

David Kotelchuck

Looking at worker health and safety over the past century, what stands out sharply is the great progress that has been made in protecting worker health and safety on the job over the past thirty years. And that progress in turn rests on the great struggles of working men and women to organize themselves into large, strong, industrial trade unions.

At the beginning of this past century, the labor movement was relatively small, with hardly more than a foothold in the great booming industries of the day: steel, textiles, automaking and electrical manufacturing. The unions that did exist were organized largely by craft and were constantly at each other's throats, arguing over whose members should perform which tasks and what union should represent them. Meanwhile, workers were dying and being maimed by the tens of thousands in the steel mills of Pittsburgh, the underground mines of West Virginia, and railroad accidents across the country.

During this period one workplace incident, the 1910 Triangle Shirtwaist Fire in New York City, took the lives of 146 workers, most of them young women. The women were trapped in the raging fire by windows that were barred, doors that opened inward, and a fire escape that melted under the heat of the flames. The resulting public outcry focused the attention of the nation on the carnage in U.S. workplaces. Among the consequences of this outcry were passage of city and state industrial fire safety laws, passage of Workers Compensation laws in states across the country, and increased unionization of textile and other industries.

But over the next few decades, from World War I through World War II, relatively little was done to improve workers' health and safety, as unions attended to their first priority—organizing and getting a foothold in the largest U.S. industries. This was highlighted by the great CIO (Congress of Industrial Organizations) organizing drives of the 1930s, which gave rise to the United Steelworkers, the United Auto Workers, the United Electrical Workers, and the Amalgamated Clothing and Tex-

Written especially for *Perspectives in Medical Sociology*, 3/E.

tile Workers, among others. These efforts were aided by passage of the federal Wagner Act in 1936, which guaranteed workers the right to petition for and conduct elections to establish unions in their plants.

Gradually, during this period, workers gained some important health and safety protections through their union contracts and through use of grievance procedures to enforce these contract provisions. But these protections were spotty and of course protected only those workers covered by union contracts.

This was to change in 1970, with the passage of the landmark federal Occupational Safety and Health Act (OSHA). This law came about by an array of circumstances: the militancy of organized coal miners following a terrible mine explosion in Farmington, West Virginia in 1978; the failure of state laws to adequately protect workers' health and safety on the job; and the sharp rise in the rates of job injuries and illnesses during the 1950s and 1960s (Levenstein, 1988). But none of these was so important or decisive as the strong, united support of the law by U.S. labor unions. Without the labor movement behind it, this law might have gone the way of much other needed federal legislation: delay, weak or no standards, lack of adequate enforcement—in short, death by a thousand cuts.

But instead OSHA was passed, largely intact, establishing minimum health and safety standards for most private-sector employees (and some public-sector employees), and a national system of inspectors with the right to enter and inspect all covered workplaces. This law has faced strong employer opposition ever since, and in almost every session of Congress since 1970 Senators and Congressmen, supported by large, unregulated corporate campaign donations, have tried to weaken the law. In most cases they have failed, thanks in large measure to the strong, steady support of OSHA by the labor movement.

A number of important worker protection standards have been issued under OSHA by the U.S. Department of Labor. Among them are standards to provide health and safety information to workers and prevent overexposure to asbestos dust, lead, noise and other chemical and physical hazards. (Details are available at www.osha.gov.) But these have been undermined by underfunding of the OSHA agency and lack of OSHA enforcement. What impact have these laws and standards had on workers' health and lives?

Worker Health and Safety in the 1990s

National statistics on work-related injuries and illnesses, compiled annually for OSHA by the federal Bureau of Labor Statistics

(BLS) and based on management (!) reports, show a decline in the annual incidence of worker injuries and illnesses during the 1990s. Indeed OSHA reported record low rates of these injuries and illnesses in 1996 and then again in 1998 (OSHA, 1999). These data reflect both lost-time and non-lost-time incidents.

Thus in 1998 OSHA/BLS reported 5.5 million work-related injuries and 392,000 work-related illnesses among U.S. workers in private industries covered by OSHA, corresponding to an incidence rate of 6.7 work-related injuries and illnesses per 100 full-time workers. In other words approximately 6.7 percent of U.S. workers—about 1 in 16—experienced a work-related incident that year, the lowest rate, remember, since OSHA began reporting such statistics.

Looking at lost-time injuries and illnesses only presents a more sobering—and probably more realistic—picture of work injuries and illnesses, since lost-time incidents are typically better documented than non-lost-time ones (e.g., through worker compensation reports and medical records). Between 1973, the first year BLS compiled national OSHA statistics, and 1980, the lost-time injury and illness rate climbed slowly from 3.4 to 4.0 work-related injuries and illnesses per 100 full-time workers (BLS, 1997a)—that is, in 1980 four workers per 100, or one in 25, suffered lost-time injuries or illnesses on the job that forced them to miss or be transferred to a lighter job for at least one full workday. This rate, already quite large, remained roughly constant during the 1980s. During the 1990s this reported rate has fallen slowly and steadily, from 4.1 per 100 workers in 1990 to 3.4 in 1996 (the same value as in 1973), and then to a record low of 3.1 in 1998. Thus over these few decades then lost-time injury and illness rate has remained remarkably constant, varying within a range of about plus or minus 15 percent around an average of about 3.6 per 100.

What this means in concrete terms, as noted by Dr. Linda Rosenstock, Director of the National Institute for Occupational Safety and Health (NIOSH), the federal health and safety research arm of the federal government, is that *every day* 9,000 U.S. workers suffer injuries that cause them to lose at least one day of work, and 16 workers die from these on-the-job injuries. NIOSH further estimates that another 137 persons lose their lives each day due to the long-term effects of occupational diseases. Furthermore, each year, 64,000 young workers under the age of 18 have to visit hospital emergency rooms to treat work injuries, and of these 70 die from the injuries (Rosenstock, 1999).

But even the reported rates of workplace injuries and illnesses may be underestimates. Currently the federal OSHA Administration is conducting record low rates of workplace inspections, and has been doing so throughout the 1990s.

In fiscal year 1996 (October 1, 1995 to September 30, 1996), the number of federal OSHA inspections fell to 24,024, *down 17.5 percent from the previous record low in fiscal year 1995*. Before last year, the lowest number of inspections conducted by OSHA was in 1972, the first year of OSHA operations.

Even more dramatic was the sharp drop in violations cited by OSHA inspectors. Nationwide, they cited only 55,093 violations in 1996, *a drop of 39 percent from the record low number of 90,555 violations cited in 1995*. The number of *willful violations* they cited fell by *14 percent* in 1996, and the number of *serious violations* by *40 percent*.

Of course, with inspections and violations down, penalties for employers also dropped. Federal OSHA assessed $66.8 million in fines for violations cited in 1996, *a drop of 23.4 percent* from the $87.2 million assessed in 1995. This was *not* a record low (!), but only the lowest value since 1990.

As a result of the sharp drop in OSHA enforcement activity in 1995, the two-year period of 1995 and 1996 represents the most drastic curtailment of federal OSHA enforcement in its 25-year history. This has continued in the years since, with the number of inspections roughly constant (Jeffress, 1999). In the fiscal years 1994–1996, following the election of the conservative Newt Gingrich-led Republican Congress, OSHA's record showed the following declines:

Enforcement Category	Percent Drop, FY 1994–1996
No. Inspections	43%
Total Violations	62%
Serious Violations	65%
Willful Violations	39%
Repeat Violations	51%
Total Penalties	44%

This is an abysmal enforcement record. Former OSHA Director Joseph Dear said at the time, "The idea of enforcement is to impose serious consequences for serious violations" (C&E News, 12/9/96). The agency's deeds don't fit his words. Citations for serious violations fell by 65 percent from FY 1994–1996. For the serious violations cited, fines went up from $822 per violation in 1994 to $928 in 1996, a 13 percent increase. In real dollars—that is, taking inflation into account—this amounts to a real *six percent increase* in fines per serious violation! "Serious consequences for serious violations?!" Who's OSHA kidding?

In 1997, President Clinton appointed Ms. Alexis Herman as Labor Secretary, and later Charles Jeffress, former Director of the North Carolina state health and safety program, as Assistant Secretary of Labor for OSHA. The weak enforcement of OSHA regulations continues, since its toothless enforcement policies and its emphasis on cooperation with management come from the top (that is, from the Clinton Administration), not from the Labor Department.

Worker Training and Education Programs

Another important, positive development in worker health and safety in recent years has been the establishment and growth of worker training and education programs. Four states—Michigan, New York, Connecticut and Maine—have created worker health and safety training funds, in most cases through a small tax (0.2–0.5%) on workers' compensation premiums. The programs distribute anywhere form $200,000 in Maine to about $4 million in New York State in training grants to labor unions, local Committees for Occupational Safety and Health (COSH groups), hospitals, local government health and safety agencies, and private employers. Efforts are currently under way to enact similar programs in other states. These could be an important stimulus to grassroots health and safety activities by union locals and in local communities.

Musculoskeletal Disorders and Ergonomics Hazards in the Workplace

The workplace injuries and illnesses caused by ergonomics hazards were one of the hot-button health and safety issues of the 1980s and 1990s, and dealing with these hazards is among the most difficult challenges of the new millennium.

Ergonomics is the science of fitting the job to the worker (*not* the worker to the job). When there is a mismatch between the physical requirements of the job and the physical demands on the worker, work-related injuries and illnesses can occur, such as carpal tunnel syndrome (a painful, often disabling wrist disorder), tendonitis, and disabling back injuries. Currently almost two-thirds (64 percent) of all work-related illnesses are repetitive strain injuries (RSIs) such as carpal tunnel syndrome—up from only a few percent of all such illnesses reported in the early 1980s (BLS, 1997b).

These hazards cause severe hand and wrist pains among auto workers, meat-packing workers and many other manufacturing workers. Recent studies show that 50 percent of all supermarket cashiers suffer from ergonomics-related disorders, as they constantly twist their hands and arms to record prices on their laser-beam cash registers. Clerical workers and others who use computers constantly, such as newspaper reporters and telemarketers, suffer high rates of these disorders.

If we add the impact of work-related back injuries to those of the repetitive strain disorders noted above—together these are called MSDs (muculoskeletal disorders)—then MSDs account for one-third of all occupational injuries and illnesses serious enough to cause lost workdays. More than 600,000 U.S. workers suffer lost-workday MSDs each year. These incidents are estimated to cost over $15 *billion* in workers' compensation costs each year (OSHA, 2000).

Much research has been carried out during the last three decades linking ergonomic hazards and work-related injuries and illnesses (NIOSH, 1997). But many major industries and their Congressional allies, especially in the conservative wing of the Republican Party, deny that the link between workplace ergonomics hazards and job injuries and illnesses has been proven scientifically. Thus they have strongly resisted efforts by OSHA to enact an ergonomics standard. Indeed, the so-called Gingrich Congress in 1995 [Rep. Newt Gingrich (R-GA) was Speaker of the U.S. House of Representatives and chief author of the Republican "Contract for America"] attached an amendment to federal budget legislation banning OSHA from enacting *or even proposing* such a standard! (U.S. Congress, 1996) This so-called "rider" amendment to the federal budget was passed annually as part of the federal budget for each of the next two years.

During this time, however, a consensus was developing among scientists about the harmful effects of ergonomics hazards. In 1997 NIOSH issued a report based on a consensus of over 40 scientists which found "a strong association between MSDs and certain work-related physical factors" (NIOSH, 1997). A 1998 report by the National Academy of Sciences (NAS, 1998) came to the same conclusions, that:

- Musculoskeletal disorders are a serious national problem.
- The scientific literature clearly demonstrates that musculoskeletal disorders in workers are caused by exposure to ergonomic hazards at work.
- For most people, their main exposure to ergonomic hazards is at their workplace.
- Scientific research clearly demonstrates that effective workplace interventions are available which can reduce ergonomic hazards.

As a result of this growing scientific consensus and political pressure by organized labor, Congress overturned the "Ergonomics Ban" in 1998, but not before awarding the National Academy of Sciences, despite its clear-cut determinations in its 1998 study (as noted above), $890,000 to conduct yet another three-year study of the impact of ergonomic hazards (BNA OSH Reporter, 1998).

Once this ban on its activities was overturned, OSHA took advantage of the opportunity to propose a new ergonomics standard in 1999, one it argued was long needed in the United States, given the large number of disabling injuries and illnesses ergonomics hazards cause (Federal Register, 11/23/99). As proposed by OSHA, the Ergonomics Standard (CFR 1910.900) would apply to all manufacturing and manual handling operations. This means that in *manufacturing companies*, assembly-line workers, inspectors, machine operators, and machine loaders and unloaders would ordinarily be covered. In *manual handling operations* patient-handling jobs such as nursing aides and orderlies would be covered, as well as jobs involving hand packing and packaging; package sorting, handling and delivery; stock handling and bagging, grocery store, and garbage collecting.

But, if workers are not in such a facility, although they may spend all day working at their computers, they are not automatically covered by the standard. Nor are workers in all other non-manufacturing general industry facilities, unless one or more work-related musculoskeletal disorder (MSD) is reported and recorded. Unfortunately, this provision is virtually an invitation to companies to put pressure on workers *not* to report their injuries. The very first MSD reported and determined to be work-related would immediately put all workers in the reported work category, and hence the company employing them, under the many requirements of this standard. Would the reporting employee consider his or her job safe, and their future for promotion in the company secure, if he/she was the first to report such an injury? And wouldn't the company have every incentive to contest and try to contravene this first reported case (e.g., it was not caused by work/it was caused at home/it is not serious)? This provision alone makes the proposed OSHA Ergonomics Standard only half a standardægood for those it covers, but almost useless for those it doesn't.

OSHA requires the following elements in any employer ergonomics program:

- *Management Leadership* —Establish a system to report and respond to signs and symptoms of these disorders

- *Employee Participation*—Worker access to information about the program, and input in developing, implementing and evaluating all program elements
- *Job Hazard Analysis Controls* —Employers must uncover and eliminate or reduce all ergonomic hazards
- *Worker Training*—Provide initial and then periodic training to all affected employees (at least once every three years)
- *MSD Management*—Provide access to a health-care professional for injured workers and *maintain workers' pay while on work restrictions*
- *Program Evaluation and Review*—At least every three years

(Further details on the standard are available from the OSHA website: www.osha-slc.gov/ergonomics-standard.)

OSHA officers hope to complete hearings on the proposed new standard, make modifications, and issue a final standard by the end of the year 2000. This is an ambitious schedule, given the many years it usually takes OSHA to enact much less controversial standards. But OSHA officials are prodded by the fact that a new presidential administration and a new U.S. Congress will take office in January 2001, hence a new cast of actors will then be on the scene, with uncertain impact on the OSHA administration.

Home-Work

Another major health and safety issue facing workers and the general public in the new century will be the issue of "home-work." The amount of paid work being done in the home has been growing dramatically since the 1980s. (Unpaid work at home, of course, is as old as human civilization.) Many textile workers, some legally and some not, now work in their homes under sweatshop conditions—often joined by their young children. Small-scale assembly operations are sent out for workers to do at home, many times by immigrant labor.

With the advent of computers and computer-based jobs, many professional and government workers work a day or two a week at home, while others work full-time at home on their computers. Many salespeople work their telephones all day at home. And of course, as people live longer, more Americans are finding work in private homes as caregivers to the elderly.

Along with these home-based jobs come health and safety hazards—back injuries from lifting, repetitive strain injuries from machine work, and occupational illnesses from chemicals used on assembly jobs. So it's not surprising that sooner or later federal OSHA would be drawn into this work arena.

In February 2000 OSHA got drawn into this issue in a big way, and OSHA emerged with egg on its face, having angered not only its corporate and small-business enemies but its friends in the labor movement as well. What happened was that in December 1999 California OSHA (CalOSHA) fined three electronics companies nearly $200,000 for violations associated with piecework assembly in homes, including chemical safety violations. Following company protests, CalOSHA asked federal OSHA to confirm that it had authority to levy these fines. In January OSHA announced that the fines were legal and these health and safety hazards in the home were violations of the OSHA Act.

After only two days of angry company protests and lots of unwanted publicity, Secretary of Labor Alexis Herman backed off, withdrew her previous letter and called for a dialogue between all involved parties— read: we're not going to do anything about health and safety of home workers, at least not until the presidential elections are over in November. This was just another in a long list of sad retreats by OSHA and the Clinton Administration. But the problem of workers being injured and made ill by home-work won't go away, and workers in these jobs deserve the protections to which the OSHA law entitles them.

The OSHA law is clear about who is and is not covered by it: Federal OSHA covers all persons employed by employers in the private sector who engage in interstate commerce (unless there are some other laws which protected particular groups of workers, such as airline pilots or nuclear workers). State plans also cover city and state public employees.

OSHA does *not* cover self-employed persons, like consultants or accountants. (But if the accountants or consultants work together in a firm of any size, they are covered). Also, household servants are specifically exempt from coverage, precisely to avoid sending inspectors into people's homes (especially rich people's homes).

It's clear then which home workers are covered by OSHA and which are not: If a worker in a home is working there as an employee of someone else, he or she is covered. So of course the workers in California who were employed by electronics companies were covered when they worked at home (and when they worked in the plant). A home health worker who is employed by a placement service is covered. A public employee who is allowed to work on his/her computer at home one day a week is covered. But a private consultant working for himself at home or anywhere else is *not* covered.

Struggles over home-work are part of a fight that has been going on for over a century. At the turn of the last century, the textile industry was hip deep into home-work. Desperate women and children were available to work long hours for low wages. But the resulting child labor and filthy living conditions gave rise to disease and ill health in the community. Labor unions and reformers such as Florence Kelly and Eleanor Roosevelt called for the abolition of home-work. In 1938, they won passage of the Fair Labor Standards Act, which banned most home production. Later, the OSHA law, passed in 1970, added to the protection of workers at all worksites.

As a noted labor historian and a women's studies expert said recently:

> Telecommuting entrepreneurs will undoubtedly claim it is absurd to compare the working conditions of a computer-literate home worker in the exurbs to the grinding labor of a tenement-house sewing-machine operator on the Lower East Side in New York City. But it is not the character of the technology alone that determines the well-being of the workers or the level of their wages. When today's computerized homebodies find themselves with a pain in their wrist, fatigue in their neck or a crick in the lower back, the cause is remarkably similar to that of their sweatshop ancestors: inadequate equipment, self-exploitation and overwork. . . . So as we open a dialogue about the workplace of the future, let's not leave behind the advances of the past. These include the guarantee of decent work in an environment that nurtures the worker instead of destroying the soul. (Nelson Lichtenstein and Eileen Boris, *Los Angeles Times* 1/20/00)

What we really need in this new century is the Fair Labor Standards Act, which is still in effect, to end illegal home-work. And for those who are legally working at home, we need OSHA health and safety enforcement for all workers who are covered there. This doesn't mean random inspections of homes by OSHA inspectors trying to find home-workers, but it does mean responding aggressively to complaints either from the workers or from others. And, yes, it might mean that OSHA will conduct occasional inspections of homes where it knows such work is being done. The alternative, after all, is unregulated, potentially abusive working conditions and a steady stream of injuries and illness on the job at home (UE News, 2000).

Looking Toward the Future

The importance of OSHA—and hence its visibility as a program—lies not in its standards or enforcement, important as they are, but in its broad base of support among working men and women and the general public. Working people today believe that among their inalienable rights is the right to a safe and healthful workplace. When employers or others try to undermine this right, they face determined opposition by working people and their labor unions, supported in broad measure by the community. And this, after all, is more important than the wording of any standard.

As long as working people with community support firmly insist on workplace protections on the job, their health and safety rights are secure, no matter what the ups and downs of the OSHA agency in different federal and state administrations. With this support, the future prospects for maintaining and improving health and safety protections on the job are bright.

References

BLS, *Bureau of Labor Statistics News* (Dec. 17, 1997a) Table 6.

BLS, *Bureau of Labor Statistics News* (Dec. 17, 1997b) Chart in BNA *Occupational Safety and Health Reporter*, Vol. 27 (1997), p. 1102.

BLS, *Bureau of Labor Statistics News* (Dec. 16, 1999) Table 6. See also <http://stats.bls.gov/news.release/osh.toc.htm>

C&E, *Chemical and Engineering News* (Dec. 9, 1996).

Federal Register, Dept. of Labor, Occ. Safety & Health Admin., Vol. 64, No. 225 (Nov. 23, 1999), pp. 66066–66078.

Levenstein, Charles, "A Brief History of Occupational Health and Safety," in B. Levy and D. Wegman (eds.), *Occupational Health*, 2nd ed. New York: Wiley (1988), pp. 11–12.

NAS, National Academy of Sciences, *Work-Related Musculoskeletal Disorders: Report, Workshop Summary, Workshop Papers*, National Academy Press (1999).

NIOSH, National Institute for Occupational Safety and Health, *Musculoskeletal Disorders and Workplace Factors: A Critical Review*, DHHS (NIOSH) No. 97–41(1997).

NY Times, *New York Times* (11/22/1999), p. 1.

OSHA, Occupational Safety and Health Administration, *Proposal for an Ergonomics Program Standard: Frequently Asked Questions* (2000), p.1. See also http://www.osha-slc.gov/ergonomics-standard/ergo-faq.html

Rosenstock, Linda (Director, NIOSH), speech to NIOSH conference on Psychosocial Costs of Work-Related Injuries and Illnesses, Denver (6/14/1999).

UE News, Health on the Job column, D. Kotelchuck, "OSHA Inspections Drop to Record Lows Again!" (Jan. 1997), p. 15.

UE News, Health on the Job column, D. Kotelchuck, "Home-Work" (Feb. 2000), p.15.

U. S. Congress, "Ergonomics Rider," *Conference Report to Accompany H.R.3019*, 104th Congress, 2nd Session, Report No. 104-537 (Apr. 25, 1996).

PART II

Being Ill and Getting Care

As noted in the general introduction, some of the central issues with which I am concerned are the ways people experience illness, and the relationships and interactions between people and their health care providers. A number of articles in other sections also underscore this theme, but in this section we put special emphasis on the topic.

The study of illness behavior and of medical interaction has pre-occupied the recent generation of medical sociologists. Through examining people's illness experience, we go beyond a concrete bio-medical *disease* to a socially experienced *illness*. This shows us how many different meanings and implications illness has for people. By studying the ways in which care-seekers and caregivers deal with one another, we are able to learn more about the lay experience of illness and to delve into the often unspoken and implicit assumptions of medical ideologies and conceptions. At the same time, studies of interaction show how medical practice often mirrors the biases that occur throughout our society, particularly those involving class, gender, and race. Because the doctor-patient relationship is a classic power relationship, it can provide a model for the study of the interpersonal dynamics and social biases which occur in other forms of social encounters.

This part of the book contains four sections. The first, Experiencing Illness and Seeking Care, examines the diverse forms of patients' experience of illness, sometimes as a result of individuals' particularities and sometimes as a result of the person's membership in a certain social group. The second section, Interaction and Negotiation Between Patients and Providers, uses both conceptual and fieldwork approaches to study the ways in which patients and providers interact. Alternatives to Formal Medicine, the third section, looks at conceptions and practices of health behavior that depart from traditional medical knowledge and professional styles. In the fourth section, Technology, Experimentation, and Social Control, we look at

193

more direct power relations and mechanisms of social control which involve illegitimate research on human beings, disclosure and withholding of medical information, and the conflicts between patients and physicians over the choice of medical procedures.

Section IV

Experiencing Illness and Seeking Care

Modern medical sociology has reframed how we look at the definition of health problems. This can be seen in particular in the discussion in the previous section of the critique of the medical model, and of social constructivism. While *disease* is the physiological condition a medical professional would observe, *illness* is the way that a person experiences that physiological condition. The same disease or condition is often experienced differently by different people. For example, the existence of pneumonia may lead one person to lie in bed and demand attention, yet lead another person to stay out of bed and to try to continue routine living. The same form of cancer may engender denial by one person, while another experiences it with active dread. Pain is perceived differently according to people's social class and ethnic cultural backgrounds.

Further, not all disease is experienced as illness, nor is all illness the result of a particular disease. Some people manage to avoid active symptoms, or to attribute them to other sources. Certain people tend to experience symptoms that are not traceable to a known cause, and some spend much time fearing they will catch any number of diseases. A large number of visits to doctors are for very minor symptoms and for psychological attention.

In many cases, popular concepts of health differ from medical concepts, due to the gulf in both knowledge and perspective between consumers and providers. Understanding this divergence in viewpoint is of central concern to medical sociologists, since it underlies many conflicts which occur in the health care system. As citizens become more educated, conscious, and active in health matters, these conflicts often increase. Differences in perception mean that people also differ in the ways that they choose to deal with their health problems.

These and many other dimensions of *illness behavior* have led sociologists to pay closer attention to patient perspectives on health, illness, and medical care. Health professionals, too, have begun to

195

alter their perspectives on such issues. A growing number of doctors and hospitals pay particular attention to specific aspects of illness behavior rather than focusing exclusively on disease.

Race, class, sex, ethnic, and national differences lead to differing degrees of self-treatment and to diverse help seeking. Irving Kenneth Zola's article, "Pathways to the Doctor—From Person to Patient," illuminates many of these issues through a study of patient help seeking in three clinics. Zola finds major differences among Italian, Irish Catholic, and Anglo-Saxon Protestants in the experience of illness and the ways that complaints were presented to doctors. Zola provides more evidence that much help-seeking behavior is not primarily a result of physiological problems, or disease as defined by the medical model. Instead, it is triggered by five major types of occurrences: interpersonal crises, perceived interference with social or personal relations, sanctioning on the part of another family member, perceived interference with work or physical activity, and temporalizing (time-bound perceptions of symptoms).

Gareth Williams's contribution, "The Genesis of Chronic Illness: Narrative Reconstruction," gives us detailed glimpses into the ways in which three people reconstruct how they believe they "got" rheumatoid arthritis. Williams' respondents employ broader viewpoints than the biomedical model. One imputes a political and economic causality; another locates etiology in a nest of social relationships and psychological makeup; another uses a mystical explanation. Each of these people produces a coherent self-analysis for their own narrative, thus providing a way to repair the rupture which chronic disease causes in their relationship with the world. This selection is valuable not only because it provides examples of individual illness experience, but also because it demonstrates the usefulness of narrative methods of research, i.e., reconstructing how people tell stories and give accounts of their life experience.

In "Life with AIDS," Rose Weitz takes us inside the daily routines of people with AIDS, sharing how they think, feel, and act about their condition. The magnitude of living with a fatal disease is difficult enough, but AIDS sufferers face further stigmatization and rejection. Indeed, Weitz writes, much of their daily life in early stages of their illness involves finding ways to avoid or reduce stigma. Later they often find their way to support groups and helping networks. For some, living with this disease enables them to reevaluate their lives, to get more politically involved, and to become more compassionate to others. Weitz's fieldwork with AIDS sufferers points out the important for medical sociology of learning about the everyday lives of people with any illness or disability, for only then can we get a more complete picture than we would from only medical and epidemiological knowledge.

Susan Zimmerman's "The Medical Management of Femininity: Women's Experiences with Silicone Breast Implants" illustrates how medical practice can be a result of social pressures and norms that have nothing to do with health and illness. The rampant use of silicon breast implants for cosmetic purposes produced much harm to women, despite prior knowledge of the dangers. Zimmerman's article is useful for showing the nature of disputes over iatrogenic effects (effects caused by medical action), since women's clear experiences of illness were countered by research that argued that implants were not dangerous. In keeping with the social movement theme, Zimmerman also shows how women's common experience of suffering brought them together to provide mutual support and to take political action against implants, leading to an FDA moratorium on implants.

10
Pathways to the Doctor—
From Person to Patient

Irving Kenneth Zola

The problem on which we wish to dwell is one about which we think we know a great deal but that, in reality, we know so little—how and why an individual seeks professional medical aid. The immediate and obvious answer is that a person goes to a doctor when he is sick. Yet, this term "sick," is much clearer to those who use it, namely the health practitioners and the researchers, than it is to those upon whom we apply it—the patients. Two examples may illustrate this point. Listen carefully to the words of a respondent in Koos' study of the Health of Regionville as she wrestled with a definition of this concept.

> I wish I really knew what you meant about being sick. Sometimes I felt so bad I could curl up and die, but had to go on because the kids had to be taken care of and besides, we didn't have the money to spend for the doctor. How could I be sick? How do you know when you're sick, anyway? Some people can go to bed most anytime with anything, but most of us can't be sick, even when we need to be [1].

Even when there is agreement as to what constitutes "sickness," there may be a difference of opinion as to what constitutes appropriate action, as in the following incident:

> A rather elderly woman arrived at the Medical Clinic of the Massachusetts General Hospital three days after an appointment. A somewhat exasperated nurse turned to her and said, "Mrs. Smith, your appointment was three days ago. Why weren't you here then?" To this Mrs. Smith responded, "How could I? Then I was sick."

Examples such as these are not unusual occurrences. And yet they cause little change in some basic working assumptions of the purveyors of medical care as well as the myriad investigators who are studying its delivery. It is to three of these assumptions we now turn: (1) the

Reprinted by permission from *Social Science and Medicine*, Vol. 7, pp. 677–89. Copyright © 1973, Elsevier Science, Ltd., Pergamon Imprint, Oxford, England.

importance and frequency of episodes of illness in an individual's life; (2) the representativeness of those episodes of illness which come to professional attention; and (3) the process by which an individual decides that a series of bodily discomforts he labels symptoms become worthy of professional attention. Together these assumptions create an interesting if misleading picture of illness. Rarely do we try to understand how or why a patient goes to the doctor, for the decision itself is thought to be an obvious one. We postulate a time when the patient is asymptomatic or unaware that he has symptoms, then suddenly some clear objective symptoms appear, then perhaps he goes through a period of self-treatment and when either this treatment is unsuccessful or the symptoms in some way become too difficult to take, he decides to go to some health practitioner (usually, we hope, a physician).

The first assumption, thus, deals with the idea that individuals at most times during their life are really asymptomatic. The extensive data pouring in from periodic health examination has gradually begun to question this notion. For, examinations of even supposedly healthy people, from business executives to union members to college profes-sors, consistently reveal that at the time of their annual check-up, there was scarcely an individual who did not possess some symptom, some clinical entity worthy of treatment [2]. More general surveys have yielded similar findings [3]. Such data begins to give us a rather uncomfortable sense in which we may to some degree be sick every day of our lives. If we should even think of such a picture, however, the easiest way to dismiss this notion is that the majority of these everyday conditions are so minor as to be unworthy of medical treatment. This leads to our second assumption; namely, the degree of representativeness, both as to seriousness and frequency, of those episodes which do get to a doctor. Here too we are presented with puzzling facts. For if we look at investigations of either serious physical or mental disorder, there seem to be at least one, and in many cases several, people out of treatment for every person in treatment [4]. If, on the other hand, we look at a doctor's practice, we find that the vast bulk is concerned with quite minor disorders [5]. Furthermore, if we use symptom-check-lists or health calendars, we find that for these self-same minor disorders, there is little that distinguishes them medically from those that are ignored, tolerated, or self-medicated [6].

With these confusions in mind, we can now turn to the third assumption. On the basis that symptoms were perceived to be an infrequent and thus somewhat dramatic event in one's life, the general assumption was that in the face of such symptoms, a rational individual after an appropriate amount of caution, would seek aid. When he does not or delays overlong, we begin to question his rationality. The innumerable studies of delay in cancer bear witness.

If we examine these studies we find that the reason for delay are a list of faults—the patient has no time, no money, no one to care for children, or take over other duties, is guilty, ashamed, fearful, anxious, embarrassed, or emotionally disturbed, dislikes physicians, nurses, hospitals, or needles, has had bad medical, familial or personal experiences, or is of lower education, socioeconomic status, or an ethnic or racial minority [7]. As the researchers might put it, there is something about these people or in their backgrounds which has disturbed their rationality, for otherwise, they would "naturally" seek aid. And yet there is a curious methodological fact about these studies for all these investigations were done on *patients*, people who *had* ultimately decided to go to a physician. What happened? Were they no longer fearful? Did they get free time, more money, outside help? Did they resolve their guilt, shame, anxiety, distrust? No, this does not seem to have been the case. If anything the investigators seem to allude to the fact that the patients finally could not stand it any longer. Yet given the abundant data on the ability to tolerate pain [8] and a wide variety of other conditions, this notion of "not being able to stand it" simply does not ring true clinically.

We can now restate a more realistic empirical picture of illness episodes. Virtually every day of our lives we are subject to a vast array of bodily discomforts. Only an infinitesimal amount of these get to a physician. Neither the mere presence nor the obviousness of symptoms, neither their medical seriousness nor objective discomfort seems to differentiate those episodes which do and do not get professional treatment. In short, what then does convert a person to a patient? This then became a significant question and the search for an answer began.

At this point we had only the hunch that "something critical" must ordinarily happen to make an individual seek help. Given the voluminous literature on delay in seeking medical aid for almost every conceivable disorder and treatment, we might well say that the statistical norm for any population is to delay (perhaps infinitely for many). The implementing of this hunch is owed primarily to the intersection of two disciplines—anthropology and psychiatry. The first question to be faced was how and where to study this "something." Both prospective and retrospective studies were rejected. The former because as Professor H. M. Murphy noted there is often an enormous discrepancy between the declared intention and the actual act. The retrospective approach was rejected for two reasons—the almost notoriously poor recall that individuals have for past medical experiences and the distortions in recall introduced by the extensive "memory manipulation" which occurs as a result of the medical interview. Our resolution to this dilemma was a way of studying the patient when he was *in the process* of seeking medical aid. This process was somewhat artificially created by (1) interviewing patients while they waited to see their physician; (2) confining our sample to new patients to the Out-Patient Clinics of the Massachusetts General Hospital who were seeking aid for their particular problem for the first time. Thus, we had a group of people who were definitely committed to seeing a doctor (i.e. waiting) but who had not yet been subject to the biases and distortions that might occur through the medical interview (though some patients had been referred, we included only those on whom no definitive diagnosis had been made). This then was where we decided to study our problem.

In what to look for we were influenced by certain trends in general psychiatry away from defining mental illness solely in terms of symptoms possessed by a single isolated individual and instead conceptualising it as a more general kind of disturbance in interpersonal behaviour and social living. (The resemblance that this bears to early classical notions of health and illness is quite striking. For then illness was conceived to be the disturbance between ego and his environment and not the physical symptom which happens to show up in ego) [9]. On the empirical level we were influenced by the work of Clausen and his colleagues at the National Institute of Mental Health on the first admission to the hospital for male schizophrenics. Most striking about their material was the lack of any increase in the objective seriousness of the patient's disorder as a factor in this hospitalisation. If anything, there was a kind of normalisation in his family, an accommodation to the patient's symptoms. The hospitalisation occurred not when the patient became sicker, but when the accommodation of the family, of the surrounding social context, broke down [10]. A translation of these findings could be made to physical illness. For, given all the data on delay, it seemed very likely that people have their symptoms for a long period of time before ever seeking medical aid. Thus one could hypothesize that there is an accommodation both physical, personal, and social to the symptoms and it is when this accommodation breaks down that the person seeks, or is forced to seek medical aid. Thus the "illness" for which one seeks help may only in part be a physical relief from symptoms. The research question on the decision to seek medical aid thus turned from the traditional focus on "why the delay" to the more general issue of "why come *now*." This way of asking this question is in itself not new. Physicians have often done it, but interestingly enough, they have asked it not in regard to general physical illness but rather when they can find nothing wrong. It is *then* that they feel that the patient may want or have been prompted to seek help for other than physical reasons.

The final issue which is essential to understanding the study concerns the nature of the sample. Here in particular there was an intersection of anthropology and psychiatry. Time and again anthropologists had called attention to the problem of designating certain behaviours as abnormal in one cultural situation but would be considered quite normal and even ignored in another. Usually, when they explained this phenomenon they did so in terms of value-orientations; namely that there was something about the fit or lack of fit of the particular problem (symptom or sign), into a larger cultural pattern which helped explain why it was or was not abnormal [11]. Why could not the same process be operating in regard to physical symptoms? Perhaps many of the unexplained epidemiological differences between groups may also be due to the fact that in one group the particular physical sign is considered normal and in the second group not. For given the enormous tolerance we have for many physical conditions, given that our morbidity statistics are based primarily on treated disorders, many of these differences may reflect differences in attention and not differences in prevalence or incidence. While anthropologists have reported their findings mostly in comparisons of nonliterate groups with a more "modern" society, we decided to translate their idea of a culture into a contemporary format. We thus speculated that ethnic groups, particularly in an area such as Boston, Massachusetts, might well function as cultural reference groups and thus be an urban transmitter and perpetuator of value-orientations. The specific ethnic groups we studied were determined by a demographic study at the Massachusetts General Hospital, from which we were able to determine the three most populous ethnic groups, Italian, Irish Catholic and Anglo-Saxon Protestant.

To summarize the methodological introduction, in our first study, the sample consisted of patients completely new to the out-patient clinics who were seeking medical aid for the first time for this particular problem, who were between the ages of 18 and 50, able to converse in English, of either Anglo-Saxon Protestant, Irish Catholic or Italian

Catholic background. The data-collection took place at the three clinics to which these groups were most frequently sent—the Eye Clinic, the Ear, Nose and Throat Clinic, and the Medical Clinic, which were, incidentally three of the largest clinics in the hospital. The interviewing took place during the waiting time before they saw their physicians with the general focus of the questioning being: Why did you seek medical aid now? In addition to many such open-ended questions, we had other information derived from the medical record, demographic interviews, attitude scales and check lists. We also had each examining physician fill out a medical rating sheet on each patient. In all we saw over two hundred patients, fairly evenly divided between male and female [12].

We first examined the presenting complaints of the patients to see if there were differing conceptions of what is symptomatic [13]. Our first finding dealt with the location of their troubles. The Irish tended to place the locus of symptoms in the eye, the ear, the nose or the throat—a sense organ while the Italians showed no particular clustering. The same result obtained when we asked what was the most important part of the body. Here too the Irish tended to place their symptoms in the eyes, ears, nose and throat with the Italians not favouring any specific location. We noted, however, that this was not merely a reflection of epidemiological differences; for Italians who did have eye, ear, nose and throat problems did not necessarily locate their chief complaint in either the eye, ear, nose or throat. We thus began to wonder if this focussing was telling us something other than a specific location. And so we turned our attention to more qualitative aspects of symptoms, such as the presence of pain. Here we noted that the Italians much more often felt that pain constituted a major part of their problem, whereas the Irish felt equally strongly that it did not. However, we had our first clue that "something else" was going on. The Irish did not merely say they had no pain, but rather utilized a kind of denial with such statements as, "No, I wouldn't call it a pain, rather a discomfort"; or "No, a slight headache, but nothing that lasts." Further analysis of our data then led us to create a typology in which we tried to grasp the essence of a patient's complaint. One type seemed to reflect a rather specific organic dysfunctioning (difficulty in seeing, inappropriate functioning, discharge, or movement etc.) while the second type represented a more global malfunctioning (aches and pains, appearance, energy level etc.). Looked at in this way, we found that significantly more Irish seemed to describe their problem in terms of a rather specific dysfunction whereas the Italians described their complaints in a more diffuse way. Thus, the Irish seemed to convey a concern with something specific, something that has gone wrong, or been impaired; whereas the Italian is concerned with or conveyed a more global malfunctioning emphasizing the more diffuse nature of their complaints.

We now had differentiated two ways of communicating about one's bodily complaints—a kind of restricting versus generalizing tendency and we thus sought evidence to either refute or substantiate it. Two "tests" suggested themselves. The first consisted of three sets of tabulations: (1) the total number of symptoms a patient had; (2) the total number of different types of malfunctions from which he suffered (the typology mentioned above actually consisted of nine codifiable categories); and (3) the total number of different parts of the body in which a patient located complaints. Each we regarded as a measure of "generalizing" one's complaints. As we predicted the Italians had significantly more complaints of greater variety, and in more places than did the Irish. Our second "test" consisted of several questions dealing with the effect of their symptoms on their interpersonal behaviour. Here we reasoned that the Irish would be much more likely to restrict the effect of their symptoms to physical functioning. And so it was, with the Italians claiming that the symptoms interfered with their general mode of living and the Irish just as vehemently denying any such interference. Here again, the Irish presented a "no with a difference" in such statements as "No, there may have been times that I become uncomfortable physically and afraid to show it socially. If I felt that way I even tried to be a little more sociable."

Perhaps the best way to convey how differently these two groups communicated their symptoms is by a composite picture. The two series of responses were given by an Italian and an Irish patient of similar age and sex, with a disorder of approximately the same duration and seriousness and with the same primary and, if present, secondary diagnosis.

The crux of the study is, however, the decision to see a doctor. One of our basic claims was that the decision to seek medical aid was based on a break in the accommodation to the symptoms, that in the vast majority of situations, an individual did not seek aid at his physically sickest point. We do not mean by this that symptoms were unimportant. What we mean is that they function as a sort of constant and that when the decision to seek medical aid was made the physical symptoms alone were not sufficient to prompt this seeking. Typical of the amount of debilitation people can tolerate as well as the considerable seriousness and still the decision to seek medical attention made on extra-physical grounds is the case of Mary O'Rourke.

> Mary O'Rourke is 49, married and is a licensed practical nurse. Her symptom was a simple one, "The sight is no good in this eye . . . can't see print at all, no matter how big." This she claimed was due to being hit on the side of the head by a baseball 4 months ago, but she just couldn't get around to a doctor before this. Why did she decide now, did her vision become worse? "Well . . . about a month ago I was taking care of his (a client's) mother . . . he mentioned that my eye-lid was drooping . . . it was the first time he ever did . . . if he hadn't pointed it out I wouldn't have gone then." "Why did you pay attention to his advice?" "Well it takes away from my appearance . . . bad enough to feel this way without having to look that way . . . the same day I told my husband to call." Diagnosis—Chorioretinitis O.S. (permanent partial blindness) "lesion present much longer than present symptoms." Incidentally, no "drooping" was noticeable to either the interviewer or the examining physician.

Case after case could be presented to make this point but even more striking is that there is a "method underlying this madness." In our data we were able to discern several distinct nonphysiological patterns of triggers to the decision to seek medical aid. We have called them as follows: (1) the occurrence of an interpersonal crisis; (2) the *perceived* interference with social or personal relations; (3) sanctioning; (4) the *perceived* interference with vocational or physical activity; and (5) a kind of temporalizing of symptomatology. Moreover, these five patterns were clustered in such a way that we could characterize each ethnic group in our sample as favouring particular decision-making patterns in the seeking of medical aid.

The first two patterns, the presence of an interpersonal crisis, and the perceived interference with social or personal relations were more frequent among the Italians. The former, that of a crisis, does not mean that the symptoms have led to a crisis or even vice-versa, but that the crisis called attention to the symptoms, caused the patient to dwell on them and finally to do something about them. Two examples will illustrate this.

> Jennie Bella was 40, single, and had a hearing difficulty for many years. She said that the symptoms have not gotten worse nor do they bother her a great deal (Diagnosis: Nonsupporative Otitis Media) and, furthermore, she admitted being petrified of doctors. "I don't like to come . . . I don't like doctors. I never did . . . I have to be unconscious to go. . . ." She can nevertheless not pinpoint

any reason for coming at this time other than a general feeling that it should be taken care of. But when she was questioned about her family's concern, she blurted out, "I'm very nervous with my mother, up to this year I've been quiet, a stay-at-home . . . Now I've decided to go out and have some fun. My mother is very strict and very religious. She doesn't like the idea of my going out with a lot of men. She don't think I should go out with one for awhile and then stop. She says I'm not a nice girl, that I shouldn't go with a man unless I plan to marry . . . she doesn't like my keeping late hours or coming home late. She always suspects the worst of me . . . This year it's just been miserable . . . I can't talk to her . . . she makes me very upset and its been getting worse. . . . The other day . . . last week we (in lowered tones) had *the* argument." Miss Bella called for an appointment the next morning.

Carol Conte was a 45-year-old, single, bookkeeper. For a number of years she had been both the sole support and nurse for her mother. Within the past year, her mother died and shortly thereafter her relatives began insisting that she move in with them, quit her job, work in their variety store and nurse their mother. With Carol's vacation approaching, they have stepped up their efforts to persuade her to at least try this arrangement. Although she has long had a number of minor aches and pains, her chief complaint was a small cyst on her eyelid (Diagnosis: Fibroma). She related her fear that it *might* be growing or could lead to something more serious and thus she felt she had better look into it now (the second day of her vacation) "before it was too late." "Too late" for what was revealed only in a somewhat mumbled response to the question of what she expected or would like the doctor to do. From a list of possible outcomes to her examination, she responded, "Maybe a 'hospital' (isation) . . . 'Rest' would be all right . . ." (and then in a barely audible tone, in fact turning her head away as if she were speaking to no one at all) "just so they (the family) would stop bothering me." Responding to her physical concern, the examining physician acceded to her request for the removal of the fibroma, referred her for surgery and thus removed her from the situation for the duration of her vacation.

In such cases, it appeared that regardless of the reality and seriousness of the symptoms, they provide but the rationale for an escape, the calling-card or ticket to a potential source of help—the doctor.

The second pattern—the perceived interference with social or personal relations—is illustrated by the following two Italian patients.

John Pell is 18 and in his senior year of high school. For almost a year he's had headaches over his left eye and pain in and around

TABLE 1

Diagnosis	Question of Interviewer	Irish Patient	Italian Patient
1. Presbyopia and hyperopia	What seems to be the trouble?	I can't see to thread a needle or read a paper.	I have a constant headache and my eyes seem to get all red and burny.
	Anything else?	No, I can't recall any.	No, just that it lasts all day long and I even wake up with it sometimes.
2. Myopia	What seems to be the trouble?	I can't see across the street.	My eyes seem very burny, especially the right eye . . . . Two or three months ago I woke up with my eye swollen. I bathed it and it did go away but there was still the burny sensation.
	Anything else?	I had been experiencing headaches but it may be that I'm in early menopause.	Yes, there always seems to be a red spot beneath this eye . . . .
	Anything else?	No.	Well, my eyes feel very heavy . . . at night they bother me most.

These cases have been chosen precisely because they are relatively minor disorders. So straightforward are they that one should expect very little difference between patients who are their "owners." And yet not only does the Italian patient consistently present more troubles than the Irish but while the Irish patient focussed on a specific malfunctioning as the main concern, the Italian did not even mention this aspect of the problem but focussed on more "painful" and diffuse qualities of his condition.

his right, artificial, eye. The symptoms seem to be most prominent in the early evening. He claimed, however, little general difficulty or interference until he was asked whether the symptoms affected how he got along. To this he replied, "That's what worries me . . . I like to go out and meet people and now I've been avoiding people." Since he has had this problem for a year, he was probed as to why it bothered him more at this particular time. "The last few days of school it bothered me so that I tried to avoid everybody (this incidentally was his characteristic pattern *whenever* his eyes bothered him) . . . and I want to go out with . . . and my Senior Prom coming up, and I get the pains at 7 or 7:30 how can I stay out . . . then I saw the nurse." To be specific, he was walking down the corridor and saw the announcement of the upcoming Prom. He noticed the starting time of 8 p.m. and went immediately to the school nurse who in turn referred him to the Massachusetts Eye and Ear Infirmary.

Harry Gallo is 41, married, and a "trainee" at a car dealer's. "For a very long time my trouble is I can't drink . . . tea, coffee, booze . . . eat ice cream, fried foods. What happens is I get pains if I do it." (Diagnosis: peptic ulcer). He becomes very dramatic when talking about how the symptoms affected him. "It shot my social life all to pieces . . . we all want to socialize . . . and it's a tough thing. I want to go with people, but I can't. Wherever we go they want to eat or there's food and I get hungry . . . and if I eat there, I get sick." Of course, he has gone off his "diet" and has gotten sick. Most of the time he watches himself and drinks Maalox. He saw a doctor once 2 years ago and has been considering going again but, "I kept putting it off . . . because I got lazy . . . there were so many things. I've just been starting a new job and I didn't want to start taking off and not working, but this last attack was *too much!*" He then told how day after day the "boys at work" have been urging him to stop off with them for a few quick ones. He knew he shouldn't but he so wanted to fit in and so "It was with the boys and the other salesmen . . . I drank beer . . . I knew I was going to have more than one . . . and . . . *it* happened on the way home. . . ." Storming into his home, he asked his wife to make an appointment at the hospital, stating almost exasperatingly, "if you can't drink beer with friends, what the hell. . . ."

In these cases, the symptoms were relatively chronic. At the time of the decision there may have been an acute episode, but this was not the first such time the symptoms had reached such a "state" but rather it was the perception of them on this occasion as interfering with the social and interpersonal relations that was the trigger or final straw.

The third pattern, sanctioning, was the overwhelming favorite of the Irish. It is, however, not as well illustrated by dramatic examples, for it consists simply of one individual taking the primary responsibility for the decision to seek aid for someone else. For many weeks it looked as if one were seeing the submissive half of a dominant-submissive relationship. But within a period of 6 months, a husband and wife appeared at the clinics and each one assumed the role of sanctioning for the other.

> Mr. and Mrs. O'Brien were both suffering from Myopia, both claimed difficulty in seeing, both had had their trouble for some period of time. The wife described her visit as follows: "Oh, as far as the symptoms were concerned, I'd be apt to let it go, but not my husband. He worries a lot, he wants things to be just so. Finally when my brother was better he (the husband) said to me: 'Your worries about your brother are over so why can't you take care of your eyes now?'" And so she did. Her husband, coming in several months later, followed the same pattern. He also considered himself somewhat resistant to being doctored. "I'm not in the habit of talking about aches and pains. My wife perhaps would say 'Go to the doctor,' but me, I'd like to see if things will work themselves out." How did he get here? It turns out that he was on vacation and he'd been meaning to take care of it, "Well I tend to let things go but not my wife, so on the first day of my vacation my wife said, 'Why don't you come, why don't you take care of it now?' So I did."

Thus in these cases both claimed a resistance to seeing a doctor, both claimed the other is more likely to take care of such problems, and yet both served as the pushing force to the other. Interestingly enough, the dramatic aspect of such cases was not shown in those who followed the general pattern, which was often fairly straightforward, but in those cases which did not. Two examples illustrate this. One was a woman with a thyroid condition, swelling on the side of the neck, who when asked why she came at this time blurted out almost in a shout, "Why did I come now? I've been walking around the house like this for several weeks now and nobody said anything so I *had to come myself*." Or the almost plaintive complaint of a veteran, kind of grumbling when asked why he came now, begrudged the fact that he had to make a decision himself with the statement, "Hmm, in the Navy they just take you to the doctor, you don't have to go yourself." It is not that these people are in any sense stoic, for it seemed that they were quite verbal and open about complaining but just that they did not want to take the responsibility on themselves.

There is a secondary pattern of the Irish, which turns out to be also the major pattern of the Anglo-Saxon group [14]. It was almost straight out of the Protestant ethic namely a perceived interference with work or physical functioning. The word "perceived" is to be emphasized because the nature of the circumstances range from a single woman, 35 years old, who for the first time noted that the material which she was typing appeared blurred and thus felt that she had better take care of it, to a man with Multiple Sclerosis who despite falling down and losing his balance in many places, did nothing about it until he fell at work. Then he perceived that it might have some effect on his work and his ability to continue. The secondary Anglo-Saxon pattern is worth commenting on, for at first glance it appears to be one of the most rational modes of decision-making. It is one that most readers of this paper may well have used, namely the setting of external time criteria. "If it isn't better in 3 days, or 1 week, or 7 hours, or 6 months, then I'll take care of it." A variant on this theme involves the setting of a different kind of temporal standard—the recurrence of the phenomenon. A 19-year-old college sophomore reported the following:

> Well, it was this way. I went into this classroom and sat in the back of the room and when the professor started to write on the blackboard I noticed that the words were somewhat blurry. But I didn't think too much about it. A couple of weeks later, when I went back into that same classroom, I noted that it was blurry again. Well, once was bad, but twice that was too much.

Now given that his diagnosis was Myopia and that it was unconnected with any other disease, we know medically that his Myopia did not vary from one circumstance to another. This imposition of "a first time, second time that's too much" was of his doing and unrelated to any medical or physical reality.

By now the role that symptoms played in the decision to seek medical aid should be clearer. For our patients the symptoms were "really" there, but their perception differed considerably. There *is* a sense in which they sought help because they could not stand it any longer. But what they could not stand was more likely to be a situation or a perceived implication of a symptom rather than any worsening of the symptom *per se*.

I now would like to note some of the implications of this work. When speaking of implications, I ask your indulgence, for I refer not merely to what leads in a direct line from the data but some of the different thoughts and directions in which it leads me. What for example are the consequences for our very conception of etiology—conceptions based on assumptions about the representativeness of whom and what we study. We have claimed in this paper that the reason people get into medical treatment may well be related to some select social-psychological circumstances. If this is true, it makes all the more meaningful our earlier point about many unexplained epidemiological differences, for they may be due more to the differential occurrence of these social-psychological factors, factors of selectivity and attention which get people and their episodes into medical statistics rather than to any true difference in the prevalence and incidence of a particular problem or disorder [15]. Our findings may also have implications for what one studies, particularly to the importance of stress in the etiology of so many complaints and disorders. For it may well be that the stress noted in these people's lives, at least those which they were able to verbalize, is the stress which brought them into the hospital or into seeking treatment (as was one of our main triggers) and not really a factor in the etiology or the exacerbation of the disorder.

Our work also has implications for treatment. So often we hear the terms "unmotivated, unreachable and resistance" applied to difficult cases. Yet we fail to realise that these terms may equally apply to us, the caretakers and health professionals who may not understand what the patient is saying or if we do, do not want to hear it. An example of this was seen in the way physicians in this study handled those patients for whose problem no organic basis could be found [16]. For despite the fact that there were no objective differences in the prevalence of emotional problems between our ethnic groups, the Italians were consistently diagnosed as having some psychological difficulty such as tension headaches, functional problems, personality disorder, etc.; whereas the Irish and Anglo-Saxon were consistently given what one might call a neutral diagnosis something that was either a Latinized term for their symptoms or simply the words "nothing found on tests" or "nothing wrong." Our explanation is somewhat as follows, namely that this situation is one of the most difficult for a physician and one in which he nevertheless feels he should make a differential diagnosis. Faced with this dilemma he focussed inordinately on *how* the Italians presented themselves—somewhat voluble, with many more symptoms, and somewhat dramatic social circumstances surrounding their decision to seek help. This labelling of the Italians is particularly interesting since as we mentioned above the Irish and Anglo-Saxons had similar psychological and social problems but presented them in a much more emotionally neutral and bland manner. There are no doubt other factors operating such as the greater social distance between the Italians and the medical staff, but that would constitute another paper.

One final remark as to treatment, again and again we found that where the physician paid little attention to the specific trigger which forced or which the individual used as an excuse to seek medical aid, there was the greatest likelihood of that patient eventually breaking off treatment. Another way of putting this is that without attention to this phenomenon the physician would have no opportunity to practice his healing art. Moreover, this problem of triggers etc. brooked no speciality nor particular type of disorder. So that being a specialist and only seeing certain kinds of problems did not exempt the physician from having to deal with this issue.

Such data alone supports those who urge more training in social and psychological sophistication for *any* physician who has contact with patients. With chronic illness making up the bulk of today's health problems it is obvious that the physicians cannot treat the etiological agent of disease and that the effect of specific therapies is rather limited. Nevertheless the physician may more intelligently intervene in the patient's efforts to cope with his disorder if he has the knowledge and awareness of the patient's views of health, sickness, his expectations and his reasons for seeking help.

This report has several different goals. To the social scientist we have tried to convey the somewhat amazing persistence of certain cultural characteristics which we in our cultural blindness have felt should have died and disappeared. The reason for their survival is that such behaviours may well be general modes of handling anxiety, sort of culturally prescribed defense mechanisms and probably transmitted from generation to generation in the way that much learning takes place, almost on an unconscious level. If this be true, then they constitute a group of behaviours which are much less likely to be changed as one wishes or attempts to become more American. Hopefully, the present research has also demonstrated the fruitfulness of an approach which does not take the definition of abnormality for granted. Despite its limitations our data seems sufficiently striking to invite further reason for re-examining our traditional and often rigid conceptions of health and illness, of normality and abnormality, of conformity and deviance. As we have contended in the early pages of this essay, symptoms or physical aberrations are so widespread that perhaps relatively few, and a biased selection at best come to the attention of official treatment agencies. We have thus tried to present evidence showing that the very labelling and definition of a bodily state as a symptom as well as the decision to do something about it is in itself part of a social process. If there is a selection and definitional process then focussing solely on reasons for deviation (the study of etiology) and the reasons for not seeking treatment (the study of delay) and ignoring what constitutes a deviation in the eyes of an individual and his reasons for action may obscure important aspects of our understanding and eventually our philosophy of the treatment and control of illness.

Finally, this is not meant to be an essay on the importance of sociological factors in disease, but rather the presentation of an approach to the study of health and illness. Rather than being a narrow and limited concept, health and illness are on the contrary empirically quite elastic. In short, it is not merely that health and illness has sociological aspects, for it has many aspects, but really that there is a sense in which health and illness *are* social phenomena. The implication of this perspective has perhaps been much better put by the Leightons (though quoted out of context):

> From this broad perspective there is no point in asking whether over the span of his adult life a particular individual should or should not be considered a medical case—everyone is a medical case. The significant question becomes how severe a case, what kind of case [17].

I myself would add—how does one become a case and since of the many eligible, so few are chosen, what does it mean to be a case. In an era where every day produces new medical discoveries, such questions are all too easily ignored. The cure for all men's ills seems right over the next hill. Yet as Dubos has cogently reminded us [18], this vision is only a mirage and the sooner we realise it the better.

Notes

[1] Koos, Earl L. *The Health of Regionville*, New York: Columbia University Press, 1954.

[2] General summaries: Meigs, J. Wistar. Occupational medicine. *New Eng. J. Med.* *264*, 861, 1961; Siegel, Gordon S. *Periodic Health Examinations—Abstracts from the Literature*, Public Health Service Publication, No. 1010, Washington, DC: U.S. Government Printing Office, 1963.

[3] See for example: Commission on Chronic Illness, *Chronic Illness in a Large City*, Cambridge: Harvard University Press, 1957; Pearse, Innes H. and Crocker, Lucy H. *The Peckham Experiment*, Allen & Unwin, London, 1954; *Biologists in Search of Material*, Interim Reports of the Work of the Pioneer Health Center, London: Faber & Faber, 1938.

[4] Commission on Chronic Illness, *op. cit.*; Pearse and Crocker, *op. cit.*

[5] Clute, Y. T. *The General Practitioner*, University of Toronto Press, Toronto, 1963, as well as many of the articles cited in Stoeckle, John D., Zola, Irving K. and Davidson, Gerald E. The quantity and significance of psychological distress in medical patients. *J. Chron. Dis. 17*, 959, 1964.

[6] Unpublished data of the author and also Kosa, John, Alpert, Joel, Pickering, M. Ruth and Haggerty, Robert J. Crisis and family life: a re-examination of concepts. *The Wisconsin Sociologist 4*, 11, 1965; Kosa, John, Alpert, Joel and Haggerty, Robert J. On the reliability of family health information. *Soc. Sci. & Med. 1*, 165, 1967; Alpert, Joel, Kosa, John and Haggerty, Robert J. A month of illness and health care among low-income families. *Publ. Hlth. Rep. 82*, 705, 1967.

[7] Blackwell, Barbara. The literature of delay in seeking medical care for chronic illnesses. *Hlth. Educ. Monographs* No. 16, pp. 3–32, 1963; Kutner, Bernard, Makover, Henry B. and Oppenheim, Abraham. Delay in the diagnosis and treatment of cancer. *J. Chron. Dis. 7*, 95, 1958; Kutner, Bernard and Gordon, Gerald. Seeking aid for cancer. *J. Hlth. Hum. Behav. 2*, 171, 1961.

[8] Chapman, William P. and Jones, Chester M. Variations in cutaneous and visceral pain sensitivity in normal subjects. *J. Clin. Invest. 23*, 81, 1944; Hardy, James D., Wolff, Harold G. and Goodell, Helen. *Pain Sensations and Reactions*, Baltimore: Williams & Wilkins, 1952; Melzack, Ronald. The perception of pain. *Scient. Am. 204*, 41, 1961; Olin, Harry S. and Hackett, Thomas P. The denial of chest pain in 32 patients with acute myocardial infection. *J. Am. Med. Ass. 190*, 977, 1964.

[9] Galdston, Iago. (editor) Salerno and the atom. In *Medicine in a Changing Society*, pp. 111–61. New York: International Universities Press, 1956.

[10] Clausen, John A. and Radke Yarrow, Marian. The impact of mental illness on the family. *J. Soc. Iss. 11*, 1, 1955.

[11] Opler, Marvin K. *Culture, Psychiatry and Human Values*, Charles C Thomas, Springfield, Illinois, 1956; Opler, Marvin K. (editor) *Culture and Mental Health*, New York: Macmillan, 1959.

[12] All differences reported here are statistically significant. Given that there are no tabular presentations in this essay it may be helpful to remember that for the most part we are not stating that all or necessarily a majority of a particular group acted in the way depicted but that at very least, the response was significantly more peculiar to this group than to any other. Moreover, all the reported differences were sustained even when the diagnosed disorder for which they sought aid was held constant. For details on some of the statistical procedures as well as some of the methodological controls, see Zola, Irving K. Culture and symptoms, *op. cit.*

[13] The findings re. symptoms are primarily a contrast between the Irish and the Italians. This is done because (1) there is a sense in which ethnicity in Boston is a much more "real" phenomenon to the Irish and the Italians than to our Anglo-Saxon Protestant, (2) these two groups are more purely "ethnic" and constitute a fairer comparison being of similar generation, education, and socio-economic status, and (3) the differences are frankly much more dramatic and clearly drawn. If you wish to picture where the Anglo-Saxons might be in these comparisons, think of them as mid-way between the Irish and Italian responses, if anything, a little closer to the Irish. Some further discussion of this issue is found both in Zola, Irving K., Culture and symptom and Illness behavior . . ., *op. cit.*

11
The Genesis of Chronic Illness: Narrative Re-Construction

Gareth Williams

We are seated in the living-room of a modern, urban council house somewhere in the north-west of England. Bill, the fifty-eight year-old man with whom I have been talking for almost an hour, leans forward. Then, in a strained voice and with a look of exasperated incomprehension on his face, he says: "and your mind's going all the time, you're reflecting . . . 'how the *hell* have I come to this?' . . . because it isn't me" (B13.6).

Bill has rheumatoid arthritis (RA), which was first diagnosed eight years ago following two years of intermittent pain and swelling in his joints; a serious heart attack has added to his difficulties. We have never met before. His words indicate the way in which a chronic illness such as RA may assault an individual's sense of identity, and they testify to the limitations of medical science in delivering a satisfactory explanation for the physical and social breakdown to which such an illness can lead.

In the *Collected Reports* on the rheumatic diseases published by the Arthritis and Rheumatism Council, and with a beguiling acknowledgement of the popular image of the scientist as Great Detective, the experts admit their limitations and pronounce RA to be "one of the major medical mysteries of our time."[1] What is striking about Bill's interrogative, however, is that it points to a concern with something more than the cause of his arthritis, and what I would like to do in this paper is to examine the nature of his question, and those of two others, and to consider the significance of the answers they provide. That is to say, I want to elucidate the styles of thought and modes of "cognitive organization"[2] employed by three people suffering from RA in making sense of the arrival of chronic illness in their lives. I will not be claiming that these three cases are "representative" in any statistical sense, but I *do* suggest that they symbolise, portray, and represent something

Reprinted by permission of Basil Blackwell from *Sociology of Health and Illness*, Vol. 6, No. 2, pp. 176–200. Copyright © 1984 by Basil Blackwell, Ltd.

important about the experience of illness. They are powerful, if idiosyncratic, illustrations of typical processes found in more or less elaborate form throughout my study group.

The fieldwork on which this study is based consisted of semistructured, tape-recorded interviews with thirty people who had been first diagnosed as suffering from RA at least five years ago prior to my contact with them. The rationale guiding selection of people at this point in their illness was that in pursuing a general interest in what might be called the structured self-image of the chronically sick person it seemed sensible to talk to those who were "seasoned professionals" rather than novices in the difficult business of living with a chronic illness. Four members of my study-group were in-patients on rheumatology wards and the rest were out-patient attenders at rheumatology clinics at two hospitals in north-west England. The in-patients were interviewed at a relatively tranquil side-room off the busy ward while the out-patients were first approached in the clinic and subsequently interviewed in their own homes. Of the 30 respondents, 19 were women and 11 were men, so my group had proportionately more men than one would expect to find in the general population.[3] Their ages ranged from 26 to 68 years at time of interview; thirteen being between 26 and 49, eleven between 50 and 64, and six were 65 years of age or over. Twenty-two were married, the rest being a mixture of single, widowed, and divorced or separated.

The interview covered a variety of themes relating to the experience of living with arthritis, and the data were elicited according to a simple checklist of topics. The duration of the interview as a whole and the sequencing of particular topics were influenced more by contingent features of the interview process than by any well-considered plans of my own. Where I had to compete with an obstreperous budgerigar[4] or a boisterous young child, the interviews would likely be short and fragmented. On better days, with a minimum of interruption and an eager and lucid respondent, the interview could last for three or even four hours.

Although my central concepts—*narrative reconstruction* and *genesis*—are, I believe, novel,[5] the issues they are designed to address— how and why people come to see their illness as originating in a certain way, and how people account for the disruption disablement has wrought in their lives—have been the subject of innumerable investigations. Sociological and anthropological research into illness behaviour and health beliefs and psychological research into processes of attribution have all, in one way or another, attended to related issues; but there is so much of it! I cannot possibly indicate all my debts, but perhaps the body of work which has had most influence on this paper is that which examines lay beliefs or folk theories about the causes of specific diseases or illness in general.[6] Although much interesting material has been collected in this line, it has tended to rest content with treating people's beliefs as simply that: beliefs about the aetiology of illness. However, it seems to me that if, in some fundamental way, an individual is a social and historical agent with a biographical identity (in the fullest sense) and if the prime sociological importance of chronic illness is the "biological disruption"[7] to which it gives rise, then an individual's account of the origin of that illness in terms of putative causes can perhaps most profitably be read as an attempt to establish points of reference between body, self, and society and to reconstruct a sense of order from the fragmentation produced by chronic illness.

In this paper, therefore, I use my three cases to illustrate the way in which people's beliefs about the cause of their illness needs to be understood as part of the larger interpretive process which I have chosen to call narrative reconstruction. Before looking at the specifics of my analysis, however, I would like to clarify the theoretical concepts which inform it.

Theoretical Prologue

The concept of "narrative" does not hold an established theoretical place in any sociological school or tradition. In general speech it is often used, in noun form, as a synonym for "story," "account," or "chronicle." When used as an adjective, as in "narrative history," it typically refers to the process of relating a continuous account of some set of events or processes. When A.J.P. Taylor, for example, refers to himself as a "narrative historian," as he often does, he implies both a concern with telling a good story and also a preference for a common-sense, empirical reading of historical events, unencumbered by any theoretical baggage be it Marxist, structuralist, or psychoanalytic.

As I see it the term has two aspects: the routine and the recon-structed. In its routine form, it refers to the observations, comments, and asides, the practical consciousness which provides essential accompaniment to the happenings of our daily lives and helps to render them intelligible. In this sense narrative is a process of continu-ous accounting whereby the mundane incidents and events of daily life are given some kind of plausible order. If "biography" connotes the indeterminate, reciprocal relationships between individuals and their settings or milieux and between those milieux and the history and society of which they are a part[8] then narrative may be seen as the cognitive correlate of this, commenting upon and affirming the multi-form reality of biographical experience as it relates to both self and society.

In his fictional, philosophical chronicle, *The Man without Qualities*, Robert Musil, speaking through his central character Ulrich, suggests that narrative order is: ". . . the simple order that consists in one's being able to say: 'When that had happened, then this happened.'"

Musil/Ulrich goes on to argue:

> In their basic relation to themselves most people are narrators. They do not like the lyrical, or at best they like it only for moments at a time. And even if a little "because" and "in order that" may get knotted into the thread of life, still they abhor all cogitation that reaches out beyond that. What they like is the orderly sequence of facts because it has the look of a necessity, and by means of the impression that their life has a "course" they manage to feel somehow sheltered in the midst of chaos.[9]

The trouble is that sometimes the "orderly sequence of facts" gets broken up. It cannot be sustained against the chaos and, for a time at least, the life-course is lost. The routine narrative expressing the concerns of the practical consciousness as it attends to the mundane details of daily life is pitched into disarray: a death in the family, serious illness, an unexpected redundancy and so forth. From such a situation narrative may have to be given some radical surgery and reconstructed so as to account for present disruptions. Narrative reconstruction, therefore, represents the workings of the discursive consciousness.[10]

In my interviews, the reason for the conversation and the excuse for the occasion was the fact of the person being ill. In this context, the aetiology of the affliction and the narrative history of the illness held a key place in the dialogue. I remarked earlier on the many studies examining lay theories about illness. In one such study comparing the beliefs of cancer and noncancer patients with regard to the aetiology of that disease, the authors suggest:

> The person without cancer can afford to be more dogmatic about cancers and likely to think in stereotypes. The closer he comes to dealing with the disease, the less clear-cut and more complex the explanations may become.[11]

The reason for such complexity, it seems to me, is that the explanations advanced by afflicted individuals have both causal and purposive or functional components. They represent not only explanations for the onset of a given disease, but also acts of interpretation, narrative reconstructions of profound discontinuities in the social processes of their daily lives. The illness is part of their story and as with any story, to borrow from George Orwell, the closer one gets to the scene of events the vaguer it becomes.[12] In some ways narrative reconstruction may be seen to involve a process of remembrance akin to R. G. Collingwood's notion of historical thinking where:

> Every present has a past of its own, and any imaginative reconstruction of the past aims at reconstructing the past of this present, the present in which the act of imagination is going on, as here and now perceived.[13]

In confronting the experience of chronic illness, then, like any unusual or disturbing experience, Musil's narrative thread—"when that had happened, then this happened"—becomes *questionable*. The individual's narrative has to be reconstructed both in order to understand the illness in terms of past social experience and to reaffirm the impression that life has a course and the self has a purpose or *telos*. It is from this viewpoint that I have read the "causes" to which my respondents refer both as delineations of putative, efficient connexions between the "dependent variable" (arthritis) and various "independent variables," and also as narratively reconstructed reference points in an unfolding historical relationship between body, self, and society. These reference points may be seen as constituents in the *genesis* of a misfortune within a narrative which imaginatively reconstructs the past so that it has meaning or purpose for the present.[14] In this way narrative reconstruction becomes a framework for teleological explanation.

Given the teleological form of narrative reconstruction, I employ the concept of "genesis" not for stylistic or rhetorical purposes, but in order to liberate myself from the semantic straitjacket imposed by the term "cause" as it has been generally understood since Hume,[15] and so as to establish a connexion with the Greek tradition of reflection on the origins of things which attained its apogee in Aristotle's doctrine of the four causes.[16] Robert Nisbet has remarked that the modern consciousness has been, inevitably, so influenced by Roman, Christian and sceptical thought about causality that it is difficult for us nowadays to tune-in to the Aristotelian schema. Nisbet argues:

> To Aristotle—and to the Greeks generally, I believe—something different is involved, something that is somewhat less "cause" in our inherited sense of the word than it is a point of reference in a self-contained, developmental process.[17]

In Aristotelian philosophy different levels of causality are conceived within an overall process of becoming which includes an account of ends as well as beginnings and purposes alongside "causes" (in the modern sense). In this regard the "causes" to which my respondents refer are seen, in part, as points of reference within the process of becoming ill, and the genesis, or mode of formation, of the illness constitutes, in a sense, the dominant theme of the account. It is an analytic construct through which the respondent can be seen to situate a variety of causal connexions as reference points within a narrative reconstruction of the changing relationships between the self and the world; a world within which the biographical *telos* has been disrupted. In this way Humean "constant conjunctions" are absorbed into an Aristotelian teleology.

The three case studies in this paper illustrate the way in which distinctive narrative forms are reconstructed to answer the question of genesis as it arises in different lives. The first two reformulate my abstract question: "Why do you think you got arthritis?" into substantive questions more suitable for interrogating the genesis-of-illness experience. Bill, as we saw at the start, wants to know "how the *hell* have I come to be like this? . . . because it isn't me." In the same vein, Gill wonders: "Where have I got to? There's nothing left of me." The third case is rather different. Betty exemplifies a situation in which both "causal" analysis and narrative reconstruction may be transcended when the *telos* of life is gently enshrouded within a powerful theodicy. She does not need to reformulate my question because: "people say: 'Why you?' Well, why not me? Better me who knows the Lord."

Bill: Narrative Reconstruction as Political Criticism

A significant portion of Bill's working life had been disrupted. In fact, he had had a tough time. He had worked as a skilled machine operator in a paperworks and, shortly before the first appearance of symptoms, was promoted to the position of "charge hand" which entailed his supervising three floors in the factory. It was shortly after assuming his expanded responsibilities as a "working gaffer" that things began to go wrong:

> I was a working gaffer . . . but, you know, they were mostly long hours and the end result, in 1972, was every time I had a session like, my feet began to swell and my hands began to swell. I couldn't hold a pen, I had difficulty getting between machines and difficulty getting hold of small things.

At this time he also had a massive heart attack and was off work for five months. A series of blood tests were done by his heart specialist who then referred him to a rheumatologist, and within the space of a couple of weeks, he was hospitalized. At the time this unpleasant sequence of events was ambiguous and confusing, but over ten years Bill had become clearer about it:

> I didn't associate it with anything to do with the works at the time, but I think it was chemically induced. I worked with a lot of chemicals, acetone and what have you. We washed our hands in it, we had cuts, and we absorbed it. Now, I'll tell you this because it seems to be related. The men that I worked with who are much older than me—there was a crew of sixteen and two survived, myself and the gaffer that was then—and they all complained of the same thing, you know, their hands started to puff up. It seems very odd.

Yes, very odd indeed. If I were simply interested in identifying his central aetiological motif no more need be said because the rest of the discussion was essentially a reiteration of this connexion. However, in order to understand the strength of his attachment to this belief, in the face of highly plausible alternatives, it is necessary to examine how his view of life has called forth this essential connexion between work and illness.

An important point about narratives, whether they be routine or reconstructed, is that they are necessarily co-authored.[18] The interview, of course, is itself a particularly clear case of co-authorship, but, more generally, narratives are bounded by and constructed in relationship with various individual people and organizations. With regard to illness, any narrative built around it needs to take account of the medical world within which the official definition of that illness has been specified. Bill described how, following the diagnosis of "rheumatoid arthritis" resulting from clinical and laboratory investigations, the doctors disclaimed any interest in his hypothesis about workplace toxicity and pursued alternative hunches:

> I was assured by them (the doctors) that this is what it was, it was arthritis. Now, it just got worse, a steady deterioration, and I put it down that it was from the works. But with different people questioning me at the hospital, delving into the background, my mother had arthritis, and my little sister, Ruth, she died long before the war, 1936/7, and she had not arthritis, just rheumatism and that naturally did for her.

From a clinical perspective and, indeed, from a common-sense appreciation of "inheritance," there appeared to be a strong case for accepting an explanation in terms of genetic transmission. Certainly, in rheumatological circles, genetic and viral hypotheses are those receiving most serious and sustained attention. Why was he not content with this?

Bill had spent many years in the military services, and had served eighteen years with the paratroopers completing 211 successful jumps. Had he suffered any joint trouble during this time?

> No, none whatever. This is why I couldn't associate it. All that time during the war we had a minimum of clothing on, we never went under shelter, we kipped in holes, slept on the deck—great stuff! You know, no problems.

What he appeared to be suggesting by reference to his life in the services was two separate but related things. Firstly, given that he had "no trouble" during a hard life in the services, he could not realistically entertain any idea of inherited weakness. On more than one occasion he said that *because* of his harsh experiences he "couldn't associate anything with it" (his arthritis). If there had been some inner predisposition surely it would have become manifest sooner? The second theme was that the absence of symptoms while he was in the services made it unlikely that those activities *themselves* were responsible for creating physical vulnerability. It all happened so much later and with such suddenness.

Bill was never entirely clear about his state of health while in the services. At a later point in the interview he mentioned that he *had* had some symptoms at that time, and that parachuting with 60 lb packs was a "probable factor" but, in clarification, he remarked that many of his mates in the services had symptoms of a similar kind and that it was put down to "fatigue." Whilst conceding that the tough life with the paratroopers must have had some effect on his body, he could not square those experiences with the debilitating development of RA: "To see myself as that, and now, from 1956, I can't accept it, it's not on."

The references to the services, like the account of the workplace, make it clear that, for Bill, the body is defined by its relationship to the world of social action not in isolation from it. The medical model, employing a reduced range of clinically ascertainable factors, has no sensible meaning in the light of his pragmatic perspective. He was never dogmatic in his beliefs, but his pragmatism would not allow him to accept the validity of the medical model which appeared to rest upon an image of biological arbitrariness and caprice:

> I was trying more or less self-analysis—where have I got it from? How has it come? And you talk to different people over all ages and you find that they are at a loss. They don't know, they don't know, nobody knows. And who do we ask? We ask the doctor (who says): 'It's just one of them things (. . .) and there's nothing to be done about it."

At this point there is no indication of the basis for Bill's refusal of medical rationality. All we have is a statement of preference for one explanation, workplace toxics, over others. A little later we returned to the workplace and to the experiences of his fellow workers as he remembered them:

> But thinking back to the way the other blokes were who are now gone, so we can't ask them, and what I remember of them, they more or less came to it in the same manner . . . I wasn't in there with them all the time, I was travelling between floors so I was coming out of it and getting fresh air and washing more frequently than they did. So this is something to do with it.

Bill had mentioned the "odd" coincidence of similar symptoms at the start of the interview, but his thinking had clearly gone beyond a simple observed correlation. Not only, it seems, was there evidence of definite patterns of symptomatology amongst the workers, but also a differential severity which he explained by reference to the amount of time spent in contact with toxic substances. In the language of classical epidemiology Bill is invoking, unwittingly, the "dose-response criterion," according to which the investigator considers: "whether the risk of disease increases commensurately with degree of exposure"[19] and then examines this in relation to characteristics of both host and environment.

It seemed then, that, notwithstanding the doctors' declared disinterest in Bill's hypothesis, there was *something* happening at the factory:

> They just complained, and I noticed their hands were getting puffy, and that was one of the things, this seemed to be a common factor for everybody. Their hands started to puff and their shoes busted. And there was one guy, Joe (. . .), he was a very tall man, walked fairly rapidly, and he became slower and slower. And he said: "That's it, I'm out, it's this. . . ." He said straight: "It's killing me, I'm getting out," and it fetched him straight down. And that's where

> it's stuck, in the back of my mind. If Joe . . . remembering the way
> Joe was, a good walker, he could nip up and down steps, seeing
> him just shuffling till he couldn't even get from the lodge to the
> workshop without coming through the lift, he just couldn't make
> the steps. Well I got that way till I couldn't make the steps, just
> couldn't make the steps.

This graphic description of the destruction of men by their work
adds little to the facts of the matter. What it does is to shift the quality
of the discussion away from a simple description of illness associations to an intimation of the sense of revolt which existed amongst the
workers in their consciousness of the situation.

Bill recognized the pressure to accept the doctors' analysis as
legitimate, but in the light of his practical knowledge he felt that their
analysis was inadequate:

> But putting it out of my mind, and having spoken to the specialists,
> they say: "No way." So you take their word for it. But it seems a bit
> . . . thinking in my mind when I go to bed. . . . I can't go to sleep
> straight away, I have to wait until I get settled and your mind's going
> all the time, you're reflecting "How the *hell* have I come to be like
> this?", you know, because it isn't me.

Bill has gone some way towards answering the question. He has
identified a causal agent which seemed to explain his arthritis as well
as symptoms in others, and he has described the milieu in which the
causal nexus was situated. He has also portrayed a critical consciousness and a feeling of revolt amongst the workers which helps to explain
his own unswerving attachment to his explanation when faced with a
plausible clinical alternative. But is this observation of work experiences also part of a far more pervasive image of the world?

At another point in the interview, echoing his observation of the
workers whose shoes "busted," Bill told me of the experience of his
wife who "busted her back" while working with the local authority
school meals service. How did this happen?

> Well, it was ridiculous because there were no men working there,
> and they had to go into a stock-room and the "veg man" had stacked
> spud bags which are 56 lb five high. And it came to a particular
> day where they had to get one off the top, and she (his wife) was
> on her own, and she stood on a chair to get one off, and as it came
> down—up to that point she was a very strong woman—it just
> pushed her over and she went right down on the table. But she
> didn't realise at the time just how badly hurt she was. It was a
> couple of days after, she just couldn't move, she was almost
> paralysed.

This episode, as well as providing an analogue with his own experience, has also led to shared involvement in a long struggle with medical and governmental bureaucracy:

> She has a pension from [her employers], but the [invalidity] allowance which was taken from me has been stopped for her, and they didn't even have to give it back. It's the usual "cock-up" at the DHSS (Department of Health and Social Security).

Whilst Bill did not cite his wife's experience as an explicit parallel, these details of his biography, it seems to me, provide the basis for analogical reasoning and are central to an understanding of the explanation he elaborates for his own affliction. Taking these details into account, the narrative reconstruction of his personal experience has expanded into a more general political criticism exposing the illusions and false consciousness purveyed by various representatives of officialdom. Within this act of interpretation, the model of causation which informs his perception of his own illness and his wife's accident is one where the origins of misfortune are seen as direct, immediate, and within the bounds of human agency, but where the sick/injured person is not culpable in the slightest degree. In both episodes the workplace is defined not in terms of neutral tasks and accidental events, but as the locus of exploitative social relations in which workers are the victims of injustice and neglect.

The increasingly political tenor of his discussion of work and illness became even clearer in a section of the interview where Bill discussed issues surrounding his wife's claim for compensation. She was refused compensation, he told me, firstly because there was no witness to her accident, and secondly because the DHSS medical advisor had diagnosed "osteoporosis" (a chronic deterioration in bone strength) antedating her accident. Bill's response to this was unequivocal:

> I think that "osteoporosis" is a cop-out. Nobody examined her or tested her, nobody took any samples from inside her bones. And this would be the only way, decalcification of the bones, because she's on calcium tablets now. But this only came up to my way of thinking because it was a cop-out, so they wouldn't have to pay a great deal of compensation. You know, so what the people at DHSS said was that everybody has this, *you* have it, I'm a liar but you've got it. They will say so without even examining you.

When issues of diagnosis are removed from the quiet location of the doctor's clinic and situated within the context of a struggle for compensation, the neutrality of the medical task and the objective validity of its procedures are thrown into doubtful relief. Bill recognised that technology and science are ideological, and that medicine can support political bureaucracy in preventing the establishment of social justice.

The tenacity of Bill's attachment to a workplace toxics explanation for the aetiology of his own arthritis takes on clearer significance in the light of these other experiences which, together, form a narrative reconstruction of the genesis of illness which carries a highly political image of the social world. Both illness, and the response of professionals to it, suggest a world of power inequality. There was much more in Bill's account that drew upon images of injustice in society. His experience of getting beaten-up by the police was introduced into the interview and recounted at some length and, as a whole, the world was presented as a place where ordinary people are exploited, conned, and manipulated by a range of social "powers" be they doctors, bureaucrats, or the police. However, it is important not to jump the gun. So far, all I have shown is that Bill locates the onset of his arthritis within the workplace, and that other features of his account suggest mistrust and scepticism with regard to the interests and intentions of people in positions of power. What we have to do now is to look further to see if this radical populist image of society *directly* influences his ideas with regard to the genesis of his own illness.

Following the excursions into the subjects of his wife's accident and the incident with the police, we returned to his own illness and disablement, and Bill related more scenes from his working life:

> 'cause there you had extremes of heat, in the tapes section, we were doing computer tapes. There was a special section, and that was quite hot up there. Your entry and exit was through the fire door, and there was no air intake, no fresh air from the outside because it had to be a particular temperature. And even the chemist down there realised that they're like ovens. It's totally enclosed, it's double thick glass, and they always had the damn things shut till we opened them. We said, "Get us a vent in here or we're not running." And he got one in—that's the chairman who is now dead—he got us an intake. But it was too late for them lads. They had been in it all the time and they were much older than me, and I think their age was against them. They had minimum resistance.

Not only, then, was there a sense of revolt amongst individual workers such as Joe, but a collective refusal by a number of workers to continue what they were doing until certain health and safety measures were instigated. It was not clear how long it was from the workers' recognition of detrimental effects to management compliance, but it was certainly too long for some of them. In this way, Bill's particular arthritic symptoms and their origin became absorbed into a public issue, the issue of health and safety at work, and the original question about the causes of his arthritis was transformed into an examination of the power struggle between workers and management.

By situating the cause of his own misfortune in this context and juxtaposing it with the experience of his wife and friends, Bill's narrative reconstruction articulated a nascent political criticism of the way of life in modern society in which the genesis of his own misfortunes and those of others could be understood as the product of malevolent social forces. Bill himself, of course, did not make such extravagant claims on behalf of his own thinking and, with an almost apologetic appreciation of the limitations of biographical evidence, he said:

> I'm just going off the way the other fellows were, that it became too much for them, and they probably had arthritis at one time, of one type or another. Because none of them walked with a proper gait apart from myself at that time.

Nonetheless, if his narrative reconstruction is read as a sort of historically rooted political criticism, his original identification of workplace toxics as the cause of his arthritis can be seen as part of a more complex attempt to define the dynamics of the relationship between illness, the individual and society. This society is seen as the locus of exploitation, bureaucratic silence and multiple frauds upon the laity, where personal troubles are also public issues requiring political intervention.

Bill's analysis did not stop at the workplace. In a final statement he located the issue of illness in the workplace in the context of societal power:

> All those other lads, all their dependents got was two and a half years pay. Probably any investigation that the company made into it had been hushed up a bit 'cause the man I worked for at that time, Sir John Smith, and he became a Lord and is now deceased, and Lord Green and Lord Black were into the company and therefore had very powerful knowledge, and they shut it up if they were giving toxics out and killing men you see. 'Cause nothing's happened since . . . nothing's happened since.

The precise extent of the damage incurred by the workers was never made entirely clear (although it is clear enough). Apparently, the company accepted liability and paid compensation, but Bill argued that the full scale of damage and responsibility was hidden within a strategy of nondecision and silence, ultimately controlled by powerful members of the ruling class who wanted to protect their economic and political interests.

The fact that Bill should have talked of all these things is not necessarily surprising. What is important is that these observations constitute essential reference points in a narrative reconstruction within which the genesis of illness and other misfortunes can be defined and rendered sensible. Within this reconstruction Bill encompassed what had happened to his body, the nature of his social roles, the quality of his immediate milieu, and the structure of power in society. In doing so, he linked his own demise with that of others, transcended the particulars of his own illness, and redefined his personal trouble as a public issue.

Gill: Narrative Reconstruction as Social Psychology

In Bill's long and detailed reconstruction, both discrete causes and biographical genesis were located essentially outside himself. Although his account encompassed social relations, it left out any reference to his identity or self; there was no sense of personal responsibility or even of any socio-psychological involvement in the development of his affliction. Social relations, however, are also the place in which a sense of identity is developed and constrained, nurtured and broken. In this regard the genesis of an illness may be seen in terms of the body's relationship to the self and the self's relationship to the world.

Gill was a middle-aged school teacher living in a wealthy and conservative suburb. She had had RA for approximately five years, and the onset of the disease took place in a twelve-month period which included a number of tragic events. In my interview with her we spent less time discussing the cause of her affliction than had been the case with Bill. Nevertheless, her ideas were interesting and they represent an illuminating form of narrative reconstruction. As with Bill, I simply asked her why she thought she had got arthritis:

> Well, if you live in your own body for a long time, you're a fool if you don't take note of what is happening to it. I think that you can make naive diagnoses which are quite wrong. But I think that at the back of your head, certainly at the back of my head, I have feelings that this is so and that is so, and I'm quite certain that it was stress that precipitated this.

Now, there is nothing unusual about the identification of "stress" as an important aetiological factor. Indeed, in my study group stress was one of the most popular factors, particularly amongst women and, as Allan Young has indicated, the "discourse on stress" is firmly entrenched in modern thinking on illness and disease.[20] However, more often than not the content of "stress" is left unspecified and, indeed, part of its attractiveness is that it can be used to designate anything from excessive noise to bereavement. Gill, however, felt it necessary to specify exactly what she meant by stress, and having suggested that it precipitated her arthritis she went on:

> Not simply the stress of events that happened but the stress perhaps of suppressing myself while I was a mother and wife; not "women's libby" but there comes a time in your life when you think, you know, "where have I got to? There's nothing left of me."

Gill did not conceptualize stress in terms of external stressors, exogenous agents which impinge upon the body in some arbitrary fashion, rather she saw her illness as the bodily expression of a suppression of herself. However, while it was not simply a question of external stressors, neither was it a question of internal psychological pathology because she saw the stress of events and the suppression of herself as merely components in the social process of being a wife and a mother. It is within this process that the genesis of bodily breakdown finds its meaning. The causal efficacy of certain events could only be understood within a purposive account of the social process of womanhood in which her personal *telos* and a sense of identity had become lost.

However, as Gill has implied, within this overall social process there were specific events that were deemed to have a causal import and which are needed to explain why arthritis supervened at this precise moment in her life-course:

> And then on top of that feeling of . . . not really discontent, but rather confusion about identity . . . to have various physical things happen like, you know, my daughter . . . I'm quite certain that the last straw was my husband's illness. So, I'm sure it was stress induced. I think that while my head kept going my body stopped.

The various "physical things" that happened to Gill were a number of life-events that followed in sequence in a twelve-month period. Her daughter went away from home in distressing circumstances (which she asked me not to reproduce), her husband became seriously ill, she suffered a rapid onset of RA (from ambulant to bedridden within 36 hours), her sick husband died, her youngest son was killed in a motorcycle accident, and finally, as a consequence, she lost her longstanding belief in God. Thus, within the social process of womanhood, which was itself stressful, aspects of that womanhood which gave meaning and definition to it—her relationships with her husband and daughter—were damaged. Her arthritis developed in the wake of these events only to be followed by the tragic losses of her husband and her youngest son and the obliteration of the cosmological framework that might have helped her come to terms with these losses: "I feel very lost now that I've lost God. I do. I feel that terribly." It was after the death of her son that she lost God, and she was left with: "A big black hole. Nothing." The symbolically reconstituted past revealed in her narrative reconstruction is one of almost total loss: the disappearance of her daughter, the loss of her physical competence, the death of her husband, the destruction of her youngest son, and, not surprisingly perhaps, the death of God. Now, one of the crucial criteria required for the ascertainment of a causal relationship is a clear time-order separating independent and dependent factors. In this regard, the loss of her husband, her son, and God can have no effective relationship to the onset of her arthritis, but they nevertheless lie within the same crucial matrix of social relationships within which her arthritis has arisen, and they thus form an essential component of her narrative reconstruction. They represent critical ruptures which have formed her present ideas about the causal role of other factors antedating the onset of her arthritis.

At this point, Gill has located the cause of her arthritis within a web of stressful events and processes: a genesis arising out of particular features of a woman's relationships in the modern world. It is a recognition of the distorting and constraining tendencies in these relationships that leads her to the question: "Where have I got to? There's nothing left of me," and to develop her narrative reconstruction around this theme of loss of self and confusion about personal identity. Gill is a good example of what Alasdair MacIntyre has in mind when he suggests:

> When someone complains—as do some of those who attempt to commit suicide—that his or her life is meaningless, he or she is often and perhaps characteristically complaining that the narrative of their life has become unintelligible to them, that it lacks any point, any movement towards a climax or *telos*.[21]

Gill did not commit suicide; her mind did not admit the problems and kept going, but her body indicated the necessity of rebellion by breaking down. Because her sense of ontological security was so firmly located within the context of conventional social relationships, the disturbance in those relationships led to an intimation of pointlessness, the development of illness, and the obliteration of all metaphysical referent.

What we have so far then is Gill's essentially sociological explanation of why she developed arthritis. But, in the years between onset of the illness and our meeting, Gill had regular contact with the medical profession and its mode of rationality. To forget this is to create an artificial abstraction. The medical model has often been disparaged by sociologists for, on the one hand, reducing the problems of the sick individual to a set of biophysical parameters and, on the other, reifying the concept of disease to a thing-in-itself.[22] In opposition to this, Mike Bury has argued that the medical model is often a useful symbolic resource which can be employed by individuals to mitigate the feelings of guilt and responsibility which often inform their response to illness, and to help them maintain some sense of integrity and autonomy in the context of meaninglessness. Whilst Gill developed a sophisticated socio-psychological model to explain her illness, she also understood that, in terms of the way illness became manifest, a general and popularized version of the medical model had a pleasing common-sense plausibility:

> I had quite forgotten until you mentioned the word virus . . . I said myself that I thought stress had precipitated this, but I would not preclude the fact that it might have been a kind of virus, because in the early stages I did feel as if I had bad "flu" . . . Do you remember when you get like that?

And, of course, I did remember. In this instance, the medical model provided us with a shared concept and a common understanding. The sociological model of "womanhood," on the other hand, was not something which I could possibly have encompassed within my social experience. But the problem with the influenza analogy is that it merely describes a sensation from which a viral aetiology may be inferred. It does not provide an adequate account of the genesis of her illness because it fails to locate it within a context of the changing relationship between herself and the social world.

Although Gill was not racked by feelings of guilt about her illness and did not feel personally responsible, she did have a sense of involvement in what had happened:

> It's the old Adam, we've all got to be ill. No . . . well, I don't know, certainly things like osteoarthrosis, you're bound to get worn out parts, like cars. . . . Mind you, I sometimes wonder whether arthritis is self-inflicted . . . not consciously. You know, your own body says, "right, shut-up, sit down, and do nothing." I feel very

strongly about myself that this happened to me, that one part of my head said, "if you won't put the brakes on, I will." Because I had had many years of very hard physical work, you know—washing and ironing and cooking and shopping and carting kids around and carrying babies and feeding babies and putting babies to bed and cleaning up their sick. It all sounds again so very self-pitying, but it's fact. Bringing up five children is hard work. That, and with the stress on top, I'm sure that I just cut out, I just blew a fuse.

In this passage from my interview with Gill, the final one relevant to the subject under consideration, the relationship of womanhood, and specifically motherhood, to illness was reaffirmed and described in the bold style of someone confident of their position. But some new elements have been introduced which elaborate that original relationship. Gill brought into play two metaphors, one religious and one mechanical, to suggest the inevitability of illness in society. The image of the Fall from Grace was introduced to account for the ubiquity of illness in human life and then, hesitatingly, wary perhaps of the fatalism in a religiosity she has lost, she rejected this in favour of the idea of an obsolescence built into the body-machine where certain kinds of mechanical degeneration are a necessary consequence of the structure and functioning of the component parts. Whilst both these images fit nicely into the teleological framework of an Aristotelian world-view, they do not explain the particular manifestation of illness in *her* life at this moment in time. Thus, following this metaphorical addendum, Gill returned to the central motif of her narrative reconstruction. Given the necessity, mechanical or metaphysical, of *some* kind of illness, the genesis of her arthritis was seen to reside in the social processes of stress and hardship which are the result of the role of women in the modern social structure. The notion of arthritis being self-inflicted implies not simply an individual flaw in a psyche brutalized by contingent events, but more the constraints placed upon the self within a social flow of essential activity.

Much of the work that has considered "lay beliefs" about the causes of particular diseases or illness in general have drawn a line between those beliefs which refer to the source of illness as outside the individual and those which see it as coming from within the individual.[23] Gill's account indicates the inadequacy of such an analytic bifurcation. In a crude sense, she located the source of her arthritis outside herself in a variety of events and processes, but the events she cites are precisely those which speak of the complex relationship between her personal *telos* and her social roles in modern society. What she was attempting to express, it seems to me, was that illness arises out of our relationship to the social world when personal identity and the social processes within which that identity is defined come into conflict. When the social self is forced to continue its everyday work and where personal revolt is impossible, the body may instigate its own rebellion. This is what Gill means when she refers to her arthritis being self-inflicted but not consciously.

In her illuminating account Gill managed to describe the relative autonomy of the body, the self, and the social world while indicating the way in which they interrelate. If her narrative is read as a simple description of cause and effect processes, it could be easily categorized as a belief model invoking social stress/life events plus (possible) virus, but this would be to violate it. As a narrative reconstruction, Gill's account can be read as an attempt to portray the genesis of illness within a socio-psychological interpretation of the relationships between personal identity and social roles in modern society, given the inevitability of some kind of illness and the ever-present possibility of viral attack. The complexity of her account results less from her concern to identify the causes of her arthritis and more from her need to reaffirm *telos* and to reconstruct a narrative order in the presence of profound disruptions in the biographical processes of daily life.

Betty: The Transcendence of Causality and Narrative Reconstruction

I have indicated that the degree of narrative embellishment or complexity in the process of reconstruction is related to the amount of biographical disruption to which the individual's life has been exposed. It could be argued, however, that since the amount of biographical disruption cannot be assessed apart from the actors' accounts of their perceptions the whole argument becomes circular. There is a horrible logic to this, and it is something which I cannot properly refute within the constraints of my present methods. Nonetheless, in partial mitigation of this objection, I would suggest that it is reasonable, if not entirely valid, to infer the amount of disruption from certain brute "facts." Bill's own premature retirement followed by his wife's accident would certainly spell disruption for the home economy of most working-class families and, in the same vein, it would be difficult to imagine the tragic chapter of accidents experienced by Gill being accepted by anyone with equanimity. Their narrative reconstructions were attempts to account for and repair breaks in the social order. I realise that there are all sorts of methodological and epistemological objections to this but, as I write, there is little else I can say in my own defence. Instead, I rest content with presenting the experiences of Betty who, in spite of inability to hold a much-needed job, to wash and dress herself, and, because of chronic pain, to sleep in the same bed as her husband, appeared remarkably composed.

There are some situations in which the central meaning of a life is defined by some transcendent principle—whether or not we accept the validity of the principle or the authenticity of the proclaimed belief in it. Where God is a powerful feature of an individual's cosmology His existence may be adduced not as a cause of the illness, as some other studies imply,[24] but as good reason why, in matters of illness and other misfortunes, the believer is not granted automatic exemption. Where God is the Cause or the Unmoved Mover, the individual may be liberated from the burdens of narrative reconstruction and causal analysis and left free to indulge their lyrical sensibility.

Betty was in her early sixties, married, and had worked full-time and then part-time in a shop until developing disablement made continuation impossible. She had had arthritis for about seven years. Her life was not a comfortable one, and she had worked, as she put it, "out of necessity," in order to supplement her husband's low wage, to pay off the mortgage, and to maintain a base equilibrium in the home economy. The loss of her wage rendered the future profoundly insecure. I asked her why she thought she got arthritis:

> The Lord's so near, and, you know, people say "why you?" I mean this man next door, He's German, and of course he doesn't believe in God or anything (sic) and he says to me, "you, my dear, why he chose you?" And I said, "Look, I don't question the Lord, I don't ask (. . .), He knows why and that's good enough for me." So he says, "He's supposed to look after . . ." [and] I said, "He is looking after his own (. . .) and he does look after me," I said, I could be somewhere where I could be sadly neglected (. . .), well, I'm not. I'm getting all the best treatment that can be got, and I do thank the Lord that I'm born in this country, I'll tell you that.

Instead of simply affirming that her arthritis originated in the mysterious workings of God's will, Betty tells a story that locates her attitude to her illness within a framework of justification that has been called forth on other occasions by nonbelievers. She suggests that her personal misfortune can only be approached within an understanding of the good fortune in other aspects of her life. The goddess Fortuna faces both ways. The secular search for cause and meaning or what Alasdair MacIntyre calls the "narrative quest"[25] is redundant because the cause, meaning, and purpose of all things is preordained by God:

> I've got the wonderful thing of having the Lord in my life. I've got such richness, shall I say, such meaning. I've found the meaning of life, that's the way I look at it. My meaning is that I've found the joy in this life, and therefore for me to go through anything, it doesn't matter really, in one way, because I reckon that they are testing times. . . . You see, He never says that you won't have these things, He doesn't promise us that we won't have them, He doesn't say that. But He comes with us through these things and helps us to bear them and that's the most marvellous thing of all.

So, for Betty, biographical robustness, narrative order, and the personal *telos* were not actually contingent upon what happened to her in the profane world. In fact the idea of a separate and vulnerable "personal" *telos* would make little sense in the context of her essential relationship with God's purpose. MacIntyre argues that teleology and unpredictability coexist in human lives and that the intelligibility of an individual life depends upon the relationship between plans and purposes on the one hand, and constraints and frustrations on the other. The anxiety to which this might give rise did not exist for Betty because the unpredictability of say, pain and illness, are part of an ulterior teleology.

This kind of interpretation of life and its difficulties is hard to appreciate in the context of a secular society with its mechanical notions of cause and effect. In talking of "God's purpose" as a component in people's understanding of the genesis of illness, it is important to think carefully about what exactly is entailed in the use of such expressions. When Betty talked about God and personal suffering, she did not imply that God's will was an efficient or proximate cause in the development of her arthritis, rather He is the cause of everything and, as such, makes narrative quests unnecessary. Nonetheless, from a sociological viewpoint, Betty's concept of "God" had similarities to Gill's image of "womanhood" and Bill's notion of "work" in that it transcended linear frameworks of cause and effect so as to define a symbolic and practical relationship between the individual, personal misfortune, social milieu, and the life-world. However, although both Gill and Bill went beyond a linear explanation of disease by placing their experiences of illness within, respectively, a socio-psychological and political narrative reconstruction of their relationships to the social world, Betty's "God" implied a principle of meaning that transcends the social world as such. Betty did not have to reconstruct order through narrative because God, existing "outside" both the individual and society, encompasses within his plans what appear to us as biological caprice and senseless biographical disruption. Physical suffering was only important insofar as it signified a feature of her essential relationship to God and so her sense of identity was not unduly threatened by the body's afflictions. The body itself is nothing as was made clear when, elsewhere in the interview, Betty aired her thoughts on donating her body to medical science:

> Your body is dust and that is what it goes to. I mean the spirit goes to the Lord, the part of me that's telling you all that I am and what goes to the Lord.

Although much that Betty said of her material life would suggest profound disruptions in socio-economic circumstances, there was no sense of disruption because her life was part of God's unfolding purpose. Moreover, "God's will" does not imply self-blame where the individual is bad and illness is retribution; at least, there is no direct relationship:

> You see, it's got nothing to do with Man's goodness. It's all to do with Christ, all to do with Him being born to save me, to suffer my sins and everything I've ever done. I'm made righteous and sanctified by the wonder of that cross and that to me is marvellous, that to me is the jewel of life (. . .). You see, there's a beauty about everything and you can sort of go through it in this way, you know, talking to the Lord and entering into it. He knows all about it. So people say, "why you?" Well, why not me? Better me who knows the Lord.

Because she did not see herself as the author of her own narrative there was nothing for her to reconstruct or explain. For Betty the course and end of her life were defined outside herself and history:

> And I think that, yes, it's helped me to understand, and even to the [point where] it can have a mental depressive [effect] on some people, because if they haven't got the Lord in their lives, of course, it must do. You know, "why am I here? why this, that and the other?" To me there's an end to it, something the Lord has for it, and He knows best what to do. I reckon, you know, that with faith I'll go through with this to an extent and that'll be it, and God will say, "well, that's it."

The interview with Betty was a particularly difficult one to conduct because my sociological questions appeared insignificant and redundant in the face of the teleological certainty of her beliefs. When interviewing someone with such a profound sense of meaning, it seemed almost meaningless to ask whether the illness had damaged her sense of self-worth or whatever. For Betty, most people live their

lives in the immediacy of personal and material interests. Their lives
follow a narrative thread defined by everyday events and happenings
and routines, and when major problems occur in their social world
their identity is bound to be threatened and it is not surprising that
they should become lost and depressed. But for her "there is an end
in it" and all analytic puzzlement and personal doubt evaporate in the
glare of God's purpose.

Conclusion

In his study of the Gnau tribe of New Guinea, Gilbert Lewis
describes how these people say of some illnesses that they "just come"
and how they say of the sick person that he or she is "sick nothingly."
In this way, sickness may be defined as having no cause or function,
and no intent. He goes on to contrast this situation with that of western
societies where illness is seen as the result of natural processes which
we can study by the scientific method. However, recognizing perhaps
the bluntness of this viewpoint, Lewis adds a crucial caveat:

> Individual people in our society may not accept it (the scientific
> view) as fully adequate to account for illness and seek religious and
> moral reasons for the illnesses of particular people, or even for
> illness in general; or individuals may feel an obscure and yet deep
> emotional dissatisfaction with explanation purely in natural terms,
> but the general view remains.[26]

The cases I have presented show a far more eclectic search than this.
It is true that Bill's account, and those of some other respondents, have
the same quality of systematic observation and inference that characterizes representations of scientific procedure. Many of their belief
models, at least in formal terms, bear a striking resemblance to the
multifactorial models of susceptibility/vulnerability/trigger employed
in sophisticated medical discourse, and a large number of respondents
resembled those women in Mildred Blaxter's study of lay beliefs in
whom:

> Their general models of causal processes, painstakingly derived
> from their experience as they saw it, were often scientifically wrong
> in detail, but were not in principle unscientific.[27]

I have tried to show that there may be more to such "causal" models
than at first meets the eye. Although in my interviews I framed the
question in terms of "what causes arthritis?" I have shown in the cases
presented that this question was explicitly translated into more sub-

stantive biographical questions. It was not just that they were "personalizing" the question they were transforming the meaning of it.

In this light, Lewis appears to be conflating two different levels of analysis—disease and illness, fact and value, science and morality. People may well draw upon some common-sense version of science and the medical model, but when Gill asks: "Where have I got to? There's nothing left of me," she is asking a question that breaks the bounds of traditional scientific discourse and shifts into a complex social psychology and practical morality. Furthermore, developments in science itself have rendered it increasingly distant from the language and perceptions of everyday life while, at the same time, forming part of the secularization of the western mind which has made overarching cosmologies less available and less plausible. As Comaroff and Maguire put it:

> In our society biomedical science and practice may provide satisfactory explanation and resolution for a wide range of afflictions often (but not always) seeming to render more thorough-going metaphysical speculation redundant. But precisely because of its apparent wide applicability in everyday life, particularly in the wake of the decline of overarching cosmological systems, we are especially bereft when we have to face events for which no rational explanation or remedy is forthcoming.[28]

This was written in relation to childhood leukaemia where the limits of rational explanation are particularly obvious, and, to paraphrase Turgenev, death may be an old jest but it comes new to everyone.[29]

RA is not a terminal illness, and therefore lacks the existential gravity of leukaemia or typhus. Nevertheless, it assaults the taken-for-granted world and requires explanation. Bill and Gill, finding no meaning in the medical view and having no overarching theodicy or cosmology, elaborated reconstructions of their experience in such a way that illness could be given a sensible place within it. These reconstructions bridge the large gap between the clinical reductions and the lost metaphysics. Once you begin to look at causal models as narrative reconstructions of the genesis of illness experience in the historical agent, moral or religious and, indeed, political and sociological factors become central to elucidating illness experience and rendering intelligible the biographical disruption to which it has given rise.

The body is not only an object amongst other objects in the world, it is also that through which our consciousness reaches out towards and acts upon the world. This is the dual nature of the body referred to by Sartre,[30] and within this duality chronic illness is a rupture in our relationship with that world. However, consciousness is itself biographically framed, so that consciousness of the body and the interpretations of its states and responses will lead us to call upon images of the private and public lives we lead. Narrative reconstruction is an attempt to reconstitute and repair ruptures between body, self, and world by linking-up and interpreting different aspects of biography in order to realign present and past and self with society. In this context, the identification of "causes" creates important reference points in the interface between self and society. My respondents were, perhaps, not so different from the *baladi* women in Evelyn Early's study for whom "The dialectic between the diagnosis and the life situation is crystallized in the illness narrative, where somatic progression and social developments are both documented."[31]

For Bill, illness developed out of a working life but where the significance of work could only be understood by elaborating an image of the kind of society in which that work was situated. His attachment to workplace toxicity as a causal factor could be understood only in terms of his image of society as a place of exploitative relationships and power inequality. In Gill's case, illness was seen to arise out of a way of life in which personal identity had been defined and constrained by essential features of womanhood. The genesis of her illness was located not solely in the person nor outside in the external world, but within the relationships constitutive of social being. For Betty, the genesis of illness was seen to reside in the transcendental realm of God's purpose. This is not to say that God was seen as an efficient cause of her illness, but rather that her illness was necessitated and justified by reference to her intrinsic relationship to a suffering God.

These accounts all speak of illness experience at one moment in time. Their pasts were the pasts of those presents in which they were interviewed, and I have no evidence for or against the proposition that their image of the past would have been substantially different in other presents. To test that would require an altogether more sophisticated piece of research. Within the constraints, what I have attempted to demonstrate is that causality needs to be understood in terms of narrative reconstruction and that both causal analysis and narrative reconstruction may be rendered redundant in the presence of an embracing theodicy. For medical sociologists such an approach suggests caution in attributing particular belief models to individuals out of relation to other aspects of their narrative, and for doctors it could alert them to reasons for the apparent resistance of some patients to clinical explanations.

Notes

[1] The Arthritis and Rheumatism Council for Research, *Reports on Rheumatic Diseases. Collected Reports 1959-1977*, London: ARC, 1978, p. 6.

[2] D. Locker, *Symptoms and Illness: The Cognitive Organization of Disorder*, London: Tavistock, 1981.

[3] P. H. N. Wood (ed.), *The Challenge of Arthritis and Rheumatism: A Report on Problems and Progress in Health Care for Rheumatic Disorders*, London: British League Against Rheumatism/Arthritis and Rheumatism Council, 1977.

[4] A small parakeet kept in a cage as a domestic pet.

[5] The term "genesis" is used by Claudine Herzlich in her monograph: *Health and Illness: A Socio-Psychological Approach*, London: Academic Press, 1979. Although I employ a somewhat different definition, I have been much influenced by both the style and substance of that excellent book.

[6] For example, J. H. Mabry, "Lay concepts of aetiology," *J. Chron. Dis.*, vol. 17, 1964, pp. 371–86; R. G. Elder, "Social class and lay explanations for the aetiology of arthritis," *J. Hlth. Soc. Behav.*, vol. 14, 1973, pp. 28–38; M. Linn, B. Linn, and S. Stein, "Beliefs about causes of cancer in cancer patients," *Soc. Sci. Med.*, vol. 16, 1982, pp. 835–39; R. Pill and N. Stott, "Concepts of illness causation and responsibility: some preliminary data from a sample of working class mothers," *Soc. Sci. Med.*, vol. 16, 1982, pp. 43–52; M. Blaxter, "The causes of disease: women talking," *Soc. Sci. Med.*, vol. 17, 1983, pp. 59–69.

[7] M. Bury, "Chronic illness as biographical disruption," *Sociology of Health and Illness*, vol. 4, no. 2, 1982, pp. 167–82.

[8] See P. Berger and B. Berger, *Sociology: A Biographical Approach*, Harmondsworth: Penguin, 1976; C. W. Mills, *The Sociological Imagination*, Harmondsworth: Penguin, 1970; D. Bertaux (ed.), *Biography and Society: The Life History Approach in the Social Sciences*, New York: Sage, 1981.

[9] R. Musil, *The Man without Qualities, Two: The Like of It Now Happens (II)*, London: Picador, 1979, p. 436.

[10] The terms "practical consciousness" and "discursive consciousness" are borrowed from: A. Giddens, *Central Problems in Social Theory: Action, Structure and Contradiction in Social Analysis*, London: Macmillan, 1979, p. 5.

[11] M. Linn et al., *op. cit.*, p. 838.

[12] G. Orwell, "Shooting an elephant," in, *Inside the Whale and Other Essays*, Harmondsworth: Penguin, 1962, p. 93.

[13] R. G. Collingwood, *The Idea of History*, Oxford: Clarendon Press, 1946, p. 247.

[14] This idea of the relationship of past to present is similar to that of G. H. Mead. For a useful exposition see: D. R. Mains, N. M. Sugrue, and M. A. Katovich, "The sociological import of G. H. Mead's theory of the past," *Am. Sociol. Rev.*, vol. 48, 1983, pp. 161–73.

[15] Probably the best version of Hume's ideas on causality and related issues may be found in: David Hume, *A Treatise of Human Nature*, Oxford University Press, 1978. This includes a helpful analytic index by L. A. Selby-Bigge.

[16] R. Bambrough, *The Philosophy of Aristotle*, New American Library, Mentor, 1963.

[17] R. Nisbet, *Social Change and History: Aspects of the Western Theory of Development*, New York: Oxford University Press, 1969, p. 27.

[18] A. MacIntyre, *After Virtue: A Study in Moral Theory*, London: Duckworth, 1981.

[19] N. S. Weiss, "Inferring causal relationships: elaboration of the criterion of 'dose-response,'" *Am. J. Epidem.*, vol. *113*, no. 5, 1981, pp. 487–90.

[20] A. Young, "The discourse on stress and the reproduction of conventional knowledge," *Soc. Sci. Med.*, vol. 14B, 1980, pp. 133–46.

[21] A. MacIntyre, *op. cit.*, p. 202.

[22] For example, M. Taussig, "Reification and the consciousness of the patient," *Soc. Sci. Med.*, vol. 14B, 1980, *op. cit.*, p. 202.

[23] For example, R. Elder, *op. cit.*; R. Pill and N. Stott, *op. cit.*

[24] M. Linn, et al., *op. cit.*

[25] A. MacIntyre, *op. cit.*

[26] G. Lewis, *Knowledge of Illness in Sepik Society*, London: Athlone Press, 1975, p. 197.

[27] M. Blaxter, *op. cit.*, p. 68.

[28] J. Comaroff and P. Maguire, "Ambiguity and the search for meaning: childhood leukaemia in the modern clinical context," *Soc. Sci. Med.*, vol. 15B, 1981, p. 119.

[29] I. Turgenev, *Fathers and Sons*, Harmondsworth: Penguin, 1965.

[30] J-P. Sartre, *Sketch for a Theory of the Emotions*, London: Methuen, 1971.

[31] E. A. Early, "The logic of well-being: therapeutic narratives in Cairo, Egypt," *Soc. Sci. Med.*, vol. 16, 1982, p. 1496.

12
Life with AIDS

Rose Weitz

To individuals who first learn that they have HIV disease, the problems this will bring can seem overwhelming. For some men and women, these problems remain overwhelming until death overtakes them. Others, however, over time, develop strategies to make living with HIV disease more manageable despite the physical, social, and emotional problems it causes. These strategies help individuals cope with the fear and the reality of social stigma, the changes in their social relationships, the impact of illness on their bodies, and their impending deaths.

Avoiding Stigma

A central part of having HIV disease is the experience of stigma. Stigma is a concern during all phases of the illness, from before diagnosis, when individuals must evaluate the risk of discrimination if they get tested for HIV, to the time when death seems inevitable and they must cope with the possibility of discrimination by funeral directors. As a result, one of the basic tasks persons with HIV disease confront is learning to avoid or reduce stigma.

A basic stratagem used by persons with HIV disease, as by those who have other stigmatized illnesses, is to hide the nature of their illness.[1] Hiding can begin at the time of diagnosis, if individuals and their doctors decide to provide false or misleading information to government disease registries or health insurance companies, and can occur in all social relationships.

Persons with HIV disease use a variety of methods to hide their illnesses. Jeremy routinely transfers his zidovudine (AZT) pills to an unmarked bottle because he fears that others might recognize the drug as one used to treat HIV disease. Those whose tongues show the tell-tale whitish spots of candidiasis (an infection that frequently accompanies this illness) close their mouths partially while smiling or talking. Others select clothing or use makeup to hide their emaciation or skin problems.

Most importantly, individuals learn to gauge how sick they look on any given day. Whenever possible, they try to look healthy when out in public. Kevin, for example, says, "Every time I go out [to a bar] I try to hide it. I try to act energetic and normal and I always have them put a squeeze of lime in my drinks so it's like a mixed drink." When their health makes it impossible to appear normal, they stay home. As David explains, "There are days that I really feel shitty and I look bad and I won't let anybody see me. I won't go around anybody. And then there are days I really force myself to put myself together so I will look decent and I'm not afraid to go out then."

This strategy is no help on days when individuals must go out despite visible symptoms. To protect their secret in these circumstances, individuals must devise plausible alternative explanations for their symptoms. In the early stages, they can claim that their weight loss is caused by stress or exercise, and that other symptoms are caused by minor illnesses, such as colds or the influenza. In the latter stages, they can claim that they have some other serious, but less stigmatized illness, such as leukemia or cancer.

Although hiding one's illness offers some protection against rejection, it carries a high price. Relationships with friends and families suffer when persons with HIV disease feel it is unsafe to discuss their illness with these others. At the same time, individuals forfeit any emotional or practical support they might otherwise receive from those who do not know of their illness. In addition, persons with HIV disease risk losing their jobs when they can offer no acceptable reason for their reduced productivity and increased absences. As a result, they eventually must disclose the nature of their illness to at least some individuals.

Following disclosure, individuals can avoid further stigma and emotional stress by reducing contact with those who prove unsupportive. As a result, however, their social lives shrink significantly. As Kevin says, "[Before getting ARC], I was out all the time. I loved to be around people. I hated to be by myself. But now, I find that I don't like to be around people that much except if it's people I know are not going to reject me because I don't want the rejection. I don't want to be hurt. I'm tired of being hurt."

To cope with losing their former social ties to friends, colleagues, and relatives, individuals can join support groups or participate in other social activities organized specifically for those who share their illness. In this way, they can garner the benefits of a social life without risking rejection or social awkwardness. Jeremy explains that he mostly socializes with others who have HIV disease "mainly because I guess I'm still afraid of people's reactions" but also "because I think they [those who have this illness] can understand more what your feelings are, what is going through your head. It's a lot easier to sit around and have a conversation with someone who is also ill with this disease, and you don't have to worry about avoiding certain topics." Persons with HIV disease also benefit from participating in these activities because everyone in these groups is stigmatized. As a result, the illness loses its "shock value" and instead becomes something that can be taken for granted. Consequently, they can engage in normal social interactions rather than interactions that are strained by the constant awareness of the illness. For example, Caleb, who was abandoned by most of his friends, tells of his pleasure at attending a potluck social for persons with HIV disease. At the potluck, he learned that he "was not alone":

> I met a lot of really beautiful people, a lot of really nice friends. They took your phone number. They call you, socialize with you. You go to the show with them. You do things with them. If you need any help or whatever, they're there. . . . I went through hiding myself in my house and every time the facial sores started I would be afraid to go out and let people see me. These people don't care. You're not the only one that's had the facial sores and they don't care. You're welcome there. . . . Nobody [at the potluck] was afraid because a person with ARC or AIDS made a dish. We all rather enjoyed the food. It was like all the barriers went down when you were with these other people.

For those who live outside of the state's two major metropolitan areas, however, this strategy is unfeasible. It is also emotionally unfeasible for those who feel uncomfortable in groups that are solely or predominantly composed of gay men. Heterosexuals who do go to these meetings often conclude that they are wasting their time because the problems the groups discuss differ too greatly from their problems. Finding and informing new sexual partners, for example, is a difficult problem for all who have HIV disease. The particular issues involved, however, and the particular strategies one can use to cope differ for gay men and for heterosexuals, because the former but not the latter function in a sexual community in which everyone is presumed to be at risk for HIV disease and many already know that they are infected.

Even for gay men, support groups are mixed blessings. Although socializing with persons who have HIV disease solves some problems, it creates others. Because these persons often have only their illness in common, the relationships they develop with each other can be superficial and unrewarding. In addition, as Brent explains, these social circles do not permit him or other persons with HIV disease "to get away from AIDS and be myself at the same time." Only with others who have the same illness can they abandon the facades they use to protect themselves from social stigma. Yet when they are with such others, they cannot avoid thinking about their illness. Moreover, those who become friends must cope with their friends' illnesses and dying as well as their own. As a result, the pleasure derived from support groups can turn to pain. Once this happens, individuals may decide to protect themselves emotionally by withdrawing from support groups and social networks made up of persons who share their illness.

Reducing Stigma

Although both hiding one's illness and restricting one's social circle can help persons with HIV disease avoid stigma, they will not reduce that stigma. Consequently, some individuals, like others who are stigmatized by society, consider these strategies inadequate and choose to attack the roots of that stigma directly.[2]

The decision to come out of the closet about their illness is not an easy one. Several men and women I interviewed would like to do so, but their doctors, husbands, friends and relatives, fearing the potential for stress and stigma, have urged them not to. These warnings are particularly effective with those who have children and who fear that their children might also be stigmatized if their diagnosis becomes known.

Nevertheless, some do choose to reveal their condition publicly. They work for community organizations that deal with HIV disease, serve as "resources" for acquaintances who have unanswered questions about the illness, or even speak to the media about their situation. Those who take these actions believe that it is the only way to truly improve their situation. For example, after his friends shunned him and his mother refused to help him obtain health insurance, Hugh decided to speak out publicly about having ARC. He explains, "The only way that I could see getting rid of that stigma is to stick up for myself and become publicly known, to say it's okay to be my friend, it's okay to hug me, it's okay to sit down on a couch with me and watch TV." Other individuals continue to conceal their own diagnoses but nonetheless try to teach those around them that persons with HIV disease should not be shunned. David, for example, describes a confrontation with a neighbor who accused him of having AIDS and asked him not to use the pool in their apartment complex. David denied that he had AIDS, but also told the neighbor that "ignorance is no excuse. You ought to read up on AIDS—you can't get it that way."

To reduce stigma, individuals not only must educate others about the biology of their illness, but also must challenge the idea that it is a deserved punishment for sin. They do so in two ways. First, gay men who have HIV disease can argue that God is the source of love and not of punishment and that God would not have created gay people only to reject them as sinners. Second, all persons with HIV disease can argue that illnesses are biological phenomena and not signs of divine judgment. They also can assert that it was simply bad luck that the first Americans affected by HIV disease were gay men or drug users. Gay men who have HIV disease seem especially likely to argue that this illness originated with heterosexuals in Africa and thus cannot be a punishment for homosexuality. As Chris says, "It didn't start out as a homosexual disease and it's not going to finish that way."

These alternative explanations for their illnesses allow Chris and others like him to reject their rejecters as prejudiced or ignorant. Others, however, themselves believe that they deserve HIV disease. Such individuals can attempt to reduce stigma through what Goffman terms "apologies."[3] Instead of offering excuses for their behavior, these men and women first accept responsibility for their drug use or, more commonly, homosexuality and affirm their belief in the social norms that label those activities immoral. Second, they claim that they have reformed and are no longer the person who engaged in these activities. On this basis, they ask their families, churches, and God to accept their apologies, forgive their former sins, and believe that the new persons they have become are their real selves.

Finally, persons with HIV disease can reduce stigma through bravado—putting on what amounts to a show to convince others of the reality of their situation, that they are, in fact, still functioning and worthwhile human beings. David describes how he and other persons with HIV disease occasionally go to a bar to "show these people that we can live with AIDS. That we can have a good time. That we can dance, that we can socialize, that we're not people with plagues." Describing a recent visit to a local bar, he says, "I just walked in, put my arms around somebody, said 'Hi, how're you doing? Everything going ok with you?' and he said, 'Well, how are you doing?' and I said,

'Well, ARC hasn't gotten me down yet. I don't think it will.' I said, 'I'm going to beat this thing.' And I just acted like nothing was wrong."

Living with HIV Disease

As their illness progresses, both the concerns of persons with HIV disease and the resources available to them shift. Stigma becomes a less critical issue, as their interactions with others necessarily become more limited and as they develop a supportive, if narrower, circle of friends, relatives, and health care workers. With time, too, the shock individuals feel at how some of their relatives and friends have reacted lessens, and they learn to accept the distance between them and those who once were close. Calvin, who was completely rejected by his family, says:

> Like anything else, any other disappointment that you have in life, you adjust. You categorize it in a fashion that's comfortable to you and you put it on the shelf with the rest of your hurts and you get on with your life. You don't let it destroy you. There's nothing wrong with hurting as long as you don't stay in that position too long and hurt for too long of a time. I can't change AIDS and I can't change my family so I accept and go forward. That's all I can do.

Time also can help individuals recover from their own feelings of shame. At the follow-up interview, Brent, whose diagnosis had changed since the first interview from ARC to AIDS, said:

> In the beginning I had horrible feelings of dirtiness. Just the "leprosy" [feeling] was just overpowering. I wanted to hide it from the world. As I've had a time to accustom myself to having this and give myself time to think and rationalize and come to intellectual ideas rather than emotional responses, the feelings are less. . . . I've changed and become accustomed to it and I'm used to the idea.

As stigma recedes as an issue, and as the physical consequences of their illness become more overwhelming, other concerns come to the forefront. With the changes in their bodies, persons with HIV disease increasingly lose the ability to meet their own expectations for how they should perform in the roles and relationships that they retain. This loss of abilities and the resulting failed performances seriously threaten individuals' self-concepts. Psychologists have documented that, whenever possible, people will avoid recognizing any evidence that might force them to change their self-concepts, especially if that evidence might result in lowering their self-esteem.[4] The desire to maintain a consistent self-concept and level of self-esteem leads people to assume that their own motives are pure, acknowledge only favorable evaluations from others, recall and take credit for successes but not failures, and perceive new data selectively so as to confirm their preexisting self-concepts. Given the overwhelming changes produced by HIV disease, however, these strategies cannot work for long. As a result, as their illness progresses, individuals must develop ways to maintain their self-concepts and self-esteem despite unavoidable evidence that their lives have changed. To do so, they must construct new philosophical frameworks that allow them to downgrade the importance of their losses and to value the persons they now are and the lives they now lead.

To begin with, persons with HIV disease can reevaluate the importance of physical appearances. Typically, those I interviewed report that whereas previously they had thought "if I lose my looks I'll lose everything," now they believe that "the important thing is that I'm alive." As a result, they can separate their ideas about their appearance from their ideas about their inherent self-worth.

Similarly, persons with HIV disease can reevaluate their ideas about the importance of sexual activity; this is especially relevant for gay men. As those activities diminish, they may learn to value relationships that provide friendship more than those that provide sexual gratification. In addition, as their social circles shrink due to both stigma and their diminishing physical abilities, individuals quickly learn who are their true friends. As a result, they often feel that their remaining relationships with friends and lovers are now better and more meaningful than ever before. They therefore are able to replace their former self-concepts as sexual beings with new and equally valued self-concepts as loving beings.

Persons with HIV disease also find worth in their lives and their selves by emphasizing past accomplishments or present joys rather than future losses. This strategy additionally aids individuals by restoring some of their sense of control over their lives, for they can assert far more control over how they conceptualize the past and experience the present than over what will happen in the future.

Chris's case illustrates how one can derive a sense of self-worth by focusing on the past rather than the future. A former alcoholic, now diagnosed with AIDS, Chris has made peace with the thought of his death by emphasizing what he has accomplished in his life. As he says, "I used to think about it all the time, that I didn't want to die. . . . But I'm proud of my life. I've changed it. I've done something with it. . . . I've stayed sober and I've passed along some sobriety to people. I've helped some people understand it, and that's important."

Other individuals deemphasize their diminished futures by stressing the benefits of focusing on the present and deriving pleasure from the wonders of everyday life. This is an especially important change for those whose previous focus on future goals had left them perennially dissatisfied with their lives. As a result, persons with HIV disease can experience greater happiness than ever before. Robert, who also has AIDS, says: "I think I just enjoy life so much more now. Everybody I come into contact with, it seems I notice the good things about them. You notice the flowers more. . . . You notice the sky more. You just notice all the things that are created in this world, and most all of them are beautiful. . . . I think I've gained life, actually [from having AIDS]. The beauty of it and what it really means, the caring, the sharing, the pretty flowers, the ugly flowers, the weeds or whatever, the sunshine, and the rain. I like all of it now."

Similarly, some individuals (especially those who used drugs) in the past had not taken their own lives very seriously. They had let things happen to them rather than trying to direct their fates. Now that they recognize that their life spans are short and finite, they are much more conscious about every choice they make—how they spend their time and with whom, what they eat and wear, how they interact with others, and the like. With this new consciousness, they can now choose how to live their remaining days so as to bring them happiness. As a result, HIV disease can seem more like a gift than a curse.

In sum, by changing their ideas about physical appearances, sexual activities, and the relative worth of past, present, and future, persons with HIV disease can limit the damage their illness can do to their self-esteem and more global self-concepts. Perhaps more surprisingly, they can develop new cognitive frameworks that enable them to use their illness not just to maintain but actually to improve their self-esteem. As individuals discover within themselves the emotional resources needed to confront illness, stigma, and dying with dignity, their self-esteem can increase. Similarly, as their experiences with HIV disease teach them a new compassion for and understanding of others, individuals can redefine themselves as less selfish and more humane than they had previously thought. Sarah, who now works for a community organization that deals with HIV disease and has begun organizing a support group for women, says, "I used to be a really stressed out, rat-raced, job-oriented person, always put my careers ahead of my relationships. I'm just not like that [anymore]. I'm a much more caring person toward other people. I just take one day at a time.

I relax. I've mellowed out and I'm a much better person for it." Clint derives similar benefits from helping others in his support group. He attends the group because he has, he says, "a very positive outlook on this thing [AIDS]. And if I can help those people that are having a very difficult time adjusting, and give them some of my energy, then I'm doing some good. I'm doing my part."

Political activism can also allow individuals to develop enhanced selves. This is especially true for those who can no longer contribute to the world through their work. David, who has appeared on the local news to describe his problems in obtaining social security, recalls, "I didn't want everybody to know. But . . . once it was over and done with, I felt good about what I had done. Because it wasn't only for me that I was doing it. It was for a lot of other people out there that got the same problem." Similarly, others I interviewed point to their participation in this and other research studies as "legacies" that they are leaving to help others.[5] Calvin, explaining why he agreed to do the interview, says, "It's important to me to try to do something for mankind. To create enough interest that somebody will do something." Activities such as these help individuals to supplant failed performances in old roles with successful performances in valued new roles, and thus to maintain their self-esteem.

In addition, persons with HIV disease believe that they can help others simply because their deaths will add to the toll from this illness. They believe that, as that toll rises, the government eventually will have to devote more resources to seeking a cure or vaccine. Calvin continues, "I feel that I am making a positive approach toward mankind with dying from AIDS. . . . I feel that with my dying from AIDS I am becoming part of the statistics. Once there is enough statistics, then somebody is going to do something about it, but they are not going to do anything until there is an emergency." This philosophy allows individuals both to find meaning in their suffering and to retain a sense of worth.

For gay men, having HIV disease can also improve their self-esteem by making them more comfortable with their sexuality.[6] Several report that in the past they had experienced considerable guilt and ambivalence about their lifestyles. Although they had engaged in gay sexual activities, they had found it difficult to embrace gay identities. Their illness has enabled them to integrate their sexual activities and sexual identities into coherent sexual self-concepts in one of two ways. For some, the process of dealing with a fatal, sexually transmitted disease has caused them to reexamine their feelings toward being gay. In this process, some have found a new self-acceptance. As Dick says, "I think

I'm more comfortable with myself, now that I've had to deal with it [being gay] again. It's almost like coming out again. You can come out feeling better about yourself and feeling better about being gay." Having HIV disease also helps some men to feel more comfortable with being gay by allowing them to see other gay men in a new and more favorable light. Tom has lived a very closeted life and has never had a serious relationship with another man. His feelings toward other gays have changed dramatically since becoming ill:

> The [gay] people I've seen caring for other persons with AIDS and so on made me realize that there can be a spiritual depth in the homosexual that I didn't realize there was before. My primary experience with homosexuals was in bars or bath houses and not a very positive experience. And to see people you might otherwise just have seen as being a hunk of meat or something like that actually caring for another person or going through all sorts of degradations in the disease process has really illuminated to me the fact that homosexuals are human beings.

In this way, their experiences with HIV disease enable some individuals who engage in gay activities to embrace gay identities for themselves.

For other gay men, HIV disease can eliminate dissonance between their sexual identities and sexual activities by ending those activities. Once concern about infecting others or worsening their own health forces them to abandon sexual activities, they no longer face contradictions between those activities and their sense of who they are or should be. Subsequently, both they and their families may stop considering them either deviant or sinful. As a result, they experience both more peace with themselves and improved self-esteem.

Dying with HIV Disease

As their health declines and death seems increasingly close and inevitable, persons with HIV disease must come to grips with the reality of their own mortality. To do so, they must once again develop a new set of cognitive frameworks which both makes their illness comprehensible to them and clarifies their options. Once they conclude that their illness will be fatal, they can make peace with their lack of control over their impending deaths by attempting to assert control over the nature of their dying.

Initially, HIV disease can seem an unfathomable mystery, which produces overwhelming uncertainties about its origins, nature, and consequences. Nevertheless, persons with HIV disease do develop explanations for why illness struck them specifically. In addition, over time, individuals develop ideas about the nature and consequences of HIV disease that enable them to understand and accept the changes in their bodies. Dick, for example, was diagnosed with ARC at the time of the initial interview and with AIDS at the time of the follow-up interview. He describes how he has come to terms with the uncertainty his illness has created:

> I remember, a little over a year ago when I was first told what I had, it was very frightening. . . . You didn't know what the future held. A lot of that has been, at least, resolved. I don't worry about it so much as I did in that respect. It's still not something I want, but I guess you learn to live with it a little better. Then, when you get a case of pneumonia you know what it is, and you don't really think anything of it, other than the fact, that, well, "We know what's caused this."

In addition, as time passes, the uncertainty persons with HIV disease feel about the consequences of their illness not only is reduced but also becomes an accepted part of life. Stress decreases as individuals learn both to assert control over some aspects of their lives and to accept that they cannot control other aspects. For example, at the time of the first interview, David had ARC. By the follow-up interview, he had been told by his doctor that he was on the border of AIDS. Comparing his feelings at the initial and follow-up interviews, he says, "All I think I've done is adjust to it. I'm not so afraid. I guess I have realized that there's nothing that I can do about it."

Although most persons with HIV disease continue to hope for a cure, eventually their frenetic search for one abates, both because they lose hope and because they learn that the constant search for a cure can be physically and emotionally damaging. Jill, for example, describes how initially she would try to "do everything":

> But you see what that means is I'd get real hyped [on] things in the newspaper, the media, you know, cures and stuff. . . . [But] I knew if I got that high I'd have to come down and get that low. Do you what I mean [sic]? So then I'd get real high about cures or ideas. Or I'd read something, you know, "This is wonderful!" And, you know, "This is going to just—this will do it. This will save my life." And, "This will make some of the things better." And then I'd get real high about that and I'd rush around and get real positive. And believe it or not, it wasn't real healthy because, you know, I'd either be so physically exhausted from just being so hyper about something that the next day I'd either sleep all day or I would have a depression. It's the highs and lows that get you.

Jill no longer will read stories about HIV disease in the newspapers, but instead relies on her doctor to let her know of any new drug she should try.

Robert, who has AIDS, describes a different set of dangers persons with HIV disease can face if they start believing in a cure. He had taken zidovudine for a while, but was forced to stop because of life-threatening loss of blood cells. He says:

> People with AIDS need to realize they are sick, deathly sick. I had got where I think you start feeling good which I guess it was because I was on AZT [zidovudine] too. It is the difference between black and white, night and day, or whatever. The first time I went on it I lasted six weeks. It was just marvelous. I just felt so good. Then the next time it didn't work for but a week and the next time it didn't work for but a week and I got scared. I had forgotten the possibility of dying.

This experience convinced Robert that he would be happier if he accepted his fate than if he continued on an emotional roller coaster of false hopes.

Those who conclude that nothing will cure them or restore their quality of life may decide to stop trying to preserve their lives. Calvin has stopped taking all medications:

> At first, I got on the bandwagon of vitamins and getting nutrition and proper meals and eating my spinach and everything. One day I finally said: "What for?" It's not going to save me. I don't know of anybody that has not died from AIDS just because they ate spinach. . . . You can't run from AIDS. There's nowhere to go. If it's any other illness, then you have hope, you have dreams, you have treatment. With AIDS you don't. You just simply don't have an alternative to dying.

Calvin, like Robert, has decided that resigning himself to his fate is less distressing than trying to fight it. By so doing, he can now feel that he is once again making choices about what will happen to his life, albeit from a limited and perhaps self-destructive set of options.

Once persons with HIV disease decide that death is inevitable—and to some extent regardless of how sick they currently are—their conception of the future narrows. A striking feature of conversation with these men and women is the telescoping meaning of the future, as their long-range perspective shrinks and they move from talking about the future in terms of years from now, to months, weeks, or even hours. Sharon, for example, who has ARC, feels that her future has been "snatched away" from her. She says, "I don't feel the future exists for me any longer. [In the past] I would think about ten or twenty years down the road when I would be at a certain point in my life. Now I don't think about that. I think about each day."

In this narrowed future, death looms increasingly close. The regrets individuals feel center on the pain their death will bring to others and on their own loss of potential experiences, as they realize that they will miss seeing various future events, from their children's marriages to the price of strawberries next year. Jeremy, for example, says, "I regret that I probably will never make it to the point where I'll be one of those old men sitting in the malls drinking coffee, watching." A wistfulness, rather than bitterness, pervades most such remarks.

The meaning of death, however, is not overwhelmingly negative. For those who have firm Christian convictions, death can take on especially positive connotations of salvation and rejoining God in heaven. Religion can become a "fortress in the storm"—a source of strength in this world and hope about the next—especially if they find sympathetic clergy who will listen to their fears and sorrows and provide "unconditional love."

As their physical pain increases, death also can come to seem a blessing. Calvin emphatically states, "I'm so miserable now I pray to the Lord every night that he takes me. I cry myself to sleep just begging to die. I want to die so bad I can't hardly stand it. Not because I'm suicidal, but because I hurt. I hurt and I want it over with."

Although death can lose its power to frighten persons with HIV disease, however, dying retains its horror. Carol echoes the sentiments of most others when she says, "I'm not afraid to die. I may be afraid of the *way* it's going to happen, but I'm not afraid to die." Similarly, Dennis, who has already suffered one agonizingly debilitating episode, says, "Death doesn't bother me. Being ill as I was terrifies me." As these quotes suggest, the greatest fears of persons with HIV disease typically center on being kept alive against their will beyond the point where pain or disability makes their lives no longer worth living.

Such feelings led Dennis, along with several others I interviewed, to make plans to commit suicide should that seem warranted so that he could maintain his sense of control over the nature of his dying. As Dennis explains, "If I'm going to die, I would rather it be my business. I guess it's a lack of control. I want to reassert as much control as I can." Others have decided to let the disease take its natural course. They have signed living wills to prohibit physicians from keeping them alive through extraordinary means, instructed relatives not to let them be placed on life-support systems, and decided to stop taking their medications once life no longer seemed worthwhile. As Calvin, who has thrown away all his medications without informing his physician, explains, "I don't want to die, but I don't have a choice. I have to—period. I mean, no question. So if I have to die, why not tackle the chore and get it over with?"

Notes

[1] See, for example: Marie I. Boutte, "'The Stumbling Disease': A Case Study of Stigma Among Azorean-Portuguese," *Social Science and Medicine* 24 (1987):209–217; Richard A. Hilbert, "The Acultural Dimensions of Chronic Pain: Flawed Reality Construction and the Problem of Meaning," *Social Problems* 31 (1984):365–378; and Joseph Schneider and Peter Conrad, *Having Epilepsy: The Experience and Control of Illness* (Philadelphia: Temple University Press, 1983).

[2] See, for example: Zachary Gussow and George S. Tracy, "Status, Ideology, and Adaptation to Stigmatized Illness: A Study of Leprosy," *Human Organization* 27 (1968):316–325; and John Kitsuse, "Coming Out All Over: Deviants and the Politics of Social Problems," *Social Problems* 28 (1980):1–13.

[3] Erving Goffman, *Relations in Public* (New York: Basic Books, 1971).

[4] This research is summarized in Viktor Gecas, "The Self-Concept," *Annual Review of Sociology* 8 (1982):1–33; and Barry R. Schlenker, *The Self and Social Life* (New York: McGraw-Hill, 1985), pp. 12–15, 89–92.

[5] See Appendix 1 [from *Life with AIDS*] for further details.

[6] My thanks to Kathy Charmaz for helping me conceptualize this section.

13

The Medical Management of Femininity: Women's Experiences with Silicone Breast Implants

Susan Zimmermann

Introduction

Silicone breast implants have been used to enhance or recon-struct the breasts of over one million women for more than thirty years. In the early 1990s, the American public learned that these devices may have a number of dangerous side effects. On December 10, 1990, *Face to Face with Connie Chung* aired a show which explored the possibility that the gel from leaking and ruptured implants can cause debilitating autoimmune symptoms and connec-tive-tissue diseases, and that the polyurethane coating on some of the devices can lead to cancer. On October 12, 1992, talk-show host Jenny Jones came forward about her own ordeal with implants, claiming that the devices had ruptured and encapsulated, leading her to endure multiple surgeries and disfigurement. Newspapers also began to disseminate information about implant-related risk, providing details about manufacturer cover-ups and anecdotes from women who claimed to be harmed by the devices (see Burton 1993; Reuter 1993; Hilts 1992a, 1992b).

On January 6, 1992, David Kessler, the Commissioner of the Food and Drug Administration (FDA), declared a voluntary moratorium on the use of silicone breast implants because manufacturers failed to provide sufficient evidence proving the safety and efficacy of the devices, and increasing numbers of women were reporting prob-lems. Kessler's decision generated even further commentary on the breast implant controversy. Marcia Angell (1992), editor of the *New England Journal of Medicine*, wrote that the decision was unfair, asserting that women have the right to make their own medical choices. Angell also believed that the decision caused unnecessary anxiety among the 1–2 million women who already were implanted

Written especially for *Perspectives in Medical Sociology*, 3/E.

with the devices. Position statements of the American Medical Association, American College of Rheumatology, American College of Surgeons, American College of Radiology, Society of Surgical Oncologists, and the American Society of Plastic and Reconstructive Surgeons also opposed the FDA's decision, stating that the benefits of implants far outweigh their risks (Fisher 1992). Consistent with this viewpoint, a panel of scientists convened by the Institute of Medicine reviewed the most recent studies on breast implants and, on June 21, 1999, concluded that breast implants do not pose a major health risk to women.

Despite the medical community's stance on the implant debate, anecdotal evidence has continued to support a causal relationship between implants and disease. By June, 1992, a total of 14,259 women reported to the FDA that they had experienced adverse reactions to their implants (HRIRSCGO 1993). Moreover, by the end of 1993, over 12,000 women had filed lawsuits against Dow Corning Corporation, the leading breast implant manufacturer. These women all alleged that their implants had caused them to develop disabling symptoms and that Dow had intentionally withheld information about these risks from the public prior to their surgeries. The number of lawsuits brought against Dow and other implant manufacturers resulted in a $4.3 billion global settlement, intended to offer compensation to any woman with diseases or symptoms associated with breast implants. Over 400,000 women filed claims, while an estimated 15,000 women opted to pursue litigation against implant manufacturers outside of the settlement.[1]

Today, breast implants continue to be the focus of several controversies: the FDA and medical associations are struggling over whether to lift the moratorium on their use; politicians and attorneys are debating whether the large number of breast implant suits are a proper avenue of justice or the latest example of the tort system gone amiss; and scientists and physicians are disputing whether they are causally linked to autoimmune diseases. While these debates have kept breast implants in the forefront of the news, there has been scant scholarly attention paid to this topic outside of medical and epidemiological journals. In this chapter, I shed light on the personal experiences that underlie these controversies. Drawing from in-depth interviews with implant recipients, I trace the course of their experiences from their initial decision to seek implants, to their encounters with the medical profession, to their ways of coping with medical problems and uncertainty. Analysis of these experiences shows how women arrive at a decision to surgically alter or reconstruct a part of their bodies that is intrinsically linked to ideas about femininity, and how they come to view this decision after learning that their way of achieving a cultural ideal has either failed or has the potential to fail.

Two conceptual themes guide this study. The first is the role of *agency*—the capacity of individuals to act upon their circumstances—in women's decision to receive breast implants (also see Davis 1995). Shedding light on the social and medical contexts that shape women's reasons for enhancing or reconstructing their breasts, and the magnitude of the personal and physical suffering they endured after being implanted with devices they believed were "perfectly safe," I question the extent to which plastic surgery can be seen as a "choice." I argue that while women participate in the medicalization of femininity by opting to undergo surgery to alter their female bodily appearances this participation is less a reflection of "agency" than it is a revelation of the specific nature of women's subordination.

The second theme guiding this analysis is *medical uncertainty*. More specifically, this analysis demonstrates how women's descriptions of their physicians' responses to the uncertainty associated with their implant-related symptoms and complications are infused with cultural assumptions about gender, science and medicine. I show how women's ways of coping with medical uncertainty can exist in tension with professional or "expert" opinions, and how women who derive knowledge from their own bodies rather than from scientific and medical evidence can, ironically, become empowered by their illness experiences. Many of the women I interviewed who had once perceived themselves as passive victims of medicalization and ideological manipulation came to view themselves as active agents, capable of taking charge over their life circumstances. This transformation occurred when women educated themselves about the risks related to their implants and learned to question both medical authority and their own ideas about female attractiveness.

Methods

Primary data for this research consists of forty in-depth interviews with women who had received breast implants. I obtained interviews by placing announcements in local newspapers, through support groups for implant recipients, through law firms handling breast implant litigation, and by word of mouth (i.e., through colleagues, friends and family members who knew women with implants). The average length of the interviews was about two hours, although one interview was less than an hour and a few of them were close to four hours. Although interviews were based on a prepared interview schedule, I made an effort to ask women open-ended questions so that they could talk about their implant-related experiences with minimal interruptions. In order to avoid taking notes and maintain eye contact, I tape-recorded all but one interview.[2] I transcribed each interview after it was completed and coded the transcripts according to themes that I developed throughout the interview process.

Twenty-six of the women I interviewed had breast implants for cosmetic reasons.[3] According to popular belief, cosmetic surgery involving breast implants enhances the size and shape of women's breasts. However, only eleven of the 26 women who deemed their surgery "cosmetic" had received implants for this purpose. Twelve women had implants not to enlarge their breasts but to lift their breast tissue after it had sagged following a pregnancy, nursing, or losing weight. Three of the 26 women had implants because their breasts were slightly asymmetrical.

Fourteen of the women received breast implants for reconstructive purposes. Generally, breast reconstruction refers to the replacement of one or both breasts following a mastectomy. However, women who have severely asymmetrical breasts or congenital deformities of the breast also undergo reconstructive mammaplasty. Of the 14 women I interviewed who had breast reconstruction, 10 had implants following a mastectomy: one because her breasts were asymmetrical from a spinal deformity, one because her breast tissue decreased in volume after nursing, one because she had "severely sagging" breasts, and one because her breasts were "tubular."

The women ranged in age between 23 and 72. Seven women had received breast implants before turning age 25; 20 more between ages 25 and 35; nine more between ages 35 and 45; and three more between ages 50 and 65. Of the forty women with whom I spoke, twenty-two were married, eight were divorced, three were separated, and seven had never been married. All the divorced or separated women had been married at the time they received breast implants. Thirty-six women identified themselves as White, one as Asian, two as Latino, and one as Native American. Seventeen women were employed, nine were homemakers, three were students, and eleven were currently unemployed. Of these unemployed, one reported that she was currently looking for a job; the remaining ten women stated that they had lost their jobs because they were too ill to work. These women were on disability insurance because they had been diagnosed with an illness that prevented them from participating in the workforce. Most of the women in my sample were well educated. Seven women had high school degrees, twenty-three had attended either a two- or four-year college, nine had advanced professional or master's degrees, and one had completed a doctoral degree.

Twenty out of the forty women had their breast implants removed because they experienced complications or symptoms associated with these devices. However, not every woman who experienced implant-related side effects had undergone this surgery. In total, 35 of the 40 women interviewed reported having experienced problems directly related to their implants, such as deflation, ruptures or encapsulation (causing a severe hardening of the breasts), leading to multiple replacement surgeries and disfigurement. Thirty-four of the 40 women believe they are now experiencing physical symptoms associated with their implants. These symptoms range in severity from minor aching joints to debilitating pain and chronic fatigue. Other symptoms included hair loss, stomach irritability, rashes, fevers, and allergic reactions to certain foods and chemicals found, for example, in perfumes and household cleansers. Twenty-five women also were diagnosed with one or more of the following diseases after they received their implants: rheumatoid arthritis, fibromyalgia, irritable bowel syndrome, chronic fatigue syndrome, lupus, Sjogren's syndrome, scleroderma, Reynaud's disease, cancer, and peripheral neuropathy. Only five out of the forty women with whom I spoke reported no symptoms and no implant-related complications.

Plastic Surgical Decisions

A number of feminist researchers and scholars have explored women's involvement with beauty practices. Most scholarship in this area has focused on the larger structural and cultural forces that shape and perpetuate a homogenous representation of femininity and female attractiveness. Some of this research, for instance, views beauty as oppression—women partake in beauty practices because they have internalized institutionalized patterns of gender inequality in the larger society, which lulls them into believing that if they change their appearances, their lives will be somehow better (Millman 1980; Baker 1984; Chapkis 1986). Other researchers who focus on the larger systemic and cultural forces which shape ideal gendered traits perceive beauty as cultural discourse (Jaggar and Bordo, 1989; Jacobus, Keller and Shuttleworth 1990; Bordo 1990, 1993). In other words, cultural representations of the female body are a site for exploring the interplay between gender and power relations that exist in our larger social world. In this way, the body can be read as a text that tells a story about patterns of control and ideas about femininity within broader social and historical contexts. Research also is beginning to explore how women themselves construct meaning around their own experiences with beauty regimes. In particular, Kathy Davis (1995) conducted in-depth interviews (with women who were either planning to have, or who already had, some type of cosmetic surgery) in order to analyze the life circumstances that lead women to seek cosmetic surgery. Davis's study included follow-up interviews with twelve women one year after they had received breast implants, enabling her "to compare women's reasons for wanting surgery with how they felt about it after the fact" (p. 9).

Based on the conclusions she draws from her own research, Davis contends that most theoretical frameworks for understanding women's beauty regimes tend to focus on how such practices work to discipline and control women. Whether the emphasis is on beauty as oppression or as cultural discourse, these frameworks perpetuate the view of women as victims who are "blinded by consumer capitalism, oppressed by patriarchal ideologies, or inscribed within the discourses of femininity" (Davis 1993, p. 24). According to Davis, these models are overly simplified since they ignore how women themselves actively participate in their own decision to undergo cosmetic surgery. Davis does not view women as "cultural dopes" who have been blinded by the promise of a new body; rather, she perceives them as moral actors who negotiate what should and should not be done to their own bodies.

Opting for a "Cosmetic" Procedure:
The Influence of Interpersonal Relationships

Many of the women I interviewed who had undergone surgery to enhance their breast size had this surgery over ten years ago, allowing them the time to reflect on their reasons for receiving breast implants. The majority of these women did not perceive their decision to reshape their bodies as a liberating experience or as a way of taking charge of their lives. In hindsight, nearly 70 percent of the women in my study who had implants for cosmetic purposes perceived this decision as an action taken under pressure from family members, spouses, and lovers who believed that women are better off with larger, more shapely breasts. For instance, twenty-six years ago, when Christine was 29, she actually thought that breast enhancement would save her marriage:

My husband and I were going though a divorce, and I asked him what the problem was because our sex life wasn't very good and we were having problems. And he said, "Well, you don't have the same figure that you had when I married you. . . . your breasts are so saggy." So, I thought maybe I should give the marriage my best effort. . . . I felt that if my husband didn't want me with sagging breasts, no other man would.

Other women explained that their parents were the ones who had influenced their decision to undergo cosmetic surgery. For instance, Karen, who is now in her early thirties, said that her mother and father gave her money for implant mammaplasty as an eighteenth birthday present. Ann, who has had her implants for 23 years, believed that her desire to have larger breasts was linked to her relationship with her father, who would "always give throw-away comments like 'This lady . . . is very nice—flat as a pancake—but so nice,'" perpetuating her belief that "if you are attractive, you are loved—if you are not, you are invalidated."

In hindsight, these women did not perceive their decision to receive implants as an act of self-determination or as a means to exercise their freedom of choice about how to present themselves to the world. Rather, they understood how their interpersonal relationships served as threads linking the gendered structure of American society to their day-to-day feelings about themselves and their bodies. Through critical comments or passing remarks, the spouses, lovers, and family members of these women conveyed to them the message that in order to be worthy of love and attention in this society, women must adhere to a rigid, narrowly defined image of femininity. Plastic surgeons hold the power to perpetuate this message by providing women with a quick surgical solution for their feelings of inadequacy and undesirability.

Getting Caught up in "Plastic Surgery Promises"

Surprisingly, many of the women I interviewed explained that they had visited their plastic surgeons without the intention of having their breasts enlarged. For instance, Jenna visited a plastic surgeon because she felt a lot of shame about the pendulous shape of her breasts after she had nursed her three children. She hoped that the surgeon could somehow "lift" her sagging breast tissue. However, her plastic surgeon responded to this inquiry by saying, "No, no, you don't want a lift, you will be too flat—you won't like it." Lulled by her surgeon into believing that she would be "better off" if she conformed to a cultural ideal of female attractiveness characterized by large breasts, Jenna was convinced that she should get implants.

Eleanor also had no intention of receiving breast implants when she visited her plastic surgeon. She explained that she had lost a tremendous amount of weight, leaving her with excess skin around her abdomen, and thought a surgeon might be able to give her a simple "tuck." However, after meeting with a plastic surgeon, she was convinced that she needed not only abdominal surgery but also breast surgery. Eleanor described her initial interaction with her plastic surgeon:

> Upon examining [my abdomen], the surgeon said to me when he looked at my breasts, "You don't have to look like that." So, that is how it all started. When he said that I didn't have to look like that, I bought it. And [this surgeon] was drop-dead gorgeous.

Both Jenna and Eleanor explained their feelings that their surgeons were "attractive" men who could make them "look beautiful." The combination of these factors influenced both patients' decision to undergo surgery, demonstrating not only how gendered assumptions infiltrate plastic surgeons' ideas about what constitutes a beautiful female body, but also how women's own self-worth is deeply connected to men's responses to their physical appearance. Jenna explained:

> You are so vulnerable. I mean, you are going to someone about your breasts—right? You are just like wide open. And [the surgeon] tells you, "That won't look good, that won't look good." And, you are thinking, "Well, this is a man talking. . . ." It is this whole spell you get under of plastic surgery promises.

Jenna and Eleanor's experiences with their plastic surgeons illustrate how women's ideas about how their bodies should look may initially diverge from plastic surgeons' conceptions of the ideal female body. Nevertheless, perceived as both "medical experts" who know what is best for their patients and "artists" who possess the skills necessary to construct ideal gendered traits, plastic surgeons hold the power to influence women's decision to undergo cosmetic surgery.[4]

Reconstructive Surgery Following Mastectomies

Several of the women who had breast reconstruction following a mastectomy also explained that physicians had influenced their decision to undergo surgery with implants. Their doctors began talking about the replacement of their real breast(s) with one(s) made of silicone immediately after they had been diagnosed with cancer. In Kate's case, she was asked to decide whether she wanted reconstructive surgery on the same day she was diagnosed with breast cancer. In hindsight, she believed that she was "more or less in a state of shock" and could not make a sound choice at that time. Brenda, too, was encouraged by her physician to make a decision about receiving breast implants soon after she was told she had cancer. Describing the circumstances under which she decided to have implants, Brenda illustrates how this "choice" was constrained by the medical context that shaped it:

> [After my diagnosis,] I was introduced to the plastic surgeon who was brought in to give me information on the reconstructive procedure. Now, when these doctors explain this surgery to you, you do not necessarily understand it. You don't understand it, your spouse doesn't understand it. . . . I am now so much against doctors encouraging this surgery because I was not mentally all there at that point to make such a decision. Not only was I not mentally correct to make it, but I did not understand what the plastic surgeon was saying to me and the terms he was using. I just went along with it.

Brenda eventually learned that reconstructive surgery involving breast implants can be a long, drawn-out process involving several weeks of physician visits and physical pain. Because women who undergo radical mastectomies are left with no breast tissue, their skin needs to be expanded before an implant can be inserted properly. An expander is placed underneath the skin where the mastectomy is performed and over the course of several weeks is slowly filled with saline solution. Once the skin is sufficiently stretched out, the expander is removed and an implant is inserted. In hindsight, Brenda was certain she would not have opted to receive implants if she had been fully aware of the time and pain involved.

The women who had implants for both reconstructive and cosmetic purposes were not "blindly" duped by the cultural image of ideal female attractiveness. They were perfectly aware of structured inequalities within the larger society as well as prevailing media norms which constrained and limited their own views of female attractiveness. However, most of the women with whom I spoke also did not perceive themselves as creative agents who knowledgeably chose to undergo plastic surgery as a means to take hold of their lives. The descriptions women provided of their reasons for seeking implants suggest that although they participated in the medicalization of femininity by undergoing surgery to reshape or reconstruct their bodies, this participation had more to do with the specific nature of their subordination than their capacity to take action over their life circumstances.

False Expectations

According to Kathy Davis (1995), cosmetic surgery provides women who feel trapped inside bodies that do not fit their sense of self a way to re-negotiate their identities. This interpretation fits with half the experiences reported to me by the women I interviewed. For instance, Joyce, who had undergone breast augmentation over ten years ago, recalled:

> After I had the surgery, for the first time in my life, I really felt like I was a whole person, like everybody else. I had self-confidence and was able to wear anything I wanted. I didn't feel threatened anymore.

According to Joyce and other women with whom I spoke, cosmetic surgery enabled them to move through life with more confidence and pride. Feeling less self-conscious about their appearances, these women conceptually incorporated their new breasts into their sense of self or being. Women who had reconstructive surgery with implants felt similarly. Suzanne, who had a bilateral mastectomy, referred to her new breasts after implantation as her "new girls." She explained that she "really embraced [the implants], taking them into [her] body" as if they truly were a part of her self.

Despite these positive responses toward receiving breast implants, twenty of the forty women I interviewed experienced mixed emotions or a sense of inner conflict soon after their surgeries. For instance, Ann, who had received her implants in the early 1970s, vividly remembered the feelings she experienced during her operation:

> I was awake for the surgery and remembered seeing my reflection in the light and sort of seeing my body cut open. It was very bizarre because they put the screen in front of you so you don't see what is going on, but I watched the surgery from above me. Then, as soon as it was done, I sat up and felt this well of anger. Like, look what *they* had done to me, *they* collectively—the collective world, the whole shebang—that *they* had to just cut up my body and stick these things in me.

As Ann watched her surgeon cut open her body and insert two shiny, silicone-filled plastic bags, she became acutely aware of her feeling that her decision to be on the operating table was not entirely her own—*society* was at fault for making her feel unimportant without larger breasts. Ann explained that she eventually overcame the initial anger she experienced after her surgery and was left with a strange curiosity about having a different body, "this sexy, attractive body." At the same time, however, she explained that she always felt like she was "faking it"—presenting herself as someone who she really was not.

Ironically, while women receive implants in an effort to conform to societal ideas about femininity, some felt uncomfortably obvious and *more* self-conscious about their bodies after receiving implants than prior to surgery. This is another finding that diverges from the results presented in Davis's research (1995). While nearly all of the women Davis interviewed one year after receiving breast implants were delighted with their new bodies, many of the women with whom I spoke felt more like sex objects. Lorraine, for instance, explained that after she received breast implants, her new breasts made her feel like she was on display: "I felt very obvious. I don't feel like they are me, you know?" Lorraine commented on how these feelings affected her social life:

> When I was single and dated fellows, I wouldn't dance close. I was always afraid that they could tell [I had implants] by getting up close, holding somebody close, or anything that gets that way. If nothing else, getting implants was the best birth control—sex shut down.

Not only were many of the women I interviewed dismayed that their breast implants failed to improve their social and sexual lives, but to make matters worse, most of them reported having experienced complications and debilitating symptoms they believe to be related to their implants. Breast implants initially may have given these women the appearance (and for some, the identity) they had always wanted—but at an expensive cost they never could have imagined. Well over half of the women I interviewed suffered extreme losses because their implant-related illnesses prevented them from participating in normal, daily-life activities. Christine's story of loss resonates with the experiences of other women I interviewed. Christine once had a lucrative career as a chiropractor and used to enjoy a number of outdoor sports and activities. She is now on disability and has had to sell her practice because she can barely get herself out of bed in the morning. She explained:

> I don't know who I am anymore, I really have changed so much. I am not the person I used to be. And, it is like—you start thinking to yourself, "I used to do this, I used to do that; I used to love this, I used to love that." Now, I just see myself as a chemically toxic person.

Davis found that her respondents, for as long as a year following their surgeries, continued to perceive their decision to undergo cosmetic surgery as an "empowering" experience. However, the respondents in Davis's follow-up study—aside from the case of "Irene," who had her implants for over 15 years and had multiple surgeries and symptoms (pp.149–153)—did not experience the extent of pain, discomfort and illness described by the women I interviewed. Do women who experience debilitating autoimmune symptoms continue to feel that they made the right choice given their circumstances? Or do they feel that perhaps they were not fully aware of the larger cultural forces at work when they made their decision? Contrary to Davis's findings, most of the women I interviewed deeply regretted their decision to reshape their bodies and felt they had, in a sense, fallen prey to a society that places more value on a woman's appearance than her health.

Responses to Medical Uncertainty

When the women I interviewed began to associate their symptoms with their breast implants in the early 1990s, they were frightened about their future health and turned to medicine, hoping to disentangle the "medical facts" from the "sensationalist media hype." They had faith in medicine and trusted their physicians to provide them with accurate and definitive answers about health, illness, and disease causation. Nevertheless, they explained that the more they approached medical "experts" with questions about breast implants and their worsening symptoms, the more disillusioned and disappointed they became—rather than providing them with "reasonable" explanations to account for their deteriorating health, physicians minimized and dismissed women's fears and anxieties as well as their physical symptoms. In particular, women claimed that their doctors tended to normalize and psychologize their implant-related troubles.

"It's No Big Deal"

Despite the fear and anxiety women endured after experiencing unforeseen complications related to their implants, such as ruptures, infections, hardening and inflammation of their breasts, physicians responded to these problems by treating them as normal and common effects of breast implants which they expected women to tolerate. For instance, when Barbara's breasts had hardened after her surgery, she returned to her plastic surgeon, who told her, "That is the way your breasts are supposed to look."

Similarly, women explained that their doctors described the procedures and surgeries that were necessary to "fix" their implant-related problems as normal, safe, and standardized forms of care when, in fact, they eventually led to further complications. For instance, Jenna explained that about a month after she had received saline implants in 1989, her left implant dislodged and shifted up into her armpit. Although she was startled, her plastic surgeon was "very unimpressed" by the problem and treated it as if it were "no big deal." He simply told Jenna that he would replace her implants with silicone devices, which he said were "less likely to move around and encapsulate." Trusting her surgeon's advice, Jenna agreed to this surgery. However, soon thereafter she began to experience a wide range of symptoms, including chronic fatigue, fevers, and hair loss. Jenna now believes that these symptoms were associated with her body's immunological response to her "new and improved" implants.

In some cases, women claimed that their physicians responded to their implant-related complications by withholding important medical information from them. For instance, Frances had received silicone implants in 1977 following a bilateral mastectomy. By 1979, her implants had encapsulated, causing her breasts to become hard, painful, and deformed. In response to this problem, Frances's plastic surgeon said not to worry, that he could replace her silicone implants with saline implants, which he said were intended to prevent the reoccurrence of encapsulation. In the 1990s, Frances learned through reading her medical records that her silicone implants had ruptured. Her surgeon had never conveyed this information to her. While most of the women with whom I spoke who experienced similar acts of miscommunication from their physicians were angry and outraged, France was not. She simply explained: "Well, you know, back then [ruptured implants] were probably no big deal."

Frances's comment implicitly points to the fact that, in the 1970s, leading medical journals had yet to address the safety of breast implants. Prior to the 1990s, only a small number of rheumatology and immunology journals had published research demonstrating a connection between silicone and rheumatic disorders. Concerned with only the latest developments in their own field of specialization, most plastic surgeons probably were unaware of these studies (Vasey and Feldstein 1993) and simply chose the type of implant they thought worked best or produced the best "cosmetic result" without rupturing or encapsulating. For instance, some surgeons used polyurethane-covered implants, since their textured envelopes (which scientists later suspected to be carcinogenic) were assumed to prevent hardening and produce a more natural feel than other implants on the market. However, by the 1990s, as scientific studies increasingly called into question the safety of these and other silicone gel-filled implants, saline implants became the preferred implant among many plastic surgeons. Now, even these devices have come under scrutiny— the FDA has launched an investigation of their safety, and consumer advocacy groups are urging the government to restrict their use.

Women's descriptions of their experiences with plastic surgeons demonstrate how the knowledge about the risks and benefits associated with different types of implants has been continuously evolving[5] (i.e., in the 1970s, Frances's surgeon replaced her encapsulated silicone implants with saline ones which, according to him, were the "greatest" implants on the market; yet, in the 1980s, Jenna's plastic surgeon dealt with her failed saline implants by replacing them with "better" silicone prostheses which he said were less likely to shift around and become hard). Moreover, they illustrate how physicians deal with the ambiguous and uncertain qualities of medicine by normalizing their patients' troubles. Rather than conveying to women that the risks associated with breast implants are indefinite and vague, plastic surgeons responded to women's implant-related complications by telling them that the troubles they were experiencing were normal and common side effects which warranted no concern. Surgeons also led women to believe that the surgeries used to treat encapsulated and ruptured implants were standardized forms of care. However, the perceived risks and benefits of these medical interventions also are uncertain.

Gendered Medical Language

When these women discovered that their "minor" implant-related complications could have been signs of serious trouble, they found fault in their physicians for "intentionally" withholding information from them. However, blaming physicians ignores the complex process through which predominating beliefs about medical science interact with cultural assumptions about gender, shaping the ways in which physicians have responded to women's problems with implants. In particular, the language physicians used to divert attention away from the uncertainty of women's problems with breast implants is infused with images of failed, degraded, and defective female bodies.

The research of a number of feminist scholars demonstrates a male-dominated perspective in modern medicine. For instance, the biologist Anne Fausto-Sterling (1992) suggests that since Western medical science traditionally has appointed the male reproductive life cycle as "normal," any aspect of female reproduction which deviates from the male's has been viewed as "abnormal" (p. 121). Consequently, a wide range of normal female bodily processes, including menopause and menstruation, have been defined by medical and scientific experts as disease states. Similarly, in her cultural analysis of reproduction, Emily Martin (1992) describes how medical textbooks depict menstruation:

> The fall in blood progesterone and estrogen "deprives" the "highly developed endometrial lining of its hormonal support," "constriction" of blood vessels leads to a "diminished" supply of oxygen and nutrients, and finally "disintegration starts, the entire lining begins to slough, and the menstrual flow begins." (Vander et al., quoted in Martin, p. 45)

This description is replete with images of failed functions, deprivation, and decline. Susan Bell (1987) found similar imagery in scientific papers on menopause that explained this natural bodily process in terms of a "deficiency disease."

Bell (1988) interviewed a woman whose prenatal exposure to diethylstilbestrol (DES) prevented her from carrying her pregnancy to term, but whose physician attributed her miscarriage to her "incompetent cervix"—a term that "blames the victim for the problem" (p.107). My respondents' descriptions of their physicians' responses to their ruptured and encapsulated breast implants were replete with similar language. For instance, when Karen's breasts hardened after receiving breast implants, her surgeon implied that her body was at fault—not her implants: "When I began to experience the hardening, the surgeon made it seem as if there was something wrong with my body."

In Jane's case, her physician not only blamed her body for her implant-related complication but, in so doing, disregarded the potential seriousness of her problem. After Jane returned home from an appointment for her annual mammogram, she received a phone call from her primary-care physician. The purpose of his call was to inform Jane that one of her implants had ruptured:

> He calls me up on the phone and he says, "Well, it looks like you sprung a leak." I said, "Excuse me, who is this?" and he says, "This is Dr. Jones." And I said, "Sprung a leak? What are you talking about?" And he goes, "Your mammogram. You have breast implants, don't you?"

Cultural assumptions about female bodies as inherently "flawed" pervade the logic which guides this description of Jane's problem:

Jane's *implant* did not "spring a leak"—her own body did. Such a description attributes blame to Jane's body. Moreover, by focusing solely on the results of her mammogram, Jane's physician treated her body as if it were separate and detached from her self.[6] Consequently, he failed to consider how Jane might react to the discovery that her implant had ruptured and that she would need additional surgery to remove it. In response, Jane was angry and upset.

"If It's Not in Your Body, It Must Be in Your Head"

The women I interviewed were angry at their physicians, not only for treating their ruptured and encapsulated implants as minor and common complications but also for failing to take seriously their strange progression of symptoms. In particular, physicians minimized their implant-related troubles by relegating them to the realms of psychological or emotional complaints. In fact, 23 percent of the 34 women in my sample who reported experiencing implant-related symptoms reported that they were referred to psychiatric care. Many of these women said that their doctors had diligently performed tests for lupus, rheumatoid arthritis, and various other immunological disorders; however, since the results of these lab reports almost always came back "normal," physicians were unable to attribute women's symptoms to any known medical or physiological condition. Consequently, they proceeded to tell their patients that that their *real* problems were in their heads, not in their bodies. Abby, who runs a support group for women with breast implants, commented:

> Everyone [in our group] was all feeling the same way, but when we went to the doctors, we were told "you are going through menopause" or "you need to see a psychiatrist." They just don't associate implants with the sickness we have.

Abby said that her doctors, too, misdiagnosed her implant-related symptoms as signs of early menopause.

The descriptions of medical mistreatment shared by the women I interviewed resonate with social science research which suggests that women patients, in general, are not taken seriously and are viewed as "overemotional," "neurotic," "difficult" and unable to understand complicated medical explanations (Wallen 1979; Todd 1989; Fisher 1986). In response to this type of treatment, the women I interviewed had become disillusioned with medical care, claiming that their physicians used their professional authority to minimize their troubles and "put them in their place" to protect their reputations. However, such an explanation fails to take into account how cultural assumptions about gender interact with predominating beliefs about medicine, continually creating tensions between doctors and their female patients.

Modern medicine is characterized by a tendency of medical specialists to focus on separate and isolated physiological processes and by the belief that disease causation can be understood in a context in which bodies are fragmented into isolated parts to be treated and cured. Women's responses to their implant-related symptoms illustrate how the cultural assumption that women are inherently overemotional interacts with this dominant medical perspective. The women with whom I spoke explained that they visited many different doctors about the symptoms they experienced after receiving breast implants; however, none of the doctors linked their worsening health to these devices. Eleanor, for instance, began experiencing numerous debilitating symptoms after her surgery with implants:

> I saw an immunologist, an internist, and was under the care of a urologist. A lot of specialized people looking at one little thing and not looking at the whole picture. All these doctors keep everything so separate. . . . You know, in hindsight, how could nobody even say, "Gee, Eleanor just had her breasts reconstructed with implants"—that was never written in these doctors' reports. They could have written that I had just had surgery and that possibly my body was having an autoimmune reaction. . . . but there was no connection made.

The inability of Eleanor's doctors to understand her health troubles outside the narrow scope of their own medical specialties resulted in their belief that Eleanor's problem must be psychological, not physical: she was subsequently referred to a psychiatrist for care.

Responses to the Scientific Evidence

To Eleanor and other women, the relationship between their exposure to silicone and their worsening health seemed all too obvious for their physicians to miss. Yet, at the same time, epidemiological and scientific studies consistently have found no evidence of a significant relationship between implants and disease. For example, the results of the Mayo Clinic study on implant-related risk "do not support an association between breast implants and connective-tissue diseases or other disorders that were studied" (Gabriel et al. 1994, p. 1702). Similarly, every investigation on the long-term health effects of silicone breast implants presented in a recent volume of the

Journal of Clinical Epidemiology found no evidence of an increased risk among implant recipients of disease.[7]

In order to explain the distinction between the results of these studies and anecdotal evidence which suggests a link between illness and breast implants, the women I interviewed alluded to a political bias in the production of scientific knowledge. For instance, some women believed that studies on implant-related risk were biased, since they were funded either by plastic surgeons' associations or implant manufacturers,[8] or were conducted by researchers who were consultants to law firms representing implant manufacturers in lawsuits brought by women who believed they had been harmed by the devices.[9] Recognizing these possible biases, one interviewee, Paula, exclaimed:

> All the studies [on implant-related risk] that are being done should not be funded by the manufacturers and plastic surgeons—they shouldn't be paying for it! Maybe the government should be putting in the money so that no strings are attached, and so that researchers can really study the *women* and not base their research on looking at their old records and seeing what their records say, because the records are false or inaccurate half the time.

This remark is directed specifically at the Mayo Clinic study, which was based on a comparative analysis of 749 medical records of women who had breast implants and 1,498 who were not implanted with these devices. Paula's criticism implies that research based solely on medical records rather than on interviews with patients may be entirely futile, since physicians tend to record only information they view as "medically relevant" and not information based on women's own descriptions of how they feel. Rebecca's description of her plastic surgeon's response to the pain she was experiencing in her chest, arms, and ribs after receiving implants further illustrates this possibility:

> Nobody really seemed to be concerned about anything—particularly the plastic surgeon, never. I don't think he ever even wrote [anything] down—you know, we would discuss it, but I never saw him write down that I was having any pains. . . . When I described this, I remember vividly his saying to me on several occasions, "No one else has ever complained of that," or "I haven't heard that problem." And it would always—I would leave his office and I would always ask myself, "How can he say that?— he isn't even writing down what I'm saying." So, if he's not documenting what I'm saying, then there's no evidence that anyone [else] has had any problems [laughs] because it's just not there.

Our culture assumes that knowledge based on scientific "facts" is more accurate and precise than knowledge based on life experiences. However, some of my interviewees believed that the scientific evidence on implants was shaped by larger political and economic contexts. Feminist scholar Evelyn Fox Keller (1992) similarly asserts that scientific knowledge is never objective but inescapably value-laden, since it is always "shaped by our choices—first, of what to seek representations *of*, and second, of what to seek representations *for*" (p. 5). Many of my respondents believed that their physicians resisted acknowledging a possible link between implants and disease because they were afraid of losing profits and jeopardizing their professional reputations. In effect, they preferred to rely on "biased" scientific evidence which consistently reported that implants are safe, rather than give credibility to women's reports of their worsening physical symptoms. Perceived as medically irrelevant, these symptoms never were recorded in women's medical evaluations and, therefore, according to certain studies, never even existed.

Another criticism of scientific research on breast implants has been that most studies have focused only on classical forms of immunological disorders or connective-tissue diseases such as rheumatoid arthritis, lupus, scleroderma, and Sjogren's syndrome.[10] Women with breast implants, on the other hand, seem to have atypical forms of autoimmune illnesses such as chronic fatigue syndrome and fibromyalgia, which are extremely difficult to diagnose.

Frank Vasey, a rheumatologist who has seen many cases of women with breast implants experiencing autoimmune-type symptoms, suggests that while implant recipients do not test positive for classical forms of disease, their symptoms are nevertheless consistent with those characterized by these conditions. In fact, many of the women I interviewed who were experiencing chronic fatigue, general achiness, hair loss, and a variety of other vague symptoms explained that their physicians diligently tested them for immunological diseases and connective-tissue diseases; however, the results of these tests almost always came back "normal." Vasey suggests that women with implants may be experiencing a new form of illness he refers to as "silicone disease." Single lab tests cannot confirm the presence of this illness, simply because the technology does not exist. As a result, "physicians have not been able to identify the disease in their patients and therefore have instituted a long chain of blind testing and trial medications" (Vasey and Feldstein 1993, p. 13). Or, as many of my respondents believe, when physicians are unable to attribute women's symptoms to any known medical condition, they relegate them to the realms of reproductive malfunctions or emotional problems.

Transforming Identities

Despite the scientific evidence which suggests that the relationship between breast implants and disease is "insignificant," the majority of the women I interviewed were convinced that their worsening health was related to their implants. After repeated visits with physicians who consistently failed to take their symptoms and implant-related complications seriously, they became angry and disillusioned with medical care, believing that the entire medical community was collaborating to keep their troubles silent. Through the help of support groups and by speaking to women with breast implants who experienced similar types of symptoms and concerns as their own, these women broke away from the dominant medical perspective which perpetuated the view that their troubles were all in their heads and not in their bodies. They learned to recognize the limitations of medical and scientific knowledge as they gradually placed trust in their own intuition about the source of their troubles. Through the process of educating themselves and taking a more active role in their health-care decisions, the women with whom I spoke ironically became empowered by their illness experiences.

Tracy, for instance, explained:

> My experience with implants has taught me an awful lot. It has changed me in many ways. It has made me feistier and not afraid of anything. . . . It has made me stronger to speak out and question—I am more self-assured. And I realize that a lot of people that I am talking to who I thought were bright, really are not—and that I am actually very bright. You know, it makes you feel differently about the way you see yourself and see others.

However, not all of the women in my sample felt "empowered" or perceived themselves as active agents capable of taking charge over their life circumstances. Some women, in fact, felt *powerless* after they began experiencing implant-related health problems. Barbara, for example, was experiencing many of the negative health effects associated with implants. However, her busy work schedule along with her poor economic situation prevented her from dwelling on the extent of her pain and discomfort. She was more concerned with how she was going to make it through each day, given her poor financial situation, than with how she was going to cope with her physical troubles. Consequently, she chose not to probe into the roots of her health troubles. Other women resisted acknowledging a possible link between their poor health and their implants because they did not want to confront the prospect of removal surgery or returning to a "flat-chested" body.

The women convinced that their implants were related to their worsening health confessed that they, too, went through periods of denial and disbelief before taking actions to improve their life circumstances. These women became "empowered" only after they had made the conscious decision to educate themselves about the long-term negative health effects of silicone and were able to find support through networking with other implant recipients. Their experiences suggest that the degree to which "agency" accounts for women's involvement with surgery to enhance the size or shape of their breasts varies among women and can change over the course of one's experiences with implants.

Bookman and Morgen (1988) argue that empowerment "begins when [women] change their ideas about the causes of their powerlessness, when they recognize the systemic forces that oppress them, and when they act to change the conditions of their lives" (p. 40). Similarly, my respondents who had decided to take their lives into their own hands and learn more about implant-related risk did so only after beginning to link their lack of knowledge to the oppressive structure of the society in which they lived. These women had developed different approaches to experiencing "empowerment." For many, empowerment involved transforming their identities from that of passive patients who once assumed that medicine was capable of providing definitive and accurate information about health, illness, and disease causation, to that of health-care activists who acknowledged the fallibility of medicine. For others, it meant reconceptualizing their sense of self as "feminine" as they began to confront the possibility of implant removal. Gayle, for example, explained how her removal surgery influenced the meaning she attributed to "femininity":

> I have to assume that part of what I used to consider feminine was tied up into how my body looked. Otherwise, I wouldn't have had the implants. Um, today, that is not where my femininity is. It is inside now. It is in my heart, in my spirituality. And my body is just a housing for that.

For many women, empowerment also involved transforming their relationships with others. Once women were able to accept themselves, despite their scarred and sometimes disfigured bodies, they began relinquishing their ties with those in their lives who had contributed to their own negative self-image. These women found more meaningful relationships with individuals who appreciated who they were, rather than how they appeared. For instance, Sophie, who mistakenly believed that receiving implants would save her marriage to a man who constantly ridiculed her about her "flat chest," eventually met a man who cared for her even after she had developed debilitating symptoms and had undergone surgery to have her implants removed. She remarked, "Now I realize that a man can still love me and still see me as a woman without my having large breasts."

Although empowerment may have been experienced differently by these women, it almost always involved their recognition of the larger cultural and systemic forces that influenced their decision to seek breast implants. At the time the women opted to receive implants, they had believed that they were taking the best course of action to relieve their personal suffering. In hindsight, however, they began to question the system of beliefs that shaped their understandings of femininity, as well as their expectations of medicine and science. These women came to the conclusion that they, in a sense, had been the passive victims of ideological manipulation—they had falsely assumed that their sexual and social lives would improve if they adhered to a cultural standard of femininity, that medical experts could provide them with a safe and simple solution for improving their self-images, and that medical and scientific knowledge is accurate, complete, and certain. Recognizing the fallibility of these assumptions, women came to view their decision to reconstruct or reshape their bodies not as a "choice" but as an action taken under cultural conditions which constrained and limited the ways in which they thought about health, illness, and the female body. This new level of awareness led women to find richer, more fulfilling and meaningful ways of leading their lives.

Conclusion

Feminist scholars have explored how natural female reproductive processes such as pregnancy, menstruation, and menopause have come under medical scrutiny (Riessman 1983; Rothman 1991; Martin 1992). Other researchers have focused on the social and historical contexts which shape prevailing beliefs about female beauty (Bordo 1993; Chapkis 1986), or on women's personal involvement with beauty practices such as cosmetic surgery (Davis 1995). However, recent scholarship has not made an extensive effort to bridge the gap between these bodies of literature. In this chapter, I have attempted to accomplish this task by describing the process through which female breast size and shape have come under medical scrutiny and the implications of this for breast implant recipients. I have shown how this process is dependent upon the prevailing system of beliefs which links a woman's bodily appearance to her self-concept as feminine, while conveying the message that medicine is capable of employing quick, simple and safe surgical solutions for her troubles.

This research also calls attention to problems inherent within the structure of modern medicine and the nature of the doctor-patient relationship. Women's descriptions of their implant-related experiences suggest that in a cultural context which perpetuates the belief that biomedicine holds all the answers about health, illness, and disease causation, misunderstandings and miscommunications between doctors and patients are inevitable. Even though medical knowledge is uncertain, ambiguous, and continuously evolving, in our society it is presumed to be infallible. Similarly, physicians who are medical "experts" are expected to possess definitive information about the devices they use and the procedures they perform. This study has demonstrated how these beliefs transcend the ways in which physicians present information about medical procedures and devices to their patients. It suggests that patients need to be educated about the limitations of medical knowledge so that they can take a more active role in making their own health-care decisions.

Women's experiences with implants also have illuminated ways in which increased specialization and technological determinism have distanced doctors' understandings of their patients' troubles. These developments have permitted physicians to focus on specific anatomical parts or single bodily processes to improve their understanding of disease etiologies. However, they also have perpetuated the idea that disease causation can be explained solely by perceiving the human body as a conglomeration of fragmented parts to be manipulated and cured, and by relying on diagnostic tests to verify whether patients are truly sick. This reliance leads to inevitable tensions between patients who are certain that something is wrong with them and physicians who base their knowledge about health and illness on quantifiable, scientific "fact."

Finally, this analysis has shown how women themselves can work toward changing the structure of modern medicine and the asymmetrical power relationship between doctors and patients. The majority of women in this study learned to question their physicians' expertise and professional authority and, in the process, began to take more responsibility over their own health-care decisions. Indeed, many of them even became active in health-care politics, writing to their legislators about the dangers of implants, organizing rallies and networking with support groups. Through actions such as these, individuals can learn to recognize the limitations of medical and scientific knowledge and trust their own ways of knowing about health and illness.

Notes

[1] The settlement eventually was deemed underfunded by at least $3 billion and eventually fell apart. Moreover, in 1995 Dow Corning Corporation filed for bankruptcy, freezing implant litigation against the company. Four years later, on December 1, 1999, a federal judge approved Dow Corning's $4.5 billion plan to emerge from bankruptcy, including a $3.2 billion settlement for breast implant recipients.

[2] One woman refused to be recorded, explaining she felt uncomfortable with the idea that I would have a tape of her private, personal experiences. In this case, I relied on note taking and memory to recall the details of the interview.

[3] Of the total population of implant recipients, an estimated 20% receive implants for reconstructive purposes and 80% receive them for cosmetic reasons (Angell 1992).

[4] See Dull and West (1991) for an interesting analysis of how surgeons who perform cosmetic surgery account for their activities.

[5] Bell (1997) develops a similar argument in relation to the risks and benefits associated with diethylstilbestrol (DES).

[6] Jane's experience also illustrates the tendency of physicians to distance themselves from daily life experiences, feelings and understandings. Mishler (1981) argues that this type of distancing is an inherent goal of medical practice.

[7] See Engel et al. 1995; Morgan and Elcock 1995; Deapen and Brody 1995; Hochberg et al. 1995; and Goldman et al. 1995.

[8] For instance, the Mayo Clinic study (Gabriel et al. 1994) was supported by grants from the Plastic Surgery Educational Foundation, and studies conducted by Goldman et al. (1995) and Hennekens et al. (1996) were partially funded by Dow Corning Corporation.

[9] Two of three authors of a study which found no evidence of a relationship between silicone and rheumatic disorders (Sanchez-Guerro et al. 1994) were consultants to law firms. See Haney (1994) for details of this possible bias.

[10] See Kolata (1996) for a discussion of this criticism.

References

Angell, Marcia. 1992. "Breast Implants—Protection or Paternalism?" Editorial. *The New England Journal of Medicine* 326:1695–1698.

Baker, Nancy C. 1984. *The Beauty Trap: Exploring Woman's Greatest Obsession.* New York: Franklin Watts.

Bell, Susan. 1987. "Changing Ideas: The Medicalization of Menopause." *Social Science and Medicine* 24:535–542.

————. 1988. "Becoming a Political Woman: The Reconstruction and Interpretation of Experience through Stories," pp. 97–123 in Alexandra Dundas Todd and Sue Fisher, eds., *Gender and Discourse: The Power of Talk*. Norwood: Ablex Publishing.

————. 1997. "Technology Assessment, Outcome Data and Social Context: The Case of Hormone Therapy," in Boyle, P., ed., *Getting Doctors to Listen*. Washington, DC: Georgetown University Press.

Bookman, Ann and Sandra Morgen. 1988. *Women and the Politics of Empowerment*. Philadelphia: Temple University Press.

Bordo, Susan. 1990. "Reading the Slender Body," pp. 83–112 in Mary Jacobus, Evelyn Fox Keller, and Sally Shuttleworth, eds., *Body Politics: Women and the Discourse of Science*. New York: Routledge.

————. 1993. *Unbearable Weight: Feminism, Western Culture and the Body*. Berkeley and Los Angeles: University of California Press.

Burton, Thomas. 1993. "Breast Implants Raise More Safety Issues." *The Wall Street Journal*, 4 Feb.

Chapkis, Wendy. 1986. *Beauty Secrets: Women and the Politics of Appearance*. Boston: South End Press.

Davis, Kathy. 1991. "Remaking the She-Devil: A Critical Look at Feminist Approaches to Beauty." *Hypatia* 6:23.

————, 1993. "Cultural Dopes and She-Devils: Cosmetic Surgery as Ideological Dilemma," pp. 23–47 in Kathy Davis and Sue Fisher, eds., *Negotiating at the Margins: The Gendered Discourses of Power and Resistance*. New Brunswick: Rutgers University Press.

————, 1995. *Reshaping The Female Body: The Dilemma of Cosmetic Surgery*. New York: Routledge.

Deapen, Dennis and Garry Brody. 1995. "Augmentation Mammaplasty and Breast Cancer: A Five-Year Update of the Los Angeles Study." *Journal of Clinical Epidemiology* 48:551–556.

Dull, Diana and Candace West. 1991. "Accounting for Cosmetic Surgery: The Accomplishment of Gender." *Social Problems* 38:54–95.

Engel, Arnold, Steven Lamm, and Sheghan Lai. 1995. "Human Breast Sarcoma and Human Breast Implantation." *Journal of Clinical Epidemiology* 48:539–544.

Fausto-Sterling, Anne. 1992. *Myths of Gender: Biological Theories about Women and Men*. New York: Basic Books.

Fisher, Jack. 1992. "The Silicone Controversy: When Will Science Prevail?" Editorial. *New England Journal of Medicine* 326:196–198.

Fisher, Sue. 1986. *In the Patient's Best Interest: Women and the Politics of Medical Decisions*. New Brunswick: Rutgers University Press.

Gabriel, Sherine, Michael O'Fallon, Leonard Kurland, Mary Beard, John Woods, and Joseph Melton. 1994. "Risk of Connective Tissue Disease and Other Disorders after Breast Implantation." *The New England Journal of Medicine* 330:1697–1702.

Goldman, John, Jesse Greenblatt, Ron Joines, Leslie White, Bruce Aylward, and Steven Lamm. 1995. "Breast Implants, Rheumatoid Arthritis, and Connective Tissue Disease in a Clinical Practice." *Journal of Clinical Epidemiology* 48:571–582.

Haney, Daniel. 1994. "Medical Editor's Role as Expert Paid by Lawyers is Scrutinized." *The Boston Globe*, 12 Dec.

Hennekens, Charles, I-Min Lee, Nancy Cook, Patricia Herbert, Elizabeth Karlson, Fran LaMotte, JoAnn Manson, and Julie Buring. 1996. "Self-Reported Breast Implants and Connective Tissue Diseases in Female Health Professionals: A Retrospective Cohort Study." *JAMA* 275:616–621.

Hilts, Philip J. 1992a. "Company to Release Data Questioning Implant Safety." *The New York Times*, 23 Jan.

———. 1992b. "Silicone: Friend or Foe?: Strange History of Silicone Held Many Warning Signs." *The New York Times*, 18 Jan.

Hochberg, Marc, Robyn Miller, and Fredrick Wigley. 1995. "Frequency of Augmentation Mammoplasty in Patients with Systemic Sclerosis: Data from the John's Hopkins-University of Maryland Scleroderma Center." *Journal of Clinical Epidemiology* 48:565–569.

Human Resources and Intergovernmental Relations Subcommittee of the Committee on Governmental Operations, (HRIRSCGO). 1993. *The FDA's Regulation of Silicone Breast Implants*. Washington, DC: Government Printing Office.

Jacobus, Mary, Evelyn Fox Keller, and Sally Shuttleworth. 1990. *Body/Politics: Women and the Discourses of Science*. New York: Routledge.

Jaggar, Alison and Susan Bordo, eds. 1989. *Gender/Body/Knowledge*. New Brunswick: Rutgers University Press.

Keller, Evelyn Fox. 1992. *Secrets of Life and Death: Essays on Language, Gender and Science*. New York: Routledge.

Kolata, Gina. 1996. "Study Cites Small Risks for Women From Breast Implants." *The New York Times*, 28 Feb.

Martin Emily. 1992. *The Woman in the Body: A Cultural Analysis of Reproduction*, 2nd ed. Boston: Beacon Press.

Millman, Marcia. 1980. *Such a Pretty Face*. New York: Berkeley Books.

Mishler Elliot. 1981. "Critical Perspectives on the Biomedical Model," pp. 153–166 in Phil Brown, ed., *Perspectives in Medical Sociology*, 1st ed. Belmont: Wadsworth.

Morgan, Robert and Maryellen Elcock. 1995. "Artificial Implants and Soft Tissue Sarcomas." *Journal of Clinical Epidemiology* 48:545–549.

Reuter. 1993. "Dow Corning Cites Subpoena for Falsified Implant Data." *The Boston Globe*, 18 Feb.

Riessman, Catherine Kohler. 1983. "Women and Medicalization: A New Perspective," pp. 190–220 in Phil Brown, ed., *Perspectives in Medical Sociology*, 1st ed. Belmont: Wadsworth.

Rothman, Barbara Katz. 1991. *In Labor: Women and Power in the Birthplace*. New York: W.W. Norton and Company.

Sanchez-Guerro, J., P. H. Schur, and M. H. Liang. 1994. "Silicone Breast Implants and Rheumatic Disease." *Arthritis and Rheumatism* 37:158–168.

Todd, Alexandra Dundas. 1989. *Intimate Adversaries: Cultural Conflict between Doctors and Women Patients*. Philadelphia: University of Pennsylvania Press.

Vasey, Frank and Josh Feldstein. 1993. *The Silicone Breast Implant Controversy: What Women Need to Know*. Freedom: The Crossing Press.

Wallen, J. 1979. "Physician Stereotypes about Female Health and Illness." *Women and Health* 4:135–146.

Section V

Interaction and Negotiation Between Patients and Providers

Although the study of doctor-patient interaction has a long tradition in medical sociology, the classic thrust was to increase patient compliance with doctor's orders, and, relatedly, to increase patient satisfaction. This earlier work tended to avoid qualitative observations and fieldwork, in favor of discrete quantitative measurement of variables such as level of comprehension, symptoms reporting, understanding of prescriptions, and anxiety. This work also also tended to focus on the microcosm of the interaction, without attention to the larger social context that affects it.

Recent approaches to interaction and negotiation take a more critical standpoint. They are not concerned primarily, if at all, with increasing the efficiency of the medical system. Rather, they are attempting to understand the social dynamics of medical interactions in their own right. The goal of the research is more likely to be empowerment of patients than greater efficiency for practitioners. In order to capture the complexity of the problem, recent studies of interaction and negotiation typically involve ethnographic fieldwork where scholars immerse themselves in the field. Qualitative observations sometimes are accompanied by coding of encounters, and even administration of standardized questionaires. Researchers focus on issues such as: who raises questions and who gives answers, what level of information is requested by patients and disclosed by providers, what linguistic devices are used to control the situation, what biases are introduced as a result of patients' social backgrounds, and if and how the parties reach agreement.

Eliot Freidson's "The Social Organization of Illness" starts off this section by noting how institutional settings impose their own organization on the social behavior of illness. He then explores various typologies of doctor-patient interaction, showing how they vary according to illness type, practice style, and lay perceptions. Fre-

283

idson concludes that medical interaction is always conflictful to some degree, and that for this reason we usually observe a *negotiation* process between the two parties. Negotiation can involve determination of symptom severity, the actual diagnosis of disease, treatment choices, and future restrictions or limitations.

In "Infantilization: The Medical Model of Care," Karen Lyman writes of the highly stressful job of caring for elderly dementia patients. Staff adapt to this task by treating the patients as if they were children, but this leads to excessive social control and has detrimental effects on the patients. In this selection we observe not only the dyadic interaction between staff and patients, but also the institutional basis of such interaction. Especially since the institution is taking care of stigmatized people, it is easy for it to allow and foster such negative forms of what should be helping relationships.

14
The Social Organization of Illness

Eliot Freidson

The Institutional Organization of Responses to Illness

Remembering that for the sociologist, medical treatment constitutes one kind of societal reaction to a type of deviance, the essential fact bearing on the organization of illness in institutions is that the staff, unlike the patient himself or his lay associates, is performing a job. For the job to be performed at all requires some administrative routine, and it requires the reduction of individual patients to administrative and treatment classes, all members in each class to be managed by much the same set of routines. If the job is to be performed to the satisfaction of the staff, procedures that minimize interference with their routine and maximize their convenience are required.

Consequently, we find that there are standard administrative courses through which a patient is likely to travel in spite of variation in his condition from others in the same treatment category. Rosengren and DeVault[1] observed that in one lying-in hospital the staff attempted to maintain a definite spatial and temporal organization of its work irrespective of individual variations in condition. In the traditional movement from admitting office, to prep room, labor room, delivery room, and finally the lying-in room, no step was skipped even when the patient was well past the need of it; instead, she was moved through the step more rapidly than otherwise. By the same token, the staff tolerated the expression of pain by the patient only in the delivery room, where it was considered appropriate to the "illness" and where it could be managed by anesthetic: elsewhere, it was deprecated and ridiculed. And in order to maintain the "routine" tempo of work flow established by the staff, laggard women were helped along (with forceps and other techniques) to get them to deliver on schedule.

Reprinted by permission of the University of Chicago Press, from *Profession of Medicine* by Eliot Freidson, pp. 312–22. Copyright © 1970, 1988 by Eliot Freidson.

Another example of the way the staff imposes standardized organization on the course of treatment (and therefore the social course of illness) is to be found in Roth's observations of the way the staff in tuberculosis hospitals has a conception of how long it "should" take to get cured that is imposed on the clinical course of the individual's illness, organizing the progressive steps of managing the illness on the basis of the normative timetable rather than on the results of laboratory tests that may be taken to reflect the biological status of the illness "itself."[2] And I cannot fail to mention, finally, that mordant analysis by Roth of the circumstances in which tuberculosis was and was not treated as infectious.[3]

In the process whereby the treatment institution can impose its own organization on the social behavior connected with illness, two prominent characteristics facilitate staff control. First, the patient may be isolated from the lay community and those of his associates who are concerned with his welfare. Contact with the lay world is rationed where possible. While there may be medical reasons for such isolation, it is frequently a matter of administrative convenience, minimizing "bother" for the staff more than protecting the patient from disturbance. The social consequences are to isolate the patient from the sources of social leverage that supported him while in ambulatory consultation and that could sustain his resistance to the therapeutic routine in the institution. Second, and more important, is the tendency of the staff of all such institutions to carefully avoid giving the patient or his lay associates much information about the illness and what is supposed to be done for it. Virtually every study of patients in hospital points out how ignorant of condition, prognosis, and the medically prescribed regimen are both the patients and their relatives and how reluctant is the staff to give such information.[4] In Davis' words, describing staff behavior toward parents of children stricken with poliomyelitis, the parent's questions were "hedged, evaded, rechannelled, or left unanswered."[5]

As Davis noted in his analysis, the staff's reluctance to give information is often explained as a desire to avoid an emotional scene with the parents. Sometimes, as Glaser and Strauss note in the case of the dying patient, the staff withholds information in the belief, based on "clinical experience," that it will protect the patient and his family from shock and excessive grief.[6] Sometimes this reluctance to give information is explained by a genuine uncertainty, so that no really reliable information is available. However, as Davis has noted in detail, "in many illnesses . . . 'uncertainty' is to some extent feigned by the doctor for the purpose of gradually getting the patient ultimately to accept or put up with a state-of-being that initially is intolerable to him."[7] Whatever the reason, however, the net effect of the withholding of information is to minimize the possibility that the patient can exercise much control over the way he is treated. If he does not know that he is supposed to have a yellow pill every four hours, he cannot comment on the fact that it is sometimes overlooked and insist on getting it regularly. And if he does not know that his condition normally responds to a given treatment in a week, he cannot insist on a consultation after several weeks have passed without change in condition or treatment.[8]

A great deal more can be said about the institutional shaping of illness, particularly in qualification of the point I have been trying to make here. Not all treatment institutions are the same, nor are all patients or treatment staffs. For example, the rehabilitation institution studied by Roth and Eddy[9] had a particularly powerful influence on the course of illness behavior because its patients were largely supported by public funds and lacked effective advocates from the community outside. They rarely, therefore, "got well enough" to leave. This helplessness is somewhat tempered by the fact that in rehabilitation, tuberculosis, and other institutions, many patients have similar illnesses and are in a position to socialize and organize each other. When these conditions exist, the patients are able to develop a common conception of the way their illness should be managed and to generate the influence required to impose some of their own conceptions on the staff.[10] Furthermore, institutions can be dominated by a staff ideology which specifies that the patient participate in his treatment. In fact, there are a number of patterns of interaction that reflect the degree of influence and activity allowed the patient in the course of his treatment and that express the meaning of his illness to himself and to those treating him.

Patterns of Interaction in Treatment

I have already suggested that when in treatment in a client-dependent practice, interaction will be fairly free between doctor and patient, the latter initiating and controlling some part of it. Conversely, when in treatment in a colleague-dependent practice, interactions will likely be lesser in quantity and less free, the physician initiating and controlling the greater part of it. By the time the patient reaches the latter practice, which often involves institutionalization, he has been rendered relatively helpless and dependent, perhaps, as Goffman suggests, already demoralized by a sense of having been stripped of some part of his normal identity.[11] In other cases he has been rendered helpless by his failure to find help on his own or by the way his physical illness has incapacitated him.

A second element that seems to be able to predict some part of the quality of the interaction between patient and physician lies in what physicians consider to be the demands of proper treatment for a given illness. This is to say, all that doctors do is not the same and does not require the same type of interaction. Following Szasz and Hollander's typology of doctor-patient relationships[12] but reversing the direction of analysis, we may note that under some circumstances—as in surgery and electroconvulsive therapy—the patient must be thoroughly immobilized and passive, wholly submissive to the activity of the physician. The work itself requires such minimal interaction: attendants, straps, anesthesia, and other forms of restraint are employed to enforce the requirement of submission. This model for interaction Szasz and Hollander call *activity-passivity*. In it, the patient is a passive object.

The second treatment situation, discussed by most writers as *the* doctor-patient relationship, is one in which the patient's consent to accept advice and to follow it is necessary. Here, the patient "is conscious and has feelings and aspirations of his own. Since he suffers . . . he seeks help and is ready and willing to 'cooperate.' When he turns to the physician, he places [him] . . . in a position of power. . . . The more powerful . . . will speak of guidance or leadership, and will expect cooperation of the other."[13] The interaction is expected to follow the model of *guidance-cooperation*, the physician initiating more of the interaction than the patient. The patient is expected to do what he is told; he assumes a less passive role than if he were anesthetized but a passive role nonetheless, submissive to medical requirements.

Finally, there is the model of *mutual participation*, found where patients are able or are required to take care of themselves—as in the case of the management of some chronic illnesses like diabetes—and therefore where initiation of interaction comes close to being equal between the two. Here, "the physician does not profess to know exactly what is best for the patient. The search for this becomes the essence of the therapeutic interaction."[14] Obviously, some forms of psychotherapy fall here.

Szasz and Hollander's scheme, however, is defective logically and empirically, for their models represent a continuum of the degree to which the *patient* assumes an *active* role in interaction in treatment without being extended to the logical point where the *physician* assumes a *passive* role. Such a defect reflects the characteristically normative stance of the medical thinker: while the existence of situations where the practitioner more or less does what the patient asks him to do may not be denied, such situations are rejected out of hand as intolerably nonprofessional, nontherapeutic, and nondignified to be conceded for mere logic and dignified by the recognition of inclusion.[15] Logic and fact do, however, require recognition, and they dictate the suggestion of two other patterns of interaction—one in which the patient guides and the physician cooperates, and one in which the patient is active and the physician passive. It is difficult to imagine an empirical instance of the latter possibility, which requires that the physician cease being a consultant, so we may label it "merely" a logical construct. For the former instance, however, we may find empirical examples in a fair number of the interactions in client-dependent practices, particularly where the practice is economically unstable and the clientele of high economic, political, and social status.[16]

As I have noted, what distinguishes Szasz and Hollander's models from those I have added is the fact that they represent patterns of relations with patients that medical practitioners *wish* to establish and maintain on various occasions for various illnesses and patients. Assuming one type of interaction pattern is necessary for the therapist's work to proceed successfully, what social circumstances are prerequisite to its existence and how are they established? When the *activity-passivity* model does not automatically exist by virtue of coma or the like, some of the physician's behavior must be devoted to soothing the patient in order to get him to submit to the straps, injections, face-masks or whatever. The basic prerequisite, however, is *power* as such—sustained by the a priori incapacity of the patient, or by *making* the patient incapacitated. Such power is created by the fact that the individual is, let us say, unconscious and in a coma. In other instances, the exercise of power to overcome resistance when the patient is not in a coma is legitimized by the social identity imputed to the patient: he is just an infant, a cat, a retardate, a psychotic, or in some other way not fully human and responsible and so cannot be allowed to exercise his own choice to withdraw from treatment. Aside from circumstances where the patient's identity legitimizes the exercise of force, this pattern of interaction is most likely to be found where cultures diverge a great deal. There, few patients voluntarily enter medical consultation: their participation may be required by political power or may be facilitated by the incapacitating force of the disease itself.

The second pattern of interaction, *guidance-cooperation*, is essentially the one most people have in mind when they speak of the doctor-patient relationship. Obviously, its existence is contingent on a process that will bring people into interaction with the therapist in the first place, the process of seeking help that leads to the choice of utilizing one service rather than another. Here, the patient must exercise his own choice. Utilization is not merely something that facilitates establishing the relationship; it constitutes one-half of the battle in interaction: to actively choose to utilize a doctor in the first place requires that one in some degree concede his value and authority in advance[17] and that one in some degree already shares the doctor's perspective on illness and its treatment. The problem of interaction in treatment lies in the details of this acceptance, in the concrete areas in which lay and professional cultures converge. The doctor's tool for gaining acceptance is his "authority," which is not wholly binding by his incumbency in a formal legal position as expert.[18] Here, to the extent that the patient's culture is congruent with that of the professional, the authority of the latter is likely to be conceded in advance and reinforced in treatment by the fact that what the professional diagnoses and prescribes corresponds with what the patient expects and that communication between the two is relatively easy, so that confidence can be established when the professional must make new or unexpected demands on the patient. In this situation, what is problematic most of all is the physician's authority as such: it must be conceded before examination can begin and if treatment is to proceed. It is the *motive* for cooperation. Only secondarily problematic but problematic nonetheless is the capacity of the physician to make his desires for information and cooperation known and the capacity of the patient to understand the physician sufficiently to do as he is told. Essentially, then, faith and confidence on the part of the patient, and authority on the part of the physician, are the critical elements.

Finally, there is the pattern of *mutual participation*. Clearly, the interaction specified by this model requires characteristics on the part of the patient that facilitate communication. Communication is essential in order to determine what is to be done in therapy. Cultural congruence is thus obviously one necessary condition for such free interaction. According to Szasz and Hollander, the relationship "requires a more complex psychological and social organization on the part of both participants. Accordingly, it is rarely appropriate for children, or for those persons who are mentally deficient, very poorly educated, or profoundly immature. On the other hand, the greater the intellectual, educational, and general experiential similarity between physician and patient the more appropriate and necessary this model of therapy becomes."[19] However, it is not only educational and experiential similarity but also a collaborative *status* that is required. Here the patient is not to merely accept the authority of the doctor; each must accept the other as an equal in the search for a solution to the problem. Deference on the part of either patient or physician is likely to destroy such mutual participation. Thus, status congruence is necessary to the relationship in order that the interaction of each *can* be fairly equal, and the influence of the doctor on the patient will hinge essentially not on physical power or professional authority but on his capacity to *persuade* the patient of the value of his views.[20]

These characterizations of different patterns of interaction may be used to distinguish (1) the needs of different kinds of medical work, (2) the way different kinds of illness are managed, and (3) the problems of practice that arise when the character of the lay community and particularly the lay referral system varies. (1) Veterinary medicine, pediatrics, and surgery are among those practices obviously prone to require the activity-passivity model, though the families of pets and pediatric patients are prone to interfere more than the model predicts. Internal medicine and general practice are among those prone to require the guidance-cooperation model. And verbal psychotherapy as well as rehabilitation and the treatment of the chronic diseases are all prone to need the mutual-participation model. (2) Stigmatized illnesses that spoil the identities of the sufferers are prone to be managed by the activity-passivity pattern, as are those with severe trauma, coma, and psychosis, and with patients who are extremely variant in culture or capacity: these characteristics prevent the patient *or* the physician from being socially responsive in treatment. In any single community, most "normal"—which is to say conditionally legitimate— illnesses are prone to be managed by the guidance-cooperation pattern; in those cases not clearly legitimized by lay culture (and so withholding authority from the physician), the mutual participation pattern is likely to be common and the pattern where the patient guides and the physician cooperates is possible. (3) I might note that the activity-passivity pattern of interaction in treatment is most likely to be found where lay culture diverges greatly from professional culture and where the status of the layman is very low compared to the professional. Where these divergences are lesser, the guidance-cooperation pattern is likely to be found, whereas where both the lay culture and status of the patient are very much like that of the professional, the mutual-participation pattern is likely to be used often.

The Conflict Underlying Interaction

In discussing interaction in treatment, I have adopted here, as elsewhere, a situational approach: I have attempted to discern whether some regularities in situations exist such that, by specifying the situation, we can predict the kinds of people likely to be in it, the kinds of illness, and the kinds and amount of interaction likely to take place. This seems to me to be an eminently useful approach, but we should not lose sight of the fact that it is merely an approach specifying regularities across arrays of individuals—statistical regularities. Furthermore, those regularities are defined as *relative*, not absolute. Nevertheless, it is unwise to assume too much regularity in the interaction in treatment settings. While the patient can be more or less excluded from assuming an active role in interaction, he can rarely be wholly excluded. He can at least, as do low-status and poorly educated patients everywhere, practice evasive techniques and act stupid in order to avoid some of what is expected of him. And while the patient can be involved in mutual participation by virtue of his similarity to the therapist, he is never wholly cooperative. Given the viewpoints of two worlds, lay and professional, in interaction, they can never be wholly synonymous. And they are always, if only latently, in conflict. Indeed, I wish to suggest that the most faithful perspective on interaction in treatment is one reflecting such conflict in standpoint, not on assuming an identity of purpose to be discovered by better education or a disposition to cooperate sometimes hidden by misunderstanding or by failure to cooperate.[21]

Hence, interaction in treatment should be seen as a kind of negotiation as well as a kind of conflict. This point is suggested in Balint's psychiatric sense that the patient is using his symptoms to establish a relationship with the physician[22] but more particularly in the sense of negotiation of separate conditions and of separate perspectives and understandings. The patient is likely to want more information than the doctor is willing to give him—more precise prognoses, for example, and more precise instructions. As Roth's study indicated, just as the doctor struggles to find ways of withholding some kinds of information, so will the patient be struggling to find ways of gaining access to, or inferring such information.[23] Similarly, just as the doctor has no alternative but to handle his cases conventionally (which is to say, soundly), so the patient will be struggling to determine whether or not he is the exception to conventional rules. And finally, professional healing being an organized practice, the therapist will be struggling to adjust or fit any single case to the convenience of practice (and other patients), while the patient will be struggling to gain a mode of management more specifically fitted to him as an individual irrespective of the demands of the system as a whole. These conflicts in perspective and interest are built into the interaction and are likely to be present to some degree in every situation. They are at the core of interaction, and they reflect the general structural characteristics of illness and its professional treatment as a function of the relations between two distinct worlds, ordered by professional norms.

Notes

[1] William R. Rosengren and Spencer DeVault, "The Sociology of Time and Space in an Obstetrical Hospital," in Eliot Freidson, ed., *The Hospital in Modern Society* (New York: The Free Press of Glencoe, 1963), pp. 266–292.

[2] Julius A. Roth, *Timetables: Structuring the Passage of Time in Hospital Treatment and Other Careers* (Indianapolis: Bobbs-Merrill Co., 1963).

[3] Julius A. Roth, "Ritual and Magic in the Control of Contagion," *American Sociological Review*, XXII (1957), 310–314.

[4] See the detailed analysis Raymond S. Duff and August B. Hollingshead, *Sickness and Society* (New York: Harper and Row, 1968), Chapter 13.

[5] Fred Davis, *Passage Through Crisis: Polio Victims and Their Families* (Indianapolis: Bobbs-Merrill Co., 1963), p. 64. For other observations on the extent to which patients are kept ignorant, see Ailon Shiloh, "Equalitarian and Hierarchal Patients," *Medical Care*, III (1965), 87–95.

[6] Barney G. Glaser and Anselm L. Strauss, *Awareness of Dying* (Chicago: Aldine Publishing Co., 1965), pp. 29ff.

[7] Davis, *op. cit.*, p. 67, and see Fred Davis, "Uncertainty in Medical Prognosis, Clinical and Functional," *American Journal of Sociology*, LXVI (1960), 41–47.

[8] See James K. Skipper, Jr., "Communication and the Hospitalized Patient," in James K. Skipper, Jr., and Robert C. Leonard, eds., *Social Interaction and Patient Care* (Philadelphia: J. B. Lippincott Co., 1965), pp. 75–77.

[9] See Julius Roth and Elizabeth Eddy, *Rehabilitation for the Unwanted* (New York: Atherton Press, 1967).

[10] For a very useful discussion of the implications of such characteristics, see Stanton Wheeler, "The Structure of Formally Organized Socialization Settings," in O. G. Brim, Jr., and Stanton Wheeler, *Socialization After Childhood* (New York: John Wiley & Sons, 1966), pp. 53–116.

[11] See Erving Goffman, "The Moral Career of the Mental Patient," in his *Asylums* (New York: Anchor Books, 1961), pp. 125–161. In the context of the succeeding discussion of interaction, it is also appropriate to cite, in the same book, pp. 321–386, "The Medical Model and Mental Hospitalization."

[12] See Thomas S. Szasz and Mark H. Hollander, "A Contribution to the Philosophy of Medicine," *A.M.A. Archives of Internal Medicine*, XCVII (1956), 585–592.

[13] *Ibid.*, pp. 586–587.

[14] *Ibid.*, p. 589.

[15] This lack of concern for being logically consistent and systematic is characteristic of virtually all writing about the doctor-patient relationship by medical men. Another interesting analysis of the doctor-patient relationship explores other facets to be found in nature but restricts itself to the "pathological." See F. W. Hanley and F. Grunberg, "Reflections on the Doctor-Patient Relationship," *Canadian Medical Association Journal*, IXXXVI (1962), 1022–1024, where nine "syndromes" are constructed out of three stereotypical patients and three stereotypical physicians. So long as medical writers persist in crippling their logic by normative considerations, they cannot expect serious intellectual considerations.

[16] See Eliot Freidson, *Patients' Views, of Medical Practice* (New York: Russell Sage, 1961), pp. 171–191 for historical and contemporary examples of such relationships.

[17] See Theodore Caplow, *The Sociology of Work* (Minneapolis: University of Minnesota Press, 1954), p. 114.

[18] See Eliot Freidson, *Professional Dominance* (New York: Dodd, Mead, 1970).

[19] Szasz and Hollander, *op. cit.*, p. 387.

[20] In this sense the influence of the expert rather than the authority of the professional is indicated.

[21] For a more extended analysis of the conflict see Freidson, *Patients' Views, op. cit.*, pp. 171–191. And see the discussion in Carl Gersuny, "Coercion Theory and Medical Sociology," *Case Western Reserve Journal of Sociology*, II (1968), 14–20.

[22] See Michael Balint, *The Doctor, His Patient and the Illness* (New York: International Universities Press, 1957), *passim*.

[23] See Roth, *Timetables, op. cit.*, and Julius A. Roth, "Information and the Control of Treatment in Tuberculosis Hospitals, in Eliot Freidson, ed., *The Hospital in Modern Society, op. cit.*, pp. 293–318.

15
Infantilization: The Medical Model of Care

Karen A. Lyman

To manage stress in caring for elderly persons with dementia, most often control is carried out and rationalized through the process of infantilization, treating older adults as if they were children (Lyman, 1988). Disease progression is conceptualized as a "regression" to a childlike state of dependency and normative violations. For example, in one day care center's training manual for in-home respite caregivers, a section on "typical" Alzheimer's behavior contains four examples, all of which are of either incontinence or innocent but inappropriate sexual behavior.

The structure of day care is borrowed from the child daycare model, and few opportunities are provided in most day care centers to continue meaningful adult activity. Many staff-client interactions involve staff treating their elders like children—"for their own good." For example, the program director at Beach City described dementia in terms of "a regression in developmental stages." At Coast, the director said the program was "too childish" for people with mild dementia, but appropriate for people who were "moderately impaired." Staff in both of these programs at times referred to and treated clients as children. At Beach City, one worker referred to the clients as "the kids." At Coast, a worker was frustrated by one client who followed her around, "like a kid you can't get rid of." A coworker at this site rewarded one client for being "a good boy" during the MMSE reassessment [a mental status exam] by offering him a lollipop.

A number of props associated with the care of children are used in caring for older adults who are cognitively impaired. For example, in one day-care program's packet of information for family caregivers, four of the eleven "tips" included reference to products designed for infants: baby gates, baby safety knobs, baby toys, baby cups with covers. The use of these props contributes to the image of older adults as childlike.

Infantilization is a strategy employed to cope with the stress of dementia care. The demands of caregiving may be eased by conceptualizing the one cared for as being childlike rather than an elder. First, much of dementia caregiving is basic custodial work: dirty work and legwork. Personal care and routine supervision are elevated to "therapy" if infantilization is viewed as part of the medical "treatment" of people who have Alzheimer's. Second, basic custodial work is made simpler if staff legitimately can "take over" in a playful manner, as one might with children who cannot complete self-care tasks. In this example from Bayview, the program director engaged in play with a client to ease the embarrassment of toileting.

> Susan is an R.N. by training, who is a very warm, affectionate companion to the people enrolled in her program. She participates with her staff in toileting and other personal care, when she is free from administrative responsibilities. She has developed a special relationship with Andrea, who can be difficult at times. She takes Andrea to the toilet, asking if she has to "pee pee," then playfully encourages Andrea to pretend that she is Susan's mom ("spank, spank"), and then assumes the adult role again: "Do you need help wiping?"

Third, staff members increase their control over working conditions and minimize some of the emotion work associated with dementia care, to the extent that they "know" what to expect and what to do. Thus, when persons with dementia "go downhill," this is taken as evidence of an "Alzheimer's disease stage." Gubrium (1987) explains this process as "ordering" the disorderly aspects of caregiving, so that dementia makes sense to caregivers.

Infantilization transforms the uncertainty concerning the nature of self-deterioration into something stereotypically familiar and manageable: older people decline to a childlike state in which it is appropriate to expect very little of them and to control their behavior. And so, dementia caregivers increase their sense of control over the conditions of their work by exercising control over their clients.

Infantilization may benefit staff, but quality of care suffers. Research in other settings has found that unnecessary control by service providers exacerbates impairment. "Excess disabilities" may result from a "highly redundant environment" in which service providers "take over" activities clients could manage themselves (Brody et al., 1971; Chappell, 1978; Kielhofner, 1983). Treating older adults with dementia as if they are children denies recognition of the older adult self, the person who is still inside, who has developed a lifetime of skills and who still has worth as an individual. Staff may very well provide for the physical security and comfort of clients they view as childlike. They are unable to meet people's emotional needs, however, if they deny the painful reality that their clients are older adults who live daily with cognitive impairment and who often are fully aware of frightening changes within themselves and depressing changes within their intimate and social relationships.

Social Control

In addition to the demands and uncertainties in caring for people with dementia, there are many stressful conditions in the organization of the work and the workplace. For service providers, many of the working conditions that contribute to the stress of dementia care may seem to be unchangeable. For example, the staff may feel powerless to override agency policies or remodel the facility. As a result, workers may compensate for powerlessness in regard to the structure of the agency or facility by establishing a power relationship in caregiving. Control over clients is rationalized by medical labels and typifications and organized as medical authority necessary "for their own good," in caring for persons with dementing illnesses.

Six methods of control are employed by staff to cope with their stress. Most are methods typically employed with children. These forms of caregiving for older adults with dementia are part of an underlying strategy of infantilization common in dementia day care.

The first form of control is by *directives*, whereby clients are simply told what to do: "Let's sit down and relax." These kinds of "Sit down" orders sometimes are successful, in persuading clients to stay in group activities or to refrain from leaving the building, but most often this form of control is unsuccessful. And so, frustrations for staff increase as clients disobey their commands.

The second form of control is by *deception*. For example, at Coast there were several inconveniences in the physical environment, which the staff managed by lying to clients. One bathroom was located outside in an unfenced area, requiring staff to accompany clients for their safety. Also, the office was an open space with no privacy, so it was difficult for the secretary to work when clients persisted in asking to use the phone. Staff often resorted to deception to minimize inconvenience and interruption, telling clients that "the bathroom [or telephone] is out of order; can you wait a few minutes?" Tales frequently told and retold among coworkers at Coast attributed the success of this strategy to short-term memory loss: "They forget" that the out-of-order explanation had been offered many times. Other humorous tales told with great delight by these coworkers revolved around successful deception. Kim, one of the program aides, shared this story about Marge, a woman who generally wore a pained, weepy look and required almost constant individual attention as she power walked around the center: "This is funny: I have Marge wait until after I tie my shoe. She says 'OK.' Of course, my shoe is untied all the time, so . . ." Similarly, at Inland workers wrote notes from a client's "spouse" indicating when he would arrive, so that a persistent client would stop asking when her husband was coming. These forms of deception involved exploitation of the clients' impairment, in the interest of stress management.

The third method of control has been referred to by Conrad and Schneider (1980) as *careful coercion*, persuasive methods used in lieu of restraints to control mental patients. These methods also are among those commonly used with children. Their transference to dementia care is symbolized by the "day care" designation and is part of the process of infantilization.

In dementia care, careful coercion includes calculated compliments ("You're *so* good at that!") or requests for help intended to persuade clients to "choose" an activity. These strategies do seem successful, at times, in drawing people into group activity and boosting morale. For example, during exercise at Coast, Sarah, the program manager, successfully encouraged several people to "lead" the group.

> Sarah was an energetic, articulate Hispanic woman in her thirties, whose enthusiasm and physical energy were contagious. She asked clients to suggest exercises that the others could do: "How about an exercise, Ryan! Just one you can do from your chair!" Ryan is a slim, attractive, usually upbeat man in his seventies, a former nuclear physicist who often is on the go, looking for the next activity
>
> *Ryan*: I suggest that we do this way and this way and then somersaults!!
> *Sarah*: Oh Ryan! How about something a little easier!
> *Ryan* dramatically simplifies his original suggestion:
> "Well. . . . wiggle one toe. Now put it down and wiggle the other one."
>
> Everyone carries out this suggestion and applauds. Then Sarah asks Steven, a retired military officer. He does a difficult crab walk across the circle, an old military exercise, he says. "Could you scale it down a little," Sarah asks, "so I won't break anything?" She

adapts Steven's exercise as a chair exercise, making it clear that it is her limitations, rather than his or the group's, that are the reason. Then she asks Mimi, who is hesitant. "I don't know exactly." Mimi says. She stands up and starts to do something vague. Someone else in the group helps her out, saying, "Dancing!"

Sarah transforms this, validating her suggestion: "OK, we're going to stand up. . . . Now one hand up, and down. . . . OK! That was hard, Mimi! Thank you!" People applaud; Mimi smiles. She has just led an exercise group.

It may not matter that these situations are staged and somewhat manipulative, if the end result is a boost for the sagging self-esteem of people suffering from cognitive impairment. Happy campers make for an easier day, both for staff and clients. However, there is a kind of dehumanization and distancing that occurs in some exchanges in which a client becomes an object of humor for the staff while being persuaded to participate in an activity. During the same exercise session at Coast this was apparent:

> Then Sarah asks Maggie to show the group an exercise. The standing joke for the staff is that she always goes to the center of the group, and she always does the same exercise, a very simple ordinary motion. Coworkers make eye contact, waiting for the inevitable repetition of this pattern. This may be staged for my benefit, or just as an inside joke for the staff.
>
> *Maggie* goes to the center of the circle, but she says: Well, I've shown you before!
> *Sarah*: Well, we'll give it a try. It's kind of hard, but we'll do it. Let's stand up and join Maggie. How many should we do?
> *Maggie*: However many you want.
> *Sarah*: How about ten. . . . Great! Let's give her a hand!
>
> Coworkers roll their eyes or share a chuckle over this favorite joke. Maggie may or may not know that she is being "a good sport."

Careful coercion also includes distraction to dissuade clients from an intended choice. Distraction, like deception, is predicated on a dementia typification, the assumption that these people, like children, will quickly forget the previous self-directed activity. Sometimes staff are surprised to find that distraction does not work, because the dementia typification was faulty: "He remembered!" But distraction often is successful.

Another form of careful coercion is "behavior modification," a term used to refer to a process of rewarding people who are coerced

successfully by compliments, requests for help, or distraction. For
example, at Coast the staff persisted in trying to persuade Marge, the
woman who often looked as if she were about to cry, to join activity
groups. Marge was almost constantly in motion; she preferred pacing
or one-on-one attention from the staff. The behavior modification
strategy was to offer her attention as a reward if she joined an activity
group: "Someone is waiting there to give you a hug!"

This strategy rarely worked. When I asked Marge about the benefits
of joining the group, she replied in a flat monotone: "It doesn't do that
for me." Although the staff received little reinforcement for their
behavior modification efforts with this client, the strategy was continued. In dementia care, where often nothing "works," behavior modification at least specifies whose behavior is to be changed and maintains
the authority of the staff.

The fourth method of control is the most extreme: *pharmacological
restraints*. According to client files from the eight day care centers, 20
to 40 percent of the clients are prescribed psychoactive drugs, administered at the discretion of the day-care staff (under a nurse's supervision) when prescribed "prn" (as required). Clients who are particularly troublesome often are "managed" by drugs, as illustrated by the
case of Judy at Inland. Judy was seen by staff as very demanding
because she pushed people, was unpredictable in her moods, and
loudly demanded attention at inconvenient times. One staff member
discussed with a sense of relief the possibility of pharmacological
restraints: "She has had her medication today so she doesn't seem as
bad. Her husband wasn't giving it to her. . . . Now we have permission
to give it to her here too, if she's getting anxiety-ed out in the afternoon."

Ironically, when medication is used as a means of control, the
"agitation" it was intended to manage often increases, resulting in
greater demands on the staff. An illustration from Coast:

> Marge, the woman constantly in motion, has been prescribed mild
> tranquilizers, sometimes several in combination. These are sup-
> posed to be "calmer downers," according to the nurse, but obvi-
> ously have the opposite effect on Marge. Penny, the nurse,
> recommends hospitalizing Marge to conduct a proper evaluation,
> to bring down the dosage or withdraw her from tranquilizers.
> Instead, the psychiatrist just substitutes one drug for another. Part
> of the problem is that Medicare will not cover hospitalization for
> this adjustment in medications. And so, the staff are required to
> cope with psychiatric incompetence and the inadequacies of na-
> tional health care policy, while providing care for individuals with

dementia. Penny says, with considerable frustration, "We'll just do the best we can while she's here."

Even though the use of pharmacological restraints sometimes is self-defeating for the staff, as well as inappropriate treatment for the client, medication for troublesome clients is favored. Prescription drugs offer a sense of control for staff, as they attempt to manage the unpredictable, uncertain aspects of dementia care. Even if they "don't work," there is less of a sense of failure for staff than if clients "don't respond" to other efforts. If medication "has no effect," the explanation can be medicalized without taking it personally: inadequate dose, change in metabolism, disease progression. However, if medication or other restraints escalate the troublesome behavior they were intended to control, the outcome may be a cycle of control by restraints (Gubrium, 1975; Mace, 1987; Pynos and Stacey, 1986), which increases the demands of the work for care providers.

The fifth method of control is *segregation by competence*. Dementia day care is a place where misbehavior is expected, explained, and managed within biomedical definitions of impairment. When people with dementia are "typed," as they are more in some programs than in others, they are assigned places in the facility on the basis of presumed levels of impairment. The practice of segregation by competence defines the separate places of staff and clients, as well as more- and less-impaired clients.

In some programs the openness of the facility indicated less segregation between staff and clients. Even staff offices remained accessible for clients to explore. But in other centers the offices were "in back," or doors were closed, or other physical features were used to define separate places. For example, at Inland staff frequently stood and talked on one side of a serving counter in the kitchen, distancing themselves from clients who sat at tables on the other side of the counter. At times the staff sat at one table and clients at others.

Segregation by competence among clients was institutionalized in some programs more than in others and was supported by facility design. In small programs, housed in smaller facilities, everyone was together as a group in one room for all activities. But in several larger centers, "higher functioning" clients were separated for special "cognitive stimulation" groups or other separate activities for part of the day. At Coast, the announcement of segregated group assignments was couched in terms such as "the talkers will be meeting in the other room," and people were strongly encouraged, though not required, to attend the suggested group. Segregation by competence allows the staff to succeed, by not expecting much from the "lower-functioning" people or from staff who work with them. These group assignments are rotated, so that all staff are able to be with the more stimulating clients at times. Thus, segregation by competence benefits all who are "higher functioning," including the staff.

At Valley, located in a remodeled house, some clients were taken "to the back room" when staff perceived that some of the "higher functioning" people would be "bothered" by their presence. This practice was viewed as benefiting the "higher" people without hurting the "lower" ones, who were thought to be less aware of the distinction. The view was that the "higher functioning" people were not simply intolerant of the misbehavior of their peers, but were experiencing a kind of anticipatory stigma as they observed people "farther along" than they were. And so, segregation by competence at Valley was sometimes practiced to control the misbehavior of people with more severe impairment, but more commonly it was used to ease the emotional burden of dementia on those who were less impaired.

In some settings, defining people's place extended to setting place names at the table for meals. Control over who sits with whom was defended by Josh, a tall lanky young program aide at Bayview. This day health care program prided itself on its well-publicized "integrated" program, which segregated people at various times, including lunch. Josh explained, "We assign places by who gets along with whom, plus dementia people versus others, so you don't have a whole table of silent people or people babbling incoherently."

In this program, staff took care of themselves, as well as clients. It is clear that assigning place names is an attempt to prevent misbehavior at mealtimes, such as one person taking another person's food. Place names help to reduce the demands of mealtime for staff. It is not so clear that all of the "dementia people" are comfortable with the categorical, segregated seating.

Segregation by competence is rationalized as necessary because of what the staff "know" about dementia, impairment, disease progression, and the potential for misbehavior. "Knowing one's place" is part of this staff knowledge, knowing what is required in caring for people with dementing illnesses.

A sixth method of control is the use of facility design features to isolate troublesome clients or discourage wanderers: *environmental control.*

Social Distance

In addition to exercising control over clients to manage stress, some Alzheimer's day-care staff become more distant and detached. Service providers are present, but not "there." This coping mechanism prevents staff from meeting the basic emotional security needs of their clients, while it may offer care providers a sense of control in facing the emotional demands of Alzheimer's care.

In research in long-term care settings, Asuman Kiyak and Eva Kahana have identified marginality and distancing by staff who experience stress in working with older adults. Whether they leave or stay, the lack of commitment of dissatisfied marginal workers reduces quality of care for clients (Kiyak and Kahana, 1983). The links between staff stress and client care also are revealed by several indicators on Maslach's Burnout Inventory: emotional exhaustion, diminished sense of personal competence, and depersonalized detached relationships (Maslach and Jackson, 1981). Burnout involves what might be called emotional absenteeism, a form of social distance that prevents high-quality care.

In several of the day-care programs included in this study, characteristics of burnout that inhibit quality of care were observed regularly. When demands were too high, when there seemed to be very little control over working conditions, and when social support was lacking, client care suffered: a client's request or apparent need for assistance was ignored; people were isolated from the group or ridiculed.

At Inland the staff ratio often was 1:10, because more privileged coworkers stayed "in back" in their offices rather than providing direct care "on the floor." The staff ratio was even worse when one of the two "floor staff" had to spend time one-on-one with clients they referred to as "heavy care," or take someone to the bathroom. As in many stressful occupations, humor relieves the tension. But for Cindy, a self-described "burned out" program aide, people with dementia sometimes became the object of insensitive ridicule, as in this example:

> Verne is in a wheelchair. He is generally cheerful and cooperative, kids around a lot, and is easy to care for. But recently Verne has had "prostate trouble," requiring frequent assistance in toileting. Often his requests have turned out to be false alarms; he has not been able to urinate at all, or much, when he is taken to the toilet. Each trip to the bathroom is not only an undesirable task for Cindy, but an interruption that requires leaving just one program aide in charge of the group. After a number of these requests on a particularly stressful day, Cindy began to loudly discuss Verne's

prostate and urination problems in front of the entire group, apparently hoping to embarrass him so that he would not ask to go to the bathroom unless it was absolutely necessary. However, it is unclear to a patient who has this problem whether or not the urge to urinate is a false alarm; it is a very uncomfortable condition. At one point Cindy raised her voice and said, "I'm announcing to the world that Verne has to GO!!!"

The uncaring caregiver also may be understood in light of Anselm Strauss's discussion (1975) of people who care for those with "stigmatic" chronic illnesses, and Kathy Charmaz's description (1980) of those who do "death work" in hospitals or mortuaries. Strauss describes the "abandonment rationales" developed by caregivers who are overwhelmed by the stress of caring for people with "terribly demanding" conditions. These rationales are similar to the dementia typifications found among Alzheimer's caregivers: "they" are going downhill, the decline is inevitable. The result is that interactions occur between caregivers and "them," rather than affirming individual self-identity. Charmaz identifies similar strategies employed by people who work with the dead, to create barriers between self and stigmatized work.

In dementia care, barriers at times are erected between workers and their stigmatized clients by avoiding meaningful conversation. Gubrium (1975) has observed administrators in a residential facility greet people with impersonal pleasantries "in passing," avoiding personal contact. Similarly, I have observed staff who dismiss or gloss over the emotional concerns of clients, as if to "move people along" and get out of the conversation without really talking with the person. Some staff members are skillful at and interested in what I would call "dementia talk," a laborious process of reflective listening to decode the personal concerns expressed by people with language impairment. But many rely upon moving people along, whenever clients begin to talk about ambiguous or personal concerns. I have heard these examples of moving people along, by various service providers in conversations initiated by people with dementia: "Oh, I see . . ." "Oh, I know . . ." "OK, I'll check on that."

This form of staff-client interaction offers superficial contact while maintaining distance. Staff stress is minimized by this strategy, but at the same time, the self-identity and emotional needs of people with dementia are ignored.

References

Brody, Elaine M., M. M. Kleban, M. P. Lawton, and H. A. Silverman. 1971. "Excess Disabilities of Mentally Impaired Aged: Impact of Individualized Treatment." *The Gerontologist* 11:124–33.

Chappell, Neena L. 1978. "Senility: Problems in Communication." In *Shaping Identity in Canadian Society*, edited by J. Haas and W. Shaffir. Englewood Cliffs, NJ: Prentice-Hall.

Charmaz, Kathy. 1980. *The Social Reality of Death*. Reading, MA: Addison-Wesley.

Conrad, Peter, and Joseph W. Schneider. 1980. *Deviance and Medicalization: From Badness to Sickness*. St. Louis: C. V. Mosby.

Gubrium, Jaber F. 1975. *Living and Dying at Murray Manor*. New York: St. Martin's Press.

_____. 1987. "Structuring and Destructuring the Course of Illness: The Alzheimer's Disease Experience." *Sociology of Health and Illness* 9:1–24.

Kielhofner, G. 1983. "'Teaching' Retarded Adults: Paradoxical Effects of a Pedagogical Enterprise." *Urban Life* 12:307–26.

Kiyak, H. Asuman, and Eva F. Kahana. 1983. "Predictors of Job Commitment and Turnover among Staff Working with the Aged." Paper presented to the Gerontological Society annual meeting, November.

Lyman, Karen A. 1988. "Infantilization of Elders: Day Care for Alzheimer's Disease Victims." In *Research in the Sociology of Health Care*, vol. 7, edited by Dorothy Wertz, 71–103. Greenwich, CT: JAI Press.

Mace, Nancy L. 1987. "Characteristics of Persons with Dementia." In *Losing a Million Minds: Confronting the Tragedy of Alzheimer's Disease and Other Dementias*. U.S. Government Office of Technology Assessment, OTA–BA–323, 59–83. Washington, DC: Government Printing Office.

Maslach, Christina, and Susan Jackson. 1981. *Maslach Burnout Inventory Manual*. Palo Alto, CA: Consulting Psychologists Press.

Pynoos, Jon, and Candace A. Stacey. 1986. "Specialized Facilities for Senile Dementia Patients." In *The Dementias: Policy and Management*, edited by M. L. M. Gilhooly, S. H. Zarit, and J. E. Birren, 111–30. Englewood Cliffs, NJ: Prentice-Hall.

Strauss, Anselm. 1975. *Chronic Illness and the Quality of Life*. St. Louis: C. V. Mosby.

Section VI

Alternatives to Formal Medicine

Traditionally, the medical establishment has frowned on varying forms of alternatives to formal Western medicine. Those who did not believe in seeing regular physicians and following their prescriptions were viewed as anti-scientific, irrational, or psychologically disturbed. Practitioners of alternative medical forms were seen as crackpots and charlatans. Yet historically, there was often a multitude of medical approaches. Paul Starr's piece, "The Growth of Medical Authority," in a later section on "Health Care Providers," talks about how mainstream medicine defeated many of those alternatives. Presently, we are rediscovering some of those legacies. People are using a wide range of methods to prevent, cure, and alleviate illness. These include folk remedies, psychologically based approaches, tai-chi, accupuncture, chiropractic, homeopathy, herbal medicine, dietary methods, and a host of other practices.

Medical sociologists have always been fascinated by the number of people who did not seek professional help, and they pioneered in understanding the alternative ways that people took care of themselves, as we read in a previous section, "Experiencing Illness and Seeking Care." People's health behavior is often complex, composed of more than one approach to their problems. Laypeople, just like medical sociologists, understand that shortcomings with mainstream medicine do not mean that we must abandon it completely—all three articles in this section deal with people combining formal, Western medicine with other approaches (e.g., self-care or Eastern medicine).

Ann Dill, Phil Brown, Desiree Ciambrone, and William Rakowski's article, "The Meaning and Practice of Self-Care by Older Adults: A Qualitative Assessment," is based on interviews with members of a senior center about how they deal with mundane symptoms. Rather than look only at immediate, time-bound self-care practices, the authors explore how self-care notions developed over time, and what they represent in the larger context of people's lives. Dill and colleagues discover that elderly people have a repertoire of self-care beliefs and practices that they often learned early in life. In addition to helping them take care of their health conditions, these self-care beliefs and practices are also ways that people frame their relationships with others, and even parts of their self-identity. One important implication is that mainstream medical professionals could benefit by eliciting from patients the ways that they take care of themselves.

In "Western Reflections on Eastern Medicine," Alexandra Dundas Todd recounts her and her son's personal triumph in using a combination of Western and Eastern medicine to treat her son's cancer. Todd weaves her family's personal experiences with the experience of others, as well as a sociological analysis of research on the effectiveness of various alternative treatments. She shows us how her son become more personally empowered about his life and his illness, and offers hope that the methods he used will become more widely used in this country.

Michael Goldstein's "The Emergence of Alternative Medicine" provides a comprehensive examination of the dramatic growth of alternative medicine, at the same time rooted in his son's experience. He contrasts the weak position of alternative medicine in 1983 when his son was badly burned, with its expansive position by 1996 when he began to write the book from which this excerpt is taken. Americans now make many visits to alternative healers and spend huge amounts on alternative care. Many HMOs now cover alternative care, and the National Institutes of Health even has a special section to examine it. Much of this is in response to flaws in the health care system and in traditional physician-patient encounters, and is accelerated by a growing body of medical research showing many significant results from alternative medicine.

16
The Meaning and Practice of Self-Care by Older Adults

Ann Dill, Phil Brown, Desirée Ciambrone,
and William Rakowski

This paper reports findings from twenty-one interviews at a senior center in which older adults examined their own understandings of how they themselves care for common physical symptoms. Most research on self-care conceptualizes such behavior as consisting of specific responses by individuals to particular symptom episodes (Dean 1986, 1992; Levin, Katz and Holst 1976; Haug, Wykle and Namazi 1989). Drawing deductively from theory on health behavior, symptom response, and illness attributions, such work limits the frame of reference of self-care to a time-bound and decisional response by an individual actor (Brody and Kleban 1981; Chappell, Strain and Badger 1988; Dean 1981, 1986, 1991; Leventhal and Prohaska 1986; Segall and Chappell 1991; Segall and Goldstein 1989). Other literature on care-seeking, particularly for chronic illness, suggests that self-care transcends the acknowledgment of discomfort and subsequent treatment of symptoms; it also involves the interpretation of present and past illness experiences (Bury 1991; Charmaz 1991; Register 1987; Williams 1984). This means that variable temporal and behavioral dimensions typify self-care practices, which thus suggests alternative meanings of self-care behavior. Looking at how individuals interpret and respond to conditions affecting their health requires an understanding of their social and economic circumstances, personal biographies, health beliefs, and self concepts. Our analysis suggests that self-care has a dynamic and interactive relationship with other sources of care and, further, that beyond its connection with specific symptoms it has a symbolic significance based in the social context and identity of the older person.

From *Research on Aging*, Vol. 7, No. 1, pp. 8–41. Copyright © 1995 by Sage Publications, Inc. Reprinted by permission of Sage Publications.

Background: Studying Self-Care

Dean (1986, p. 276) provides a fairly comprehensive definition of self-care:

> Self-care in illness is the range of individual behavior involved in symptom recognition and evaluation, and in decisions regarding symptom responses, including decisions to do nothing about symptoms, to treat the symptoms by self-determined actions or to seek advice regarding treatment. Self-care thus includes consultation in the lay, professional and alternative care networks as well as evaluation of decisions regarding action based on the advice obtained in consultation.

Self-care is frequently discussed as the antithesis of formal medical care, subsumed under positively regarded rubrics such as the professional, Western, modern, expert or scientific model. In contrast, self-care often bears an association with what are deemed less informed and more conventional systems—those termed traditional, lay, folk or non-Western (Segall and Chappell 1991). Due to negative connotations accompanying the latter headings, self-care may be seen as inferior and, thus, an inadequate substitute for formal health care; at the least, the efficacy of self-care is likely to be evaluated with that of formal medicine used as a point of reference. On the other hand, there is recognition that most persons find useful a combination of self- and formally provided care and further that the two differ in their approach and functions. Professional medicine concerns itself with defining and treating physiological malfunction or disease. Conversely, through self-care, individuals express lay conceptions of sickness, attach personal meaning to the state of being sick, and "structure the social experience of illness" (Segall and Chappell 1991, p. 116).

Older people may be particularly likely to use self-care in response to illness due to the higher probability of having health problems, especially chronic conditions which are less amenable to professional intervention (Chappell 1987; Haug 1984). Despite this, the study of self-care among the elderly has been relatively neglected (Chappell 1987; Haug, Wykle and Namazi 1989).

Most research has examined the immediate response to a discrete symptom experience, seeking to identify predictors of a choice of self-care behavior. Studies have thus examined the impact of socio-demographic characteristics, health beliefs and other attitudinal variables, and symptom attributes. Results have yielded only moderate explained variance and few consistent predictors. Two factors that have been regularly found to influence symptom response (though with complex consequences for self-care) are the perceived seriousness of the symptom and whether it is attributed to aging. Symptoms viewed as more serious appear to invoke more and different types of care-seeking (including self-care) than those less serious (Leventhal and Prohaska 1986; Prohaska et al. 1987; Chappell et al. 1988). On the other hand, individuals may be more likely to use *only* self-care for symptoms perceived as less serious than for more serious ones (Haug et al. 1989). Attributions of symptoms to old age appear in some studies to lead to more passive responses, such as denying or mini-mizing it or monitoring its progress without seeking care (Prohaska et al. 1987; Brody and Kleban, 1981). Asserting, conversely, that "wait-ing" or "doing nothing" can be important self-care strategies, Haug et al. (1989) found that attributing a symptom to aging was the only attitudinal variable significantly related to a higher rate of self-care for both serious and nonserious symptoms.

Problems with the Paradigm

Despite variability in concept and method, most work on self-care among the elderly shares a set of assumptions as well as a particular logic; it derives from a common paradigm. As noted above, the key aspect of this paradigm is the definition of self-care as comprised of immediate responses to symptom experiences and, in some studies, preventive or health maintenance activities. Embedded in this defini-tion is the biomedical model of disease, in which the individual is the locus of infirmity, and disease (as well as responses to it) occurs in more or less bounded temporal episodes (see Kleinman 1988; Mishler 1981). Even work focused on subjective responses to perceived illness, rather than disease states, (e.g., Haug et al. 1989; Verbrugge and Ascione 1987) assumes that self-care behavior is a time-bound and decisional response by an individual actor.

Locating self-care in this way has implications and limitations for the ways in which individuals' health-related behaviors are studied. First, like the biomedical model, self-care studies assume a dualism between mind and body. Psychological and emotional attributes (e.g., aging attributions, perceived symptom seriousness, or self-perceived health status) therefore become either hypothetical predictors of self-care, or they are part of the response to a symptom episode (e.g., emotional reactions or psychological distress). This approach thus does not attempt to represent, nor to problematize, a more holistic "self" inclusive of mind and body, nor a dynamic self which *simultaneously* is an active agent, reactive object and reflexive subject.

The common definition of self-care similarly segments the individual from his or her social nexus. Properties of social networks and social relations become either predictors or consequences of self-care action. In a more complex model of illness behavior, as proposed by Dean (1992), social networks are treated as interactive and mediating forces. Satisfaction with one's social support network, for example, appears to have an effect on professional care seeking, independent of age and health status. Even this more elaborate conceptualization, however, investigates the triggers of care behavior while neglecting the social factors involved in learning and/or creating self-care responses and making care-related decisions. While not antithetical, there is little room in this approach to study how self-care might involve or reflect decisions made within primary groups, nor how individuals might use social network resources in their quest for self-care strategies.

Finally, self-care, informal caregiving, and formal medical care constitute alternative outcomes in the common model. While studies do explore how individuals might choose different forms of care in sequence or in combination, they do not explore other possible linkages among the forms of care. Some self-care might, for example, derive entirely from medical recommendations; conversely, it might represent a reaction against previously received informal or formal care. The present model thus permits a very restricted view of the meaning of self-care in terms of overall health behavior.

Because illness (again, especially chronic illness) disrupts daily life processes, it forces the individual to formulate some account of that disruption and its consequences. The result can be a reformulation of the personal biography, a "narrative reconstruction" which tries to "reconstitute and repair ruptures between body, self, and the world" (Williams 1984, p. 287). Living with symptoms over time may further transform a person's social and psychological identity or sense of self, and the changed sense of self may in turn affect reactions to the experience of symptoms (Charmaz 1991; cf. Bury 1991).

Towards an Alternative Model

Broader work on illness behavior thus suggests the need for a more dynamic view of self-care, one which examines the repertoire of self-care behaviors individuals develop over time, identifies the sources of particular symptom responses in the context of that repertoire, and explores diverse linkages among sources of care. Such a perspective should, furthermore, assess the personal meanings of self-care responses and their relationship to issues of self identity.

Data and Methods

We interviewed twenty-one older adults attending a large New England senior center on their understandings of their self-care. Although questions center on responses to specific symptoms and symptom episodes, the interview also elicits a more holistic view of self-care behavior. Thus, respondents are asked to describe the range and typicality of their responses to symptoms, including emotional as well as behavior reactions; the origins of these responses; factors that might influence their willingness to alter care responses; and actions or thoughts that occur between symptom episodes but are related to self-care strategies. These inquiries seek to portray the dynamic nature of self-care. They also facilitate descriptions of the social contexts in which self-care occurs, an area tapped more directly by questions on formal provider contacts, informal social networks, and the influence of both on self-care behavior.

The sample consists of eighteen females and three males. Age of respondents ranges from 63 to 82, with a mean of 76 years. The majority (N=9), as expected in the case of older women, are widowed. Of the remaining respondents, seven are currently married, two separated, two never married, and one person divorced. The vast majority cite having at least one major medical condition, with the most frequently reported health conditions being hypertension, arthritis, problems concerning the eyes (e.g., cataracts and glaucoma), and heart conditions.

Findings presented below focus first on linkages between self-care and other forms of care-seeking behavior and secondly on the social context of self-care. From this material it will then be possible to analyze the relationship of self-care to systems of meaning centered on the self for whom care is being provided.

Forms of Caring

Findings suggest that self-care relates in various ways to care provided by others, whether medical professionals or members of informal social networks. Consistent with existing literature, respondents report seeking different types of care simultaneously as well as sequentially during symptom episodes. Consultation with others also commonly accompanies self-care; indeed, self-care decisions are seldom made without such discussion.

The impact of other forms of care on self-care is not, however, limited to the time of the symptom episode. Both formal and informal care providers are sources of learning of self-care strategies; they may provide this through direct instruction, role modeling, sanctioning, or more suggestive, symbolic means, as seen below. In addition, past consultations can significantly impact present care-related decisions. There is, as well, a future-related influence, since individuals project their symptom responses in advance and can anticipate what might cause a change in those responses.

Analysis of interview material produced a classification of respondents into three groups depending upon the sources guiding their self-care actions: 1) *individual self-care* refers to actions reported as care decisions arrived at by the individual's own knowledge and experience; 2)*formally guided self-care* refers to actions undertaken on the recommendation, or under the supervision, of a health or medical professional; 3) *combination self-care* strategies refers to cases where respondents base self-care actions on advice or direction of people in social networks (including family, peers, and acquaintances) as well as physician recommendations.

Individual Self-Care

One-third (N=7) of respondents report caring for symptoms primarily by themselves, relying on methods that have been part of their care repertoires for many years. Mrs. A, a seventy-six-year-old widow, for example, relies on home remedies to relieve leg and knee pain. She describes her care strategy in this way:

> When I have it [leg] elevated, after I have an old sweater that I cut the sleeves off and I put it over my knee to keep it warm, and I figured the heat is good for it.

Mrs. A learned of the "sweater treatment" from her parents:

> Well I knew it was wool and the sweaters nowadays, some of them are not all the real wool and it was an old sweater so I cut it off and put it like an old stocking.

She continues to explain her parents' choice of wool:

> Well they figured if it was a pain that had to do with joints, they figured it had to be rheumatism, or what they called it in the old days, and the heat would do it.

Mrs. P's care repertoire further illustrates the generational link respondents often draw when discussing their symptoms. Mrs. P is an eighty-two-year-old widow who, in addition to hypertension, migraine headaches and allergies, often experiences pain in her fingers and toes. To ease arthritic pain, Mrs. P reports taking aspirin and exercising her fingers. When asked from whom she learned these actions she states:

> Well I remember my mother having problems with her fingers and I keep the fingers warm because I bought her a pair of mittens at the time and they seemed to be a great help to her. That was only when she was inactive. She was a very busy lady, she had nine children. I took it from my mother so to speak because she had the same problem.

The exercises she learned from her husband. She explains:

> My husband had a little, well he was a baseball player and he had a little squeegee ball and we decided to use that for exercising my fingers. It had to be longer than that because my husband has been dead for twenty years.

Another respondent, Mrs. B, describes the cold symptoms she experiences in the winter time as "no big thing." The seventy-year-old woman tends to her symptoms by taking over-the-counter medications and cough syrup, resting, and increasing fluid intake. Mrs. B cites these actions as things she "learned from way back," as things she "always did." She is unwilling to try new ways of dealing with symptoms because her present treatments prove effective. Moreover, Mrs. B feels that common symptoms can be successfully treated without professional care:

> I take care of it at home. I take care of it myself. I go to the doctors myself because I have a little high blood pressure and he checks me for the pressure and for pulse and the heart and whatever, and everything is fine. But with this here [cold], I do it on my own. If it gets worse I have to go to the doctor.

Formally Guided Self-Care

Other respondents' symptom responses are shaped primarily by consultation with health care professionals, overwhelmingly physicians. A few people demonstrate a strong reliance on professional care, refusing to take action to relieve symptoms without consulting their physicians. In dealing with bone and joint pain, Mrs. C, for example, reports that she usually takes non-prescription pain relievers. When asked from whom she learned this, she clearly demonstrates her dependence on physician care:

> I don't do nothing without the doctor. If I go to have a tooth pulled I go ask him . . . If I have a tooth pulled I have to call him, stop the aspirin and they can't put me to sleep. They give me Novocaine and I have a cancerous tumor in the bladder and they put me to sleep. They gave me a spinal and I have to be very careful and I can't take a chance.

When asked if she might consider trying a new way of dealing with aches and pain Mrs. C further exhibits her dependence on professional care:

> Well there isn't anything because the doctors said they wouldn't give it to me. They said it would go away as time goes by.

When asked if a new method would have to be doctor recommended, Mrs. C states:

> Oh yes, I can't do nothing without him. Even if I have a cold I have to ask him what to take.

Like Mrs. C, when Ms. D experiences discomfort due to bone and joint pain she consults her physician. While she also restricts her activity and applies heat to aching bones, she looks to her doctor in hopes of receiving medication that will alleviate her pain. Acknowledging that she then tailors the taking of medicine to her own preferences, Ms. D nonetheless evaluated her self-care in the biomedical terms of compliance:

> I call my doctor and ask him what happened and he usually tells me to come into the office and then what medication. I do have medication to take and I haven't been taking it as regular as I should have been because I know there are some side effects on it. But when I am in great pain, but they tell me I shouldn't take it when I need it, I should take it all the time and maybe that is my mistake. I don't know but I'll start taking it everyday.

When asked if taking medication is the usual way she deals with aches and pains, Mrs. D replies, "Yes, it is about the only way you can." In addition to these actions, all of which she learned from her physician, Ms. D reports that she is quite willing to try a new method to deal with aching bones. She, however, like most of the respondents in the present sample, is not inclined to attempt a new treatment without obtaining professional confirmation. When asked from whom she would learn of a new treatment, she cites either "a doctor or a pharmacy":

> I would check with my doctor before I did it. If someone would say, "I have some medication would you take that?" I would say, "no way. Just 'cause you can take it doesn't mean I can."

More typical than the extreme reliance demonstrated in the above cases is respondents' making use of physicians as sources of information. This could involve the application to present symptoms of advice gleaned some time earlier; it could also involve an expectation that a medical recommendation would have to warrant any future changes in care strategies.

Respondents commonly retain self-care techniques taken or adapted from physicians' recommendations some time in the past. Mrs. M, for example, identifies her children's pediatrician as the origin of her symptom response of drinking fluids in large quantities:

> I remember my kids were small, you know . . . the doctor used to give me those written down things. I used to always let him write the things cause I get confused. For the children he used to say, never mind the food, push fluids.

Mrs. M also takes self-initiated actions, such as "dressing properly" and taking her temperature, but she prefers to employ doctor-suggested treatments. Of trying a new technique to deal with cold symptoms, she states:

> I don't. Why should I look for new ways if these are the ways that are helping us up to now . . . No I can't think of [anything] you could do, unless the doctor would suggest it. Other than that he tells me, you're doing fine.

Mrs. L's reply also typifies formally guided self-care. She usually exercises and takes an over-the-counter medication to relieve bone and joint pain. Of the exercises she remarks:

> The acupuncturist advised me always to keep my joints moving, waking, walking was the best thing. I walked around the block every morning, came down the stairs. All that helped because if you get a frozen joint it is the worst thing that can happen.

Mrs. L is willing to try a new technique to deal with aches and pains, but would first consult her physician:

> Well if it was suggested on my surgeon's advice. [Asked whether she would be influenced by word of new treatment through the

media or friends:] Well I would listen to that part, but I would immediately ask my doctor if he knew of this new [thing], and if it would benefit me in any way.

These respondents are not alone in their preference for doctor-suggested or scientifically proven treatment modes. In fact, even of those who did not seek formal care for symptom treatment, the vast majority of respondents are highly skeptical of other "less informed" sources. One way to interpret this apparent inconsistency is that both reliance on home remedies and faith in biomedicine reduce uncertainty for respondents in responding to illness symptoms: the former, through the validation of personal experience and the latter, through the imprimatur of science.

Combination Self-Care Strategies

The majority of respondents (N=11, 47%) demonstrate both formally and informally guided self-care in tending to symptoms. For the most part, these respondents take care of their symptoms on their own, utilizing methods learned from those in their informal networks. Yet professional care, specifically physician care, is also part of their coping strategy. Mrs. G, for example, is a seventy-three-year-old recent widow who rates her overall health as "very good." She has not been hospitalized in the past five years, but she has experienced pain in her legs and knees, especially on "damp days." One way in which she relieves her aches and pain is with a hydroculator (moist heating pad) which she learned about from her therapist and her mother. Following dinner in a "very cold" restaurant, Mrs. G began to experience "terrible pain in the back." She explains how she coped with the pain:

> I went to an orthopedic and he said it was arthritis and so he gave me a different kind of medication. Anyway I took that and I broke out and it gave me a rash, and so then he tried the medicine. I think I took three bottles and he finally said I needed therapy, so then I went to a therapist who was the one that did the brace and the hydroculator. My mother had to a have a hydrolic [sic], so she gave me hers because my father had fallen and hurt his back. So they told him to use that, and that is about all.

When asked if she would consider trying a new way to deal with bone and joint pain, Mrs. G replies:

> Yes I think I would, but I am afraid of, not medication, but I am afraid of it. [In response to what could persuade her to try

something new, she states,] I think a doctor, I wouldn't take it from anyone else.

Mrs. T, a seventy-seven-year-old widow, also demonstrates a mixture of lay and professional care in dealing with cold symptoms which she experiences annually. She tends to her cold and flu symptoms with the use of an "old remedy" that she learned from her grandmother:

> I usually stick to hot toddies. Hot lemonade with honey or maybe brandy. Lots of liquids and that is about it.

She also cites "seeing the doctor" as an action she takes to deal with cold and flu symptoms:

> Gee I would see a doctor. When you get a cold you usually see the doctor.

Mrs. T, like other respondents, later says she only consults her physician "if it gets bad or if it lasts too long," echoing the use of "temporalizing" as a trigger in decisions to seek medical aid (Zola 1973). When asked if she would consider trying a new way to deal with cold and flu symptoms, Mrs. T maintains that she would not as long as her present methods continue to prove effective. In the event that her remedies ceased working, she would contact the doctor for "something stronger."

Summary: A Mixed Model of Self-Care

The present analysis suggests several ways in which professional care, informal care, and self-care intersect. First, no one in the present sample could be categorized as solely engaging in individual self-care. All of the respondents either report consultation with a lay or professional consultant prior to action, or relied on treatments that they learned from previous encounters. Even those who do not seek professional care to deal with these common symptoms utilize formal health care for their "more serious" ailments; thus their coping strategies include formal care *a priori*. Few fail to cite physicians as information sources regarding new ways to deal with symptoms.

These results indicate the power of biomedicine in the lives of these older adults. Respondents, including those who credit their relief to non-medical interventions, prefer a medically approved method or treatment. However, they often prefer to use their own methods, or versions of formal methods, as long as possible. Furthermore, very few respondents rely exclusively on professional care for symptom relief. Contributions of informal social networks to self-care are apparent in the origins of learned responses as well as in the shaping of self-care behavior by its social context, as described further below. Psychosocial aspects of self-care further reveal themselves in the commonly observed continuity of self-care strategies over the life course. This suggests that the dichotomization of self-care into mutually exclusive professional and lay care categories oversimplifies and limits the description of the symptom experience. Older persons appear to approach and interpret their symptoms within both a biomedical framework and a psychosocial context.

The Social Contexts of Self-Care

Symptom experience not only shapes the individual's account of illness, but more importantly, it elucidates the link between the self, body and society (Williams 1984), reinforcing self-care behavior as a social phenomenon. That is, symptom response represents behavior that is shaped by interaction with self and others (either formally or informally). Symptoms typically affect an individual's physical, psychological (i.e., self-esteem) and social self (Charmaz 1991)—realms that are interactive as they affect symptom responses. Respondents frequently described their symptoms and care strategies in terms of present or past relationships with significant others. This section shows how, in making reference to past and present relations to describe a recent phenomenon or state, respondents linked their sense of self with their social context. More abstractly, it illustrates how individuals draw upon social experiences and relationships to help make sense of symptoms and, at times, health and illness more generally.

The Role of Significant Others in Self-Care

For many older people, sickness is part of their "reality." In tending with common symptoms, those not necessarily attributed to aging, some of our respondents discuss significant others as part of their caring strategies. For example, Mrs. M, a seventy-year-old woman who experiences cold symptoms about three times a year, explains how her daughter plays a crucial role in maintaining her physical and psychological health. Mrs. M considers herself extremely fortunate to have her daughter's support, because her spouse is unsympathetic to her ailments. She describes her husband as "bitter" and "selfish," while her daughter is her "doctor" and "morale builder." Of her husband, Mrs. M says:

> Then I have this husband that doesn't understand. Well he's had extreme illness, he's had open heart surgery, he's had aneurysms, he's had an ulcer operation so he's very bitter. Since he's got this heart attack, I think it's eight years ago, he became very, very bitter. Even if you're dying he doesn't want to hear it because he's being mistreated the worst and I wait on him hand and foot . . . because if I get sick who's gonna take care of him, selfish.

It is not surprising that Mrs. M attributes the cause of cold/flu symptoms to "stress," "nerves," and "misunderstandings"—emotion-laden factors that apparently reflect her sometimes troubling relationship with her husband. In response to how she usually deals with cold and flu symptoms, Mrs. M replies:

> Well my daughter calls me and she says, are you resting Ma, are you drinking Ma? Yes I am. I'm gonna check up on ya at noon time, you better tell me, I'm keeping track of your temperature and how much did you drink. Did you drink half a gallon. Yes I did. Very good, you're doing good. She kinda, you know, you need a little something like that.

Similarly, Mrs. K, a seventy-nine-year-old widow, explains how her daughter helps her comply with the "doctor's orders":

> Well the doctor tells you to rest and so on and so forth you know because I always like to keep going and sometimes that doesn't help, so that is why I rest and I live with my daughter and naturally she helps me out, to make sure that I rest . . . I am not supposed to exert myself, Diane don't want me to, my daughter is the type that doesn't want me to do too much.

Later she comments:

> Well I tell you, a lot of people my age live alone and it makes them depressed and I feel bad for them. I am lucky I have a family.

At the close of the interview, the interviewer remarks that Mrs. K. seems "very happy." In response Mrs. K offers a fairly long narrative comparing her attitude to her daughter's. She states:

> Well, you know what is the use of complaining, you know what I mean, if something happened and my daughter is the same way. She doesn't feel too good, but she runs a, she just opened up a preschool in September and a lot of things she had to go through, but she managed to get it done. And she had what they call sprue

and can't eat anything and then she has swollen glands and that effects her breathing . . . And she is another one who you would never think she is sick.

In addition to her supportive family, Mrs. K attributes her relatively good health to caring for her ill husband. She says that prior to the death of her husband she did not give much thought to the return of cold and flu symptoms:

No because I haven't experienced too much illness in my life. I guess I was too busy taking care of my husband for fifteen years. He was an invalid . . . he needed all the care I could give him. Plus he couldn't talk, but I had help, my son-in-law, my daughter helped me and I was alright for all those years, then I got this angina attack and I think that weakened me.

Mrs. W, who relies on her physician for treatment advice, also cites her husband as a source of relief:

I have a husband that can treat me better than a doctor . . . I don't know, but he knows just what to do. He should have been a doctor or a lawyer or an Indian Chief. He missed his profession . . . He takes better care of me than a doctor or nurse, but now he is sicker than I am.

Caring and Caregiving

Situating symptoms and care in relation to ill significant others is particularly common among elderly caregivers. A seventy-six-year-old man, Mr. G, places his symptoms in this context as well. Mr. G has Crohns disease, two detached retinas, and cataracts. He also underwent a prostate operation approximately two years ago. Mr. G cares for his seventy-nine-year-old wife, who is "incapacitated," and his thirty-nine-year-old son, who is mentally ill. When asked if his wife is presently alive, Mr. G says of his spouse:

She is living but she [is] incapacitated. She goes to adult day care three days a week . . . she does require quite a bit of care and I am the caregiver, and it takes up a good deal of my time.

Asked about his home ownership, Mr. G continues to elaborate on his wife's condition:

She has severe arthritis and it has affected her ambulation. Also, she had a major depression and was hospitalized for two months in a psychiatric unit in 1987, so she is on a lot of medication.

When asked if he rates his overall health as "good," Mr. G places his health in the context of caregiving.

> Yes, in the sense that caring for two ill people in the house and just the three of us, having to do all the cooking and cleaning, the shopping and all that is quite a job. Not that I am complaining, but this is one of the things when you asked about the cold, I really couldn't afford to be that sick, to be incapacitated.

Mrs. B, age seventy, also discusses her health status in terms of her caregiving role. She rates her own health as "very good," but also explains the toll on her of caring for her husband, who suffers from "confusion" and presently resides in an area nursing home. Of her health status Mrs. B notes:

> When you have lack of sleep and you have to get up the next morning and start from scratch all over again, what you are doing for him, it knocks you out. When he went I got my sleep, I really did, I got a good night's sleep for a week and I went out and took a walk and got in the air and let the air get you. With a little bit of rest you feel much better. When you are closed in and you have these surroundings it is not that great.

Generational Linkages

Drawing upon past care scenarios involving themselves and significant others, some respondents make references to generational linkages in describing their care strategies. Two instances of this are noted above: Mrs. A's "sweater treatment" (copied from her parents) and Mrs. P's use of mittens (which she bought for and then "took" from her mother).

Similarly, in describing his response to pain in his hands, Mr. H refers to a response developed in young adulthood as part of the profession he shared with his father:

> I rubbed it [finger]. My fingers are very flexible so when I get a pain I just go to work with my fingers. Massage, yes. It is the best medicine in the world, like a good chiropractor. When you go to them that is what his main thing is, using his fingers, massaging the part that is hurt . . . My father was in the hatter business and our fingers were our main source of livelihood. I was talking to a fellow from East Germany who is in the same business. We were talking about it one day at the store, that is how he brought up the subject [hand massage].

Later Mr. H states that he knew of this technique long before his encounter with the East German colleague: "Getting right out of school. Getting right out of school, standing out on a wooden box and doing it."

Problematic Pasts and Troubling Presents

Other respondents express how past experiences in their own lives have helped to shape their present self and view of symptoms and/or illness. For example, one respondent, Ms. D, reports that she experiences bone/joint pain quite frequently and it causes her a great deal of pain. Ms. D is separated from her husband and has two children (a son and a daughter) with whom she no longer maintains contact. She reports that bone and joint pain make her feel angry and frustrated. Ms. D expresses that her frame of mind appears unrelated to her illness, but to a fear of death.

> And what I can't understand, it has nothing to do probably with the rheumatoid. But what I can't understand is why now that I am sixty-three years old and I think more of dying than I did before. Now I stop and think, you know, will it be today, tomorrow, how am I going to go, am I going to be in a lot of pain.

When asked if her preoccupation with death is due to her age or health, Ms. D reveals that her attitude has much more to do with life satisfaction at different points in time. Her narrative clearly reveals a retrospection of her "young," undesirable life:

> It just comes to me and I got ten years, I am sixty-three, seventy-three most people are dying at seventy-three or am I going to keep living till I am about ninety. Yeah I would like to even if I am the way I am. I would like to live as long as I possibly can 'cause right now this is the best part of my life. My older times have been better to me. My young life was nothing but trouble. I would get into trouble and stuff like that, not because I wanted to, I was trying to get back at other people, try to get back. I hurt me and my family, life stunk, you know you are pushed from this home to that home, I wanted to get back at everybody. That was my young life, now my old life I can do what I want, say what I want, come in and go out when I want, no husband either to tell me what to do. I lived nine years of hell married so it's just great to be just me and I would like to live, now I can enjoy what I got . . . in my younger life I thought of committing suicide, but that quickly went over.

Ms. L, another of the younger respondents at age sixty-five, draws upon a significant prior life experience as well as a generational linkage to explain her symptom reality. Ms. L has been experiencing pain in her legs which she attributes to falling off some slippery rocks. When asked if she thought her pain was due to aging, Ms. L recreates her mother's level of activity and compares it to her own:

> You know too I thought like psychosomatic or like if you tell me you have a pain then I have one. I recently lost my mother and she used to say all the time that one of her legs, she couldn't walk. And of course I would say "come on Ma let's go outside" and she would say "I can't walk from here to there, I can't even imagine that your body would," then she would start and she used the walker and all those things. But lo and behold I got the same damn pain over here like she had and I cried even more and said, gee, I can't explain it to you. [Interviewer: "Well I understand I think you are getting at the pain represented more than just I fell down and I have this pain, it could have affected your frame of mind."] I associated it with sadness and . . . guilt. [Interviewer: "Because you thought you could prevent it?"] No, but I thought I could have told my mother I loved her.

A few respondents explain their frame of mind in terms of grief and loss. For example, Mrs. G explains her frame of mind when dealing with bone/joint pain in terms of the grief she has experienced within the past year. Prior to the death of her husband, Mrs. G would get "angry" when experiencing symptoms, now she becomes more depressed. When asked to describe her frame of mind when faced with bone/joint pain, she notes:

> Kind of depressed a little bit. Right now, you know, I lost my husband eight months ago, so it doesn't make it very easy because I miss him so much. We were very close. We were married for forty-six years. He died a week before Christmas.

In addition to her husband, Mrs. G has recently lost her mother. To prepare for symptoms Mrs. G exercises and has tried to lose weight—an "accomplishment" she also credits to her sorrow.

> I lost weight from stress 'cause of I am all alone and now I don't eat. I used to like to bake but I don't now. I just have one son, and I don't have anyone else . . . That is why I come here and try to forget. 'Cause if I am home all I will do is cry. You can tell by my eyes.

In a similar vein, asked about the extent of her discomfort caused by bone/joint pain, Mrs. N reports taking a nightly sleeping pill for the past twelve years, since the death of her husband. Mrs. N, seventy-seven years old and without children, experiences "stiffness in her bones" quite regularly, during which time she becomes "nervous." In addition to exercising and taking an analgesic, Mrs. N has this to say about self-care actions:

> Such as getting away from it all. Well I think a lot of my problem is that I am not happy where I am living. Ever since I sold my home I am not happy where I am. [So you think it affects your health?] I think so, yes. And I can't seem to stay home alone. I want to get out, so I come here and go to the mall and there are people there. I can't seem to stay alone.

Indeed, Mrs. N expresses that moving into an apartment was "the sorriest thing [she] ever did" and it is "always on the back of [her] mind." Thus, aside from chronic bronchitis, inner ear problems, and cataracts, Mrs. N places her physical pain in social context. Her reality is mediated by what appears to be loneliness and a clear dissatisfaction with her current living arrangement.

Mrs. H, at age sixty-two, experiences severe, or in her words "massive," back pain that, at times, is incapacitating. In the course of discussing common problems, such as headaches and colds, the interviewer asks, "Do you think there's any physical complaints or problems that are particularly related to being a woman?" In response, Mrs. H says:

> Oh. Yeah. The main thing is . . . women nowadays are independent and are able to take care of themselves more than women of my generation . . . I was left with three children, I had a boy in college, a daughter and a baby ten days old; my husband left . . . And I raised the three of them, but I had to do it with physical work, which I had done all my life. And I went back to school and got my education and thought, well gee whiz, now I'm going to do something easy. I went to secretarial school and all that, but then I fell and hurt my back. So I had to raise them alone and work two jobs, but then they found out that my back, . . . one morning I got up and couldn't move. It started a chain reaction, a complete disintegration of my spine. But then they found out that I had scoliosis as a child, and I had rheumatic fever, which all led up to the whole condition, one is hurting the other, and the other's hurting the other one . . . I was orientated . . . my whole was divided into worlds . . . I had to earn a living but yet I had to take care of the kids too. I found it harder being a woman . . . if I had been a man I feel like I would've still had the career part without the physical part of it.

The interviewer then asks "Are you feeling that this caused some of your physical problems?" Mrs. H responds:

> Yeah, because I had the responsibility and if I hadn't been, ya know, a woman I wouldn't have had the responsibility of the children and the home and the breadearning and all that by myself and sometimes I felt like I had been, you know, a man it would have been much easier but I had to assume the role of a man, which I didn't like.

As illustrated by this fairly lengthy narrative, Mrs. H situates her health in a difficult past—a time in which she was struggling to meet the demands of family, school, and employment. Interestingly, unlike other respondents, Mrs. H speaks of a gendered self. Her past social context is discussed in terms of being a woman and having to tend to both the private and public spheres, a role that was much less common and, perhaps for many, less desirable than it is today.

Summary: The Social Self

This section has shown how relationships with children and significant others, the role of caregiving, and problematic pasts are all part of the older adult's reality and help construct and/or alter the sense of self. While social networks clearly shape symptom responses, those responses themselves also express social meanings incorporated into the individual's present identity and longer term personal biography. When investigations of self-care restrict their focus to the actions older adults take when experiencing discomfort or whether or not aged respondents seek formal care, they overlook how the individual's social worlds affect present symptom responses. This analysis suggests that these effects will differ in degree and in kind for each individual.

Discussion: Caring for the "Self"

In the course of describing what they do to care for common symptoms, respondents also display who they are: the terms they use to represent their behaviors and feelings encapsulate representations of themselves. They depict various roles such as worker, parent, child, or spouse, caregiver or care recipient. They also appear in different capacities. As active agents they invent, adapt, and implement care decisions and strategies. They react to the instructions, signals, sanctions and needs of others. Finally, they are reflexive, objectifying their symptoms and symptom episodes and using their accounts of them as occasions for life review.

These reports thus contain many types of self representation, with respondents signalling diverse and often inconsistent selves. In some cases the inconsistency derives from the incompatibility of role requirements, as when being a caregiver makes it impossible also to become a care recipient. There is also a more general inconsistency in cognitions about self-care, the clearest example of which is the constant reliance on home remedies coupled with proclaimed faith solely in biomedical expertise. In other instances the inconsistency comes from the juxtaposition of different dimensions of reality. Many accounts fracture time, with the present self contrasted in one sentence with the self in the past, in the next with a future projection. Representations of space, context and social others shift in corresponding manner.

As narratives, these accounts echo anthropologist Katherine Ewing's (1990, p. 251) description of the self as a multiple entity:

> In all cultures people can be observed to project multiple, inconsistent self-representations that are context-dependent and may shift rapidly. At any particular moment a person usually experiences his or her articulated self as a symbolic, timeless whole, but this self may quickly be displaced by another quite different 'self', which is based on a different definition of the situation. The person will often be unaware of these shifts and inconsistencies and may experience wholeness and continuity despite their presence.

Thus, while selves shift, the individual experiences his/her present identity as "whole and continuous" (Ewing 1990, p. 252). Maintaining this sense of coherence is possible, Ewing maintains, because individuals develop flexibility in shifting among multiple self-presentations and fail to examine inconsistencies those contain. In times of stress or conflict, however, such flexibility may become strained, or confronting inconsistencies may become inescapable.

Symptom experiences appear to act precisely as this form of disjunction, denoting not merely the possibility of physical breakdown, but that of temporal plans, spatial habitation, social relations, and personal biography (Williams 1984, Charmaz 1991). Symptoms are precisely "ab- [out of] normalities," and individuals appear to take action in response only when temporal, spatial and/or social dimensions of their normal realities are sufficiently threatened (Zola 1973). Self-care thus involves the attempt to re-establish a sense of wholeness, to regain the ability *not* to attend to inconsistencies, present or potential, in one's life.

Metaphorically speaking, caring strategies must pull the self and/or selves together again, and it is largely through metaphor and other semiotic devices that they do so. Describing the concept of organizing images or metaphors used to examine life review narratives of older adults, Luborsky (1993, p. 448) notes,

> An image or metaphor, by referencing a larger orienting construct . . . is integral to constituting a sense of wholeness and identity . . . Metaphors serve as orienting constructs that sustain a sense of wholeness. They do so by the dissolving of prior images or disparate elements . . . to give a fresh coherence to the multitude events of a lifetime. Guiding metaphors . . . cross-reference separate domains of meaning to supply information from a familiar to a lesser known domain, thus merging them to form a new one.

The most common use of metaphor by respondents in this study is the way they interpret past and present social relations to frame their interpretation of bodily symptoms and care responses. In some cases they merge the relationship and the symptom directly (e.g., "I took it from my mother, so to speak," Mrs. P; "lo and behold I got the same damn pain over here like [her mother] had," Mrs. L). In other cases, caring for others, or loss and grief form the domains linked to self-care strategies. Social roles more generally form the metaphoric context for Mrs. H's discussion of her back pain as a "woman's problem."

The linkage of self to other people and to past times merges present (or recent) self-care with a broader domain of meaning. It creates a metaphoric distance from the concrete experience of symptoms, sheltering that experience within a "powerful orienting image" (Luborsky 1993, p. 448). It is this transcendent quality of metaphor that particularly instills a sense of wholeness (Luborsky 1993; cf. Ewing 1990).

Other narrative and semiotic devices achieve similar results. Noting that medical encounters objectify patients in a realm where their own sense of self is lost, Katherine Young posits that stories told by patients in medical interviews act to provide an "enclave" for the self (Young 1989, p. 153). Asking individuals to describe symptom experiences may instill the same sense of objectification of the body, an exhortation to see the body from the outside and in parts, rather than as a whole connected with the self. Weaving stories of past selves and past generations, as well as representations of others into the account of self thus acts as a narrative enclave, protecting against a sense of "ontological abandonment" (Gergen and Gergen 1983, p. 271) and reestablishing a coherent orientation.

Asking about past sources of learning and possible changes in self-care strategies creates openings for respondents to describe prior and future events. Their responses go beyond those questions, however, both substantively and symbolically, as when they contrast their present selves with troubled pasts or trace the use of a strategy across the courses of their lives. These discussions thus provide a dialogic context in which respondents organize and present multiple self-representations based in past, present and future (cf. Ewing 1990).

A final semiotic device apparent in these responses is the use of metonymy, figurative speech in which the name of one thing is substituted for another closely associated with it. Much like the psychological process of displacement, metonymy may provide a defense of the self by focusing on a peripheral detail that comes to represent a wider experience in a way that is not affectively charged (Ewing 1990). In the several cases where respondents reveal broader pains in their lives, symptom descriptions may have provided this type of focus. Mrs. M's discussion of cold symptoms, for example, garners the wider realm of a cold husband and caring daughter. The way in which she describes "pushing" fluids (a strategy associated with a doctor caring for her children) is a more specific distillation of that social environment. Similarly, Mrs. N's nightly sleeping pill, taken on a doctor's advice for stiffness in her bones, recalls the death of her husband.

While biomedicine has been criticized for failing to live up to its claim to operate with affective neutrality (cf. Mishler et al. 1981), the lesser affective charge that "fluids" have compared with "husband," or "sleeping pill" compared to "grief," may make formal medical prescriptions useful metonymic elements, whatever their physiological properties. That is, they allow the formulation, use and recall of self-care strategies to proceed while lessening the impact of emotionally painful or threatening associations. Going one step farther, this may be one reason people look so consistently to biomedicine to certify something new for common symptoms, even as they continue to rely on informally learned and experientially tested self-care strategies. Clearly the "cultural authority" of medicine (Starr 1982), its control over the social construction of disease, is at work here. In addition, however, biomedicine may possess metonymic power in being able to provide affectively neutral means of focusing and treating diffuse, highly charged complaints. As individuals combine biomedical and lay strategies in their self-care, they thus merge rational and emotional elements of self, yielding a treatment more holistic (at least on a symbolic level) than either could provide alone.

Conclusions

The focus of this analysis has been on how elderly individuals devise self-care practices for mundane symptoms and the meanings they attach to them. Accounts of this type of self-care reveal in action the semiotic processes used to organize and interpret the sense of self. While the intent here has been to assess how self-care works symbolically, the discussion suggests the possibility of psychologically therapeutic properties deriving from the use of metaphor and metonymy.

The continuity of self-care practices over a long period of one's adult life course implies that individuals may perceive a personal history of "things that work" and "things that don't." In all likelihood, these personal successes and failures with various self-care strategies are embedded in a context of the experiences of other persons in the social network. Perhaps there is also a belief that certain self-care strategies work "sometimes, but at least they do not make the situation worse," as opposed to those which have produced unpleasant side effects or simply were not effective at all. Therefore, a specific self-care strategy can be avoiding a definite negative as much as it is assuring a positive outcome whenever it is used.

References

Brody, Elaine M. and Morton H. Kleban. 1981. "Physical and Mental Health Symptoms of Older People: Who Do They Tell?" *Journal of the American Geriatrics Society* 29:442–49.

Bury, Michael. 1991. "The Sociology of Chronic Illness: A Review of Research and Prospects." *Sociology of Health & Illness* 13:451–68.

Chappell, Neena L. 1987. "The Interface Among Three Systems of Care: Self, Informal, and Formal." Pp. 159–179 in *Health in Aging: Sociological Issues and Policy Directions*, edited by R. A. Ward and S. S. Tobin. New York: Springer.

Chappell, Neena L., Laurel A. Strain, and Mark Badger. 1988. "Self-Care in Health and Illness." *Comprehensive Gerontology* 2:92–101.

Charmaz, Kathy. 1991. *Good Days, Bad Days: The Self in Chronic Illness and Time.* New Brunswick, NJ: Rutgers University.

Dean, Kathryn. 1986. "Lay Care in Illness." *Social Science and Medicine* 2 2:275–84.
_____. 1992. "Health-Related Behavior: Concepts and Methods." Pp. 27–56 in *Aging, Health and Behavior*, edited by M. G. Ory, R. P. Abeles, and P. D. Lipman. London: Sage.

Ewing, Katherine P. 1990. "The Illusion of Wholeness: Culture, Self, and the Experience of Inconsistency." *Ethos* 18:251–78.

Gergen, Kenneth J. and Mary M. Gergen. 1983. "Narratives of the Self." Pp. 254–73 in *Studies in Social Identity*, edited by T. R. Sarbin and K. E. Scheibe. New York: Praeger.

Haug, Marie. 1984. "Doctor-Patient Relationships and Their Impact on Elderly Self-Care." Paper presented at the Annual Meeting of the Gerontological Society of America.

Haug, May L. Wykle and Kevan H. Namazi. 1989. "Self-Care Among Older Adults." *Social Science and Medicine* 29:171–83.

Leventhal, Elaine A. and Thomas R. Prohaska. 1986. "Age, Symptom Interpretation, and Health Behavior." *Journal of the American Geriatrics Society* 34:185–91.

Levin, Lowell S., Alfred H. Katz, and Erik Holst. 1976. *Self-Care: Lay Initiatives in Health*. New York: Prodist.

Luborsky, Mark R. 1993. "The Romance with Personal Meaning in Gerontology: Cultural Aspects of Life Themes." *The Gerontologist* 33:445–52.

Mishler, Elliot G., Lorna Amara Singham, Stuart T. Hauser, Ramsay Liem, Samuel D. Osherson, and Nancy E. Waxler, editors. 1981. *Social Contexts of Health, Illness, and Patient Care*. Cambridge: Cambridge University.

Prohaska, Thomas R., Mary L. Keller, Elaine A. Leventhal, and Howard Leventhal. 1987. "Impact of Symptoms of Aging Attribution on Emotions and Coping." *Health Psychology* 6:495–514.

Register, Cheri. 1987. *Living with Chronic Illness*. New York: Free Press.

Segall, Alexander and Neena L. Chappell. 1991. "Making Sense Out of Sickness: Lay Explanations of Chronic Illness Among Older Adults." *Advances in Medical Sociology* 2:115–33.

Segall, Alexander, Neena L. Chappell, and Jay Goldstein. 1989. "Exploring the Correlates of Self-Provided Health Care Behaviour." *Social Science and Medicine* 29:153–61.

Starr, Paul. 1982. *The Social Transformation of American Medicine*. New York: Basic Books.

Verbrugge, Lois M. and Frank J. Ascione. 1987. "Exploring the Iceberg: Common Symptoms and How People Care for Them." *Medical Care* 25:539–69.

Williams, Gareth. 1984. "The Genesis of Chronic Illness: Narrative Reconstruction." *Sociology of Health and Illness* 6:176–200.

Young, Katharine. 1989. "Narrative Embodiments: Enclaves of the Self in the Realm of Medicine." Pp. 152–165 in *Texts of Identity*, edited by J. Shotter and K. J. Gergen. London: Sage.

Zola, Irving K. 1973. "Pathways to the Doctor—From Person to Patient." *Social Science and Medicine* 7:677–89.

17
Western Reflections on Eastern Medicine

Alexandra Dundas Todd

In the fall of 1992, "The CBS Evening News" ran a five-part series on alternative medicines. The subject matter, increasingly in the news, is not unusual, but CBS's respectful treatment of these innovative methods is surprising. Acupuncture and relaxation, hypnotherapy and herbal remedies, chiropractics and macrobiotics were all investigated. Although no claims to absolute proof were made, the commentators expressed enthusiasm for success stories and preliminary data. Edie Magnus, the reporter covering the series, introduced the week with the statement "Proven or not, alternative treatments are now being used by more than half of all Americans, so conventional medicine finds itself forced to consider the unconventional."[1] And in concluding: "It seems the medical profession is learning to never say never."[2]

Similarly, in the spring of 1993, PBS ran the phenomenally popular series "Healing and the Mind," hosted by Bill Moyers. Acupuncture, herbal remedies, therapeutic support groups, biofeedback, visualizations, and more were reviewed through Moyers's own fascinated eyes. Experts and studies were quoted, and although it was made clear that no one has all of the answers, the obvious message was that to ignore such offerings meant mistaken medicine. The success of the series was followed by best-seller sales of the program's complementary book.[3] Concurrently, popular magazines such as *Time* and *Consumer Reports*, as well as MIT's *Technology Review*, ran favorable articles on new ways of expanding our understanding of health and healing.[4]

Such popularity shouldn't surprise us. After all, according to an article in the *New England Journal of Medicine*, many of us have sought help from a variety of nonmainstream providers. One in three respondents in a study of 1,539 adults in the United States "reported using at least one unconventional therapy in the past year, and one-third of these saw providers for unconventional therapy" (an average of 19 visits each).[5]

Given this growing interest, the call by Ralph W. Moss (editor of *Cancer Chronicles* and author of various books on health care) for more research on alternatives continues to be timely. He claims we need to weed out the useful from the false, the helpers from the harmers. The stakes are too high not to widen our visions and definitions.

> ... the continuing failure of orthodox medicine to deal satisfactorily with the major forms of cancer guarantees the growth of nonconventional approaches. Some of these approaches are possibly fraudulent or even harmful; others are doubtlessly inert. Yet among them all may well be some methods of great benefit to cancer patients. It is the job of the true scientist ... to take a serious and open-minded look at all methods and claims. . . . A million new cases [of cancer] a year demand no less.[6]

The alternative methods used by Drew [John Andrew Todd, Jr., son of Alexandra Dundas Todd, and whose triumph over cancer is the subject of the book from which this is excerpted]—especially acupuncture, relaxation techniques, and macrobiotics—though still considered exotic (particularly by him) are not so uncommon. Numerous stories and some studies suggest, amid controversy, that combining Eastern with Western medicines may be good for your health. Drew thought so. He felt that exactly the remedies now seeping into mass media discussions had helped him to help himself, to heal faster and feel better in the process.

Nutrition and Cancer

I met Rachel at my first natural-foods cooking class in 1991. A trim, elegant woman in her late fifties, dressed in a stylish jogging suit, her head wrapped in a silk turban, she looked like someone who would be whipping up nouvelle this or that, not studying healthy cooking.

"What brought you here?" I asked, looking for reassurance that I wasn't joining a cult of brown rice grazers.

"Cancer," she replied.

She had started with surgery, moving on to chemotherapy.

"When the doctors told me the cancer was still there, that it was spreading, and they couldn't do anything more, I figured what's to lose."

Rachel had read an article years before about people curing themselves of cancer with diet and had filed it away in the back of her mind. She'd been on a healing foods diet for about six months when I met her. Soon after starting she felt better than she had for some time. She traveled with her husband and kept up her busy social life, taking her own dinner to elegant dinner parties.

"I put my dinner in a lovely casserole and ask whoever's in the kitchen to warm it in the oven for me."

"Really? What are people's reactions?" I asked.

"Well, if they're close friends, it's understood; if not, I tell them in advance. What are they going to say? Besides people don't like to talk about cancer. They don't inquire past the word."

Rachel, like many seemingly self-cured cancer recoverers, is someone who believed in modern medicine. Like everyone I've talked to or read about, she learned of her illness from a doctor. In Rachel's case she did what they told her to do; it didn't work. There was nothing more medicine could offer. She was considered terminal. Ann Fawcett and Cynthia Smith's book *Cancer Free* includes numerous personal stories similar to Rachel's. Kit Kitatani, for example, underwent surgery for stomach cancer. The surgery was followed by chemotherapy. The cancer was still there, along with a new problem: bone marrow damage from the chemotherapy. When the doctor explained that he had nothing more to offer, Mr. Kitatani was furious.

"Don't be silly. You can't just drop me like this. Isn't there anything you can do?"

"Nothing," replied the doctor.[7]

Mr. Kitatani was lucky to run into a friend who claimed she had cured herself of terminal cancer with macrobiotics. He tried it. Seven years later, recovered, Mr. Kitatani is still a development specialist with the United Nations. He has used his influence to form the International Macrobiotic Society of the United Nations, introducing health information to agencies around the world.

A more famous example is Anthony Sattilaro, chief executive officer of Methodist Hospital in Philadelphia. A conventional doctor and administrator, after learning that he had metastasized prostate cancer, he turned to the best modern medicine had to offer. It was, after all, just down the hall from his office. But nothing worked for him, either. He was planning his funeral when he learned about macrobiotics from two hitchhikers. He never let go of medicine, clinging to bone scan results and consulting his team of specialists regularly. He would have gone the full medical course had it offered him the hope of a cure. But it hadn't. So, continuing to discuss his alternative path with skeptical doctors, he found help elsewhere.[8]

Rachel, Kit Kitatani, and Anthony Sattilaro did not reject modern medicine. Modern medicine rejected them. They are examples of one way that people happen upon an alternative route. Equally common in the literature are people who start out on the conventional route, reject it at varying points, and introduce their own game plan. They are, for the most part, conventional people who accepted their doctors' diagnoses and treatments. But somewhere along the way they lose faith; the cure is worse than the cancer, or the odds are so slim, the remedies so drastic, it doesn't seem worth it.

When Michael Shanik, in his early forties, was told he had a malignant melanoma, he and his wife did some research. His chances of survival, whether treated or not, were between 10 and 20 percent. The Shaniks discovered macrobiotics, changed their diet, slowed down their lives, and, over the strenuous objections of their physician, turned down the suggested surgery. Mr. Shanik received a chilling letter from his doctor: "I need for you to be aware of the high risk you're taking by choosing your present course of action, which appears limited to using a macrobiotic diet. I trust that I have made myself clear."

To Mr. Shanik, "it was like receiving a death notice." After agonizing considerations he decided to stay with the diet. "We were unsure of macrobiotics because we didn't know much about it. One thing we were sure of though was that Michael's chances were slim to none, according to the doctors, where macrobiotics offered us some hope," his wife Mickey recalls.[9]

Michael Shanik thinks he made the right choice. Today he has no diagnosable cancer. He feels terrific.

A third, smaller group rejects medicine altogether. Dirk Benedict, the TV and film star, in his *Confessions of a Kamikaze Cowboy*, takes the solitary wrangler approach. A Montana boy, steeped in all the American West loner trappings, he rides off to Michio Kushi's remote New Hampshire cabin, with only his miso soup and a few other sundries, to tough it out—alone. Tough it out he does. He, unlike Dr. Sattilaro, has no use for doctors and their "shot in the dark" approach to illness in general, his prostate cancer in particular. Unlike Dr. Sattilaro, who is careful to commend modern medicine despite its inability in his case to save his life, Benedict launches tirades against the whole profession: "There's an old saying that goes, 'The only two things you can't escape are death and taxes.' I disagree. The only two things you can't escape are death and doctors! And if you have enough to do with the latter, you increase your chances of the former."[10] But escape death and doctors he does. At least this time around.

Like the other riveting and inspiring stories in print, from such sources as Ann Fawcett and Cynthia Smith's book to individual accounts like Elaine Nussbaum's *Recovery* and Anthony Sattilaro's *Recalled by Life*, the prognosis is promising. The data, although anecdotal, are ample enough to warrant attention and more scientific study.

Drew's story is different. Unlike the survivors described above, he stayed with conventional medicine. Western techniques of surgery and radiation played the biggest part in his recovery. Unlike the other cases, no one suggested that Drew forgo the recommended procedures and rely solely on macrobiotics. I wanted them to. It's not that Drew would have done so or that I would have urged him to. But I craved the reassurance of "Oh that, yes I've seen that a lot; people recover without surgery or radiation. My friend X is just fine." That would have been comforting, less serious. No one said anything of the sort. No one in any field claims everyone can be cured of cancer. Macrobiotic counselors are no exception. Anthony Sattilaro reports that Michio Kushi, when confronted with people who seemed past hope, would say, "It is very difficult. We won't know for a few months."[11]

At a dinner in honor of Herman Aihara, probably in his early seventies and considered one of the great macrobiotic theorists and practitioners in this country, along with Michio Kushi, I got this same message. My friend Karin told him about Drew. What did he think? He looked at me sadly.

"Very serious," he said and then looked down.

I felt the conversation was over. Karin persisted.

"He's had the first surgery. The second is scheduled for next week."

"Yes, of course he must have the surgery," agreed Mr. Aihara.

What! Of course he must have the surgery? This from a man who had devoted his life to curing the incurable, fixing the unfixable through macrobiotics. Mr. Aihara wanted to eat his dinner; he was at a party. I wanted a miracle. I wanted macrobiotics, at least in theory, to be that miracle. I knew we would not reject Dr. T's advice, but I wanted Mr. Aihara to reject it. He wouldn't either.

Just as Drew did not reject medical science, the doctors did not reject him. They were cautiously optimistic. The word *terminal* was never used; the procedures were based on successful results. The statistics, the same old 1 percent odds (now 5 percent) that had let us down repeatedly, were still being pulled out to give reassurance. We let them. But not completely. After all, we, like the people whose case studies I had read, were trying a variety of other modalities. But we weren't taking an either/or approach. We were hoping West would meet East, that they would complement each other, one technique bolstering another. We were combining what Hugh Faulkner calls "complementary [alternative] medicines" with orthodox (conventional) medicine.

Hugh Faulkner, a retired English doctor, was diagnosed in 1987 with pancreatic cancer. Firmly entrenched in the medical model, he followed his doctor's advice.

"When Marian [his wife], assuming that I had a cancer which was likely to be inoperable, asked what would happen if I didn't have the operation, Mr. Cochrane said that I would almost certainly obstruct. Naturally I decided to have the operation."[12]

Despite all that could be done, Dr. Faulkner knew his chances were slim. Pancreatic cancer, on the increase, is considered inevitably fatal. In a study of 196 cases, done at Yale, the average survival was seven months. One person lived six years. All died.

Dr. Faulkner had the surgery. He also had shiatsu massage and started a macrobiotic diet. Today he feels well and continues to work in retirement on what interests him most, health care and writing about his own cancer experience.[13] He sums up his situation as follows:

> Today, well over two years after the initial diagnosis, I feel extremely well. I can't claim conclusively that my cancer is regressing, though ultrasound and a CAT scan suggest some shrinking and liquefaction in the center of the tumor area. Nor can I prove that my present state is the result of macrobiotics. This story is just another example of the anecdotal accounts that many physicians quite properly find unconvincing. However, it has persuaded me that further dialogue is desirable between orthodox Western medical science and complementary medicine. The situation in the United States where both sides appear to hurl insults at one another across a Berlin Wall of misunderstanding is deplorable.[14]

Dr. Faulkner is right; his story is an anecdote, not something to base a medical practice on. He's also right that this should not stand in the way of further dialogue. And perhaps this metaphorical Berlin Wall is crumbling, just as the real one did. There are, in fact, many intriguing studies that help this dialogue. In earlier chapters [also from *Double Vision*, not reprinted here], I discussed studies on radiation and diet as well as a growing literature on nutrition and general health. The studies I list in this chapter, the ones directly related to cancer and its possible cure and prevention, were the ones that Drew found most convincing. And he, like everyone else with cancer who turns to alternatives, needed to be convinced.

Drew may not love leafy greens or brown algae in his soup, but the more he read, the more he too was intrigued. He stopped saying "there's nothing to lose" and started talking about all there was to gain.

The growing use of alternative medicines by so many people is perhaps easier to understand once cancer statistics in America are considered. According to the American Cancer Society one in three Americans alive today "will eventually have cancer." The National Cancer Institute figures show that between 1988 and 1990 lifetime *risk* for developing cancer (of any kind) was 42.5 percent for men, 38.8 percent for women. Between 1973 and 1990, cancer *rates* rose 18.3 percent.[15]

Of those afflicted, only roughly one in three survive, the same survival rate as in 1950. Furthermore, Dr. Steven A. Rosenberg of the National Cancer Institute, while applauding modern medical techniques in the treatment of some cancers, concludes: "Except possibly in selected patients with cancer of the stomach, there has been no demonstrated improvement in the survival of patients with the ten most common cancers when radiation therapy, chemotherapy, or both have been added to surgical resection."[16] In fact, these therapies can wreak damage from toxic effects.

Far from winning the "war on cancer," other reports, such as one by John Cairns of the Harvard School of Public Health, show heavy losses: "[A]part from the success with Hodgkin's disease, childhood leukemia and a few other cancers, it is not possible to detect any sudden change in death rates for any of the major cancers that could be credited to chemotherapy."[17] And John C. Bailar, who has worked for the National Cancer Institute and the *New England Journal of Medicine* and currently holds a faculty position at McGill University, told the President's cancer panel, "Whatever we have been doing, it is not working."[18]

With newer radiation techniques, greater precision in the use of chemotherapy, and better understanding of mutations in the chemical makeup of genes, some argue that these statistics are improving. I hope so, Drew certainly hopes so, but more time is needed to know. It's no wonder Americans find cancer the most frightening disease around.

But if these statistics overwhelm and frighten, others offer hope. As early as 1964, the World Health Organization stated that cancer could be 80 percent preventable with dietary and life-style changes. More recently, a few cancer specialists have been calling for a change in emphasis from cure to prevention. John C. Bailar and Elaine M. Smith write: "[W]e are losing the war against cancer, notwithstanding progress against several uncommon forms of the disease. . . . A shift in research emphasis, from research on treatment to research on prevention, seems necessary if substantial progress against cancer is to be forthcoming."[19] John Cairns too, in *Scientific American*, calls for prevention, citing history as our teacher. Historically, all of our major public health problems, from smallpox to tuberculosis to polio, have been overcome with prevention, not after-the-fact treatments.

In the absence of a vaccine against cancer, the emphasis on prevention is primarily on nutritional and life-style changes. Most dietary recommendations are similar to a macrobiotic diet—increase whole grains and vegetables, decrease animal fats and sweets, eat fresh, nonprocessed foods. A decrease in fats and chemicals especially increases health. Toxic chemicals are stored in fats in the body; thus, a diet high in both presents a double liability. (Since breast tissue is so high in fat, perhaps the escalating use of chemicals and of breast cancer rates are related.)

Despite the call for prevention from many medical experts and promising news on a variety of alternative approaches, some in medicine cry quackery at anything that veers from conventional treatment. Some of these dissenters find the public's interest in alternatives disturbing. The cited concerns of lack of proof, the proliferation of strange remedies that hark back to snake oils, and a fear that the public, even when well educated, is too gullible[20] all raise legitimate questions. But the answer to these questions is to find research to study new popular methods, not to dismiss them. Orthodox understandings must include what the public clearly wants and is pursuing, often in the face of dashed hopes by conventional cures.

Today new studies are being done on alternative medicines. National centers like the National Institutes of Health and the American Cancer Society, as well as medical centers around the country, are slowly opening their research agendas to include prevention and innovative medicines. But completed studies that meet scientific criteria are not yet common. Studies in progress may be promising but are rarely or only recently publicized. However, when a study with negative results is done, it is heralded as a landmark, proof that danger lurks in all "unproven" techniques, not just the one researched. (Victor Herbert, for example, lumps together and blasts what he terms "lucrative holistic practices" from "acupuncture to iridology, chiropractics, homeopathy, holistic psychotherapy . . . [to] therapeutic touch, and the hazards of herbal medicine.")[21]

The much noted study by Barrie R. Cassileth and colleagues received lavish attention.[22] Cassileth's elegantly designed research compares seventy-eight advanced cancer patients undergoing conventional treatments with seventy-eight similar patients participating in an alternative program at a center in San Diego, California. This center dispensed a mostly raw-foods diet, injections of bacille Calmette-Guerin and an immunity-enhancing vaccine, and coffee enemas. (Some participants at the alternative center were also using conventional treatments.) No differences were found in lengths of survival between the two groups. The San Diego group reported a decreased quality of life based on factors such as feelings of hunger (no doubt a result of a diet of raw foods).

Subsequent articles have used this study as a warning siren against "unproven" methods of cancer treatment[23] (a warning that assumes incorrectly that conventional always means proven). Actually, this study merely shows that people receiving care at one specialized alternative center fared no better (and in terms of length of survival, no worse) than those undergoing routine treatments. To generalize from this study (unless the same alternative procedures are used) is misleading and unscientific.

The most startling implication of this study, however, goes unmentioned in the reporting article, the subsequent citations, and the popular press: To find no differences in length of survival between those receiving conventional therapies and those receiving coffee enemas seems extraordinary to me and as telling about the former modes of treatment as the latter.

The macrobiotic diet (not included in the above-mentioned programs) also seems to strike a negative chord in some areas of medicine. Like my own first mistaken assumptions, articles against macrobiotics assume that the diet is rigidly brown-rice-dominated. Cassileth and Berlyne, in another article warning against alternative therapies, incorrectly claim that a macrobiotic diet "includes only whole grains, some specially cooked vegetables, and miso."[24] In 1984 the American Cancer Society cautioned, "The more restrictive macrobiotic diets pose a serious hazard to health."[25] And in *Oncology Nursing Forum*, nurses are told to counsel cancer patients away from macrobiotics to avoid nutritional deficiencies.[26] Despite lack of data to support such warnings, valid concerns do emerge from the articles. Macrobiotics has not been systematically studied, with proper controls and conclusions.[27] But just as yet no studies definitively prove macrobiotics works, none proves it doesn't. *All* cancer therapies, conventional and alternative, need more rigorous study. The current evidence for macrobiotics is largely personal testimony with some suggestive studies on foods included in the diet. More research is needed. The second concern is that macrobiotics can lead to nutritional deficiencies (for example, the vitamin B's and iron) in those most at risk from such a lack—the ill. This is a danger. As with any new food regimen, especially one that is exotic to the preparer, great care must be taken. Grains, beans, nuts, and seeds should be combined to create enough complementary proteins. It is also important to include fish (twice a week was recommended for Drew) and daily servings of sea vegetables to ensure that minerals and vitamins are sufficiently provided. Finally, consumers of all health care need to find qualified practitioners to guide them, and macrobiotics is no exception. We should ask a lot of questions, take nothing on faith, call umbrella organizations for referrals, ask to speak to others who have tried suggested programs. Demand to be convinced before accepting advice from any consultant, whether conventional or alternative.

Despite the critics, a congressional publication on health and long-term care supports the view that a careful macrobiotic diet is nutritionally sound.

> . . . the current macrobiotic diet . . . appears to be nutritionally adequate if the mix of foods proposed in the dietary recommendations is followed carefully. There is no apparent evidence of any nutritional deficiencies among macrobiotic practices. The diet is consistent with the recently released dietary guidelines of the National Academy of Sciences and the American Cancer Society in regard to possible reduction of cancer risks.[28]

And Michael Lerner, in a review (and careful critique) of Cassileth and Berlyne's article (both appeared in the same issue of *Oncology*) suggests that "engaging in health-promoting behaviors may improve general health and functional status, which are sometimes associated with better outcomes in cancer. There are frequently benefits in terms of quality of life. . . . Improvement in quality of life in cancer is, after all, of extraordinary significance in itself."[29] Lerner includes in his long list of "health promoting behaviors" the remedies Drew found so beneficial: Chinese medicine such as acupuncture, relaxation exercises, and a balanced vegetarian diet.

Controversy over macrobiotics, still evident, is nonetheless decreasing. As noted doctors such as Dean Ornish and Benjamin Spock speak on it at conferences, as dietary changes are increasingly recommended, macrobiotics—perhaps not always labeled as such—becomes more acceptable, at least in theory.

As the emphasis begins to shift to prevention through individual life-style changes, I would argue again that responsibility extends out from the individual to the environment and society for prevention. Once someone is ill, however, cure is an individual road. Drew didn't have time to work on cleaning up the smoggy air or polluted waters of New England as a means to rid himself of a malignant tumor—that's something for him to think about when well. But he could change his own care and work on his own cleanup. The available evidence suggested that he would be foolish not to. There are no nutritional studies of chondrosarcoma, grade 2, under the optic chiasm in the sphenoid sinus. In fact, there are probably not enough people in the world in this category to study it. But other studies focusing on other cancers are useful.

Breast cancer struck one in twenty American women in 1940, one in eleven in 1981, one in eight today, and is still rising. In Massachusetts, where it is declared an epidemic, breast cancer rose 26 percent between 1982 and 1988.[30] Once considered a disease of older women, usually postmenopause, today it strikes all ages.

Controversy rages over whether fats in the diet and/or estrogens accumulated in the body encourage breast cancer. Studies done on people, difficult to control, show conflicting results about a fat/fiber component in the cause of this disease.[31] Even those most critical of the diet/breast cancer link, however, recommend that women adhere to a low-fat diet to prevent other cancers, such as cancer of the colon, as well as heart disease.

More numerous are the laboratory animal studies. Rats injected with mammary cancer fared better with a high-fiber diet,[32] miso soup,[33] and sea vegetables.[34] A recent University of Wisconsin study linked fermented soy sauce (on the same principle as miso soup) to reduced chances of stomach cancer.[35] The connections go on and on. Colon, lung, esophageal, ovarian, and stomach cancers, leukemia, and lymphoma have all been linked to diet. The same basic habits seem to apply—the more fiber in the form of fresh vegetables and grains and the fewer animal products such as dairy and meats, the better. If you throw in some fish, beans, and, if you're adventurous, tofu (shown to help prevent stomach cancer in a Japanese study[36]), your chances of preventing cancer or helping to cure it may increase.

Doctors have been slow to embrace disease/diet connections in general and cancer/diet linkages in particular. They are beginning to change. The evidence, although preliminary, is suggestive. Especially in the area of heart disease and fat, the news is everywhere. Cancer/food relationships are less understood and accepted, but evidence is growing. These studies, however tentative, are intriguing. But dietary change is difficult, and when it comes to such oddities as miso soup, tofu, or seaweeds, there is much resistance.

- Vivian Newbold, a physician on the staff of Holy Redeemer Hospital in Philadelphia, wrote a paper on her study of six patients diagnosed with various advanced cancers, including metastasized pancreatic cancer and malignant melanoma. The common thread was that all underwent some conventional medical treatment and all were considered terminal. One woman died; the other five people did not. This story is as interesting for its politics as for its health news.

Newbold's paper is written in the form of case histories (six patients are too few for a formal study). Each person's case was deemed hopeless by her or his doctors. All six, however, adhered to a macrobiotic diet, individually tailored to their particular illness. The five who recovered are thriving after five years or more, with no sign of cancer. When one woman, apparently recovered, gave up macrobiotics, the cancer returned, and she died. She might have died anyway. Vivian Newbold at no time claims to have proved her case. Rather, she calls on the medical community to ask more questions, look more closely, do the studies that could provide more definite knowledge. Drawing on her own and other case studies, as well as preliminary controlled research, she concludes, "in view of the many remissions of cancer and other serious diseases that have occurred in connection with this alternative approach, the medical community would serve itself well to investigate these phenomena seriously."[37]

In the Office of Technology Assessment report *Unconventional Cancer Treatments*, a congressional investigator writes, "If cases such as Newbold's were presented in the medical literature, it might help stimulate interest among clinical investigators in conducting controlled prospective trials of macrobiotic regimens, which could provide valid data on effectiveness."[38] But the medical journals were *not* interested. No one would publish Newbold's work. She was told that the readership wouldn't find it interesting. Help in the endless, time-is-running-out, heavy-losses "war on cancer" not interesting to doctors?

Perhaps this is changing. In the summer of 1993, Newbold, with five other doctors, published a retrospective study on diet and cancer in the *Journal of the American College of Nutrition*. The authors suggest that a macrobiotic diet extended life and quality of life in a sample of people with pancreatic, prostate and other nutrition-related cancers. The authors call for more systematic research to follow up their own small study.[39] In the meantime more and more people are doing their own experiments—experiments on themselves. After all, as Drew kept saying as he held his nose and drank miso soup, "At least this stuff can't hurt me."

Visualizations and Cancer

Dr. Newbold is careful to point out that other alternative modalities are also important. The meditation and visualization exercises that Drew practiced before, during, and after the surgeries helped to keep him steady in the face of emotional and physical chaos. These techniques are also being researched. Once again, controversy abounds in this area. Even if connections among mind, body, and stress do exist, the relationship of these connections to actual illness, and possible benefits from meditation and relaxation exercises, are more uncertain.[40] Striving for scientific certainty, research units in hospitals all around the country are conducting studies on the usefulness of meditation and visualization for panic attacks, diabetes, multiple sclerosis, AIDS, heart disease, cancer, and other illnesses. Although behavioral medicine is still considered a fringe medical area, researchers like Herbert Benson and Jon Kabat-Zinn in Massachusetts, Martin Rossman in California, and Janice Kiecolt-Glaser and Ronald Glaser in Ohio are lending legitimacy to this field.

Jon Kabat-Zinn has gained acceptance by many mainstream practitioners with a relaxation video used in hospitals. At the University of Massachusetts Medical Center, where he runs a stress-reduction clinic, all inpatients are told about his video, which is shown on the hospital channel throughout the day. More than one hundred hospitals around the country currently offer this tape to patients in their rooms. One patient at New York University Medical Center wrote Kabat-Zinn about how much his voice had meant to her:

> "[W]ords of yours have stayed with me through two frightening cancer surgeries. So many other comforting thoughts that you offer on your video have helped me keep my sanity. . . . So many other patients during my hospital stay were taking comfort from your

voice. . . . I am still hurting from my most recent surgery, and I am
still scared, but I have too many good, in fact wonderful, moments
because of your help."[41]

Despite the growing awareness of the usefulness of relaxation
techniques, no doctor we saw suggested that Drew could benefit from
such exercises, and few people we knew were aware of them. As with
macrobiotics, the gains could be enormous, but first we needed to
learn about the techniques and potential benefits through our own
review of the scientific literature.

No one working in the field of behavioral medicine claims conclusive
proof. As in most of medicine, whether conventional or alternative,
certainty is more elusive than we realize, and good research with
steady results is hard to find. But a growing mixture of case studies,
extensive clinical experience, and new scientific information on
mind–nervous system–immune system connections is worth attention.

The relatively new field of psychoneuroimmunology is clearly examined by Steven Locke, of Harvard Medical School, in his book *The
Healer Within*.[42] He explains the scientific findings on how white blood
cells, crucial to immune function, receive messages from the brain
through the nervous system. If the immune system is vital to identifying
foreign matter in the body, whether it be a virus or a cancer cell, and
the mind can influence that function in some way as yet not fully
understood, then yet another avenue toward recovery is at least
explorable.

Researchers have shown that immunity can fluctuate under stress.
Medical students' "natural killer cells" (immune cells that kill viral
cells) went down during exams and back up when the stress had
passed.[43] Separation, divorce, loss, unemployment, and so forth have
been shown to lower immunity. The central question here is whether
lowered immunity leads to poorer health. Logically, one might say that
of course it does, but to date there is no evidence that gives definite
answers to these questions. In numerous studies, Janice Kiecolt-
Glaser and Ronald Glaser show a relationship between stress and
lowered immune function. They stop short, however, of asserting a
correlation between these dynamics and the development or cure of
diseases such as cancer. They don't deny the connections but argue
for more research.[44] Others, such as Kabat-Zinn, have found emerging
evidence that chronic stress and impaired immune function can lead
to bodily breakdown, not as a single causal agent but as one possible
factor among many.[45] They claim that visualizations can help to heal
this breakdown.

It's not clear at what point meditating or visualizing changes patterns of stress, immune dysfunction, and the possibility of disease. If you do relaxation exercises regularly, perhaps bolstering your immunity, making stresses more manageable, will you avoid getting sick in the first place? Are these techniques good prevention against the ills of modern life? Can I avoid getting cancer if I keep myself calm in the face of whatever comes my way in the last years of this rather beat-up century? Or is it best applied as one of a series of solutions to illness once present? Can it help cure cancer or heart disease?

These questions probably pose too simple either-or scenarios that no two researchers or practitioners in the area would agree on. But meditations do seem to help people cope with a variety of problems, from day-to-day stress to heart disease. Jon Kabat-Zinn, focusing on healing and coping rather than curing, would argue that the ends don't matter; it's the means, the moment-to-momentness of life, that we need to concentrate on. He has people practice mindfulness, a focus on each second as important. If you live only another day, at least that day has been experienced to the fullest.

Dean Ornish, after working with cardiovascular patients in a more cure-oriented framework, argues that diet, walking, yoga, and meditation are crucial in the reversal of heart disease. The one man in his study who died ate the prescribed diet but insisted on too vigorous exercise, ferociously competing against the clock, ignoring the more meditative yoga exercises and the visualizations. In the PBS documentary on this study, Ornish suggests to this man that he work on relaxing, encouraging him to do more meditation and yoga exercises, to no avail. Ornish concludes, after the man's death, that the meditative skills must be emphasized, taught, and encouraged more strongly. Perhaps he would have died anyway. It's dangerous to generalize from one case, and not everyone can be cured or cure themselves all of the time. But the excellent results of the other participants, as opposed to degenerative conditions in the control group, which followed careful conventional heart association medical guidelines, are hopeful.

Hope is what Drew derived from these exercises. Whether stress is a factor in the cause of cancer or not, once you have cancer, it is inevitable. Hopelessness runs rampant. Control or any illusion of it is out the window. Relaxation exercises helped Drew counteract these sensations. They helped him sleep and feel less passive in the face of illness and the patient role. Visualizing the tumor shrinking, the cells healing and returning to normal, delivering his body back to him well and as he had known it, gave him a sense of hope. He was not helpless in the face of an unknown. He knew that tumor. The illness was his own, reclaimed from the pages of medical textbooks, taken back from the abstract categories mulled over in disease talk by his doctors. The unfamiliar became familiar. The foreign became part of him, a part he could recognize and work with. Fear decreased; confidence grew.

Perhaps these exercises improved his immune function. Perhaps they made him physically and psychologically stronger. Perhaps not. What did happen was that he felt better from doing them, and when it comes to illness, feeling better is crucial. The images Drew used changed during the course of his illness. They always, however, involved gentle healers making his head glow with health.

A young, six-year-old boy with a tumor in his brain stem visualized a different scenario. His mother told me his story on the phone one day. Her son was uninterested in gentle healers. He sought high adventure with a crew of Ninja Turtles. His mother explained to me, "When he was diagnosed, we tried to remove violent images from his life, and so we were against his watching the Ninja Turtle videos. But in the hospital that's what he wanted to watch. And he watched them over and over. The Ninja Turtles became for him the good guys fighting the tumor."

Once home she found her four-year-old son and her ill six-year-old son dancing the "Ninja Turtle fighting the tumor" dance. She took this image, created by her son, and used it when guiding him through relaxation/visualization exercises.

She and I marveled at her son's insights into what he needed, his ability to create his own healing stories. It reminded us both, as caretakers, how important it is to listen to the person you're helping, how wise we all are about the choices we make to feel better, regardless of how young or how old.

Stress centers around the country, usually in hospitals, offer classes or programs to teach people how to cope with stress and live with illness. When these stress centers exist in hospitals, doctors become more aware of them, and many refer their patients. At the University of Massachusetts Hospital, the expected referrals for chronic pain occur regularly. Increasingly, however, even the more skeptical specialists, such as oncologists and cardiovascular physicians, recommend people. Some doctors, so impressed with the results, sign up for themselves.

Kabat-Zinn's comprehensive book, with the ominous title *Full Catastrophe Living*, gives a detailed introduction to mind/body connections as well as the step-by-step, how-to approach taken in his stress-reduction clinic. He reminds us not to think of single causes and simple solutions. In his discussion of stress and the immune system he notes that larger forces can also be at work: "Of course it is possible for a person to be exposed to such massive levels of carcinogenic substances that even a healthy immune system would be overwhelmed . . . toxic dumping . . . Love Canal . . . Hiroshima, Nagasaki . . . Chernobyl. . . . In short, the development of any kind of cancer is a multistage, complex occurrence involving our genes and cellular processes, the environment, and our individual behavior and activities."[46]

Equally important in a growing literature that can be too simply interpreted, Kabat-Zinn debunks the idea of blaming the ill person for negative emotions. If we are to embrace alternative methods, it is crucial that they not be presented as a palliative for all of the supposedly bad things people did to themselves to get sick. Brain surgery should not be considered an antidote to negativity or overemotionalism. Mind-altering exercises shouldn't be either. In the controversy over whether bad thoughts, negative mind-sets, or personality types encourage disease, Kabat-Zinn doesn't take sides. Rather, he says it doesn't really matter. It's how the person is treated that matters.

> Even if it turns out that there is a statistically important relationship between negative emotions and cancer [not shown to date], to suggest to a person with cancer that his or her disease was caused by psychological stress, unresolved conflict, or unexpressed emotions would be totally unjustified. It amounts to subtly or not so subtly blaming the person for his or her disease. . . . This attitude is far more likely to result in increased suffering than in healing.[47]

Not only is a blame-and-guilt cycle unjustified, it's illogical. The idea that certain personality types get cancer is ungrounded. One out of three Americans get cancer; are they all similar in character? I think not. Besides, babies get cancer. Dogs get cancer. Is this because of their negative emotions? Did they cause their illnesses? Seems unlikely. In any case, Drew used these exercises not to overcome negativity or to change his personality type, whatever that may be. He used them to relax, to feel better. To feel better. It's that simple.

Acupuncture and Cancer

There are many alternative approaches to disease available worldwide today that Drew did not try. To cite a few of the many respected healing methods used here and in other countries: First, the Queen of

England employs a personal homeopathic doctor as well as an allopathic (conventional medicine) one. Second, Ayurvedic medicine, increasingly popular in the United States, is a healing method from India. Ayurvedic practice combines meditation, diet, herbs, minerals, and aromas to create balance, and thus health, in the individual and thus in nature. And third, Germany has a network of cancer rehabilitation health spas where all who have cancer can go for six-week stays, once a year for five years. The spas are located in mountainous settings, with all of the amenities of hotels combined with the medical care of hospitals. Diet and exercise are tailored to the individual with an emphasis on low-fat, natural foods. People on chemotherapy are given injections of vitamins and minerals to counteract side effects. Herbal remedies, massage, and spa baths are available to pamper the clientele, and people report feeling indulged and energized. It is a humane gesture to those with an inhumane disease. And it is free of charge as part of the national health plan.

Any of these approaches might have helped, but we didn't know much about them or they were not available to us and time was short. Drew relied on what those close to him already knew. Nutrition was the most known, experimented with, and thus focused on. Complementary to diet and relaxation exercises was acupuncture. Drew had no phobias about needles, and once reassured that it was not painful in the sense of shots all over the body (ultrathin disposable needles barely pierce the skin; blood is not drawn), he agreed to try it. After all, he said, once you've eaten seaweed, anything goes.

In her letters, Rebecca [his partner at the time] encouraged Drew by describing how ubiquitous acupuncture was in China. She found it to be the taken-for-granted treatment for a variety of ills and procedures. She reported that her professor of ancient Chinese history at the University of International Business and Economics in Beijing had undergone a cesarean birth with acupuncture as the sole anesthetic. She had felt no pain during the surgery, and at its end she got up from the operating table, picked up the baby, and walked home. Furthermore, my mother's and my own experiences pointed Drew toward acupuncture. Once again I was able to provide him with a broader database to strengthen our anecdotal stories—data that rarely furnished precise, scientific verification but did offer suggestive evidence.

In the late 1980s I had introduced Chinese medicine as a topic in my medical sociology classes. I had become increasingly dissatisfied with the standard curriculum based on explorations of Western medicine, its definitions, strengths, and deficiencies. I decided to add readings and discussions of alternative visions of what health and illness meant in a variety of cultures. Students met lecturers on Chinese medicine with enthusiasm. The topic's foreignness opened their eyes to more diverse interpretations of other cultures as well as their own.

Acupuncture, like macrobiotics and relaxation therapies, through different means strives to correct imbalances, restoring equilibrium to a person, body, and mind. It is based on a complicated system of meridians and energy flows that run throughout the body. Chi, the vital energy, moves freely through those open meridians or pathways when all is well. Illness is understood as an imbalance in the meridian system. Energy may be blocked, deficient, or excessive, creating what is understood to be conditions of disharmony. Each person's pattern is unique. Acupuncture needles, when placed on specific points along the meridians, work to restore balance and vitality, thus health. Herbs are often prescribed in addition to acupuncture treatments. Philosophically, Chinese medicine is rooted in a balance between opposites that also blend into each other—yin and yang. As with macrobiotics, extremes in either direction swing one out of line. Careful work through food or pressure points is suggested to restore harmony.

This overly simplistic explanation is akin to explaining nuclear physics in a paragraph. Excellent books and articles abound that explain in more detail what is in fact difficult for the Western mind to grasp, for one cannot see meridians, Chi, or pressure points under a microscope. Practitioners do not conduct extensive tests, lab workups, and so on. Rather, an acupuncturist will take all six pulses in each wrist, to assess the depth, pace, length, strength, and quality of each pulse as a means to consider organ health and energy flow. Practitioners will also observe facial color, examine the tongue for coatings, color, and so forth, and, like Western doctors, take a detailed history.

Acupuncture, widely practiced in the United States under regulations differing from state to state, is increasingly studied in hospitals by doctors. One source cites 6,500 accredited acupuncturists in the United States today, and many more are unregistered. Numerous schools of acupuncture exist throughout the country, with more in the making.[48] In Austria, acupuncture as well as homeopathy are now part of conventional medical training.

But in America much of the public finds acupuncture confusing. A friend in search of an acupuncturist for her debilitating carpal tunnel problems in both wrists reported, "It's not exactly easy to find a specialist here. It's not like I can look for the best acupuncturist in town to treat carpal tunnel syndrome. They don't use those terms. They're likely to think it's the liver or something."

Regardless of its strangeness to Westerners, however, people are going to acupuncturists in increasing numbers. It is U.S. medicine that remains the most skeptical. Despite acupuncture's growing acceptance in other countries and a three-thousand-year history in China, "Where's the proof?" is the most common question established medicine asks.

It may be a long time before these attitudes change. Scientific studies here and abroad are underway. Proof, as we understand it, is difficult, however. For example, if someone has colon cancer, in Western medicine you do tests and come up with a diagnosis. Surgery and chemotherapy can be done, and the person may live or die, but once you have a sufficient number of people—and there is no shortage here—you can try different dosages of a drug until it starts to work or fails. You can set up control groups, and you will learn what works, what doesn't. Over time, with enough rats or enough people, you may be able to show something conclusive. The process is linear—one problem, one set of symptoms, one cure. In Chinese theory this is not possible. Two people with colon cancer could be diagnosed quite differently. One person's system might be "damp," another's "dry." The phases and blockages could be opposite. Treatment points would be different in each case. To find enough people who need the exact points treated over the course of the disease is rare. To conduct Western-style studies with large test and control groups becomes complicated. It can be done, as discussed below; but to date, acupuncturists, like most Eastern (and in fact, Western) practitioners, use case histories and clinical practice as the basis for what works.

Studies do exist, despite the difficulties, in international and national medical journals, explaining in scientific terms the usefulness of acupuncture for a variety of ills from depression and pain to inflammation and paralysis. For example, Margaret Naeser, associate research professor of neurology at Boston University Medical School, uses acupuncture to treat paralysis in those who have suffered strokes. She first observed such treatment in China. Impressed by the improvements in strength and mobility, she came home to conduct her own research. Her study "compared real versus sham acupuncture in the treatment of paralysis in acute stroke patients, and examined the results in relationship to CT scan lesion sites." Improvement was significant in the real acupuncture patients. There was no change in patients receiving sham acupuncture. Naeser is currently publishing information on these promising techniques.[49]

The benefits of Chinese medicine most widely recognized in the United States today, however, are in the areas of pain and anesthesia. The results here are more easily discernible. Whereas doctors in the 1970s, when acupuncture was first introduced here, claimed that the results were placebo effects (thinking it will work and thus it does), such attitudes over time and with observation are harder to maintain in the face of surgery. If you cut someone's abdomen open without anesthesia, you can count on their feeling it no matter what they're thinking. In China, acupuncture needles were used on specific points to block pain during surgery, with few or no drugs. Today acupuncture and small amounts of drugs are more likely to be combined.

Curious American teams have witnessed this, filmed it, and imported it. One journalist experienced it firsthand. James Reston of the *New York Times* some years ago needed emergency surgery for a ruptured appendix while in China. Imagine his surprise when he found that he was to receive acupuncture as part of the treatment for pain. His surprise changed to interest in a good story when he experienced the benefits firsthand.[50] Some skeptics still claim a placebo effect. But when the evidence of drug-free, painless surgery on dogs is presented, a skeptical posture is harder to sustain.

Thus, acupuncture to block pain, whether surgical or dental, headaches or cramps, is slowly finding acceptance, if not regular use, in mainstream medicine. Another use is in our continuous battle against drug and alcohol addiction. This is the use that most intrigues students in my classes. Terry Courtney, who launched the first detox acupuncture clinic in Boston in the late 1980s, learned of this approach from the Lincoln Hospital program in the South Bronx. This detox clinic, started in the 1970s, reports remarkable success rates with addicts. No one gets or expects 100 percent triumphs in this complex endeavor, but studies on acupuncture treatments are showing higher detox and lower recidivism than any other approach, including the dominant one of methadone. Other clinics have opened in the Boston area, as well as around the country.

Milton L. Bullock and colleagues conducted a placebo-controlled, single-blind study (the practitioners knew who were receiving specific points versus nonspecific, sham points; the participants did not) of eighty severe recidivist alcoholics. In the treatment group, twenty-one of the forty people finished the program with significant detoxification effects still present at the end of six months. In the control group (sham points) only one of the forty completed the program, with more than twice the number expressing a need for alcohol.[51]

Judge Stanley Goldstein, of Miami Beach, Florida, offers all first-offense drug offenders acupuncture detox treatment rather than jail. In the three years that he's made this offer, only 3 percent have been rearrested, compared with 33 percent in regular court. Length of treatment averages seventeen months. Goldstein reports: "What we've ended up with is nothing short of amazing." Other cities, too, have found it amazing. Portland, Oregon; Dayton, Ohio; and Oakland, California, have patterned drug courts on Judge Goldstein's model, and interest is growing.[52] In Portland, acupuncture is required before addicts can try methadone. Previously the first line of defense against addiction, methadone is now the last resort.[53]

When Terry Courtney comes to my classes, she brings pictures and videos explaining the treatment for an addict: once a day for forty-five minutes, five days a week for several weeks, followed by a varying schedule based on the individual's progress. As in all drug rehabilitation programs, counseling is recommended.

The treatment consists of five slim, short needles inserted in detoxification and relaxation points of each ear. One journalist, Nancy Waring, found the success rate, even with those who had "tried everything," impressive. One of her interviewees reports: "After years of failing at other things, I just wanted to give acupuncture a try."[54] Like many clients, this man, a crack addict, is more than pleased with the results, even though no one fully understands how it works. Waring notes:

> Exactly how stimulating these points eases drug withdrawal and reduces cravings is not fully understood, but studies show that the release of endorphins, the body's own pain relieving, relaxation-inducing opiates is partly responsible. . . . [But] even those enthusiastic about acupuncture detox are aware that it may not be the best course of treatment for everyone. Skeptics, for their part, cite the lack of long-term studies. But with no sure cures and many more addicts than there are spaces in treatment programs, no one disputes that acupuncture detox is worth watching.[55]

And watched it is. Judge Goldstein is content with his short-term success rates. Others are accumulating statistics, watching the results with keen interest. In fact, it is through the back door of drug treatment that acupuncture may find its way into general health care, especially for chronic diseases, those diseases with which conventional medicine has the least success.

Anesthesia and drug detoxification speak a language of process and results graspable by Western doctors even if not fully understood. Using needles to block pain folds in with current research in medicine on blocking pain in general, whether through drugs or needles. Furthermore, to watch acupuncture accomplish this during surgery is impressive. Similarly, in detox the concentration is on endorphins, a hot medical topic, something the medical profession can understand.

A current theory is that heroin addicts lack endorphins and thus crave drugs to fill this void. Acupuncture, unlike methadone, revives the body's own ability to create endorphins, a natural high, decreasing the need for heroin. This is a concept medicine can work with. Unlike Chi or meridians, endorphins are familiar. Thus, it is through these two avenues that acupuncture is slowly working its way into medical and public imagination in the United States.

Perhaps it is stories like that of Tim Fortugno, a pitcher for the California Angels, that in the end will sway the public. In college, signed by the Oakland Athletics, Fortugno "blew out" his pitching arm. Nothing helped. Orthopedists, along with every known specialist, were sought, to no avail. His contract was canceled before he even began. A friend talked him into trying acupuncture. It worked. Today, in his thirties, his arm intact, he's pitching his best games. What could be more compelling than the return to form of a top athlete? Forget the drug addiction and chronic pain stories. Tim Fortugno may be all that's needed to mainstream acupuncture in North America.[56]

In England, more open to acupuncture, the popular view is different. In London a famous acupuncturist treats skin diseases. People line up around the block, waiting their turn for the unfixable to be fixed. Ask North Americans what acupuncture does best, and Tim Fortugno notwithstanding, they will probably answer, "Pain relief." Ask the English the same question, and they may be more likely to say, "Skin disease."

In fact, in both England and America acupuncturists treat a wide variety of health problems, from arthritis to cancer, from fatigue to the flu, from constipation to heartburn. Despite the wide applications to detox and pain prevention in the United States and skin diseases in the United Kingdom, the majority of an acupuncturist's work, like that of a conventional general practitioner or family practice physician, covers a broad range, from acute to chronic illnesses, mild to severe diseases.

Drew, like my students, was fascinated that a few needles in the ears could relax and detox long-term, hardened crack and heroin addicts.

He was equally impressed with acupuncture used as anesthesia. But, he pointed out, he had a tumor; he wasn't a drug addict. He didn't feel well, but he wasn't in a lot of pain, and he knew he didn't want his head cut open without conventional anesthesia. So what did acupuncture have to offer him? These were excellent questions. The answers weren't so clear. Traditional acupuncturists would have responded that a tumor was a sign of major imbalance. Surgery, drugs, and radiation might alleviate the obvious problems but would stress his already out-of-whack body further. Do the surgery, have the radiation, but rely on other modalities to restore harmony, to strengthen the body, calm the mind.

Coming from a Western orientation, my explanations focused on acupuncture as a means to boost his immune system and release endorphins to give him a natural, calming high amid all of the frenzied lows he faced each day. He had talked with Val, my acupuncturist, and decided for himself. Probably I was pushier than I remember. In any case he had gone, at least to ask.

After his initial interview with Valerie, Drew was amenable. He liked her approach to his illness. He liked her open, supportive manner, and he liked her. Val worked with a physician in his office. Drew, making so many new adjustments, enjoyed at least some familiarity there—a doctor's office with the usual accoutrements.

In the first week home from his first surgery, I took my weak and bundled-up son to Val. Her approach was to work aggressively on strengthening him, physically and emotionally, so that his body could do the healing. She chose not to work on the cancer. She explained that in China a practitioner, when treating cancer with Chinese medicine, might see the patient five or six times a week. Accompanying the treatments would be extensive use of Chinese herbs. The process would be aggressive, sometimes painful, and time-consuming. It would be the primary force toward a cure. Just as Drew's life revolved around the hospital, his numerous doctors, and lab visits, an Eastern approach would have him equally busy with the Chinese methods. Since Western medicine was dominant here, she acted as supplementary care. Further, Val felt that if Drew were to take herbs, she would refer him to an herbal specialist. There are remarkable success stories for a variety of illnesses using herbal remedies, but Drew couldn't face another practitioner. He was doing enough.

Val treated the cancer indirectly by enhancing Drew's general health. From the beginning she said his pulses showed a strong constitution. Working from this base, she enhanced his chances of recovery by first treating his immune system. Her aim was to safeguard his system by working to block new cancer cells and keep him strong against other illnesses, such as the endless round of New England winter flus. Throughout the two surgeries and radiation she worked to counteract the invasiveness of these lifesaving but weakening procedures by keeping his metabolism steady and his energy flowing smoothly.

During the radiation she concentrated on detoxification from the radiation itself, as well as from the breakdown of cancerous cells. As the body rejects toxic waste, whether drugs or cells, the elimination process stresses the body and can mirror the symptoms of the illness itself.

An extreme example of too rapid detoxification can be seen in bird migration. When birds feast on pesticide-poisoned grass or insects, the toxins store in their body fat and muscles. When they migrate south, they burn fat and exercise muscles, often resulting in death—literally falling from the sky—poisoned by toxins in their bodies being released too quickly. Thus, although detox in Drew's case was not life-threatening, Val worked to minimize the side effects of radiation by trying to release slowly the excess toxins before they could build up.

Val's approach was at the general level of immunity, strengthening, and detoxification. She also attended to the specific. On each visit she focused on points relevant to what Drew reported that day. He occasionally had hovering headaches and later, during the radiation, she intervened to stop nausea and fatigue when they were on the verge of happening. Drew also experienced hormonal fluctuations as varied supplemental levels were being tried to replicate his defunct pituitary gland. Hot flashes, fatigue, and other symptoms were corrected by regulating his hormone supplements, bolstered by on-the-spot acupuncture.

Another important, less tangible area of treatment was emotional help. Like Eastern practitioners in general, acupuncturists do not separate the mind from the body. The emphasis is on restoring a quality of life that encompasses a healthy body and a calm, strong mind. Thus, in acupuncture the practitioner-patient relationship is part of the cure. Val explained, "The quality of my interactions with patients is important. I try to establish a good relationship. I've never met an acupuncturist who wasn't interested in dealing with a patient as a person rather than a cluster of symptoms. It's intrinsic to the approach. I have to know what kind of mood someone is in, background about the person's family life and professional life to round out my assessment of them."

The psychoemotive level in a person is defined as the finer, subtler level on a continuum on which the physical is seen as the grosser, more obvious manifestation of a person's health. To understand a person's condition and to treat that condition, these different elements have to be considered. "Symptomatically, most of the time patients will have emotional tendencies consistent with physical disharmonies in our system of classification," Val noted.

In Drew's case, Val felt he was well adjusted on the psychoemotive level. His main problems were physically displayed. "He came to acupuncture very clear and ready to deal with his emotions around his health—different from many people who have emotional difficulty facing it all." Talking with Val helped Drew remain emotionally steady.

She offered support during each acupuncture visit. Drew could talk with her openly, and she was available to him both as a listener and as a practitioner. She worked with acupuncture to relax him. Part of every treatment was to generate a calm energy, an endorphin high, something he could feel immediately and keep with him to face the rest of his troubling life. It was this part that hooked Drew to acupuncture. He went two or three times a week, lay down on a comfortable examining table, and talked with Val about his symptoms, concerns, and fears. She placed the needles in the appropriate places and left him to relax for fifteen to twenty minutes. With soft classical background music, Drew went into a deep relaxation, often falling asleep.

Counseling and Cancer

Illness allows you to be self-centered, to put yourself first. Many become drenched with self-pity, an understandable but debilitating mood. While concentrating all of his energies on recovery, Drew never exhibited the understandable "why me?" attitude, with which we all would have sympathized. His focus was on getting well, not wallowing in being sick. That didn't mean painful questions didn't reside just under the surface. Although Val felt his emotional health was good, Drew decided to see a counselor, a psychotherapist, to explore these fumblings. Better to deal with them now and learn from them than have to rediscover them, more deeply entrenched, years later. Once again, my university offered support through its counseling center. Drew went to a wonderful man, Paul, who encouraged him to indulge himself for this one hour a week in whatever he wanted to talk about.

Drew didn't have to worry about distressing Paul with his fears. He could open the wounds and let them rip, with a less involved but gentle man to guide him, a man who cared a lot yet wasn't going to weep with him or feel his pain as searingly as he (or Stephen and I) did. This relationship lasted for six months. It started when radiation began and ended in May with the close of school. Drew found it a reprieve from the physical: We all felt he had handled having cancer too well. Counseling gave him an avenue to explore the seamier side of cancer, the weaknesses and the loathings. Drew also explored with Paul the effects his having cancer had on his relationships with others. He was, after all, deeply changed. Drew now, for example, faced renewing his relationship with Rebecca. Rebecca returned from China in December 1991, three days before radiation was to begin. (She had offered to come home before the first surgery. Drew talked her out of it.) Both had been through the most profound experiences of their lives; but those experiences were very different, and they went through them separately. Rebecca, age twenty, from a small, close-knit family in small-town and rural Vermont, had traveled around the world, geographically and metaphorically, to China. Drew had undergone two major surgeries for a malignant tumor bordering his brain. Neither could fully understand the vast dimensions of the other's changes. Drew had never been out of the Western world. Rebecca had never been seriously ill.

By the time Rebecca returned, Drew looked and felt quite well. His hair flopped over his scull scar. He was gaining weight and energy. He didn't look like a cancer patient. Rebecca, relieved to see him so well, presumed his illness was mostly over. Drew, in an emotional sense, had waited for Rebecca's return for it to really begin. His expectations were higher, more grandiose, than possibility allowed. All of those hours in MRI chambers holding onto Rebecca's image, all of the fantasies; nothing in real life could match those dreams. Paul helped Drew sort this out.

Drew and Rebecca held on. At age twenty-one and twenty, they did what many people of any age can't do in a crisis—they talked to each other and to friends, they wrote their thoughts and expectations down, they spent time apart, they came together. Rebecca could have walked away. She didn't. Drew could have withdrawn, claiming he had been through enough. He didn't. They struggled with the beast and beat it. Paul helped with this complicated journey.

Counseling and acupuncture combined with diet and relaxations to make Drew feel rested and calm, with renewed energy to face the struggles of getting well. He liked these strange new strategies. His friends and family loved hearing about them. Many wanted to try them.

Once again, everyone but the doctors was curious. But no doctor was against Drew's healing methods. Universally, their attitude was that if Drew wanted to do them, if he thought they helped—fine, then do them.

Drew wanted to do them, and he indeed did do them; he did them all. And just in case Norman Cousins and the *Reader's Digest* were right, that laughter is the best medicine, he watched hilarious movies, covering all bases.

Notes

[1] Edie Magnus, "CBS Evening News," October 21, 1992.

[2] Ibid., October 25, 1992.

[3] Bill Moyers, *Healing and the Mind*. (New York: Doubleday, 1993).

[4] For example, Anastacia Toufexis, "Dr. Jacobs' Alternative Mission," *Time*, March 1, 1993, pp. 43–44. "Can Your Mind Heal Your Body?" *Consumer Reports*, January 1994, pp. 51–59. Arielle Emmet, "Where East Does Not Meet West," *Technology Review*, November/December 1992, pp. 50–56.

[5] David M. Eisenberg, M.D., et al., "Unconventional Medicine in the United States: Prevalence, Costs, and Patterns of Use," *New England Journal of Medicine* 328 (1993): 246–52.

[6] Ralph W. Moss, *The Cancer Industry: Unravelling the Politics* (New York: Paragon Press, 1989), p. xxi.

[7] Kit Kitatani, "Stomach Cancer," in Ann Fawcett and Cynthia Smith, eds., *Cancer Free: 30 Who Triumphed over Cancer Naturally* (New York: Japan Publications, 1991), p. 107.

[8] Anthony J. Sattilaro, M.D., *Recalled by Life* (New York: Avon Books, 1982).

[9] Michael Shanik, "Malignant Melanoma," in Ann Fawcett and Cynthia Smith, eds., *Cancer Free* (New York: Japan Publications, 1991), pp. 47, 51.

[10] Dirk Benedict, *Confessions of a Kamikaze Cowboy* (Garden City, NY: Avery Publishing Group, 1991), p. 64.

[11] Sattilaro, *Recalled by Life*, p. 182.

[12] Hugh Faulkner, M.D., "Pancreatic Cancer," in Ann Fawcett and Cynthia Smith, eds., *Cancer Free* (New York: Japan Publications, 1991), p. 144.

[13] Dr. Hugh Faulkner, *Physician Heal Thyself* (Becket, MA: One Peaceful World Press, 1992).

[14] Faulkner, "Pancreatic Cancer," in Ann Fawcett and Cynthia Smith, eds., *Cancer Free* (New York: Japan Publications, 1991), p. 148.

[15] American Cancer Society, *Cancer Facts and Figures*, 1992. National Cancer Institute, interview by author with Angela Harris, February 7, 1994.

[16] Steven A. Rosenberg, "Combined-Modality Therapy of Cancer," *New England Journal of Medicine* 312 (1985): 1512–14.

[17] John Cairns, "The Treatment of Diseases and the War Against Cancer," *Scientific American*, November 1985, pp. 51–59. See also Moss, *The Cancer Industry*.

[18] Richard Knox, *Boston Globe*, January 26, 1994.

[19] John C. Bailar III and Elaine M. Smith, "Progress against Cancer," *New England Journal of Medicine* 314 (1986): 1226–32.

[20] The majority of people using alternative medicines are likely to be well educated, a fact that puzzles critics of unorthodox procedures. There is no mystery here, however. Well-educated people are more likely to have the resources to pursue treatments that are not covered by private insurance or public funding. The two-tiered health care system in the United States, where the haves get the best and the have-nots don't, applies to alternative care as well.

[21] Victor Herbert, M.D., J.D., "Unproven (Questionable) Dietary and Nutritional Methods in Cancer Prevention and Treatment," *Cancer* 58 (1986): 1930–41.

[22] Barrie R. Cassileth, Ph.D., et al., "Survival and Quality of Life among Patients Receiving Unproven as Compared with Conventional Cancer Therapy," *New England Journal of Medicine* 324 (1991): 1180–85.

[23] For example, Johanna T. Dwyer, "Unproven Nutritional Remedies and Cancer," *Nutritional Reviews* 50 (April 1992): 106–109.

[24] Barrie R. Cassileth, Ph.D., and Deborah Berlyne, Ph.D., "Counseling the Cancer Patient Who Wants to Try Unorthodox or Questionable Therapies," *Oncology* 3 (April 1989): 29–33.

[25] Editors, "Unproven Methods of Cancer Management—Macrobiotic Diets," *CA* 34 (January/February 1984): 60–63.

[26] Cathy Arnold, "The Macrobiotic Diet: A Question of Nutrition," *Oncology Nursing Forum* 11 (May/June 1984): 50–53.

[27] This is changing. The National Institutes of Health has awarded a research grant to study macrobiotics and cancer. Lawrence Kushi, Sc.D., an epidemiologist at the University of Minnesota School of Public Health, is principal investigator. He will conduct the research with a team of doctors, nutritionists, and fellow scientists.

[28] U.S. House, Subcommittee on Health and Long-Term Care, "Quackery: A $10 Billion Scandal" (Washington, DC: U.S. Government Printing Office, 1984): pp. 66–68, 107. (Committee Publication No. 94–435).

[29] Michael Lerner, Ph.D., "The Article Reviewed," *Oncology* 3 (April 1989): 34, 40–41.

[30] *Boston Globe*, May 20, 1992.

[31] Paolo Toniolo, et al., "Calorie-Providing Nutrients and Risk of Breast Cancer," *Journal of the National Cancer Institute* 81 (1989): 278–86; Walter Troll, "Prevention of Cancer by Agents That Suppress Oxygen Radical Formation," *Free Radical Research Communications* 12–13 (1991): 751–57; Walter C. Willet, M.D., et al., "Dietary Fat and Fiber in Relation to Risk of Breast Cancer," *Journal of the American Medical Association* 268 (1992): 2037–44 (see also accompanying editorial, pp. 2080–81).

[32] L. A. Cohen, et al., "Modulation of N-nitrosomethylurea-induced Mammary Tumor Promotion by Dietary Fiber and Fat," *Journal of the National Cancer Institute* 83 (1991): 496–501.

[33] J. E. Baggott, et al., "Effect of Miso (Japanese Soybean Paste) and NaCl on DMBA-induced Rat Mammary Tumors," *Nutrition and Cancer* 14 (1990): 103–9.

[34] Ichiro Yamamoto, et al., "The Effects of Dietary Seaweeds on 7,12-dimethyl-benz[a]anthracene-induced Mammary Tumorigenesis in Rats," *Cancer Letters* 35 (1987): 109–18; J. Teas, M. L. Harbison, and R. S. Gelman, "Dietary Seaweed and Mammary Carcinogenesis in Rats," *Cancer Research* 44 (1984): 2758–61.

[35] J. Raloff, "A Soy Sauce Surprise," *Science News* 139 (1991): 357.

[36] T. Hirayama, "Epidemiology of Stomach Cancer," in T. Murakami ed., *Early Gastric Cancer*, Gann Monographs on Cancer Research, no. 11 (Tokyo: University of Tokyo Press, 1971), pp. 3–19.

[37] Vivian Newbold, M.D., "Remission of Cancer Patients on a Macrobiotic Diet," unpublished paper.

[38] Office of Technology Assessment (OTA), "Unconventional Cancer Treatments" (Washington, DC: Government Printing Office, 1990).

[39] James P. Carter, et al., "Hypothesis: Dietary Management May Improve Survival from Nutritionally Linked Cancers Based on Analysis of Representative Cases," *Journal of the American College of Nutrition* 12 (1993): 209–26.

[40] Barrie R. Cassileth, et al., "Psychosocial Correlates of Cancer Survival: A Subsequent Report 3 to 8 Years after Cancer Diagnosis," *Journal of Clinical Oncology* 6 (1988): 1753–59; Laurence T. Vollhardt, "Psychoneuroimmunology: A Literature Review," *American Orthopsychiatric Association* 61 (1991): 35–47.

[41] Jon Kabat-Zinn, Ph.D., *Full Catastrophe Living: Using the Wisdom of Your Body and Mind to Face Stress, Pain and Illness* (New York: Dell, 1990), pp. 181–82.

[42] Steven E. Locke, M.D., and Douglas Colligan, *The Healer Within: The New Medicine of Mind and Body* (New York: E. P. Dutton, 1986).

[43] Janice K. Kiecolt-Glaser et al., "Modulation of Cellular Immunity in Medical Students," *Journal of Behavioral Medicine* 9 (1986): 5–21.

[44] Ibid.; Janice Kiecolt-Glaser and Ronald Glaser, "Major Life Changes, Chronic Stress, and Immunity," in T. Peter Bridge et al., eds., *Psychological, Neuropsychiatric, and Substance Abuse Aspects of AIDS* (New York: Raven Press, 1988); Janice Kiecolt-Glaser and Ronald Glaser, "Psychoneuroimmunology: Past, Present, and Future," *Health Psychology* 8 (1989): 677–82.

[45] Kabat-Zinn, *Full Catastrophe Living*, J. Bernhard, et al., "Effectiveness of Relaxation and Visualization Techniques as an Adjunct to Phototherapy and Photochemotherapy of Psoriasis," *Journal of the American Academy of Dermatology* 19 (1988): 572–73.

[46] Kabat-Zinn, *Full Catastrophe Living*, p. 209.

[47] Ibid.

[48] *One Peaceful World*, no. 10, Spring 1992, "Medical-Scientific Update," p. 3.

[49] Margaret A. Naeser, Ph.D., Dip. Ac., et al., "Real versus Sham Acupuncture in the Treatment of Paralysis in Acute Stroke Patients: A CT Scan Lesion Site Study," *Journal of Neurologic Rehabilitation* (forthcoming).

[50] Kabat-Zinn, *Full Catastrophe Living*, p. 192.

[51] Milton L. Bullock et al., "Controlled Trial of Acupuncture for Severe Recidivist Alcoholism," *Lancet*, June 24, 1989, pp. 1435–39.

[52] Christopher Boyd, *Boston Globe*, April 17, 1992.

[53] *One Peaceful World*, no. 10, Spring 1992, "Medical-Scientific Update," p. 3.

[54] Nancy Waring, *The Boston Globe Magazine*, June 17, 1990.

[55] Ibid.

[56] *Boston Globe*, August 7, 1992.

18
The Emergence of Alternative Medicine

Michael Goldstein

In 1983 when Joshua, my oldest son, was eighteen months old, a hot iron fell on his foot and remained there until the person watching him discovered it. Most of the skin on the top of his tiny foot was gone. The emergency room doctor, his pediatrician, and three or four physician friends who examined him all agreed this was a "third-degree burn." There was no way it could ever heal by itself. The only reasonable course of action was a skin graft. The well-known surgeon at a highly regarded burn center concurred. Laura (his mother) and I both felt lucky that the surgery could be scheduled very quickly. But our feelings changed when we found out that our son would have to be tied to his bed for the entire lengthy hospitalization to prevent him from scratching at the graft, and that the sight of this would be so upsetting that we would be restricted to a brief visit each day.

There had to be something else we could try before subjecting our little baby, no less ourselves, to such an ordeal. Laura's brother had a suggestion. He knew that in Japan, after the atomic bomb was dropped, the juice of the aloe vera plant had been used to treat people with much more severe burns. When we decided to try this ourselves, the Japanese proprietor of a nearby nursery offered helpful advice on which parts of the plant to use and how to start growing our own supply so as not to be dependent on him. Three times a day I carefully dripped the freshly cut aloe vera onto the wound. As I did, I drew on my own knowledge about how imagery affects the body. I would speak to my son in a soothing voice, pointing his finger at his foot and describing over and over what I wanted to happen: "The white part of your skin at the edge is a tiny bit bigger than it was yesterday, the dark part is a tiny bit smaller. . . . Good, good. Your skin is getting stronger. Let's think about how the juice is helping your skin grow." In about three months the foot had healed. By the time Joshua was six, only the slightest outline of the burn could be detected.

As soon as it was clear that the burn had healed, Laura proposed that we get in touch with all the physicians who had advised a skin graft for our son. Surely they would want to know about a less intrusive and less costly alternative. Those we spoke with were all happy about the outcome. But not a single one was willing to say that they might suggest our solution to someone else in a similar predicament. It wasn't only their fear of a malpractice suit. Most were frank: treating a third-degree burn with aloe vera was just too far removed from what they had learned, and what their colleagues would find acceptable. Our experience, no matter how important for us, meant little or nothing to them.

By 1996, when I started to write this book, the situation was vastly different. In September of that year, a *Life Magazine* cover story, "The Healing Revolution," predicted that health care in America was about to be "completely transformed" by the integration of "ancient medicine and new science to treat everything from the common cold to heart disease." The first page featured a dramatic photograph of cardiac surgery being performed at New York City's Columbia-Presbyterian Hospital, with an "energy healer" laying on hands alongside the surgeon. Anyone who frequents a newsstand would hardly have been surprised to come upon this cover story. During the few months prior, stories about alternative medicine had appeared on the covers of both *Newsweek* and *Time*.

These prominent cover stories are but one manifestation of the immense amount of attention that the mass media have given to something that is variously referred to as "alternative medicine," "holistic medicine," or "complementary medicine." A visit to any large chain bookstore will reveal an abundance of books about alternative medicine; they fill the large sections devoted to health, medicine, self-care, and self-help. Just one of Deepak Chopra's books on alternative medicine, *Ageless Body, Timeless Mind: The Quantum Alternative to Growing Old*, has sold more than seven million copies since it was first published in 1993. Sales figures for this book and similar ones by physician-authors like Larry Dossey, Bernie Siegel, and Andrew Weil have consistently placed them atop the bestseller lists. To the extent that the American public reads nonfiction books, they are likely to be about alternative medicine.

Some of the media attention and popular concern comes from the vivid personal testimony offered on behalf of various alternative treatments. Celebrity accounts have received a good deal of attention. Shirley Maclaine, who has abandoned Western medical pharmacology for "the healing powers to be found in acupuncture, spirit messages and crystal rocks," now teaches that we can all learn to heal ourselves by visualizing colors specific to each area of the body. The powerful description by cultural critic Norman Cousins of his battle with "an incurable illness," ankylosing spondylitis, was particularly influential. Cousins attributed his success in recovering from what doctors thought to be an irreversible illness to his alternative approach to healing. He reasoned that "if negative emotions produce negative chemical reactions in the body, wouldn't the positive emotions produce positive chemical changes?" On this basis he stopped his medication, checked himself out of the hospital, began an innovative regimen of massive doses of vitamin C and amusing movies, and sought "love, hope, faith, laughter, confidence, and the will to live. . . ." His successful recovery made him a crusader for his views. Since he was well connected and widely respected for his probing intellect, those who may have scoffed at the anecdotes of others were less likely to dismiss Cousins's story. Although his experience became widely known through his book, the initial account (upon which the book is based) appeared in the highly prestigious *New England Journal of Medicine* (*NEJM*) and included his assertion that "the hospital was no place for a person who was seriously ill." Cousins spent the remainder of his years on a medical school faculty trying to persuade academic medical researchers to take his ideas seriously.

Vivid stories detailing all sorts of personal battles and triumphs over life-threatening diseases through the use of alternative healing practices have become common. *Double Vision: An East-West Collaboration for Coping with Cancer* is among the most impressive. This book details how when twenty-one-year-old Drew Todd was diagnosed with a rare form of aggressive cancer, his mother Alexandra set out on an unrelenting quest to discover what was available beyond conventional care. Their story and similar accounts not only acquaint readers with many of the specific alternative techniques (Todd used a macrobiotic diet, relaxation, visualization, and acupuncture, among others), but deliver powerful messages about the possibility of personal transcendence and the shortcomings of the mainstream health care system.

For the most part, however, the media has paid attention to alternative medicine not merely because of the triumphs of the famous. Rather, a consistent stream of well-researched academic reports has emerged over the past several years, portraying the American population as actively engaged in alternative practices and as believing in the ideas that underlie many such techniques.

The most frequently cited of these accounts, a 1990 survey of a national sample of American adults, found that about one-third had used what was termed "unconventional medicine" in the past year to treat a medical problem. In 1997, when the researchers repeated the survey, those who reported using alternative therapies in the past year had jumped to over 42 percent. In both years affluent, highly educated whites were the most typical users. Although almost all the users of these unconventional techniques were using mainstream care at the same time, in both surveys over two-thirds of the users did not discuss the unconventional therapy with their physician. The authors speculate that this "deficiency in patient-doctor relations" might "derive from medical doctors' mistaken assumption that their patients do not routinely use unconventional therapies for serious medical problems." Those who used unconventional treatments made an average of nineteen visits per year to "alternative providers" to receive care. By extrapolation the authors conclude that the 427 million visits Americans made to alternative practitioners in 1990 had grown by 47.3 percent to 629 million visits in 1997. This far exceeds the 336 million visits made to all primary-care physicians that same year. The total out-of-pocket cost of all this alternative care was estimated to have increased by a similar proportion to more than 27 billion dollars in 1997, well in excess of what was spent out of pocket on all physician services. Yet the methodology of the study specifically excluded any visit or use of unconventional medicine for the purpose of prevention or health promotion, considered by many advocates to be the primary strengths of unconventional medicine. Therefore, these findings should be seen as very conservative estimates of the magnitude of the alternative medicine phenomenon. In fact, two other national surveys reported in 1998 also found that 42 percent of households polled had used some type of alternative care within the past year.

Research on specific forms of alternative care consistently presents a similarly impressive picture of extensive use. For example, approximately a third of all those who suffer from back pain—an extremely common, chronic condition—chose chiropractic rather than mainstream medicine for treatment. Depending on the study, between a quarter and a half of all individuals with a terminal illness seek alternative care at some point in the course of their disease. The prevalence of alternative medicine appears to be widespread regardless of the severity of the medical problem. Studies have indicated that socioeconomic status is either independent of the use of alternative medicine, or that higher status and more highly educated individuals are overrepresented among alternative medicine users.

Alternative health care is not always easy to define, however, or to distinguish from broader health promotion activities. This can make specific statistical findings difficult to interpret. For example, *Natural Foods Merchandiser* reports that sales of "natural foods" totaled $9.17 billion in 1995. But it is unclear how much of this sum can reasonably be considered to have been spent on alternative medicine. The $1.5 billion reported by the *Los Angeles Times* that Americans spent on "medicinal herbs" in that same year might be a better estimate, although to use this value assumes that we know how these herbs are being used. Thousands of people use "cat's claw" (a vine from the Amazon, long used by Peruvians for many types of healing) because they believe it will strengthen their immune systems. Are they practicing alternative medicine even if they are in good health? What if the user is HIV positive? Does using herbs for weight loss qualify as "alternative medicine?" Attempting to resolve these ambiguities leads to the matter of defining precisely what is meant by the term "alternative medicine," as well as the terms "prevention" and "cure," along with the most basic notions of "health" and "illness" themselves.

However these conceptual matters are resolved, the media, the public, policymakers, and many people in the established health professions have already begun to act in ways that break down whatever distinctions exist between alternative and conventional care. Just a few years ago, it would have been difficult to imagine an "energy healer" working side by side with a cardiac surgeon in the operating room at one of the nation's leading academic medical centers, much less the hospital allowing the scene to be photographed for *Life Magazine.* The growing trend of many health maintenance organizations (HMOs) to develop or "contract out" for "spiritual healing" programs could be dismissed as purely a marketing device, a public relations stunt, or even a cynical substitution of a very inexpensive form of care for one more costly. But a 1997 survey of three hundred HMO executives found that 94 percent believe personal prayer or other spiritual practices can aid medical treatment and accelerate healing. Recent reports have depicted numerous examples of conventional health care organizations recognizing alternative medicine. For example, in 1996 a panel of 114 leading scientists and representatives of academia, drug companies, and community groups appointed by the National Institutes of Health (NIH) to review the nation's AIDS research effort issued a blistering report that recommends a greater focus on alternative medicine in future HIV/AIDS research. In the same year, Oxford Health Plan, which provides care to 1.4 million people in the eastern United States, announced that it would add alternative medicine to some of its health plans. The initial group assembled by Oxford included approximately one thousand chiropractors, acupuncturists, naturopathic doctors, massage therapists, and yoga instructors, with plans already underway to add practitioners of T'ai Chi and reflexology. In the wake of such reports, it is becoming increasingly difficult to ignore the possibility that a more fundamental change in society's orientation to health and healing is taking place.

Mainstream medicine's growing openness to various forms of alternative care is just beginning to have an impact on daily medical practice. In Europe, fairly high proportions of the established medical community either accept or practice alternative medicine to some degree. For example, in Britain about 40 percent of general practitioners state that they find homeopathy to be effective in some situations, and either refer clients or practice it themselves. In the United States, there has always been a small number of physicians who have practiced some form of alternative treatment. For the most part they have restricted their work to one or a few specific modes of treatment, and have been shunned by most other M.D.s and the major medical organizations. Today, however, medical schools openly hold courses on many forms of alternative care, along with support groups for holistic and alternative physicians. There is even a national organization, the American Holistic Medical Association, that restricts its membership to M.D.s and medical students.

By any measure of the number of people involved, money spent, professional regard, or public opinion, alternative medicine has taken on a significant and growing presence in America. Thus, it should be no surprise that the popular media are filled with news about alternative medicine. The national media have long given attention to developments in medicine and health care. Until recently, the media considered innovation and scientific or technical advances to be the essence of what was "newsworthy." It is striking, then, that the media, hundreds of newsletters, Internet sites, and other sources devoted to alternative medicine actually contain very little that is "new." The techniques and approaches to health and healing that are extolled (or condemned)—such as acupuncture, massage, homeopathy, chiropractic, naturopathy, and herbal medicine—are almost all therapeutic systems and modalities that have existed for hundreds or even thousands of years. Any long-time observer of alternative medicine in America would wonder, why this glut of attention *now*?

Understanding alternative medicine's position within the broader health-care scene requires some description of how perceptions of health and health care among the general public and policymakers have changed over the past several decades. The successes and domination of "scientific" medicine have helped foster a climate of high costs, unreasonable expectations, distance, and distrust. These factors have combined with more longstanding critiques of the biomedical model of American health care to create what might be described as a popular "grievance" against Western medicine.

The career of Ralph Moss is a good example of how this "grievance" develops and interacts with the field of alternative medicine. Moss was a well-regarded science writer who eventually became assistant director of Public Affairs at the Sloan-Kettering Cancer Center in New York. His growing public disenchantment with the effectiveness of conventional cancer therapies, especially chemotherapy, led to his firing, and a new view of himself as a muckraking crusader whose articles and books like *The Cancer Industry* and *Questioning Chemotherapy* would give patients and their families an "insider's perspective." Over the past twenty years his writing has come to include more and more information about alternative cancer therapies, and he was asked to serve on the original advisory board of the federal government's Office of Alternative Medicine (OAM). Currently he supports himself by producing a regular journal on cancer therapy (*The Cancer Chronicles*) both in print and on-line, as well as reports on treatment options for people with cancer. He charges $275 each for each of these "Moss Reports."

The ambiguities that surround alternative medicine inhere in the term itself. Does "alternative medicine" indicate cohesion around some underlying conceptual framework, or is it merely a phrase of convenience? The popular media and many practitioners often speak of a "paradigm shift" or a "revolution" in understanding disease and healing. At the same time, other practitioners stress that alternative approaches can and should be integrated into mainstream health care. Is there truly a paradigm shift that underlies these techniques and approaches? If there is, what is it? If a "new paradigm" exists, can it coexist with mainstream doctors and hospitals, no less the rapidly changing health care system, as it moves toward "managed care?" It seems clear that there is a coherent underlying set of commonalties that justifies viewing alternative medicine as a single, if broad and diverse, phenomenon. It would be a mistake to think of alternative medicine as merely a name for a residual list of techniques omitted from the standard medical school curriculum.

To find that alternative medicine is a conceptually coherent category does not necessarily imply that there is a corresponding empirical or organizational reality. There is no doubt that a plethora of professional associations, conferences, publications, support groups, and commercial enterprises devote themselves to "alternative medicine." But it is still not clear to what extent "alternative medicine" exists as an empirically verifiable social reality and how it relates to mainstream medicine. Do the people who practice some form of alternative medicine, and those who utilize some facet of it for real health problems, see it as a cohesive entity? The answer here is not at all clear-cut. However, an organizational reality increasingly is emerging and gaining acceptance among the public, the government, and the health-care establishment. The extension of third-party insurance coverage to alternative therapies, the decision of some HMOs to develop networks of alternative medicine practitioners, and the opening of the Office of Alternative Medicine at the National Institutes of Health all indicate that the climate in the late 1990s is far more open to alternative medicine than it was just a few years ago.

The central role of religion and spirituality in many forms of alternative medicine is one factor that complicates the future of alternative medicine in America. Many health professionals have a difficult time accepting spirituality as a core component of health and healing. Understanding this tension is vital to predicting the future relationship between alternative and mainstream medicine.

Another potentially pivotal characteristic of alternative medicine is that it draws on ideologies associated with both the political "right" and "left," thereby transcending common political categories. Many of its basic criticisms of mainstream medicine emerge from a left perspective that opposes the dominance of professionals as well as excess profit making in medicine. Alternative medicine also encompasses a strong countercultural component whose roots are on the left. Yet, the strong focus on enhanced individual responsibility for health, along with an emphasis on nongovernmental solutions to health problems, often gives alternative medicine a distinctly rightward cast. Examining a number of "political" struggles, such as the formation of the Office of Alternative Medicine at the National Institutes of Health and the efforts of alternative providers to gain licensure and third-party reimbursement, is the best way to understand the relationship of various political ideologies to alternative medicine.

Mainstream medicine in the United States is being fundamentally altered by nationwide efforts to hold down the costs of care and increase corporate control (usually referred to as "managed care"). In addition, there is ongoing debate about the escalating cost of health care to the government. These developments have significant implications for the future of alternative medicine. Both contain the potential for fostering its integration into the broader health-care system and imposing restraints on the form and content of that integration. Any predictions about the future of alternative medicine will need to keep this new economic context in mind.

There is ample evidence that alternative medicine is assuming a greater role in the currents of American life. This will no doubt require more interaction, if not cooperation, with the medical mainstream, bringing with it the potential for co-optation and assimilation of that which is truly distinctive. The powerful economic forces changing mainstream medicine will likely exacerbate this possibility. At the same time, alternative medicine may be developing into an "identity movement" that offers a new understanding of what is possible both to its adherents and to society at large.

Today my son Joshua is a teenager with no real memory of his badly burned foot or of how it healed. His injury and recovery in 1983 has become only one of the many stories all families tell about themselves. It has much in common with the story the Todd family tells about Drew's cancer, and the stories Ralph Moss, Deepak Chopra, Andrew Weil, and many others offer their readers. All of these stories suggest that with some knowledge and effort you can harness the resources to triumph over much illness, suffering, and disability. This is a powerful message.

Bibliography

Altman, L. K. 1996. Panel Offers Sharp Criticism of AIDS Research Programs. *New York Times* 14 March: A1.

Astin, J. A. 1998. Why People Use Alternative Medicine: Results of a National Study. *Journal of the American Medical Association* 279:1548–1553.

Brooks, N. R. 1996. From Gooch to High Gloss: Change Signals Shift for Natural Foods Industry. *Los Angeles Times* 24 July: D1.

Carry, T. S., et al. 1995. Care-Seeking Among Individuals with Chronic Low-Back Pain. *Spine* 21:312–317.

Cassileth, B. R., and H. Brown. 1988. Unorthodox Cancer Medicine. *Ca—A Cancer Journal for Clinicians* 38:176–196.

Colt, G. H. 1996. The Healing Revolution. *Life Magazine* September:35–50.

Cousins, N. 1976. Anatomy of an Illness: As Perceived by the Patient. *New England Journal of Medicine* 295:1458–1463.

Cowley, G. 1995. Melatonin Mania. *Newsweek Magazine* 6 November 60–63.

Eisenberg, D. M., et al. 1998. Trends in Alternative Medicine Use in the United States, 1990–1997: Results of a Follow-up National Survey. *Journal of the American Medical Association* 280:1569–1575.

Hilts, P. J. 1995. Health Maintenance Organizations Are Turning to Spiritual Healing. *New York Times* 27 December: B10.

John Templeton Foundation. 1997. Press Release. Survey Reveals HMO Executives Overwhelmingly Recognize Role of Spirituality in Health Care. Available: http://www.templeton.org/sandh/course97/release3.htm

Kleinjen, J., et al. 1991. Clinical Trials of Homeopathy. *British Medical Journal* 302:316–323.

Landmark Healthcare. 1998. The Landmark Report on Public Perceptions of Alternative Care Report. Sacramento, CA.

Langone, J. 1996. Alternative Therapies: Challenging the Mainstream. *Time Magazine* Fall Special Issue: 40–43.

Moss, R. 1993. *Cancer Therapy. The Independent Consumer's Guide to Non-Toxic Treatment and Prevention.* Brooklyn, NY: Equinox Press.

Moss, R. 1996. *The Cancer Industry: The Classic Exposé on the Cancer Establishment.* Brooklyn, NY: Equinox Press.

Shekelle, P. G, 1994. Spine Update—Spinal Manipulation. *Spine* 1980:858–861.

Wallis, C. 1991. The New Age of Alternatixe Medicine. *Time Magazine* 4 November: 68–76.

Wallis, C. 1996. Faith and Healing. *Time Maqazine* 24 June: 58–64.

Yates, P. M., et al. 1993. Patients with Terminal Cancer Who Use Alternative Therapies: Their Beliefs and Practices. *Sociology of Health and Illness* 15:199–216.

Section VII

Technology, Experimentation, and Social Control

Medicine constantly seeks to develop new understandings and treatments of diseases. This involves new drugs, new procedures, and new forms of surgery. While it is true that some medical advances can help people and save lives, a good deal of high-tech medicine is harmful or ineffective. More importantly, at the macro-level, changes in mortality rates have historically been determined by non-medical interventions such as sanitation, diet, and economic development. As we have already learned, our country excels in medical technology yet fares poorly in major indicators such as infant mortality.

Often, in its quest to expand its scientific boundaries, medicine enters the realm of social control. The concept of medicine as an institution of social control has received much support in recent years. Social control in the medical sphere is, in part, a result of *medicalization*, the claim of medical professionals to power and clinical authority in more and more areas of everyday life (e.g., sexuality, family relations, child rearing, crime). Our society has a technological imperative which often favors scientific sophistication at the expense of humane interpersonal caregiving, and this imperative lends credence to medicalized approaches.

Social control also stems from the inequality in most medical relationships, with the patient having too little control over decision making. Social control is exacerbated by the tendency for physicians to act rather than not to act; they are more likely to find illness than not to find it, and, if they are surgeons, to perform surgery rather than recommending against it. In addition, social control can result from the application or withholding of medical techniques by political and economic power holders, a situation quite common in reproductive issues such as contraception and abortion.

The articles in this section portray medical coercion and control on a variety of levels. James Jones writes about "The Tuskegee Syph-

373

ilis Experiment," an experiment ended as recently as 1972, which many commentators have likened to Nazi medical experimentation in concentration camps. For forty years the federal Public Health Service had been conducting a project in which black men with syphilis were deliberately left untreated so that researchers could view the results of the disease's natural progress. Poor Southern black men had been tricked into believing that they were getting medical attention, and the nature of the Tuskegee study was widely known in medical circles. Jones shows the clear racism which underpinned such endeavors, and he further emphasizes that the Tuskegee experiment was in some ways a logical outgrowth of a system in which medical and scientific research can transcend the bounds of normal morality in its frequently unmonitored and allegedly value-free search for knowledge.

Renee Fox and Judith Swazey,'s contribution, "Transplantation and the Medical Commons," take up one of the most intriguing forms of medical technology, organ transplants, a phenomenon largely begun in the 1980s. They look at the way that organs are allocated, the debates over whether transplantation is a wise use of finite medical resources, and the ethical and social values that arise in these endeavors. We already know that transplantation is often uncovered or only partly covered by insurance, and many Americans lack insurance anyway. Further, there have been many examples of special consideration to people not on the official waiting list or lower down the order; some organs are even exported to wealthy people abroad. In 1995, former baseball great Mickey Mantle received a liver transplant, apparently way ahead of the waiting list. Many believed his fame was responsible for special treatment.

Genetic technology has been another recent development that has grabbed the attention of medicine and the public. Dorothy Nelkin and Susan Lindee's "The DNA Mystique: The Gene as a Cultural Icon" discusses the enormous power of "genetic essentialism," the notion of reducing human life to a series of genetic structures. Public symbols and metaphors make the gene appear to be the fundamental building block of human life, with little regard for the social surroundings. Medical science seeks to use this biotechnology to intervene in many biological processes, some with the promise of preventing serious disease. But genetic-driven approaches have made many errors, such as in associating homosexuality with a genetic cause. Presently, insurance companies are denying coverage to people who only have a slight chance of contracting a disease, based on their genetic makeup. So too are employers keeping people from jobs. These are but two of the dangerous implications of an uncontrolled genetic essentialism.

In "Prenatal Diagnosis in Context," Barbara Katz Rothman examines the political and ethical issues involved in prenatal diagnosis. As physicians have expanded their intervention into pregnancy and fetal development, they have frequently asserted that there are conflicts between pregnant women and their fetuses, based on the diagnosis of actual or potential disorders in the fetus. This leads to a rise in cesarean sections, sometimes by physician-obtained court order. It also places legal abortion in the forefront of medical and social options for women with diseased fetuses. But women are not always in control of abortion or other reproductive concerns. Rothman, like many others, worries that prenatal diagnosis may perpetuate the legacy of eugenics, an approach beginning early in the century that attempted to preserve white, Anglo-Saxon dominance in the gene pool. Given this considerable baggage, it is no surprise that the genetic counseling sessions Rothman audits are fraught with lack of clarity about whose needs are met and who really makes choices.

19
The Tuskegee Syphilis Experiment

James Jones

In late July of 1972, Jean Heller of the Associated Press broke the story: for forty years the United States Public Health Service (PHS) had been conducting a study of the effects of untreated syphilis on black men in Macon County, Alabama, in and around the county seat of Tuskegee. The Tuskegee Study, as the experiment had come to be called, involved a substantial number of men: 399 who had syphilis and an additional 201 who were free of the disease chosen to serve as controls. All of the syphilitic men were in the late stage of the disease when the study began.[1]

Under examination by the press the PHS was not able to locate a formal protocol for the experiment. Later it was learned that one never existed; procedures, it seemed, had simply evolved. A variety of tests and medical examinations were performed on the men during scores of visits by PHS physicians over the years, but the basic procedures called for periodic blood testing and routine autopsies to supplement the information that was obtained through clinical examinations. The fact that only men who had late, so-called tertiary, syphilis were selected for the study indicated that the investigators were eager to learn more about the serious complications that result during the final phase of the disease.

The PHS officers were not disappointed. Published reports on the experiment consistently showed higher rates of mortality and morbidity among the syphilitics than the controls. In fact, the press reported that as of 1969 at least 28 and perhaps as many as 100 men had died as a direct result of complications caused by syphilis. Others had developed serious syphilis-related heart conditions that may have contributed to their deaths.[2]

The Tuskegee Study had nothing to do with treatment. No new drugs were tested; neither was any effort made to establish the efficacy of old forms of treatment. It was a nontherapeutic experiment, aimed at compiling data on the effects of the spontaneous evolution of syphilis on black males. The magnitude of the risks taken with the lives of the subjects becomes clearer once a few basic facts about the disease are known.

Syphilis is a highly contagious disease caused by the *Treponema pallidum*, a delicate organism that is microscopic in size and resembles a corkscrew in shape. The disease may be acquired or congenital. In acquired syphilis, the spirochete (as the *Treponema pallidum* is also called) enters the body through the skin or mucous membrane, usually during sexual intercourse, though infection may also occur from other forms of bodily contact such as kissing. Congenital syphilis is transmitted to the fetus in the infected mother when the spirochete penetrates the placental barrier.

From the onset of infection syphilis is a generalized disease involving tissues throughout the entire body. Once they wiggle their way through the skin or mucous membrane, the spirochetes begin to multiply at a frightening rate. First they enter the lymph capillaries where they are hurried along to the nearest lymph gland. There they multiply and work their way into the bloodstream. Within days the spirochetes invade every part of the body.

Three stages mark the development of the disease: primary, secondary, and tertiary. The primary stage lasts from ten to sixty days starting from the time of infection. During this "first incubation period," the primary lesion of syphilis, the chancre, appears at the point of contact, usually on the genitals. The chancre, typically a slightly elevated, round ulcer, rarely causes personal discomfort and may be so small as to go unnoticed. If it does not become secondarily infected, the chancre will heal without treatment within a month or two, leaving a scar that persists for several months.[3]

While the chancre is healing, the second stage begins. Within six weeks to six months, a rash appears signaling the development of secondary syphilis. The rash may resemble measles, chicken pox, or any number of skin eruptions, though occasionally it is so mild as to go unnoticed. Bones and joints often become painful, and circulatory disturbances such as cardiac palpitations may develop. Fever, indigestion, headaches, or other nonspecific symptoms may accompany the rash. In some cases skin lesions develop into moist ulcers teeming with spirochetes, a condition that is especially severe when the rash appears in the mouth and causes open sores that are viciously infectious. Scalp hair may drop out in patches, creating a "moth-eaten" appearance. The greatest proliferation and most widespread distribution of spirochetes throughout the body occurs in secondary syphilis.[4]

Secondary syphilis gives way in most cases, even without treatment, to a period of latency that may last from a few weeks to thirty years. As if by magic, all symptoms of the disease seem to disappear, and the syphilitic patient does not associate with the disease's earlier symptoms the occasional skin infections, periodic chest pains, eye disorders, and vague discomforts that may follow. But the spirochetes do not vanish once the disease becomes latent. They bore into the bone marrow, lymph glands, vital organs, and central nervous systems of their victims. In some cases the disease seems to follow a policy of peaceful coexistence, and its hosts are able to enjoy full and long lives. Even so, autopsies in such cases often reveal syphilitic lesions in vital organs as contributing causes of death. For many syphilitic patients, however, the disease remains latent only two or three years. Then the delusion of a truce is shattered by the appearance of signs and symptoms that denote the tertiary stage.

It is during late syphilis, as the tertiary stage is also called, that the disease inflicts the greatest damage. Gummy or rubbery tumors (so-called gummas), the characteristic lesions of late syphilis, appear, resulting from the concentration of spirochetes in the body's tissues with destruction of vital structures. These tumors often coalesce on the skin forming large ulcers covered with a crust consisting of several layers of dried exuded matter. Their assaults on bone structure produce deterioration that resembles osteomyelitis or bone tuberculosis. The small tumors may be absorbed, leaving slightly scarred depressions, or they may cause wholesale destruction of the bone, such as the horrible mutilation that occurs when nasal and palate bones are eaten away. The liver may also be attacked; here the result is scarring and deformity of the organ that impede circulation from the intestines.

The cardiovascular and central nervous systems are frequent and often fatal targets of late syphilis. The tumors may attack the walls of the heart or the blood vessels. When the aorta is involved, the walls become weakened, scar tissue forms over the lesion, the artery dilates, and the valves of the heart no longer open and close properly and begin to leak. The stretching of the vessel walls may produce an aneurysm, a balloonlike bulge in the aorta. If the bulge bursts, and sooner or later most do, the result is sudden death.

The results of neurosyphilis are equally devastating. Syphilis is spread to the brain through the blood vessels, and while the disease can take several forms, the best known is paresis, a general softening of the brain that produces progressive paralysis and insanity. Tabes dorsalis, another form of neurosyphilis, produces a stumbling, foot-slapping gait in its victims due to the destruction of nerve cells in the spinal cord. Syphilis can also attack the optic nerve, causing blindness, or the eighth cranial nerve, inflicting deafness. Since nerve cells lack regenerative power, all such damage is permanent.

The germ that causes syphilis, the stages of the disease's development, and the complications that can result from untreated syphilis were all known to medical science in 1932—the year the Tuskegee Study began.

Since the effects of the disease are so serious, reporters in 1972 wondered why the men agreed to cooperate. The press quickly established that the subjects were mostly poor and illiterate, and that the PHS had offered them incentives to participate. The men received free physical examinations, free rides to and from the clinics, hot meals on examination days, free treatment for minor ailments, and a guarantee that burial stipends would be paid to their survivors. Though the latter sum was very modest (fifty dollars in 1932 with periodic increases to allow for inflation), it represented the only form of burial insurance that many of the men had.

What the health officials had told the men in 1932 was far more difficult to determine. An officer of the venereal disease branch of the Centers for Disease Control in Atlanta, the agency that was in charge of the Tuskegee Study in 1972, assured reporters that the participants were told what the disease could do to them, and that they were given the opportunity to withdraw from the program any time and receive treatment. But a physician with firsthand knowledge of the experiment's early years directly contradicted this statement. Dr. J. W. Williams, who was serving his internship at Andrews Hospital at the Tuskegee Institute in 1932 and assisted in the experiment's clinical work, stated that neither the interns nor the subjects knew what the study involved. "The people who came in were not told what was being done," Dr. Williams said. "We told them we wanted to test them. They were not told, so far as I know, what they were being treated for or what they were not being treated for." As far as he could tell, the subjects "thought they were being treated for rheumatism or bad stomachs." He did recall administering to the men what he thought were drugs to combat syphilis, and yet as he thought back on the matter, Dr. Williams conjectured that "some may have been a placebo." He was absolutely certain of one point: "We didn't tell them we were looking for syphilis. I don't think they would have known what that was."[5]

A subject in the experiment said much the same thing. Charles Pollard recalled clearly the day in 1932 when some men came by and told him that he would receive a free physical examination if he appeared the next day at a nearby one-room school. "So I went on over and they told me I had bad blood." Pollard recalled. "And that's what they've been telling me ever since. They come around from time to time and check me over and they say, 'Charlie, you've got bad blood.'"[6]

An official of the Centers for Disease Control (CDC) stated that he understood the term "bad blood" was a synonym for syphilis in the black community. Pollard replied, "That could be true. But I never heard no such thing. All I knew was that they just kept saying I had the bad blood—they never mentioned syphilis to me, not even once." Moreover, he thought that he had been receiving treatment for "bad blood" from the first meeting on, for Pollard added: "They been doctoring me off and on ever since then, and they gave me a blood tonic."[7]

The PHS's version of the Tuskegee Study came under attack from yet another quarter when Dr. Reginald G. James told his story to reporters. Between 1939 and 1941 he had been involved with public health work in Macon County—specifically the diagnosis and treatment of syphilis. Assigned to work with him was Eunice Rivers, a black nurse employed by the Public Health Service to keep track of the participants in the Tuskegee Study. "When we found one of the men from the Tuskegee Study," Dr. James recalled, "she would say, 'He's under study and not to be treated.'" These encounters left him, by his own description, "distraught and disturbed," but whenever he insisted on treating such a patient, the man never returned. "They were being advised they shouldn't take treatments or they would be dropped from the study," Dr. James stated. The penalty for being dropped, he explained, was the loss of the benefits that they had been promised for participating.[8]

Once her identity became known, Nurse Rivers excited considerable interest, but she steadfastly refused to talk with reporters. Details of her role in the experiment came to light when newsmen discovered an article about the Tuskegee Study that appeared in *Public Health Reports* in 1953. Involved with the study from its beginning, Nurse Rivers served as the liaison between the researchers and the subjects. She lived in Tuskegee and provided the continuity in personnel that was vital. For while the names and faces of the "government doctors" changed many times over the years, Nurse Rivers remained a constant. She served as a facilitator, bridging the many barriers that stemmed from the educational and cultural gap between the physicians and the subjects. Most important, the men trusted her.[9]

As the years passed the men came to understand that they were members of a social club and burial society called "Miss Rivers' Lodge." She kept track of them and made certain that they showed up to be examined whenever the "government doctors" came to town. She often called for them at their homes in a shiny station wagon with the government emblem on the front door and chauffeured them to and from the place of examination. According to the *Public Health Reports* article, these rides became "a mark of distinction for many of the men who enjoyed waving to their neighbors as they drove by." There was nothing to indicate that the members of "Miss Rivers' Lodge" knew they were participating in a deadly serious experiment.[10]

Spokesmen for the Public Health Service were quick to point out that the experiment was never kept secret, as many newspapers had incorrectly reported when the story first broke. Far from being clandestine, the Tuskegee Study had been the subject of numerous reports in medical journals and had been openly discussed in conferences at professional meetings. An official told reporters that more than a dozen articles had appeared in some of the nation's best medical journals, describing the basic procedures of the study to a combined readership of well over a hundred thousand physicians. He denied that the Public Health Service had acted alone in the experiment, calling it a cooperative project that involved the Alabama State Department of Health, the Tuskegee Institute, the Tuskegee Medical Society, and the Macon County Health Department.[11]

Apologists for the Tuskegee Study contended that it was at best problematic whether the syphilitic subjects could have been helped by the treatment that was available when the study began. In the early 1930s treatment consisted of mercury and two arsenic compounds called arsphenamine and neoarsphenamine, known also by their generic name, salvarsan. The drugs were highly toxic and often produced serious and occasionally fatal reactions in patients. The treatment was painful and usually required more than a year to complete. As one CDC officer put it, the drugs offered "more potential harm for the patient than potential benefit."[12]

PHS officials argued that these facts suggested that the experiment had not been conceived in a moral vacuum. For if the state of the medical art in the early 1930s had nothing better than dangerous and less than totally effective treatment to offer, then it followed that, in the balance, little harm was done by leaving the men untreated.[13]

Discrediting the efficacy of mercury and salvarsan helped blunt the issue of withholding treatment during the early years, but public health officials had a great deal more difficulty explaining why penicillin was denied in the 1940s. One PHS spokesman ventured that it probably was not "a one-man decision" and added philosophically, "These things seldom are." He called the denial of penicillin treatment in the 1940s "the most critical moral issue about this experiment" and admitted that from the present perspective "one cannot see any reason that they could not have been treated at that time." Another spokesman declared: "I don't know why the decision was made in 1946 not to stop the program."[14]

The thrust of these comments was to shift the responsibility for the Tuskegee Study to the physician who directed the experiment during the 1940s. Without naming anyone, an official told reporters: "Whoever was director of the VD section at that time, in 1946 or 1947, would be the most logical candidate if you had to pin it down." That statement pointed an accusing finger at Dr. John R. Heller, a retired PHS officer who had served as the director of the division of venereal disease between 1943 and 1948. When asked to comment, Dr. Heller declined to accept responsibility for the study and shocked reporters by declaring: "There was nothing in the experiment that was unethical or unscientific."[15]

The current local health officer of Macon County shared this view, telling reporters that he probably would not have given the men penicillin in the 1940s either. He explained this curious devotion to what nineteenth-century physicians would have called "therapeutic nihilism" by emphasizing that penicillin was a new and largely untested drug in the 1940s. Thus, in his opinion, the denial of penicillin was a defensible medical decision.[16]

A CDC spokesman said it was "very dubious" that the participants in the Tuskegee Study would have benefited from penicillin after 1955. In fact, treatment might have done more harm than good. The introduction of vigorous therapy after so many years might lead to allergic drug reactions, he warned. Without debating the ethics of the Tuskegee Study, the CDC spokesman pointed to a generation gap as a reason to refrain from criticizing it. "We are trying to apply 1972 medical treatment standards to those of 1932," cautioned one official. Another officer reminded the public that the study began when attitudes toward treatment and experimentation were much different. "At this point in time," the officer stated, "with our current knowledge of treatment and the disease and the revolutionary change in approach to human experimentation, I don't believe the program would be undertaken."[17]

Journalists tended to accept the argument that the denial of penicillin during the 1940s was the crucial ethical issue. Most did not question the decision to withhold earlier forms of treatment because they apparently accepted the judgment that the cure was as bad as the disease. But a few journalists and editors argued that the Tuskegee Study presented a moral problem long before the men were denied treatment with penicillin. "To say, as did an official of the Centers for Disease Control, that the experiment posed 'a serious moral problem' after penicillin became available is only to address part of the situation," declared the *St. Louis Post-Dispatch*. "The fact is that in an effort to determine from autopsies what effects syphilis has on the body, the government from the moment the experiment began withheld the best available treatment for a particularly cruel disease. The immorality of the experiment was inherent in its premise."[18]

Viewed in this light, it was predictable that penicillin would not be given to the men. *Time* magazine might decry the failure to administer the drug as "almost beyond belief or human compassion," but along with many other publications it failed to recognize a crucial point. Having made the decision to withhold treatment at the outset, investigators were not likely to experience a moral crisis when a new and improved form of treatment was developed. Their failure to administer penicillin resulted from the initial decision to withhold all treatment. The only valid distinction that can be made between the two acts is that the denial of penicillin held more dire consequences for the men in the study. The *Chicago Sun Times* placed these separate actions in the proper perspective: "Whoever made the decision to withhold penicillin compounded the original immorality of the project."[19]

The human dimension dominated the public discussions of the Tuskegee Study. The scientific merits of the experiment, real or imagined, were passed over almost without comment. Not being scientists, the journalists, public officials, and concerned citizens who protested the study did not really care how long it takes syphilis to kill people or what percentages of syphilis victims are fortunate enough to live to ripe old age with the disease. From their perspective the PHS was guilty of playing fast and loose with the lives of these men to indulge scientific curiosity.[20]

Many physicians had a different view. Their letters defending the study appeared in editorial pages across the country, but their most heated counterattacks were delivered in professional journals. The most spirited example was an editorial in the *Southern Medical Journal* by Dr. R. H. Kampmeir of Vanderbilt University's School of Medicine. No admirer of the press, he blasted reporters for their "complete disregard for their abysmal ignorance," and accused them of banging out "anything on their typewriters which will make headlines." As one of the few remaining physicians with experience treating syphilis in the 1930s, Dr. Kampmeir promised to "put this 'tempest in a teapot' into proper historical perspective."[21]

Dr. Kampmeir correctly pointed out that there had been only one experiment dealing with the effects of untreated syphilis prior to the Tuskegee Study. A Norwegian investigator had reviewed the medical records of nearly two thousand untreated syphilitic patients who had been examined at an Oslo clinic between 1891 and 1910. A follow-up had been published in 1929, and that was the state of published medical experimentation on the subject before the Tuskegee Study began. Dr. Kampmeir did not explain why the Oslo Study needed to be repeated.

The Vanderbilt physician repeated the argument that penicillin would not have benefited the men, but he broke new ground by asserting that the men themselves were responsible for the illnesses and deaths they sustained from syphilis. The PHS was not to blame, Dr. Kampmeir explained, because "in our free society, antisyphilis treatment has never been forced." He further reported that many of the men in the study had received some treatment for syphilis down through the years and insisted that others could have secured treatment had they so desired. He admitted that the untreated syphilitics suffered a higher mortality rate than the controls, observing coolly: "This is not surprising. No one has ever implied that syphilis is a benign infection." His failure to discuss the social mandate of physicians to prevent harm and to heal the sick whenever possible seemed to reduce the Hippocratic oath to a solemn obligation not to deny treatment upon demand.[22]

Journalists looked at the Tuskegee Study and reached different conclusions, raising a host of ethical issues. Not since the Nuremberg trials of Nazi scientists had the American people been confronted with a medical *cause célèbre* that captured so many headlines and sparked so much discussion. For many it was a shocking revelation of the potential for scientific abuse in their own country. "That it has happened in this country in our time makes the tragedy more poignant," wrote the editor of the *Philadelphia Inquirer*. Others thought the

experiment totally "un-American" and agreed with Senator John
Sparkman of Alabama, who denounced it as "absolutely appalling"
and "a disgrace to the American concept of justice and humanity."

Memories of Nazi Germany haunted some people as the broader
implications of the PHS's role in the experiment became apparent. A
man in Tennessee reminded health officials in Atlanta that "Adolf Hitler
allowed similar degradation of human dignity in inhumane medical
experiments on humans living under the Third Reich," and confessed
that he was "much distressed at the comparison." A New York editor
had difficulty believing that "such stomach-turning callousness could
happen outside the wretched quackeries spawned by Nazi Germany."[23]

The specter of Nazi Germany prompted some Americans to equate
the Tuskegee Study with genocide. A civil rights leader in Atlanta,
Georgia, charged that the study amounted to "nothing less than an
official, premeditated policy of genocide." A student at the Tuskegee
Institute agreed. To him, the experiment was "but another act of
genocide by whites," an act that "again exposed the nature of whitey:
a savage barbarian and a devil."[24]

Most editors stopped short of calling the Tuskegee Study genocide
or charging that PHS officials were little better than Nazis. But they
were certain that racism played a part in what happened in Alabama.
"How condescending and void of credibility are the claims that racial
considerations had nothing to do with the fact that 600 [all] of the
subjects were black," declared the *Afro-American* of Baltimore, Maryland. That PHS officials had kept straight faces while denying any
racial overtones to the experiment prompted the editors of this influential black paper to charge "that there are still federal officials who
feel they can do anything where black people are concerned."[25]

The *Los Angeles Times* echoed this view. In deftly chosen words,
the editors qualified their accusation that PHS officials had persuaded
hundreds of black men to become "human guinea pigs" by adding:
"Well, perhaps not quite that [human guinea pigs] because the doctors
obviously did not regard their subjects as completely human." A
Pennsylvania editor stated that such an experiment "could only happen
to blacks." To support this view, the *New Courier* of Pittsburgh implied
that American society was so racist that scientists could abuse blacks
with impunity.[26]

Other observers thought that social class was the real issue, that
poor people, regardless of their race, were the ones in danger. Somehow people from the lower class always seemed to supply a disproportionate share of subjects for scientific research. Their plight, in the

words of a North Carolina editor, offered "a reminder that the basic rights of Americans, particularly the poor, the illiterate and the friendless, are still subject to violation in the name of scientific research." To a journalist in Colorado, the Tuskegee Study demonstrated that "the Public Health Service sees the poor, the black, the illiterate and the defenseless in American society as a vast experimental resource for the government." And the *Washington Post* made much the same point when it observed, "There is always a lofty goal in the research work of medicine but too often in the past it has been the bodies of the poor . . . on whom the unholy testing is done."[27]

The problems of poor people in the rural South during the Great Depression troubled the editor of the *Los Angeles Times*, who charged that the men had been "trapped into the program by poverty and ignorance."[28]

Yet poverty alone could not explain why the men would cooperate with a study that gave them so little in return for the frightening risks to which it exposed them. A more complete explanation was that the men did not understand what the experiment was about or the dangers to which it exposed them. Many Americans probably agreed with the *Washington Post*'s argument that experiments "on human beings are ethically sound if the guinea pigs are fully informed of the facts and danger." But despite the assurances of PHS spokesmen that informed consent had been obtained, the Tuskegee Study precipitated accusations that somehow the men had either been tricked into cooperating or were incapable of giving informed consent.[29]

An Alabama newspaper, the *Birmingham News*, was not impressed by the claim that the participants were all volunteers, stating that "the majority of them were no better than semiliterate and probably didn't know what was really going on." The real reason they had been chosen, a Colorado journalist argued, was that they were "poor, illiterate, and completely at the mercy of the 'benevolent' Public Health Service." And a North Carolina editor denounced "the practice of coercing or tricking human beings into taking part in such experiments."[30]

The ultimate lesson that many Americans saw in the Tuskegee Study was the need to protect society from scientific pursuits that ignored human values. The most eloquent expression of this view appeared in the *Atlanta Constitution*. "Sometimes, with the best of intentions, scientists and public officials and others involved in working for the benefit of us all, forget that people are people," began the editor. "They concentrate so totally on plans and programs, experiments, statistics—on abstractions—that people become objects, symbols on paper, figures in a mathematical formula, or impersonal 'subjects' in a scientific study." This was the scientific blindspot to ethical issues that was responsible for the Tuskegee Study—what the *Constitution* called "a moral astigmatism that saw these black sufferers simply as 'subjects' in a study, not as human beings." Scientific investigators had to learn that "moral judgment should always be a part of any human endeavor," including "the dispassionate scientific search for knowledge."[31]

Notes

[1] *New York Times*, July 26, 1972, pp. 1, 8.

[2] Because of the high rate of geographic mobility among the men, estimates of the mortality rate were confusing, even in the published articles. PHS spokesmen in 1972 were reluctant to be pinned down on an exact figure. An excellent example is the Interview of Dr. David Sencer by J. Andrew Liscomb and Bobby Doctor for the U.S. Commission on Civil Rights, Alabama State Advisory Committee, September 22, 1972, unpublished manuscript, p. 9. For the calculations behind the figures used here, see *Atlanta Constitution*, September 12, 1972, p. 2A.

[3] During this primary stage the infected person often remains seronegative: A blood test will not reveal the disease. But chancres can be differentiated from other ulcers by a dark field examination, a laboratory test in which a microscope equipped with a special indirect lighting attachment can view the silvery spirochetes moving against a dark background.

[4] At the secondary stage a blood test is an effective diagnostic tool.

[5] Dr. Donald W. Prinz quoted in *Atlanta Journal*, July 27, 1972, p. 2; *Birmingham News*, July 27, 1972, p. 2.

[6] *New York Times*, July 27, 1972, p. 18.

[7] Dr. Ralph Henderson quoted in ibid.; *Tuskegee News*, July 27, 1972, p. 1.

[8] *New York Times*, July 27, 1972, p. 2.

[9] Eunice Rivers, Stanley Schuman, Lloyd Simpson, Sidney Olansky, "Twenty Years of Followup Experience in a Long-Range Medical Study," *Public Health Reports* 68 (April 1953): 391–95. (Hereafter Rivers et al.)

[10] Ibid., p. 393.

[11] Dr. John D. Millar quoted in *Birmingham News*, July 27, 1972, pp. 1, 4; *Atlanta Journal*, July 27, 1972, p. 2.

[12] Prinz quoted in *Atlanta Journal*, July 27, 1972, p. 2.

[13] Millar quoted in *Montgomery Advertiser*, July 26, 1972, p. 1.

[14] Ibid.; Prinz quoted in *Atlanta Journal*, July 27, 1972, p. 2.

[15] Millar quoted in *Montgomery Advertiser*, July 26, 1972, p. 1; *New York Times*, July 28, 1972, p. 29.

[16] Dr. Edward Lammons quoted in *Tuskegee News*, August 3, 1972, p. 1.

[17] Prinz quoted in *Atlanta Journal*, July 27, 1972, p. 2; Millar quoted in *Montgomery Advertiser*, July 26, 1972, p. 1.

[18] *St. Louis Dispatch*, July 30, 1972, p. 2D.

[19] *Time*, August 7, 1972, p. 54; *Chicago Sun Times*, July 29, 1972, p. 23.

[20] Their reactions can be captured at a glance by citing a few of the legends that introduced newspaper articles and editorials that appeared on the experiment. The *Houston Chronicle* called it "A Violation of Human Dignity" (August 5, 1972, Section I, p. 12); *St. Louis Post-Dispatch*, "An Immoral Study" (July 30, 1972, p. 2D); *Oregonian*, an "Inhuman Experiment" (Portland, Oregon, July 31, 1972, p. 16); *Chattanooga Times*, a "Blot of Inhumanity" (July 28, 1972, p. 16); *South Bend Tribune*, a "Cruel Experiment" (July 29, 1972, p. 6); *New Haven Register*, "A Shocking Medical Experiment" (July 29, 1972, p. 14); and Virginia's *Richmond Times Dispatch* thought that "appalling" was the best adjective to describe an experiment that had used "Humans as Guinea Pigs" (August 6, 1972, p. 6H). To the *Los Angeles Times* the study represented "Official Inhumanity" (July 27, 1972, Part II, p. 6); to the *Providence Sunday Journal*, a "Horror Story" (July 30, 1972, p. 2G); and to the *News and Observer* in Raleigh, North Carolina, a "Nightmare Experiment" (July 28, 1972, p. 4). The *St. Petersburg Times* in Florida voiced cynicism, entitling its editorial "Health Service?" (July 27, 1972, p. 24), while the *Milwaukee Journal* made its point more directly by introducing its article with the legend "They Helped Men Die" (July 27, 1972, p. 15).

[21] R. H. Kampmeir, "The Tuskegee Study of Untreated Syphilis," *Southern Medical Journal 65* (1972):1247–51.

[22] Ibid., p. 1250.

[23] Roderick Clark Posey to Millar, July 27, 1972; Tuskegee Files, Centers for Disease Control. Atlanta, Georgia. (Hereafter TF-CDC); *Daily News*, July 27, 1972, p. 63; see also *Milwaukee Journal*, July 27, 1972, p. 15; *Oregonian*, July 31, 1972, p. 16; and Jack Slater, "Condemned to Die for Science," *Ebony* 28 (November 1972), p. 180.

[24] *Atlanta Journal*, July 27, 1972, p. 2; *Campus Digest*, October 6, 1972, p. 4.

[25] *Afro-American*, August 12, 1972, p. 4. For extended discussions of the race issue, see Slater, "Condemned to Die," p. 191, and the three-part series by Warren Brown in *Jet* 43, "The Tuskegee Study," November 9, 1972, pp. 12–17, November 16, 1972, pp. 20–26, and, especially, November 23, 1972, pp. 26–31.

[26] *Los Angeles Times*, July 27, 1972, Part II, p. 6; *New Courier* also stated, "No other minority group in this country would have been used as 'Human Guinea Pigs,'" and explained, "because those who are responsible knew that they could do this to Negroes and nothing would be done to them if it became known," August 19, 1972, p. 6.

[27] *Greensboro Daily News*, August 2, 1972, p. 6; *Gazette-Telegraph*, Colorado Springs, August 3, 1972, p. 8A; *Washington Post*, July 31, 1972, p. 20A. See also *Arkansas Gazette*, July 29, 1972, p. 4A.

[28] *Los Angeles Times*, July 27, 1972, p. 20A.

[29] *Washington Post*, July 31, 1972, p. 20A.

[30] *Birmingham News*, July 28, 1972, p. 12; *Gazette-Telegraph*, August 3, 1972, p. 8A; *Greensboro Daily News*, August 2, 1972, p. 6A.

[31] *Atlanta Constitution*, July 27, 1972, p. 4A.

20
Transplantation and the Medical Commons

Renée C. Fox and Judith P. Swazey

"The dilemma confronting us," Dr. Howard Hiatt wrote in 1975, "is how we can place additional stress on the medical commons without bringing ourselves closer to ruin" (Hiatt 1975, p. 235). Hiatt's exploration of the nature of the medical commons and who is responsible for protecting its limited resources drew on an earlier paper by Garret Hardin, which used population growth to illustrate the types of human problems that, he argued, are not amenable to technical solutions (Hardin 1968). Both authors addressed the perennial ethical and social policy questions of how we should guard against the depletion of finite resources and how those resources should be most justly distributed. They did so through the analogy of a common pasture, shared by a group of herdsmen who, as their cattle increase, must decide how to balance their self-interests with the need to protect the land from overgrazing and ultimate destruction.

Drawing on Hiatt's image of medical care as a common ground that contains a finite amount of resources, we examine three sets of issues posed by the expanding effort to prevent death and hopefully restore health by replacing failing organs. These issues actually involve several "commons." First, within the sphere of transplantation, we look at the ways scarce vital organs are being allocated to potential recipients and the range of policy and human value issues posed by these means of distribution. Second, we consider the question of whether we ought to be committing more and more of our finite material and nonmaterial medical resources to organ replacement; or, as some analysts of health care needs and services have suggested, is organ replacement a pursuit that is forcing us to confront the possibility of protecting the medical commons through nonprice rationing? Third, thinking of medical care in relation to other societal needs and resources, the transplantation endeavor raises, in particularly dramatic and stark form, perhaps the most difficult social values and social policy question we need to confront about the nature and ends of medicine. That question, in the words of philosopher Daniel Callahan, is "What kind of medicine is best for a good society, and what kind of society is best for a good medicine?" (Callahan 1990, p. 29). How does transplantation speak to what we mean by "medical progress," and is it the type of progress we want to continue to pursue?

The Transplantation Commons

The 1980s saw an extensive growth in the range, number, and combination of tissues and solid organs that were transplanted, fostered by the introduction of newly developed immunosuppressive drugs and improved surgical techniques and methods for procuring and preserving donor organs. One of the major concomitants of this "boom" has been the way it has exacerbated the imbalance between the supply of transplantable organs and the demand for them.

At least by publicly visible yardsticks such as professional and popular literature and transplant-related policy debates and actions, the transplant community has been far more preoccupied with ways to significantly increase the number of organs available for transplantation than with the thorny distributive justice problem of who, among those in need, should receive these scarce potentially life-saving resources.

Despite the variety of attempted or proposed strategies to obtain more organs from both the living and the dead, however, the expanding scope and quickening pace of transplantation has meant that the demand far outstrips the supply, forcing transplant teams and organ procurement agencies to grapple with the question of how, in principle and practice, these scarce resources should be distributed. In terms of the principles of equity that, most believe, ideally should govern access to health care resources and their use in the United States (President's Commission 1983), sociomedical policy and value questions permeate two major decision-making stages in allocating organs. First, what criteria do or should determine access to the system; that is, how are patients referred to transplant centers, accepted as transplant candidates, and placed on a waiting list for an organ? Second, once potential recipients are in the system, what criteria do or should govern who receives donor organs?

Social policies concerned with equitable access to vital organs and tissues have been promulgated by the National Transplantation Act of 1984 (Public Law 98–507), the recommendations of the federal Task

Force on Organ Transplantation in 1986, and by the policies adopted by the United Network for Organ Sharing (UNOS), our national Organ Procurement and Transplantation Network. To date, the framers of transplantation policies have largely bypassed the question of how access to waiting lists should be handled and focused instead on who receives organs once they have been accepted as transplant candidates (Childress 1987; McDonald 1988; Task Force 1986). James F. Childress, a prominent medical ethicist and religionist, Vice-Chairman of the Task Force, and a member of UNOS' board, holds that concerns about patient access to waiting lists "probably cannot be directly addressed by UNOS and will require attention from other social institutions" (Childress 1989, p. 108). Yet, Childress continued, as the task force, UNOS, and others involved in transplantation have recognized,

> There is evidence that women, minorities, and low-income patients do not receive transplants at the same rate as white men with high incomes. The primary source of the unequal access . . . appear[s] to be . . . in the decisions about who will be admitted to the waiting list. . . . More research will be required to determine the extent to which unequal access to kidney transplantation, for example, hinges on patient choices and legitimate medical factors rather than on physician sequestration of patients in dialysis units, physician failure to inform and refer some groups of patients, or bias in the selection of patients seeking admission to waiting lists. (Childress 1989, p. 108; see also Eggers 1988; Kjellstrand 1988; Task Force 1986; U.S. DHHS 1987)

In addition to particularistic types of selection factors, the major barrier to equitable access at this point of entry into the organ replacement system, as for virtually all other areas of health care in the United States, is the "green screen" of ability to pay. The passage of Public Law 92–603 in 1972, providing Medicare coverage for most of the treatment costs for end-stage renal disease (ESRD), exempted most patients eligible for kidney transplantation or dialysis from the financial criterion for access (Fox and Swazey 1978, chs. 7, 11; Rettig 1976). However, as detailed in a 1991 report by the Institute of Medicine (IOM) on "kidney failure and the federal government," Medicare funding has not completely removed finances as a significant factor (Levinsky and Rettig 1991a). Transplantation is "unequivocally the best treatment for most patients with chronic renal failure, and over time far less costly to the federal government: excluding copayments and deductibles, it currently costs Medicare approximately

$32,000 a year for each dialysis patient, compared to an average of $56,000 for the first year of a kidney transplant and $6,000 a year thereafter" (Levinsky and Rettig 1991b, pp. 1145, 1144). However, Medicare coverage for kidney transplants has two major restrictions: Eligibility is confined to a 3-year period after a successful transplant, and the costs of the expensive, lifelong immunosuppressive drugs that must be taken to prevent rejection of the transplanted organ are reimbursed for only 1 year.

Dialysis patients eligible for Medicare coverage also encounter costs they must pay themselves, especially for home treatment. Moreover, some 7 percent of ESRD patients—"concentrated disproportionately among the poor and minorities"—are ineligible for any Medicare coverage because of their insurance status under Social Security (Levinsky and Rettig 1991b, p. 1145).

The Institute of Medicine study committee, believing that "access to life-saving therapy should not be limited on any basis other than status as a citizen or resident alien," recommended two major changes in the Medicare "entitlement" for ESRD patients. First, all citizens and resident aliens should receive Medicare coverage for dialysis; second, kidney transplant patients should "be granted a lifetime entitlement comparable to that available to patients on dialysis," including the cost of immunosuppressive drugs (Levinsky and Rettig 1991b, pp. 1145–1146). At the same time, the IOM committee, like many previous analysts, have recognized that the mounting cost of the ESRD program, which now provides Medicare benefits to some 150,000 patients at a price that approaches $4 billion a year, has been a matter of growing concern and controversy in light of efforts to contain the costs of health care. These individual and aggregate costs, generated primarily by dialysis, have escalated far beyond the estimates made when Public Law 92–603 was enacted for two primary reasons: (1) the increasing numbers of persons beginning treatment; and (2) the fact that, in terms of age distribution and severity of illness, there have been marked shifts toward older patients with renal failure secondary to other diseases, particularly diabetes (Cummings 1989; Levinsky and Rettig 1991a,b; Rettig 1980).

Candidates for organs other than kidneys find that the high costs of a transplant and the annual costs of immunosuppressive drugs and medical care thereafter make the green screen an even greater determinant of access to a waiting list. The financing of transplants, as we discuss in the next section, has become a controversial political and policy issue for federal and state policy-makers and third-party payers.

Decisions about coverage have been made on organ-by-organ, disease-by-disease, and patient-by-patient bases, resulting in substantial socioeconomic disparities in who gains access to transplant programs and great stress and uncertainty for patients and their families.

Although ability to pay has the greatest impact on transplant candidates who are among the millions of medically indigent or underinsured, it also can be an insuperable barrier to those with normally adequate health insurance, who still may have to pay many thousands of dollars in out-of-pocket expenses. As is attested by frequent stories in local and national media, when patients or their families cannot meet the costs of a transplant, beginning with an initial "down-payment," which for a liver transplant usually is about $100,000, they often resort to desperate fund-raising efforts. Among the newspaper stories in our files, for example, are headlines such as: "Our Towns. Rallying to Help Pay for a Transplant;" "Glen Campbell to Aid Baby in Need of Liver;" "White House Intervenes to Get Mom a Liver;" and "Reagan Call Brings Aid to Boy." As these headlines indicate, attempts to secure funds range from local community efforts spearheaded by families, friends, churches, and civic groups, to special events by celebrities, to engaging the power of the White House.

During the Reagan years the personal involvement of the Presidency was brought to bear not only on federal transplant policy decisions but on interventions for particular individuals, usually children, whose plight caught the attention of the President, his wife, or a special White House aide, Michael Batten. "The involvement of . . . Batten," health policy writer John Iglehart reported in 1983, "has led to an unusual series of federal interventions on behalf of families, including pressuring private health insurers, state Medicaid directors, and the DHHS to pay for organ transplants; making arrangements with the Air Force to ferry organs and patients; and assisting in local fundraising efforts. . . . Batten conceded that his activities amount to 'events in search of a policy'" (Iglehart 1983, pp. 126–127). However humanitarian the motivation for Batten's interventions may have been, the zeal with which he carried them out and the kind of "I represent President Reagan" pressure that he used raised serious questions about his mandate and if he had overstepped it.

Batten's apt characterization of the financing of transplants and other determinants of access to waiting lists as "events in search of a policy" is also applicable to many aspects of the ways that organs are distributed to potential recipients. If transplant candidates do gain access to a donor organ waiting list, they begin an often long period of "many sleepless nights" (Gutkind 1988), playing a waiting game for a suitable organ in which they must "compete" with other candidates who also are hoping for a gift of life. Potential recipients must play this "game," which many of them lose because they die before an organ is procured not only because of the "organ shortfall," but also because of persisting ambiguities and strife about the medical, ethical, and operational criteria for allocating these scarce resources. As a matter of moral principle and social policy, Childress has written,

> The federal Task Force on Organ Transplantation (1986) held that donated organs belong to the community, and this fundamental conviction undergirded all of its "recommendations for assuring equitable access to organ transplantation and for assuring the equitable allocation of donated organs among transplant centers and among patients medically qualified for an organ transplant." From this perspective, organ procurement and transplant teams receive donated organs as trustees and stewards for the community as a whole, and they should determine who will receive available organs according to public criteria that have been developed by a publicly accountable body with public representation and that reflect principles of justice as well as medical standards. (Childress 1989, p. 102)

In practice, however, there is still a long way to go before these ideals are realized at national, regional, state, or institutional levels. To begin with, at the basic level of medical criteria, the importance of HLA tissue-type matching between a cadaveric organ and a candidate recipient remains, after several decades, a major problem of uncertainty and controversy (Fox and Swazey 1978, ch. 2; Starzl and Fung 1990). Despite the uncertainty about the relevance of HLA antigen matching for the outcome of cadaveric organ grafts, it is an important element in the use of a "multifactorial point system" for deciding who, on local or national waiting lists, should receive an available organ. This system, initially proposed by Starzl in 1987 for kidney transplants and now used by UNOS for kidney, heart, and liver allocation decisions, assigns a set number of points to a candidate based on factors such as length of time on a waiting list, medical urgency, the logistics (ease and speed) of the transplant, and antigen matching between the donor organ and the patient (Starzl et al. 1987). Although the system's developers saw it as providing a neutral, medically determined way to ensure the equitable distribution of organs, it is not, in fact, value-free. For example, "the vigorous debate about how much weight each criterion should have . . . is to a great extent ethical . . . the points assigned to [the] various factors . . . reflect value judgments about the relative importance of patient [medical and nonmedical] need, probability of success, and time of waiting" (Childress 1989, pp. 104–105).

In addition to the problematic nature of certain medical criteria, as Childress pointed out, distribution based on the concept of donor organs as belonging to "the community" is at best ambiguous. In both principle and practice, it is unclear whether "community ownership" or "stewardship" of a donated organ means it should "belong" to and be used by the local community or region where it was procured, or that it is a national resource that should be assigned according to a country-wide distribution system (Childress 1989, p. 102).

Without clear and agreed-upon normative and medical standards for the equitable distribution of organs, their allocation, like the prior stage of access to waiting lists, has invoked controversy. Dramatic personal appeals for an organ by parents or spouses who can gain the attention of the media or of powerful intermediaries such as the President of the United States, clash with the norms of equity that most people believe should govern the allocation of this or other scarce resources. When identified life appeals are successful, they result in a designated donation, which also undercuts the notion of organs as belonging to "the community." These recurring situations raise questions about whether organ procurers or the family of a cadaver donor should have the "distributional authority" to stipulate who shall receive the gift being made.

The concept of scarce organs as "community property" and a "national resource" also gave rise to a politically and emotionally charged allocative debate during the mid-1980s about "the access of foreign nationals to U.S. cadaver organs" (U.S. DHHS 1986). The controversy and nationalistic demands for an "Americans first" organ distribution policy concerned transplanting organs into foreign nationals at U.S. transplant centers and exporting donor organs to other countries. Somewhat paradoxically, the controversy was rooted in the fact that the organ shortage in the United States is a relative one compared to that in other countries, as Americans donate more organs than persons in any other nation or society and have the world's largest organ procurement system (Prottas 1985).

The nature of the issues and the character of the divisive debate were dramatically publicized in a series of stories in 1985 in the *Pittsburgh Press*. Several of the stories, which themselves generated controversy and acrimony in terms of the accuracy of some of their facts and sources, focused on the policies and practices of the country's largest kidney transplant program, then headed by Dr. Thomas Starzl, at Presbyterian-University Hospital in Pittsburgh (Pierce 1985; Schneider and Flaherty 1985a-c). The tone and substance of the series are captured by the following excerpts from the first two articles in May 1985.

Favoritism Shrouds Presby Transplants

Since January 1984, transplant surgeons at Presbyterian-University Hospital have given some foreign citizens—especially Saudi Arabians—preference over Americans for kidney transplants . . . bypass[ing] . . . the hospital's formal policy of transplanting "locals first, hard-to-match patients second, and then foreign nationals." (Schneider and Flaherty 1985a)

Woman Passed Over After 3-Year Wait

Doctors say that a 60-year-old Pennsylvania woman who has been waiting for a kidney transplant in Pittsburgh for 3 years may be running out of time. . . . The woman was one of three Americans who matched a pair of donor kidneys that became available May 4, but she was bypassed in favor of a foreigner. . . . [H]er case is the latest example of a practice that has been a pattern for 17 months for the kidney transplant team headed by Dr. Thomas Starzl. (Schneider and Flaherty 1985e)

In July 1985, responding in part to the attention generated by the *Pittsburgh Press*, the Presbyterian-University Hospital trustees issued new guidelines for the allocation of organs to U.S. and Canadian citizens and to foreign nationals. The guidelines established an annual quota system, allowing 5 percent of the kidneys and hearts and 10 percent of livers obtained by the hospital's transplant services "to be used for foreign patients" (Pierce 1985).

The newspaper's stories about Pittsburgh's allocation of organs to foreign nationals was followed by a Pulitzer Prize-winning series that detailed various facets of "selling the gift," ranging from the worldwide black market trafficking in organs to another facet of the "Americans first" controversy: the exportation of kidneys from the United States to other countries. In 1984, wrote investigative reporters Andrew Schneider and Mary Pat Flaherty, about 5 percent of the cadaver kidneys donated by families in the United States were exported, "usually to wealthy patients overseas."

Foreign surgeons say the kidneys, deemed useless by American doctors, were transplanted at success rates that rival or exceed those at the best U.S. centers. Virtually every export broke a covenant made with donor families who had faith that if their gift of organs were usable, it would be for the sickest patients—not merely the richest or the most influential. (Schneider and Flaherty 1985d)

The ethical, economic, and policy pros and cons of providing foreign nationals with donor organs captured in these and other press accounts were debated at length within the ranks of the federal task force and the directors of UNOS and its Committee on Foreign Relations. Moreover, they became the subject of a DHHS Inspector General's report, a UNOS-commissioned public opinion poll, a Congressional inquiry, and analyses in bioethical publications such as the *Hastings Center Report* (Case studies 1986; Task Force 1986; UNOS 1988a,b; U.S. DHHS 1986).

In the end, at least in terms of the official policies adopted by UNOS, arguments favoring principles of humanitarianism, egalitarianism, and accountability prevailed over those favoring strict quotas for nonresident aliens, "foreigners last," or Americans only for transplants at U.S. centers, as well as a flat prohibition against exporting organs. As summarized by Childress,

> [The policy adopted by UNOS in 1988] establishes some limits and directions but relies mainly on a procedure of accountability in the transplantation of nonresident aliens. The policy requires UNOS members to charge the same fees for [all] patients, to treat all patients accepted on . . . waiting lists according to UNOS policies for the equitable distribution of organs [i.e., the multifactorial point system], and to arrange any exportation of organs . . . only after it has been impossible to find a suitable recipient in the U.S. or Canada. . . . On the local level, UNOS member centers that accept nonresident aliens . . . are expected to establish a mechanism for community participation and review. On the national level, the UNOS committee on foreign relations has a right to audit all transplant center activities relating to the transplantation of nonresident aliens and will automatically review any center that has more than 10 percent of its . . . recipients from foreign nationals. (Childress 1989, pp. 106–107)

The mounting scarcity of donor organs has intensified uncertainty and debate about a number of other aspects of organ distribution. As the following four examples suggest, several of these matters reflect broader societal tensions about the relative importance we place on individual liberty and equality as standards governing equitable access to scarce resources. First, the growing number of multiple organ transplants, using two to five organs from one or more donors, has raised the question of "whether a single individual should be allowed to receive several organs while thousands of other dying patients are unable to obtain any" (Altman 1989). Second, similar questions about "the one versus the many" have been evoked by the estimated one-third of recipients who receive one or more retransplants—in some cases six or more—when their graft is lost due to rejection, infection, or other complications. As transplant nurse-specialist Patricia M. Park pointed out, retransplants also pose questions about "the need and criteria for responsible decisions about when to stop, when to say 'enough is enough' to the transplant process."

> Although noble in its conception, the nonabandonment policy is the root of many of transplantation's problems. . . . Statistically, retransplants have nowhere near the functional success rate of primaries, so each retransplant has a lesser chance of increasing life expectancy.

> Retransplants also reduce the number of organs available to patients who are still waiting for their first. . . . While it may make us uncomfortable to think of rationing organs like gasoline, they are, like energy resources, both limited and exceedingly valuable. If the public had a clearer understanding of what can happen when transplantation goes wrong, I suspect they would support . . . legislation [limiting the number of transplants a person can have] without hesitation. (Park 1989, p. 30)

Third, debate about the equity of transplant "multiples" for one person also exists with respect to waiting lists: To wit, is it fair for one candidate to be registered on as many lists as she or he has the knowledge and resources to access? The UNOS Board has switched its policy back and forth in terms of allowing and prohibiting multiple listings by patients. The Board's ambivalence, its Vice-Chairman recollects, "reflect[s] in part . . . uncertainty about whether [UNOS'] underlying philosophy is national or federal." It also reflects the tension between "the dominant argument for permitting [multiple listings, which] stresses maximum freedom of choice and access [and the] main argument against multiple listing [which] centers on the unfair advantage it provides for [those] patients" (Childress 1989, p. 107).

A fourth set of issues, generated by the progressive expansion of eligibility criteria and concomitant decrease in contraindications for transplants, recalls the controversies about the mixture of medical, psychosocial, and behavioral criteria used to select chronic dialysis patients during the 1960s and early 1970s (Fox and Swazey 1978, chs.

7, 8). During those years, before the Medicare ESRD Program, dialysis facilities such as the Northwest Kidney Center in Seattle formed committees to decide who among the medically qualified dialysis candidates would be chosen to receive one of the limited number of treatment slots available. The Northwest Kidney Center's Committee, dubbed "the God Squad" by its critics, was composed of responsible middle class and upper-middle class members of the community whose selection criteria were, at times, shaped by their largely sub-liminal views of "social worth," as well as their judgments about a candidate's likely "success" on dialysis given his or her medical, psychological, and behavioral profile.

Today, both the shortage of organs and the human and financial resources that must be committed to a transplant and subsequent care are posing analogous questions and debate. Whether people with end-stage liver disease due to alcoholic cirrhosis (by far the leading cause of such disease) should receive liver transplants is currently a focus of these medical-moral issues in organ replacement. Starzl and colleagues reported that patients with alcohol-related end-stage liver disease (ARESLD) have 1- and 2-year transplant survival rates, com-parable to patients with other causes of end-stage liver disease, and seem to have a low recidivism rate (Altman 1990; Starzl et al. 1988). Based on these data, HCFA recommended in 1990 that patients with alcoholic cirrhosis be included in Medicare coverage for liver trans-plantation, with the proviso that such patients abstain from drinking; it adopted such coverage as part of its April 1991 ruling that, for purposes of Medicare reimbursement, adult liver transplants are no longer experimental if programs and patients meet a list of specified criteria (Medicare coverage 1991).

Though it may represent a carefully selected patient population, the Pittsburgh data coupled with HCFA's ruling have transformed the question of whether we can obtain "acceptable results" in patients with ARESLD to the question, "Should we?" (Moss and Siegler 1991, p. 1295). Many difficult ethical and sociological questions are involved. For example, is alcoholism a disease, a behavioral deficit that leads people to engage in self-destructive behavior, or a moral failing; and what difference does, or should, the answer make with regard to the alcoholic patient's eligibility for a scarce resource—a liver transplant? Are transplanters justified medically and ethically in requiring that alcoholics stop drinking and pledge not to drink after transplant before they will be accepted as transplant candidates? Does it mean that persons seeking transplants for other diseases, such as smokers who need heart transplants, should be held to the same standards (Altman 1990a)? When allocating scarce organs to persons with alcohol-induced liver failure, are transplanters explicitly or implicitly trying to show that their work is "value free"? As happened with kidney dialysis and transplant decisions of an earlier era, are they assuming that the "gift of life" they are bestowing will cause major, enduring changes in a recipient's behavior—in this case, "converting" him or her to an alcohol-free life (Fox and Swazey 1978a, ch.9)?

Physicians and bioethicists are beginning to engage in a sharply divided debate as to whether, given the "dire, absolute scarcity of donor livers," patients with ARESLD should be allowed to "compete equally" with other end-stage liver failure patients for a transplant (Moss and Siegler 1991, p. 1298). One position is represented by the Ethics and Social Impact Committee of the Transplant and Health Policy Center in Ann Arbor, Michigan. In terms of principles of fairness and justice, they argued, "there are no good grounds at present—moral or medical—to disqualify a patient with end-stage liver disease from consideration for a liver transplant simply because of a history of heavy drinking" (Cohen and Benjamin 1991, p. 1300). Considering the same types of issues and evidence, Moss and Siegler, from the University of Chicago's Center for Clinical Medical Ethics, come to the opposite conclusion. "Considerations of fairness suggest that a first-come, first-served approach for liver transplantation is not the most just approach. . . . [S]ince not all can live, priorities must be established and . . . patients with ARESLD should be given a lower priority for liver transplantation than others with ESLD" (Moss and Siegler 1991, p. 1298). Both sides in this burgeoning debate agree that their positions may be tempered by further clinical and psychosocial research focusing on alcoholic patients and other candidates for or recipients of liver transplants. Despite such research, however, so long as organs, like dialysis machines in an earlier era, are a scarce resource, we can expect that debate will flourish over assigning them to individuals whose behavioral patterns raise questions about their clinical outcomes and, explicitly or implicitly, invoke questions and judgments about "deservingness" and "social worth."

Transplantation and the Medical Commons

During their deliberations and policy actions relevant to transplantation, members of the transplantation community, the broader medical community, and health policy-makers, with few exceptions, have studiously avoided dealing with the distributive justice question of how the financial and human resources invested in organ replacement endeavors bear on our society's ability and willingness to meet other needs in the medical commons. Rather, as we have indicated, the sociomedical policy thrust has dealt, more narrowly, with how more organs can be procured and, secondarily, how they should be distributed to those who can meet the costs of a transplant. A third major allocative issue, the costs of transplantation and who should or will pay for them, has been avoided as much as possible by federal and state health care policy-makers. They have dealt with the financing of organ replacement when pressured to do so, largely on situational bases, and have only rarely faced it as a matter demanding reasoned policy analysis and action with respect to these procedures per se and their impact on other areas of medical needs and services.

Political scientist Richard Rettig has commented that the ways the intertwined issues of financing, distributive justice, and the rationing of medical resources have been handled in the transplantation "domain" constitute "a parable of our time" (Rettig 1989). Organ transplantation, as we, Rettig, and other of its chroniclers and analysts have shown, has been a parable or paradigmatic case because of the phenomena and issues it embodies, not because of the aggregate size and costs of the enterprise. Because the numbers and thus the overall expenditures for transplants are constrained by the limited supply of donor organs, the total monetary costs of transplantation, which have yet to be calculated, probably represent a relatively small percentage of our total health care expenditures. To date, as Cate and Laudicina pointed out, "available data on transplant costs [are] incomplete and far from perfect"; actual costs are significantly understated by calculating only average hospital charges, not items such as organ procurement charges, physician fees, and post-hospital expenses such as immunosuppressive drugs (Cate and Laudicina 1991, pp. 9, 14–15). Estimates, however, clearly show why the costs of a transplant can be staggering for the individual recipient and a nontrivial item in the increasingly strained Medicare and Medicaid budgets. The median cost of a heart-lung transplant, for example, "is $240,000 for initial care and approximately $47,000 a year for follow-up medications and care" (Theodore and Lewiston 1990, p. 773).

It is these individualized costs of transplants that starkly pose ethical and policy questions about "the trade-offs involved between basic care for the many and expensive, even though [potentially] lifesaving, care for the few" (Rettig 1989, p. 218). These questions are magnified by the oft-raised possibility that the number of transplants could increase dramatically if advances in immunosuppression someday permit the successful use of organs from other species, making it possible, in principle, to offer transplants to all who might benefit medically. Under this scenario, the aggregate costs of transplantation could mount enormously, mirroring, if not exceeding, the fiscal history of chronic dialysis since the government became the chief financer of treatment costs. Thus Rettig observed that one of the factors that has kept the financing of transplantation "off the [federal policy agenda] table has been the dominance of what might be called 'the ESRD metaphor.' The administration and Congress have tended to see transplantation as a fiscal blockbuster due to high unit costs and very high estimates of need" (Rettig 1989, p. 218).

Because policy-makers, particularly at the federal level, have tried to avoid dealing with the individual and aggregate costs of transplantation, it is not surprising that they have shied away from the even more ethically and politically volatile questions about transplantation in relation to other health care needs and costs. Many writers have examined the inevitability of allocation decisions and the temporizing maneuvers we recurrently engage in to avoid the difficult and often "tragic" choices involved in making rationing decisions on ethically and medically explicit grounds (Calabresi and Bobbit 1978). For two decades or more the costs of health care and how to contain them have been a dominant leitmotif in the United States at the levels of individual patients, providers, and institutions and of state and federal policy arenas. By and large, the many cost-containment strategies employed have involved an incrementalist, tinkering approach based on the hope that "quick fixes" might work well enough to avert far more basic decisions about health care needs, how they can be addressed more effectively and equitably, and which theories and principles of social justice should undergird those decisions. As philosopher Norman Daniels pointed out,

> Saying no to [potentially] beneficial treatments or procedures in the United States is morally hard because providers cannot appeal to the justice of their denial. . . . Economic incentives such as those embedded in current cost-containment measures are not a substitute for social decisions about health care priorities and the just design of health care institutions. (Daniels 1986, p. 1383)

The difficulties we have faced in placing fiscal or other limits on transplantation epitomize two of the cardinal, interrelated features of health care in the United States that Daniels addressed. The first is the fragmented and increasingly chaotic nature of what we call our health care "system," whose long-standing signs and symptoms of malaise have been exacerbated by debates over costs and their control. On this point, as Shortell and McNerney have pointedly written, "it would be tempting to suggest that the U.S. health care system is now in disarray were it not for the fact that it has never really been otherwise. There is increasing anger and frustration among employers, consumers, uninsured people, payers, and providers, all of whom are struggling with what are perceived to be competing demands to contain costs while trying to improve productivity, increase quality, and expand access to services" (Shortell and McNerney 1990, p. 463). Second, as Americans reluctantly face the fact that our society does indeed ration health care based on ability to pay and even more reluctantly begin to consider the possibility of nonprice rationing, our lack of any broad sociopolitical consensus about the values that might provide a foundation for a more just mode of rationing becomes more glaringly apparent.

References

Altman, L. K. 1989 . With new boldness, surgeons create patchwork patients. *New York Times* (12 December): C1, C14.

_____. 1990. A question of ethics: should alcoholics get transplanted hearts? *New York Times* (April 3): C3.

Calabresi, G., and Bobbit, P. 1978. *Tragic Choices*. New York: Norton.

Callahan, D. 1990. Modernizing mortality: medical progress and the good society. *Hastings Center Report* 20(January/February): 28–32.

Case studies: in organ transplants, Americans first? 1986. *Hastings Center Report* 16(October): 23–25.

Cate, F. H., and Laudicina, S. S. 1991. Transplantation white paper: current statistical information about transplantation in America. Washington, DC: The Annenberg Program in Communication Policy Studies of Northwestern University and the United Network for Organ Sharing.

Childress, J. F. 1987. Some moral connections between organ procurement and organ distribution. *Journal of Contemporary Health Law and Policy* 3: 85–110.

_____. 1989. Ethical criteria for procuring and distributing organs for transplantation. In *Organ Transplantation Policy: Issues and Prospects*, eds. J. F. Blumstein and F. A. Sloan, pp. 87–113. Durham, NC: Duke University Press.

Cohen, C., and Benjamin, M. 1991. Alcoholics and liver transplantation. *Journal of the American Medical Association* 265(13 March): 1299–1301.

Cummings, N. B. 1989. Social, ethical, and legal issues involved in chronic maintenance dialysis. In *Replacement of Renal Function by Dialysis*, ed. J. F. Maher, pp. 1141–1158. Dordrecht, The Netherlands: Kluwer Academic Publishers.

Daniels, N. 1986. Why saying no to patients in the United States is so hard: cost containment, justice, and provider autonomy. *New England Journal of Medicine* 314(22 May): 1380–1393.

Eggers, P. 1988. Effect of transplantation on the medicare end-stage renal disease program. *New England Journal of Medicine* 318(28 January): 223–229.

Fox, R. C., and Swazey, J. P. 1978. *The Courage to Fail: A Social View of Organ Transplants and Dialysis* (2nd ed. rev.). Chicago: University of Chicago Press.

Gutkind, L. 1988. *Many Sleepless Nights*. New York: W. W Norton & Company.

Hardin, G. 1968. The tragedy of the commons. *Science* 162(13 Dec.): 1243–1248.

Hiatt, H. 1975. Protecting the medical commons: who is responsible? *New England Journal of Medicine* 293(31 July): 235–241.

Iglehart, J. K. 1983. Transplantation: the problem of limited resources. *New England Journal of Medicine* 309(14 July): 123–128.

Kjellstrand, C. M. 1988. Age, sex, and race inequality in renal transplantation. *Archives of Internal Medicine* 148: 1305–1309.

Levinsky, N. G., and Rettig, R. A., eds. 1991a. *Kidney Failure and the Federal Government*. Washington, DC: National Academy Press.

Levinsky, N. G., and Rettig, R. A. 1991b. The Medicare end-stage renal disease program: a report from the Institute of Medicine. *New England Journal of Medicine* 324(18 April): 1143–1148.

Medicare coverage is approved for liver transplant operations. 1991. *New York Times* (14 April): A24.

Moss, A. H., and Siegler, M. 1991. Should alcoholics compete equally for liver transplantation? *Journal of the American Medical Association* 265(13 March): 1295–1298.

Park, P. M. 1989. The transplant odyssey. *Second Opinion* 12(November): 27–32.

Pierce, H. W. 1985. Presby has new transplants policy. *Pittsburgh Post Gazette* (18 July): 1, 14.

President's Commission for the Study of Ethical Problems in Medicine and Biomedical and Behavioral Research.

_____. 1983. *Securing Access to Health Care: The Ethical Implications of Differences in the Availability of Health Services* (Vol. 1: Report). Washington, DC: U.S. Government Printing Office.

Prottas, J. M. 1985. Organ procurement in Europe and the United States. *Milbank Memorial Fund Quarterly/Health and Society* 63(1): 94–126.

Rettig, R. A. 1976. The policy debate on patient care financing for victims of end-stage renal disease. *Law and Contemporary Problems* 40(4): 196–230.

_____. 1980. The politics of health cost containment: end-stage renal disease. *Bulletin of the New York Academy of Medicine* 56: 115–137.

Schneider, A., and Flaherty, M. P. 1985a. Favoritism shrouds Presby transplants. *Pittsburgh Press* (May 12): A1, A10–11.

_____. 1985b. Foreigners get kidneys with flaws. *Pittsburgh Press* (8 July): A1–A2.

_____. 1985c. Selling the gift [six articles in the Challenge of a Miracle series]. *Pittsburgh Press* November 3–8.

_____. 1985d. U.S. kidneys sent overseas as Americans wait. *Pittsburgh Press* (6 November): A1, A24.

_____. 1985e. Woman passed over after 3-year wait. *Pittsburgh Press* (12 May): A10.

Shortell, S. M., and McNerney, W. J. 1990. Criteria and guidelines for reforming the U.S. health care system. *New England Journal of Medicine* 322(15 February): 463–466.

Starzl, T. E., and Fung, J. J. 1990. Transplantation. *Journal of the American Medical Association* 263(16 May): 2686–2687.

Starzl, T. E., Groth, C-G., and Makowka, L., eds. 1988. *Liver Transplantation*. Clio Chirugica. Austin, TX: Silvergirl, Inc.

Starzl, T. E., Hakala, T. R., and Tzakis, A., et al. 1987. A multifactorial system for equitable selection of cadaver kidney recipients. *Journal of the American Medical Association* 257(12 June): 3073–3075.

Task Force on Organ Transplantation. 1986. *Organ Transplantation: Issues and Recommendations*. Washington, DC: Department of Health and Human Services.

Theodore, J., and Lewiston, N. 1990. Lung transplantation comes of age. *New England Journal of Medicine* 322(15 May): 772–774.

United Network for Organ Sharing. 1988a. *Policy Proposal Statement: UNOS Policies Regarding Transplantation of Foreign Nationals and Exportation and Importation of Organs*. Richmond, VA: UNOS.

_____. 1988b. *Policy Proposal Statement: UNOS Policy Regarding the Listing of Patients on Multiple Transplant Waiting Lists*. Richmond, VA: UNOS.

U.S. Department of Health and Human Services. Office of Analysis and Inspections, Office of Inspector General. 1986. *The Access of Foreign Nationals to U.S. Cadaver Organs*. Washington, DC: U.S. DHHS. Publ. no. P-01-86-00074.

21
The DNA Mystique:
The Gene as a Cultural Icon

Dorothy Nelkin and Susan Lindee

A full-color advertisement boasts that a new BMW sedan has a "genetic advantage"—a "heritage" that comes from its "genealogy."[1] A *U.S. News and World Report* article on the Baby M custody dispute states that it will not make much difference which family brings up the child since her personality is already determined by her genes.[2] A cartoonist lists genetically linked traits: "excessive use of hair spray, bottomless appetite for country-western music, right wing politics."[3] A critic reviewing a play about the persistence of racism says, "it's as if it has a DNA of its own."[4] The term "gene pool" appears as the name of a comedy group, the title of a TV show, and in the captions of comic books and the lyrics of rock music. Indeed, in the 1990s "gene talk" has entered the vernacular as a subject for drama, a source of humor, and an explanation of human behavior.[5]

In supermarket tabloids and soap operas, in television sitcoms and talk shows, in women's magazines and parenting advice books, genes appear to explain obesity, criminality, shyness, directional ability, intelligence, political leanings, and preferred styles of dressing. There are selfish genes, pleasure-seeking genes, violence genes, celebrity genes, gay genes, couch-potato genes, depression genes, genes for genius, genes for saving, and even genes for sinning. These popular images convey a striking picture of the gene as powerful, deterministic, and central to an understanding of both everyday behavior and the "secret of life."[6]

What is this crucial entity? In one sense, the gene is a biological structure, the unit of heredity, a sequence of deoxyribonucleic acid (DNA) that, by specifying the composition of a protein, carries information that helps to form living cells and tissues.[7] But it has also become a cultural icon, a symbol, almost a magical force. The biological gene—a nuclear structure shaped like a twisted ladder—has a cultural meaning independent of its precise biological properties. Both a scientific concept and a powerful social symbol, the gene has many powers.

We explore those powers, showing how the images and narratives of the gene in popular culture reflect and convey a message we will call genetic essentialism.[8] Genetic essentialism reduces the self to a molecular entity, equating human beings, in all their social, historical, and moral complexity, with their genes.

DNA in popular culture functions, in many respects, as a secular equivalent of the Christian soul. Independent of the body, DNA appears to be immortal. Fundamental to identity, DNA seems to explain individual differences, moral order, and human fate. Incapable of deceiving, DNA seems to be the locus of the true self, therefore relevant to the problems of personal authenticity posed by a culture in which the "fashioned self" is the body manipulated and adorned with the intent to mislead.[9] In many popular narratives, individual characteristics and the social order both seem to be direct transcriptions of a powerful, magical, and even sacred entity, DNA.

Increasing popular acceptance of genetic explanations and the proliferation of genetic images reflects, in part, highly publicized research in the science of genetics. Such research, however, occurs in a specific cultural context, one in which heredity and natural ability have often seemed important to formulations of social policy and social practice.[10] Old ideas have been given new life at a time when individual identity, family connections, and social cohesion seem threatened and the social contract appears in disarray.

Changing technologies for the manipulation and assessment of DNA have, moreover, dramatically changed the social implications of these revived ideas. It seems imperative, therefore, to examine these trends critically at a time when diagnosis and prediction based on DNA analysis have so many new applications. In the laboratory, DNA can be used to detect unseen conditions of risk and predict future conditions of disability or disease. Within the family, DNA can be used to define meaningful relationships and make reproductive decisions. In the larger culture, DNA can be used to locate responsibility and culpability, as well as to justify social and institutional policies. Those on all sides of the political spectrum can proclaim that specific biological properties of DNA lend support to their policies or goals. And their claims all build on the DNA mystique.

Yet in the history of biology there are few concepts more problematic than that of the gene. It began as a linguistic fiction, coined by Danish geneticist Wilhelm Johannsen in 1909 to describe a presumed cellular entity capable of producing a particular trait. He drew the term from German physiologist and geneticist Hugo DeVries's "pangenes," a term derived from Charles Darwin's "pangenesis," a theory of the origins of biological variation. For the first generation of experimental geneticists (in the early twentieth century), a "gene" was, in practice, a physical trait—the wing shape or eye color of the fruit fly *Drosophila*, for example—which seemed to derive from a substrate of hereditary material, the actual constitution and functioning of which were unknown at the time.[11]

In the post–World War II era, the increasing elucidation of the gene as a molecular entity has both clarified its physical form—a double helix of deoxyribonucleic acid (DNA)—and complicated its biological meaning.[12] As contemporary genomics science has demonstrated, DNA does not produce bodily traits in a simple, linear way. It interacts with itself and with its larger environment: Identical sequences of DNA in different locations on the genome (the entire complement of DNA in any given organism's cells) can have different biological meanings. And different genes can have identical effects in different people. Genomes also have large regions, so-called "junk DNA," that seem to have no function at all.

For contemporary molecular geneticists, "gene" is convenient shorthand, referring generally to a stretch of DNA that codes for a protein. In the sense that some sections of DNA produce specific biological events, genes are real entities, but their workings are not simple. While increasing scientific knowledge of molecular processes has clarified some questions, it has also raised new and unexpected ones. Why is so much of the genome without obvious function? Why do many genetic diseases become more severe from generation to generation as a consequence of reduplication of short coding sections? And what does the ambiguity of the genome—its biological indeterminism—mean for our understanding of evolution and evolutionary processes? Much of this complexity disappears when the gene serves its public roles as a resource for scientists seeking public support and as a popular explanation for social problems and human behavior, and a justification for policy agendas.

The point of our analysis is not to identify popular distortions of science or to debunk scientific myths. The interesting question is not the contrast between scientific and popular culture; it is how they intersect to shape the cultural meaning of the gene. Some of the images we explore draw on well-established scientific ideas, some on findings that geneticists continue to question, while others seem to be independent of biological research. The precise scientific legitimacy of any image, however, is less important than the cultural use that is made of it. How do scientific concepts serve social ideologies and institutional agendas? Why do certain concepts gain social power to become the focus of significant popular and scientific attention? And what role do scientists play in shaping the appropriation of such concepts?

Science and Culture

It is not a coincidence that the popular appropriation of genetics has intensified just as scientists around the world have begun an effort to map and sequence the entire human genome, for in presenting their research to the public, scientists have been active players in constructing the powers of the gene. The cutting edge of this scientific exploration is the Human Genome Project, an international scientific program to map and sequence not only the genes but also the noncoding regions of all the DNA contained in the 24 human chromosomes.

Although gene mapping began in the 1910s with studies of the common fruit fly, *Drosophila*, large-scale mapping of human genes was not technically feasible until the development of greater computer capacity and a variety of new laboratory techniques in the 1980s. Building on these techniques, the human gene mapping program began in 1989 in the United States, where it is funded through the National Institutes of Health (NIH) and the United States Department of Energy (DOE) at a total anticipated cost of more than $3 billion over 15 years. Similar projects are underway in Great Britain, Japan, Russia, the European Community, and other industrialized nations.

Genome researchers hope to locate and determine the exact order of the base pairs in the estimated 100,000 human genes, as well as in the many sections of DNA with no known function. As of the summer of 1994 geneticists had identified over 2500 of the 3000 genetic markers (sections of DNA that can be used as signposts along the genome) needed to create a genetic map. Many single gene disorders—diseases caused by a known form of a particular gene—are already located on the map, either directly or through the identification of genetic markers that "follow" the disease through large, well-characterized family groups. These included cystic fibrosis, retinitis pigmentosa, one form of Alzheimer disease, and more rare conditions such as Huntington's disease, Gaucher disease, malignant hyperthermia, and epidermolysis bullosa.[13]

Geneticists are also exploring the patterns of inheritance of conditions with apparent multiple gene involvement, suggesting familial predispositions to some forms of cancer and Alzheimer's, emphysema, juvenile diabetes, cleft palate, heart disease, and mental illness. Researchers have identified the genetic markers for certain kinds of breast and ovarian cancer and have located the gene causing the mutation responsible for some colon cancers. One goal of such research is to identify susceptible individuals before their symptoms appear.[14]

Seeking to assure continued public funding of a long-term, costly project, genome researchers have been writing for popular magazines, giving public talks, and promoting their research in media interviews. They contribute to popular imagery as they popularize their work in ways that resonate with larger social concerns. Indeed, many of the values and assumptions expressed in popular representations of genes and DNA draw support from the rhetorical strategies of scientists—the promises they generate and the language they use to enhance their public image.[15]

Three related themes underlie the metaphors geneticists and other biologists use to describe work on the human genome. These are a characterization of the gene as the essence of identity, a promise that genetic research will enhance prediction of human behavior and health, and an image of the genome as a text that will define a natural order.

Some scientists borrow their images from the computer sciences: The body is less a conscious being than a set of "instructions," a "program" transmitted from one generation to the next. People are "readouts" of their genes. If scientists can decipher and decode the text, classify the markers on the map, and read the instructions, so the argument goes, they will be able to reconstruct the essence of human beings, unlocking the key to human ailments and even to human nature—providing ultimate answers to the injunction "know thyself." Geneticist Walter Gilbert introduces his public lectures on gene sequencing by pulling a compact disk from his pocket and announcing to his audience: "This is you."[16]

Other metaphors used by scientists imply the possibilities of prediction, encouraging the use of their science for social policy. They call the genome a "Delphic oracle," a "time machine," a "trip into the future," a "medical crystal ball." Nobelist and first director of the U.S. Human Genome Project James Watson says in public interviews that "our fate is in our genes."[17] Futuristic scenarios promise that genetic prediction will enhance control over behavior and disease. Thus, a geneticist promises that "present methods of treating depression will seem as crude as former pneumonia treatments seem now."[18] A food scientist writes that food companies will sell specialized breakfast cereals to consumer targets who are genetically predisposed to particular diseases. "Computer models in the home will provide consumers with a diet customized to fit their genetic individuality, which will have been predetermined by simple diagnostic tests."[19] And a biologist and science editor, describing acts of violence, editorializes that "when we can accurately predict future behavior, we may be able to prevent the damage."[20]

Scientific illustrations, too, glamorize DNA and promote the notion of genetic essentialism. The logo for the joint NIH-DOE publication, *Human Genome News*, portrays a human figure in silhouette, standing inside two swirling ribbons of DNA, contained within a circle. Inscribed around him are the names of scientific disciplines: "Chemistry, Biology, Physics, Mathematics, Engineering." The twisted double helix of DNA surrounding the figure suggests the imprisonment of the human being, who will be released through scientific knowledge. This logo conveys the power of science and its promise for the future.

Geneticists also refer to the genome as the Bible, the Holy Grail, and the Book of Man. Explicit religious metaphors suggest that the genome—when mapped and sequenced—will be a powerful guide to moral order. Other common references to the genome as a dictionary, a library, a recipe, a map, or a blueprint construct DNA as a comprehensive and unbiased resource, an orderly reference work. The population geneticist Bruce Wallace has compared the human genome to "the torn pages of a giant novel, written in an unknown language, blowing about helter-skelter in an air-conditioned, enclosed space such as Houston's Astrodome."[21] Wallace's chaotic image of the genome implies the promise that scientists engaged in mapping the human genome will (eventually) capture all the pages, put them in proper order, translate the language, and analyze the meaning of the resulting text.

The apparent precision of a map may make invisible the priorities and interests that shaped it. As forms of knowledge, all maps reflect social perspectives on the world at the time of their making; they are the products of cultural choices. Maps select and link features of the world, in effect transforming those features by making them part of a coherent, single landscape. The selectivity of maps is a part of their visual power, of course, for they are also instruments of persuasion. As one curator put it, "Every map is someone's way of getting you to look at the world in his or her way."[22] Map imagery suggests that once a gene is located, its interpretation will be objective and independent of context. But as molecular biologist Christopher Wills has observed, "simply determining the sequence of all this DNA will not mean we have learned everything there is to know about human beings, any more than looking up the sequence of notes in a Beethoven sonata gives us the capacity to play it."[23] A mapped gene may appear to be a straightforward detail, to be extracted and understood without reference to culture and experience. Yet the language of the genome, like the language of a dictionary, must be contextualized to be understood. Genes are, like words, products of (evolutionary) history, dependent on context, and often ambiguous, open to more than one interpretation.[24]

Meanwhile, the successes of molecular genetics and the high profile of the Human Genome Project are shaping the assumptions underlying research in other scientific fields. Behavioral geneticists and psychologists, working with human twins and extrapolating from animal models, have attributed shyness, intelligence, criminality, even religiosity and other complex human traits to heredity. The Minnesota Center for Twin and Adoption Research has provided percentage estimates of the extent to which certain personality traits are determined by heredity: extroversion, 61 percent; conformity, 60 percent; tendency to worry, 55 percent; creativity, 55 percent; aggressiveness, 48 percent.[25] While human genome research has been promoted as a way to find disease genes, many within the scientific community believe that a map of the genome will also document the inheritance of these complex, socially important human traits. Indeed, some scientists believe this is a major goal. Nobelist David Baltimore has commented that the genome project "will allow us to examine human variability, for example, variations in mathematical ability, or what we call intelligence. . . . The rationale is not to find human disease genes, because we're doing moderately well at finding them right now. But the only way to study the genetics of the higher perceptual, higher integrative human functions is by actually studying human beings. . . . The genetic and physical maps are designed for that."[26]

The emphasis on genes for specific behaviors, however, is controversial. Some scientists argue that efforts to measure the relative effects of heredity and environment on behavior systematically misconstrue the two as independent rather than interactive forces, underestimating the influence of environmental forces on gene expression.[27] Critics point out that the heritability of any trait is simply a statistical construct that may suggest variations between populations but may have no simple meaning for the individual.[28] Stephen Jay Gould has observed that efforts to distinguish the relative effects of nature and nurture propose a false dichotomy by confusing correlation with causation: "Genes influence many aspects of human behavior, but we cannot say that such behavior is caused by genes in any direct way. We cannot even claim that a given behavior is, say, 40% genetic and 60% environmental. . . . Genes and environment interact in a nonadditive way."[29]

Some critics question the motivation behind efforts to measure the relative effects of nature and nurture on behavior. Psychologist Douglas Wahlsten, for example, believes that "the only practical application of the heritability coefficient is to predict the results of a program of selective breeding."[30] And African American organizations, sensitive to the racist implications of deterministic explanations of deviance, attacked plans, for a scholarly conference on "genetic factors in crime."[31]

Despite continued controversy over methods and motives, efforts to determine the genetic basis of human behaviors such as alcoholism and crime draw legitimacy from the rising fortunes of molecular biology. These efforts have captured public attention, for such research addresses critical social questions—about the basis of human identity and individual differences, the nature of deviance, and the location of responsibility for social problems.

Scientists often dismiss as oversimplified and distorted the way their work is appropriated. But the relationship between scientific and public culture is far more complex. As historian Robert Young put it, it is often "impossible to distinguish hard science from its economic and political context and from the generalizations which serve both as motives for the research and which are fed back into social and political debate."[32]

Genetic Essentialism Applied

As a broadly accepted science-based concept, genetic essentialism has become a resource for many institutions, helping them resolve ambiguous and difficult problems. Institutions routinely gain legitimacy by grounding their policies and practices in what are taken to be natural categories.[33] Scientifically sanctioned, such categories are assumed to be impersonal, rational, and value-free.[34] At the same time, popular images of the gene make the use of genetic information socially acceptable. Media images channel public perceptions and help define "normal" social relationships. They frame ideas about appropriate behavior, thereby facilitating these institutional uses of genetic information.[35] The popular powers of the gene seem to promise that DNA, if comprehensively known and accurately understood, could explain both past performance and future potential. Individuals, moreover, are less likely to challenge practices that conform to mass expectations and accepted cultural beliefs.

Popular perceptions of genetics—the assumptions of genetic essentialism—are played out with practical consequences in many contemporary institutional settings. They serve as a basis for important decisions about family relationships, influence legal interpretations of criminal culpability, and help institutions to anticipate future risk by identifying individuals who are predisposed to health or behavior problems.[36]

Predicting and Avoiding Risk

Many institutions and organizations—schools, motor vehicle bureaus, immigration authorities, sports teams, organ transplant registries, adoption agencies, the military, even university tenure committees—have significant interest in predictive information. Pressured to maintain economic viability, efficiency, and accountability, such institutions need to anticipate future contingencies and to avoid risks. Genetic tests can differentiate individuals on the basis of ostensibly natural categories by identifying predispositions. Their results, applied by institutions seeking to control costs, appear to resolve ambiguities while limiting the role of arbitrary interpretation.[37] They can end up defining the competence of individuals, controlling their access to social services, educational programs, insurance, or jobs.

Medical institutions, especially health insurers, face economic pressures that encourage interest in predictive information. Genetic information can help health care providers conform to the reimbursement constraints of third-party payers, control access to medical facilities, and plan for future demands in a system increasingly preoccupied with cost containment and economic accountability. Insurance underwriters, favoring "preferred" customers who are expected to incur fewer medical expenses, welcome genetic information as a means to cut their costs. People with a genetic predisposition to a costly disease may be denied insurance coverage or expected to pay exorbitant rates.[38] Some health insurers have already tried to refuse coverage for children born with birth defects after the mothers, warned through prenatal testing, refused to abort.[39]

The threat of malpractice litigation also drives the interest in genetic information. The courts have recognized "wrongful birth" claims, awarding damages to parents of children born with genetic disorders that could have been identified in time for a fetus to be aborted. This encourages the use of genetic testing as a way to protect physicians against malpractice suits.

As the scope and sophistication of testing for genetic characteristics increases and their use becomes widely accepted, companies could justify routine testing of prospective employees for their predisposition to personality disorders and to traits that may affect their ability to work. Some corporate wellness programs offer genetic tests to employees in order to help them (and the company) anticipate future problems. Job application procedures could add genetic tests to the existing battery of pre-employment examinations, enabling employers to hire workers with genetic profiles that suggest they are likely to stay healthy and perform well.[40] Just as psychological tests are now used to predict potential productivity, honesty, and special skills, so biological tests could be used to anticipate future failure or success.

At present, genetic screening techniques are mainly used to identify and exclude workers with specific traits that may predispose them to illness from exposure to certain chemical agents in the workplace.[41] Justified in the first instance as a way to protect employee health, tests that identify vulnerable individuals can also be used to control compensation claims and avoid costly changes in the workplace environment, reducing a company's burden of responsibility to provide safe working conditions. It is the employee, excluded from the workplace, who assumes the burden and the blame for the risk.

Different corporations have stakes in genetic explanations for quite diverse reasons. Information about genetic predispositions can be used to deflect a company's legal responsibility for doing harm by blaming the damage on the victim. For example, when a behavioral modification clinic was sued following the suicide of a young man who had been attending its program, the clinic defended its procedures by arguing that the man was genetically predisposed to mental illness. It called in geneticists as expert witnesses to attest to the importance of genes as causes of suicidal tendencies.

The Ernest Gallo Clinic and Research Center, staffed by neuroscientists at the University of California at San Francisco and funded by the eighty-five-year-old wine mogul, has another stake in genetic explanations. Created in 1984, the center has worked to identify the biological causes of alcohol abuse. In 1993, Gallo Center scientists found what they believed to be a gene for alcoholism. They hypothesized that this gene produced a protein that "jams the signals" that would normally warn a person to stop drinking. Those born without this internal warning system, they suggested, might be prone to drink too much. Critics of the Gallo Center, which has received millions in research funding from the manufacturer of inexpensive wines such as Thunderbird, argue that a genetic explanation for alcoholism might be extremely useful to the liquor industry. A biological cure for alcoholism could "increase the potential market for their product," while also locating responsibility for alcoholism in an individual's DNA.[42]

Economic pressures on government agencies can also drive genetic testing. Take, for example, the Fragile-X testing program in Colorado. Fragile-X is a genetic disease that can, but does not always, cause mental impairment. To justify genetic testing for the disease, proponents of the Colorado program provided an estimate of the public cost of caring for Fragile-X patients. They concluded that the economic burden called for improved identification of carriers—"even mildly affected carriers of normal IQ"—so as to reduce the number of affected births. "The savings for the state would be tremendous."[43]

Similarly, on Long Island (in New York State), members of an organization seeking to reduce school taxes have campaigned against the school system program of special education classes for learning-disabled children. Their argument is that learning disabilities are of genetic origin; therefore the responsibility falls to the medical system, not the schools.[44]

Genetic assumptions, focusing attention on the aberrant individual and away from the social context, also have strategic value for educational institutions facing demands for accountability and pressures to establish more rigorous standards for classifying students. During the 1960s, explanations of academic success or failure centered on environmental sources of behavioral and educational problems, calling attention to the influence of family deprivation or a child's socioeconomic situation. But in the 1980s, social explanations were gradually replaced by explanations drawing on the biological sciences. Learning disabilities and behavioral problems became defined as biological deficits, with problems located less in a student's social situation than in the biological structure of his or her brain.

Schools, having access to most children in the society, are traditionally responsible for assessing, categorizing, and channeling them toward future roles. Educators' interest in biological causes, therefore, has broad social impact, and their widespread acceptance of genetic essentialism legitimatizes the use of tests in the schools to define and measure what is normal or pathological in individuals, to assess their potential, and to predict their intrinsic limits.

The Blueprint of Destiny

The popularity of the Human Genome Project, with its almost weekly discovery of new genes and promises of new cures, encourages the institutional use of genetic information and, at the same time, discourages serious public scrutiny. According to the media and other sources of popular information, science provides objective, certain knowledge of genetic processes, which seem to predict, unfailingly, the future health of individuals. Yet these popular expectations of objectivity, predictability, and certainty may not be borne out when scientific studies are applied to specific social or institutional policies.

Objectivity is a norm in the practice of science, but the history of science demonstrates how cultural forces and institutional needs can shape the choice of research topics, the nature of scientific theories, and the representation of research results. Scientific fields are influenced by institutional agendas and defined to reflect the priorities and assumptions of given societies at particular times.[45] Historian Nikolas Rose, for example, has traced how the development of psychology as a credible scientific discourse in the early part of the century was driven less by curiosity about the human psyche than by the needs of the schools, the reformatories, the army, the factories, and the courts. Faced with rapid social change, these institutions sought to identify individual differences and to predict future pathologies in order to meet evolving demands. The field of psychology developed, therefore, as the "science . . . of individual differences, of their conceptualization and their measurement, . . . and of the prognosis of future conduct in terms of them."[46]

The recent interest in genetic perspectives stems not solely from dramatic advances in research, but also from the appeal of a scientific explanation that seems to justify social agendas. And our continued fascination with the criminal brain—currently reflected in the efforts to visualize the brain as a way to identify the biological basis of criminal tendencies—reflects the hope for simple, scientifically based solutions to the complex problem of understanding and managing crime. One criminologist, writing on the insanity defense, claimed that new genetic and imaging technologies will provide "direct scientific evidence of the defendant's brain . . . and we need not rely on verbal reports and questions such as 'Did the defendant know right from wrong?'"[47]

The promise of prediction is seductive. In recent years, growing perceptions of risk have encouraged the development of several fields of study—technology assessment, risk analysis, social forecasting, and even "futuronics"[48]—devoted to predicting and controlling risks. Actuarial reasoning has become a guiding principle, a way to anticipate future contingencies. The popular appeal of genetics—focusing on the "oracle of DNA," the "blueprint of destiny"—lies partly in its image as a predictive science: a means to uncover predispositions.

Predisposition, however, is a malleable concept that changes when exported from clinical genetics to social policy.[49] The scientific concept of genetic predisposition assumes the existence of a biological condition signaling that an individual may suffer a future disease or behavioral aberration. But predisposition in the clinical sense is a statistical risk calculation, not a prediction. A person "predisposed" to cancer, for example, may have biological qualities that heighten the odds that he or she will develop cancer, in the same way that driving many miles each day heightens one's odds of involvement in an automobile accident. But many variables influence whether a person will actually suffer from cancer. Terms such as "predisposed" or "at risk" are understood by scientists to mean that the individual is vulnerable to a disease that may *or may not* be expressed in the future. In the quest to identify genetic predispositions, however, the statistically driven concept of correlation is often reduced to "cause." And possible future states, calculated by statistical methods, are often defined as equivalent to current status. A genetic predisposition to alcoholism, for example, becomes an "alcohol gene." And an individual "at risk" may be regarded as deserving differential treatment long before it is known whether or not the risk will materialize.

People diagnosed as predisposed to a behavior or disease may find themselves treated as if their fate were certain, even when the relationship between genetic defects and their manifestation in actual behavior or illness is conditional and poorly understood. Take, for example, the middle-aged man who in 1992 discovered that he had a genetic predisposition to a particular neuromuscular condition. He experienced no obvious symptoms and, in particular, had never had an automobile accident or traffic violation in twenty years of driving. But when his insurance company learned (through his medical records) about the predisposition, it refused to renew his automobile insurance policy.[50]

Research in molecular biology is yielding powerful new information that may reduce ambiguity in some areas and define meaningful constraints in others. Institutions are understandably attracted to the predictions promised by a genetic "map" and to the certainties implied by genetic essentialism. But predictive information that helps institutions control uncertainty and contain costs can also have devastating effects on individuals.

Genetic information can extend discrimination to new categories of persons. Those who carry the traits for certain disorders can be reconceptualized as the "predisposed," as "persons at risk" whose potential condition differentiates them from the "normal" and labels them unsuited for normal opportunities.[51] If an employer, educator, or insurer can make the case that the "predicted" future status of their client matters, then discrimination—denial of opportunity for medical care, work, or education—can occur with impunity. Indeed, predictive genetic typing may create an underclass of individuals whose genes seem to have marked them for the nowhere track.

Some of the more discriminatory applications of genetic information are limited by legislation. The Americans With Disabilities Act, implemented in January 1992, limits pre-employment testing to the assessment of a person's actual ability to perform a job. The act will help to limit the abuse of tests that indicate genetic predisposition in a person with no symptoms. But the legislation does not preclude the use of "sound actuarial data" as a basis on which to limit health care benefits. The standard underwriting assumptions of the insurance industry are not affected. And while laws may curb specific institutional abuses, attitudes that support informal discrimination are harder to control through regulatory schemes.

The social value placed on privacy could also help to limit institutional abuses of genetic information. But a recent public opinion poll suggested that, to many Americans, genetic information does not appear to be "private." A 1992 survey by the March of Dimes Birth Defects Foundation found that most Americans believe genetic information is public property and that those with a right to information about a person's genetic characteristics include not only those family members who could be immediately affected, but insurers and employers as well.[52] The survey also found that 43 percent of Americans approved of using gene therapy to enhance the physical and behavioral traits of their children as well as for treatment of disease. The survey respondents clearly understood little about the details of genetics and the potential for harm.

In this context of public naïveté, popular assumptions about the powers of the gene make it more difficult to control institutional abuses of genetic information. Laws prohibiting discrimination may, in practice, prove less important than public acceptance, fed by ubiquitous images and appealing stories, of the essentialist premises underlying institutional decisions. So long as persons continue to be conceptualized as aggregates of physical attributes and as gene-transmitting agents, biology can be used as both a standard for opportunity and a justification for discrimination.

In the rush to apply the latest research, institutions may oversimplify the complex and poorly understood relationship between genetics and environment. And in the urgency to find solutions to social problems, they may compromise or obscure important values of equality, justice, and privacy. Genetic screening intended to assess intelligence, criminality, or predisposition to learning or behavioral problems can affect the quality of education, the functioning of the legal system, and the fairness of the work environment. Placing responsibility for social problems on the traits or predispositions of certain individuals can justify policies of discrimination or exclusion in the interest of enhancing efficiency or maintaining social control. Ultimately, the world view of genetic essentialism leads to policies that restrict the reproductive rights of individuals, for it suggests that order in a society depends on the genetic qualities of its population.

Notes

[1] Advertisement, BMW of North America Inc., 1983.

[2] John S. Long, "How Genes Shape Personality," *U.S. News and World Report*, 13 April 1987, 60–66.

[3] Cartoon by R. Chast, *Health*, July/August 1991, 29.

[4] Mervyn Rothstein, "From Cartoons to a Play about Racists in the 60s," *New York Times*, 14 August 1991.

[5] Henry Howe and John Lynn, "Gene talk in sociobiology," in Stephen Fuller and James Collier, eds., *Social Epistemology* 6:2 (April-June 1992), 109–164.

[6] "The Secret of Life" is the name of an eight-hour "NOVA" series, directed by Graham Chedd and aired on public television on 26–30 September 1993. The phrase is widely used in descriptions of DNA.

[7] The gene is the fundamental unit of heredity. Each gene is arranged in tandem along a particular chromosome. A chromosome, the microscopic nuclear structure that contains the linear array of genes, is composed of proteins and deoxyribonucleic acid (DNA), the "double helix" molecule that encodes genetic information. Each gene generates, as the "readout" of its specific DNA sequence, a particular protein—its functional product in building the cell or organism. The 24 chromosomes in the human genome contain about 100,000 genes.

[8] This term is used by Sarah Franklin in "Essentialism, Which Essentialism? Some Implications of Reproductive and Genetic Technoscience," in John Dececco and John Elia, eds., *Issues in Biological Essentialism versus Social Construction in Gay and Lesbian Identities* (London: Harrington Park Press, 1993), 27–39. She defines genetic essentialism as "a scientific discourse . . . with the potential to establish social categories based on an essential truth about the body" (34).

[9] Joanne Finkelstein, *The Fashioned Self* (Philadelphia: Temple University Press, 1991). See particularly 177–193.

[10] Anthropologists describe cultural differences in bodily skills that have far less to do with inherent biological limits than with social expectations. They find that bodily

and mental capacities are shaped by social organization. They depend in great measure on and vary with social beliefs, practices, and techniques. Paul Hirst and Penny Woolley, *Social Relations and Human Attributes* (London: Tavistock, 1982), Chapter 2.

[11] On the gene and its changing meaning, see Elof Axel Carlson, *The Gene: A Critical History* (Ames: Iowa State University Press, 1989), 23–38, 124–130, 166–173, and 259–271. To quote Carlson, "The gene has been considered to be an undefined unit, a unit-character, a unit factor, a factor, an abstract point on a recombination map, a three-dimensional segment of an anaphase chromosome, a linear segment of an interphase chromosome, a sac of genomeres, a series of linear subgenes, a spherical unit defined by a target theory, a dynamic functional quantity of one specific unit, a pseudoallele, a specific chromosome segment subject to position effect, a rearrangement within a continuous chromosome molecule, a cistron within which fine structure can be demonstrated, and a linear segment of nucleic acid specifying a structural or regulatory product. Are these concepts identical? . . . For some of these problems, the findings from different organisms are contradictory; for others, the agreements [between organisms] may be analogous rather than a reflection of identical genetic organization" (259). See also L. C. Dunn, *A Short History of Genetics: The Development of Some Main Lines of Thought 1864–1939* (1965; reprint, Ames: Iowa State University Press, 1991), 33–49 and 175–191; also, James D. Watson's treatment of the complexities surrounding the concept of the gene in his *Molecular Biology of the Gene*, 2nd ed. (Menlo Park, CA: W. A. Benjamin, Inc., 1970), 230–254 and 435–466. Watson notes that "even now it is often hard to identify the protein product of a given gene" (240) and "now . . . we realize that the rate of synthesis of a protein is itself partially under internal genetic control and partially determined by the external chemical environment" (435). Our point is that this is a complicated concept with a long, contentious history.

[12] The corn geneticist and Nobelist Barbara McClintock once began a presentation at Cold Spring Harbor that captured the complexities of the gene in the molecular age. She proclaimed that "with the tools and knowledge, I could turn a developing snail's egg into an elephant. It is not so much a matter of chemicals, because snails and elephants do not differ that much; it is matter of timing the action of genes." Cited in Bruce Wallace's colorful reconstruction of the history of the gene, *The Search for the Gene* (Ithaca and London: Cornell University Press, 1992), 176.

[13] The status of genetic disease and genetic therapy is reviewed in *Science*, 8 May 1992. In that issue, see Daniel E. Koshland, "Molecular Advances in Disease," 717; F. S. Collins, "Cystic Fibrosis: Molecular Biology and Therapeutic Implications," 774–779; K. S. Kosik, "Alzheimer's Disease: A Cell Biological Perspective," 780–783; C. T. Caskey et al., "Triplet Repeat Mutations in Human Disease," 784–788; D. H. MacLennan and M. S. Phillips, "Malignant Hyperthermia," 789–793; E. Beutler, "Gaucher Disease: New Molecular Approaches to Diagnosis and Treatment," 794–798; E. H. Epstein, Jr., "Molecular Genetics of Epidermolysis Bullosa," 799–803; P. Humphries et al., "On the Molecular Genetics of Retinitis Pigmentosa," 804–807; and W. F. Anderson, "Human Gene Therapy," 808–813.

[14] Neil Holtzman, *Proceed with Caution* (Baltimore: Johns Hopkins University Press, 1989), 88–105.

15 See the discussion of rhetorical strategies by Jeremy Green, "Media Sensationalism and Science: The Case of the Criminal Chromosome," in Terry Shinn and Richard Whitley, eds., *Expository Science*, Sociology of the Sciences Yearbook 9(1985), 139–161.

[16] See e.g. Walter Gilbert, "Current State of the H.G.I.," Harvard University Dibner Center Lecture, 15 June 1990.

[17] Leon Jaroff, "The Gene Hunt," *Time*, 20 March 1989, 62–67.

[18] Lois Wingerson, "Searching for Depression Genes," *Discover*, February 1982, 60–64.

19 Fergus M. Clydesdale, "Present and Future of Food Science and Technology in Industrialized Countries," *Food Technology*, September 1989, 134–146.

20 Daniel Koshland, "Elephants, Monstrosities and the Law," *Science* 255(4 February 1992), 777.

21 Bruce Wallace, *The Search for the Gene* (Ithaca: Cornell University Press, 1992), 199.

22 Lucy Fellows, cited in John Noble Wilford, "Discovering the Old World of Maps," *New York Times*, 9 October 1992. See also Dennis Wood, *The Power of Maps* (New York: Guilford Press, 1992). The geographer Mark Monmonier has observed that "a good map tells a multitude of little white lies. It suppresses truth to help the user see what needs to be seen": *How to Lie with Maps* (Chicago: University of Chicago Press, 1991), 199.

23 Christopher Wills, *Exons, Introns and Talking Genes: The Science Behind the Human Genome Project* (New York: Basic Books, 1991), 10.

24 See discussion in Marga Vicedo, "The Human Genome Project," *Biology and Philosophy* 7(1992), 255–278.

[25] See Thomas J. Bouchard, Jr., David T. Lykken, Matthew McGue, Nancy Segal, and Auke Tellegen, "Sources of Human Psychological Differences: The Minnesota Study of Twins Reared Apart," *Science* 250 (12 October 1990), 223. Also Val Dusek, "Bewitching Science," *Science for the People*, November/December 1987, 19.

[26] "Mapping the Genome: The Vision, the Science, the Implementation: A Roundtable Discussion," 18 February 1992, published in *Los Alamos Science* 20(1992), 68–85.

[27] Douglas Wahlsten, "Insensitivity of the Analysis of Variance to Heredity-Environment Interaction," *Behavioral and Brain Sciences* 13(1990), 109–161.

[28] Peter McGuffin and Randy Katz, "Who Believes in Estimating Heritability as an End in Itself?" 141–142, in Douglas Wahlsten, op. cit.

[29] Stephen Jay Gould, "The Confusion Over Evolution," *New York Review of Books*, 19 November 1992, 48. See also Richard Lewontin, *Biology as Ideology* (New York: Harper, 1992) and Ruth Hubbard and Elijah Wald, *Exploding the Gene Myth* (Boston: Beacon Press, 1993).

[30] Douglas Wahlsten, op. cit.

[31] In 1992 African American groups attacked plans for a University of Maryland conference on "Genetic Factors in Crime," perceiving this as racially motivated. The controversy resulted in the withdrawal of NIH funds. See David Wheeler, "University of Maryland Conference That Critics Charge Might Foster Racism Loses NIH Support," *Chronicle of Higher Education*, 2 September 1992, A6–A8.

[32] Robert Young, "Evolutionary Biology and Ideology," *Science Studies*, 1 (1971), 177–206.

[33] Mary Douglas, *How Institutions Think* (Syracuse, NY: Syracuse University Press, 1986), 63, 92.

[34] Yaron Ezrahi, *The Descent of Icarus: Science and the Transformation of Contemporary Democracy* (Cambridge: Harvard University Press, 1990). For cases that illustrate this pattern, see Dorothy Nelkin, ed., *Controversy: The Politics of Technical Decisions* (Newbury Park, CA: Sage Publications, 1992).

[35] The agenda-setting role of the media has been widely documented. See Gaye Tuchman, *Making News* (New York: Free Press, 1978).

36 For a fuller development of these ideas, see Dorothy Nelkin and Laurence Tancredi, *Dangerous Diagnostics: The Social Power of Biological Information* (New York: Basic Books, 1989).

[37] Dorothy Nelkin and Laurence Tancredi, *Dangerous Diagnostics*.

[38] Benjamin Schatz, "The AIDS Insurance Crisis: Underwriting or Overreaching?" *Harvard Law Review* 100 (1987), 1782; Katherine Brokaw, "Genetic Screening in the Workplace and Employers' Liability," *Columbia Journal of Law and Social Problems* 23(1990), 317, 327 cites cases in which genetic diseases have been excluded from coverage as "pre-existing conditions."

[39] Larry Thompson, "The Price of Knowledge: Genetic Tests that Predict Conditions Became a Two-Edged Sword," *Washington Post*, 10 October 1989.

[40] See U.S. Congress, Office of Technology and Assessment, Genetic Monitoring and Screening in the Workplace" (Washington, DC: USGPO, 1990), 10–12.

41 Mark A. Rothstein, "Employee Selection Based on Susceptibility to Occupational Illness," *Michigan Law Review* (1983), 1379. Also see Elaine Draper, *Risky Business* (New York: Cambridge University Press, 1991).

42 Michael W. Miller, "In Vino Veritas: Gallo Scientists Search for Genes of Alcoholism," *Wall Street Journal*, 8 June 1994.

[43] David Lauria, Mark Webb, Pamela McKenzie, M.D., and Randi Hagerman, M.D., "The Economic Impact of Fragile-X Syndrome on the State of Colorado," *Proceedings of the International Fragile-X Conference*, 1992, 393–405.

[44] Laura Lesch, personal communication to authors, June 1994.

[45] Robert Proctor, *Value-Free Science* (Cambridge: Harvard University Press, 1991), 5.

[46] Nikolas Rose, *The Psychological Complex* (London: Routledge and Kegan Paul, 1985), 5.

[47] C. R. Jeffery, *Attacks on the Insanity Defense: Biological Psychiatry and New Perspectives on Criminal Behavior* (Springfield, IL: Charles C Thomas, 1985), 82.

[48] Theodore Modis, *Predictions: Society's Telltale Signature Reveals the Past and Forecasts the Future* (New York: Simon and Schuster, 1992).

49 Laurence Tribe, "Trial by Mathematics: Precision and Ritual in the Legal Process," *Harvard Law Review* 84(1971), 1329.

50 Paul R. Billings et al., "Discrimination as a Consequence of Genetic Testing," *American Journal of Human Genetics* 50 (1992), 476–482.

[51] Abby Lippman argues that "[d]isorders and disabilities are not merely physiological or physical conditions with fixed contours. Rather, they are social products

with variable shapes and distributions." "Prenatal Genetic Testing and Screening: Constructing Needs and Reinforcing Inequities," *American Journal of Law & Medicine* 17(1991), 15, 17.

[52] Louis Harris and Associates, "Genetic Testing and Gene Therapy: National Survey Findings," March of Dimes Birth Defects Foundation, September 1992.

22
Prenatal Diagnosis in Context

Barbara Katz Rothman

There are many different histories one can write for the new reproductive technology, and specifically for prenatal diagnosis. As I pick and choose my way back, following different strands of the story, I realize that each history casts its own light on the present. Whichever history I present here will provide a context for understanding prenatal diagnosis—and different histories give very different contexts. These histories are not only different; at times they are quite contradictory. Prenatal diagnosis is part of the history of the loss of medical mystique and control, as physicians lost the exclusive power over the abortion decision. But prenatal diagnosis is also part of the history of medicalization, as physicians sought to gain control over pregnancy and the fetus. This is not simply a shifting of ground, but, as I will show, the outcome of two very separate movements. There is another, more fundamental contradiction. Prenatal diagnosis is part of feminist history, woman's increasing right to control her own reproductive capacity. But prenatal diagnosis is also very much part of the history of patriarchy, men's struggle to gain control over their "seed," and thus men's control over women's reproductive capacities. So I will not, cannot, present *the* history of prenatal diagnosis—I will present some of the many histories.

The History of Abortion

Legalized abortion is a necessary part of prenatal diagnosis as we now know it. For the overwhelming majority of conditions that are prenatally diagnosable, there are no prenatal treatments. While an individual woman might consider prenatal diagnosis worthwhile just for the benefit of preparation, the social support, including the funding of programs, has come for prenatal diagnosis as a preventive measure. Since the prevention can occur only after conception, and most of the conditions themselves can be neither treated nor modified in pregnancy, abortion is the preventive measure taken. In the unlikely event that abortion were to become illegal, it is hard to envision the continued existence of legal prenatal diagnosis programs. It is possible, maybe even likely, that these services, like abortion itself, would continue to be available outside of the law.

Because of their dependence on legalized abortion, and because of the strong links between legalized abortion and the contemporary women's movement, those engaged in prenatal diagnosis can and often do lay claim to a feminist basis for their services. Using these services, in turn, is sometimes seen as a "feminist" or "liberated" thing to do. But as I found when I spoke to women using prenatal diagnosis, nothing is all that simple. But because the connections are drawn, and because the dependency on legalized abortion certainly does exist, it is important to look at the history of abortion for the light it casts on prenatal diagnosis. Much of the discussion that follows draws upon Kristen Luker's fine book, *Abortion and the Politics of Motherhood.*[1]

Physicians in the nineteenth century used abortion as a wedge toward gaining their own professional status. Abortions were apparently widely available in America at that time, advertised in newspapers, and performed by people with a variety of backgrounds. In driving out the "quacks," physicians were in one sense doing what they were doing in other areas of practice. They replaced midwives at childbirth and a host of other practitioners who were supplying services that only later became defined as "medical" in nature. But with abortion, another dimension was added. Physicians argued that their knowledge of embryonic and fetal development (really quite minimal at that time) enabled them to know what the women having abortions presumably did not know: that the embryo was a baby. Having made this claim, doctors were able to say that the abortionists were not only incompetent, dirty, backward—all the charges they leveled at midwives and other competitors—but also that what they were doing was fundamentally wrong, immoral.

The physicians, however, did not want an absolute ban on abortion. What the doctors claimed, a contradiction highlighted by Luker, was that abortion was wrong, but physicians, and only physicians, could determine when it was *necessary*. Abortion was *necessary* when pregnancy threatened the life of the mother—a determination over which the physicians claimed technical expertise. Thus there were two kinds of abortions: the ones the doctors did not do, which were "immoral" and "criminal," and the ones that the doctors did do, which were both moral and, almost by definition, "therapeutic."

As the overall health of the population improved, and as medical technology improved, abortions literally to save the life of the mother became increasingly rare—but abortion itself did not become correspondingly rare. Rather, it seems, the categories of therapeutic abortion broadened to take into consideration the woman's general health: physical and, eventually, emotional health. While some physicians and hospitals were doing abortions only to preserve the life of the mother in the strictest interpretation of that phrase, others did them based on broader definitions of life and health. A gap opened between what Luker calls the "strict constructionists" and the "broad constructionists," in the way they defined the preservation of the mother's life. In one of life's stranger ironies, it was these "broad constructionist" physicians who opened the can of worms that abortion reform meant, which eventually lost the medical profession its control over abortion. They did so by seeking legislation to legitimize their broad interpretation of the law. They did so, Luker argues, without realizing that their view of abortion was not universally held, without even realizing that strict constructionists still existed, let alone existed as a potentially powerful political force.

It is not all that uncommon for a reform to open the door to an out-and-out rebellion, and that is what seems to have happened with abortion. Once a "broad" interpretation, or "liberal" abortion law was allowed, the inherent and often arbitrary power of physicians to do the interpreting was laid bare. And thus what Luker claims to be a new force entered the abortion discussion: women, as women; claiming abortion as a *right*, not dependent upon the approval of their physicians, but as a basic human right to control their own bodies.

The rest, as they say, is history.

Part of the legacy of the history of abortion is the rather strange language with which we are left. Abortions that are most clearly "medical"—that is, abortions based on medical considerations of *any* sort—are called "therapeutic." Still. That includes those abortions that are based not at all on the condition of the woman's health, but on the health of the fetus. This language itself makes abortion following prenatal diagnosis an easy target for attack by those opposed to abortions: it is hard to claim that abortion for genetic defect is "therapeutic" for the fetus aborted, and the mother is not sick. The more the "right-to-life" movement attacks abortions for fetal indication, the more the "pro-choice" movement feels called upon to defend such abortions.

For those who are neither in the right-to-life movement, nor particularly concerned with abortion as a specifically *feminist* concern, other considerations come into play. Fears of disability, extreme repugnance toward the mentally retarded, and deeply embedded cultural ideas about health combine to make abortions when the fetus would be "defective" among the most acceptable of abortions to most Americans.

Politics, as they say, does make strange bedfellows. Those in the disability rights movement are courted by those in the right-to-life movement. The feminist movement, loudly proclaiming that biology need not be destiny, calls upon notions of biology as destiny, disability as doom, to support the continued availability of abortions. It is perfectly understandable that people would call upon "worst-case" scenarios to defend abortion, the "what if your 14-year-old daughter was raped and got pregnant" variety of argument. Given social attitudes toward disability, the temptation to call upon abortions following prenatal diagnosis as support for all abortions is also clear: what if you or your wife were pregnant and going to have a "cripple," a "retard," a "defective" child? What if she had taken thalidomide, a "teratogenic" drug? Teratogenic means "causing fetal abnormality," but it comes from the root meaning "monster." Very deep feelings are being called upon.

The Fetus as Patient

The early part of the history of abortion which I just presented, abortion in the 1800s, is part of the history of the *medicalization* of reproduction. In spite of having lost its control over abortion, the power of medicine as a profession is still considerable. In her book on the new reproductive technology, *The Mother Machine*, Gena Corea writes of the "pharmocrats," the physicians and biotechnicians who control reproductive technologies.[2] Just as "theocracy" refers to political rule by a priesthood, "pharmocracy" refers to political rule by medicine. As more and more aspects of our lives have come under medical supervision—i.e., are "medicalized"—medicine has become even more clearly an institution of social control.[3] Reproduction has come under medical control, as first abortion was seen as a medical decision and childbirth as a surgical event, and then pregnancy as a disease, and now the fetus has attained the status of patient.

Control over reproduction is not quite like other forms of medicalization. Compare the medicalization of pregnancy with the medicalization of alcoholism. Declaring that people who drink too much alcohol are ill and therefore "patients" has not the same far-reaching effects as declaring fetuses to be patients. One can negotiate the "alcoholic" label, argue about who is and who is not "really" an alcoholic. But declaring fetuses to be patients, as medicine now does, is the most inclusive categorization possible: we have all been fetuses, and there is no other entry into life but passage through the status of fetus; in the beginning, we are all fetuses. As medicine gains control over fetalhood, it controls the gates of life; in the beginning, we are all patients.

How has this view of the fetus as a patient come about, and what does it mean for women—women as the people in whom fetuses grow?

Perhaps it really began in earnest with the by-now familiar techniques for fetal monitoring in labor. Not all that long ago, just back in the 1970s, the way that medicine "monitored" or to put it simply, *watched* a labor, was to watch the laboring woman. Her heart rate, blood pressure, the frequency and intensity of her contractions, and the rate at which her cervix, the neck of the uterus, was opening up, provided the information on how the labor was going. In addition, there was one other measure that was taken, one that was more directly a measure of the fetus: by putting a stethoscope to the mother's abdomen, one could hear the heartbeat of the fetus.

Electronic fetal monitoring was introduced for use with "high-risk" pregnancies, but as is so often the case, it rapidly came into widespread use. Electronic monitoring was used to provide more direct information about the status of the fetus in three ways: (1) externally, by ultrasound monitoring of the fetal heart rate and uterine contractions; (2) internally, by fetal electrocardiogram obtained with electrodes attached to the fetal head and uterine monitoring by means of a catheter passed into the uterus through the cervix; and (3) by direct sampling of fetal scalp blood, obtained from an electrode screwed into the fetal head.[4] As it turns out, electronic fetal monitoring may not really provide all that much more information on the condition of the fetus than does good nursing care. It certainly does look like more information, though, with endless strips of printout for the duration of the labor.

But I think more important than the sheer quantity of the data, impressive though that was, was that the information came in a new context. Instead of having to approach the woman, to rest your head near her belly, to smell her skin, to feel her breathing, you could now read the information on the fetus from across the room, from down the hall. While there was still one being on the bed, medical personnel came to see the woman and the fetus as separate, as two different patients. The continued development of a technology that renders the fetus visible, that gives obstetricians more and more direct access to the fetus itself—the fetal tissue, blood, and the direct observation of the fetal movements that sonography allows—exacerbated the problem. More and more doctors developed a relationship with the fetus, the separate patient within.

This technology came at just that point that women were rejecting the patient role for themselves in pregnancy, often to the irritation and even distress of their doctors. As pregnant women increasingly declared themselves healthy and rejected the label of pregnancy as an illness, the doctors were looking more and more closely at the fetus within, the tiny, helpless, dependent fetus.

In part as a response to this new technology that enables the obstetrician to see, and perhaps diagnose, and perhaps even treat the fetus; and in part as a response to the changes in the status of women as patients; and in part as a continued growth of men's domination of reproduction—because of all of these, pregnancy is increasingly becoming seen, as Ruth Hubbard has pointed out, as a conflict of rights between a woman and her fetus. With the fetus seen as a separate patient, the obstetrician has come to see the mother as a potential adversary, a potential barrier to the optimum medical care of the fetus. The special irony introduced in the case of prenatal diagnosis, as it is used in early to mid-pregnancy, is that there is as yet no medical care available for the fetus. Still physicians may claim the right of the fetus to diagnosis, or conversely, may feel their right as physicians to diagnose their patient, the fetus. Some physicians see the development of diagnostic techniques as just the first step toward ultimately developing treatment techniques. What happens when treatments are developed that are experimental, that may be harmful to the woman?

The potential conflict in this situation has recently been dramatized in court-ordered caesarean sections. When women in labor or late pregnancy have disagreed with their physicians (or who they thought were *their* physicians) over how to manage labor, the physicians have turned to the court.[5] In several bedside juvenile court hearings, with a lawyer appointed to represent the unborn fetus, another representing the pregnant woman, and yet others representing the hospital, women have been ordered to submit to caesarean sections, the fetus within them claimed by the state as a "dependent and neglected child."[6] In

1981, *Obstetrics and Gynecology*,[7] writing to an audience of obstetricians, carried an article reporting one such case in which the woman, although found to be psychiatrically competent, was forced to undergo a caesarean section very much against her will. The article quoted the current edition of one of the classic obstetrics textbooks, *Williams*, which states that the fetus has "rightfully achieved the status of the second patient, a patient who usually faces much greater risk of serious morbidity and mortality than does the mother."

Caesarean section is one of the most common operations done on women. Caesareans are very, very occasionally done to save the life or the health of the woman herself. Much more commonly, caesareans are done in response to fetal indications, because obstetricians, rightly or wrongly, believe that the laboring uterus is potentially quite dangerous to the fetus. Major abdominal surgery is conducted on the body of the woman to help her fetus. In the crisislike situation of a labor going poorly, or which doctors believe is going poorly, the conflict of rights and interests between the mother and fetus may well be blurred.

The situation becomes more dramatically fraught with possibilities when surgery is suggested on the fetus itself, with the mother opened up only to gain access to the fetus. Several procedures of this sort have been done, including placing a shunt in a hydrocephalic fetus to prevent fluid from building up in the brain of the fetus. The procedures are experimental and have had little real success. Doctors, lawyers, and philosophers have somehow anticipated women's possible objections to such procedures, and begun to talk about "fetal advocates," people who can make decisions on behalf of the fetus, represent the fetus's interests, presumably particularly in those cases where the mothers resist experimental surgery.

But is that the way it really works? I was amused—no, I laughed out loud—at a presentation by a noted ethicist at a meeting of the Society of Law and Medicine.[8] The topic was experimental fetal surgery, and the ethicist was holding forth on the intense feelings of all those involved in such procedures: the prayerful, beseeching mothers, trying to save the babies dying within them; the pioneering, new-frontier excitement of the doctors repairing a fetus and replacing it in the womb. Someone asked the ethicist: but what about those fetal advocates you have called for in the past? Ah, he said, there seemed no need. The doctors and ethicists were surprised to see that the mothers were acting as advocates for the fetus. The mothers themselves were pleading for the surgery—the ethicists found themselves, he said, reminding the mothers of how dangerous the surgery was for them, for the mothers, trying to prevent mothers from risking their lives and health without good cause.

He discovered motherhood! Mothers are fetal advocates! Mothers will risk sacrificing themselves for their babies! Whatever will science discover next?

To be surprised by the willingness of mothers to risk themselves for their children—this takes a special kind of training. It takes the kind of context that medicine has been developing, a context in which mothers and their fetuses are separate patients, with separate needs and separate rights.

While the most recent roots of this perspective may lie in the development of a new technology that enables, and indeed encourages, us to see the fetus and the mother as two separate patients, the roots truly go much deeper. The roots go to the very history of patriarchy. In an earlier work[9] I discussed the way that patriarchal ideology has influenced the provision of modern maternity care. But it is not only in our management of pregnancy as a "stress" or "risk" condition, in our management of childbirth as a surgical event, that the influence of patriarchal ideology can be seen. That perspective or ideology, which takes men as the dominant group, and men's views as the dominant view of the world, influences all of our reproductive technology, and all of our ideas about reproduction.

Patriarchy

Someone recently said to me, as if it were a generally recognized principle, that abortion was "inherently" feminist. So closely have these two movements been linked that she could only see abortion—the actual procedure itself—in the context of a woman's right to control her own body.

But what have been the conditions under which women have had abortions? It has certainly not been, invariably, out of their own needs and wishes. At the extreme, we have the situation of women forced to abort female fetuses because their husbands want sons. While rare among Western populations, with the introduction of amniocentesis Eastern women do face just this situation.[10] *No* technology can be "inherently" feminist; all technologies exist in a social context. In our own society, one of the most widely recognized reasons for abortion, a reason we see as basis for abortion "on demand," or the more "liberated" woman's abortion, is pregnancy in an unmarried woman. A woman without a man *needs* an abortion. Abortion prevents "illegitimate" births. This, like abortions of unwanted females, is hardly an inherently feminist justification for abortion, even if it does indeed meet the needs of women in the system.

Obviously, reproduction can be controlled not only to meet the needs of women but also to meet the needs of men, both men as individuals and men as a class. Thus prenatal diagnosis and the new reproductive technology can also be seen in the light of the history of patriarchy. Patriarchy has meant many things, but at its core is the recognition of paternity, the concept that children grow out of men's seeds. Recognition of paternity changes the way men and women see themselves and see each other, changes the way we see the world. Without paternity, the distinction between seed and soil hardly matters: plants spring forth from the earth, children from the mother. With paternity, with the primitive "seed" concept of paternity, seed and soil separate: the farmer sows the field; Daddy plants a seed in Mommy. The seed is the source of life, and the soil, now "dirt," is only the receptacle; the woman, the vessel for men's seed.

Patriarchy begins with paternity, but it moves beyond, to an encompassing world view. With recognition of the seed, people are seen as *on* but not *of* the earth. The seed penetrates the soil, breaks into the crust of the earth, but is not drawn from the earth. With patriarchy, man rules over the earth. Unlike the earth goddesses, the God of patriarchy is the God of all the world, the one God, above whom there is none other, and below whom lies the earth and all its inhabitants. The God of patriarchy gives hierarchical order to the world. That which was interconnected and interdependent becomes hierarchical and ranked.

From a cycle of being comes a great chain of being, a line of domination and hierarchy—from God to man, from King to subject, from Man to beast. The cycle of the world straightens out into a line, and time itself, no longer cyclical, straightens up and marches on. Tomorrow is not yesterday again, the earth continually reborn, but each day a step forward, a progression.

In such an ordered world, different ways of thinking develop. Erich Fromm, in his analysis of myths and fairy tales, contrasts the matriarchal with the patriarchal principles:

> The matriarchal principle is that of blood relationship as the
> fundamental and indestructible tie, of the equality of all men [*sic*],
> of the respect for human life and of love. The patriarchal principle
> is that the ties between man and wife, between ruler and ruled,

take precedence over ties of blood. It is the principle of order and authority, of obedience and hierarchy.[11]

It is this principle that determined that to be worthy of God, Abraham had to be willing to sacrifice his son Isaac, to place obedience before blood. Abraham may have experienced anguish, but he was willing to do it, willing to sacrifice Isaac, and patriarchal religion praises him for that willingness and obedience. Echoes of Abraham's dilemma can be heard in the voices of the women in this book [*The Tentative Pregnancy,* from which this article is reprinted].

The History of Eugenics

What is a seed? A seed is potential, pure potential. Given the right environment, the seed can *become*: the acorn, the oak tree; the bulb, the tulip; and the sperm, the man. One of the earliest uses of the microscope was to look at sperm, to see the little "homunculus," the tiny little man the scientists believed they saw curled up inside each sperm. Spilled on inhospitable ground, the seed becomes nothing. Planted in a welcoming, nurturing soil, the seed can become all it was meant to be.

The more we focus on genetics, on the seedlike qualities, the more we think of potential: what the person can become. One effect of the focus on potential has been to see the mother not as a source of nourishment, a source of energy and strength, a protector, but the mother as a barrier to full potential. The seed has in it all it can become—but the very idea of a seed as potential tells us that it cannot become more, only less than its full potential. Is the infant less than its seed might have been? Then how has the mother harmed it, how has she failed it?

But there is another thing that happens when we focus on the seed: we think of different seeds as having different potentials. The history of prenatal diagnosis has roots in the eugenics movement, in various attempts to "improve the race." It is certainly one of the less flattering lights in which to view prenatal diagnosis, but part of its history has been an attempt to control the gates of life: to decide who is, and who is not, fit to make a contribution to the "gene pool," whose seed is worth passing on. Thus began eugenics.

The study of eugenics in the United States attracted a large number of prominent scientists and physicians, including Alexander Graham Bell, and crystallized in the activities of a eugenics movement, whose headquarters was The Eugenics Records Office at Cold Spring Harbor,

Long Island, established in 1904 by Charles B. Davenport. From this early eugenics movement came the impetus and the scientific rationale for legislation permitting forced sterilization of certain kinds of "undesirables" and, later, limiting immigration. Indiana passed the first state sterilization laws in 1907, requiring compulsory sterilization of inmates of state institutions who were insane, idiotic, imbecilic, or feeble-minded, or were convicted criminals, upon recommendation of a board of experts. By 1931 thirty states had similar legislation, to include such "hereditary defectives" as sexual perverts, drug fiends, drunkards, diseased, and degenerate persons.[12] Harry Laughlin, Davenport's assistant, was the most active eugenicist in the sterilization campaign.

The Immigration Restriction Act of 1924 extended the eugenics concept to racial differences. The act contained a eugenics provision, again argued for by Laughlin, the appointed "expert eugenics agent" of the House Committee on Immigration and Naturalization. This provision for selective restriction dramatically limited the entry of individuals from Southern and Eastern Europe, the "biologically inferior," in favor of the "Nordics." And in Germany in 1933 Hitler decreed the Hereditary Health Law, or Eugenic Sterilization Law.

One of the people influenced by the eugenics movement was a physician, Charles F. Dight, who in a 1927 will left his estate to the University of Minnesota, "To Promote Biological Race Betterment—Betterment in Human Brain Structure and Mental Endowment and therefore in Behavior." The university was to "maintain a place for consultation and advice on heredity and eugenics for the rating of people, first, as to the efficiency of their bodily structure; second as to their mentality; third, as to their fitness to marry and reproduce."[13]

The Dight Institute for Human Genetics began to function in 1941, with family consultations used more as the basis for future studies than as a eugenics program. In 1947 a man named Sheldon Reed began working at Dight, and genetic counseling was born. Reed rejected the older names for his work, such as "genetic hygiene," and substituted *genetic counseling* "as an appropriate description of the process which I thought of as a kind of genetic social work without eugenic connotations."[14]

Reed's claim was that he could divorce genetic counseling from eugenics, and could put the clients' needs at the center:

> Genetic counseling, in my conception at least, is a type of social work contributing to the benefit of the whole family without direct concern for its effect upon the state or politics.

By 1951 there were ten genetic counseling centers in the United States. Through the 1950s genetic counseling developed as a form of preventive medicine. As such it moved from the academic centers to the major medical centers. Genetic counseling became medicalized, and physicians began claiming turf. The bulletins of the Dight Institute shifted title from "Counseling in Human Genetics" to "Counseling in Medical Genetics."

Genetic Counseling: The Contemporary Context

All of these historical strands come together in modern genetic counseling: the medicalization of reproduction and reproductive decision-making, the availability of abortion, the world view of patriarchy, and perhaps, some fear, the remnants of eugenic thinking.

Genetic counseling and genetic testing are rapidly becoming a routine part of prenatal care. It began with women who were at high genetic risk, including women over 40. The age has moved down to 35, and is now inching its way down to the early thirties. I think genetic counseling of some sort will ultimately reach everyone who seeks prenatal care.

As genetic counseling has become more widespread, more routine, physicians are beginning to turn the work over to lower-status, and very much lower paid, workers. As genetic counseling becomes a more standard part of prenatal care, these counselors take over more and more of the counseling from physicians, "freeing" the physicians for other work. Counseling is not high-status, technical work: it is "just talking." We now consider what it is that is discussed, and how counselors talk to clients.

The Genetic Counseling Session

Genetic counseling sessions are most often initiated by the obstetrical services. The private obstetrician or the clinic refers the woman, uniformly called "the patient," for genetic counseling based on information gathered in the obstetrical history. Most commonly the only indication is "advanced maternal age," standardly taken to mean 35 years or older at "e.d.c.," estimated date of confinement. Occasionally someone is referred because of a history of birth defects in previous pregnancies or because of some specific familial indication, but far and away the most common referral nowadays is for advanced maternal age.

Genetic counselors are one of those specialty service providers that most people see only once, and so no ongoing relationship is established. But because the topic under consideration has the potential for becoming intensely personal and emotional, it is important to establish some rapport right away. Like people in any other occupation that has to "meet the public," counselors develop their own style for breaking the ice. Some begin with chit-chat about the weather, the location of the office (usually in some hard-to-find place, it seems), or some other neutral topic. Others plunge right in with a question like "Do you know why you have been sent here?" That question is mostly reserved for clinic patients, who might very well *not* know why they are there, having gotten used to going where they are sent in the hospital system. While some counselors prefer to counsel a couple together, the fact is that more often than not the woman is there alone, or accompanied by her children. In more than one session where I came to observe, I found myself babysitting for a preschooler, so the mother could devote her attention to the counselor. Non-English-speaking patients have to bring their own interpreter in many medical settings. That can get awkward, particularly when the interpreter is a near-adolescent child, as I observed on occasion. Once everybody has been settled in, with appropriate introductions and translations arranged as needed, the session begins.

There are three basic parts to a genetic counseling session for advanced maternal age: genetic/medical history; information about the test; and making the decision whether or not to have prenatal diagnosis. Some counselors begin with the first, some with the second, but each session ultimately has to cover all three parts.

The paperwork involved—particularly the medical history forms and the informed consent forms—in some ways structures the interaction, becoming as one observer of medical record-keeping has called it, "a third participant in the interaction."[15] Sometimes the forms do seem intrusive. One group of counselors, for example, was working with a family history form which had them asking, "How many children do your brothers have?" and "How many children do your sisters have?" because it listed these separately. That required people to sort out their nieces and nephews in an unfamiliar way. ("Let's see, my older brother has two and my younger brother has three and my baby brother has none. That's five. Now my sisters . . .") Some counselors stick more closely to the forms, trying to get things filled in "right," and others deviate and skip over things that do not seem pertinent.

The "information giving" part of the session, as opposed to the history, or "information taking," has the most room for variation between counselors and between patients with the same counselor. When I asked counselors what they typically covered, some specifically said that they had "short versions" and "long versions" of explanations for things like "what sonograms are," and then, depending on the patient and the amount of time available, they presented one or another version. Language barriers naturally tend to shorten explanations. The essential information to be conveyed was summed up by one counselor as:

> What the amnio can tell you. The risks of the procedure. The fact that we can come up with an ambiguous result—we may not be able to tell them in black and white. For me, these are the high points.

Most counselors would probably agree with her first sentence, but most do not seem to want to raise the issue of ambiguous results. Most do not want to raise *any* ambiguous issues. When I asked counselors what they covered in a typical pre-amnio session, asking specifically about the major topics, almost all agreed that they described what the amnio feels like (not painful); what Downs Syndrome is (sometimes with pictures of people with Downs Syndrome if the client seems unsure); what neural tube defects are (with frequent reference to the March of Dimes poster children or occasional pictures again if it seems necessary); what the test can and cannot tell; what the miscarriage rate or complication rate is after amnio (some give the figure of 3 in 1,000 additional miscarriages due to the amnio; others give the "less than one-half of one percent complications" rate); and what chromosomes are, also sometimes with pictures. Almost always the risk rate for Downs Syndrome, as it increases with age, is presented.

Of equal or greater significance are the issues that are not or may not be raised. Some counselors say they "always these days" discuss what sex chromosome abnormalities are, including XXX, XXY, XYY, and XO. Most said they "rarely," "never," or "maybe never" raise these, or raise them "only if asked." One said, "Never—it scares people."

I asked if they discussed "what the choices are if Downs is found." Some always raise that, saying things like:

> They can continue the pregnancy knowing it has Downs or they can terminate, but there's nothing we can do to change the status of the fetus.

That it cannot be cured. That the parents have the choice to decide if they want to keep the pregnancy and raise a Downs child or terminate, and either way the staff will support their decision.

I also asked "Do you raise the issue of termination or do you wait for them to?" Some do:

Always—it comes at the end of the session, with reference to when the results are ready. I ask if they've discussed what they would do if the results were abnormal.

I do, at the beginning, because I want it clear to them that we cannot cure these diseases.

And some don't:

Sometimes it's assumed, and I don't push it.
I initiate it enough so they would ask.
I just say that if we find anything that needs explanation they will see a medical geneticist.

While observing sessions, a number of times I got the distinct impression that the client had no idea what this was about. This was particularly a problem when there was a language barrier, but not limited to that. For example, right near the end of a session with a middle-class, intelligent, competent-looking couple, the father finally asked, "So, tell me, what if you do find something? What can you do about it?" And another woman, there by herself, also quite bright and articulate with no language barrier, asked toward the end of a session, "I'm just so curious—if something is wrong, what could I do at this point?" In both cases the counselors (two different counselors, with quite different styles) gave the answer that the choices were between continuing or terminating the pregnancy. But the information was not given until it was requested.

Similarly, almost no counselors discuss how the abortion would be done in a pre-amnio session, "unless they ask," and a number added that "most people don't want to know." The one counselor I interviewed who does raise it routinely says she asks the client if they would like to know, and "75 percent ask to know." It is not easy to raise a discussion of how a late abortion would be done with a pregnant woman who wants her baby. And it is not easy for the pregnant woman to raise the discussion with the counselor.

Sessions end by coming back to the forms. The informed consent, with its descriptions of all that can go wrong, needs to be read and signed, which is a "downer," "a bad way to have to end the session."

The "informed consent" forms repeat some of the information of the session. They vary somewhat from institution to institution, but typically cover the possibility that a second tap might be needed, that there are conditions that the tests cannot predict, that if there is more than one fetus present the results might pertain to only one of them, and that in any case the results might be wrong or "not accurately reflect the status of my fetus." Consent to the amniocentesis tap includes the awareness that the tap itself might cause damage, including a miscarriage. Most clients seem to decide whether or not to have the amnio before they ever come in, and some decide during the session. By the time the forms come out, the decision is usually made. But some do go home to think about it, or go home to discuss it with their husbands, partners, or families.

In almost all cases the results are normal, go to the patient through her obstetrician three to four weeks later, and the client and the counselor never see each other again.

On Nondirective Counseling

What is the point of prenatal genetic counseling? Is it to prevent birth defects? If your initial response is yes, then you are thinking of what is called "directive counseling." That is not the dominant mode of genetic counseling in America today. The value is on "nondirective" counseling, counseling that presents information, but allows the patients/clients to reach their own decisions. Only one of the counselors I interviewed said she was a directive genetic counselor: "Without any question. A firm believer in directive counseling." The others might have said that they have become a little more or a little less directive over time, but nondirectiveness was a strongly shared value: "I'm not going to be taking that baby home—they will," said one. And another: "I can't make their decision. I would never presume."

Many expressed an awareness of the impossibility of being totally nondirective; as one of the counselors I interviewed said, "I am aware that I can do a very subtle thing, and make a decision for somebody, and I really work at not doing that—it's really terrible. It's not appropriate."

In the early days of genetic counseling, when genetic counselors were physicians, the situation was different:

> Neutrality is unusual in medical practice and is a difficult attitude
> for many physicians to adopt, and may even be confusing to some
> patients who expect to be guided by their physicians.[16]

Eighty-five percent of the genetic counselors interviewed in 1973,[17] most of whom were physicians, considered it important that counseling achieve prevention of disease or abnormality, and "64 percent felt it was 'always appropriate' to inform counselees in a way that would 'guide them toward an appropriate decision.'" But what *is* an "appropriate" decision? The counselors I interviewed kept stressing that the decision must be one that is "right for that woman." So many of them told me, "I'm not an amnio saleslady." Asked about what reasons people have for refusing amniocentesis, and how they (the counselors) feel about it, most echoed the counselor who told me, "Whatever their reason, I respect it."

But of course many of them were uncomfortable with some reasons: being afraid of the needle was not a good enough reason to refuse. Nor was simple faith that "God would not give me an abnormal baby." Nor was "My mother/sister/friend had a baby at 43 and it was okay." And certainly some things just seem wrong to the most nondirective of counselors: one told a couple whose fetus was diagnosed as having Downs Syndrome that no, they couldn't go on vacation and then have the abortion when they got back.

Because nondirectiveness is a value among the counselors that is supported at so many levels—the medical consumerism movement, the feminist movement, the American value of individualism—giving examples of their directiveness looks like muckraking. But counselors are bound to be directive sometimes—avowedly so in some circumstances, perhaps unwittingly so in others. If I write now about the times and ways in which they are directive, please do not lose sight of the fact that most of them do truly value nondirectiveness, do truly seek it as a goal. But they are faced by women who are making decisions that may change the course of their lives:

> When I see a woman who is genetically considered to be at high risk in her pregnancy, who has two children she loves and adores, there's no father, there's no means of support, no money, and she's looking at me and saying, "Should I keep this pregnancy?"—what do you do?

What this counselor does is say things like, "Well, let's look at this," and "Let's think about that," pointing out the problems to the woman until she comes to her decision. Others talk about building scenarios, "How are you going to feel if?" or "trying to act as the devil's advocate—'what if? what if?'"

It would be naive to think that the women are free agents with only the counselors' directiveness to worry about. Some women want the amnio but their husbands "won't let them" have it. Others are pressured by family into having the test. As a result, one counselor said, "When I feel that a patient really wants to do something but they're getting pressure from their families to do otherwise, then I feel that if I'm more directive they'll do what they really want to do."

This is the thing about the counselors' directiveness—they are trying, if directing at all, to steer the woman in the direction they think she wants to go. Mostly that is toward amnio and ultimately toward aborting affected fetuses. But sometimes it is the other way: "What bothers me is when young women come in here having the test because their doctors said they have to have it whether they want it or not. . . . Most make up their mind to do what the doctors say anyway."

A number of counselors said that they tried to steer women with a history of infertility or repeated miscarriages away from the amnio, or from doing anything that might disrupt the pregnancy; and some said that they were most clearly directive when it came to Tay Sachs disease. Tay Sachs is a kind of touchstone for genetic counseling. A normal-looking baby deteriorating over a period of years to an inescapable but lingering death is so horrifying that nondirectiveness tends to fly out the window. They feel: *of course* the couple should be tested for carrier status. What follows is that if a carrier married to a carrier is now pregnant, *of course* she should have amnio, and *why ever not* abort an affected fetus?

These are the extremes, the conditions under which many counselors feel most justified in saying what a client should do. Most everything else falls somewhere between, where the stakes are lower and the pressures more subtle. When counseling for advanced maternal age, just how old the woman actually is is probably going to have an effect on how the counselor conducts the session: 46 is not 35. As one counselor said, "When they're forty, then I'm putting much more pressure on them."

Probably when forty was the starting age for amnio, it was women in the mid-to-late forties who got the pressure.

The larger concept of riskiness, not just age, comes into question here—just how much of a risk is "high risk?" Partly it is the disease: "For Tay Sachs, one in a million is high." But there is some general understanding of what "high risk" and "low risk" means, and here, too, there has been change over time. The current counselors see riskiness somewhat differently than did those physicians doing genetic counseling in 1973. Risk rates of one-in-two, or one-in-four—the risk rates found for genetic diseases for which parents can be carriers, like Tay

Sachs or hemophilia—are seen definitely as "very high," just as they were by the earlier counselors. But even by one-in-ten a shift in perception begins, with more of the current counselors seeing higher riskiness at every risk rate. A risk rate of one-in-fifty is called high or very high by almost half of the counselors I interviewed—and by only 20 percent of the earlier group of counselors. Twice as many now call one-in-100 high or very high (21 percent vs. 9 percent) and twice as many now call one-in-200 high or very high (13 percent vs. 6 percent). And look at the flip side: what is a low risk? Among the earlier counselors, three-fourths called one-in-100 low or very low. Among the counselors I interviewed, less than half thought that low or very low. In fact, only three-fourths of the counselors I interviewed thought one-in-*400* was low or very low. In 1973 the researcher never even asked about risk levels lower than one-in-200. Perhaps in the 1990s one-in-400 will seem like a very high risk.

The implications are striking. One counselor, for example, said that she was most directive when "I feel that a couple is at very high risk and they don't realize it or if they're at very low risk and don't realize it." This counselor considered a one-in-200 risk to be moderate, one-in-300 or -400 to be low, and *nothing* to be "very low" risk.

When counselors feel their clients are at high risk, I believe it inevitable that there will be some direction given, some subtle pressures exerted. What then are the techniques available to counselors who will not say "you should"? One of the ways they can direct their clients is by separating the decision to have the amnio from the decision to have an abortion if an affected fetus is found. While the two tend to go together, the decision to have an amnio can be separated out. Some counselors say that people who say they will not abort for any fetal abnormality should not have amnio. For one thing, why take the risk of interfering with the pregnancy? The miscarriage rate, while small, is there. For another, the knowledge that something is wrong could make the pregnancy very difficult for the woman and her family.

But others saw that as precisely the reason why even women who do not plan on aborting for abnormalities should have the amnio: once the woman actually knows she is carrying a fetus with Downs or some other disabling condition, she may think differently about abortion.

Some counselors also feel that the test is likely to be reassuring, and so should be done on that basis. They think of pregnancy as a time of great anxiety, and themselves as relieving anxiety. This viewpoint can coexist with the idea of being "nondirective," because the counselor is not trying to influence the more crucial decision to abort, just the decision to have the amnio. In part, how a counselor sees this issue depends on how safe she feels the amnio itself is. Some counselors are concerned about the risks of causing a miscarriage, and that does discourage them from leading a woman toward having an amnio if she will not make use of the results. Others are much less concerned with the risks of the test itself: they feel that "miscarriages after the test probably would have happened anyway."

By avoiding the whole issue of abortion, and instead focusing the session on the test, how it works and what it does, counselors can separate the decision to have an amnio from deciding about abortion, and preserve their feeling of nondirectiveness. Unfortunately, when a bad result comes through the counselor often loses control of the situation as the physician steps in.

In addition, this pressure toward skirting the issues is offset somewhat by the very real desire counselors have to help their clients make decisions. They *like* "helping people through problems, helping them make decisions," and "making a difference in people's lives." This creates a very different kind of directedness: trying to make the client feel the need of the counseling. A number of counselors complained about clients "who think they know it all," clients who do not want the counseling but just the laboratory services, or who have very limited needs for counseling. These clients were primarily drawn from the well-educated, professional women, the women who are making up the widely publicized "baby boomlet" among older women. They certainly do not know as much genetics as the counselors, but the information that needs to be communicated from counselor to client has been made widely available in the popular press. The "what chromosomes are" and "how neural tube defects occur" and other standard "raps" are old-hat for women who, as a group, have been said to take pregnancy as a reading assignment. Similarly, spending time on family history may be just as unnecessary among this population: more often than not the Jews know about Tay Sachs, the blacks about sickle-cell, and they've all thought about family history and asked more questions of their parents than the counselors ask of them. They don't even need to hear the details of the procedure, having heard that from friends. And the decision-making is over before it began: for many of these women, amnio is already an expected, accepted part of the pregnancy experience. All that is left then is signing the forms.

At the other end of the spectrum, sometimes the counseling sessions are irrelevant not because of overpreparation, but because the ship has sailed. Clients sometimes come in *after* they have had the amnio—either because their pregnancies have not been recognized until very late, or because they have not felt the need of, or do not have access to, medical services in early pregnancy. Because of the inherent deadline imposed by the progressing pregnancy, a woman who presents herself for prenatal care for the first time at eighteen or nineteen weeks may be scheduled for an amnio virtually at once: test first and talk later. The doctors thus display their priorities: the test is important, the counseling superfluous, a nicety if time permits.

Observing a session like that, it was a little unclear just what was supposed to be accomplished. Which brings us back to the point of prenatal counseling in general: it has to have effects on decision-making or indeed there is no point. The counselors, if not trying to influence the decision, are at least trying to influence the decision-making process.

But how *can* one influence the process without directly influencing the decision? Can it be done by how one defines the decision to be made? Is this a case of a woman deciding whether or not there is a reason to risk a miscarriage, or is she deciding whether or not she "should learn everything you can about your baby"? Is she deciding whether or not she could face a twenty-one-week abortion, or is she deciding how frightened she is of having a needle poked into her pregnant belly?

The counselors shape the session, and thus the decision-making process, by directing the woman's attention toward some questions, and away from others. The counselors themselves, as one might imagine, mostly think that amnio and selective abortion is a good thing, something that expands women's control of their lives:

> I honestly do believe and I share with the patient (after a bad result) that they are lucky to get this information at this time, at a time when they can make a choice. I see a child with Downs Syndrome, or another recognizable syndrome—I don't think I ever see such a child without thinking of a couple with that diagnosis who made the decision not to be so burdened.

Most of the counselors I interviewed would have the test themselves. More than half would have, or want their daughter to have, an amnio even at 25, a "low-risk age." They would want the information. Most would have abortions for most abnormalities; half said they would abort for *any* abnormality.

> If there was any abnormality diagnosed I would terminate the pregnancy.
> All circumstances—any chromosome abnormality.

> I wouldn't have anything that was not perfect, not normal, anything with ifs, ands, or buts.

And while that does *not* mean that the counselors think their clients should do the same—they value nondirectiveness too much for that—how clearly can they make the distinction? If your experience with genetic abnormalities is such that you can say, as one counselor did about why she went into prenatal counseling, "I've had enough freaky kids throw up on me. I want to get it before it happens"; if you can say about Downs Syndrome, as another counselor said to me, "Sure they can be sweet children. And they grow up to be ugly adults"; if this is how you see it, how can you *not* influence? If the counselor thinks this woman sitting across from her is going to do something she will deeply regret for the rest of her life, how can she *not* influence her? Just what kind of person would she be if she saw someone heading off a cliff and sat back "nondirectively"?

With all of these provisos, with all these warnings and disclaimers, let me end this chapter with my notes of a session I observed. It was not "typical," and I do not present it as such. It was indeed one of the more disturbing sessions I went through. But this is what can happen, this is what does happen, when people try to help people for their own good:

Notes of Observations, 1/83

A 39-year-old Hispanic woman arrives for counseling accompanied by her sister, who also serves as translator. She had been married for 13 years, separated for the last four. This is her first pregnancy. The sister says this several times, adding, "Nothing, not even any abortions." They told her she was sterile. The woman sits quietly. Answers questions about herself in monosyllables. Quietly but firmly refuses to answer any questions about the father. The counselor does not press the point. The counselor does a lot of talking—the chromosome stuff, neural tube defects, etcetera. She explains how the test cannot guarantee everything, just the things that they are testing for. At 39 years the risk of Downs is one-in-140. The counselor puts it that "One-in-140 will have mongolism and we want to make sure you're not that one." The woman does not want the test. She sits, mostly silent, looking down. The counselor spends a great deal of time reassuring her that the test is not painful, that the needle will not hurt. The woman never mentions pain. She says nothing. She never brings up the fear of the needle, it's just the counselor saying she understands she is afraid, but there is nothing to fear, it's just a little pressure, no pain. The sister repeats, she doesn't want the test. The sister is shaking her head, aligning herself with the counselor. The counselor says, "Tell your sister to think of the benefits, the advantages of the test. She would know that the baby doesn't have mongolism, doesn't have an opening in the spine." The woman says, for the first time in English, that she's afraid. She doesn't say of what. The counselor doesn't ask. The counselor says: "You have to think of the advantages." The sister jumps in in Spanish, obviously trying to talk her into it, obviously irritated with her unreasoning silence. The sister is young, has a child. The counselor interrupts the sister's argument: "A woman has to decide for herself. No one can decide for her. It has to be a very personal decision."

At the end of the session, after fifty minutes of listening to this, I do not know if this was a deeply wanted pregnancy—a miracle thirteen years in the making—a pleasant surprise, or an unwanted accident. The sisters get up and leave. We don't know if she will have the amnio.

Notes

1 Kristen Luker, Abortion and the Policies of Motherhood. Berkeley: University of California Press, 1984.

2 Genoveffa Corea, The Mother Machine: Reproductive Technologies from Artificial Insemination to Artificial Wombs. New York: Harper and Row, 1985. I am grateful to Genoveffa Corea for making this book available to me in manuscript.

3 Irving Kenneth Zola, Sociomedical Inquiries: Recollections, Reflections, and Reconsiderations. Philadelphia: Temple University Press, 1983. Zola states that he coined the term "medicalization" in a graduate course (p. 243). The term refers to the sociopolitical process of "making medicine and the labels 'healthy' and 'ill' relevant to an ever-increasing part of human existence" (p. 247).

4 Barbara Katz Rothman, In Labor: Women and Power in the Birthplace. New York: W. W. Norton and Co., 1982, pp. 45–47.

5 For a discussion of the changing legal status of the fetus and the pregnant woman, see Janet Gallagher, "The Fetus and the Law—Whose Life Is It Anyway?" Ms., September 1984, pp. 62–135.

6 For a fuller discussion, see Ruth Hubbard, et al., Biological Woman: The Convenience Myth. Cambridge, MA: Schenkman, 1982, pp. 201–28.

7 Watson A. Bowes, Jr., and Brad Selgestad, "Fetal Versus Maternal Rights: Medical and Legal Perspectives." Obstetrics and Gynecology, 58:209–14, August 1981.

8 Genetics and the Law: Third National Symposium co-sponsored by the American Society of Law and Medicine and Boston University Schools of Medicine, Law and Public Health, Boston, April 2–4, 1984.

9 Rothman, op. cit.

10 For a discussion of the abortion of female fetuses, see Rita Arditti, Renate Duelli-Klein, and Shelley Minden (eds.), Test Tube Women: What Future for Motherhood? Boston: Pandora Press, 1984. In that volume, see Hoskins and Holmes, "Technology and Prenatal Femicide"; Sangari, "If You Would Be the Mother of a Son"; and Roggencamp, "Abortion of a Special Kind: Male Sex Selection in India."

[11] Erich Fromm, *The Forgotten Language: An Introduction to the Understanding of Dreams, Fairy Tales and Myths*. New York: Grove Press, 1956.

[12] Sources for history of the eugenics movement include: Kenneth Ludmerer and Marc Lappe, "Eugenics," *Encyclopedia of Bioethics*, vol. 1, 1978; and Daniel J. Kevles, "Annals of Eugenics," a four-part series in *The New Yorker*, October 1984.

[13] Sheldon C. Reed, "A Short History of Genetic Counseling," *Social Biology*, vol. 21, no. 4, 1971, pp. 332–39.

[14] Ibid., p. 335.

[15] Richard M. Frankel and Howard B. Beckman, "Between Physician and Patient: The Medical Record and the Construction of Clinical Reality." Paper presented to the Society for the Study of Social Problems, Detroit, August 1983.

[16] Cited in Seymour Kessler, *Genetic Counseling: The Psychological Dimension*. New York: Academic Press, 1979.

[17] James R. Sorenson, "Counselors: A Self Portrait." *Genetic Counseling*, vol. 1, no. 5, October 1973.

PART III

The Health Care System

Health costs in the United States now exceed $1 trillion, amounting to nearly 15 percent of the Gross Domestic Product (GDP). This money goes to hospitals, nursing homes, insurance companies, doctors, health workers, drugs, dentists, medical supplies, government research and support, administration, construction, and various providers. Health spending is thus a central facet of the U.S. economy. This country spends a far larger percentage of its GDP on health care than many other countries, yet it does not post better health indicators as a result. Many European countries have lowered their health spending in the 1980s, while still surpassing the United States in measures such as infant mortality and maternal health. However, no other country has such a large amount of profit made in the health care business.

There is much money to be made by the producers of drugs and medical supplies. During the 1980s and early 1990s, drug prices rose by 128 percent, compared to only 22 percent for all products. Drug firms claim they have high expenses for research, but that is an exaggeration. More than half of new drugs introduced to the market are "me-too" drugs that duplicate existing drugs. The industry spends far more on promotion ($10 billion) than on research ($9 billion), and actually much of the research budget includes routine business operating expenses. Doctors, laboratories, home care providers, and medical suppliers combine to create $100 billion in fraud, abuse, and waste each year, according to federal inspectors. At the worst end is completely fraudulent billing. We find ethically suspect behavior even in more "respectable" practices—for example, the most prestigious medical centers form partnerships with service suppliers (such as ultrasound laboratories and home infusion services) and then prompt all their doctors to refer to that supplier.

It may be hard to consider that such a thing as the "health care system" exists, since it is comprised of such a diversity of segments: organizational (e.g., organizations of professionals and institutions), institutional (e.g., health facilities and the interrelations between facilities), regulatory (e.g., government agencies such as the Food and Drug Administration), manufacturing (drugs, equipment, supplies), and financial (e.g., insurance companies and large manufacturers who carry out self-insurance programs). It is often hard to trace the relationships between these segments. Those who work in one part of the healthcare system may be unclear about the impact of their actions on the other parts of the system. Indeed, we often see *unintended consequences* of policies instead of the expected outcomes. For example, the expansion of federal reimbursements for nursing home care was partly responsible for the unintended consequence of deinstitutionalization of state mental hospital patients. Above all, members of one component of the system rarely have a worldview that takes into account the overall structure of the system.

One task of medical sociology is to provide an integrated view of the health care system. Such a view not only makes logical and necessary connections between parts of the system, but it also provides linkages between the health care system and the deeper social structure of the society at large. One example of such linkages is the relationship of reproductive health services (contraception, abortion, sterilization) with general social values and restrictions on reproduction, sexuality, and family structure.

Part 3 contains four sections. In the first section on The Health Care Industry we look at the growing role of profit-making hospital chains, the phenomenal growth of health maintenance organizations (HMOs), and the power of managed care to transform the health care system. These structures exert increasing control over many clinical practices. The next section, Institutional Settings, contains material on hospitals, both historically and in the present. The third section, Health Care Providers, offers articles on physicians and nurses, both historically and at present. The final section, Social Movements, Social Change, and Health, contains four articles about the importance of political organizing around health issues. It has often been the case that health problems and methods to prevent and treat them have come from outside the medical system As we read earlier in the section on "Experiencing Illness and Seeking Care" and in the Ann Dill et al. article on self-care, individuals often play a central role in detecting and treating illness. On a larger level, it is often the case that the detection and treatment of illness comes from groups organized to deal politically with health and illness. One excellent example is how AIDS sufferers and their supporters have been central in expanding knowledge and treatment of AIDS. Social movements in health care have been major impacts in many other diseases and conditions as well.

Section VIII

The Health Care Industry

The health care industry follows tendencies found throughout capitalist society for profit maximization and monopolization. To be sure, much health care is provided in the public sector, but even in that sector the same mechanisms often operate. Further, a good deal of the private sector is supported by public sector financing through government reimbursement of Medicare and Medicaid patients (one-third of the nation's health bill is paid by Medicaid, Medicare, and other government programs). A recent addition to this legacy is interesting: the federal government is now paying private HMOs to take care of many Medicare and Medicaid recipients, yielding a new boon to HMO profits.

The health care system faced pressure for change from the large government units and businesses that spent growing amounts on insurance premiums for workers. They began to put pressure for change in the system. Overall, "managed care" approaches were developed, whereby insurers maintained a much tighter grip on people's utilization of health services. The growth of health maintenance organizations (HMOs) was part of this process. The HMO is a form of prospective payment: people pay in a monthly premium (a per capita cost called "capitation"), and all their care is paid from that, rather than from a fee-for-service model. In these arrangments, individuals have far less choice of who is their doctor and what hospital they go to, doctors have more controls and restrictions on their practice, and the corporate owners have lower payrolls as they substitute nurses and physician assistants for doctors. When federal regulations and private insurers' reimbursement policies cut down on length of hospital stay, hospitals were left with many empty beds. Hospital chains sold off their least profitable hospitals and bought or started HMOs, which could control costs all across the health care continuum. The large insurance companies and the hospital chains are rapidly buying up other hospitals, clinics, and even doctors' group practices in order to set up HMOs and related managed care organizations. Whereas HMOs were once largely non-profit, for-profit HMOs overtook the non-profits in the early 1990s. In 1994, only one of the ten largest HMO chains was non-profit, and it had zero growth over two years, while for-profit chains grew from 15 to 139 percent in that period. HMOs continually find ways to cut back on payrolls and services, in order to maximize their profits. Yet they are quite generous with their executives—each of the chiefs of the seven largest for-profit HMOs received an average $7 million in compensation in salary, bonuses, and stock options in 1994 (the range was $2.8 to $15.5 million). Arnold Birenbaum's "What is Managed Care?" provides an overview of the origins and structures of HMOs and managed care approaches, and also touches upon issues of equity in access to care, ethical considerations, and use of medical technology that are increasingly raised in discussions of managed care.

The medical landscape is populated by a growing degree of monopolization, as major hospital chains expand their operations. To a large degree, these chains are filling the gap left behind by many public hospitals that closed in the period of fiscal crisis starting in the 1970s. What may have seemed astounding 20 years ago—the development of massive private hospital chains and nationwide managed care organization—is now taken for granted as a basic component of the health care system. This *proprietarization* (private ownership) raises a number of concerns. In particular, the poor population as well as the many uninsured people in the working class have little or no access to these private facilities. Doctors and other health professionals are very concerned that the profit-maximization practices of these chains will limit their ability to serve patients in the best possible way. Examples of the harmful practices of proprietarization include turning away acutely ill indigent cases from emergency rooms and early discharge of ill patients.

In "The Evolution of Investor-Owned Hospital Companies," Bradford H. Gray analyzes one of the most significant health care developments in recent decades—the growth of for-profit hospitals. Early in the century, many small proprietary hospitals existed, but they were typically run by a few doctors, and served a fairly small population. As the health industry expanded in the post-World War II era, federal financing and private insurance led to a dramatic growth in non-profit community hospitals and academic medical centers. The advent of Medicare and Medicaid in the mid-1960s heightened this process. With hospitals able to collect almost unlimited reimbursements from government and insurers, for-profit hospitals had a field day, and large chains came to own hundreds of hospitals and related health facilities like nursing homes. This burgeoning industry was concerned solely with bottom-line profits, rather than with serving the health needs of the population. Local community hospitals and even large city hospitals were hurt by the process, often being forced to close up by the hospital chains which restricted services to many poor and underserved people.

The federal government started to cut down on rising costs in 1983, with diagnosis-related groups (DRGs), a form of *prospective payment*, by which the U.S. government pays hospitals a fixed amount per Medicare patient, based on their diagnostic category. This replaced the older system of *retrospective payment*, whereby a hospital simply charged the government for whatever costs it incurred. This new system arose in part due to inflationary pressures since hospitals were able to bill Medicare and Medicaid for a virtually unlimited amount of money. Private insurers learned from DRGs, and began to impose strict length of stay requirements as well. While this did cut down on the expansion of the hospital chains, Gray reminds us that there is a major lesson here in the way that the health business operates very much like any other profit-seeking enterprise.

Donald Light's article, "The Origins and Rise of Managed Care," expands the above material, situating it in a broad context of a long history of health care system changes. He points out that rising costs led many large employers to set up self-insurance programs to avoid dealing with external insurers and managed care organizations. This "buyers' revolt" led insurers to rethink their approaches to health insurance, and they turned to acting more like a contractor than an insurer, in setting up packages of services for large buyers. As with previous stages, this brought health care services one step further away from a direct medical relationship. Light also discusses how these changes in the health care system led to major public attention, including President Bill Clinton's 1993 proposal for national health insurance. He shows how the flawed proposal, as well as the corporate response to it, accelerated the efforts of managed care firms to solidify their financial and political power.

Lynn Etheredge, Stanley Jones, and Lawrence Levin continue this discussion in "What is Driving Health System Change?", showing how the attempts at a market-driven health care system do not result in a sensible market model. Managed care firms engage in roughhouse competition to gain market share, without an underlying purpose that is centered on improving health. Selective "creaming" of healthier populations leaves sicker people with less access to care. Health plans continue their encroachment of physicians' autonomy and income, leading to many conflicts between doctors and the hospitals in which they work. Managed care firms have often pressured physicians to act as financial gatekeepers, using the threat of excluding them from the health plan if they order too many specialists or laboratory services. In response, some physicians are even organizing their own health plans to provide what they see as better care. Consumers, too, are organizing to keep the health care system from operating on a purely market-based model. Government has often been slow to engage in the effort to control what Etheredge et al. term "amoral market forces." In sum, these authors give us a portrait of a complex, multifactorial set of forces that act on the health care system.

23
What Is Managed Care?

Arnold Birenbaum

Health Maintenance Organizations

It has often been observed that the real consumers of health care services are physicians rather than patients. When doctors order up tests or hospitalize patients, they encounter no financial risk in traditional fee-for-service medicine; and third-party payment softens the economic blow to the patient who might question the absolute necessity of a procedure or a hospital stay. Under third-party payment, patients freely choose providers, and there is no advance agreement to serve a particular panel of patients. Integrating payment and provider in the same plan is a key innovation in American health care because it makes discipline over physicians possible.

A health maintenance organization (HMO) is both a financial plan and an organization of services for a specific population of subscribers. In this arrangement, a fiscal agent agrees to be accountable for all stipulated health services for the subscribers at a fixed price. This combination payer and provider assumes financial risk for those covered by the plan. Unlike straight indemnity insurance, HMOs exercise various kinds of control over providers and members. Those who enroll in the plan do so voluntarily and pay this price regardless of whether or not they use the services available. An advantage for the covered is they have no first dollar or deductible obligations and generally pay only a modest co-payment when they see a doctor. In some HMO arrangements providers do not even collect the small co-payment because it generates so little in the way of revenue and incurs an overhead cost to handle. A major component of the economic arrangements of HMOs is that all major hospital costs are paid for out of the combined capitation fees. Hospitals agree to make beds available in advance to the HMO at a discounted price or the HMO owns hospitals. Either way, HMOs try to limit hospital utilization because it is a major proportion of costs that will be taken from income.

From Birenbaum, Arnold, *Managed Care* (Praeger Publishers, an imprint of Greenwood Publishing Group, Inc., Westport, CT), pp. 15–29. © 1998 by Arnold Birenbaum. Reprinted with permission.

HMOs contract with providers in various ways to get them to deliver services. In staffed HMOs, such as Kaiser Permanente and Puget Sound, the physicians and other providers are salaried and work directly for the HMO, which also provides all nonmedical services. Doctors assume no financial risk in this model. Other arrangements use various financial incentives for either groups of physicians or solo practitioners to keep costs down.

> The group-model HMO usually provides the hospitals and other physical facilities and employs the nonphysician clinical staff. It also provides the administrative support staff. The HMO contracts with one large (professionally autonomous) multiple-specialty medical group practice for physician services. The HMO pays the medical group a monthly amount per member to provide services. (Freeborn and Pope, 1994, p. 21)

Within each group, usually physicians work only for that HMO, are salaried, but with monetary incentives and penalties, and are at some financial risk. These groups are made up generally of a very large number of physicians and provide a comprehensive set of medical services.

An expansion of the group model is called the network model, wherein an HMO contracts with several physician groups, but with the same capitation arrangements to cover members. Nonphysician services are provided by the group, which also assumes financial risk.

Finally, the fastest-growing model in the 1990s is one where individual physicians, forming an independent practice association (IPA), contract to care for covered individuals, usually on a heavily discounted fee-for-service basis. There is use of risk-capitation in some IPAs. In this model the physician often belongs to several HMOs at the same time. Located throughout a region, IPAs permit consumers to make choices from a larger number of primary care providers and specialists than are generally found in the other models. Additionally, providers are not subject to an integrated health service system. Enrollment growth in 1994–95 showed a 22 percent increase in networks and IPA model HMOs, compared with an 8 percent increase in staff and group model HMOs (American Association of Health Plans, 1996, p. 2).

HMOs are said to have a competitive advantage over traditional fee-for-service and third-party coverage because the enrolled achieve financial security as far as their medical expenses are concerned. In addition, capitation charges are considered to be lower than straight indemnification insurance policies, whether group or individual, because there is no incentive to the provider to do unnecessary

work. Primary care doctors or physician extenders (nurse practitioners or physician assistants) act as "gatekeepers" to specialty care.
Physician extenders are much less expensive to employ than doctors
and do excellent work in primary care, particularly in doing routine
but highly important tasks necessary to keeping people well. A
United States Office of Technology Assessment (1986) review of all
studies comparing the work of nurse practitioners with physicians
confirms this view.

Doctors who tend patients in managed care are driven by the concern to avoid unnecessary resource utilization. HMOs encourage
patients to have regular examinations while not overusing expensive
kinds of interventions. Managers of HMOs try to establish primary
care as the front line of service and have an incentive to get providers
to do preventive interventions and early detections through simple
tests (e.g., the Pap smear) in order to avoid more complex interventions and hospitalization later on. Sometimes providers also are
given financial incentives to follow this model of service rigorously.

While HMOs have been around for 60 years in the United States,
federal legislation that provided financial incentives to start up for-
profit prepaid programs initiated a rapid and enormous expansion
of members in the 1980s. The Tax Equity and Fiscal Responsibility
Act of 1982 expanded the market by making it easier for Medicare
and Medicaid beneficiaries to enroll in HMOs. Marketing was
intense. I recall that in 1984 the Chicago radio airwaves were full of
advertisements for HMOs, aimed at the senior citizen set. Today
HMOs increasingly serve a larger and larger proportion of the over-
65 population, with HMOs reporting in 1996 the development of
many new Medicare risk contracts or plans to do so. Similar trends
for contracts were found with regard to the Medicaid-eligible population, with many new programs coming on line.

Finding resources to deliver managed care became a less serious
problem for HMOs as the market favored buyers rather than sellers
of health services. The oversupply of hospital beds and physicians
during the 1980s and 1990s created a strong impetus for providers
to sign on with profit-making and nonprofit HMOs, guaranteeing a
predictable and large volume of resources. Even august institutions
found HMOs attractive. In response to losing patients, teaching hospitals with affiliations with prestigious medical schools began to create
joint ventures with HMOs. In the last decade, insurance companies
and state-organized Blue Cross programs began to sell HMO services
to subscribers. In sum, a great transformation in the organization of
providers came about with these new market considerations.

HMOs were believed to be economically viable because of their success in keeping people out of hospitals. In addition, the nonprofit HMOs essentially catered to young and healthy families, who needed routine care but rarely had the need for hospitalization. Large employers led the way in encouraging their workers to join HMOs. The financial advantage to subscribers—no deductible and no serious copayment for office visits—was a major selling point in getting conversions from traditional insurance coverage.

Growth in HMO membership has been phenomenal during this decade. Research centers and professional associations followed these trends keenly. In 1989, InterStudy, a Minneapolis-based research organization, reported that HMO membership was at 32 million. The *American Medical News* (1991, p.33), a publication of the American Medical Association, noted that an American Association of Health Plans study found that HMOs appear to be most successful in the nation's largest cities and those where they have been available the longest. The cities of San Francisco (46%) and Minneapolis-St. Paul (44%) led the way with the highest numbers of HMO members among all residents.

For employers, however, some of the HMOs' great economic appeal appears to be wearing out. Even if the enrollee gives them high marks, the corporations have found that annual increases in costs can approximate those of traditional indemnification plans or even those with managed care provisions. In some cases, businesses have dropped one or more of the several HMO plans available to their employees and dependents. However, with 545 HMOs operating nationally, as reported by the Group Health Association of America (GHAA) in 1993, there seemed to be no difficulty shopping for substitute plans. Moreover, reflecting both growth and diversity, this trade association has merged with the American Managed Care and Review Association to form the American Association of Health Plans (AAHP). By late 1996 the AAHP had more than 1000 member health plans, providing coverage for over 100 million Americans nationwide.

Where did this concept come from? Is this just another foreign import, another Volkswagen or Honda? No—HMOs are truly an American product. One of America's major industrial magnates, Edgar Kaiser, will probably earn a place in American social history for his contribution to the extension of affordable health care to millions on the West Coast. In fact, Kaiser himself suggested that his proudest achievement was in starting the Kaiser-Permanente Health Care Partnership (Keene, 1971).

This Partnership came from the modest need to provide modern health care in locations where such services were minimal. The urban development and agribusinesses of southern California were dependent on getting water from remote mountain areas, far distant from the coastal locations where cities were being built. Teams of construction workers were employed in the 1930s to build reservoirs and pumping stations, and to lay pipe for the aqueducts that carry water to the coastal areas and valleys. Sidney Garfield, a young physician, had tried to establish a private practice in towns near this construction. He found plenty of demand for his services among the construction crews but no way to receive adequate compensation. As a result, Garfield developed a scheme whereby each worker would contribute a small amount every week on a contract basis, paying in advance for any medical care he provided. In exchange for these payments, he agreed to provide all medical care, no matter how often required. Garfield even built a small mobile field hospital that could be moved on skids to follow the crews as the project advanced (Cutting, 1971, pp.17–18).

In 1937, some five years after Dr. Garfield started this program, Edgar Kaiser was building the Grand Coulee Dam in the state of Washington. This massive undertaking was financed out of public monies and employed large numbers of construction workers. Kaiser asked Garfield to create a health care program for the workers and their families. This program was jointly paid for by employee and employer contributions, and it was considered a great success.

Kaiser Industries did not specialize only in dam construction. During World War II, it built cargo and troop carriers, popularly known as liberty ships. In 1942, this massive effort employed 90,000 workers in the San Francisco Bay area. Garfield was called upon once again to create a new program. After the war, the shipyard was closed and workers were dispersed. Garfield was left with a substantial group medical practice and a few thousand patients still employed by Kaiser Industries. Rather than reduce the size of the practice, he sought to keep it going by soliciting subscribers throughout the community, depending mainly on referrals (Cutting, 1971, p. 19). This recruitment drive was successful enough to keep the Kaiser-Permanente program going. Still known by the name of the original employer (and the site of one of his cement factories), it had 970,000 members in several states in 1970.

A similar program, the Health Insurance Program or HIP, was created in New York City in the 1940s, primarily for municipal employees. Kaiser and HIP became the models for creating financial incentives for the Health Maintenance Organizations found in Federal legislation enacted in 1973. The formation of HMOs was supported in planning grants for medical groups and loans to cover losses during the early period when subscribers were being acquired. In addition, through this legislation companies with 25 or more employees are required to offer what was called group-practice services if they have group health insurance as a fully or partially paid fringe benefit, provided an approved HMO is available in the community where the corporation is located. This enabling legislation initially created some legal problems, some having to do with the right of a union to bargain collectively over the fringe benefits available to members, and others having to do with the costs involved in meeting federal guidelines for planning grants and loans. Yet from these humble beginnings and encouragement from government-employed health-policy experts, the groundwork was established for the vast changes in health care delivery we are now experiencing.

Managed Care Explained

Because it is based on rationing of services, managed care must get providers to agree to do only what is medically necessary. This does restrict the autonomy of the professional but it is supposed to be based on outcome studies that show the efficacy of interventions. Ideally, peer review determines what is permitted and what is not, and the decision to restrict access is not made by administrators who are untrained in medical matters. The creators of contemporary managed care plans sought to eliminate the anarchy of the medical workplace, with doctors evaluating, testing, and treating in many different ways. The goal of rationing is to eliminate ineffective procedures and the unnecessary treatment from the health care system, especially if they are very costly. According to the founders of managed care, this goal can be accomplished only through the participation of providers under the same management.

Providers are linked directly to the plans that agree to deliver all medical and health services to a subscriber. Uniformity of services are necessary in order to keep costs down, and the plan, or health maintenance organization, can deliver the services at the rate they charge their customers or subscribers. Health plans hire actuaries to figure out what it will cost to deliver services to a given population, including the sick as well as the healthy. Plans are capitalized to meet state insurance commission requirements so that rationing or the HMO's closing does not occur because the plan simply miscalculated its expenditures in covering lives. While most of the original health maintenance organizations were nonprofit, this is no longer the case. Health plans are part of the commercial free enterprise system and are also run by organizations like Kaiser-Permanente, Puget Sound, and Blue Cross/Blue Shield. The plan makes profits when the monetary value of the resources expended is less than the revenue taken in to cover the lives of subscribers and their dependents. In financial terms, what is expended on patient care is known as the medical-loss ratio. The value of the stock of a publicly offered HMO may plunge when news gets out that a great deal more hospitalization of patients has occurred during the last quarter of the year than anticipated (Freudenheim, 1996). These losses reverberated in the financial markets because of the nature of financing health care in for-profit HMOs.

Whether profit making or nonprofit, the plan is paid up front, and it must live within the budget of what it takes in when it contracts to provide all medical and health services to a subscriber and dependents. Individuals who are covered by the plan pay a capitation fee, a fixed amount that provides medical services for a given period of time, regardless of the frequency of use, rather than paying fees for each service delivered. This capitation or prepayment creates an incentive on the part of the providers to be cost conscious. A change in the composition of the patients recruited to the plan, known as the "case mix," can throw off the predicted service utilization.

Plans try to get as many healthy patients in their plans as they can so that they can deliver services at the lowest cost possible. Patients are also recruited on the basis of a contract that stresses cost containment. Under capitation, they agree to use only the panel of doctors made available by the plan. In exchange for this agreement, they have no deductible payments before their insurance becomes activated. The co payments they make when using the doctor are very modest—usually under ten dollars per visit.

Providers are paid on either a capitation basis if they are primary-care providers, or, sometimes on a discounted fee-for-service basis. Under capitation, patients are encouraged to go as frequently as they want, while providers attempt to discourage unnecessary visits. Plans often feature a great deal of preventive services in order to avoid more expensive treatment services. Providers who deliver primary care under capitation are encouraged to see the patients with as little frequency as possible, to limit testing, and to make as few referrals to specialists as they can since they assume some financial risk. Providers who are paid on a fee-for-service basis are giving deep discounts to the plans they belong to and often have part of their fees withheld until an audit agrees that the actual visit rate and use of tests and other resources are within expected limits.

Sometimes the rules are suspended in recognition of unusual circumstances. If physicians have a disproportionately sick panel of patients, they may not be judged the same way as all other primary-care providers; or some formula adjusted for adverse risk may be introduced to make comparisons possible with other doctors.

When hospitalization is needed, the patients must go to the hospitals approved by the plan because it has a contract with that hospital. The contract usually calls for the hospital to give a deep discount to the plan because it guarantees the hospital that a certain number of beds will be occupied. Discounting is also required of other suppliers such as pharmaceutical houses or surgical supply companies.

The new way of delivering care, through health maintenance organizations, has turned health care into a purchasable commodity. Moreover, it is produced in a more uniform and controlled work environment where there is little room for teaching and research—two of the missions of medicine—along with patient care. Each health maintenance organization is attempting to deliver a standardized product that would be recognizable by patients in any part of the world. In turn, the increasing emphasis on rationing makes it difficult for any patient to have any control in the market place. Since each plan is different, consumers cannot easily make careful comparisons. Moreover, consumers do not have the expertise that benefits officers in large corporations, through training and experience, have to make comparisons as to which is the better value.

HMOs operate according to standard business practices. As is the philosophy of American manufacturing, managers exhibit autocratic behavior in the workplace, and in turn, there is a kind of anarchy in the marketplace as the plans increasingly try to outdo each other in claiming they are the best. The advertisements for HMOs are starting to look like automobile ads, and this is not an accident since the marketing of these health plans has become similar to marketing any mass-produced product in the United States.

How did managed care come to be the *plat de jour* in American health care? The table has been set by the large multinational corporations that have become intolerant of the continued rise in the cost of health care in a system of third-party payment. Today almost 60 million are covered in HMOs, and almost every group benefit package purchased by employers and paid for jointly by employees and employers has managed care features to reduce the use of health-care services. For example, a benefits plan which allows the person covered to go directly to a specialist for a consultation will still require prior authorization if that specialist decides it is in the patient's best interest to remove a gall bladder.

With the exception of prior authorization to do an expensive procedure, the original approach to financing health care in the United States, fee-for-service, is still reproduced in the encounter between a patient and a doctor outside of the HMO. Some existing plans, called preferred provider organizations, continue to use the fee-for-service system but limit the person covered to their list of providers. You can go to a specialist without seeing a generalist first and the providers on the list agree to give a deep discount to the plan. Furthermore, members pay a smaller co-payment when they use a physician who participates in the plan. At the end of 1995, the AAHP estimated that 91 million enrollees and dependents were in PPOs, an increase of 12 million from 1994.

Americans continue to be very price sensitive when it comes to health care. What managed care in its various forms has accomplished is the introduction of new reward systems for physicians and hospitals, and consumers as well, making it possible to deliver services at lower costs. These are significantly different ways of paying the doctor than are found in the American fee-for-service system. Each method of paying for medical services has incentives to providers and patients to do certain things and avoid other things. The fee-for-service system *without* third-party payment kept the charges down because physicians were afraid to scare away patients with high fees. Patients, in turn, were careful users of the system because their post-tax income went to pay for services. Besides, many of the encounters with physicians before the advent of antibiotics, such as penicillin, did not produce an effective or desired outcome. The technology of medicine didn't begin to get sophisticated until the 1960s. Consequently, most encounters with providers were not very expensive.

For those who could afford them as a regular source of care, doctors were attentive, courteous, and warm. In an age where physicians depended on a limited market for their services they had to demonstrate their devotion to the few patients they had. They wished to retain patients as much as possible and they wanted their patients to say good things about them in their neighborhoods, churches, and clubs. And by keeping their fees low, doctors sought to cast as wide a net as possible to capture paying patients. In fact, general practitioners were reluctant to part with a patient through a referral to a specialist if they felt they could continue to help. Naturally, specialists knew this and expressed a great deal of gratitude for a referral because it was so hard won.

These arrangements worked to establish medicine as the major provider of health care services to the middle classes in the United States and promote the development of the modern acute-care voluntary hospital as we know it today (Rosenberg, 1987). By the 1930s this system was threatened as the middle classes' purchasing power declined. During the Great Depression, patients could pay neither their hospital nor doctor bills. First, in order to keep voluntary hospital beds filled and their doors open, group hospital insurance policies were underwritten and premiums collected from subscribers. Usually these policies were available to a workforce that expected to be steadily employed, such as school teachers. Blue Cross hospital insurance was developed by the hospital industry itself as a way to keep generating income during those gloomy days. What worked in a mutually advantageous way for provider and consumer alike during hard times was even more popular during good times when more people wished to share in what became known in our popular culture as the good life. But first they were used as a way of keeping valued workers happy. Health insurance policies were offered as an across-the-board fringe benefit during World War II when wage and price freezes, compounded by a labor shortage, made it hard to retain employees without offering some reward. Then, during the post-war 1940s and 1950s, an era of substantial increases in real earnings and high progressive taxation, unionized workers sought to gain health benefits in collective bargaining agreements, sometimes in preference to increases in wages, because they were considered to be untaxed income.

The health insurance industry was off and running now, and health care providers were beneficiaries. First, hospital bills were paid by insurance policies and it was not too long before major medical care was also covered by indemnification policies. Benefits permitted potential patients and their providers to interact more; some of the real financial barriers to receiving medical care had been broken.

Insurance had major consequences in changing the behavior of patients and their doctors. Known as third-party payers, private insurance coverage made it possible for patients to seek doctors with great frequency, resulting in larger patient panels and more appointments per day. In fact, under these new financial conditions, which produced more patient volume, general practitioners were less reluctant to refer to specialists. The presence of coverage enhanced doctor-patient contact. For patients, insurance protected their assets since third parties paid their medical bills and they became less price sensitive. At the other end of the relationship, doctors found that increased access generated more revenues. And because their operating costs were more or less fixed, it meant more income, both relatively and absolutely, since with each additional patient seen during the day it become an increasingly profitable consultation. Moreover, access to specialists was no longer restricted by economic considerations, and each referral was less essential to their practices, but as with general practitioners, also more economically valuable than in the past. The advent of Medicare and Medicaid merely accelerated the process of growth in the industry rather than initiating them.

The explosion in health care inflation was exacerbated by the growth of technology generated by new markets for its use. Third-party payment made consumers less price conscious in the health care marketplace. The development of new technology means greater profits for their manufacturers so long as their products are accepted as a standard tool in the doctor's arsenal. Precisely because physicians in fee-for-service medicine become partners in owning this technology, health-policy analysts and benefits officers became unwilling to underwrite the seemingly unlimited inflation in health-care services.

The plan is fairly simple: Manufacturers of diagnostic equipment, monitoring devices, and pharmaceuticals all need to get the *real* consumer, that is, the physician, to use their products. Getting these products accepted involves efforts of persuasion comparable to the selling to any target audience of consumers. The manufacturers do have a built-in advantage, given the nature of fee-for-service medical practice in the United States. Physicians are more highly rewarded, both materially and professionally, by performing procedures rather than engaging in educational efforts with patients. Third-party payers regard these procedures as more complex than patient education and reimburse claims more handsomely when technology is used. In addition, the more procedures performed with *physician-owned* diagnostic equipment, the more financially rewarding these procedures are. Recent studies point to the differences in the use of diagnostic equipment according to ownership by the examining physician. Moreover, the task can usually be delegated to a technician who can gain increasing proficiency at doing these tasks unsupervised while the physician can be doing other things. Reporting in 1991, The Florida Health Care Cost Containment Board, a state agency, found that when doctors owned their own laboratories, almost twice as many tests were performed for each patient as other laboratories. Similar results were found in this comprehensive study of the Sunshine State where the frequency of scheduled visits to physical therapy centers was higher when these facilities were owned in joint ventures by doctors (*New York Times*, Aug. 11, 1991, p. E9). According to the report, 45 percent of the state's doctors were involved in such arrangements. Over 90 percent of the diagnostic imaging centers in Florida were wholly or partly owned by doctors.

The Florida report also concluded that the poor and rural residents did not have improved access to these diagnostic and clinical services resulting from their proliferation around the state. This kind of finding is not limited to areas where senior citizens abound. Around the same time, a more systematic state-wide study of almost 38,000 patients at 100 hospitals, reported in the *Journal of the American Medical Association*, found that patients with the same symptoms receive more diagnostic testing when they are covered by insurance than when they are not (Wenneker, 1990). Massachusetts patients with chest pains or circulatory problems who were insured were more likely to be diagnosed or treated for heart disease than those patients without insurance or who were covered by Medicaid. Equipment and staff time are sometimes used selectively so that the procedures ordered up will yield revenues. Similarly, patients who are Medicaid eligible yield lower returns for the same diagnostic procedures as those who are insured or covered by the Medicare program and, consequently, also receive less testing.

Paralleling the extension of technology as part of the relationship with patients was the development of life-extending technology for those near death. Respirators were originally designed for and used with patients who had lung surgery, allowing these organs to recover slowly. Additional uses were found in intensive care units for this equipment, and patients who were in critical condition with multiple organ failures were placed on respirators.

Following the scholarly exposé in a major medical journal on involuntary clinical experimentation initiated by Beecher (1966), in which he cited numerous studies where patients never gave informed consent to participate in dangerous experiments, federal legislators and patient rights advocates began to wonder about how much choice patients had in undergoing clinical procedures or treatment regimens that might be futile, invasive, or even have adverse side effects. The development of informed consent for standard clinical care followed on the heels of similar protocols to protect the rights of subjects in experiments. Not surprisingly consumers began to wonder whether they were being told everything or whether doctors knew how to communicate with patients. However, it was undoubtedly the crisis of rising costs of health care that spurred medical ethicists to begin to see that patients had little choice to refuse these invasive procedures with questionable efficacy.

Now device manufacturers face harder times, as the HMOs take a close look at how much they need in the way of expensive technology. Where once technology was moved quickly into office and hospital-based practice, today providers and payers want to know what is necessary and what works (Borzo, 1996, p.4). The reduction in fee-for-service medicine, combined with third-party payment, is finally reducing the demand for new technology.

When third-party payment augments but does not replace the classic fee-for-service relationship between doctors and patients, it still means some out-of-pocket costs for routine office visits. The concept of insurance was a way to protect against major economic catastrophes that could befall a family, such as resulting from the death of the major wage earner, the loss of a home, or the loss of a business. Some consumers and a few providers became concerned about the high cost of services rendered. Models for how to rein in out-of-pocket expenditures did exist, although the American Medical Association severely disapproved of doctors who worked for a salary—the keystone of the first generation HMOs that provided comprehensive care for a single fee paid up front. Kaiser and other early health maintenance organizations delivered good services at moderate cost to the membership. And in so doing, consumers "locked in" their health care costs for an entire year through this prepayment arrangement with specific providers. Not only were doctors' services available under these plans, but hospital care was also provided for a single fee, with the provider assuming the financial risk if there was an unexpected utilization.

Ever since the 1960s employers have been concerned about controlling their expenditures for health care and have looked for ways to avoid increases in the costs of services. In addition, consumers have tried to lock in their annual costs for health care. Today in HMO programs, a group of doctors, including specialists, provide all the medical specialties and services by contract to a number of patients who will be cared for, no matter how frequently or infrequently they use the services. In addition, hospital-based services are also part of the contracted benefits and are pre-arranged by contracts between HMOs and hospitals or by outright purchase or building of hospitals exclusively dedicated to care for subscribers.

Skills learned in business schools and cost-based planning drive HMOs today. Contemporary HMOs are less likely to be staffed by salaried physicians who work in HMO-owned offices and hospitals, and are more likely to be part of a network of providers. The overcapacity of the hospital system has made it possible for HMOs to drive hard bargains with community hospitals and academic medical centers to admit their patients, when appropriate, at well below the rate charged the indemnity insurance companies.

Cost-consciousness is raised to a high art in managed care organizations. Managed care will pay for low-cost preventive medicine, early detection and treatment of disease, and health promotion activities such as smoking-cessation programs. Marketing is toward those already healthy, focusing on health promotion activities such as discounted memberships in fitness centers, rather than showing how well they care for stroke victims. It limits benefits where decision makers regard the care as pure comfort and not always medically necessary, as in the case of hospital stays for psychiatric care and unlimited psychotherapy. Care coordination for complex cases may also be part of an HMO's way of making sure that physicians do not order unnecessary care. Service substitution also takes place, as when nurse practitioners and physician assistants provide primary care under the supervision of a physician, or when outpatient care is given instead of hospitalizing the patient.

In sum, managed care means that the providers are watched carefully to make sure that they do not provide unnecessary care. Medical care is also rationed through prior authorization mechanisms, a form of micromanagement that professionals thoroughly resent. Even before a sick person gets to the point of needing some expensive specialty-based procedure, the primary-care provider is performing gate-keeping functions in the HMO, making sure that when a specialist is seen it is truly for something that the primary-care provider cannot do.

References

American Association of Health Plans. 1996. *1995–1996 AAHP HMO and PPO Trends Report*. Available: http://www.aahp.org/LI/RESEARCH.

American Medical News. 1991. "HMOs successful in big cities, old markets." *American Medical News*, February 18, p.33.

Beecher, H. K. 1966. "Consent in clinical experimentation: Myth and reality." *Journal of the American Medical Association* 195 (January 3): 34–35.

Borzo, G. 1996. "Managed care and technology assessment: Who should pay? *Technology News* (March): 3–4.

Cutting, C. 1971. Historical development and operating concepts. Pp.17–22 in Anne R. Somers, ed., *The Kaiser Permanente Medical Care Program*. New York: Commonwealth Fund.

Freeborn, D. K., and C. R. Pope. 1994. *Promise and Performance in Managed Care: The Prepaid Group Practice Model*. Baltimore: Johns Hopkins University Press.

Freudenheim, M. 1996. "Market Place: HMOs are having trouble maintaining financial health." *New York Times*, Wednesday, June 19, p. D12.

Keene, C. 1971. Kaiser Industries and Kaiser-Permanente health care partnership. Pp.13–16 in Anne R. Somers, ed., *The Kaiser-Permanente Medical Care Program*. New York: Commonwealth Fund.

New York Times. 1991a. "When doctors own their own labs." *New York Times* (August 11): E9.

Rosenberg, Charles 1987. *The Care of Strangers: The Rise of America's Hospital System*. New York: Basic Books.

U.S. Office of Technology Assessment. 1986. *Nurse Practitioners, Physician Assistants and Certified Nurse-Midwives: A Policy Analysis*. Technology Case Study 37. Washington, DC: U.S. Government Printing Office.

Wenneker, M. B. 1990. "The association of payer with utilization of cardiac procedures in Massachusetts." *Journal of the American Medical Association* 264 (10) (September 12): 1255–60; (October): 6–11.

24
The Evolution of Investor-Owned
Hospital Companies

Bradford H. Gray

Although the investor-owned hospital companies emerged in the mid-to-late 1960s, for-profit health care organizations were by no means new. In fact, early in the twentieth century half of U.S. hospitals were small proprietary institutions,[1] mostly established by doctors to provide facilities for themselves and for the community. The number of these proprietary hospitals declined throughout the century. Many closed, while others became nonprofits.[2] This decline has continued in recent years even as for-profit ownership has become more common elsewhere in health care. By 1989 only 258 independent proprietary hospitals remained in the United States, an enormous decrease from the estimated 2,400 proprietary institutions in 1910.[3]

Although the difficulty of generating profits in health care before the advent of Medicare and Medicaid undoubtedly contributed to the decline of the proprietary hospitals, other factors were also involved. Many, perhaps most, proprietary hospitals were established before technological change and improving standards (reflected, for example, in more stringent Life Safety Codes for buildings) dramatically increased the amount of capital required to establish hospitals and keep them up to date. In addition, the life span of some proprietary hospitals was linked to the professional careers of their physician-founders. In explaining the decline of proprietary hospitals in the 1940s, the American Hospital Association's director of research noted that their small size (an average of thirty-seven beds at that time) limited their ability to offer the services and facilities that modern practice demanded. He also mentioned two other explanatory factors that resonate in today's marketing-oriented, cost-competitive health care system: "the patients' appreciation of the advantages of a large, well-equipped, specialist-staffed hospital, [and] tax freedom and other immunities that give the voluntary hospital a competitive cost advantage."[4]

Reprinted by permission of the publishers from *The Profit Motive and Patient Care: The Changing Accountability of Doctors and Hospitals* by Bradford H. Gray, Cambridge, MA: Harvard University Press, copyright © 1991 by the Twentieth Century Fund.

It is not clear, however, just how important the tax advantages of the nonprofits were in explaining trends among for-profit hospitals. Much of the decline of proprietary hospitals took place at a time when corporate taxes (and, therefore, the nonprofits' advantages) were comparatively low, and much of the growth of the investor-owned hospital companies occurred during a period of relatively high corporate taxes.

The Rise of Investor-Owned Hospital Companies

In the late 1960s and 1970s the continuing decrease in the number of independent proprietary hospitals came to be mirrored by the rise of hospitals owned by investor-owned companies. The companies that came to assume dominance—American Medical International (AMI), Hospital Corporation of America (HCA), Humana, Inc., and National Medical Enterprises (NME)—either had their origins in the late 1960s or began their period of rapid growth at that time. The willingness of investors to put equity capital into health care companies was one of many consequences of the enormous infusion of federal dollars into the health care system by way of the Medicare and Medicaid programs. When added to the existing employment-related health insurance coverage, Medicare and Medicaid meant that 80 to 90 percent of the population had hospitalization insurance that either paid on the basis of hospitals' charges for services provided or reimbursed hospitals for allowable costs of services to beneficiaries.[5] It became possible for hospitals to make a great deal of money.

The growth of the hospital companies was facilitated by key details in the ways that Medicare and other "cost-paying" purchasers of care (primarily Blue Cross plans) determined allowable costs, most notably capital costs. Medicare's payments to hospitals included reimbursement for the cost of interest on borrowed funds, depreciation expenses, and, for for-profit institutions, return on equity.[6] Cost payers covered their share of institutions' capital costs; the remainder was included in the charges for which other payers reimbursed hospitals.

One consequence of Medicare's payment rules was that the flow of dollars to an institution generally increased when it was acquired by a new owner.[7] Some of this cash flow was just reimbursement for out-of-pocket expenses (interest), but much of it was for a noncash expense—depreciation—which was calculated on the basis of the purchase price. Return-on-equity payments also created additional cash flow. All of this meant that hospitals became more valuable to new owners than to sellers and stimulated acquisition activity.

The reimbursement environment from the late 1960s until the early 1980s made it difficult *not* to make money operating hospitals, so long as they were located away from concentrations of low-income populations and in states that did not regulate hospital income. As the companies prospered in this environment, their ability to grow was limited primarily by their ability to find suitable hospitals that could be acquired or locales where necessary governmental approval could be obtained for construction of new hospitals. The companies' attraction to areas with relatively high rates of population growth and low levels of regulation[8] resulted in a concentration in particular states, mainly in the South and the West. The willingness of the investor-owned hospital companies to acquire struggling hospitals and to build new hospitals even when the need for beds was marginal helps to explain why their occupancy rates have persistently been 10 to 15 percent lower than those in nonprofit hospitals.

The acquisition patterns of the hospital companies changed over time as the targets of opportunity for growth shifted. The purchase of proprietary hospitals was the primary source of the early growth of investor-owned companies.[9] Such hospitals had long been the least stable type, opening and closing with particular frequency.[10] They had been established by physician-owners for a variety of reasons—sometimes as a business venture, sometimes as a response to disputes with other hospitals, sometimes because needed facilities were not conveniently available. Given an opportunity to obtain a good price for their investment, many owners of proprietary hospitals were willing to sell.

By the early 1970s the construction of new facilities emerged as a second source of growth. Overall, 20 percent of the growth of the six largest hospital companies was eventually due to construction.[11] In some instances the opportunity for entry into a new market was a result of physician dissatisfaction with existing hospitals.[12] Construction as a source of growth peaked in the period 1970–1974.[13] The decline thereafter was probably a result of both new regulatory restrictions on entry, such as certificate-of-need requirements, and competing demands on capital which resulted from the next growth strategy—acquisition of entire companies rather than individual institutions.

The acquisition of other companies was the largest single source of growth of the surviving investor-owned firms after the mid-1970s. Some of the largest companies were acquired by others—most notably when Humana acquired American Medicorp in 1978 and when the Hospital Corporation of America (HCA) acquired Hospital Affiliates

International (HAI) in 1981. Making wholesale acquisitions of operating hospitals was inadvertently encouraged and facilitated by the Medicare capital-payment methods described earlier. The HCA-HAI transaction brought governmental attention to those policies and, as later discussion will show, led to their change in the 1980s.

The final source of hospitals for the investor-owned companies was nonprofit and public hospitals. The six major companies, which had acquired only thirty-one such institutions between 1965 and 1980, bought sixty-five between 1980 and 1984.[14] The fact that there were relatively few such acquisitions during the early growth years of the investor-owned companies was probably due less to the fact that the companies had little interest in such institutions than in the fact that such institutions were not available for sale. There was much suspicion of for-profit ownership among trustees of nonprofit hospitals and local government officials. Also, the reimbursement environment meant that the institutions that were financially strained tended to be small rural hospitals or hospitals that, because of mission or location, treated large numbers of uninsured patients. Even in a generous reimbursement environment, such hospitals were not attractive to acquisition-oriented hospital companies. Legal complications presented by the sale of nonprofit organizations' assets to for-profit organizations were also a barrier. In some cases, however, paths were found around this problem, for example, through the creation of a new nonprofit organization with the proceeds of the sale. (For example, the Wesley Foundation in Wichita, Kansas, was created with $200 million of the proceeds of the sale of Wesley Hospital to HCA in 1985.)

By the 1980s mergers and acquisitions had resulted in consolidation of many of the investor-owned companies, and few independent proprietary hospitals remained. If the growth of such companies was to continue, nonprofit or public hospitals would have to be acquired. Some such institutions were finding the regulatory and reimbursement environments to be increasingly complex and difficult, and some had capital needs that could not readily be met. The same forces led certain institutions into management contracts or multi-institutional arrangements and caused others to consider closure or sale of the facility. The investor-owned companies were still interested in growth, had capital, and had become less of an unknown factor. For the first time the companies were able to acquire institutions of real prominence in their communities.[15]

By 1983 the investor-owned hospital companies owned more than 13 percent of the general hospitals in the United States and managed another 6 percent.[16] The Hospital Corporation of America alone owned or managed 7 percent of the hospitals in the United States at one point. The merger and acquisition activity of the late 1970s and early 1980s had concentrated ownership in a handful of companies. As of September 30, 1984, 59 percent of the investor-owned hospitals were owned by six chains—Hospital Corporation of America (200 hospitals), American Medical International (115 hospitals), Humana (87 hospitals), National Medical Enterprises (47 hospitals), Charter Medical Corporation (41 hospitals), and Republic Health Corporation (24 hospitals). Many of those companies had extensive other holdings as well, such as hospital management subsidiaries, nursing homes, and ambulatory care centers.

The major companies had experienced consistent earnings increases of 20 percent or more per year, attracting large amounts of relatively inexpensive equity capital as a result. Medicare's reimbursement rules for interest expenses and depreciation effectively made debt capital cost-free. Various companies successfully sought and obtained capital through means that had never been seen before in health care—sale of stock, convertible debentures, the Eurodollar market.

The merger and acquisition activity fueled by the availability of capital created the impression that those few chains might take over the entire health care system, a prospect that many found alarming.

Executives from the investor-owned companies spoke with considerable certainty about two matters. One was that their steady increases in earnings and corporate growth were due to the managerial ability and incentives that came from their organizational form. The other was that the bulk of their business came from sources of payment that were solid and predictable. The federal government, it was said, would never be able to walk away from the Medicare program, and labor unions would never relinquish the health benefits that they had won. This meant, investors were told, that the for-profit hospital business was about as solid as anything could be.

Moreover, it was suggested that for-profit hospitals gained economic protection from the fact that most hospitals were nonprofit. This was so, the argument went, because nonprofit hospitals were less "efficient" than for-profits, and the payment environment would always have to be generous enough to accommodate them. Congress could never withstand the political heat that would come from taking actions that would harm large numbers of these important if inefficient entities. The investor-owned hospitals were swimming in the same protected waters, so investment in them could hardly be safer.

Forgotten by the early 1980s was the fact that hospitals had historically been unprofitable institutions. When the American Hospital Association (AHA) began its National Hospital Panel Survey in 1963, the average community hospital was losing $6 for every $100 of patient care revenue that it took in.[17] Even though implementation of Medicare and Medicaid reduced the loss, the average community hospital continued to report that patient care expenses exceeded patient care revenues throughout the 1960s and 1970s.[18] During that period the average hospital was able to report a positive *total* margin only because it had nonpatient revenues with which to offset the losses on patient care. The financial picture for hospitals improved steadily, if slowly, after the passage of Medicare and Medicaid, but it was not until the 1980s that the AHA reported that the average hospital generated more revenues than expenses from patient care. By 1984, when the average net patient margin reached the unprecedented level of 2 percent, the total net margin had increased to 6.2 percent of revenues.

Thus, the growth period for the investor-owned hospital sector was one of unprecedented prosperity for hospitals. As might have been expected, however, annual double-digit increases in health care costs finally produced multiple reactions by public and private third-party purchasers of care. What had not been understood before then became apparent: these companies had grown not because of managerial magic but as a result of the skilled use of the incentives that had been built into payment systems for hospitals. As those incentives were changed in the early 1980s, it became clear that the companies' growth strategies were now obsolete.

The End of the Golden Era

By the early 1980s the federal government's interest in controlling health care expenditures had led to significant changes in the flow of money to health care providers. Medicaid programs in various states also adopted methods to reduce the amounts paid for care of their beneficiaries. And, as the decade moved forward, employers began to take a wide variety of steps to control their health care costs. Attention focused particularly on hospitals as the major source of expenditures. As the payers' reforms started to hit, the largest investor-owned companies began to diversify into new lines of business and to sell more hospitals than they acquired.

Three changes in reimbursement rules and methods in the federal Medicare program contributed most heavily to these changes in strategy. The first pertained to depreciation expenses, a significant source of cash flow under Medicare's payment rules. The immediate stimulus for the change was HCA'S 1981 acquisition of the third-largest hospital chain, Hospital Affiliates International, in a complex merger transaction. HAI's fifty-four hospitals, eighteen nursing homes, and ten office buildings, a subsidiary that managed almost one hundred hospitals, and some forty other corporate entities were purchased by HCA from HAI's parent company, the Insurance Company of North America, for $425 million in borrowed cash, 5.39 million shares of stock valued at $190 million by HCA, and $270 million of HAI debt assumed by HCA. Although other large-scale acquisitions had previously taken place among the hospital companies, the HCA-HAI deal generated serious questions. After learning that Medicare costs had risen by $50 a bed per day at an HAI hospital in Richmond, Virginia, after its acquisition by HCA, Congressman Willis Gradison asked the General Accounting Office (GAO) to study the impact of HCA's acquisition of HAI on health care costs.[19] The resulting study revealed much about how Medicare capital-reimbursement policies had been fueling the growth and consolidation of the investor-owned hospital companies.

The GAO found that the interest and depreciation expenses associated with the HCA-HAI transaction had raised costs in the acquired hospitals by $55 million for the first year alone, over and above any costs that might have been associated with improvements or changes in hospitals' services or facilities.[20] HCA disputed several aspects of the GAO's analysis and conclusions[21] and argued that Medicare was paying too little for depreciation, not too much. Nevertheless, legislation was quickly passed to change the rules that had based Medicare's payment of depreciation expenses on the cost of the asset to the organization that acquired it rather than on the original cost of the asset.[22] Henceforth, Congress decided, Medicare would pay only once for the depreciation of an asset no matter how many times it changed hands.[23] This reduction in payments for depreciation expenses diminished the attractiveness of making acquisitions.

The second change, which also reduced the flow of dollars to for-profit hospitals, was in Medicare's return-on-equity (ROE) payments. The ROE formula paid hospitals a percentage of their equity each year. The percentage was originally set at 1.5 times the rate of return earned by Medicare's Hospital Insurance Trust Fund on its investments. Though long a bone of contention for nonprofit hospitals, which did not receive such payments, return on equity became a political issue when the annual percentage rate for ROE payments exceeded 20 percent owing to the high interest rates in the early 1980s.

Legislation ensued that reduced the formula by one-third—to the equivalent of the rate of return on the Trust Fund.

The third change was the passage in 1983 of Medicare's so-called prospective payment system (PPS), which replaced the cost reimbursement system that was widely seen as the primary culprit in the persistent inflation of hospital costs. Under PPS, the most significant change in the health system since the passage of Medicare, hospitals are paid on the basis of prospectively set per-case rates. Cases are defined in terms of the patient's diagnosis and other patient-related factors that affect cost (such as the patient's age or presence of complications). When paid a set amount based on which diagnosis-related group (DRG) a patient fits into, hospitals have an economic incentive to reduce their expenses, since they can keep the difference between their costs on a case and the DRG payment for that case.

The level at which the rates were first set, and the hospitals' initial success in reducing their expenses, largely by shortening hospital stays, produced an increase in the margin of profits for the average hospital.[24] With experience and mounting budgetary pressure, however, it became apparent that the PPS system not only had reversed the inflationary incentives of cost-based reimbursement but also was a vehicle of unprecedented effectiveness for Congress and the Health Care Financing Administration (HCFA) to limit Medicare's expenditures by squeezing hospitals economically.

Once PPS was implemented, the profitability of hospitals quickly became a policy concern in a way that it had never been as long as Medicare was reimbursing for allowable costs. By early 1987 several congressional hearings had been held on hospital profitability, and analyses had been carried out by the Office of the Inspector General, the Prospective Payment Assessment Commission, the American Hospital Association, and the Congressional Budget Office, among others.[25] Hospital margins on Medicare patients in the initial year under prospective payment were reported in different analyses and for different subgroups of hospitals to have ranged from 12 to 18 percent. The direct relationship between one year's decision on adjustments of Medicare payments and the next year's hospital profitability figures was there for the Health Care Financing Administration, the Office of Management and Budget, and Congress to see.

Hospital associations argued that the profitability picture had already changed in the two to three years that it had taken to compile the data. They also argued that to base yearly rate adjustments on past profitability figures would violate the spirit of the prospective payment system under which hospitals were supposed to be allowed to benefit from the profits that they could generate when paid a fixed price. Nevertheless, Congress inevitably found things on which it would rather spend tax revenues than on paying hospitals amounts that exceeded their costs by 15 or 20 percent. To justify this decision, it was argued that the high profits were never intended, that they resulted from flaws in the ways that the rates were originally set, and that they were partly a result of past inefficiencies that hospitals were only now correcting.

In any event, the reports of initially high profit margins among hospitals were an invitation for the federal government to adjust payment levels accordingly, and annual payment rate increases thereafter trailed inflation. Thus, the 30 to 40 percent of revenues from Medicare that were once seen as providing a highly secure source of income for the hospital industry became a problem with which hospitals had to cope. Rate adjustments began to constrict the profit that could be made in serving Medicare patients in acute care hospitals. The American Hospital Association reported that profit margins in the hospitals studied in its National Hospital Panel Survey had begun to "dip sharply" by 1986.[26] A study released by the Healthcare Financial Management Association in early 1987 said that patient care margins for services to all patients had dropped by 75 percent in the four years since the onset of Medicare's PPS system. The study also projected that the average hospital would lose money (down 1.1 percent) on Medicare patients in 1988.[27] (The political uses of the data on hospital profits may explain why the AHA had difficulty in collecting such data from hospitals and why it finally stopped trying to do so in its annual survey of hospitals.)

At the same time that hospital profits began to attract the attention of federal budget cutters, many other payers were developing and implementing new approaches to limiting their own expenditures for hospital care, either by reducing the use of hospitals or by cutting the amount they paid to hospitals, for example, by negotiating discounts.

The results of those actions by payers in both the public and private sectors, as well as of technological changes and changes in physicians' practice patterns, quickly became apparent in reduced hospital admissions, shorter lengths of stay, and, as a consequence, sharply lower hospital occupancy rates. Within a very few years a hospital-controlled economic environment was becoming an environment characterized by administered Medicare prices and price competition for the business of other payers.

Responses of the Investor-Owned Hospital Companies

As early as the fall of 1985 announcements began to emerge from one investor-owned hospital company after another that previously declared profit expectations were being revised downward. Since most of these companies had never reported anything but increases in earnings, this was shocking news indeed. Furthermore, as quarterly report followed quarterly report, companies announced declines from the previous year's earnings, and in some cases even showed losses. By mid-1986 the clear consensus among observers was that the era of high profitability in the business of running general hospitals had passed.

In anticipation of, or in response to, the changes in the hospital market, the major investor-owned companies all developed new strategies. Although these strategies varied from company to company, they all shared one purpose: to lessen company reliance on hospital ownership for income. Broadly speaking, two approaches have been used. One was entry into new lines of business, such as psychiatric and substance-abuse services. The second strategy was more surprising—the sale of hospitals.

By 1987 the four major companies (HCA, AMI, Humana, and NME) had all become net sellers of hospitals, owning fewer hospitals in the United States than in earlier years. Humana's net sales of hospitals began in the early 1980s. The other three companies became net sellers in 1985.[28]

Some hospitals were sold outright, usually to smaller and newer investor-owned companies. (Several of these companies subsequently experienced severe financial problems; a few have gone bankrupt.) Such sales were usually explained as reflecting a decision that a particular hospital did not fit into the company's overall plans, although it is likely that few were profitable.

Another method of selling hospitals (adopted by NME and AMI) involved the creation of separate organizational entities, called real estate investment trusts (REITs), to which hospitals were sold and then leased back by the company. This approach allowed the company to pull its capital out of hospitals while continuing to operate them.

A third method, announced by HCA in 1987, involved the "transfer" of 104 hospitals to a new company owned by employees (through an employee stock ownership plan) and by certain members of HCA's top management. This transaction left HCA with 80 acute care and 50 psychiatric hospitals, plus its management contracts in 215 hospitals.

As a result of the efforts of the hospital companies to extract themselves from hospital ownership, the six largest companies that had owned a total of 519 hospitals in the early 1980s owned only 320 by late 1987. With one exception, the companies were smaller still by 1989.

Conclusion

This brief review of the evolution of the investor-owned hospital companies shows that in the for-profit world, capital can move quickly from areas of low return to areas where higher returns are expected (or hoped for). This goes far beyond the examples that can be cited on the nonprofit side and appears to result from the accountability structure of for-profit organizations. This characteristic may be an advantage in some circumstances, but it can be a disadvantage in situations in which patient populations or groups of physicians have become dependent on the organization.

Because government will continue to be a vital source of income for providers of health services, the government's policies as payer (and also as regulator) deeply affect the return on capital invested in health care. Just as policies in public programs inadvertently created the circumstances that led to the formation of investor-owned hospital companies with billions of dollars in revenues, public policy has more recently stimulated moves in other directions. In neither case was an impact on investor ownership the goal of the policy.

The growth of investor-owned hospital companies stimulated much of the concern in the early 1980s that for-profit organizations might take over the health care system. By the middle of the decade they had halted their aggressive pattern of acquisitions, and by the end of the decade they were no longer the object of much discussion in health policy circles.

Understanding their behavior nevertheless remains vital. For-profit enterprise plays a large role in health care, with for-profit ownership either predominant or growing among many types of health care organizations. The mid-1980s found all of the major investor-owned health care companies making major strategic changes in a search for new sources of revenues. Companies continue to emerge and to seek their own niches.

Finally, the experience with for-profit hospitals has had a number of spillover effects—most obviously on the behavior of non-profit hospitals and, arguably on the assumptions of payers and regulators about the extent to which providers can be trusted.

Notes

[1] Bruce Steinwald and Duncan Neuhauser, "The Role of the Proprietary Hospital," *Law and Contemporary Problems* 35 (Autumn 1970): 817–838.

[2] Ibid.; Warren P. Morrill, "Proprietary to Nonprofit," *Trustee* 1 (October 1947): 30.

[3] Steinwald and Neuhauser, "Role of the Proprietary Hospital"; Federation of American Health Systems, *1990 Directory of Investor-Owned Hospitals, Hospital Management Companies, and Health Systems* (Little Rock: FAHS Review, 1989), p. 22.

[4] Morrill, "Proprietary to Nonprofit," p. 30.

5 Data from the 1977 National Medical Care Expenditure Survey, National Center for Health Services Research, cited in Gail R. Wilensky, "Underwriting the Uninsured: Targeting Providers or Individuals," in Frank A. Sloan, James F. Blumstein, and James M. Perrin, eds., *Uncompensated Hospital Care: Rights and Responsibilities* (Baltimore: Johns Hopkins University Press, 1986), p. 149.

[6] Return-on-equity payments, designed to compensate investors for the use of their capital, were based on a company's investment in plant, property, and equipment related to patient care plus net working capital maintained for necessary and proper patient care activities.

[7] The same dynamic stimulated sales of nursing homes. See Bruce Vladeck, *Unloving Care: The Nursing Home Tragedy* (New York: Basic Books, 1980), pp. 111–112.

[8] J. Michael Watt et al., "The Effects of Ownership and Multihospital System Membership on Hospital Functional Strategies and Economic Performance," pp. 260–289 in Bradford H. Gray, ed., *For-Profit Enterprise in Health Care* (Washington, DC: National Academy Press, 1986); Ross Mullner and Jack Hadley, "Interstate Variations in the Growth of Chain-Owned Proprietary Hospitals, 1973–1982," *Inquiry* 21 (Summer 1984): 144–151. Marmor, Schlesinger, and Smithey show similar patterns among other types of for-profits. Thus, for-profit psychiatric hospitals are disproportionately found in states whose laws mandate coverage of inpatient psychiatric services by private insurance; for-profit home health agencies are found in disproportionate numbers in states with relatively generous Medicaid programs; and for-profit dialysis centers are slightly more common in states that have special Medicaid coverage for end-stage renal disease patients. Theodore R. Marmor, Mark Schlesinger, and Richard W. Smithey, "Nonprofit Organizations and Health Care," in Walter W. Powell, ed., *The Nonprofit Sector: A Research Handbook* (New Haven: Yale University Press, 1987), p. 231.

9 Elizabeth W. Hoy and Bradford H. Gray, "Growth Trends of the Major Hospital Companies," pp. 250–259 in Gray, *For-Profit Enterprise in Health Care*, Table 5.

10 Steinwald and Neuhauser, "Role of the Proprietary Hospital," for example, found that proprietary hospitals, which represented 13 percent of community hospitals in 1968, accounted for 59 percent of hospital closures and 37 percent of openings between 1960 and 1986. One-third of all proprietary hospitals closed during that period (p. 825).

[11] Hoy and Gray, "Growth Trends," p. 253.

12 Jessica Townsend, "Hospitals and Their Communities: A Report on Three Case Studies," pp. 458–473 in Gray, *For-Profit Enterprise in Health Care*.

[13] During this period the forty-six hospitals built by the companies studied by Hoy and Gray, "Growth Trends," accounted for 35 percent of their growth; by the period

1980–1984 the twenty-seven hospitals built accounted for 11 percent of the six largest companies' growth.

[14] Hoy and Gray, "Growth Trends," p. 255.

[15] Examples include Wesley Medical Center in Wichita, Presbyterian Hospital in Oklahoma City, Presbyterian–Saint Luke's in Denver, Saint Joseph's Hospital in Omaha, University of Louisville Hospital, and Scripps Memorial Hospital in La Jolla, California.

[16] *1985 Directory of the Federation of American Hospitals* (Little Rock: Federation of American Hospitals, 1984); and American Hospital Association, *Hospital Statistics* (Chicago: American Hospital Association, 1985).

[17] Data come from the American Hospital Association, as reported in Gray, *For-Profit Enterprise in Health Care*, p. 99.

18 This does not necessarily mean that the average hospital was insolvent during this period. Many hospitals that had the ability to generate enough revenue to cover expenses tended to spend slightly beyond those revenues.

19 Comptroller General, *Hospital Merger Increased Medicare and Medicaid Payments for Capital Costs* (Washington, DC: General Accounting Office, 1983).

20 "Hospital Corp. Says GAO Report Assails Its 1981 Purchase of Health-Care Concern," *Wall Street Journal*, November 2, 1983, p. 12.

[21] "HCA Comments on GAO Study," press release, Hospital Corporation of America, Nashville, January 18, 1984. Among other things, HCA pointed to the capital gains taxes generated by the sale of HAI's assets.

[22] Section 2314 of the Deficit Reduction Act of 1984, Public Law 98–369.

[23] It should be noted that this change in policy did not address the largest source of costs in transactions such as the HCA-HAI example: interest expenses for the borrowed money. This use of Medicare money to help finance acquisition activity in health care seems likely to be addressed only when the decision is made on how to incorporate capital expenses into the rates that Medicare pays hospitals.

24 Hospital Research and Educational Trust, *Economic Trends* 2 (Spring 1986): 11. In a series of reports the Inspector General's Office in the Department of Health and Human Services called attention to the fact that the cost reports filed by hospitals showed that their profit margins on Medicare patients during the early experience with the prospective payment system (PPS) were in the vigorously healthy range of 14 to 18 percent of revenues, instead of being zero, as they supposedly had been under the cost-based reimbursement system. A later analysis by the Congressional Budget Office reported that 1984 hospital operating margins on Medicare PPS payments were 13.1 percent for urban hospitals and 6.6 percent for rural hospitals. From U.S. Congress, Senate Finance Committee, testimony by Nancy M. Gordon, Congressional Budget Office, 100th Cong., 1st sess., April 7, 1987. Total hospital margins (that is, not just on Medicare patients) were much lower (averaging approximately 5 to 6 percent) during this period.

25 Senate Finance Committee, Gordon testimony, April 7, 1987.

[26] "Net patient margin dropped by more than half, from 1.5 percent in 1985 to 0.7 percent in 1986, while total net margin fell from 6 percent to 5.1 percent." Mary Gallivan, "Margins Fall Despite Slower Inpatient Declines," *Hospitals*, May 5, 1987, p. 42. Hospital margins continued to fall, and by late in the 1980s the American Hospital Association reported that the average hospital was losing money on Medicare patients.

[27] *Hospitals*, May 5, 1987, p. 38.

[28] The 1986 and 1987 directories of the Federation of American Hospitals—which changed its name to the Federation of American Health Systems in 1987—showed that the number of U.S. hospitals owned by HCA declined from 230 in 1985 to 224 in 1986; AMI's ownership declined from 116 to 101; NME dropped from 50 to 41.

25
The Origins and Rise of Managed Care

Donald W. Light

Health care today in the United States is largely organized into plans, which consist of an insurer, who also administers the plan, and a number of contracts with physician groups, hospitals, clinics, laboratories, and other parts needed to make up a comprehensive health-care plan. These plans, like Aetna-U.S. Healthcare, compete to be selected by an employer or other purchaser and offered to employees or eligible members. While many heath-care insurers are for-profit, most of the managed-care plans rated highest in quality are not-for-profit, like Allina or Kaiser. Many people are disturbed about having their health care pitted against the pressure of the corporation to make a good profit, and by corporate managed care jeopardizing the future of academic medicine. Yet corporate managed care is so prevalent today that we often assume it is "natural" or "inevitable." Actually, few other countries with advanced health-care systems use managed care, and it is very recent in our own history. How did this sweeping transformation of American health care come about?

Professional Dominance and the Rise of Corporate Health Care

Early in the twentieth century, as scientific medicine developed, the American Medical Association and the state and county medical societies worked tirelessly to raise standards and eliminate competing sects that emphasized herbal and natural remedies, and spinal and other forms of physical manipulation, as well as numerous unschooled doctors who developed their home-brewed concoctions. By World War I they had persuaded state legislatures to pass strict licensing laws and regulatory bodies for the practice of medicine, laws prohibiting the corporate practice of medicine, and laws giving them control over prescription drugs. They fought off an early widespread effort to create national health insurance, and when unpaid bills mounted during the Depression, they created a form of health

Written especially for *Perspectives in Medical Sociology*, 3/E. Copyright © Donald W. Light, 2000.

insurance that passively reimbursed patients for their fees, so that their relationship with their patients would be as undisturbed as possible. In short, organized medicine attained legal and institutional dominance and created the American health-care system in its own image. This triumph, however, was like the warning, "Be careful what you wish for—you just might get it!"

During the 1950s, insurance coverage spread rapidly and was particularly oriented towards hospital and specialty care. Health-care costs doubled during the 1950s and tripled during the 1960s. The medical profession made sure that Medicare and Medicaid only passed after they had the same passive, specialty-oriented structure of reimbursing physician and hospital charges. Costs tripled again during the 1970s, as payers (i.e., employers and Congress) got increasingly upset.

Meanwhile, the irony of professional dominance creating protected markets for physicians with reimbursed charges was that it created investors' heaven. Corporations flourished in every medical market—hospital supply, hospital construction, medical devices, laboratories, and insurance—until the only large sector left untouched was medical service itself. The profession somehow thought that it could allow corporations to dominate every other sector of medicine without their invading health care itself. All these corporations commercialized professional judgments and decisions in numerous ways, by persuading physicians to use the medical device or drug made by a company that paid for them to go to a resort for an "educational seminar" or offered scores of other inducements. Studies showed that salespersons became a major source of new medical information for physicians.

By the 1970s, corporations invaded medical care itself, and large chains of hospitals and nursing homes developed. This greatly disturbed the medical profession. Leading physicians saw these corporations as alien invaders that threatened everything they stood for (Relman, 1980), and indeed many physicians still do not realize that the rise of corporate *providers* was an integral part of the system which the profession put in place. The irony of professional dominance was corporate dominance.

The Buyers' Revolt

During the 1960s and 1970s, all the tendencies of the professionally driven health-care system we have described increased. Finally, corporate buyers, other employers, and legislators became alarmed at the sharp rise in medical expenses and a number of related problems. The 1970s opened with a burst of criticisms against unnecessary surgery, excessive drug prescriptions, inefficient hospitals, too many specialists who did not care about the patient as a person, the lack of primary care, and the neglect of the poor despite Medicaid. From every sector of society arose cries for national health insurance and a total revamping of what was seen as a chaotic, wasteful system (Fortune, 1970; Greenberg, 1971; Ehrenreich, 1971; Bodenheimer, Cummings & Harding, 1972; Kennedy, 1972; Ribicoff, 1972). Numerous proposals for national health insurance, combined with reforms to contain costs, were made. President Nixon proposed a national network of health maintenance organizations (HMOs). Following the advice of Paul Ellwood, Nixon took these long-despised, anti-American hotbeds of "socialist medicine" and presented them as being the ideal business system that integrated all levels of care under one management and managed all aspects of health care in a cost-effective manner. This may be the greatest rhetorical reversal in the history of American health care.

The struggle for national health insurance and reform brought to the surface how deeply entrenched the American system was in a commercial, profit-making industry. Hospital supply, medical technology, and pharmaceutical companies, health insurance companies, hospitals, physicians, and the nursing home industry all mounted intensive campaigns against any bill that would slow down their growth or profits. Of course, universal health insurance would increase their markets, but it came with government regulations, if not governmental administration, that were ideologically offensive. Different groups of politicians dug in their heels over different measures. For example, a tax-based system was simply unacceptable to a significant bloc, regardless of its fairness to the working class and its much lower administrative costs. Endless politicking over amendments made the choices even more tortured. In the end, nothing passed (Davis 1975).

Meanwhile during the1970s, Congress, as the buyer behind Medicare, passed several bills to control costs through regulation. They focused on planning (Health Systems Agencies), regionalizing expensive facilities and equipment (Certificates of Need), and reviewing physicians' orders (Professional Standards Review Organizations). These and similar measures, however, lacked the powers of enforcement, and they had loopholes which health-care administrators and consultants quickly learned to exploit. By the end of the 1970s, policy makers concluded that "regulation doesn't work." It would have been more accurate to conclude that weak and partial regulation does not work. The 1970s ended with health care from the medical-industrial complex costing about three times what it had in 1970 and consuming 9.5 percent of GNP rather than 7.5 percent in 1970. Compared to people in other countries who faced similar budgetary crises and brought health-care expenditures under control, Americans were not really serious about cost containment—for those costs were the revenues to the medical-industrial complex, one of the strong growth areas in the American economy.

The legal basis of provider dominance and suppressed competition that the medical profession had so carefully built up faced new challenges. In a landmark case about the Virginia Bar Association issuing a schedule fee, the U.S. Supreme Court ruled for the first time that "learned professions" were exempt from antitrust laws (*Goldfarb* 1975). The Court even dismissed the fact that the fee schedule had been approved by the Supreme Court of Virginia and was therefore exempt as a state action. It was judged to be price fixing, plain and simple.

The Federal Trade Commission realized that the *Goldfarb* ruling applied to the practice of medicine. Within months, it began gathering evidence against medical societies and several specialty societies for restricting advertisement by members and restraining price competition (Pollard 1981). Soon the dominance of physicians and hospital administrators on Blue Cross and Blue Shield boards came under scrutiny. Laws that the medical profession had put through against the corporate practice of medicine and against prepaid health care plans came under attack. In short, the entire structure of legal protections against competitors began to crumble (Havighurst 1980; Weller 1983; Gee 1989). Moreover, many states began to pass new laws to facilitate the creation of HMOs and PPOs.

If one believes that shifts in the law usually reflect shifts in the body politic, then the *Goldfarb* case and several other key cases reviewed by the Supreme Court and other senior courts must be seen as part of the profession's fall from grace, and the rise of institutional buyers (Havighurst 1980). It also reflects the almost sacred status which competition holds in American culture. Competition is assumed in most textbooks and conversations to foster high quality at the lowest price, efficiency, productivity, democracy, and liberty. One does not hear about the cases of competition producing dislocation, waste, higher prices, inefficiency, deception, or inferior quality. The Supreme Court captured the competition ethos when it wrote:

> The Sherman act was designed to be a comprehensive charter of economic liberty aimed at preserving free and unfettered competition as the rule of trade. It rests on the premise that the unrestrained interaction of competitive forces will yield the best allocation of our economic resources, the lowest prices, the highest quality and the greatest material progress, while at the same time providing an environment conducive to the preservation of our democratic political and social institutions. (356 U.S. 4 1958)

However, evidence for competition doing all these things in health care is scant, except under quite specific circumstances (Light 1993).

During the 1980s, institutional buyers went into open revolt against the professionally driven system under the banner of "competition." Increasingly, they insured themselves and as a consequence managed the health-care services for their employees or enrollees more actively. They soon discovered facts about health care that shaped their thinking and have changed the course of medicine. First, evidence had been mounting for years that health care did not improve people's longevity much; the major factors were genetics, social class, environmental hazards and pollutants, and people's health habits. This interpretation of the evidence can be challenged, and certainly if a vice president of benefits discovered he had cancer, he would not hesitate to start intensive radiation or chemotherapy. Nevertheless, doubts about the value of medicine raised the question: What are we getting for our money?

Second, evidence had been mounting that doctors vary greatly in how much they hospitalize or operate on patients with the same kinds of problems, after controlling for many variables that might explain the differences. This further discredited the medical profession and raised the question of whether the high users were wasting other people's money and profiting from it. Given numerous studies indicating that 20–40 percent of many kinds of tests and procedures were unnecessary, buyers suspected that doctors and hospitals were running up bills for overtreatment.

Third, when employers and other buyers brought in specialists to ask them which of several treatments they should be paying for to relieve, for example, lower back pain (a rather common occupational disorder) or to treat breast cancer, they got a roomful of conflicting answers. The implication was that physicians, even board-certified specialists, did not know what worked and what did not. When employers asked their health-insurance carrier the same questions, they found that insurance companies did not have any answers either. The issues about the relative efficacy of alternate interventions are in fact subtle, but the message that buyers took away was not.

As a consequence of these rude awakenings, and the goals, values and policies of institutional buyers (summarized in figure 1), the buyers' revolt led to several new actions.

Figure 1 The Buyers' Revolt: Axes of Change in the 1980s

Dimensions	From Provider-Driven	To Buyer-Driven
Ideological	Sacred trust in doctors	Distrust of doctors' values, decisions, even competence
Clinical	Exclusive control of clinical decision making	Close monitoring of clinical decisions, their cost and efficacy
Economic	Carte blanche to do what seems best: power to set fees; incentives to specialize	Fixed prepayment or contract with accountability for decisions and their efficacy
	Emphasis on state-of-the-art specialized interventions; lack of interest in prevention, primary care, and chronic care	Emphasis on prevention, primary care, and functioning; minimize high-tech and specialized interventions
	Informal array of cross-subsidizations for teaching, research, charity care, community services	Elimination of "cost shifting" pay only for services contracted
Political	Extensive legal and administrative power to define and carry out professional work without competition, and to shape the organization and economics of medicine	Minimal legal and administrative power to do professional work but not shape the organization and economics of services
Technical	Political and economic incentives to develop new technologies in protected markets	Political and economic disincentives to develop new technologies
Organizational	Cottage industry	Corporate industry
Potential disruptions and dislocations	Overtreatment; iatrogenesis; high cost; unnecessary treatment; fragmentation; depersonalization	Undertreatment; cuts in services; obstructed access; reduced quality; swamped in paperwork
Source: Light, 1988		

Congress, as the largest buyer of all, got so frustrated that it inaugurated large-scale studies on the outcomes of alternate treatments. Employers were ready to accept any set of criteria by utilization review firms that seemed reasonable for identifying unnecessary tests and procedures. In both responsible and irresponsible ways, these initiatives meant that buyers were taking over the core clinical function of medicine, of deciding what tests and procedures were clinically useful and which patients needed which ones.

Buyers also campaigned to dismantle and reshape the laws, customs, and institutions so that buyer choice and competition could take place. No longer was there the sacred trust in physicians that prevailed up through the mid-1960s. Buyers demanded detailed accounts of what services were being rendered at what cost. To most people's surprise, providers did not know what their services actually cost (only what they *charged*) and did not have good data of the services they gave. Detailed clinical data systems are inherently intrusive; they lead to buyer control through monitoring systems. The battle over the control of data intensified. Even more significant, the demand for accountability shifted from measuring *inputs* (supplies, equipment, facilities, and medical procedures) to *outcomes* (whose patients get better faster and cheaper).

Employers also started to restructure their contracts to cover all or large portions of health-care services. What they sought were organized provider groups that would bid on a package for a price and then deal with these issues of excessive and unnecessary services. This prompted providers to restructure into forms that offered coordinated care. Large group practices, joint ventures between hospitals and physician groups, managed-care systems, and many other kinds of organizational arrangements emerged. The practice of medicine began to change from cost-plus treatment to results-oriented managed care.

Medicare and the Power of Buyer Dominance

Meanwhile, Medicare was by far the largest institutional buyer, and its administrators at HCFA (the Health Care Financing Authority) sponsored a wide range of research projects and experiments in payment schemes, competitive delivery systems, and methods for monitoring costs. Behind them, as the voice of taxpayers, Congress has steadfastly pressed them to find ways to keep Medicare expenses from rising so fast that they would bankrupt the Medicare Trust Fund. Using its capacity as a dominant buyer to make long-term investments in research and development, HCFA funded a project for over ten years at Yale to design a system for allocating resources within hospitals by diagnostically based utilization rather than by procedure. A bold commissioner of health in New Jersey, Joanne Finlay, proposed using this system to pay hospitals—a radical departure from the way that hospitals had ever been paid, but one that promised to reward hospitals for getting a job done within budget rather than for doing as many procedures as possible. With the support of HCFA, New Jersey imposed this radical payment system by diagnosis related groups (DRGs) on almost all of its hospitals (Widman & Light 1988), and in 1983 Congress adopted a stricter version of this system for paying hospitals for Medicare patients. Called the prospective payment system (PPS), the federal version meant that when a patient was admitted, Medicare knew in advance that they would pay only a fixed amount, unless it was a costly outlier. Given Medicare's dominance in the market, almost all hospitals agreed to comply. Subsequently, insurance companies, large employers, and large health-care systems adopted it.

PPS had a tremendous impact on the hospital industry and on the health care system in general. Hospital administrators seemed so concerned about PPS that they quickly cut staff, reduced inventory, and had briefing sessions with physicians to encourage shorter stays. They established internal monitoring systems to weed out or re-educate those providers who ran up expenses with too many tests or procedures. Secondary industries arose around maximizing payments and around clinical management systems. Profits (or surpluses) subsequently reached an all-time high, but the era of dehospitalization had begun. Congress responded to the profits by paying less. They did not give the hospitals an increase as large as overall medical inflation until 1989. As a result, profits and surpluses quickly dropped to razor-thin levels, and many hospitals ran deficits. Admissions and length of stay continued to decline.

Medicare and HCFA have developed stronger, more unified programs than the private sector in other areas as well. They restructured and strengthened a national network of peer review organizations and developed specific targets of overuse in each region of the nation. They made another long-term investment in developing a relative value scale based on actual costs of training, time, and resources for paying physicians. The resulting payment system, RBRVS, is the first nationally used fee schedule in the United States. Finally, Medicare and HCFA have steadfastly sponsored research on risk factors and how to adjust payments to providers for the risks of their patients.

Each of these tools for cost management is rife with politics and controversy, making it is easy to forget from an historical perspective what large advances they were. Medicare has also been slow to develop and structure managed-care contracts in a sensible way; so that in the mid-1990s it is the object of severe criticism. But for twenty years, Medicare led the private sector in cost controls and developed several tools for controlling costs.

Ironically, these strong measures were taken in the name of "competition" under Ronald Reagan. Yet they constituted "the most intrusive government intervention since Medicare . . . by the most conservative President since Herbert Hoover" (Goldfield 1994:78). One could see the same irony in strong actions taken by large companies that dominated their local markets. Americans believe deeply in competition, but when as buyers they can use their anti-competitive muscle, they will. Likewise, competitive sellers will dominate or control their markets when they can do so in the name of competition. Alan Maynard (1993:195), the leading health economist in Britain, where belief in competition is less ideological, points out that the goal of capitalists is to "ensure that they restrict competition, maintain market share and enhance profits: capitalists always and everywhere are the enemies of capitalism!"

The Rise of Managed-Care Systems

Besides developing the DRG and RBRVS systems as powerful forms of fiscal management, the federal government strongly supported HMOs. At the time, HMOs were proclaimed to deliver all health care for 10–40 percent less money than fee-for-service providers and hospitals, and the HMO Act of 1973 *required* employers to offer HMOs as an alternative to regular health insurance (Falkson 1980). One might call this forced competition, but it did create a national market for cost-effective managed-care systems.

The medical and hospital lobbies also weighed the HMO Act down with requirements and stipulations that became burdens to growth, and by the early 1980s the Act was considered an obstacle to HMO development—another example of how government regulations keep private markets from developing cost-effective delivery systems. But in fact it was an example of private practitioners using the government to advance their (anti-competitive) goals—it was the beneficiaries of the cost-plus private market that loaded up the HMO Act with obstructive regulations.

Besides offering HMO options and fostering other forms of managed care, employers increasingly limited their premium contribution for benefits and then let each employee choose from a "cafeteria" of alternate-benefit health plans that varied in choice, coverage and price. That is, employers increasingly went from "defined *benefit*," which guaranteed a certain level of coverage for health care (usually very comprehensive), to "defined *contribution*," which only guaranteed a certain amount of money for health insurance and other benefits. While the "cafeteria plan" approach gave the employee great choice and fostered intense competition among providers, it protected the company from the relentless increase in health care premiums. Employees thought the cafeteria plans were giving them more benefits, when in the long run they were getting less. In this context, managed-care systems that had few or no charges to patients became increasingly attractive.

During the 1970s, both HMOs and employers pressed for amendments and changes in administrative rules that would make HMOs more competitive. One can see a gradual relaxing of requirements right on through the 1980s to allow HMOs to respond to a wide array of market demands by employers. In addition, PPOs (preferred provider organizations) were invented to provide still more alternatives and flexibility. Essentially, a PPO is any group of providers who agree to discounted fees in return for an employer giving employees incentives to use them. Typically, an employer would cover through health insurance all or most of treatment by a PPO, but if the employee chose another physician, s/he would pay anything billed above that discount level.

Through the 1980s, the boundaries between PPOs and HMOs began to blur. On one hand, some PPOs agreed to capitated payments, like HMOs. On the other hand, some HMOs did not provide comprehensive care but were targeted to certain types of medical service, like PPOs. The basic point, however, is that buyers from Medicare on down to mid-sized companies in local markets were hiring managed-care companies to tell providers what services they wanted and what prices they thought were reasonable. The buyers' market was greatly aided by a surplus of sellers, that is, by an excess number of hospital beds and an increase in physicians that greatly exceeded population growth.

Paradoxically, these managed-care systems, and competition between them and traditional medical services, did not save money. While business leaders proclaimed success at using competition to end professional dominance and spiraling costs, HMOs were attracting healthier employees and shadow-pricing the premiums for traditional plans. This meant healthy profits for the HMOs and rising costs for employers as they paid for their sicker employees (or dependents) in the open-ended traditional plan. The syndrome feeds on itself: the more sicker employees got left in the traditional plan, the faster its premiums would rise, and thus the faster HMO premiums could rise as a slightly lower shadow price, and the more the employer would pay overall. When the dust settled, the costs of health benefits had risen as fast in the 1980s as in the 1970s, despite the greatest effort in history to use competition in health care.

Crisis and Paradigm Shift in Health Insurance

Several aspects of the buyer's revolt shook the health insurance industry and forced it to rethink its purpose—even what business it was in. After enjoying several decades of an expanding market, the health-insurance industry found itself facing a saturated market in the 1970s. Getting new business meant taking it away from a competitor, and the use of risk selection expanded (Light 1992). When employers started to self-insure, insurance companies not only faced a shrinking market but were also reduced to being third-party administrators. No longer did they hold huge reserves of funds on which they could earn investment income. Rather, they became little more than claims processors.

Certain insurers took the lead in redefining their business and their services by developing managed-care services. Initially, some of them served as packagers who would put together a health-care network for a large employer. They also developed capacities to do prospective, concurrent and retrospective utilization review, to do quality assessment, and to assess providers. During the 1980s, these skills and capacities came together to form a paradigm shift from writing insurance to owning or operating managed-care systems. Profits, they discovered, were much greater for them as middlemen who could keep the difference between premiums and the deep discounts they could extract from providers. The surplus of doctors and hospitals has meant that each year they could drive down what they paid providers still further. Given that contracts in these systems pass nearly all the risk on to the providers, the new business and its sources of profit have little to do with traditional insurance.

National Health Care Reform as a Watershed?

After twenty years of buyers' efforts through competition and direct efforts at regulating medical practices, the United States was the only first-world nation that still had not restrained the health-care costs of the medical-industrial complex (MIC). Rather, revenues to the MIC (and costs to citizens) had risen from $75 billion or 7.6 percent of GNP in 1970, to $250 billion or 9.2 percent of GNP in 1980, to $666 billion or 12.1 percent of GNP in 1990 (Burner, Waldo & McKusick 1992). Employers' costs equaled 100 percent of their post-tax profits. Meanwhile, fewer and fewer working people had health insurance. The "inverse coverage law" of private health insurance (Light 1992) meant that through exclusion clauses, coverage limits, waiting periods, and reimbursements limited to what the insurance company determines are "reasonable" or "customary" or "prevailing" charges, those with insurance who most needed comprehensive coverage had less coverage.

Dismantling the legal, institutional and economic features built earlier in the century to minimize price competition and cost containment by institutional buyers has been slow. Through the 1980s and into the 1990s, medical schools still trained largely specialists and provided leadership for the entire profession in state-of-the-art clinical medicine, subspecialization, and new technology—the core values of the professional model and a chief cause of escalating costs (Light 1989). Licensing and certification rules form a battlement around this core of the professionally driven health-care system. The high pay to physicians and great differential between pay for surgeons and pay for primary-care physicians remained largely in place. Despite notable savings by some large corporations in some places, the spiraling cost of health care did not slow down, even though politicians proclaimed that it did (Light 1994).

Almost twenty years after everyone demanded national health insurance and reform, everyone demanded it once again. The range of reform proposals was much narrower than twenty years earlier, so that Clinton's 1993 proposal was less comprehensive than Nixon's in 1971 (Goldfield 1994). Nevertheless, 1993 felt like 1973, because the institutional and economic structure of the health-care system that had been set during the first half century created entrenched interests against reform. The only difference was that the size of the medical-industrial complex was much greater, and the corporations involved had much more to lose. The major beneficiaries would be the large insurance companies and the managed-care corporations, because all the major reform bills except McDermott-Wellstone would place the nation's health care in their hands. By the end of 1993, however, they realized that the Clinton plan, at least, would close up the loopholes they were so profitably exploiting, and they turned against it. They realized they could do better without it.

Once again, ideological convictions played a major role. Some parties again wanted only a tax-based system; others passionately opposed a tax-based system. Some thought that government intervention was essential to make health care fair and cost-effective; others thought only private markets could do that. The lobbying effort was far larger than in 1973, with far more distorted and erroneous information (Kolbert 1995; Carlson & McLeod 1994; Reinhardt 1995). Most interesting is that employers opposed bills that would relieve them from spiraling costs. Insiders claim that employers' opposition was due to three factors. First, employers are wedded to the 50 percent tax break they get on health benefits, even though every economist agrees tax-exempt benefits have been a powerful engine driving costs up. Second, national reform would greatly reduce the size and power of corporate benefits departments, and their directors were the chief advisers to their presidents and chairmen. Third, employers wanted to keep control of benefits as a way to control labor, even though the cost of that control had risen from 50 percent to 100 percent of after-tax profits. This thinking is oddly American, for employers in no other industrialized country want to add the headaches of health benefits to the complexities of running their businesses. To put it another way, health benefits is itself a big business inside of big business.

A long view leads one to conclude that the Clinton reform effort was not a watershed but rather one more turn in the cycle of spiraling costs and shrinking coverage leading to demands for reform that threaten the institutional, economic and ideological sources of these opposing tendencies.

Corporate Medicine in a New Guise

The Clinton reforms seemed to have accelerated efforts by managed-care companies and insurance companies born again as managed-care corporations to buy, build, merge, and otherwise attain market control as oligopolies or monopolies in their principal markets before any die were cast. Thus, in the 1990s, things looked different. As the drive for national health reform was collapsing, managed-care corporations and insurance companies made a fierce and successful effort to win deep discounts and drive down hospital admissions and bed days per thousand. In areas where they had high market penetration, they succeeded and saved billions of dollars. These savings, however, went largely to executive officers, management teams, and investors' profits, not to the employers and employees who foot the bill.

Employers in a few areas have empowered their health-care coalitions to do collective buying; but this is hard to do when each employer has a somewhat different health plan, is structured in a somewhat different way, and has a different board of directors. As always, a few large buyers report impressive savings for themselves, but how much these savings are being shifted to others is unknown. One needs to look at declines in real (inflation-adjusted) growth for an entire region, not just for the big buyers.

In short, the principal force behind reducing use and cost in the 1990s has been for-profit middlemen and packagers as agents of employers. Princeton professor of health economics Uwe Reinhardt characterizes them as "bounty hunters." Once national health insurance collapsed, employers in effect hired managed-care companies and paid them a handsome bounty to go out and shoot down as many costs as they could! Many of the major HMO corporations actually provide no health care. These are the new-breed HMOs that are *packagers*, not health-service organizations. They take fixed premiums in the front door, pay provider groups under deep-discount contracts out the back door, and keep 13–23 percent for themselves. Managerial and marketing costs are high, but there was plenty left for profits in the early years.

Corporate managed care worked, or so it seemed, and by the mid-1990s business leaders were celebrating its success as their premium increases slowed from 12–16 percent a year, a decade earlier, to only 0–2 percent. A more sober analysis would start by noting that underlying general inflation had greatly slowed down to 2–3 percent a year. Since health-care costs tend to increase 50 percent faster, a slowdown to 3–4.5 percent would have happened just because of this one factor. In addition, when employers cracked down on medical inflation, they also began to reduce coverage and to make employees pay more and more of their premiums and bills. This cost shifting can give the false impression that cost increases are being controlled. A third factor is that premiums tend to fluctuate for about three years more than actual costs and then for about three years less than actual costs, and the mid-1990s were a temporary period during which premiums were increasing less than costs. When you add all these up, it becomes much less clear that the bounty hunters were really shooting down costs, even if premium increases had dropped to nearly zero. Harvard's health economist, Joseph Newhouse, saw little evidence of expenditures slowing down (Huskamp & Newhouse 1994). Rather, most of the 30 percent discounts that the managed-care companies negotiate from providers just about matched what they kept. In other words, the managed-care revolution of the 1990s may have been largely a matter of managed-care corporations transferring billions of dollars from doctors, nurses, hospitals and other providers to themselves and their investors.

Three-quarters of the new HMOs are for-profit, and consolidation has led to ten firms controlling 70 percent of the HMO market. In mature metropolitan markets like San Francisco, Los Angeles, or Minneapolis, five or fewer firms dominate the market. The larger they are, the deeper discounts they can negotiate, the more reserves they have to drive out smaller competitors, and the more political clout they have to structure markets to their advantage.

Even more than the early HMOs, which ended up with healthier patients through self-selection, the new breed used tactics that defy regulation to avoid sicker subscribers. According to two physician-researchers, they "place sign-up offices on upper floors of buildings with malfunctioning elevators; refuse contracts to providers in neighborhoods with high rates of HIV infection (an example of medical redlining); structure salary scales to assure a high turnover among physicians—the longer they are in practice, the more sick patients they accumulate; provide luxurious services (even exercise club memberships) for the well, and shabby inconvenience for those with expensive chronic illnesses [so that they will disenroll]" (Woolhandler & Himmelstein 1994:586).

Given that just 10 percent of the population consumes 72 percent of all medical costs, risk avoidance is the quickest and easiest way to make money. "As a result, society pays twice: once for the high-risk people concentrated in high-cost plans, and again for the excess profits in plans that succeed in risk selection" (p. 586). Meantime, the number of people with no insurance kept rising by about one million per year from the late 1980s into the twenty-first century. Given the economic boom of the 1990s and high employment rates, it would appear that employers are walking away from their historic role of providing health-care insurance, even with the inducement of writing off premiums as a tax-deductible business expense. This form of corporate welfare is worth about $110 billion a year, easily enough to provide health insurance to all the uninsured.

By the end of the 1990s, discounting prices paid to physicians, hospitals, and other providers had run its course, and profits of managed-care companies dropped sharply. The question, then, is whether they will extract profits from direct clinical services. Evidence indicates that this is happening already. A national survey of all managed-care enrollees found that they were 2.5 times more likely to rate the quality of services as just fair or poor, and over four times more likely to rate their doctors as fair or poor compared to enrollees in traditional plans (Commonwealth 1995). Remarkably, people in managed-care plans were just as likely to report not having a regular source of care, not getting preventive services, and post-poning needed care—the very problems that managed care is sup-posed to solve. Concerning access, managed-care enrollees were much more likely to rate ease of changing doctors, choice of doctors, access to emergency care, and waiting time as only fair or poor. Forty percent had to change their doctors when they joined their current managed-care plan. Discontinuity of care was directly related to dis-satisfaction. Yet employers and employees are constantly pressured by plans to switch for short-term gains or inducements.

A more telling 1995 survey sponsored by the Robert Wood Johnson Foundation (RWJ 1995) focused only on patients sick enough to be seeing a specialist. Compared to those in traditional unmanaged care, sick patients in managed care were 3.3 times more likely to report that they received inappropriate care, 4.0 times more likely to report that their examination was not thorough, 2.5 times more likely to report they had inadequate time with their physician, and 2.1 times more likely to report that the doctor did not care. The out-of-pocket expenses of these sick patients were not zero, as many imagine to be the case in managed-care systems, but $1,502. This is only slightly less on average than the out-of-pocket expenses of sick patients in fee-for-service care ($1,735). The picture that emerges is that managed-care corporations are already providing worse care for the sick for very little savings to either employers or employees in return for high salaries, large management expenses, and high profits.

The Rhetoric vs. Reality of Competition in Health Care

American business leaders and politicians continue to believe unquestioningly in the power of competition to make health care effi-cient and hold down costs. They always refer to the "free market," although no market is free. Even the market for street vendors is structured by city ordinances, informal but powerful rules about ter-ritory, and norms about practices. In fact, health-care markets are among the most structured and least free of any on earth. Moreover, competition was widely regarded as impossible in health care until the current period, because there are so many problems of market failure in health care as outlined in figure 2 (Light 1993).

Figure 2 Conditions for Beneficial Competition vs. Conditions in Health Care

Conditions for Beneficial Competition	Conditions in Health Care
1. Many buyers and sellers	1. Few buyers and/or sellers
2. No relation to each other	2. Close, long ties
3. Can purchase from full array of providers	3. Often only a selected array
4. No barriers to enter or exit	4. Very high barriers to entry and exit
5. Full information on prices, quality, services	5. Partial, incomplete, untrustworthy data
6. Information is free	6. Information is costly
7. Buyers seek greatest gain/best deal available	7. Buyers often don't seek much
8. Market signals quick; markets clear quickly	8. Market signals and market change slow, muddled
9. Price conveys all that buyers need to know	9. Price conveys little that buyers need to know
10. No externalities; buyers experience consequences of their choices fully	10. Extensive externalities, often by construction
Source: Light, 1998	

There is little evidence that competition can really save money after biased selection, cost shifting, and significantly higher transaction costs are taken into account. It seems like once again the United States is not learning how to contain costs from nations that have done so without sacrificing high-quality care for everyone, but rather has come up with another policy innovation that will not achieve its stated goals. Health care will continue to take money from education, housing, industrial development, and welfare as it consumes an increasing percentage of state and federal budgets.

What makes American health-care policy fascinating is that alongside an undying faith in competition, employers and the government impose unilateral changes that are anti-competitive just to be sure competition works! The Reagan administration, for example, talked about the Prospective Payment System as being "competitive," but it was basically price fixing on a grand scale, and it worked. Just to be sure competition works, employers are cutting benefits. We have already described the continued thinning of coverage for working Americans, and the number with no insurance is rising by about a million a year.

Congress is acting out the same ironic syndrome. On one hand, they are rapidly pushing the elderly and the poor into managed-care systems, while on the other hand, they are poised to make historically large cuts in the budgets for both Medicare and Medicaid. Put these together and it means that for-profit organizations with an unclear track record of saving money but a good track record of making money are in charge of rationing health care for the elderly and the poor to fit within reduced budgets. But even more interesting is the conflict between buyer dominance and competition as two different strategies for keeping costs in line. Strong restraining actions by monopoly *buyers* are as anti-competitive as are restraining actions by sellers, even though the buyers may say they are fostering competition.

Given all the difficulties in creating competitive conditions in health care, competition also fits health care poorly because a competition strategy may destroy professional altruism, commercialize medical care for the sick, and induce providers to play elaborate games in the marketplace without saving much money. Is it buyer dominance we want or competition? And if the answer is competition, are we ready for the change from buyer dominance to provider dominance as the baby-boom generation grows old and the current surplus of doctors becomes a shortage?

My own analysis is that we are in the middle of a shakedown period in which there is fierce competition between managed-care systems for control of large markets in each region. Most of the "savings" will go to the 15–30 cents they take out of every premium dollar to run their systems. But in the end, there will be only a few major health-care corporations in most metropolitan or regional markets, and as oligopolies they will not compete much on price. Overall savings occurred largely during the shakedown period, and the United States will be stuck with ever hungrier, multibillion-dollar corporations in control.

On the positive side, the managed-care corporations will have cut out (with a hatchet) more fat, faster, than any other approach, and they will have put a large percentage of Americans into capitated delivery systems. They will have restructured the medical profession towards primary care and hospitals towards community care. That is, the excesses of professional dominance over the past sixty years will have been greatly reduced. Does this mean that the medical profession is becoming deprofessionalized or proletarianized, as John McKinlay and others contend (McKinlay & Arches, 1985; Haug, 1973; 1975)? That is a question which requires separate treatment (Light & Levine, 1989; Light, 1995).

These changes are very useful for universal health insurance, if Congress decides to do it. In fact, an obvious question may arise: why pay these corporations 15–30 percent to run managed-care systems when a universalized version of Medicare would cost less than 5 percent to run? In fact, as profits thin out, the corporations running the managed-care systems may be happy to get out of the business and do something else. If something like this happens, then the American health-care system will end up having close to an ideal structure for maximizing people's health and dealing with the tidal wave of chronic disease disorders that will roll in with the twenty-first century.

Acknowledgments

This essay is based on a policy research project to analyze the restructuring of American health care and its consequences for society. Support is gratefully acknowledged from The Twentieth Century Fund. I also wish to thank Howard Freeman, Sol Levine, Odin Anderson, Theodore Litman, and Adrian Wagner for their suggestions and critical remarks.

References

Bodenheimer, Tom, Steve Cummings, & Elizabeth Harding, eds. 1972. *Billions for Bandaids*. San Francisco: Medical Committee for Human Rights.

Bruner, S. T., Waldo D. R., & McKusick D. R. 1993. "National Health Expenditures Projections through 2030." *Health Care Financing Review* 14:1–29.

Carlson, E. & D. McLeod. 1994. "The 'Big Lie' vs. Health Reform: Direct-mail Firms 'Raised Millions' with Scare Letters." *AARP Newsletter* 35(1) Nov. 9.

Commonwealth (The Commonwealth Fund). 1995. *Managed Care: The Patient's Perspective*. New York: The Commonwealth Fund.

Davis, Karen. 1975. *National Health Insurance: Benefits, Costs, and Consequences*. Washington, DC: The Brookings Institution.

Ehrenreich, Barbara & John Ehrenreich. 1971. *The American Health Empire: Power, Profits and Politics*. New York: Vintage.

Falkson, Joseph L. 1980. *HMOs and the Politics of Health System Reform*. Chicago: American Hospital Assn. and Robert J. Brady Co.

Fortune. January 1970. Special issue, "Our Ailing Medical System."

Gee, M. Elizabeth. 1989. FTC Antitrust Actions in Health Care Services. Washington, DC: Federal Trade Commission, typescript.

Goldfarb v. Virginia State Bar 95 S. S. Ct. 2004 (1975).

Goldfield, N. 1994. "The Looming Fight over Health Care Reform: What We Can Learn from Past Decades. *Health Care Management Review* 19(3):70–80.

Greenberg, Selig. 1971. *The Quality of Mercy: A Report on the Critical Condition of Hospital and Medical Care in America*. New York: Atheneum.

Haug, Marie. 1973. "Deprofessionalization: An Alternate Hypothesis for the Future." *Sociological Review Monograph* 20:195–211.

———. 1975. "The Erosion of Professional Authority: A Cross-cultural Inquiry in the Case of the Physician." *Milbank Memorial Fund Quarterly/Health and Society* 54: 83–106.

Havighurst, Clark C. 1980. "Anti-Trust Enforcement in the Medical Services Industry: What Does It All Mean?" *Milbank Memorial Fund Quarterly* 58:89–123.

Huskamp, H. A. & Newhouse, J. P. 1994. "Is Health Spending Slowing Down?" *Health Affairs* 13(5):32–38.

Kolbert, E. 1995. Special Interests' Special Weapon: A Seeming Grass-Roots Drive Is Quite Often Something Else. *New York Times* March 26:20.

Kennedy, Edward. 1972. *In Critical Condition*. New York: Simon & Schuster.

Light, Donald W. 1986. "Corporate Medicine for Profit." *Scientific American* 255(6):38–45.

———. 1988. "Toward a New Sociology of Medical Education." *Journal of Health and Social Behavior* 29:307–322.

———. 1992. "The Practice and Ethics of Risk-Rated Health Insurance." *Journal of the American Medical Association* 267:3503–3508.

———. 1993. "Escaping the Traps of Postwar Western Medicine." *European Journal of Public Health* 3:223–231.

———. 1994. Medical Prices Outrun the Rate of Inflation. *The New York Times* Feb. 18: A23.

———. 1995. "*Homo Economicus*: Escaping the Traps of Managed Competition." *European Journal of Public Health* 5.

Light, Donald W. & Sol Levine. 1989. "The Changing Character of the Medical Profession." *The Milbank Quarterly* (forthcoming).

Maynard, A. 1993. "Competition in the UK National Health Service: Mission Impossible?" *Health Policy* 23:193–204.

McKinlay, John and Joan Arches. 1985. "Toward the Proletarianization of Physicians." *International Journal of Health Services* 15(2):161–195.

Pollard, Michael R. 1981. "The Essential Role of Antitrust in a Competitive Market for Health Services." *Milbank Memorial Fund Quarterly* 59:256–268.

Reinhardt, Uwe E. 1995. "Turning Our Gaze from Bread and Circus Games." *Health Affairs* 14(1):33–36.

Relman, A. S. 1980. "The New Medical-Industrial Complex." *The New England Journal of Medicine* 303(17): 963–970.

Ribicoff, Abraham with Paul Danaceau. 1972. *The American Medical Machine*. New York: Saturday Review Press.

Rosner, David. 1982. *A Once Charitable Enterprise: Hospitals and Health Care in Brooklyn and New York, 1885–1915*. New York: Cambridge University Press.

Rosoff, Arnold J. 1984. "The 'Corporate Practice of Medicine' Doctrine: Has Its Time Passed?" *Health Law Digest* 12(12) Supplement.

Rothstein, William G. 1972. *American Physicians in the 19th Century: From Sects to Science*. Baltimore: The Johns Hopkins University Press.

RWJ (The Robert Wood Johnson Foundation). 1995. "Sick People in Managed Care Have Difficulty Getting Services and Treatment, New Survey Reports." Princeton, NJ: News from the Robert Wood Johnson Foundation.

Weller, Charles D. 1983. "The Primacy pf Standard Anti-Trust Analysis in Health Care. *Toledo Law Review* 14:609–637.

Widman, Mindy & Donald W. Light. 1988. *Regulating Prospective Payment*. Chicago: Health Administration Press.

Woolhandler, Steffie & David U. Himmelstein. 1994. "Clinton's Health Plan: Prudential's Choice." *International Journal of Health Services* 24:583–592.

26
What Is Driving Health System Change?

Lynn Etheredge, Stanley B. Jones, and Lawrence Lewin

Introduction

Trying to understand what is going on in the rapidly changing U.S. health care system, and why, is a daunting challenge. Any assessment must be partial and open to differing experiences and views. Both the public and private sectors need to better understand the drivers of health system change—and their implications. In this paper we nominate our candidates for key motivators of change in each of four health care sectors: employers, health plans, providers, and consumers. These candidates were identified through our own experience and, in particular, with the assistance of a group of leading health care experts who met to discuss drivers of change. We invite others to contribute their views as well.

An Evolving, Imperfect Market

The dynamics of health system change today are quite different from those of recent decades. During the period of open-ended, fee-for-service insurance payments, factors such as technology, demographics, physician and hospital supply, and physician decision making were usually identified as key drivers of change. Today's dynamics involve a new set of powerful influences such as the purchasing power of buyers vis-à-vis providers, the role of price competition, the managed care industry and its practices, the drive for market share, assumption of insurance risk, the impact of investment capital, and new roles of employers and patients. This does not mean that health care today approaches any theoretically desirable market system, nor that its consequences are all desirable. Indeed, today's health care market is flawed by the inability to measure quality (value) and by inadequate social cost financing, and it is mostly driven by socially amoral economic forces.

In this paper we describe the new, fundamental forces of change

Published by *Health Affairs*, 15(4) (Winter, 1996), pp. 93–101. Copyright © 1996, The People-to-People Health Foundation, Inc., Project HOPE. http://www.projhope.org/HA

for employers, health plans, providers, and consumers and identify trends that will shape future changes. We discuss government's role, as well as possible "wild cards" that could emerge as important influences. Although we recognize that there are differences among local health care markets, we aim here to present a generalized description to highlight fundamental market forces. A "terrain map" to illustrate the paradigm shifts at work was used in the group discussion for this paper (see appendix).

Employers/Purchasers

Private-sector employers have become key drivers of health system change. They have achieved this influence by shifting their purchasing power from paying for open-ended, fee-for-service health insurance benefits to buying health care, on a capitated basis, from managed care plans. The percentage of workers in private firms who are enrolled in some form of managed care grew from 29 percent in 1988 to 70 percent in 1995.[1] Employers now have a firm conviction that enormous savings are possible in health spending without reducing quality of care. They now expect (and demand) that rather than the annual double-digit premium increases of the insurance era, managed care premiums should fall, or rise only modestly. This strategy has succeeded in slowing the rise of national health care costs to its lowest rate in three decades. [2]

Health Plan Purchasing Strategies

Employers drive the health care market through a tough, price-focused competitive process to select the plans offered to workers. Most employees (48 percent) have only a single plan available or may choose among only two plans (23 percent) or three plans (12 percent). In this environment, health plans must control their health care spending; price competition is intense and effective. A recent Department of Labor study indicated that employer health benefit spending rose only 0.1 percent from June 1995 to June 1996.[3]

Employee Satisfaction

Employers seek, through a number of strategies, to allay workers' concerns about plans that are too restrictive. Many employers select health plans with out-of-network options, which has made such plans the fastest-growing insurance product. Larger employers, with more geographically dispersed and diverse employees, also tend to offer a greater choice of plans; smaller employers offer fewer choices. The need for cost control has driven employers away from purchasing fee-for-service insurance, while the need to satisfy their workers is driving them away from purchasing tight, closed-panel health maintenance organization (HMO) plans. The employer health plan market is now filling in with a whole continuum of health plan options.

Employers' new purchasing strategies, with their price-based selection of health plans, are driving changes throughout the health system, in both organization of care and cost cutting. By purchasing from health plans, employers accord plans great influence over health care providers.

Future Influences

We expect price (premium)–driven purchasing by employers to dominate the health care system for the foreseeable future. Employers also will make use of better information and watch the effectiveness of new purchasing strategies.

First, better information for employers will give them a basis for more sophisticated purchasing of health care. Employers would like to go beyond price-based comparisons to purchase health plans on the basis of value added, such as improved health and productivity of their workforce. The National Committee for Quality Assurance's (NCQA's) accreditation and the Health Plan Employer Data and Information Set (HEDIS) are widely viewed as steps in the right direction. But these indicators still leave many aspects of quality unmeasured and a large burden for consumers and purchasers to carry in trying to assess quality. Only as better measures of value are available will employers have a persuasive basis for purchasing health care other than by price comparisons.

Second, pragmatism may lead to new purchasing arrangements. Employers have evolved their purchasing strategies mostly by emulating the successes of leading companies. In many areas, excessive hospital overuse and excessive specialists' incomes remain a problem. In other areas, employers are already questioning whether there is much value added from health plans beyond their ability to aggregate purchasing power and impose unsophisticated utilization controls.

Employer initiatives that will be watched include direct contracting and health care purchasing alliances. Large employers in the Twin Cities market are now aggregating their purchasing power through a business purchasing coalition and are seeking direct contracts with organized delivery systems; this purchasing strategy bypasses managed care plans, with their large overheads and profits. Providers' interest in fostering such arrangements is reflected in the "provider service network" options included in recent Medicare reform legislation. Most large employers already "carve out" mental health and pharmacy services to specialized benefit management firms.

Employers also are evolving ways to make better use of purchasing alliances and multi-employer purchasing arrangements. These organizations offer greater purchasing power than individual companies offer alone; they can be particularly attractive options for small firms. Larger firms, if they judge that a more effective health plan market has been created by such mechanisms, may disengage from their own purchasing efforts and allow workers to purchase through such arrangements.

Health Plans

As health plans compete in the new employer market for managed care, price competition drives their business strategies. Pressures and uncertainties of the market require plans to prepare to quote future prices that are lower than those they offer today.

This price discipline is driven by competitors as well as by employers. New health plans employ aggressive pricing to get started in the market; existing insurers must respond to hold on to market share. A substantial market share enhances a health plan's negotiating leverage with providers and is a telling factor in its success or failure vis-a-vis competitors. Indeed, price competition among health plans that are seeking to gain market share is getting tougher, as early gains at the expense of fee-for-service insurers are now giving way to a market fight among managed care plans for a declining number of privately insured individuals. Acquisitions and mergers among health plans also enhance market share.

New Plan Models

Today's health plans include many new hybrid models of varied structure, sponsorship, financial relationships, out-of-plan options, and other features. Old verities, such as that Kaiser-type organizations will be the most successful, are being challenged with views that such organizations are, for now, at a disadvantage because of their ownership of hospitals and salaried physicians, and that service capacity can be purchased less expensively in the market. In a rapidly changing marketplace, health plans recognize the need to be nimble, operate through many contractual and other relationships, and be ready to change rapidly.

Cost Control

The managed care industry, in today's price-competitive environment, is placing high priority on its cost control strategies. Most managed care plans now use the aggregated purchasing power of employer and worker premiums, through contracted networks, to leverage price discounts from the oversupplied hospital sector and specialists. They also use various "triage" approaches to control utilization through tighter controls over specialist referrals and hospital use. Only a few companies thus far are actively managing clinical care quality through improved disease management.

In the face of tough market pressures, leading plans are quite confident that in most markets they will be able to realize economies for years to come. This confidence, in itself, is a key motivator as health plans develop their strategic plans and investment strategies. The confidence is based on a track record of realizing large economies while still having high consumer ratings, particularly through reducing hospital use. Both health plans and employers cite hospital use rates achieved by managed care (days of care per thousand population), compared with much higher levels that prevail in most markets, as the single most persuasive predictor for future savings. Other major savings opportunities are seen in reducing specialists' fees and use in oversupplied fields. Such easy savings mean that health plans could prosper without having to take on more challenging issues, such as improving health status, unless purchasers and competitors forced them to do so.

Venture Capital

A plentiful supply of venture capital for innovators and entrepreneurs is another key factor driving the managed care industry's growth. Wall Street has noted the profitability of managed care plans. Investment capital repeatedly destabilizes the status quo to capture excess profits throughout the health care system. Investment capital is also attracted to relentless growth in revenues and profits, thus creating a voracious appetite for rises in market share that are driven by mergers and acquisitions.

Risk Selection

Today's health plan strategies also are driven by risk selection, particularly in markets for small-group and individual coverage. It is much easier for health plans to price their premiums competitively by avoiding high-risk populations than by achieving real economies. About 10 percent of the population uses 70 percent of health care. Marketing strategies are usually designed primarily to attract good risks and to avoid patients on whom a plan would lose money. Why do health plan ads show happy, healthy babies? Will we ever see health plans advertising for patients with congestive heart failure, cancer, or cerebral palsy on the grounds of their clinical excellence in treating them?

Medicare and Medicaid Managed Care

The major public fee-for-service insurance programs, Medicare and Medicaid, have lagged behind the private sector in the shift from traditional insurance to managed care. However, they control one-third of today's $1 trillion national health care economy, enroll sixty-seven million people, and are already starting to influence market developments. With Medicare enrollees switching to managed care at roughly 100,000 enrollees per month, about a half-billion dollars of new annual premium revenue flows into managed care plans each month. States also have been moving their Medicaid populations into managed care; more than one-third of the thirty-five million Medicaid enrollees, primarily women and children, are now enrolled in private health plans.

Future Influences

We think that the health plan market will continue to be driven by today's major influences for the foreseeable future, but there will also be new influences. First, the Medicare market, with its enormous size and explosive growth potential, is the most important future market for managed care, now that most insured workers have already been enrolled in managed care. The insurance industry is working hard to enact new Medicare legislation to offer to private health plans, with the new point-of-service plans, broader network options, and organized "open-season" enrollment periods. The 70 percent of workers who are already enrolled in managed care are likely to continue in managed care as they reach Medicare eligibility, which will, by itself, raise the current 12 percent managed care enrollment rate. Health plans believe that the market power they will gain from new Medicare revenues will advance their ability to leverage future savings from health care providers. Competition for Medicare enrollees will be an important development over the next few years.

We also expect new consumer protection legislation. The abuses reported as "horror stories" in the news media may not be representative, and some proconsumer legislation is being pushed by providers and others who are opposed to managed care. Nevertheless, the managed care industry has not dealt effectively with its shortcomings and thus has come to be seen as adversarial to the interests of consumers. Legislators are being called upon to enact regulations with respect to clinical care of high-cost populations, grievance procedures, disclosure of clinical guidelines, financial incentives for underservice, and other areas.[4]

The health plan market is likely to become more competitive as a result of growth of multi-employer purchasing arrangements, cooperatives, and alliances, particularly among small employers. A number of the remaining small indemnity insurers are likely to leave the market over the next few years, which will enhance the purchasing clout of the larger health plans that acquire them. The next few years also will likely see the breakup of the Blue Cross and Blue Shield system, but the arrangements of the pieces and their partnerships and alliances are difficult to foresee, as are the effects.

Competition among health plans also is likely to change as better quality measures and improved disease management technologies expand the ability of plans and providers to differentiate themselves on the basis of value (particularly health outcomes) and to manage for improved health status. So far, such efforts have been hampered by enormous gaps in the research literature on clinical effectiveness (and cost-effectiveness) and by inadequate development and use of quality measures. As a result, simplified practice guidelines developed by actuarial consulting firms, such as Milliman and Robertson, now play a substantial role in managed care but have relatively low acceptability among physicians. Investment by health plans in better clinical care for high-cost patients has been slowed because health plans are averse to being known as market leaders in offering centers of excellence and other features that could attract high-risk and thus money-losing populations. Also, few health plans, providers, or professional groups have the financial resources and incentives to invest in this kind of patient care research. Medical groups that are adversely affected by practice guidelines research have been able to curtail federal financing for such activities.[5]

Finally, purchasers, health plans, and providers are likely to work out better risk adjustment methods to appropriately pay providers that excel in serving chronically ill and other high-cost patients. Direct contracting between purchasers and providers seems the most promising avenue for developing such methods, given the reluctance of health plans to be market leaders.

Providers

Price competition for contracts from health plans is the primary driver for health care providers. Most providers confront the stark reality of being an oversupplied resource in a market with aggressive purchasers and with little basis for distinguishing the quality or value of their services from those of other competitors. As managed care takes hold, providers' expectations have shifted toward a future of unrelenting pressures on pricing and for downsizing. Whereas physicians were turning down offers of Medicare fees plus 10 percent a few years ago, they now are accepting Medicare fee schedules of minus 20 or 30 percent. Fear is now said to be a major driver of change among health care providers, and a particularly influential one.

Partnership Strategies

Most providers are trying to control their futures by joining various partnerships.[6] Despite these mergers, acquisitions, joint physician/hospital ventures, and alliances, such strategies usually rearrange resources that are still in oversupply, even after significant reductions, and may not offer long-term stability.

Venture Capital

The drivers of change for health care providers also include a large amount of investment capital to back new ventures. There are many business opportunities in downsizing the health care system. Such capital is largely amoral; that is, it seeks financial opportunity but not social good. A significant amount of capital from hospital surpluses and reserves has gone into deficit-financing mergers and partnerships among health care providers, but this financing source may be eroding.

Future Influences

These current drivers of change among health care providers are likely to continue to be major influences for the foreseeable future. We expect financial pressures on providers to increase. In addition to these existing influences, the most important new driver of changes will be the rapid movement of Medicare enrollees into managed care. This will shift tens of billions of dollars to the bargaining power of health plans, while reducing providers' fee-for-service revenues and social-cost payments for charity care, graduate medical education, and rural hospitals. Many providers still live in a market that is split between fee-for-service (Medicare) and managed care revenues, and the "reverse cost shift" to Medicare is a critical factor propping up current overcapacity. Rapid shifts of Medicare enrollees to managed care will hasten the collapse of the "house of cards" that providers have built and sustained with open-ended fee-for-service insurance.

The turning of economic screws on providers' incomes by health plans is likely to generate increasing rivalry between hospitals and physicians for control of the health care delivery system. These new pressures may dissolve the glue of many hospital/physician alliances, as physicians come to see that their interests diverge from those of hospitals. There also are likely to be more physician-centered ventures, which include the acceptance of risk in return for clinical autonomy. Examples include cancer care networks and California physicians' willingness to organize and accept risk. There may also be increasing carveouts of care to provider organizations by health plans. Many of the hospital/physician ventures launched during the past several years could fail under these conditions, or there may be a realignment of control within such ventures.

Finally, market pressures on providers inevitably will drive out the cross-subsidies that have funded health care for more than forty million uninsured persons and have financed graduate medical education. Providers that have borne these costs face dire consequences; government action will be required to provide other financing.

No one really knows where the "bottom" is in the future health care system. After decades of fee-for-service reimbursement, in which providers were not called on to justify what they did or to measure quality, a strong clinical science base for resisting demands for economizing is hard to find. Providers thus find themselves in very insecure positions when, as oversupplied resources, they are asked by managed care companies to change their practices. Many providers and their patients face years of market-driven change.

Consumers

Consumers drive health care market trends today primarily through their willingness to purchase health plans on the basis of price comparisons. The evidence shows that individuals tend to select lower-price plans from employers' multiple-choice offerings and that even small premium differences can drive enrollment shifts among health plans. Thus, consumer choice and employer purchasing both drive price-based competition in the health plan market.

Consumers report, on many surveys, that they have a high degree of overall satisfaction with health care providers and with managed care plans. At the same time, experts portray consumers as being relatively uninformed and unsophisticated purchasers in the health care market who often are confused about how to choose among plans and providers. As with employers, consumers would like to be informed about quality differences but now have little basis for making valid comparisons. Satisfaction reports need to be qualified, because the vast majority of enrollees are healthy; whether there are equally high satisfaction ratings from high-need/high-use populations has yet to be clarified.

Access And Choice

Consumers are also driving the health care system to respond to their concern about access to care and providers. Consumers' inherent distrust of health plans' quality is fueled by media "horror stories." In response to pressure from workers, employers have been broadening networks and out-of-network options. Consumers' concerns, particularly those of disabled and chronically ill patients, also have been strongly felt in state legislatures. There has been an explosion of consumer protection legislation; for example, more than a thousand consumer protection bills were introduced in 1995.[7] Not much of this legislation has passed yet, but much of it reflects legitimate complaints and real problems that have not been addressed by the industry.

Future Influences

The rapid shift of Medicare enrollees into managed care plans will be the most important consumer-choice influence in the near future. Health plans are offering large price savings, about $1,000 per person compared with traditional Medicare, as well as better benefits and less paperwork, and enrollment is already growing 25–30 percent annually.[8] As a new system of choice for Medicare enrollees offers more attractive plans and quality assurance, even more elderly persons are likely to shift to managed care.

More consumer advocacy and assistance activities seem likely in both the public and private sectors. The growing numbers of elderly managed care enrollees alone will intensify pressures for consumer protection regulation. Starting with relatively healthy populations, HMOs have only recently become mainstream providers, and many of their protocols, operating methods, and organizations are not well suited to populations with higher needs, including the elderly. But many consumer groups, particularly those working with disabled and chronically ill populations, also realize that it is going to be up to knowledgeable consumers, and those working on their behalf, to drive quality of care in this new market-driven environment.

Finally, there will be improved information for consumers about health plans, providers, and treatments. Many of the early information efforts, such as HEDIS, have aimed at employer purchasing; consumers usually have different sets of concerns. Consumers often are much more interested in information about physicians and hospitals than in health plan data; they tend to view health plans as bill-paying organizations that hassle consumers and physicians. Better information will help to move the broader consumer movement along.

Government's Future Role

In recent years neither the federal government nor most state governments have had major roles in shaping the forces that drive health system change. Nevertheless, their future actions may be particularly influential. The implications of Medicare's shift toward managed care will be felt throughout the health care system. Medicare's health plan standards, market rules, quality assurance, grievance procedures, and consumer information, as well as its national consumer-choice system for thirty-seven million enrollees, may provide models for national reforms. Both federal and state governments will be considering proconsumer regulation of health plans.

We believe that a great deal of social distress lies ahead, however, if government does not recognize the adverse consequences of the socially amoral economic forces that are now driving change in the health care system. Today's elaborate cross-subsidy financing for care provided to uninsured persons will be unsustainable, and new public financing sources must be found to assist these populations and the providers that serve them. The dumping of more patients onto public hospital systems is not a feasible option; many public hospitals face steadily deteriorating finances, and their demise will be hastened by the movement of Medicaid to managed care. (Community health centers, however, may be viable elements in Medicaid managed care plans.) A majority of academic health centers, located in areas where they are not essential for health plan networks, also face grim financial futures in competitive markets, as well as reduced Medicare financing for graduate medical education.

The nature of market competition is to drive out cross-subsidies, which have been the hallmark of our health care system's way of financing such social costs. Government will need to step in with direct financing and/or regulation to pay for social costs. As a single optimistic note, however, evolution of the market likely will present government with purchasing opportunities for the nation's forty million uninsured persons that cost much less than universal coverage would have cost even a few years ago.

Wild Cards

Finally, it is interesting to speculate about various "wild-card" initiatives, other than comprehensive government reforms, that could sharply alter the outlook for the health care system. A number of such initiatives are already being tested.

Role of Physicians

A rapid rise in the number of physicians who are organizing to take on clinical management and risk is one of the factors that could alter the course and speed of health system change. Physicians used to control an estimated 70–80 percent of health care decisions, but they have recently been moved "down the food chain" by well-capitalized insurance companies and hospital-backed ventures. Physician-organized systems could shift the balance in the health care system far more toward competition among providers and away from competition among health plans and could foster organizations based on treatment of various conditions (for example, cancer, diabetes, or heart ailments).

While some speculators can see physicians moving to the top of the health care system, others suggest that physicians' role might be in jeopardy as team approaches and protocol-driven treatments make greater use of other professionals to provide value to the patient. Such arrangements might become common in much of primary care, as well as for the chronically ill.

Consumer Activism

Another speculation is that a national consumer movement could become a powerful force for shaping the health care system. This movement would be generated by consumers' recognition that they can no longer trust their physicians to work solely in their best interests, along with a mistrust of their employers and health plans. A major new consumer-focused "helper" industry could emerge that includes "front-end" services, such as an Internet-based system for patient contact, information, advice, and referrals.

Expert Systems

The health care system also could organize to rapidly advance the scientific basis of clinical care and health care management. All major actors now recognize their enormous information deficiencies, but no one actor or professional society is now organized to address this problem. An improved capacity to measure and demonstrate value could change the basis of competition and clinical management. Similarly, expert systems (software that structures medical diagnoses and treatment decisions into computerized step-by-step processes based on best practices and clinical evidence) also could affect the content of medical care and relationships within the health care system.

Financial Failures

Several developments might slow the pace of market-driven changes. Catastrophic financial failures of some large investment-financed enterprises or uninsured health plans could drop high-flying stock prices. A failure of health plans to deal with legitimate complaints could lead to slow growth of Medicare enrollments and to regulation that limits the industry's discretion. Chaos brought on by the coupling of rapid market change and government's unwillingness to finance social needs directly could bring on price regulation to protect vulnerable institutions, providers, and population groups.

New Employer Strategies

Finally, the nation's employers could affect future developments by making major changes in their purchasing strategies. Possibly, small employers will recognize the advantages of multiemployer health care purchasing and move aggressively to support legislation for purchasing cooperatives and alliances. Another possible development is more direct purchasing, whereby self-insured employers contract with provider-organized systems, without insurers in the middle. Others think that employers—once accreditation, report cards, and other measures are in place for a well-functioning market—will disengage from active health care purchasing and move to a strategy of fixed contributions, close their health benefits staffs, and allow their employees a broad choice among qualified plans.

Who 'Owns' the Consumer?

As we have discussed the health sector's evolution with many colleagues, the question "Who 'owns' the consumer?" has emerged as one of the key issues shaping the future of the health care market. Much of today's competitive market clout of health system actors— employers, physicians, health plans, and community hospitals—lies in their capacity to attract or deliver patients, premium dollars, and market share to others with whom they contract. As health plans offer more point-of-service options, and as consumers slowly gain better information for exercising choice, it is not clear that there will be many secure franchises "owning" patients. Market-driven insecurity, perpetual change, and competition to satisfy the consumer is the way of life in most markets. In this paper we have offered our take on today's drivers of change and suggested new influences over the next few years. For the longer term, however, we conclude that answers to such fundamental questions as "What will consumers and employers choose to reward?" and "How will the supply side be organized, who will determine its clinical practices, and on what basis will it compete?" are now open for resolution in an evolving, highly imperfect market.

Appendix

Paradigm Shift in the U.S. Health Care Market: A Terrain Map

Employers and Government

Shift from	To
Defined benefits	Defined contributions
Expanding large purchaser roles	Expanding consumer role
Self-insured	Paying premiums
Fee-for-service and managed care plans	Purchased health plans
Multiple choice with fee-for-service	Managed care plan(s)
Access to all providers	Networks, carve-outs (prescription drugs, behavioral care, chronic illness)
Buying comprehensive benefits	Contributing what's affordable
Employers/government at financial risk	Individuals/providers/plans at financial risk
Buy for/protect the employee/beneficiary	Inform the consumer
Quality review of services	Private "credentialing" of plans
Provide access to high-quality care	Access to "satisfactory" care
Providers drive purchasers' expenditures	Purchasers drive providers' incomes
Individual employer purchasing	Employer purchasing alliances
Seek social consensus on access/coverage	Leave it to the market

Physician, Hospital, and Insurer Business Environment

Expanding markets	Downsizing markets
Rapidly rising expenditures/premiums	Slowly rising expenditures/premiums
Market share desirable	Market share essential
Cost-driven prices	Price-driven costs
Stability/predictability	New competitors, products, markets
Cottage industry	Horizontal/vertical integration, mergers, consolidations, alliances
Independence	Owners, managers, bosses
Mutual prosperity	Top of food/risk chain prospers most
Provider profits	Health plan profits
Nonprofit/bond financing	For-profit/equity financing
Revenue growth from service expansion	Revenue growth from mergers and alliances
Profits from revenue increases	Profits from cost control
Selling value	Selling price

Physicians and Hospitals

Rewards for overservice	Rewards for risk carrying/underservice
Accountable to professional standards	Accountable to health plan standards
Merck manuals	Milliman and Robertson manuals
Hospital use declines	Hospital use really declines
Specialist physicians ascendant	Primary care physicians ascendant
Seller's market	Buyer's market

Physicians and Hospitals (cont.)

Shift from	To
Physician as clinical manager	Physician as clinical and cost manager
Referrals at physician's discretion	Referrals to network providers
Providers as patient advocates	Providers with divided responsibilities
"Appropriate" care determined by physician	"Appropriate" care determined by group/plan protocols
More and newer is better	Outcomes/technology assessment
Gaming health plans	Partners with/owners of health plans
Financial gains from "high-cost" patients	Avoid bad risks
Cost shift for uninsured	Avoid uninsured
Episodic care	Disease management, carve-outs, chronic care management
Patients come from professional reputation	Patients come from health plan networks
Health care as a profession	Health care as a business

Health Insurers/Health Plans

Market to large/small employers, individuals	Market to large/small employers, employees, Medicare beneficiaries, individuals
Selling comprehensiveness	Selling price, satisfaction
Financial intermediary	Health plan
Purchasers' administrative agent	Providers' partner
Risk carrier (fee-for-service)	Risk shifter (capitation, global fees)
Pay bills/manage costs	Manage clinical care and costs
Rating/estimating	Budgeting
Fee-for-service/procedure	Incentive arrangements, capitation
Charges	Negotiated payments
Unmanaged care	Managed care, disease management
All providers	Selected providers/networks
Accept existing referral patterns	Channel referrals
Compete by empaneling marry providers	Compete by selective contracting
Compete by discounting	Compete by "protocoling"
Bill payment systems	Information systems
Compete with other insurers	Compete with managed care plans, providers, and others

Employee/Individual Buyers

Standard benefits and premiums	Choices of benefits and premiums
Choice of doctors and hospitals	Choice of health plans
What the doctor ordered	What the health plan approved
Paperwork, bill-paying hassles	Bureaucracy, prior-approval hassles
Beneficiary/patient	Buyer
Trusting patient	Informed consumer
Physician as patient advocate	Patient as purchaser from physician
Employers/government as advocate	Employers/government as subsidizers
Anxiety about costs	Anxiety about cost control

Employee/Individual Buyers (cont.)

Shift from	To
Buy based on benefits	Buy based on price
Lower premium/cost sharing	Rising premium/cost sharing
Family coverage	Worker coverage
Everyone should pay same premium	Sicker and older can pay more
"Fair" is equal access and cost	Fair" is what the market determines
Complain about health insurers (not doctors)	Complain about managed care plans (not doctors)
Talk about need for system reform	Health plans as target for dissatisfaction

Source: S. Jones and L. Etheredge

Notes

[1]   KPMG Peat Marwick, *Health Benefits in 1995* (Washington: KPMG Peat Marwick, 1995).

[2]   K. R. Levit et al., "National Health Expenditures, 1994," *Health Care Financing Review* (Spring 1996): 205–242.

[3]   U.S. Department of Labor, *A Look at Employers' Cost of Providing Health Benefits* (Washington: Department of Labor, July 1996).

[4]   See Families USA, *HMO Consumers At Risk: States to the Rescue* (Washington: Families USA, July 1996).

[5]   M. W. Serafini, "The Unkindest Cut," *National Journal* (19 August 1995): 2108.

[6]   W. A. Zelman, *The Changing Health Care Marketplace: Private Ventures, Public Interests* (San Francisco: Jossey-Bass, 1996).

[7]   Families USA, *HMO Consumers at Risk.*

[8]   C. Zarabozo et al., "Medicare Managed Care: Numbers and Trends," *Health Care Financing Review* (Spring 1996): 243–261.

Section IX

Institutional Settings

Despite the recent growth of non-hospital institutions like hospices, freestanding clinics, and neighborhood health centers, the hospital continues to play a dominant role in the health care system. Hospitals are still the place where most people are born, suffer serious illness, and die. They are the location for essential work activities of many medical professionals and personnel. Hospitals are the site of major discoveries and innovations in health services. Hospital costs are the major component of rising overall health costs, which is why the diagnosis-related group (DRG) method of financing Medicare reimbursement has been so powerful. Even when many services are removed from inpatient hospital settings—as with the dramatic rise of day surgery—those services are typically done in units of hospitals. State-level regulations of the health care system usually center on control of hospital expansion and acquisition of major items. Yet, even while regulators and the public seek more controls on hospitals, organized lobbying groups of the hospital trade associations exert tremendous pressure on many public decisions about health care.

Charles Rosenberg's "The Rise of the Modern Hospital" places the hospital as we know it today into historical context. Rosenberg complements his history of the institutional development of the hospital with his emphasis on the interwoven development of the professions of medicine and nursing. Although the modern hospital is vastly different than its predecessors, Rosenberg reminds us that this historical viewpoint shows us concerns that always return: conflicts over the work roles and ethical responsibilities of health professionals, the ways that we handle the ethic of responsibility to care for those in need, and the biases of race, class, and gender that affect hospital services.

"The Patient in the Intensive Care Unit," by Robert Zussman, gives us a glimpse of the sociological fieldworker's skills at analyzing the human dimension of institutional life. In research at two intensive care units (ICUs), Zussman shows us how this setting eliminates the usual sort of expected interaction between patient and doctor, as staff treat people as if they were inert bodies. While we might expect staff to deny personhood to people unable to communicate because of serious injury, Zussman notes that they do it even to aware, communicative patients. Such behavior is not, he reminds us, due to meanness or a lack of caring but is rather a seemingly logical outcome of crisis management in a limited-time setting.

27
The Rise of the Modern Hospital

Charles Rosenberg

When Thomas Jefferson was inaugurated as president in 1800, there were only two American hospitals—one in Philadelphia and the other in New York. And these novel institutions played only a minor role in the provision of medical care; the great majority of inpatient beds were provided in almshouse wards, and even these were comparatively few in number. Most Americans still lived on farms and in rural villages.

Although in this demographic sense marginal, the hospital was nevertheless a characteristic product of the society that nurtured it. The hospital could not help but reproduce fundamental social relationships and values in microcosm. Early national America was a society in which relationships of class and status prescribed demeanors and specified the responsibilities of individuals and the community. It was a society in which bureaucracy and credentials meant little—bearing and social origin much. Even in America's largest cities, traditional views of Christian stewardship shaped assumptions of a proper reciprocity between rich and poor. It was an urban world in which benevolence could still be imagined—if not always realized—in a context of face-to-face interaction between the giver and receiver of charity.

Allied with medicine's limited technical resources, these demographic and attitudinal realities produced a medical system minimally dependent on institutional care and in which dependence and social location, not diagnosis, determined the makeup of institutional populations. Sickness in itself did not imply hospitalization—only sickness or incapacity in those without a stable home or family members to provide care.

Late eighteenth- and early nineteenth-century hospital advocates felt two kinds of motivation. One was the imperative of traditional

Christian benevolence in urban communities already burdened with large numbers of "unsettled" individuals needing care. The other sort of motivation grew out of the clinical and educational goals of an elite in the medical profession. Both lay and medical supporters of private hospitals contended that there could be no conflict between the hospital goals of laymen and physicians, for citizens of every class would ultimately benefit from the clinical instruction that could be most effectively organized around the aggregated bodies of the poor.

But such bland assurance of a necessary consistency between the professional needs of physicians and the benevolent goals of lay trustees were not enough to banish conflict. From its earliest years, the American hospital was marked by a structured divergence of interest between those of the pious laymen who bore the moral and legal responsibility for the institution and the doctors who practiced and taught within it. Drawn largely from the same social circles, attending physicians and lay authorities shared most values and assumptions, but in regard to professional matters such as autopsies, for example, or admission policies they could and did differ. Where they did not, however, was in their assumption of stewardship and the mingled authority and responsibility that constituted it; wealth, gender, and social position implied both the right and duty to direct the lives of dependent fellow citizens.

And the hospital was—insofar as its trustees and attending physicians could manage—a reflection of such relationships and responsibilities. Patients, nurses, attendants, and to an extent the junior house officers were considered moral minors in need of direction and guidance. Trustees felt a personal responsibility for every aspect of the institution and regularly inspected its wards and interviewed patients just as they personally oversaw admissions and settled accounts.

Poverty and dependence were the operational prerequisites for hospital admission. Sickness was a necessary but insufficient condition; aside from the occasional trauma victim, even the laborer or artisan preferred to be cared for at home—if he had a home and family to provide that care. It was only to have been expected that men should have far outnumbered women among nineteenth-century hospital patients. Urban America's abundant supply of single laboring men provided the bulk of admissions.[1] If age and sex justified the father's authority in an ordinary home, so gender and class identity legitimated that authority in the hospital and implied the unquestioned deference that patients were supposed to show toward superintendent, attending physicians, and trustees.

The intimate scale of early nineteenth-century hospitals provided a context in which these more general social realities could reproduce themselves. It was expected that the superintendent would see every patient every day, that he would know all their names and be aware of their personal situations, just as he knew the cook and laundress and coachman, all of course resident in the hospital. Not surprisingly, many of these employees worked for long years at their jobs and were paid on a quarterly or semiannual basis. Like the patients they cared for, the hospital's workers bartered independence for security. This harsh quid pro quo provided nevertheless a measure of stability in a world that offered few such choices for the great majority of Americans who worked with their hands.

The hospital was part of an institutional world that minimized cash transactions, subsisting instead through a network of less tangible interactions. Physicians were paid in prestige and clinical access; trustees in deference and the opportunity for spiritual accomplishment; nurses and patients were compensated with creature comforts: food, heat, and a place to sleep. Patients offered deference and their bodies as teaching material. Few dollars changed hands, but the system worked in its limited way for those who participated in it.

In part this was possible because the antebellum hospital was not burdened by a capital-intensive technology. There was little that could be done for a patient in the hospital that could not and, in practice, was not provided equally well at home—at least if that home could provide food, warmth, and care. Just as medical treatment was not segregated in the hands of a licensed and trained corps of practitioners, so the provision of acute care was not limited to a specific institutional setting. The domain of antebellum medicine was ill defined. Domestic and irregular practice were a significant part of medical care—a vital reality even in families well able to employ trained physicians.

Boundaries between hospital and home were similarly indistinct. A limited technology as well as traditional attitudes blurred the practical distinctions between home and hospital. In architecture as well as in terms of their social organization, America's early hospitals differed little from any large home or welfare institution. As late as the Civil War, much surgery was still done on the wards—laboratories, x-ray units, and sterile operating theaters were far in the future. The rationale for construction of early nineteenth-century surgical amphitheaters was primarily pedagogic.[2] Many antebellum hospitals did not even have specific spaces adapted to the treatment of emergencies or the evaluation of individuals for admission. A limited technology demanded little in a way of functionally differentiated space. A socially undifferentiated patient population similarly implied no need for class-distinct accommodations. Most nineteenth-century hospitals did have a few private rooms, but they were generally insignificant in terms of space or numbers of occupants. The large open ward seemed appropriate to the presumably blunted sensibilities of those sort of individuals who became hospital patients—and to the hospital's own need to minimize costs. Until the twentieth century, hospital current expense budgets were dominated by the cost of food, heat, light, and labor—costs little different from those of an orphanage, boarding school, or rich man's mansion.

Medical ideas and skills were widely disseminated in the community as well and not segregated in the profession, justifying in part the hospital's marginality and paralleling its lack of internal differentiation. Every educated gentleman was presumed to know something about medicine, every woman was something of a general practitioner. Medicine provided a striking example of a still-traditional society's more general lack of specialized roles. In terms of authority, class relations, technology, administration, and even architecture, the hospital was very much a microcosm of the community that produced it. The boundaries, in fact, between community and hospital, between medicine and its clients, remained indistinct in American cities until mid-nineteenth century—and in rural areas until much later. Even ideas of disease causation reflected, incorporated, and legitimated social values generally; this was an era in which disease was still a holistic and nonspecific phenomenon. It could be caused by poor diet, stress, alcoholism, constitutional weakness, or more frequently, some plausible combination of several such factors. Laymen could understand as well as manipulate these ideas—medicine was still practiced in the home in terms mutually understandable to medical men and their patients.

A New Kind of Hospital

All of this had changed drastically by 1920. The hospital had become a national institution, no longer a refuge for the urban poor alone. On January 1, 1923, there were 4,978 hospitals in the United States, 70 percent of them general hospitals. (In 1873, the first American hospital survey had located only 178 hospitals.)[3] By the early 1920s, few enterprising towns of any size had failed to establish a community hospital; it had become an accepted part of medical and especially surgical care for most small town Americans as well as their urban contemporaries. Diagnosis and therapeutic capacity as well as an individual's social location had begun to determine hospital admission. Technology had provided new tools and, equally important, a new rationale for centering acute care in the hospital. Medical men and medical skills were playing an increasingly important part in the institution—gradually supplanting older norms of lay control. Bureaucracy had reshaped the institution's internal order: a trained and disciplined nursing corps, a professionalizing hospital administration, as well as an increasingly specialized medical profession had all played a role in transforming the nineteenth-century hospital.

But certain older aspects of the hospital remained tenaciously intact. One was the stigmatizing distinction between public and private sectors. Municipal or county hospital care—like its almshouse predecessor—was clearly the less desirable, less adequately founded sibling of the private sector. In some ways, however, the formal boundary between public and private remained indistinct; all hospitals were clothed with the public interest, yet not easily subjected to the control of public authority. Decentralized funding and decision making continued to characterize the hospital. The lack of formal planning did not deter long-term trends from acting themselves out in parallel ways in institution after institution and locality after locality. But collective decision making was not easily imposed on an array of institutions that jealously guarded their autonomy and often associated independence with the prestige of localities, of ethnic and religious groups. This competitiveness was, in fact, one of those trends that manifested itself in parallel fashion in city after city; planners could deplore but do little to moderate its effects.

A first generation of hospital reformers had already discovered the structural rigidities beneath the seemingly inconsistent assortment of autonomous institutions that constituted the universe of early twentieth-century American hospitals. Regional planning for the most effective use of available resources was sought after as early as the first decade of the present century. Yet, despite polite words of support, few individual institutions were willing to change their normal priorities or concede any meaningful aspect of their operational independence to some larger group. By 1910, the hospital had already begun to appear to some of its critics as a monolithic and impersonal medical factory.[4]

Many social functions were moving from the home and neighborhood to institutional sites in late nineteenth- and early twentieth-century America—but none more categorically than medical care. And in no other case was the technical rationale more compelling. From a late twentieth-century perspective, the resources of hospital medicine in the period of the First World War may seem primitive, but they were impressive to contemporaries. Antiseptic surgery, the x-ray, and the clinical laboratory seemed to represent a newly scientific and efficacious medicine—a medicine necessarily based in the hospital. Few practitioners could duplicate these resources in their offices or make them easily available in the homes of even their wealthiest patients. Successful physicians had come to assume, and had convinced their patients, that the hospital was the best place to undergo surgery and in fact to treat any acute ailment.

But none of these events could have taken place without changed expectations—on the part of both physicians and their patients. Each decision by a middle-class American to enter a hospital reflected the attitudes and needs of both, even if it was the physician who ultimately referred his case to a hospital bed. Although attitudinal changes are difficult to document, respectable Americans would not have begun to enter hospitals had their perceptions of the institution not changed.

Not only the hospital, but the image of medicine itself had changed radically in the last third of the nineteenth century. The establishment of the germ theory, the advances of diagnosis and therapeutics made possible by immunology and serology, and the x-ray provided a dramatic series of highly visible events that cumulatively recast traditional attitudes toward the physician. It not only raised patient expectations, but also identified medicine's new-found efficacy with the laboratory and the image of science. Few would or could have agreed on what that science might be, but such assumptions nevertheless invested medical men with a new identity, one that based its legitimacy and claims to authority on something called science.[5]

Physicians were hardly immune to the attractions of scientific medicine. A cadre of bright young men had begun in the 1880s and 1890s to orient their careers in terms of the exciting new possibilities in surgery and the specialties. Reputations would be won or lost in these areas—reputations for hospitals as well as their staff members. The stakes were high for ambitious clinicians. Technical virtuosity was being inextricably related to status for institutions as well as individuals.

By the 1920s, surgery had become the acknowledged key to hospital growth and status. Although most patients still saw physicians in their own homes or the practitioner's office, major surgical procedures had shifted to the hospital. Not surprisingly, costs rose steadily; although simple and technologically unadorned by contemporary standards, the hospital of the 1920s was a capital-intensive institution, certainly by comparison with its mid-nineteenth-century predecessors. An increasingly sophisticated technology, both medical and nonmedical, implied higher capital and operating costs and thus a ceaseless quest for reliable sources of income and endowment. Yet only a minority of proprietary hospitals could entirely dispense with the institution's traditional mission of caring for the needy. And treating the poor and lower middle class threatened unending deficits. Administrators of nonprofit hospitals thus energetically sought to maximize private patient income. Competition in terms of elegant rooms and restaurant quality food began in the 1890s, but few institutions filled enough of these private rooms to provide a comfortable cash flow—let alone underwrite costs of treating the indigent. There were simply not enough well-to-do patients.[6]

A far greater number of Americans found themselves unable to afford private rates, yet were unwilling to enter charity wards in voluntary hospitals or their even more stigmatizing counterparts in municipal institutions. America's first generation of hospital planners had, as we have seen, grown acutely aware of this group—shut off by income or place of residence from private hospitals, consultants and specialists. The hospital had become an indispensable element in American health care, yet just as it achieved that status experts decried its failure to provide optimum care at reasonable cost.

Within the hospital itself, physicians and medical values had become increasingly important in decision making. Although there was no abrupt or categorical shift, the general trend was clear enough; even where lay authorities still controlled public or private governing boards, they deferred to doctors in a way that would hardly have been approved by their self-confidently intrusive predecessors a century earlier. The growing complexity and presumed efficacy of medicine's tools seemed to make the centrality of physicians in hospital decision making both inevitable and appropriate. More than technical judgments were relevant. Once hospitals became dependent on patient income, they became dependent as well on the doctors who could fill their private beds. Similarly, increasing scale and an ever larger and more specialized house and nursing staff also distanced laymen from the institutions they formally—and formerly—controlled.[7]

In most hospitals, the influence of attending staffs did not go uncontested, however. Like many other institutions in this period, the hospital was becoming increasingly bureaucratic, governed by a new kind of chief executive officer with the aid of a middle management of nursing superintendent, senior residents, and comptroller. Authority was negotiated as well as imposed.

No single change transformed the hospital's day-to-day workings more than the acceptance of trained nurses and nurse training schools, which brought a disciplined corps of would-be professionals into wards previously dominated by the values and attitudes of work-class patients (and attendants originally recruited from the same strata of society). In a period when few careers were open to women, trained nursing attracted a far greater variety of women, many of them rural and only a minority from the urban working class. Professional ambition and social origin set these first generations of credentialed nurses apart from the ward's accustomed occupants as much as any specific aspect of their schooling.

The status of trained nurses reflected but could not rival the growing influence of a male-dominated medical profession. In the hospital, as in the world outside its walls, female-identified occupations tended to become exclusively female and subordinate to male authority. Central to the professional identity of trained nursing was a relentless emphasis on discipline and efficiency, paralleling medicine's newly scientific self-image. This emphasis and the trained nurses who embodied and enforced it helped impose a new social order in the wards and rooms of the hospital. Nursing added an additional layer to hospital management—yet on balance enhanced rather than undermined the growing power of medicine within the hospital.[8]

The increasing prominence of technology and the physicians who employed these impressive new tools expressed itself in another and particularly tenacious way. This was the prominent role of acute care in the nonprofit hospital, and a parallel lack of interest in the chronically ill, who tended to pile up in county, municipal, and state institutions. In a good many rural areas in the 1920s, the county almshouse continued to serve as the community's repository for "chronics and incurables." Such patients were expensive and fit uncomfortably into the priority of an increasingly self-confident medical profession. Most chronic facilities, for example, found it difficult to attract housestaff; the duties were depressing and the cases "uninteresting."[9]

Surgery in particular had helped shorten voluntary hospital stays, attracted a new mix of patients and reinforced an already well-established emphasis on acute care. Diagnosis had become self-consciously scientific, determined increasingly by medical men and medical categories. By the 1920s, diagnosis had replaced dependency as the key to hospital admission (although *which* hospital one was admitted to still reflected class and ethnic factors). Socially oriented critics of the early twentieth-century hospital were already contending that the patient was in danger of being reduced to his or her diagnosis—to a biopathological phenomenon.

The hospital had been transformed not only socially and technically, but physically as well. New medical tools coupled with a new industrial and building technology had made the early twentieth-century hospital a physical artifact very different from its forerunners a century earlier. The needs of radiology and clinical pathology, of hydrotherapy and electrotherapy, and, most importantly, of antiseptic surgery demanded reorganization of the hospital's interior so as to minimize steps for its medical and nursing staff. The growth of fee-for-service practice in the hospital implied examining and consulting rooms more private than facilities previously available in ward and outpatient departments. The presumed needs and desires of valued pay patients led to the creation of more and more private and semi-private accommodations.[10] And like every other large institutional structure at the time, hospitals were being built with electric lights, dynamos, elevators, partially mechanized kitchens and laundries. Added to the cumulative impact of a mid-century reform movement that had underlined the need for improved modes of heating and ventilation, these technological necessities were turning the early twentieth-century American hospital into a capital-intensive and internally differentiated physical entity—mirroring in a different sphere the changes in professional organization and the distribution of knowledge that were reshaping medical care more generally.

Medical knowledge, like medical practice, was gradually but inexorably being segregated in professionally accredited hands. No longer was it assumed that an educated man would understand something of medicine (or law, classics, and theology). No longer was it assumed that midwives would provide the bulk of care during childbirth and early infancy. Drugs were purchased not gathered—and even in rural areas, most Americans turned sooner to physicians than they would have several generations earlier.[11] Within the medical profession too, knowledge was gradually being segregated so that ordinary practitioners were no longer presumed to be omnicompetent (even if they might have to ignore such limitations in rural areas or choose to ignore them in cities). Practitioners as well as educated laymen assumed that the hospital was and must be the site for medicine's most advanced and specialized care.

Although laymen were certainly impressed by the scientific style and seeming efficacy of medicine, it was physicians who in fact determined the content of that medicine. The medical community shaped professional expectations and defined career patterns. And if the optimum relationship between science and its clinical applications remained unclear, the place of the hospital did not. It was central to every aspect of medicine by 1920. The hospital's wards and rooms were the place to learn clinical skills, to master a specialty, often a place to practice, and, for an increasingly influential academic minority, a place to pursue research.

If the hospital had been medicalized, the medical profession had been hospitalized in the years between 1800 and 1920. This intraprofessional development has attracted far less attention from contemporary historians than the hospital's social and economic evolution—but it is no less significant. They are in fact inseparable; the structure of medical careers and changing medical perceptions and priorities are fundamental elements of hospital history.

Hospital service had always been central to the ambitions and careers of America's medical elite. By the First World War, it had become central to the education and practice of a much larger proportion of the profession, which was itself becoming more tightly organized, uniformly trained, and systematically licensed. Since the eighteenth century, hospitals had played a key role in disseminating as well as accumulating medical knowledge, helping to communicate ideas and techniques from a metropolitan elite to a new generation of practitioners. With an ever-larger proportion of physicians serving as interns and residents, the twentieth-century hospital became an increasingly effective tool for the diffusion of ideas and skills. By the 1920s, hospital experience had become an accepted part of medical training. With the national accreditation of hospitals and internship programs and the integration of residency and fellowship programs into board certification, the hospital had become with each passing decade more tightly integrated into the career choices and aspirations of the medical profession.[12]

With consulting and surgical practice moving increasingly into the hospital in the 1920s, interest as well as intellect united in emphasizing its importance to the practitioner. Cash transactions had become increasingly important, not only to the individual physician, but to the hospital as it sought to maximize income in the face of growing demands and rising costs. Older commitments to the provision of gratuitous care allied with institutional rivalries implied that most hospitals would not tolerate falling too far behind in their efforts to provide first-rate staff and facilities. Costs would inevitably increase.

The American hospital can be seen as having moved by the 1920s into a marketplace of discrete and impersonal cash transactions—to a style of benevolence that would have seemed inappropriate to the sort of men who managed hospitals in the first third of the nineteenth century. Efficiency, not stewardship, threatened to dominate the early twentieth-century hospital—as it did the school, state, government, and factory.

But the hospital never assumed the guise of rational and rationalized economic actor during the first three-quarters of the twentieth century. It was never managed as a factory or department store. The hospital continued into the twentieth century, as it had begun in the eighteenth, to be clothed with the public interest in a way that challenged categorical distinctions between public and private. Private hospitals had always been assumed to serve the community at large—treating the needy, training a new generation of medical practitioners, and attracting a varied and eclectic assortment of subventions from city, county, and state authorities.[13] The late eighteenth and early nineteenth centuries had in any case never been comfortable with absolute distinctions between the public and private sphere; the idea of commonwealth subsumed collective responsibility for that community's health. It was natural for most hospital authorities to assume that they should continue to receive public funds, just as they assumed they should be free of local taxes and the constraints of tort law.

The hospital's transactions involved pain, sickness, and death, as well as the public good. An insulating sacredness surrounded the activities of the twentieth-century hospital; its "products" were, in a literal sense, beyond material accounting. The newly intensified expectations of scientific medicine were, that is, both material and transcendent. A growing number of Americans hoped and expected that this new institution could provide a refuge from the sickness and premature death that had always seemed immanent in man's corporeal body. It is not surprising that (except for a minority of proprietary, for-profit institutions) the private hospital's operations have never been entirely disciplined by the logic of profit maximization or easily bent to communally determined demands for planning and cost control. A deficit could be construed as a sign of worthiness and not culpable administrative failure.

Nor is it surprising that transactions within the hospital continued until the Second World War to be structured in part around the exchange of labor and status. The hospital was in but not of the marketplace. Nurses and house staff still exchanged labor for credentials; attending physicians bartered their ward services for prestige and admission privileges in private services. Nonprofessional workers traded a measure of autonomy and the higher wages they might have received on the commercial labor market for the security and paternalism that, presumably, characterized the hospital. Thus, even as it was being transformed into an increasingly technical and seemingly indispensable institution, the hospital remained clothed with a special and sacred quality that removed it from both normal social scrutiny and the market's discipline.

Even if the hospital could not turn itself into a income-maximizing marketplace actor, it did serve as an equity-maximizing vehicle for many of those connected with it. I use the word equity advisedly, for the hospital provided rewards in several forms. To private practitioners, it could provide income; to attending physicians, income and status; to lay trustees, it offered prestige and, in many cases, affirmation of individual or group status; to hospital suppliers, it constituted an increasingly voracious customer; to academic physicians, it provided "clinical material" for teaching and research; to nurses, workers, and attendants, it offered security; and to some, a measure of status. Even the Depression-era hospital reflected and incorporated all these, sometimes conflicting, motives as it struggled with limited budgets.

The late twentieth-century hospital already existed in embryo, waiting only the nutrients of third-party payment, government involvement, technological change, and general economic growth to stimulate a rapid and in some ways hypertrophied development. New and abundant sources of support after the Second World War only intensified well-established patterns. They provided funds on the provider's terms without fundamentally changing the provider's orientation; cost-plus contracts and outright grants are hardly ideal mechanisms for the enforcement of external control.[14]

The Past in the Present

If the hospital in Thomas Jefferson's or Andrew Jackson's America had been a microcosm of the community that nurtured it, so is the hospital of the 1980s. Although we live in a very different sort of world, the hospital remains both product and prisoner of its own history and of the more general trends that have characterized our society. Class, ethnicity, and gender have, for example, all shaped and continue to shape medical care, and the hospital has become a specialized, bureaucratic entity of a kind that has come to dominate so many other aspects of contemporary life. National policies and priorities have come to play a significant role in affairs that had been long thought of as entirely and appropriately local. The origins of America's hospitals are hardly recognizable in their quaint forerunners in a handful of early nineteenth-century port cities.

The hospital is a necessary community institution strangely insulated from the community; it is instead a symbiotically allied group of subcommunities bound together by social location and the logic of history. This insulated character is typical of a good number of social institutions: the schools, the federal civil service, the large corporations. But there are some special aspects of the hospital that have facilitated its ability to look inward, to pursue its own vision of social good. This institutional solipsism developed in ironic if logical conjunction with the hospital's defining function of dealing with the most intimate and fundamental of human realities.

Like the U.S. Defense Department, the hospital system has grown in response to perceived social need—in comparison with which normal budgetary constraints and compromises have come to seem niggling and inappropriate. Security, like any absolute and immeasurable good, legitimates enormous demands on society's resources. Both health and defense have, moreover, become captives of high technology and worst-case justifications. In both instances, the gradient of technical feasibility becomes a moral imperative.[15] That which might be done, should be done. In both cases, cost-cutting could be equated with penny-pinching—inappropriate to the gravity of the social goals involved. Absolute ends do not lend themselves to compromise, and the bottom line is that there has been no bottom line.

In both areas, material interests obviously play a role; hospitals, doctors, and medical suppliers like defense contractors and the military have interests expressed in and through the political process. But ideas are significant as well. It is impossible to understand our defense budget without factoring in the power of ideology; it is impossible to understand the scale and style of America's health care expenditures without an understanding of the allure of scientific medicine and the promise of healing. Both the Massachusetts General

Hospital and the General Dynamics Corporation operate in the market, but they are not entirely bound by its discipline; both also mock the categorical distinction between public and private that indiscriminately places each in the private domain.

This analogy can, of course, be carried too far. The hospital has, as we have emphasized, a special history incorporating and reflecting the evolution of medicine and nursing, and the parallel development of our social welfare system. The high status of medicine has been built into the hospital, not only in the form of an undifferentiated social authority, but in the shape of particular, historically determined techniques and career choices. The ideas that rule the world-view of medicine and its system of education and research have very practical connections with the pragmatic world of medical care and medical costs.

An increasingly subdifferentiated specialization, an emphasis on laboratory research and acute care, for example, have all played an important role in the profession and thus, in the hospital. So complex and intertwined are these interrelationships that changes in any one sphere inevitably impinge on other areas. Some aspects of modern medicine seemed at first unrelated to the marketplace. One, for example, was the increasing ability of physicians to disentangle specific disease entities. This was an intellectual achievement of the first magnitude and not unrelated to the increasingly scientific and prestigious public image of the medical profession. Yet, we have seen a complex and inexorably bureaucratic reimbursement system grow up around these diagnostic entities; disease does not exist if it cannot be coded. It was equally inevitable that efforts to control medical costs should have turned on these same diagnostic categories. Thus the 1980s controversy surrounding Diagnosis Related Groups can be seen in part as a natural outcome of the intellectual and institutional history of the medical profession—and of the hospital as well.

To most contemporary Americans, rising costs have been the key element in transforming the hospital into a highly visible social problem. And it is true that an apparent crisis in hospital finance may well be creating the conditions for fundamental changes. After all, it was not until after the Second World War that the hospital gradually emerged from the world of paternalism. Unions and a more assertive nursing profession, ever-increasing capital costs, a growing dependence on federal support, and rising insurance rates, even the need to pay house staff in dollars have moved the hospital system into the market—and exposed hospitals to the prospect of increasing external control.[16] Still clothed with the public interest and promising immeasurable equities, the hospital remains a rigid and intractable institution.

As we contemplate its contentious present and problematic future, we remain prisoners of its past. The economic and organizational problems that loom so prominently today should not make us lose sight of fundamental contradictions in the hospital's history, contradictions that have fueled two decades of critical debates.

Scientific medicine has raised expectations and costs, but has failed to confront the social consequences of its own success. We are still wedded to acute care and episodic, specialized contacts with physicians. There is a great deal of evidence that indicates widespread dissatisfaction with the quality of care as it is experienced by Americans. Changes in reimbursement mechanisms will not necessarily alter that felt reality. Chronic and geriatric care still constitute a problem—as they always did. We cannot seem to live without high-technology medicine; we cannot seem to live amicably with it. Yet, for the great majority of Americans, divorce is unthinkable. Medical perceptions and careers still proscribe or reward behaviors that may or may not be consistent with the most humane and cost-effective provision of care. And despite much recent hand-wringing, it still remains to be seen whether physicians will be edged aside from their positions of institutional authority.

There are many equities to be maximized in the hospital, many interests to be served, but the collective interest does not always have effective advocates. The discipline of the marketplace will not necessarily speak to that interest; the most vulnerable will inevitably suffer. In any case, I see little prospect of hospitals in general becoming monolithic cost minimizers and profit maximizers. Social expectations and well-established interests are both inconsistent with such a state of things. We will support research and education, we will feel uncomfortable with a medical system that does not provide a plausible (if not exactly equal) level of care to the poor and socially isolated. Health care policy will continue to reflect the special character of our attitudes toward sickness and society.

Notes

[1] Sex ratios were most disproportionate in large urban municipal and voluntary hospitals. Disparities were not so marked in a growing number of community hospitals founded at the end of the century or at many religious and ethnic

institutions. Both social and technical factors, especially antiseptic surgery, made a hospital stay in these institutions less stigmatizing.

[2] And to an extent esthetic, removing the patient from the eyes and ears of ward mates.

[3] This not entirely complete survey did include mental hospitals. U.S. Dept. of Commerce, Bureau of the Census, *Hospitals and Dispensaries, 1923* (Washington: Government Printing Office, 1925), p. 1; J. M. Toner, "Statistics of Regular Medical Associations and Hospitals of the United States," *TAMA* 24 (1873):287–333. For a useful discussion of late nineteenth-century hospital growth patterns, see: Jon M. Kingsdale, "The Growth of Hospitals: An Economic History in Baltimore" (Ph.D. diss., Univ. of Michigan, 1981).

[4] Medicine was hardly alone in clothing itself in the garb of science—this was an era in which domestic science, library science, and political science, among other disciplines and would-be disciplines, reached self-consciously for "scientific" status and academic acceptance. In the case of medicine, of course, connections with the scientific disciplines was particularly significant and increasingly relevant to care. On the other hand, medicine experienced organizational changes paralleling those undergone by other professions and occupations at the same time, suggesting that its ultimate social form and prerogatives were more than logical and necessary consequences of cognitive change alone.

[5] For useful case studies illuminating the economic difficulties of hospitals in the period before 1930, see: David Rosner, *A Once Charitable Enterprise, Hospitals and Health Care in Brooklyn and New York, 1885–1915* (Cambridge, London, New York: Cambridge University Press, 1982) and (on Baltimore) Kingsdale, "The Growth of Hospitals."

[6] The growing influence of professional administrators was apparent in politically colored municipal institutions as well as in their private peers. The pattern was apparent in other cultural and benevolent institutions as well where professional managers gradually came to mediate between wealthy directors and the objects of their benevolence. See, for example: Kathleen D. McCarthy, *Noblesse Oblige. Charity and Cultural Philanthropy in Chicago, 1849–1929* (Chicago: University of Chicago Press, 1982).

[7] The professionalization of nursing did provide supervisory positions for women, but the great majority of such posts remained subordinate to male superintendents, medical boards, and trustees. In a small minority of women's hospitals, this was not the case and, as we have suggested, the Catholic hospitals also provided a setting in which women could exert a greater degree of real authority. They were insulated by their sex and vocation from the will of medical boards and by their orders from the unfettered control of diocesan administrators.

[8] For a useful discussion, see Ernst P. Boas and Nicholas Michelson, *The Challenge of Chronic Diseases* (New York: Macmillan, 1929).

[9] For a survey of the hospital's internal architectural history, centering on room and ward arrangements, see John D. Thompson and Grace Goldin, *The Hospital: A Social and Architectural History* (New Haven and London: Yale University Press, 1975). Cf. Adrian Forty, "The Modern Hospital in France and England." In: A. King, ed., *Buildings and Society* (London: Routledge & Kegan Paul, 1980), 61–93.

[10] Hospital facilities were seen by contemporary observers to be inadequate particularly in poor or isolated areas as evidenced by the interest of a number of private foundations in the 1920s and 1930s.

[11] The influence of a developing specialism on the hospital and of the hospital on special practice is an extremely important part of hospital history, but one that has been on the whole neglected by historians.

[12] New York, Massachusetts, Connecticut, and Pennsylvania, for example, had all found ways to support voluntary hospitals throughout the nineteenth century. For a general discussion, see Rosemary Stevens, "'A Poor Sort of Memory': Voluntary Hospitals and Government before the Depression," *Milbank Memorial Fund Q.* 60(1982): 551–84; Stevens, "Sweet Charity: State Aid to Hospitals in Pennsylvania, 1870–1910," *Bulletin of the History of Medicine* 58 (1984): 287–314, 474–95.

[13] Hill-Burton did specify conditions, but they seem not to have greatly constrained institutional politics. The intra-institutional effects of externally supported research have been significant but are difficult to evaluate.

[14] And the carrying out of that imperative has created economic and bureaucratic interests committed to existing procurement patterns and thus another source of rigidity in both areas.

[15] The similarities between for-profit hospitals and the great majority of their not-for-profit peers are at least as significant as their differences. Both are prisoners of the same attitudes, expectations, technology, and funding realities and must pursue a good many parallel strategies.

28
The Patient in the Intensive Care Unit

Robert Zussman

"A Little Bit of a Science Project"

In their now classic article "The Basic Models of the Doctor-Patient Relationship," Thomas Szasz and Marc Hollander argue that the degree to which medical care involves the patient as a participant in his or her own treatment depends heavily on the quality of illness.[1] In cases of chronic illness (ranging from diabetes to psychoneuroses), they argue, the very "notions of disease and health lose most of their relevance" and are replaced by concepts of behavior and adaptation.[2] By consequence, the character of the patient—the patient's willingness to reform long-held patterns of behavior, to accommodate to an often difficult medical regimen—becomes an essential part of treatment. In contrast, in cases of acute disease, which make up much of the practice of contemporary hospital medicine, the notion of disease consists of specific signs and symptoms while treatment consists primarily of what the doctor does to the patient. The patient may be asked to cooperate with a specific regimen, to follow "doctor's orders," but the demands on the patient typically fall far short of a total reorganization of a way of life. Finally, in cases in which the patient is unconscious, in a coma or during surgery, the patient is entirely passive. Diagnosis and treatment alike, Szasz and Hollander argue, take place "irrespective of the patient's contribution."[3] Treatment consists entirely of what the doctor does to the patient, and the patient's participation is beside the point.

The bearing of all this on the matters at hand is that it is the third model of the doctor-patient relationship that predominates in intensive care. "In the unit," one resident explained, "it is a little bit of a science project. . . . That's basically what people are reduced to. It's blood pressure, temperature, respirations, and their cardiogram." In this sense, if we are to follow Szasz and Hollander, the patient vanishes in intensive care—not, of course, as an object of treatment but, in any meaningful sense, as a participant.

In other settings, diagnosis begins as a doctor takes a patient's history. The taking of a history may not exactly make the patient a coparticipant in medical care, but it is a process in which the character of the patient is expressed, in which the patient's own narrative is the starting point for medical treatment. In intensive care, however, doctors and nurses are often called on to treat patients who cannot give histories. There are extreme cases, as one resident explained: "At least one of those a month, an unknown male found on the street by EMS [Emergency Medical Service], with an overdose or unresponsive. There's no history. . . . Basically you are depending on the exam and the numbers and there's no human interaction at all." Even when physicians and nurses do know a patient's history, at least in basic outline, that history often becomes little more than a secondary source, replaced by the objective measures of laboratory-generated data. "Good doctors never look at the history of the patient," Ken, the Countryside unit's medical director, explained one day during rounds: "They just look at the numbers." Even the physical exam, the literal laying on of hands that implies at very least an acknowledgement of the patient's physical presence, becomes less important in the setting of intensive care. "I don't talk to patients," Ken insisted on another day, after a woman's private physician reported that the patient had said she was feeling fine. "This is the patient," the private physician answered, perhaps only half joking as he held up the flow sheet that listed the woman's laboratory values. An Outerboro resident explained:

> I think you don't have to look at a patient here, basically. You don't have to really examine a patient. . . . Someone has a PA [pulmonary artery] line in, you don't have to listen to their lungs. . . . In that respect, with technology you don't have to deal with a patient, examine a patient. The numbers, I feel, they are more reliable.

And as another put it, in a striking image in which the irrelevance of the patient's personhood becomes altogether apparent, "In a way it's almost like veterinary medicine."

Of the 237 patients whose admissions I observed at Outerboro, 35 (15 percent) were admitted with, in the language of the unit, "no mental status"—unable to speak and unresponsive to voice, apparently unaware of place or person.[4] Of 111 admissions at Countryside, nineteen (17%) were unresponsive. These are patients who cannot, in any sense, participate in their own care. To the doctors and nurses who work in the unit, they are, by result of the very conditions that bring them to the unit, objects of treatment. An additional 65 patients at Outerboro (27 percent) and 29 patients at Countryside (26 percent) entered the unit stuporous or lethargic, able (in some cases) to speak and respond but usually unaware of where they were, let alone why (see table 1).

Table 1   Mental Status of ICU Patients

	Outerboro		Countryside	
No Mental Status	15%	(n = 35)	17	(19)
Stuporous	27	(65)	26	(29)
Alert	58	(137)	57	(63)
Intubated	18	(43)	28	(31)
Not Intubated	40	(94)	29	(32)
Total	100	(237)	100	(111)

Moreover, to the conditions the ICU is intended to treat are added the character of the treatments themselves. At Outerboro and Countryside, as at most hospitals, a basic service of intensive care is to support patients in respiratory distress, whether from pneumonia, severe asthma, heart disorders, or any number of other conditions. This is done by supporting the patient with a mechanical respirator, a process which usually requires "intubation," the placement of a tube leading from the respirator through the patient's nose or mouth and then through the esophagus. Intubation is not only painful, but also prevents the patient from speaking. An intubated patient cannot give a history, cannot register complaints, cannot communicate, except by shakes of the head and laboriously written notes—and this only when the sedatives used to control the pain of the process are not too heavy.[5] Thus, many of the patients who enter the unit alert are soon faced with an added handicap to their participation in their own care. Of the 137 patients who entered the Outerboro unit alert, 43 (31 percent of alert patients, 18 percent of all patients) were intubated within twenty-four hours of admission. Of the 63 patients who entered the Countryside unit alert, 31 (49 percent of alert patients, 28 percent of all patients) were intubated within twenty-four hours of admission. In all, then, only 94 of the 237 (40 percent) of the Outerboro patients and 32 of the 111 (29 percent) Countryside patients whose admission I observed were neither stuporous nor intubated.

Yet even these figures understate the degree to which intensive care is occupied by unresponsive patients. Patients who are neither stuporous nor intubated are healthier than those who are. As a result, their ICU stay is usually shorter (an average of 3.7 days, compared to 8.3 days for those who were intubated or not alert at Outerboro; 1.6 days compared to 4.5 at Countryside). Put a little differently, patients who entered the unit alert and who were not quickly intubated accounted for less than one-quarter of all patient days in the unit at Outerboro and less than one-seventh at Countryside. Moreover, many patients decline over the course of their ICU stay. The result, then, is often a unit caring almost entirely for unresponsive patients.

Consider one day at Outerboro. Seven of the eight beds in the open ward were full.

Bed 1: Irving Krickstein had been stuporous on admission, five days earlier, and unresponsive to questions. He was intubated and sedated soon after his admission. Although the ICU staff had lightened up on his sedation, he was still intubated and "doing badly" when asked to answer questions.

Bed 2: Empty

Bed 3: Peter Edwards had been intubated and sedated on admission, nine days earlier. Although one of the interns described him as "clear" when she reduced his sedation, he was still intubated.

Bed 4: Jack Reilly, intubated early in his ICU stay, had been in the unit for forty-eight days. Initially, according to a note in the chart, he had been "very agitated" but, for the last month, had been "minimally responsive—even to needle sticks." According to one of the residents, he did squeeze his wife's hand when she visited but was otherwise unresponsive.

Bed 5: The only new admission of the day was an unidentified, unresponsive man who had been brought to the hospital from a men's shelter by Emergency Medical Service. "The only history we got," an intern explained during his presentation, "was from his chest, which showed multiple surgery."

Bed 6: Edith Green had been brought to the hospital unresponsive "except to deep pain" and had remained so for thirteen days.

Bed 7: Max Kohler had been admitted with slurred speech. He had been intubated and sedated since his admission five days earlier.

Bed 8: Lotte Baer, in her fourth day in the ICU, was the only patient on the ward who was alert and oriented.

All six of the beds in the back section of the unit were full:

Bed 9: Max Rosenberg had been brought to the hospital with an "altered mental status" and was intubated in the Emergency Room even before his admission to the ICU. Although his mental status had improved over the course of his five-day stay, and he was now "totally there," he had not responded to attempts to wean him from the respirator and remained intubated.

Bed 10: Alberto Rodriguez had been intubated on the second of his seven days in the ICU. Over the course of the week, his alertness had waxed and waned. He was now alert but still intubated.

Bed 11: Angel Santiago had been brought to the unit the day before in a diabetic coma. "He was tubed within ten minutes of coming up," one intern explained, "so we don't have much history." Although the same intern described Santiago's mental status as now improved, he remained intubated and unresponsive to commands to open and close his eyes.

Bed 12: Georgia Johnson had been admitted to the unit fifty-six days earlier following a respiratory arrest and was later diagnosed as having fatal esophageal cancer. Intubated even before her ICU admission, she was now alert and able to sit up in a chair but unable to speak and able to communicate at all only with great difficulty through a few signs.

Bed 13: Allan Lerner had been admitted to the unit the same day as Georgia Johnson and also intubated immediately for the chronic lung disease that would result in his death. In addition to his intubation, he had been "morbidly depressed" even before his admission. It was not clear to the ICU staff how much he understood, although one of the nurses did report that he squeezed her hand in response to questions.

Bed 14: Audrey Roland had been admitted to the unit fifteen days earlier, intubated and sedated a few days later. Although alert, frequent notes she wrote showed little understanding that she was in a hospital.

Such patients are poor candidates for participation in their own care.

"There can be," one Outerboro resident insisted, "a very nice relationship . . . if you have an awake and alert patient who's not intubated." But, he quickly acknowledged, this is not usually the case.

> The relationship with the patient . . . who comes in comatose and debilitated, unable to speak for themselves or respond to you . . . is a difficult one. You're often left with a sense of, What am I doing here? That is, the patient has been dehumanized, not by any act of people but just by the disease that's happened. Here we are with a mass of protoplasm.

"They have names," another resident added, "but we speak of the patient in that bed with this problem." Because a lot of people are intubated, they can't talk. And so you've got to just deal with them not as a person but as a problem, a set of numbers and dynamics. We're not dealing with a walking, talking person.

Good Medicine

Only the most determined sociological reductionist would deny the brute force of disease and disability in denying ICU patients their personhood. But if it is physiology that denies personhood to many ICU patients, it is a distinctive notion of what constitutes good medicine that denies personhood to the rest. Intensive care, in particular, is organized around a notion that medicine at its best—at its most heroic, its purest—is about physiology and physiology alone.[6]

The mission of intensive care is, explicitly and without apology, to deal with medical crises. "The unit," according to one Outerboro resident,

> is really a place to get people over a kind of medical disaster. It's a place you just try to get them out of alive, and you don't worry about [other things]. You treat the immediate problem. You don't necessarily deal with the other underlying chronic problems or what is this person going to do when they go home or any of that stuff. You deal with the acute problem.

Intensive care addresses acute physiological problems. Other considerations are simply crowded out. "All we care about in the unit," a Countryside resident stressed, echoing the sentiments of his counterpart at Outerboro, "is making sure somebody is alive."

If, in other settings, as medicine's critics complain, the patient is reduced to a disease, in intensive care physicians may focus on a particular physiological process in which even the underlying disease is forgotten. "Usually," an Outerboro resident explained, the reason a patient is in the unit "is because of an infection superimposed [on something else] or a GI [gastrointestinal] bleed superimposed [on something else]. . . . We try and stop that. But the underlying problem often doesn't make any difference." Thus, the ICU physicians treat the respiratory distress that results from cancer but often not the cancer itself; they treat the gastrointestinal bleed that results from underlying liver disease, but not the liver disease itself.

If ICU physicians sometimes ignore underlying disease in favor of treating immediate problems, they are even less attentive to the broader context of that disease. To be sure, even in the abbreviated histories characteristic of intensive care, some physicians remain acutely aware of social, environmental, and emotional components in the etiology of disease. In discussing the ethnically diverse patients at Outerboro, most housestaff, even in the ICU, routinely mention at least something about the patient's social background as a possible diagnostic clue. At both hospitals, many housestaff often mention something about the patient's living situation and, where relevant, histories of drug use, alcohol use, and cigarette smoking as well as occupational hazards to which the patient might have been exposed. Yet, however interested in such factors as explanations of the origins of disease, physicians in the ICU remain indifferent to them factors in its treatment. "When they get to the floor," a Countryside resident explained, drawing a contrast with the unit, "then you start with, do they have nurses at home to take care of them, are they getting home oxygen. . . . Here we do what we have to do [to] get the patient better." With his characteristic bluntness Ken, the unit's medical director, drove home a similar point when one of the interns raised questions about psychogenic components in the treatment of a 72-year-old woman who had been brought to the unit pulseless: "We don't talk about psychiatric disorders here." Put simply, it is specific, discrete treatments, abstracted from any social or emotional context, that constitute good medicine in intensive care. The physician's job, at least as physicians themselves understand it, is to treat acute physiological conditions and little else.

The narrowing of the ICU physicians' interest is perhaps most apparent in the suicide attempts they are occasionally called on to treat. Consider, for example, the case of Matt Flowers, an eighteen-year-old with a severe learning disability, seriously depressed for two months, and admitted to the Outerboro ICU after having taken an overdose of drugs. While the presentation of Flowers's case made due reference to emotional strains, the medical staff were quick to reassert their primary focus. The "major concern," the intern in charge of the case explained, "is damage to the liver." And the "only mysterious thing about him," an attending added, "is why he's still asleep." That evening Flowers's sister brought in his suicide note, written in a childish scrawl. The next day it was exhibited at rounds: "Dear Mommy, I love you. I don't want to rember [sic] no one or anything at all." Seeing the note, one resident said simply, "It's very sad." But the attending physician was quick to remind him of the proper focus: "This suggests there's impaired functioning."

None of this is to say that the ICU physicians and nurses are indifferent to human suffering. They are not. Indeed, there are many instances of small kindnesses. The ICU nurses and physicians constantly reassure patients, sometimes even when they are not sure the patients understand, but just on the off chance that they might. A nurse goes out of her way to tie a bow in the hair of a depressed, elderly woman. For the rare patient who lingers in the ICU for many days, alert and conscious, the physicians and nurses often provide a few extras—making sure, for example, that such a patient has a television or radio (not standard in the Outerboro unit) or, at Countryside, decorating the walls with pictures brought from home. But such kindnesses are incidental. They are kindnesses precisely because they are voluntary, something extra that individual members of the ICU staff may (or may not) do, apart from the unit's primary task of treating acute physiological disruptions. They are meant to get the patient— and, perhaps, the doctor or nurse—through the day as comfortably as possible and with as little disruption of the real business of treatment as possible.

The Limits of Moral Judgment

In one curious sense, doctors and nurses do show an interest in their patients as persons. Despite their focus on physiology, the doctors and nurses who staff the intensive care units at Outerboro and Countryside do not shy away from moral judgment. When Tommy Jackson, a 26-year-old drug user on chronic dialysis, was admitted to the Outerboro unit, the unit physicians were quick to take me aside. "Here's a sociological problem," one told me. "It's not medical." And another explained, "He's been in the unit seven times and in the CCU three times. His basic stance is to whine. He's very dependent. . . . His mother is part of the problem. She thinks, my little Tommy. She doesn't believe he's ever done drugs." During the presentation of Jackson's case, the rest of the staff laughed when one of the interns reported that Jackson was claiming he no longer used drugs. And an attending physician, concerned about Jackson's hepatitis, suggested nothing less than that he should be given a visible stigmata of that high infectious disease: "I think they should be tattooed, frankly."

Tommy Jackson is an extreme case, but by no means unique. The language of intensive care is filled with terms of derision. Perhaps the best known of these is GOME or GOMER, short for "get out of my emergency room," for a patient "who has lost—often through age—what goes into being a human being."[7] Even more starkly, I have heard comatose patients described as "dead meat" or "pets." Claims by drug users that they are no longer using drugs or by alcoholics that they are no longer drinking are dismissed routinely: "You never believe that," one resident announced during rounds. And one of the few times that I heard such a claim accepted, it was with high sarcasm: "I believe him. He's got no peripheral veins left." One demanding patient is described, with mock scientism, as "a roaring bear personality." Another patient, unemployed for five years and living in a men's shelter, is "absolutely pathetic." Yet others are "ornery," "crotchety," "crabby."

To be sure, the moral judgments cut both ways. Patients are characterized as "a nice lady," a "gentleman," "intelligent," "well educated," "a charmer," "patient," "a class act," "brave," and "cute." Occasionally, a resident will insist on the good standing of a patient: "He's a real citizen type. He works as a tailor. . . . He has a real job. He's not like Unknown Male." In one case, an intern was insistent even on distinguishing one drug user from the rest: "He was kind of a spiritual leader of the drug community."

Nonetheless, it is the negative characterizations which predominate. Like police officers preoccupied with crime or clergy preoccupied with sin, the physician's view draws disproportionately from the seamy side of life. Particularly in urban hospitals, and particularly in intensive care, a large proportion of the patients suffer from self-induced illness. Of admissions I observed at Countryside, physicians included reports of drug use (9 percent), alcohol use (11 percent), or both (an additional 3 percent) in over one-fifth. Among 237 admissions at Countryside, the totals were even higher, with alcohol use reported in 8 percent of the cases, drug use in 8 percent, and both in an additional 3 percent. And none of this is to mention the suicide attempts, the frequent patient who had failed to follow a medically prescribed regimen, or the very frequent smoker. As medically relevant aspects of the patient's life, such behaviors are mentioned routinely in the initial presentation of the patient's social history. Although these presentations are usually quite matter of fact, their language insistently invokes the language of "abuse" and, by implication, evaluation: "social history notable for ethanol abuse," "a 53-year-old man with a history of alcohol abuse," "IV [intravenous] drug abuser with shortness of breath," "five-year history of IV drug abuse." Yet, even without the language of "abuse," the evaluative implications of such presentations are perhaps inevitable. Like the police and the clergy, physicians are not only licensed to view the seamy side of life but positively enjoined to seek it out. If, from this, there emerges a baleful, even cynical view of human life and human nature, it should not surprise us.

What might surprise us, however, is how little relevant the moral judgments of physicians and nurses are to life in intensive care. For the most part, the ICU staff neither demeans patients nor tries to reform them nor, most important, treats them differently on the basis of such judgments. Occasionally, a nurse or an intern may sit down with a patient and try to explain the health consequences of heavy drinking or drug use. So, too—and considerably less benignly—an occasional patient may be rushed out of the unit because the housestaff find him or her unusually distasteful. One patient, for example, according to an outraged Outerboro resident, had been sent out of the ICU "inappropriately" because, the resident thought, "she's an incredible pain in the ass . . . an alcoholic, active IV drug abuser, noncompliant with meds. . . . We don't like noncompliant people." But both differential treatment and efforts at reform are episodic and unsystematic. More frequent is a remarkably thoroughgoing tolerance, born perhaps of resignation. With all their complaints about Tommy Jackson, the ICU physicians nonetheless provided him with the hemodialysis he had come to the unit for and, finding his condition improved, at least temporarily, discharged him from the hospital. Doctors and nurses may make jokes among themselves about the wealthy patient whose cirrhosis of the liver was the result of too much Remy Martin Cognac or that one of the "drinking buddies" of a comatose woman was named "Jack Daniels." They may disbelieve the comatose man who, on awakening, insisted that he had never before used cocaine. But for the most part, they keep their jokes and disbeliefs to themselves. They address patients, except for the occasional ones who have lingered in the unit long enough to have assumed a first name, as "Mister" or "Mrs." or "Miss." Overwhelmed by acute medical crises, the ICU staff is simply too busy—and too little interested—to bother with reforming character. If they do not treat the liver disease that is a frequent source of gastrointestinal bleeding, they certainly do not even attempt to treat the alcoholism that is often the source of liver disease. If their job is to treat respiratory distress in a crisis situation, it matters little if the distress is the result of a cancer for which the patient is, to all appearances, blameless or the result of a drug-induced coma for which they would happily blame the patient.

Consider, for example, Naismith Brown. Brown is precisely the sort of patient who is frequently the butt of medical humor and the object of moral judgment. A 44-year-old single man with a long history of alcoholic cirrhosis, Brown was brought to Outerboro by the Emergency Medical Service with falling blood pressure, the result of a gastrointestinal bleed, itself brought on by too many drinks over too many years. In the Emergency Room, Brown was intubated for airway protection and sent almost immediately to the Intensive Care Unit. In the unit, Brown's doctors ordered an endoscopy, found the proximate source of his bleed, provided him with transfusions, prescribed pitressin to help control his bleeding, and, after a one-night stay, sent him to the wards for continued medical management.

Brown himself was alert and conscious throughout his ICU stay. But if anyone had spoken to him about his use of alcohol, if anyone had demeaned him, tried to reform him, or in any way distinguished him from the "solid citizens" who are the ICU staff's patients of preference, he could not remember:

> Up there is strictly business place. What I mean by business place, you know, fast going place. But business place. So after they finish, after up there they finish the most important part of the job, they send you down, get your treatment. . . . They're very fast up there and they know what they're doing. They know their work.

In Brown's vision of intensive care and in the vision of others like him, moral judgment has no part.

Moreover, it is a vision ICU physicians and nurses themselves whole-heartedly share. One addressed the situation of patients like Naismith Brown directly, comparing the practice of medicine in intensive care to that in other parts of the hospital:

> We don't get very much involved with either their social problems or how they've responded to their disease or how they've gotten to the point that they're at. The classic is the alcoholic who's GI bleeding. We don't address the fact that, is there anything that we can correct about their home situation or their social situation to

stop them from drinking? Not that we could on the floor, but . . .
that question isn't even addressed in the unit. What's addressed
in the unit is how fast they're bleeding and where they're bleeding
from.

Drugs and alcohol may bring patients to intensive care. And the
physicians who treat those patients may disapprove, sometimes
deeply, of the behaviors which are the underlying causes of the
conditions they are called on to treat. But their job, at least as they see
it, is not to reform behavior or even to distinguish among patients of
widely varying character and imputed worth. The physicians in intensive care are not—and do not imagine themselves—as priests or cops,
as ministers to the soul or guardians of decency. If anything, they are
rather more like repairmen. If, in some circumstances, many of
medicine's critics find such an image cold and impersonal, they must
also recognize that it is, in other circumstances, egalitarian and even
liberating.

The Patient Vanishes

In settings other than intensive care, what Anselm Strauss and his
colleagues have called "sentimental work" assumes a prominent place
in medical treatment. Successful treatment depends, integrally, on the
physician's or nurse's ability to build trust, to help patients maintain
their composure, to maintain or rebuild personal identities in the face
of debilitating illness.[8] In such settings, a recognition of the patient's
personhood is essential. But intensive care is different.

In intensive care, patients vanish. Patients do not, of course, vanish
in the sense of disappearing physically. But they do vanish in two other
senses. First, they vanish in the sense that disease itself robs them of
many of the capabilities we associate with full personhood. Second,
they vanish in the sense that the doctors and nurses who work in the
unit are largely indifferent to matters of identity or character. "I have
almost no relationship with the patients in the unit," an Outerboro
resident explained. "If they're nice people, it's great. You kind of wave
hello, whatever, but you don't have a whole lot of time . . . for small
talk." This vanishing act is not a matter of design. Doctors and nurses
do not start out with the intention of ignoring patients. Rather, other
issues are simply more pressing.

The ICU staff live in a moral universe of limited liability. What
happens before the patient enters intensive care may be of diagnostic
interest, but it is not the housestaff's responsibility. What happens after

the patient leaves the ICU may also be of interest, but neither is it part of the ICU's responsibility. Doctors and nurses attempt to restore their patients' personhood by medical treatment. But the restoration of personhood is, at best, an outcome of medical treatment. Personhood has little to do with the tasks at hand. Doctors and nurses—perhaps themselves overwhelmed by their patients' disease—do not imagine it as part of the process of treatment.

Notes

1. Thomas Szasz and Marc Hollander, "Basic Models of the Doctor-Patient Relationship," *Archives in Internal Medicine* 97(1956): 585-92. There is an ambiguity in the Szasz and Hollander article on whether the basic models are meant as models of appropriate behavior or models of actual behavior. I have treated them here as models of actual behavior.

2. Ibid., p. 589.

3. Ibid., p. 586.

4. The concept of "no mental status," as it is used at Outerboro and elsewhere, is not limited to patients who are "brain dead," a relatively rare condition. Patients are said to have "no mental status" when they are unresponsive except to pain. In general, "no mental status" refers to patients who are unable to take part in any meaningful human interaction.

5. See Ingered Bergbom-Engberg and Hengo Haljame, "Patient Experiences during Respirator Treatment—Reason for Intermittent Positive-Pressure Ventilation Treatment and patient Awareness in the Intensive Care Unit," *Critical Care Medicine* 17 (1989): 22–25.

6. For discussions of intensive care that proceed along similar lines, see Stuart J. Youngner, ed., *Human Values in Critical Care Medicine* (New York: Praeger, 1986); Joel E. Frader and Charles L. Bosk, "Patient Talk at Intensive Care Unit Rounds," *Social Science and Medicine* 15 (1981):267–74; Renee R. Anspach, "Notes on the Sociology of Medical Discourse: The Language of Case Presentation," *Journal of Health and Social Behavior* 29(1988): 357–75.

7. Samuel Shem, *The House of God* (New York: Dell, 1978), p. 424.

8. Anselm Strauss, Shizuko Fagerhaugh, Barbara Suczek, and Carolyn Wiener, *The Social Organization of Medical Work* (Chicago: University of Chicago Press, 1985), especially pp. 129–50.

Section X

Health Care Providers

Although other sections of this book look at various kinds of inter-actions between health providers and their clients, it is important to spend time looking at the structural makeup of the health care work-force. These are the people who provide direct patient care in offices, clinics, and hospitals. If we saw patient care as the sole or primary goal in health care delivery, we might expect that members of the health workforce would have a unified agenda. But professional and non-professional groups have different, and often conflicting, goals. These goals include groups' particular needs for control of the work process, control of relations with other groups, and general advance-ment of the profession or group. Even when different groups do agree that patient care is central, they might have drastically differ-ent points of view, as we know from classic tales of discrepancies of patient care practices between nurses and physicians, and between different physicians. If we understand the background and interests of the groups that make up the health workforce, we can better understand their actions in the health care system.

If health and illness are so salient because of their life-and-death nature, then it is no surprise that doctors are held in such importance, since they are often the people who exercise that control over life. Yet physicians are viewed in a curiously ambivalent way by the public. They are often endowed with great power and authority, even with magical qualities. Yet at the same time, they are blamed for our per-sonal misfortunes and for situations that may well be outside of their control. To be sure, contemporary culture questions the authority of the doctor. Doctors have faced changes in salaried vs. self-employed status, in the centrality of the hospital as a location for medical prac-tice, in the growth of for-profit hospital chains, in the control over who pays their bills, in the degree to which their medical work is monitored and regulated by state and federal governments, and in ethical and legal challenges to their practice decisions. Yet it would be incorrect to say, as some theorists do, that medical authority has eroded.

Physicians have always been a group that serves as a focus for the study of professions. Our definitions of what a profession is, notions of professional socialization, and beliefs about professional-lay relations often stem from our observation of physicians. Physicians provide a basis upon which to study how professionals codify a body of knowledge, certify a method of training, determine a model of legal licensure and control, police themselves, and define their relationship to the society at large. As many sociologists note, physicians are the profession *par excellence*, and this has strongly influenced medical sociologists, who have studied medical education, diagnostic conceptualization, practice styles, and professional group behavior. Sociologists have also been interested in the political clout of physicians, ranging from legislative lobbying to cultural and ideological commentary.

Paul Starr's contribution, "The Growth of Medical Authority," takes a historical look at how organized medicine grew, and how this growth went hand in hand with the growth of hospitals (a look back to Charles Rosenberg's article on the development of hospitals would be a valuable complement to the Starr piece). Starr shows the interconnection between social mobility and the struggle for cultural authority, placing this in the context of both internal professional development and larger changes in the sociocultural realm. We see here the development of the previously mentioned elements of professionalism, in Starr's discussion of personal versus institutionalized authority, mechanisms of legitimation, and physicians' historical maneuverings to gain power and authority. In their professional development, physicians have achieved what sociologists call *medical dominance*, their control over other health care professions and groups. Of special interest is Starr's notion that physicians' expansion both created a new marketplace for their services, while at the same time restricting the marketplace due to the social need to regulate the medical world.

From the perspective of a physician attuned to patients' unique experiences of illness, Rita Charon writes in "To Listen, To Recognize" about how doctors need to listen for the *stories* that patients tell, rather than to proceed with a traditional mode of questioning and diagnostic workup. Charon goes further in recommending that doctors write their own stories about medical encounters so that they can better understand both their patients and themselves. This emphasis on the narrative approach to disease and illness brings us back to the earlier piece by Gareth Williams, "The Genesis of Chronic Illness."

When we study the history of Western medicine, we see many examples of physician advances built upon the defeat of other healing professions. Witness the case of midwifery. The Flexner Report of 1910 capped an era in which doctors were influential in chasing out midwives, homeopaths and naturopaths, and in forcing osteopaths to be more like the modern Western doctors, termed at the time "allopaths."

Physicians' power and authority gives them control over other professions. This holds not only for lines of authority within the hospital or clinic, but also for external control such as regulation and licensing of other professionals. Although *medical dominance* sometimes yielded better medicine education and care, early nineteenth-century doctors were quite open about their fear of competition from other providers. Modern approaches to medical sociology have placed much importance on the ways in which medical dominance has operated. These more recent scholars have been very interested in the medical and social roles of other types of providers and in the different insights those providers have on disease, illness, and patient care.

Efforts of other health providers to improve their status often involve defining their own group or profession as central to fulfilling the needs of the medical practice as a whole. What we see is a generalized attempt at *professionalization* by the other health professions, an attempt which mirrors the past efforts of physicians. There are pitfalls in this occupational strategy, since the public and the state are not that eager to accept the argument that everyone is a professional and therefore deserving of special privileges. Certainly the hospitals and the financing apparatus of the health care industry are not eager to pay higher salaries and fees to other professionals. Nor do administrators wish to have additional parties with any claim to power and authority in health care settings.

Clearly there are economic and career gains to be made by the other health professions, but we must understand them in the appropriate context. For example, some nurses have risen in power and status, but often at the expense of others. The RN (registered nurse) has supplanted the LPN (licensed practical nurse). The RN with a baccalaureate degree has supplanted the RN with a certificate. The RN with a master's degree has supplanted the RN with a BS. Most recently, the nurse practitioner has replaced the master's level nurse. This process of upgrading professional credentials, requirements, and responsibilities is part of the ongoing *restratification* of the health field. Much of this process is driven by the goal of saving costs by replacing physicians in the routine daily work of nonserious medical visits, especially in HMOs and other managed care settings.

In "A Caring Dilemma: Womanhood and Nursing in Historical Perspective," Susan Reverby traces the development of nursing, pointing to the many conflicts between female nurturing roles and medical professionalism. Reverby argues that in order to develop professionally over time, nurses were forced to professionalize their altruism, at the expense of their own autonomy. The duty to care became merely the duty to follow physicians' orders in the medical hierarchy. Recent changes in nursing ideology, as well as in the structure of health service settings, have opened the doors to greater autonomy. Ultimately, Reverby asserts, the historical conflict experienced by nurses can be resolved by adopting a political ideology which links altruism with autonomy in nursing as well as in other spheres of social life.

Daniel Chambliss's contribution, "Nurses' Role: Caring, Professionalism, and Subordination," complements the Reverby article with his fieldwork of present-day nursing. He examines the various ways in which nurses' caring roles are played out, how their professional identities are shaped, and how their subordination to physicians detracts from their work. Chambliss shows how these three components of nursing work—caring, professionalism, and subordination—produce conflicting requirements, and that nurses' work requires much attention to managing these conflicts.

29
The Growth of Medical Authority

Paul Starr

The rise of the professions was the outcome of a struggle for cultural authority as well as for social mobility. It needs to be understood not only in terms of the knowledge and ambitions of the medical profession, but also in the context of broader changes in culture and society that explain why Americans became willing to acknowledge and institutionalize their dependence on the professions. The acceptance of professional authority was, in a sense, America's cultural revolution, and like other revolutions, it threw new groups to power—in this case, power over experience as much as power over work and institutions.

In a society where an established religion claims to have the final say on all aspects of human experience, the cultural authority of medicine clearly will be restricted. But this was no longer the principal barrier to medicine in the early nineteenth century. Many Americans who already had a rationalist, activist orientation to disease refused to accept physicians as authoritative. They believed that common sense and native intelligence could deal as effectively with most problems of health and illness. Moreover, the medical profession itself had little unity and was unable to assert any collective authority over its own members, who held diverse and incompatible views.

Authority, as I've indicated, involves a surrender of private judgment, and nineteenth-century Americans were not willing to make that surrender to physicians. Authority signifies the possession of a special status or claim that compels trust, and medicine lacked that compelling claim in nineteenth-century America. The esoteric learning, knowledge of Latin, and high culture and status of traditional English physicians were more compelling grounds for belief in a hierarchically ordered society than in a democratic one. The basis of modern professionalism had to be reconstructed around the claim to technical competence, gained through standardized training and evaluation. But this standardization of the profession was blocked by internal as well as external barriers—sectarianism among medical practitioners and a general resistance to privileged monopolies in the society at large.

From *The Social Transformation of American Medicine*, by Paul Starr, pp. 17–24. Copyright © 1982 by Paul Starr. Reprinted by permission of Basic Books, a member of Perseus Books, L.L.C.

The forces that transformed medicine into an authoritative profession involved both its internal development and broader changes in social and economic life. Internally, as a result of changes in social structure as well as scientific advance, the profession gained in cohesiveness toward the end of the nineteenth century and became more effective in asserting its claims. With the growth of hospitals and specialization, doctors became more dependent on one another for referrals and access to facilities. Consequently, they were encouraged to adjust their views to those of their peers, instead of advertising themselves as members of competing medical sects. Greater cohesiveness strengthened professional authority. Professional authority also benefited from the development of diagnostic technology, which strengthened the powers of the physician in physical examination of the patient and reduced reliance on the patient's report of symptoms and superficial appearance.

At the same time, there were profound changes in Americans' way of life and forms of consciousness that made them more dependent upon professional authority and more willing to accept it as legitimate. Different ways of life make different demands upon people and endow them with different types of competence. In preindustrial America, rural and small-town communities endowed their members with a wide range of skills and self-confidence in dealing with their own needs. The division of labor was not highly developed, and there was a strong orientation toward self-reliance, grounded in religious and political ideals. Under these conditions, professional authority could make few inroads. Americans were accustomed to dealing with most problems of illness within their own family or local community, with only occasional intervention by physicians. But toward the end of the nineteenth century, as their society became more urban, Americans became more accustomed to relying on the specialized skills of strangers. Professionals became less expensive to consult as telephones and mechanized transportation reduced the cost of time and travel. Bolstered by genuine advances in science and technology, the claims of the professions to competent authority became more plausible, even when they were not yet objectively true; for science worked even greater changes on the imagination than it worked on the processes of disease. Technological change was revolutionizing daily life; it seemed entirely plausible to believe that science would do the same for healing, and eventually it did. Besides, once people began to regard science as a superior and legitimately complex way of explaining and controlling reality, they wanted physicians' interpretations of experience regardless of whether the doctors had remedies to offer.

At a time when traditional certainties were breaking down, professional authority offered a means of sorting out different conceptions of human needs and the nature and meaning of events. In the nineteenth century, many Americans, epitomized by the Populists, continued to believe in the adequacy of common sense and to resist the claims of the professions. On the other hand, there were those, like the Progressives, who believed that science provided the means of moral as well as political reform and who saw in the professions a new and more advanced basis of order. The Progressive view, always stated as a disinterested ideal, nevertheless happily coincided with the ambitions of the emerging professional class to cure and reform. The cultural triumph of Progressivism, which proved more lasting than its political victories, was inseparable from the rise in status and power of professionals in new occupations and organizational hierarchies. Yet this was no simple usurpation; the new authority of professionals reflected the instability of a new way of life and its challenge to traditional belief. The less one could believe "one's own eyes"—and the new world of science continually prompted that feeling—the more receptive one became to seeing the world through the eyes of those who claimed specialized, technical knowledge, validated by communities of their peers.[1]

The growth of medical authority also needs to be understood as a change in institutions. In the nineteenth century, before the profession consolidated its position, some doctors had great personal authority and they pronounced on all manner of problems, by no means restricted to physical illness. Indeed, in the small communities of early American society, where the number of educated men was relatively small, some physicians may have possessed even broader personal authority than do most of their counterparts today. What I am talking about here, on the other hand, is authority that inheres in the status of physician because it has been institutionalized in a system of standardized education and licensing. The establishment of such a system reproduces authority from one generation to the next, and transmits it from the profession as a whole to all its individual members. Before the profession's authority was institutionalized in the late nineteenth and early twentieth centuries, physicians might win personal authority by dint of their character and intimate knowledge of their patients. But once it was institutionalized, standardized programs of education and licensing conferred authority upon all who passed through them. The recognition of authority in a given doctor by laymen and colleagues became relatively unambiguous. Authority no longer depended on individual character and lay attitudes; instead, it was increasingly built into the structure of institutions.

"Built-in" dependence on professional authority increased with such developments as the rise of hospitals. I do not mean only the development of mental hospitals and procedures for involuntary commitment, though the asylum is obviously an important and radical form of institutionalized medical authority. Even the voluntary shift of seriously ill patients from their homes to general hospitals increases the dependent condition of the sick. At home, patients may quite easily choose to ignore the doctor's instructions, and many do; this is much more difficult in a hospital. For the seriously ill, clinical personnel subordinate to the doctor have, in effect, replaced the family as the physician's vicarious agent. They not only administer treatment in the doctor's absence, but also maintain surveillance, keep records, and reinforce the message that the doctor's instructions must be followed.

Other institutional changes have also made people dependent on medical authority regardless of whether they are receptive or hostile to doctors. As the various certifying and gatekeeping functions of doctors have grown, so has the dependence of people seeking benefits that require certification. Laws prohibiting laymen from obtaining certain classes of drugs without a doctor's prescription increase dependence on physicians. "The more strategic the accessories controlled by the profession," Eliot Freidson writes, "the stronger the sanctions supporting its authority."[2] In the twentieth century, health insurance has become an important mechanism for ensuring dependence on the profession. When insurance payments are made only for treatment given by physicians, the beneficiaries become dependent on doctors for reimbursable services. A doctor's authorization for drugs and prosthetics has become necessary for a host of insurance and tax benefits. In all these ways, professional authority has become institutionally routine, and compliance has ceased to be a matter of voluntary choice. What people think about doctors' judgments is still important, but it is much less important than it used to be.

In their combined effect, the mechanisms of legitimation (standardized education and licensing) and the mechanisms of dependency (hospitalization, gatekeeping, insurance) have given a definite structure to the relations of doctors and patients that transcends personalities and attitudes. This social structure is based, not purely on shared expectations about the roles of physicians and the sick, but on the institutionalized arrangements that often impose severe costs on people who wish to behave in some other way.*

The institutional reinforcement of professional authority also regulates the relations of physicians to each other. The doctor whose personal authority in the nineteenth century rested on his imposing character and relations with patients was in a fundamentally different situation from the doctor in the twentieth century whose authority depends on holding the necessary credentials and institutional affiliations. While laymen have become more dependent on professionals, professionals have become more dependent on each other. Both changes have contributed to the collective power of the profession and helped physicians to convert their clinical authority into social and economic privilege.

---

*Role expectations are the heart of what was once the most influential schema in the sociology of medicine—that of Talcott Parsons. according to Parsons, the social structure of medical practice can be defined by the shared expectations about the "sick role" and the role of the doctor. On the one hand, the sick are exempt from normal obligations; they are not held responsible for their illness; they must try to get well; and they must seek competent help. On the other, the physician is expected to be "universalistic," "functionally specific," "affectively neutral," and "collectivity-oriented" These complementary normative rules have a functional relation to the therapeutic process and the larger society.[3]

While useful as a point of departure for understanding doctor-patient relations, Parsons' model is open to severe objections as a model of medical practice. It fails to convey the ambivalence of doctor-patient relationships and the contradictory expectations with which each party must contend.[4] It also accepts the ideological claims of the profession—for example, to be altruistic ("collectivity-oriented")—and ignores evidence of contrary rules of behavior, such as tacit agreements to ignore colleagues' mistakes.[5] Parsons' approach concentrates almost entirely upon the system of norms in purely voluntary doctor-patient relations. That such relations are not wholly voluntary both because of dependency conditions and the historical process that lies behind the professional dominance is a point Parsons simply overlooks. The distribution of power, control of markets, and so on do not enter significantly into his analysis. Parsons also neglects other relations important to medical practice, such as those among doctors and between doctors and organizations. The more important these collegial and bureaucratic relations become, the less useful Parsons' approach appears.

From Authority to Economic Power

The conversion of authority into high income, autonomy, and other rewards of privilege required the medical profession to gain control over both the market for its services and the various organizational hierarchies that govern medical practice, financing, and policy. The achievement of economic power involved more than the creation of a monopoly in medical practice through the exclusion of alternative practitioners and limits on the supply of physicians. It entailed shaping the structure of hospitals, insurance, and other private institutions that impinge on medical practice and defining the limits and proper forms of public health activities and other public investment in health care. In the last half century, these organizational and political arrangements have become more important as bases of economic power than the monopolization of medical practice.

The emergence of a market for medical services was originally inseparable from the emergence of professional authority. In the isolated communities of early American society, the sick were usually cared for as part of the obligations of kinship and mutual assistance. But as larger towns and cities grew, treatment increasingly shifted from the family and lay community to paid practitioners, druggists, hospitals, and other commercial and professional sources selling their services competitively on the market. Of course, the family continues even today to play an important role in health care, but its role has become distinctly secondary. The transition from the household to the market as the dominant institution in the care of the sick—that is, the conversion of health care into a commodity—has been one of the underlying movements in the transformation of medicine. It has simultaneously involved increased specialization of labor, greater emotional distance between the sick and those responsible for their care, and a shift from women to men as the dominant figures in the management of health and illness.

What sort of commodity is medical care? Do doctors sell goods (such as drugs), advice, time, or availability? These questions had to be worked out as the market took form. To gain the trust that the practice of medicine requires, physicians had to assure the public of the reliability of their "product." A standardized product, as Magali Sarfatti Larson points out about the professions, requires a standardized producer.[6] Standardization of training and licensing became the means for realizing both the search for authority and control of the market.

Through most of the nineteenth century, the market in medical care continued to be competitive. Entry into practice was relatively easy for untrained practitioners as well as for medical school graduates; as a result, competition was intense and the economic position of physicians was often insecure. Toward the end of the century, although licensing laws began to restrict entry, many doctors felt increasingly threatened by the expansion of free dispensaries, company medical plans, and various other bureaucratically organized alternatives to independent solo practice. In the physicians' view, the competitive market represented a threat not only to their incomes, but also to their status and autonomy because it drew no sharp boundary between the educated and uneducated, blurred the lines between commerce and professionalism, and threatened to turn them into mere employees.

The contradiction between professionalism and the rule of the market is long-standing and unavoidable. Medicine and other professions have historically distinguished themselves from business and trade by claiming to be above the market and pure commercialism. In justifying the public's trust, professionals have set higher standards of conduct for themselves than the minimal rules governing the marketplace and maintained that they can be judged under those standards only by each other, not by laymen. The ideal of the market presumes the "sovereignty" of consumer choices; the ideal of a profession calls for the sovereignty of its members' independent, authoritative judgment. A professional who yields too much to the demands of clients violates an essential article of the professional code: Quacks, as Everett Hughes once defined them, are practitioners who continue to please their customers but not their colleagues. This shift from clients to colleagues in the orientation of work, which professionalism demands, represents a clear departure from the normal rule of the market.

When fully competitive, markets do not obey the organized judgment of any group of sellers. A market is a system of exchange in which goods and services are bought and sold at going prices. In the ideal case cherished by economists, each buyer and seller acts independently of every other, so that prices are set impersonally by levels of supply and demand. There are no relations of dependency in the ideal market: Any individual buyer is supposed to have a free choice of sellers, any seller a free choice of buyers, and no group of buyers or sellers is supposed to be able to force acceptance of its terms. Nor are there supposed to be any relations of authority in the market, except those necessary to provide rules of exchange and the enforcement of contracts. Whereas the household and the state both allocate resources according to decisions made by governing authorities, the distinctive feature of a market is the absence of any such authoritative direction. The absence of power is, paradoxically, the basis of order in a competitive market. Collectively, sellers might wish to keep the prices of commodities higher than their marginal cost, but so long as they act individually, they are driven to bring them down into equilibrium to secure as large as possible a share of the market for themselves.

This is not a prospect that sellers usually enjoy and, whenever the means are available, it is one they quickly subvert. Power abhors competition about as intensely as nature abhors a vacuum. Professional organization is one form resistance to the market may take. Similarly, concentrations of ownership and labor unions are other bases of market power. These cases are parallel. Just as property, manual labor, and professional competence are all means of generating income and other rewards, so they can be used by a monopolistic firm, a strong guild or union, or a powerful, licensed profession to establish market power. This was what the medical profession set about accomplishing at the end of the nineteenth century when corporations were forming trusts and workers were attempting to organize unions—each attempting, with varying success, to control market forces rather than be controlled by them.

Doctors' increasing authority had the twin effects of stimulating and restricting the market. On the one hand, their growing cultural authority helped draw the care of the sick out of the family and lay community into the sphere of professional service. On the other, it also brought political support for the imposition of limits, like restrictive licensing laws, on the uncontrolled supply of medical services. By augmenting demand and controlling supply, greater professional authority helped physicians secure higher returns for their work.

The market power of the profession originated only in part from the state's protection. It also arose from the increasing dependence of patients on physicians. In the ideal market no buyer depends upon any seller, but patients are often dependent on their personal physicians, and they have become more so as the disparity in knowledge between them has grown. The sick cannot easily disengage themselves from relations with their doctors, nor even know when it is in their interests to do so. Consequently, once they have begun treatment, they cannot exercise that unfettered choice of sellers which characterizes free markets.

One reason that the profession could develop market power of this kind was that it sold its services primarily to individual patients rather than organizations. Such organizations, had they been more numerous, could have exercised greater discrimination in evaluating clinical performance and might have lobbied against cartel restrictions of the physician supply. The medical profession, of course, insisted that salaried arrangements violated the integrity of the private doctor-patient relationship, and in the early decades of the twentieth century, doctors were able to use their growing market power to escape the threat of bureaucratic control and to preserve their own autonomy.

Notes

[1] For an excellent account of the struggle for authority and its relation to changing social organization, see Thomas L. Haskell, *The Emergence of Professional Social Science* (Urbana: University of Illinois Press, 1977).

[2] Eliot Freidson, *Professional Dominance: The Social Structure of Medical Care* (New York: Atherton, 1970), 117.

[3] For Parsons's classic statement, see *The Social System* (Glencoe, IL: Free Press, 1951), Chap. 10.

[4] See Robert K. Merton and Elinor Barber, "Sociological Ambivalence," in *Sociological Theory, Values and Sociocultural Change*, ed. Edward A. Tiryakian (New York: Free Press, 1963), 91–120.

[5] See Freidson, *Profession of Medicine*, esp. Chap. 7.

[6] Magali Sarfatti Larson, *The Rise of Professionalism* (Berkeley: University of California Press, 1977), 14.

30
To Listen, To Recognize

Rita Charon

The practice of medicine requires powerful instruments for visualizing patients' bodies. We now know that we must see clearly the lives of patients as well as their bodies. This article describes instruments for visualizing and comprehending the lives of patients. These instruments are stories and the imagination. Let me describe some of the stories we tell each other and then suggest ways in which different kinds of stories may enrich our practice by allowing us to recognize our patients more fully.

"This is the first Presbyterian Hospital admission for this seventy-two-year-old woman with a chief complaint of shortness of breath." So begins a story that a student tells about a patient. "The patient was well until two weeks prior to admission when she noted gradually increasing dyspnea on exertion. She denies chest pains, palpitations, cough, or fever." As the attending listening to this story, I pay attention to the content and to the form of the story. I await the unfolding of the narrative according to the rules of the literary genre of the presentation. The student who offers me lab data before giving me the vital signs bewilders me. The student who mishandles the dramatic structure of the story, who does not build suspense toward climax and then deftly turn to denouement, disappoints the drama coach in me. In our work storytelling is a powerful instrument that defines our concerns and allows us to share them. Our genres also define us. By following our own literary rules, we accept each other into a circle.

We tell other kinds of stories for many different reasons. An internist tells me, "The guy with the neck from last week, it was Hodgkins." All I might have to say to a hematologist is, "85K," and he will know that our patient with idiopathic thrombocytopenic purpura is getting better on steroids. We go through our days telling stories to each other in these truncated, elliptical, telegraphic forms, and it is through that kind of exchange that we grow in our knowledge, that we aid each other in our work, that we take care of patients. The scraps of information are legal tender among us. They satisfy our curiosity; they resolve our uncertainty; and they bind us to each other in very special ways.

It is in the stories we tell and how we tell them that we learn the basic lessons of medicine. Our genres limit us in significant ways. By telling our stories in the way that we do, we impose limits on admissible data; we insist on a particular stance toward the material. The formal medical presentation is stunning in its control, its precision, its flatness. There is for sure an intellectual playfulness about it—Why does the presenter choose those negatives to include? Is that historical fact a clue or a red herring? Listeners derive joy from following along an inventive and dense presentation. Yet, the genre prohibits certain behaviors and observations. Has a presenter ever mentioned his or her own response to the patient in question, or explained what sense the patient makes of the symptoms? The genre, in the end, is the distillation of many medical lessons, and by teaching our students how to tell this type of story, we teach them deep lessons about the realms of living that are included and excluded from patient care.

But there are other, more complex stories to hear, to tell, and to write. These are the stories that will give us great rewards. John Berger wrote in *A Fortunate Man* of a family doctor in rural England.[1] He says that patients think of the doctor as the "clerk of their records," the one who recognizes patients in fraternity. He writes eloquently about the physician who acknowledges narratives by patients, narratives that will be heard by no one else. He casts the doctor in the fairly humble role of clerk. In fact, clerking is what we all do. The doctor witnesses and documents meaningful events in his or her patients' lives. Medical charts are journals, chronicles of lives and of times. Doctors are allowed to recognize the events and the people who dwell in them, and patients come to them for that recognition. Our work is centered on telling stories and on hearing stories, and by choosing one kind of story over another, we can transform our practice of medicine.

Eudora Welty says in *One Writer's Beginnings*, an autobiography, "Long before I wrote stories, I listened for stories. Listening *for* them is something more acute than listening to them. I suppose it's an early form of participation in what goes on."[2]

When I sit in my examining room with patients, I use my writer instincts. A woman came to see me because of back pain. She was an obese middle-aged woman with multiple vague complaints. She seemed sad. When I examined her, I discovered surgical evidence of a breast reduction procedure and tiny vertical scars behind each ear. This was a woman who cared deeply about her personal appearance.

She had gained fifty pounds in the past four years. My literary curiosity was aroused. There was a gap in this character's motivational history. "You're an attractive woman," I said, "and you care about your appearance. What happened four years ago to change you?"

She started to cry. Four years ago her daughter was found to have breast cancer. "I can't tell anybody about this," the patient said. "They talk, they talk, and if they know somebody has cancer, they won't pick up a cup if that person touched it." As she spoke, she picked up an imaginary coffee cup and then spat it away from herself. "They're all afraid, so it stays inside me like a secret." Had I not listened for her story, I would have made the mistake we all dread: I would have missed something.

Listening for stories is the first step in developing respect for their power. The next level in approaching stories is to write them, and to write them in genres different from the clinical presentation. When I teach second-year students how to interview patients, I ask them to write histories of present illness using the patient's narrative voice.[3] They write in the first person from the patient's point of view. Some complain about these assignments. "This isn't a creative writing class, is it?" they'll mumble. Most have never tried writing stories before. When they sit down to find the voice of the patient, they find the feelings and perspective of the patient as well. By taking on the patient's stance, they experience events as the patient might have. They discover the remarkable powers of writing, and I suggest, of empathy.

I use the writing of fiction to clarify my own feelings and understandings about patients. When I am confused or distressed about a patient, I write that patient into a short story. I give myself full license of the novelist. I start with known details, often scanty, about the patient's life. I fill in with fiction the gaps there are in fact. I find ways in which to tie together the events, complaints, and actions of the patient. I also place myself in the story, and this is a crucial element of my exercise. I describe myself from the patient's point of view. I play with the distance between myself as doctor and the patient, as well as the distance between myself as author and the patient.

What does this exercise do for me or for the patient? I am not surprised when details that I imagine about a patient turn out to be true. There is, after all, a deep spring of knowledge about our patients that is only slightly tapped in our conscious work. We know more about our patients than we think we do. This intuition is the basis for diagnosis as well as for interpersonal aspects of patient care. As scientists and as artists, and I submit that we are always both when we act as doctors, we rely on hints, guesses, and connections that are made not so much by our minds as by our imaginations.

Writing stories about my patients does something more important for me and my patients than discover things that I know about them. It gives me appropriate distance. Aesthetic distance, it turns out, is akin to clinical distance. Both writers and doctors have to find that perfect middle ground between identification and objectification. They neither merge with their subjects nor separate from them. They do not expropriate the subjects' experience as if it were theirs. Rather, they experience the events through the character. They let go of the characters and allow them to act, trying only to keep up with them. They open themselves to the weight and the meaning of the stories they receive.

Doctors struggle to find that middle ground. They overshoot into passive helpless sympathy with patients only to overshoot in the opposite direction into intellectual detachment. They look for a place to stand. Writing helps to find the foothold, for it allows the writer to partake of the context of that patient's life. It makes the patient become kindred without becoming self.

Michael Balint observed that a diagnosed disease is not simply "out there" in the patient, but is the result of negotiation between physician and patient. Clinical history taking and diagnosing are active processes through which a disease is constructed rather than found.[4]

This process points to the physician's part in defining the problem and deciding what is wrong. A patient does not approach us saying, "I have congestive heart failure." Rather, she approaches saying, "I feel tired all the time, and I have a hard time breathing if I work too hard." She may add, for clarity, "It all started when my daughter moved in with her three kids, and ever since then I just can't keep up with everything."

What is the problem? What is the relationship between the symptoms of shortness of breath and being overwhelmed with family responsibilities? The physician chooses an avenue of questioning and excludes data that do not belong to that line of thought. We frame patients' complaints, we array them in our minds in ways that make sense to us. Perhaps the patient would have included different material in her frame. Elliot Mishler described medical encounters as conversations between the "voice of medicine" and the "voice of the lifeworld." He suggested that effective patient care rests on both languages being heard.[5] We have to be alert to the patient's frame as well as to our own.

The point, then, is that the patient's story is coauthored by doctor and patient. They share in drawing that frame; together they select the subplots and the minor characters. They agree through practice on the relevant data to be included. When a doctor-patient relationship breaks down, it is usually because this tacit agreement was not reached and one or the other participant is uncomfortable with the frame that has been drawn.

In order to hear patient's stories, we have to acknowledge the subtexts of those stories. Patients come to doctors for trivial or tragic problems. We occupy a peculiar position for them. We are the ones who diagnose and treat their physical problems, but we also stand for a level of the transcendent in their lives. We preside at scenes of human crisis—pain, loss, death, as well as joyous ones like birth and recovery. Members of few other occupations can stand on the ground that we do—clergy perhaps, police officers in a different way. Like ministers or rabbis or police officers, we are granted entrance into private, sometimes horrifying, often sad, and always significant worlds. We are the interpreters for patients' dealings with dark and troubling events. We as physicians embody patients' hopes that they will live forever, and they expect that we can intercede with the gods or the fates when their time comes.

We are the gatekeepers not only to services of subspecialists and fancy technology but also gatekeepers to the land of the living. Susan Sontag in *Illness As Metaphor* talks about the kingdom of the well and the kingdom of the sick, and says that one is born with a citizenship in both kingdoms.[6] "Illness is the nightside of life," she says, and we, because we know about that territory, are the guides for travelers in it.

Some readers will recognize my last name from Greek mythology. Charon is the boatman who ferries souls of the dead across the river Styx to Hades. During my medicine rotation when I was a third year student, a patient recognized my name. The patient was a twenty-six-year-old man with metastatic hepatocellular carcinoma. He looked at my name tag and said, "So this is it?" He died two days later of pulmonary hemorrhage. I seriously considered changing my name, until I realized that my task is to accompany people ultimately to their deaths, and that my name was most appropriate for medicine.

Because of the nature of the work we do with patients, we are in touch with deep levels of meaning in their lives. A forty-year-old woman tries to decide whether or not to have a child. Another patient tries to decide whether the time has come to place an elderly parent in a nursing home. Another has to choose his resuscitation status.

These are the conversations that we have to train ourselves to listen for. The hesitant glance, the inarticulate sigh, or, as William Carlos Williams says, "the hunted news I get from some obscure patients' eyes"[7] carry with them profound challenge about the meaning of lives and the meaning of deaths. Even if the problem at hand is a trivial one, it will cascade through these other thoughts, because we doctors are the ones who deal in that stuff, and any brush with us connotes a brush with it.

I suggested earlier that the doctor and the patient coauthor the story. What part should the doctor play in the patient's narrative? We are taught not to get personally involved in our patients' care, that we are not to allow our personal biases or values to interfere in the care of patients. We are warned not to take friends or relatives as patients. This is all true. Yet, when a doctor sits in a room with a patient, that doctor is an active presence. The personal history of that man or woman cannot help but be involved in an encounter as fragile and as powerful as the one between doctor and patient.

A physician said to me recently, "My mother died last year, and I had to place my father in a home; he has Alzheimer's. And you know, it was my patients who saw me through it. They knew what was happening, and they were the ones who supported and comforted me through the whole thing." Another physician told me of a patient who was dying of lung cancer, a young woman. The doctor got to know the patient's family quite well. This doctor had recently lost a sister in a hiking accident. She was able to sit with the sister of this dying woman, to cry with her, to share the depth of a sister's loss.

Mr. Glade is an eighty-two-year-old patient of mine with hypertension, diabetes, and mild renal insufficiency. When I first examined him, I discovered a prostatic nodule that turned out on biopsy to be prostatic cancer. He went through surgery and radiation therapy, and suffered uncomfortable and personally shameful side-effects of the treatment. I rued the day that I had found that mass.

He is a jazz musician who had been active in the thirties jazz scene in Harlem, and he would tell me about clubs to go to in New York, and releases of Bessie Smith records. He came in to see me recently. He was feeling sick, had a urinary tract infection; his diabetes was out of control. I looked behind him as he sat in the chair in my examining room, and I saw a vision of him in hospital johnny with a 40 percent face mask, Foley in place, cefoxitin dripping in. In my vision, his creatinine was 7, his BUN 93. He was not able to respond to my voice; he was slipping away.

When I snapped back to the present tense, I was distant, coolly efficient with my questions and physical exam. I resented his being sick. I know for sure that he will die soon, and that my vision is an accurate prediction of how he will die. I was feeling prematurely my anger at his leaving. I was angry that he planned to abandon me. I know that I shall miss him once he is gone. I found a way to tell him that I wanted him to get better; I treated his UTI; and he is now doing well.

Were we physicians overstepping the boundaries between professional and personal relationships? By accepting the support of patients, by reflecting on our own losses, by forming bonds with patients that then hurt us when they die, were we being naive and maudlin?

Quite the opposite. We were appropriately using human skills and responses in human settings. We were using our own personal histories in comprehending and embracing the narratives of our patients. We did more. We increased the effectiveness of our therapeutic interventions with our patients and their families by offering our own experience into the encounter.

We all know on some level that medicine has to do with personal relationships. We chose this life because it lets us know people, lets us help them. However acute may be our interest and skill in the biotechnical aspects of medicine, we chose to become doctors because we would have patients.

A remarkable thing happens after we have known a patient for a while. We allow ourselves to sit back in the chair with peace and receptivity, to not dawdle over the Aldomet and the Inderal, but to ask with true interest, "How's it going?" It becomes clear over time that people have few opportunities to be asked those kinds of questions. Because we have been clerking the records, we know about the daughter who has been in trouble with the law, about the son who is graduating with honors from Bronx Science, about the beautician course that the patient is just finishing up, hoping to open up her own shop in the neighborhood. We follow each subplot with interest, and with interest that contributes to that patient's health. It is in these subplots that we recognize the patient in his or her uniqueness and strength. Virginia Woolf says that "the body is a sheet of plain glass through which the soul looks straight and clear. . . . The creature within can only gaze through the pane—smudged or rosy."[8] We never take care of the body without peering through it to the soul.

It turns out that there is much less difference between the sick and the well than any of us imagine. The brutal and isolating aspects of medical training and practice can be transformed into the most humanizing experience if we allow ourselves to see our fellowship with our patients. Medicine lets us glimpse the nobility, the strength, the tenacity of our fellow human beings. If we can open to the journeys of our patients, we are rewarded with a stunning landscape of the human spirit.

Doctors have an important gift to offer to people in crisis. We have seen this before. We have seen people in pain; we have seen people die. We have made it our business to learn about these things, these terrible moments for people. They rely on our having been there before.

This is our offering—to recognize. We recognize symptoms, emergencies, the need for action. If we couple this with a recognition of the people in the midst of their distress, we become complete doctors.

The stories of patients fill us with joy. It is at times a black joy, to use the words of Richard Selzer,[9] a joy incomprehensible because it is rooted in tragedy and loss. Yet there is tremendous joy in sharing meaningful events with people, strangers even, and making of those events something that can transcend the accidents of life. Our presence and recognition can endow events with grace. By entering into the deep experiences that people have within our field of vision, we can first of all learn of them ourselves, and then give wisdom to others going through them. If we allow ourselves to be instruments of hope, of resourcefulness, and of acceptance, we shall have fulfilled our oaths, we shall have used our knowledge well, and we shall be rewarded in the way only a physician can: we shall have healed.

Notes

[1]Berger, J, and Mohr, J: A Fortunate Man. New York: Pantheon Books, 1967, pp. 69, 109.

[2]Welty, E: One Writer's Beginnings. Cambridge: Harvard University Press, 1984, p. 14.

[3]Charon, R: To render the lives of patients. Literature and Medicine 5: 39–48, 1986, in press.

[4]Balint, M: The Doctor, His Patient and the Illness. New York: International University Press, 1957, p. 18.

[5]Mishler, E: The Discourse of Medicine: Dialectics of Medical Interviews. Norwood, New Jersey: Ablex Publishing Corporation, 1984, p. 192.

[6]Sontag, S: Illness as Metaphor. New York: Vintage Books, 1979, p. 3.

[7]Williams, WC: The Autobiography of William Carlos Williams. New York: New Directions Books, 1967, p. 360.

[8]Woolf, V: On being ill. In The Moment and Other Essays. London: The Hogarth Press, 1947, pp. 14–24, p. 14.

[9]Selzer, R: Letters to a Young Doctor, New York: Simon & Schuster, 1982, p. 125.

31
A Caring Dilemma: Womanhood and Nursing in Historical Perspective

Susan Reverby

"Do not undervalue [your] particular ability to care," students were reminded at a recent nursing school graduation.[1] Rather than merely bemoaning yet another form of late twentieth-century heartlessness, this admonition underscores the central dilemma of American nursing: The order to care in a society that refuses to value caring. This article is an analysis of the historical creation of that dilemma and its consequences for nursing. To explore the meaning of caring for nursing, it is necessary to unravel the terms of the relationship between nursing and womanhood as these bonds have been formed over the last century.

The Meaning of Caring

Many different disciplines have explored the various meanings of caring.[2] Much of this literature, however, runs the danger of universalizing caring as an element in female identity, or as a human quality, separate from the cultural and structural circumstances that create it. But as policy analyst Hilary Graham has argued, caring is not merely an identity; it is also work. As she notes, "Caring touches simultaneously on who you are and what you do."[3] Because of this duality, caring can be difficult to define and even harder to control. Graham's analysis moves beyond seeing caring as a psychological trait; but her focus is primarily on women's unpaid labor in the home. She does not fully discuss how the forms of caring are shaped by the contexts under which they are practiced. Caring is not just a subjective and material experience; it is a historically created one. Particular circumstances, ideologies, and power relations thus create the conditions under which caring can occur, the forms it will take, the consequences it will have for those who do it.

The basis for caring also shapes its effect. Nursing was organized under the expectation that its practitioners would accept a duty to care rather than demand a right to determine how they would satisfy this duty. Nurses were expected to act out of an obligation to care, taking on caring more as an identity than as work, and expressing altruism without thought of autonomy either at the bedside or in their profession. Thus, nurses, like others who perform what is defined as "women's work" in our society, have had to contend with what appears as a dichotomy between the duty to care for others and the right to control their own activities in the name of caring. Nursing is still searching for what philosopher Joel Feinberg argued comes prior to rights, that is, being "recognized as having a claim on rights."[4] The duty to care, organized within the political and economic context of nursing's development, has made it difficult for nurses to obtain this moral and, ultimately, political standing.

Because nurses have been given the duty to care, they are caught in a secondary dilemma: forced to act as if altruism (assumed to be the basis for caring) and autonomy (assumed to be the basis for rights) are separate ways of being. Nurses are still searching for a way to forge a link between altruism and autonomy that will allow them to have what philosopher Larry Blum and others have called "caring-with-autonomy," or what psychiatrist Jean Baker Miller labeled "a way of life that includes serving others without being subservient."[5] Nursing's historical circumstances and ideological underpinnings have made creating this way of life difficult, but not impossible, to achieve.

Caring as Duty

A historical analysis of nursing's development makes this theoretical formulation clearer. Most of the writing about American nursing's history begins in the 1870s when formal training for nursing was introduced in the United States. But nursing did not appear de novo at the end of the nineteenth century. As with most medical and health care, nursing throughout the colonial era and most of the nineteenth century took place within the family and the home. In the domestic pantheon that surrounded "middling" and upper-class American womanhood in the nineteenth century, a woman's caring for friends and relatives was an important pillar. Nursing was often taught by mother to daughter as part of female apprenticeship, or learned by a domestic servant as an additional task on her job. [It was] embedded in the seemingly natural or ordained character of women's expression of love of others, and was thus integral to the female sense of self.[6] In a society where deeply felt religious tenets were translated into gendered virtues, domesticity advocate Catharine Beecher declared that the sick were to be "commended" to a "woman's benevolent ministries."[7]

The responsibility for nursing went beyond a mother's duty for her children, a wife's for her husband, or a daughter's for her aging parents. It attached to all the available female family members. The family's "long arm" might reach out at any time to a woman working in a distant city, in a mill, or as a maid, pulling her home to care for the sick, infirm, or newborn. No form of women's labor, paid or unpaid, protected her from this demand. "You may be called upon at any moment," Eliza W. Farrar warned in *The Young Lady's Friend* in 1837, "to attend upon your parents, your brothers, your sisters, or your companions."[8] Nursing was to be, therefore, a woman's duty, not her job. Obligation and love, not the need of work, were to bind the nurse to her patient. Caring was to be an unpaid labor of love.

The Professed Nurse

Even as Eliza Farrar was proffering her advice, pressures both inward and outward were beginning to reshape the domestic sphere for women of the then-called "middling classes." Women's obligations and work were transformed by the expanding industrial economy and changing cultural assumptions. Parenting took on increasing importance as notions of "moral mothering" filled the domestic arena and other productive labor entered the cash nexus. Female benevolence similarly moved outward as women's charitable efforts took increasingly institutional forms. Duty began to take on new meaning as such women were advised they could fulfill their nursing responsibilities by managing competently those they hired to assist them. Bourgeois female virtue could still be demonstrated as the balance of labor, love, and supervision shifted.[9]

An expanding economy thus had differing effects on women of various classes. For those in the growing urban middle classes, excess cash made it possible to consider hiring a nurse when circumstances, desire, or exhaustion meant a female relative was no longer available for the task. Caring as labor, for these women, could be separated from love.

For older widows or spinsters from the working classes, nursing became a trade they could "profess" relatively easily in the marketplace. A widow who had nursed her husband till his demise, or a domestic servant who had cared for an employer in time of illness, entered casually into the nursing trade, hired by families or individuals unwilling, or unable, to care for their sick alone. The permeable boundaries for women between unpaid and paid labor allowed nursing to pass back and forth when necessary. For many women, nursing thus beckoned as respectable community work.

These "professed" or "natural-born" nurses, as they were known, usually came to their work, as one Boston nurse put it, "laterly" when other forms of employment were closed to them or the lack of any kind of work experience left nursing as an obvious choice. Mehitable Pond Garside, for example, was in her fifties and had outlived two husbands—and her children could not, or would not, support her—when she came to Boston in the 1840s to nurse. Similarly Alma Frost Merrill, the daughter of a Maine wheelwright, came to Boston in 1818 at nineteen to become a domestic servant. After years as a domestic and seamstress, she declared herself a nurse.[10]

Women like Mehitable Pond Garside and Alma Frost Merrill differed markedly from the Sairy Gamp character of Dickens' novel, *Martin Chuzzlewit*. Gamp was portrayed as a merely besotted representative of lumpen-proletarian womanhood, who asserted her autonomy by daring to question medical diagnosis, to venture her own opinions (usually outrageous and wrong) at every turn, and to spread disease and superstition in the name of self-knowledge. If they were not Gamps, nurses like Garside and Merrill also were not the healers of some more recent feminist mythology that confounds nursing with midwifery, praising the caring and autonomy these women exerted, but refusing to consider their ignorance.[11] Some professed nurses learned their skills from years of experience, demonstrating the truth of the dictum that "to make a kind and sympathizing nurse, one must have waited, in sickness, upon those she loved dearly."[12] Others, however, blundered badly beyond their capabilities or knowledge. They brought to the bedside only the authority their personalities and community stature could command: Neither credentials nor a professional identity gave weight to their efforts. Their womanhood, and the experience it gave them, defined their authority and taught them to nurse.

The Hospital Nurse

Nursing was not limited, however, to the bedside in a home. Although the United States had only 178 hospitals at the first national census in 1873, it was workers labeled "nurses" who provided the caring. As in home-based nursing, the route to hospital nursing was paved more with necessity than with intentionality. In 1875, Eliza Higgins, the matron of Boston's Lying-In Hospital, could not find an extra nurse to cover all the deliveries. In desperation, she moved the hospital laundress up to the nursing position, while a recovering patient took over the wash. Higgins' diaries of her trying years at the Lying-In suggest that such an entry into nursing was not uncommon.[13]

As Higgins' reports and memoirs of other nurses attest, hospital nursing could be the work of devoted women who learned what historian Charles Rosenberg has labeled "ad hoc professionalism," or the temporary and dangerous labor of an ambulatory patient or hospital domestic.[14] As in home-based nursing, both caring and concern were frequently demonstrated. But the nursing work and nurses were mainly characterized by the diversity of their efforts and the unevenness of their skills.

Higgins' memoirs attest to the hospital as a battleground where nurses, physicians, and hospital managers contested the realm of their authority. Nurses continually affirmed their right to control the pace and content of their work, to set their own hours, and to structure their relationships to physicians. Aware that the hospital's paternalistic attitudes and practices toward its "inmates" were attached to the nursing personnel as well, they fought to be treated as workers, "not children," as the Lying-In nurses told Eliza Higgins, and to maintain their autonomous adult status.[15]

Like home-based nursing, hospital nurses had neither formal training nor class status upon which to base their arguments. But their sense of the rights of working-class womanhood gave them authority to press their demands. The necessity to care, and their perception of its importance to patient outcome, also structured their belief that demanding the right to be relatively autonomous was possible. However, their efforts were undermined by the nature of their onerous work, the paternalism of the institutions, class differences between trustees and workers, and ultimately the lack of a defined ideology of caring. Mere resistance to those above them, or contending assertions of rights, could not become the basis for nursing authority.

The Influence of Nightingale

Much of this changed with the introduction of training for nursing in the hospital world. In the aftermath of Nightingale's triumph over the British army's medical care system in the Crimea, similar attempts by American women during the Civil War, and the need to find respectable work for daughters of the middling classes, a model and support for nursing reform began to grow. By 1873, three nursing schools in hospitals in New York, Boston, and New Haven were opened, patterned after the Nightingale School at St. Thomas' Hospital in London.

Nightingale had envisioned nursing as an art, rather than a science, for which women needed to be trained. Her ideas linked her medical and public health notions to her class and religious beliefs. Accepting the Victorian idea of divided spheres of activity for men and women, she thought women had to be trained to nurse through a disciplined process of honing their womanly virtue. Nightingale stressed character development, the laws of health, and strict adherence to orders passed through a female hierarchy. Nursing was built on a model that relied on the concept of duty to provide its basis for authority. Unlike other feminists at the time, she spoke in the language of duty, not rights.

Furthermore, as a nineteenth-century sanitarian, Nightingale never believed in germ theory, in part because she refused to accept a theory of disease etiology that appeared to be morally neutral. Given her sanitarian beliefs, Nightingale thought medical therapeutics and "curing" were of lesser importance to patient outcome, and she willingly left this realm to the physician. Caring, the arena she did think of great importance, she assigned to the nurse. In order to care, a nurse's character, tempered by the fires of training, was to be her greatest skill. Thus, to "feminize" nursing. Nightingale sought a change in the class-defined behavior, not the gender, of the work force.[16]

To forge a good nurse out of the virtues of a good woman and to provide a political base for nursing, Nightingale sought to organize a female hierarchy in which orders passed down from the nursing superintendent to the lowly probationer. This separate female sphere was to share power in the provision of health care with the male-dominated arenas of medicine. For many women in the Victorian era, sisterhood and what Carroll Smith-Rosenberg has called "homosocial networks" served to overcome many of the limits of this separate but supposedly equal system of cultural division.[17] Sisterhood, after all, at least in its fictive forms, underlay much of the female power that grew out of women's culture in the nineteenth century. But in nursing, commonalities of the gendered experience could not become the basis of unity since hierarchial filial relations, not equal sisterhood, lay at the basis of nursing's theoretical formulation.

Service, Not Education

Thus, unwittingly, Nightingale's sanitarian ideas and her beliefs about womanhood provided some of the ideological justification for many of the dilemmas that faced American nursing by 1900. Having fought physician and trustee prejudice against the training of nurses in hospitals in the last quarter of the nineteenth century, American nursing reformers succeeded only too well as the new century began. Between 1890 and 1920, the number of nursing schools jumped from 35 to 1,775, and the number of trained nurses from 16 per 100,000 in the population to 141.[18] Administrators quickly realized that opening a "nursing school" provided their hospitals, in exchange for training, with a young, disciplined, and cheap labor force. There were often no differences between the hospital's nursing school and its nursing service. The service needs of the hospital continually overrode the educational requirements of the schools. A student might, therefore, spend weeks on a medical ward if her labor was so needed, but never see the inside of an operating room before her graduation.

Once the nurse finished her training, however, she was unlikely to be hired by a hospital because it relied on either untrained aides or nursing student labor. The majority of graduate nurses, until the end of the 1930s, had to find work in private duty in a patient's home, as the patient's employee in the hospital, in the branches of public health, or in some hospital staff positions. In the world of nursing beyond the training school, "trained" nurses still had to compete with the thousands of "professed" or "practical" nurses who continued to ply their trade in an overcrowded and unregulated marketplace. The title of nurse took on very ambiguous meanings.[19]

The term, "trained nurse," was far from a uniform designation. As nursing leader Isabel Hampton Robb lamented in 1893, "the title 'trained nurse' may mean then anything, everything, or next to nothing."[20]

The exigencies of nursing acutely ill or surgical patients required the sacrifice of coherent educational programs. Didactic, repetitive, watered-down medical lectures by physicians or older nurses were often provided for the students, usually after they finished ten to twelve hours of ward work. Training emphasized the "one right way" of doing ritualized procedures in hopes the students' adherence to specified rules would be least dangerous to patients.[21] Under these circumstances, the duty to care could be followed with a vengeance and become the martinet adherence to orders.

Furthermore, because nursing emphasized training in discipline, order, and practical skills, the abuse of student labor could be rationalized. And because the work force was almost entirely women, altruism, sacrifice and submission were expected, encouraged, indeed, demanded. Exploitation was inevitable in a field where, until the early 1900s, there were no accepted standards for how much work an average student should do or how many patients she could successfully care for, no mechanisms through which to enforce such standards. After completing her exhaustive and depressing survey of nursing training in 1912, nursing educator M. Adelaide Nutting bluntly pointed out: "Under the present system the school has no life of its own."[22] In this kind of environment, nurses were trained. But they were not educated.

Virtue and Autonomy

It would be a mistake, however to see the nursing experience only as one of exploitation and the nursing school as a faintly concealed reformatory for the wayward girl in need of discipline. Many nursing superintendents lived the Nightingale ideals as best they could and infused them into their schools. The authoritarian model could and did retemper many women. It instilled in nurses idealism and pride in their skills, somewhat differentiated the trained nurse from the untrained, and protected and aided the sick and dying. It provided a mechanism for virtuous women to contribute to the improvement of humanity by empowering them to care.

For many of the young women entering training in the nineteenth and early twentieth centuries, nursing thus offered something quite special: both a livelihood and a virtuous state. As one nursing educator noted in 1890: "Young strong country girls are drawn into the work by the glamorer [sic] thrown about hospital work and the halo that sanctifies a Nightingale."[23] Thus, in their letters of application, aspiring nursing students expressed their desire for work, independence, and womanly virtue. As with earlier, nontrained nurses, they did not seem to separate autonomy and altruism, but rather sought its linkage through training. Flora Jones spoke for many such women when she wrote the superintendent of Boston City Hospital in 1880, declaring, "I consider myself fitted for the work by inclination and consider it a womanly occupation. It is also necessary for me to become self-supporting and provide for my future."[24] Thus, one nursing superintendent reminded a graduating class in 1904: "You have become self-controlled, unselfish, gentle, compassionate, brave, capable—in fact, you have risen from the period of irresponsible girlhood to that of womanhood."[25] For women like Flora Jones, and many of nursing's early leaders, nursing was the singular way to grow to maturity in a womanly profession that offered meaningful work, independence, and altruism.[26]

Altruism, Not Independence

For many, however, as nursing historian Dorothy Sheahan has noted, the training school, "was a place where . . . women learned to be girls."[27] The range of permissible behaviors for respectable women was often narrowed further through training. Independence was to be sacrificed on the altar of altruism. Thus, despite hopes of aspiring students and promises of training school superintendents, nursing rarely united altruism and autonomy. Duty remained the basis for caring.

Some nurses were able to create what they called "a little world of our own." But nursing had neither the financial nor the cultural power to create the separate women's institutions that provided so much of the basis for women's reform and rights efforts.[28] Under these conditions, nurses found it difficult to make the collective transition out of a woman's culture of obligation into an activist assault on the structure and beliefs that oppressed them. Nursing remained bounded by its ideology and its material circumstances.

The Contradictions of Reform

In this context, one begins to understand the difficulties faced by the leaders of nursing reform. Believing that educational reform was central to nursing's professionalizing efforts and clinical improvements, a small group of elite reformers attempted to broaden nursing's scientific content and social outlook. In arguing for an increase in the scientific knowledge necessary in nursing, such leaders were fighting against deep-seated cultural assumptions about male and female "natural" characteristics as embodied in the doctor and the nurse. Such sentiments were articulated in the routine platitudes that graced what one nursing leader described as the "doctor homilies" that were a regular feature at nursing graduation exercises.[29]

Not surprisingly, such beliefs were professed by physicians and hospital officials whenever nursing shortages appeared, or nursing groups pushed for higher educational standards or defined nursing as more than assisting the physician. As one nursing educator wrote, with some degree of resignation after the influenza pandemic in 1920: "It is perhaps inevitable that the difficulty of securing nurses during the last year or two should have revived again the old agitation about the 'over-training' of nurses and the clamor for a cheap worker of the old servant-nurse type."[30]

First Steps toward Professionalism

The nursing leadership, made up primarily of educators and supervisors with their base within what is now the American Nurses' Association and the National League for Nursing, thus faced a series of dilemmas as they struggled to raise educational standards in the schools and criteria for entry into training, to register nurses once they finished their training, and to gain acceptance for the knowledge base and skills of the nurse. They had to exalt the womanly character, self-abnegation, and service ethic of nursing while insisting on the right of nurses to act in their own self-interest. They had to demand higher wages commensurate with their skills, yet not appear commercial. They had to simultaneously find a way to denounce the exploitation of nursing students, as they made political alliances with hospital physicians and administrators whose support they needed. While they lauded character and sacrifice, they had to find a way to measure it with educational criteria in order to formulate registration laws and set admission standards. They had to make demands and organize, without appearing "unladylike." In sum, they were forced by the social conditions and ideology surrounding nursing to attempt to professionalize altruism without demanding autonomy.

Undermined by Duty

The image of a higher claim of duty also continually undermined a direct assertion of the right to determine that duty. Whether at a bedside, or at a legislative hearing on practice laws, the duty to care became translated into the demand that nurses merely follow doctors' orders. The tradition of obligation almost made it impossible for nurses to speak about rights at all. By the turn of the century necessity and desire were pulling more young women into the labor force, and the women's movement activists were placing rights at the center of cultural discussion. In this atmosphere, nursing's call to duty was perceived by many as an increasingly antiquated language to shore up a changing economic and cultural landscape. Nursing became a type of collective female grasping for an older form of security and power in the face of rapid change. Women who might have been attracted to nursing in the 1880s as a womanly occupation that provided some form of autonomy, were, by the turn of the century, increasingly looking elsewhere for work and careers.

A Different Vision

In the face of these difficulties, the nursing leadership became increasingly defensive and turned on its own rank and file. The educators and supervisors who comprised leadership lost touch with the pressing concern of their constituencies in the daily work world of nursing and the belief systems such nurses continued to hold. Yet many nurses, well into the twentieth century, shared the nineteenth-century vision of nursing as the embodiment of womanly virtue. A nurse named Annette Fiske, for example, although she authored two science books for nurses and had an M.A. degree in classics from Radcliffe College before she entered training, spent her professional career in the 1920s arguing against increasing educational standards. Rather, she called for a reinfusion into nursing of spirituality and service, assuming that this would result in nursing's receiving greater "love and respect and admiration."[31]

Other nurses, especially those trained in the smaller schools or reared to hold working-class ideals about respectable behavior in women, shared Fiske's views. They saw the leadership's efforts at professionalization as an attempt to push them out of nursing. Their adherence to nursing skill measured in womanly virtue was less a conservative and reactionary stance than a belief that seemed to transcend class and educational backgrounds to place itself in the individual character and work-place skills of the nurse. It grounded altruism in supposedly natural and spiritual, rather than educational and middle-class, soil. For Fiske and many other nurses, nursing was still a womanly art that required inherent character in its practitioners and training in practical skills and spiritual values in its schools. Their beliefs about nursing did not require the professionalization of altruism, nor the demand for autonomy either at the bedside or in control over the professionalization process.

Still other nurses took a more pragmatic viewpoint that built on their pride in their work-place skills and character. These nurses also saw the necessity for concerted action, not unlike that taken by other American workers. Such nurses fought against what one 1888 nurse, who called herself Candor, characterized as the "missionary spirit . . . [of] self-immolation" that denied that nurses worked because they had to make a living.[32] These worker-nurses saw no contradiction between demanding decent wages and conditions for their labors and being of service for those in need. But the efforts of various groups of these kinds of nurses to turn to hours' legislation, trade union activity, or mutual aid associations were criticized and condemned by the nursing leadership. Their letters were often edited out of the nursing journals, and their voices silenced in public meetings as they were denounced as being commercial, or lacking in proper womanly devotion.[33]

In the face of continual criticism from nursing's professional leadership, the worker-nurses took on an increasingly angry and defensive tone. Aware that their sense of the nurse's skills came from the experiences of the work place, not book learning or degrees, they had to assert this position despite continued hostility toward such a basis of nursing authority.[34] Although the position of women like Candor helped articulate a way for nurses to begin to assert the right to care, it did not constitute a full-blown ideological counterpart to the overwhelming power of the belief in duty.

The Persistence of Dilemmas

By midcentury, the disputes between worker-nurses and the professional leadership began to take on new forms, although the persistent divisions continued. Aware that some kind of collective bargaining was necessary to keep nurses out of the unions and in the professional associations, the ANA reluctantly agreed in 1946 to let its state units act as bargaining agents. The nursing leadership has continued to look at educational reform strategies, now primarily taking the form of legislating for the B.S. degree as the credential necessary for entry into nursing practice, and to changes in the practice laws that will allow increasingly skilled nurses the autonomy and status they deserve. Many nurses have continued to be critical of this educational strategy, to ignore the professional associations, or to leave nursing altogether.

In their various practice fields nurses still need a viable ideology and strategy that will help them adjust to the continual demands of patients and an evermore bureaucratized, cost-conscious, and rationalized work setting. For many nurses it is still, in an ideological sense, the nineteenth century. Even for those nurses who work as practitioners in the more autonomous settings of health maintenance organizations or public health offices, the legacy of nursing's heritage is still felt. Within the last two years, for example, the Massachusetts Board of Medicine tried to push through a regulation that health practitioners acknowledge their dependence on physicians by wearing a badge that identified their supervising physician and stated that they were not doctors.

Nurses have tried various ways to articulate a series of rights that allow them to care. The acknowledgment of responsibilities, however, so deeply ingrained in nursing and American womanhood, as nursing school dean Claire Fagin has noted, continually drown out the nurse's assertion of rights.[35]

Nurses are continuing to struggle to obtain the right to claim rights. Nursing's educational philosophy, ideological underpinnings, and structural position have made it difficult to create the circumstances within which to gain such recognition. It is not a lack of vision that thwarts nursing, but the lack of power to give that vision substantive form.[36]

Beyond the Obligation to Care

Much has changed in nursing in the last forty years. The severing of nursing education from the hospital's nursing services has finally taken place, as the majority of nurses are now educated in colleges, not hospital-based diploma schools. Hospitals are experimenting with numerous ways to organize the nursing service to provide the nurse with more responsibility and sense of control over the nursing care process. The increasingly technical and machine-aided nature of hospital-based health care has made nurses feel more skilled.

In many ways, however, little has changed. Nursing is still divided over what counts as a nursing skill, how it is to be learned, and whether a nurse's character can be measured in educational criteria. Technical knowledge and capabilities do not easily translate into power and control. Hospitals, seeking to cut costs, have forced nurses to play "beat the clock" as they run from task to task in an increasingly fragmented setting.[37]

Nursing continues to struggle with the basis for, and the value of, caring. The fact that the first legal case on comparable worth was brought by a group of Denver nurses suggests nursing has an important and ongoing role in the political effort to have caring revalued. As in the Denver case, contemporary feminism has provided some nurses with the grounds on which to claim rights from their caring.[38]

Feminism, in its liberal form, appears to give nursing a political language that argues for equality and rights within the given order of things. It suggests a basis for caring that stresses individual discretion and values, acknowledging that the nurses' right to care should be given equal consideration with the physician's right to cure. Just as liberal political theory undermined more paternalistic formulations of government, classical liberalism's tenets applied to women have much to offer nursing. The demand for the right to care questions deeply held beliefs about gendered relations in the health care hierarchy and the structure of the hierarchy itself.

Many nurses continue to hope that with more education, explicit theories to explain the scientific basis for nursing, new skills, and a lot of assertiveness training, nursing will change. As these nurses try to shed the image of the nurse's being ordered to care, however, the admonition to care at a graduation speech has to be made. Unable to find a way to "care with autonomy" and unable to separate caring from its valuing and basis, many nurses find themselves forced to abandon the effort to care, or nursing altogether.

Altruism with Autonomy

These dilemmas for nurses suggest the constraints that surround the effectiveness of a liberal feminist political strategy to address the problems of caring and, therefore, of nursing. The individualism and autonomy of a rights framework often fail to acknowledge collective social need, to provide a way for adjudicating conflicts over rights, or to address the reasons for the devaluing of female activity.[39] Thus, nurses have often rejected liberal feminism, not just out of their oppression and "false consciousness," but because of some deep understandings of the limited promise of equality and autonomy in a health care system they see as flawed and harmful. In an often inchoate way, such nurses recognize that those who claim the autonomy of rights often run the risk of rejecting altruism and caring itself.

Several feminist psychologists have suggested that what women really want in their lives is autonomy with connectedness. Similarly, many modern moral philosophers are trying to articulate a formal moral theory that values the emotions and the importance of relationships.[40] For nursing, this will require the creation of the conditions under which it is possible to value caring and to understand that the empowerment of others does not have to require self-immolation. To achieve this, nurses will have both to create a new political understanding for the basis of caring and to find ways to gain the power to implement it. Nursing can do much to have this happen through research on the importance of caring on patient outcome, studies of patient improvements in nursing settings where the right to care is created, or implementing nursing control of caring through a bargaining agreement. But nurses cannot do this alone. The dilemma of nursing is too tied to society's broader problems of gender and class to be solved solely by the political or professional efforts to one occupational group.

Nor are nurses alone in benefiting from such an effort. If nursing can achieve the power to practice altruism with autonomy, all of us have much to gain. Nursing has always been a much conflicted metaphor in our culture, reflecting all the ambivalences we give to the meaning of womanhood.[41] Perhaps in the future it can give this metaphor and, ultimately, caring, new value in all our lives.

Notes

[1] Gregory Wticher, "Last Class of Nurses Told: Don't Stop Caring," *Boston Globe*, May 13, 1985, pp. 17–18.

[2] See, for examples, Larry Blum et al., "Altruism and Women's Oppression," in *Women and Philosophy*, eds. Carol Gould and Marx Wartofsy (New York: G.P. Putnam's, 1976), pp. 222–247; Nel Noddings, *Caring*. Berkeley: University of California Press, 1984; Nancy Chodorow, *The Reproduction of Mothering*. Berkeley: University of California Press, 1978; Carol Gilligan, *In a Different Voice*. Cambridge: Harvard University Press, 1982; and Janet Finch and Dulcie Groves, eds., *A Labour of Love: Women, Work and Caring*. London and Boston: Routledge, Kegan Paul, 1983.

[3] Hilary Graham, "Caring: A Labour of Love," in *A Labour of Love*, eds. Finch and Groves, pp. 13–30.

[4] Joel Feinberg, *Rights, Justice and the Bounds of Liberty* (Princeton: Princeton University Press, 1980), p. 141.

[5] Blum et al., "Altruism and Women's Oppression," p. 223; Jean Baker Miller, *Toward a New Psychology of Women* (Boston: Beacon Press, 1976), p. 71.

[6] Ibid; see also Iris Marion Young, "Is Male Gender Identity the Cause of Male Domination," in *Mothering: Essays in Feminist Theory*, ed. Joyce Trebicott (Totowa, NJ: Rowman and Allanheld, 1983), pp. 129–146.

[7] Catherine Beecher, *Domestic Receipt-Book* (New York: Harper and Brothers, 1846) p. 214.

[8] Eliza Farrar, *The Young Lady's Friend—By a Lady* (Boston: American Stationer's Co., 1837), p. 57.

[9] Catherine Beecher, *Miss Beecher's Housekeeper and Healthkeeper*. New York: Harper and Brothers, 1876; and Sarah Josepha Hale, *The Good Housekeeper*. Boston: Otis Brothers and Co., 7th edition, 1844. See also Susan Strasser, *Never Done: A History of Housework*. New York: Pantheon, 1982.

[10] Cases 2 and 18, "Admissions Committee Records," Volume I, Box 11, Home for Aged Women Collection, Schlesigner Library, Radcliffe College, Cambridge. Data on the nurses admitted to the home were also found in "Records of Inmates, 1858–1901," "Records of Admission, 1873–1924," and "Records of Inmates, 1901–1916," all in Box 11.

[11] Charles Dickens, *Martin Chuzzlewit*. New York: New American Library, 1965, original edition, London: 1865; Barbara Ehrenreich and Deirdre English, *Witches, Nurses, Midwives: A History of Women Healers*. Old Westbury: Glass Mountain Pamphlets, 1972.

[12] Virginia Penny, *The Employments of Women: A Cyclopedia of Women's Work* (Boston: Walker, Wise and Co., 1863), p. 420.

13 Eliza Higgins, Boston Lying-In Hospital, *Matron's Journals, 1873–1889*, Volume I, January 9, 1875, February 22, 1875, Rare Books Room, Countway Medical Library, Harvard Medical School, Boston.

[14] Charles Rosenberg, "'And Heal the Sick': The Hospital and the Patient in 19th Century America," *Journal of Social History* 10 (June 1977): 445.

[15] Higgins, *Matron's Journals*, Volume II, January 11, 1876, and July 1, 1876. See also a parallel discussion of male artisan behavior in front of the boss in David Montgomery, "Workers' Control of Machine Production in the 19th Century," *Labor History* 17 (Winter 1976): 485–509.

[16] The discussion on Florence Nightingale is based on my analysis in *Ordered to Care*, chapter 3. See also Charles E. Rosenberg, "Florence Nightingale on Contagion: The Hospital as Moral Universe, in *Healing and History*, ed. Charles E. Rosenberg. New York: Science History Publications, 1979.

17 Carroll Smith-Rosenberg. "The Female World of Love and Ritual," *Signs: Journal of Women in Culture and Society* 1 (Autumn 1975): 1.

[18] May Ayers Burgess, *Nurses, Patients and Pocketbooks*. New York: Committee on the Grading of Nursing, 1926, reprint edition (New York: Garland Publishing, 1985), pp. 36–37.

[19] For further discussion of the dilemmas of private duty nursing, see Susan Reverby, "'Neither for the Drawing Room nor for the Kitchen': Private Duty Nursing, 1880–1920," in *Women and Health in America*, ed. Judith Walzer Leavitt. Madison: University of Wisconsin Press, 1984, and Susan Reverby, "'Something Besides Waiting': The Politics of Private Duty Nursing Reform in the Depression," in *Nursing History: New Perspectives, New Possibilities*, ed. Ellen Condliffe Lagemann. New York: Teachers College Press, 1982.

[20] Isabel Hampton Robb, "Educational Standards for Nurses," in *Nursing of the Sick 1893* (New York: McGraw-Hill, 1949), p. 11. See also Janet Wilson James, "Isabel Hampton and the Professionalization of Nursing in the 1890s," in *The Therapeutic Revolution*, eds. Morris Vogel and Charles E. Rosenberg. Philadelphia: University of Pennsylvania Press, 1979.

[21] For further discussion of the difficulties in training, see JoAnn Ashley, *Hospitals, Paternalism and the Role of the Nurse*. New York: Teachers College Press, 1976, and Reverby, *Ordered to Care*, chapter 4.

[22] *Educational Status of Nursing*, Bureau of Education Bulletin Number 7, Whole Number 475 (Washington, DC: Government Printing Office, 1912), p. 49.

23 Julia Wells, "Do Hospitals Fit Nurses for Private Nursing," *Trained Nurse and Hospital Review* 3 (March 1890): 98.

[24] Boston City Hospital (BCH) Training School Records, Box 4, Folder 4, Student 4, February 14, 1880, BCH Training School Papers, Nursing Archives, Special Collections, Boston University, Mugar Library, Boston. The student's name has been changed to maintain confidentiality.

[25] Mary Agnes Snively, "What Manner of Women Ought Nurses to Be?" *American Journal of Nursing* 4 (August 1904): 838.

[26] For a discussion of many of the early nursing leaders as "new women," see Susan Armeny, "'We Were the New Women': A Comparison of Nurses and Women Physicians, 1890–1915." Paper presented at the American Association for the History of Nursing Conference, University of Virginia, Charlottesville, October 1984.

[27] Dorothy Sheahan, "Influence of Occupational Sponsorship on the Professional Development of Nursing." Paper presented at the Rockefeller Archives Conference on the History of Nursing, Rockefeller Archives, Tarrytown, NY, May 1981, p. 12.

[28] Estelle Freedman, "Separatism as Strategy: Female Institution Building and American Feminism, 1870–1930," *Feminist Studies* 5 (Fall 1979): 512–529.

[29] Lavinia L. Dock, *A History of Nursing*, volume 3 (New York: G.P. Putnam's, 1912), p. 136.

[30] Isabel M. Stewart, "Progress in Nursing Education during 1919," *Modern Hospital* 14 (March 1920): 183.

[31] Annette Fiske, "How Can We Counteract the Prevailing Tendency to Commercialism in Nursing?" *Proceedings of the 17th Annual Meeting of the Massachusetts State Nurses' Association*, p. 8, Massachusetts Nurses Association Papers, Box 7, Nursing Archives.

[32] Candor, "Working and Wages," Letter to the Editor, *Trained Nurse and Hospital Review* 2 (April 1888):167–168.

[33] See the discussion in Ashley, *Hospitals, Paternalism and the Role of the Nurse*, pp. 40–43, 46–48, 51, and in Barbara Melosh, "The Physician's Hand": Work Culture and Conflict in American Nursing (Philadelphia: Temple University Press, 1982), passim.

[34] For further discussion see Susan Armeny, "Resolute Enthusiasts: The Effort to Professionalize American Nursing, 1880–1915." Ph.D. dissertation, University of Missouri, Columbia, 1984, and Reverby, *Ordered to Care*, chapter 6.

[35] Feinberg, *Rights*, pp. 130–142; Claire Fagin, "Nurses' Rights," *American Journal of Nursing* 75 (January 1975): 82.

[36] For a similar argument for bourgeois women, see Carroll Smith-Rosenberg, "The New Woman as Androgyne: Social Disorder and Gender Crisis," in *Disorderly Conduct* (New York: Alfred Knopf, 1985), p. 296.

[37] Boston Nurses' Group, "The False Promise: Professionalism in Nursing," *Science for the People* 10 (May/June 1978): 20–34; Jennifer Bingham Hull, "Hospital Nightmare: Cuts in Staff Demoralize Nurses as Care Suffers," *Wall Street Journal*, March 27, 1985.

[38] Bonnie Bullough, "The Struggle for Women's Rights in Denver: A Personal Account," *Nursing Outlook* 26 (September 1978): 566–567.

[39] For critiques of liberal feminism see Allison M. Jagger, *Feminist Politics and Human Nature* (Totowa, NJ: Rowman and Allanheld, 1983), pp. 27–50, 173, 206; Zillah Eisenstein, *The Radical Future of Liberal Feminism*. New York and London: Longman, 1981; and Rosalind Pollack Petchesky, *Abortion and Women's Choice* (Boston: Northeastern University Press, 1984), pp. 1–24.

[40] Miller, *Toward a New Psychology*; Jane Flax, "The Conflict between Nurturance and Autonomy in Mother-Daughter Relationships and within Feminism," *Feminist Studies* 4 (June 1978): 171–191; Blum et al., "Altruism and Women's Oppression."

[41] Claire Fagin and Donna Diers, "Nursing as Metaphor," *New England Journal of Medicine* 309 (July 14, 1983): 116–117.

32
Nurses' Role: Caring, Professionalism, and Subordination

Daniel Chambliss

Nurses Care For Patients

"Care" is the key term in nursing's definition of itself, and crucially defines what nurses believe is their task. Anytime a group of nurses talk with an outsider about their work or its meaning, someone will certainly utter this most positive of nursing words. Important books about nursing use it in their titles;[1] job advertisements in nursing journals depict nurses holding small children, or smiling at an elderly patient, and promise job applicants to their hospital the unrestricted opportunity truly to "care." Care, some nurses say, distinguishes nursing from medicine: "Nurses care, doctors cure"; and while physicians might dispute the moral connotations of that slogan, few would completely deny its message. "Caring" figures centrally in the stories nurses tell of their own best work experiences. It may be true, as historian Susan Reverby says, that "a crucial dilemma in contemporary American nursing" is "the order [to nurses] to care in a society that refuses to value caring,"[2] but among nurses, the willingness to care when that is difficult is the distinguishing mark of the nurse.

As nurses use the term, "care" seems to include four meanings: face-to-face working with patients, dealing with the patient as a whole person, the comparatively open-ended nature of the nurse's duties, and the personal commitment of the nurse to her work. All of these are included in what nurses mean by "caring." To a moderate degree, "caring" describes what nurses actually *do;* to a great degree, it describes what nurses believe they *should* do.

1. *Nursing care is hands-on,* a face-to-face encounter with a patient. Unlike in medicine, in nursing there can be no quick review of lab reports, a scribbling of orders, and then a fast exit down the hall. Nurses carry out the scribbled orders, deliver the medications, pass the food trays, monitor the IVs and the ventilators. Nurses give

From Daniel Chambliss, 1996, *Beyond Caring* (Chicago: The University of Chicago Press), pp. 63–79. Reprinted with permission.

baths, catheterize patients, turn patients who cannot move themselves, clean bedsores, change soiled sheets, and constantly watch patients, writing notes on their patients' progress or deterioration. Close patient contact, with all five senses, is nursing's specialty. ("I could never be a nurse," says one unit clerk. "I couldn't stand all those smells.") Nurses are constantly talking with, listening to, and touching their patients in intimate ways; the prototypical, universal dirty work of nursing is "wiping bottoms." One nurse explains why in her unit nurses no longer wear the classic white uniform:

> It wouldn't stay white very long: there's red blood, feces of various colors, green bile, yellowish mucous, vomit, projectile defecations. [Field Notes]

Physicians visit floors to perform major procedures (inserting tubes into the chest, bronchoscopies); but most of what is said and physically done to patients is said and done by bedside nurses.

The nurse works primarily in a contained space, on one floor or unit; if the patients are very sick, she stays in one or two rooms. She is geographically contained and sharply focused, on this room, this patient, perhaps even this small patch of skin where the veins are "blown" and the intravenous line won't go in. She remains close to this small space, or on the same hallway, for a full shift, at least eight hours and in intensive care areas twelve hours; often she is there for two or even three shifts in a row. With the chronic shortage of nurses she frequently stays and works overtime. I have known a sizable number of nurses, in different hospitals, who worked double and triple shifts—up to twenty-four straight hours—on both floors and in ICUs. One such nurse enjoys double shifts because "I don't have to rush [to finish paperwork] . . . if it isn't done in the first shift, I'll get it done in the evening." So nurses have close contact with their patients over time, hour by hour if not minute by minute, for an extended period of time—"around the clock," they say, and sometimes this is precisely true. This close contact, over time, in a confined space, can give nurses the sense that they know better than anyone else what is happening with their patients; and they may resent any other view:

> Doctor, commenting on geriatric patient: "She looks better today."
> Nurse: "You haven't had to fuck with her all morning."
> Doctor (pause, then tentatively): "She looks better than when she came in." [Field Notes]

No doubt, the "continuity of care" by nurses can be exaggerated by nurses themselves. In fact, with rotating nursing schedules, shifting assignments, the short turnaround time of many nursing tasks, and the constant turnover of nursing personnel, it is not clear that nurses provide continuity at all. Few nurses are actually on the scene "around the clock," and only occasionally is one nurse responsible for the total care of a particular patient. Nevertheless, the geographical restriction of a nurse to one area does enhance her knowledge of the condition of those patients, even when she isn't personally caring for them.

To care for patients, then, first means that one works directly, spatially and temporally, with sick people.

2. *Care means that the patient should be treated not merely as a biological organism* or the site of some disease entity, but as a human being with a life beyond the hospital and a meaning beyond the medical world. Nurses certainly handle the physiological treatment of disease, but they also spend time teaching patients (on dialysis units, e.g., this may be their major task), answering the family's questions, listening to the patient's worries, calling for social service consultations, helping fill out insurance forms, or even, to use a fairly common example, helping an old person find a pair of glasses lost somewhere in the sheets or under the bed. In caring for AIDS patients, nurses often manage negotiations between families and lovers, or among relatives and friends, when families often don't know the true diagnosis. In all these ways, nurses seem focused on the personal experience of illness:

> [N]ursing appears to be directed to more immediate and experiential goals than medicine: a compassionate response to suffering is more closely identified with nursing than with medicine. Nurses also more often express an interest in disease prevention and health maintenance than physicians. Nurses are less wedded to the physiological theories and diagnostic modes of medical practice. And nursing has a more global and unified science approach to health care.[3]

"Care," then, includes a broad range of the patient's concerns, not just the physical disease itself.

3. *The nurse's duties are open-ended.* Perhaps because of the nurse's sheer physical availability, her job often expands to fill the gaps left by physicians, orderlies, or even families. Some duties are prescribed, but many are not. "To care" for a nurse comes to mean that the nurse will handle problems that arise, whether or not they are part of her official tasks. This occurs for practical reasons. "The nurse," in the words of Anselm Strauss, "comes and stays while others come and go . . . *The role of the nurse is profoundly affected by her obligation to represent continuity of time and place.*"[4] Being on

the scene, around the clock, means that nurses are there to integrate the different aspects of hospital work: "Since there's no general agreement about what a nurse is, there are no obvious limits to the job."[5]

Thus the nurse takes on more and more tasks, cleaning up the physical and social messes left by others. When doctors don't explain a diagnosis to the patient, when a unit clerk isn't there to answer the phone, when housekeeping has left a sink unwashed or a floor unmopped, when administration hasn't provided the staff to cover the unit, when chaplains aren't around to listen to a family, when the transportation aide hasn't shown up to take a patient to X-ray—then, often, nurses take over and do these jobs themselves, probably grumbling in the process but realizing that it must be done and that nurses will have to live with the results if they don't:

> Everybody else says: "What do you do as a nurse?" And I say, "I do everything that nobody else wants to do." [Interview]

Nurses might say they do this work *because* they "care"; but here there is no distinction between doing and caring. To care is to *do* the leftover work, to take that responsibility, whether ordered to or not.[6]

4. *Caring requires a personal commitment of the nurse to her work.* It requires a commitment of the nurse herself, as a person, to her work. There is an intertwining of professional skills and personal involvement; in a sense, the involvement is the work, in a way not true of more technical occupations. Nurses would say that some excellent surgeons are horrible human beings; but perhaps it is not theoretically possible to be simultaneously an excellent nurse and a despicable person.[7] The job itself seems to call for decency.

In practice, nursing often elicits a deep personal involvement. In the best cases, nurses give and receive with their patients, first giving of themselves and then receiving, in turn, an unusual intimacy and personal satisfaction from helping another person in his or her most difficult time. Patients can be more open with nurses than with their own families, for a variety of reasons: to spare loved ones the truth of suffering, to maintain the dignity of one's body with a spouse, or to protect children from the reality of their mother's imminent death. The caring professional hears of these things without falling apart, so patients often tell nurses what they wouldn't tell anyone else.

> It's the nurse who's there when the patient is upset and crying, especially on those long, dark nights. It's also the nurse who develops a day-to-day rapport with the patient. Patients can feel comfortable sharing their physical and emotional pain. There is a lot of intimacy involved; it's the same intimacy found with any-

one who is terminal. For some reason, people who are dying tend to lessen their barriers. It's a sad phenomenon that we wait until that time to establish those relationships. But it's a privilege for nurses to work in this area [with AIDS patients and dying patients generally], because in no other type of work are you invited into another's soul.[8]

So the first imperative of nursing is to give care—direct, person-to-person, relatively open-ended care. When nurses tell of their best moments in nursing, they tell of giving such care—not of their technical expertise, or their ability to follow complicated orders without bungling, but of care. This is what nurses identify as the meaningful heart of nursing.

Obviously "caring" is also an ideological term, an idealized way of talking about nursing. It is openly used as a weapon in nurses' conflicts with physicians, to distinguish what nurses do ("care") from what doctors do ("cure"), and to assert the nurse's moral superiority. The more challenging "care" is, the greater the moral prestige of the nurse. So when nurses say they "care," this is more than an empirical description of duties; it is a defense of their own importance.

Nurses don't live up to this high ideal of caring all the time. Not at all. But they do accept it as the ideal, and enjoy achieving it now and then, and talk about it as the noblest mission of nursing. Perhaps this is changing with the increasing emphasis on professionalism, a somewhat different principle; but nursing is still, at its center, about caring.

Nurses are Professionals

So nurses care—but others care as well. Parents care for their children, lovers for their beloved, children for their pets. For nurses, though, caring is a *job*, an economically rewarded task. And it is a certain *kind* of job, one with high demands for education and responsibility and a claim to a special status, commonly called "professional." The first imperative of nursing is to care; the second imperative of nursing is to behave like a *professional*.

The term "professional" is notoriously ambiguous, both to nurses and to social scientists. For nursing, "professional" is an occupational goal and a term of status, indicating feelings that "our work is important," and "our work takes an advanced degree of training; not just anyone can be a nurse and do nursing tasks." It is a claim to high status. For sociologists, the matter of professionalism is more complicated, and first-rate scholars have spent entire careers exploring it.[9] Here I will try to describe what practicing nurses mean by "being a professional"; I will neither defend nor debunk their claim, nor will I argue whether nursing is "really" a profession. I am trying to understand what it means to be a nurse, and the nurse's own notion of "being a professional" is a major part of that self-image.

Being a professional means (1) doing a job (2) that requires special competence and (3) that deserves special status.

1. *Most basically, a profession is a job*—and a good one at that. The most accurate generalization about nurses is not that they care for patients; it is that they are *paid* to care for patients. For many, ideology aside, this is the primary motivation. Nurses typically have little trouble finding work in America, or almost anywhere in the world. It is easy to move in and out of the nursing workforce, taking time out for raising a family, pursuing other careers, or just taking vacations. The unemployment rate for nurses in the United States is typically close to zero, and nurses' salaries rose significantly during the 1980s in the United States, so that by 1990 their typical starting income was close to $30,000. It is certainly a field open to women, requiring no overcoming of the traditional barriers that have kept women out of medicine or other professions. In a wide variety of settings—hospital, home health care, school offices, physicians' offices, etc.—a nurse enjoys work options available to very few other employees. She works for a living and probably would not be nursing were it not for the paycheck.

Since nursing is a job, the nurse is frequently required to deal with unpleasant colleagues, uncooperative patients, frustrating bureaucracies, and the routine difficulties of paid work. Even when nurses hate their patients or disapprove of their identities (casualties of gang wars, drug dealers shot in a deal gone bad), or feel that patients are to blame for their own predicament (smokers with emphysema, or alcoholics with gastrointestinal bleeding), they claim to care for them fully. In a sense, I believe, nurses' talk about disliking certain patients reinforces the pride of professionalism. Whoever the patients are, the nurse still goes to work, delivers meal trays, fills out forms, listens to supervisors, delivers medications, and cleans up messes. She can't just walk away, as a volunteer could, or care only for loved ones, as a mother could. Professionalism, then, first means performing the job.

2. Second, *professionalism requires special competence.* Nursing work is often neither simple nor easy; it can be intellectually, emotionally, and physically demanding. So sheer competence is a value, perhaps the central value in nursing.[10] Some people just can't do the work, aren't organized or responsible enough, lack the manual dexterity to insert IVs or give injections, or don't understand the necessary physiology. Nurses can quickly differentiate the good nurses

from the bad based on their ability to do the job, finish the assigned tasks, and not make the disastrous mistakes that can so easily happen. They know which nurses can be trusted and which ones can't:

> "If my baby comes in here," said one pregnant neonatal nurse to her colleague, "swear to me that you'll take care of him. I don't want R— [another nurse] taking care of my kid." [Field Notes]

Professional competence is most challenged in those emergencies when routines break down. Normally, the professional cares for her clients in the form of a "detached concern"[11]—holding her personal feelings in check while remaining open to the feelings of the patient. A special effort is required for a nurse to keep this "professional" detachment when a critically ill patient, after coming close to recovery, suddenly codes and dies:

> Right after the code had started, Madge, laughing nervously as the team worked on Mrs. B—, said to me, "Oh, God, I'd just written her assessment" [saying she was improving].
>
> After Mrs. B.'s code was over, and they'd declared her dead, Madge (who had nursed her for the past week) immediately sat at the rolling desk outside the room and wrote notes for at least 1/2 hour, very persistently, almost through tears—her face was flushed—when people said anything to her, she answered only vaguely, kept her head down writing. [Field Notes]

"Being professional" here may mean, as it often does, going into a bathroom to cry, then cleaning up and coming back out to continue working for the rest of the shift, trying to act as if nothing happened. "Competence" includes technical expertise as well as the personal fortitude to maintain that expertise under pressure.

3. *A professional deserves special status.* A professional, nurses feel, deserves respect. Nurses typically feel that they deserve more respect than they receive, from their colleagues (especially physicians) and from laypersons. They are paid for their work, but good pay is not sufficient.

> No amount of money is worth what you have to do and what you have to put up with. That's it: what you have to put up with . . . patients throwing full urinals at you, slapping you, biting, fighting, swearing. [Interview]

As professionals, nurses feel they deserve an improved status and better treatment: polite treatment by doctors, the listening ear of administrators, the respect of outsiders who too often treat nurses like maids or waitresses.

In trying to be professionals, nurses strive to differentiate themselves in the public eye from other occupations. A nurse, they emphasize, is *not* a maid, *not* a waitress, *not* a servant.[12] Nurses commonly mention these "antiroles" in talking about their work, to distinguish nursing from those jobs, even if the tasks themselves may sometimes be similar: answering patient call bells, changing sheets, emptying bedpans, helping patients dress or turn over. Nurses do some things maids do. How then does one change sheets "professionally"? The public, they feel, doesn't understand:

> It bothers me, the chronic stupid image of the nurse, the handmaid-to-the-doctor thing. I don't take well to people who kiddingly say, "You just empty bedpans all day long." The public has no idea what nursing really is all about. They can see you giving baths, carrying bedpans, taking blood pressures, temperatures, whatever. And they think that's all nurses do. [Interview]

A major part of nursing's effort to improve its status has come in changing the educational requirements for becoming an R.N. Initially, such requirements were more vocational than academic. From the late nineteenth century until the middle of the twentieth, most nurses were trained by hospitals, often the Catholic hospitals run by religious orders of nuns, and after three years they were awarded a diploma. These nursing students worked as poorly paid apprentices and received, in turn, the skills to go out and practice on their own. The training was rigorous, often notoriously so, and very applied. The nurses received training, the hospitals had cheap labor.[13]

But since the 1960s, many of the hospital schools have closed down, replaced by academic university or community-college programs. With this change, the tone of nursing has changed.

> Nursing is no longer the calling it once was, says P.W.; the influence of nuns, so pervasive when she was younger, is now fading, being replaced by the university-trained academic model of nursing. [Interview]

The collegiate nurse has come, perhaps unfairly, to represent the ascendance of education, of science, of classroom training, and of the increased social status of higher education. By comparison, the older, hospital-trained nurse represents more traditional values, the more ready subservience to doctors, the hands-on experience, the "school of hard knocks." As can easily be imagined, this split in the profession, and in what counts as a "real" nurse's education, makes a truly unified effort to improve nursing's status difficult. In addition, social class divisions in nursing between the typically middle-class B.S.N. nurses and the more working-class A.A. or diploma nurses are themselves the basis of much contention.[14] Even nurses' caps, which once symbolized a nurse's status, are now considered by most to be outdated and symbolic of lesser prestige; nurses are abandoning the traditional white uniform dress in favor of scrub suits or even civilian clothes.[15]

Many younger nurses see such changes as good; they mark the path to professionalism. Their formal education is longer, their occupational class is higher, their pay is greater, and their expectations for respect and individual initiative have increased. Professionalism is an ideal, but one which, especially through increased education, can improve their social standing.

Nurses Are Subordinates

Finally, nurses are subordinates in the hospital hierarchy. Not surprisingly, nurses see this feature of nursing less positively than the injunctions toward care and professionalism. Nurses want to care, and they want to be professionals. They don't always want to be subordinates but without doubt they are, and for the most part they accept this as part of their role. The old hospital-based nursing schools actively taught this: "under the dominance of male doctors and administrators, schools of nursing grew; and they were not noted for their development of independent, thoughtful nurses. Students entered nursing schools already expecting that women would defer to men, and, therefore, that nurses would defer to doctors."[16] Nurses' daily work is guided by others: by administrators, some of whom come from nursing; by head nurses who assign them patients; and by physicians, whose detailed orders structure their medical tasks. Nurses arrive at work at an ordered time, on an ordered shift, on specified days. They report at rounds when scheduled, read reports according to custom, answer beepers, fill out charts, and deliver medications as ordered. It is nurses who prepare the patients before procedures and who clean up afterward, changing the sheets, mopping blood, counting sponges, and calming the patients. Nurses may also see themselves as "cleaning up" in a moral sense: "[T]hese second-rank professions explicitly emphasize their role as saviors of both patient and physician from the errors of the latter."[17] The nurse is thus a stage manager for the dramatic stars, limited by the whims of those stars and by the financial and organizational requirements of the owners and managers.

Nurses aren't always directly under the orders of others, of course. In ICUs, nurses frequently make quick decisions on their own, when no physician is available; in dialysis units, it is nurses who teach patients how to dialyze themselves, who write the manuals for patients to use at home, who decide how long dialysis will continue, and who evaluate the patient's tolerance of the side effects. The nurse's subordination, then, is situational: it is almost total in the operating room, where the entire staff is under the command of a surgeon; in long-term nursing home care, by contrast, nurses are in charge. Nurses often supervise other workers, such as aides, orderlies, and therapists of various sorts. And as nurses climb the status hierarchy, other workers fill the lower positions and are subject to the abuse nurses themselves have long known:

> A nurse made a passing comment to L—, a respiratory therapist (and an older, black woman), about how she, the nurse, would have to do some procedure: as a therapist, L. wasn't supposed to do it. Over the next ten minutes, L. kept saying when spoken to, "Don't talk to me, I'm just a therapist," or "You don't want to ask me anything, I'm just a therapist," or "You asking me? A *therapist???*" etc. [Field Notes]

If there is it single dominant theme in nurses' complaints about their work, it is the lack of respect they feel, from laypersons, from coworkers, and especially from physicians. It is nearly universally felt and resented. "The docs never listen to us," they say, "you don't get any recognition from doctors"; doctors don't read the nurse's notes in the patients' chart, don't ask her what she has seen or what she thinks, they don't take her seriously. The daily evidence for this is truly pervasive; I was genuinely surprised at how common the obvious disrespect is. One day I was talking with several staff nurses in a conference room when a young male physician—probably an intern—walked in and asked what a drug was for. Immediately, the assistant head nurse explained quickly and in detail. "Oh yeah," said the doctor, "that's right," and walked out. The nurses began to laugh, and one said to the advisor, "You get an A." And doctors also often ignore nurses' opinions:

> Attending not present today, so the Fellow took charge of doc's rounds in the ICU. In discussing one patient, a resident asked the nurse taking care of this pt if she had anything to add. Before the N finished her first sentence, the Fellow was looking away, visibly uninterested; by the second sentence he had started talking with the other intern. [Field Notes]

Sometimes such ignoring of the nurse's view can have serious consequences:

At Tuesday's conference on Geriatric floor, with residents, attending, social workers, etc., all present, Asst HN said repeatedly, "You should look at Mr. F.'s foot, it will be a big problem," etc. She didn't seem to make an impression on the docs.

They did nothing about it. Saturday morning, the residents called an emergency surgery consultation because the foot was badly necrosed. Surgeon looked, said had to amputate above the ankle, maybe even above the knee, to check the sepsis. The Asst Head Nurse, who had warned them on Tuesday, was standing off to one side during this discussion, visibly exasperated. [Field Notes]

Even medical students put down nurses in small ways.

In psychiatry unit: during nursing rounds, one nurse reads aloud, written on chart, as doctor's order: "Make sure patient voids [urinates]."

"Who wrote that"

"Doctor R.'s little med. student." A good laugh about this, as if the nurse would overlook something so obvious. Getting no respect from docs—even future docs—is a source of aggravation and sometime laughs. [Field Notes]

Here, then, may begin a cycle: doctors don't trust nurses; nurses, not trusted even when they are correct, slack off. The mutual lack of respect shows in various ways. Some nurses complain that doctors doing research projects try to recruit nurses as unpaid research assistants—"You're charting this anyway, can't you just keep another copy of it for my data, too?"—and then become angry if the nurse misses six hours of this charting and the data are lost. Generally, nurses' time is considered less valuable, her work less pressing, her opinions less worthy of consideration.

Outside the door of a middle-aged woman patient, with a steady stream of visitors going in, two nurses and the resident are arguing about acidosis and ventilator settings and what Respiratory Therapy should be doing to suction the patient, all in very technical jargon, decreasing this and increasing that. The nurse who takes care of this patient is very angry, with a constant forced smile she puts on in these situations, and repeating, "I don't really want to discuss it anymore," and "It's obvious what we should do. Just sedate her, that's all you need to do." But the resident isn't sure at all, and the nurses are at the end of their rope. [The patient died within days.] [Field Notes]

There are, then, pervasive problems in nurses' work relationships with doctors.[18] In part, the difficulty results from different views of what the nurse's task actually is. To doctors, the nurses are there to carry out physicians' orders.[19] Indeed, many doctors (and many nurses) regard nursing as a sort of "lesser" medicine, with the subordination of nursing dictated by the shorter period of training.

> Dr. M., explaining why he should make the DNR decisions—and why the nurses should not—explains that the difference between him and the nurses is "years of training—I have 6 or 10, depending on how you count, and they have 2 or 4—I just understand things better." [Interview]

Dr. M. here assumes that nursing is essentially the same as medicine but with less training. He assumes that nurses share medicine's basic theory of disease (a physiological disturbance with psychosocial ramifications) and share medicine's ideas of the goals of treatment. For many physicians, laypersons, and even nurses, nursing is basically second-tier medicine, and nursing education consists of watered-down physiology courses, using textbooks written by physicians, teaching nurses how to be "the doctor's helper."

In recent years, this position is formulated in a description of nurses as "physician extenders," a cost-effective substitute in arms where there aren't enough physicians—a kind of "Hamburger Helper"[20] who does the same work for less money. So the nursing viewpoint is not merely subordinated; indeed, it is often invisible as a distinct approach. Irving Zola comments aptly on

> the term "physician's extender." It conveys the image of a gross medical appendage—a Rube Goldberg invention. In function, it implies only an extension of the physician's work—no new alternative to the care so greatly needed in chronic disease. In responsibilities, it tells the patient that anything of importance is to be left to the doctor. And in potentiality, it says to the holder that he/she is in a job with limited mobility and possibility for growth.[21]

Some nurses feel this notion that they simply practice introductory medicine is insulting; and the general public, not knowing what nurses do beyond following the doctor's orders (which is in fact a large part of the nurse's job), unintentionally disparages nursing as a profession all the time:[22]

> I don't know how many times I've heard people say, "Oh, you're so smart, you should have gone to medical school" . . . I wouldn't be a doctor for all the tea in China . . . but, I would just like a little human respect. [Interview]

But many, if not most, staff nurses accept the assumption that medicine is superior and that nursing is simply a lesser form of medicine.

They try to enhance their own prestige by a kind of "drift to medicine": by going into the more "medical" areas of nursing, like emergency work, or ICUs; by appropriating the scientific and pathophysiological model of disease; and by getting into the "medical macho" of high technology, invasive procedures, and massive pharmacological interventions, all the while setting aside the lower status "dirty work" of nursing. Although nursing as a profession tries to distance itself from medicine, establishing its own expertise, the typical nurse takes respect where she finds it, from her close association with doctors.[23]

To some extent, nurses' subordination lessened, or at least changed its character, during the period of my research from the late 1970s to the early 1990s. Nurses now more often will openly confront physicians rather than practice subterfuge; they have more ready support from independent nursing schools; perhaps because of the women's movement, nurses are somewhat more likely to expect to be treated with respect, if not really as equals. Still, despite some movement in these directions, nurses remain fundamentally unequal to doctors in their power and status. They are clearly subordinates, much more than their professional leaders or even staff nurses would like to believe. They do important work, and many of them do it with deep personal commitment and a high degree of skill. Yet their subordinate position, more than professionalism and perhaps even more than "caring," is a crucial component of most hospital nursing.

Here we see the dilemma of the nurse's role. On the one hand, she would like to raise her status by both differentiating her work from medicine ("we care, doctors cure") and by claiming to be a professional. On the other hand, by being a necessary member of the medical team she can borrow some of the prestige of medicine. The three components of the nurse's role—caring, professionalism, subordination—all represent in some degree what nurses empirically do and how they interpret what they do. In some ways they are conflicting requirements, fortified by conflicting parties: nursing schools with their admonition to professionalism, administrators with their efforts at controlling nurses, journals with their calls to "care." In some ways, managing these conflicts is inherent in the job of being a nurse.

Notes

[1] For instance, Patricia Benner and Judith Wrubel, *The Primacy of Caring: Stress and Coping in Health and Illness* (New York: Addison-Wesley Publishing Co., 1989); or Susan M. Reverby, *Ordered to Care: The Dilemma of American Nursing, 1850–1945* (New York: Cambridge University Press. 1987).

[2] Reverby, *Ordered to Care*, p. 1.

[3] Jameton, *Nursing Practice: The Ethical Issues*, p. 256.

[4] Anselm Strauss, "The Structure and Ideology of American Nursing: An Interpretation," in Davis, *The Nursing Profession: Five Sociological Essays*, pp. 117, 120; italics in the original.

[5] Anderson, *Nurse*, p. 31.

[6] For further elaboration, see Hughes, *Men and Their Work*, p. 74.

[7] "The one-caring, in caring, is present in her acts of caring. Even in physical absence, acts at a distance bear the signs of presence: engrossment in the other, regard, desire for the other's well being." Nel Noddings, *Caring: A Feminine Approach to Ethics and Moral Education* (Berkeley: University of California Press, 1984), p. 19.

[8] Janet Kraegel and Mary Kachoyeanos, *"Just a Nurse"* (New York: Dell Publishing, 1989), p. 16.

[9] Eliot Freidson, *Profession of Medicine: A Study of the Sociology of Applied Knowledge* (New York: Harper & Row, 1970); Andrew Abbott, *The System of Professions: An Essay on the Division of Expert Labor* (Chicago: University of Chicago Press, 1988); Hughes, *Men and Their Work*; Amitai Etzioni, *The Semi-Professions and Their Organization* (New York: Free Press, 1969).

[10] Jameton, *Nursing Practice*, chap. 6.

[11] Robert K. Merton, *Sociological Ambivalence and Other Essays* (New York: Free Press, 1976); the concept is discussed in a number of places in the text.

[12] I once made the mistake, in a lecture to a nurses' association, of comparing nurses' work to that of these other stereotypically female occupations. The audience didn't actually jeer, but they were visibly displeased by the comparison.

[13] Jo Ann Ashley, *Hospitals, Paternalism, and the Role of the Nurse* (New York: Teacher's College Press, 1977). See also Barbara Melosh, *The Physician's Hand: Work Culture and Conflict in American Nursing* (Philadelphia: Temple University Press, 1982); and Reverby, *Ordered to Care*.

[14] "[C]lass divisions within the nursing culture made a feminist politics difficult to achieve," Reverby, *Ordered to Care*, p. 6.

[15] The shift in number of registered nurses coming from diploma programs versus associate and baccalaureate (college-based) programs is dramatic: "More than 90 percent of the nurses [practicing in 1984] who graduated before 1960 were graduates of diploma schools . . . During the period 1980 to 1984, only 17 percent of all registered nurse graduates were graduated from a diploma program." *Facts about Nursing* 86–87, p. 21.

[16] Benjamin and Curtis, *Ethics in Nursing*, p. 79.

[17] Hughes, *Men and Their Work*, p. 97.

[18] The classic article on how the nurse "plays the game" is C. K. Hofling et al., "An Experimental Study in Nurse-Physician Relationships," *Journal of Nervous and Mental Disorders* 143 (1966), p. 171–180.

[19] Crane, *The Sanctity of Social Life*; Anderson, Nurse, pp. 246–248.

[20] I borrow the characterization from Gretchen Aumann, R.N.

[21] Irving Zola, *Socio-Medical Inquiries: Recollections, Reflections, and Reconsiderations* (Philadelphia: Temple University Press, 1983), p. 301 See also Zussman, *Intensive Care*, p. 77: "It is by virtue of their technical skills that nurses win the respect of physicians."

[22] See also Kraegel and Kachoyeanos, *"Just a Nurse,"* p. 262: "Nursing is a hard job if you have a strong ego. People assume that if you're a nurse, you're doing it because you couldn't be a doctor . . . I know I didn't want to be a doctor . . . yet it still hurts to have people think I wasn't capable of it."

[23] Perhaps to the long-term detriment of nursing's effort to independent status. See W. Glasen, in Davis, *The Nursing Profession*, p. 27.

Section XI

Social Movements, Social Change, and Health

You have probably heard at some time the saying that the health status of a country is an indicator of its overall strength and well-being. Data on infant mortality, overall mortality, and disease rates are often cited to indicate a nation's place in the world hierarchy. Changes in health data are often used to measure a country's progress and modernization. Given such a common approach, it is reasonable to conceive of health and illness as central components of the overall social structure of a society. Taking this idea further, it also makes sense to see health reform as part of overall social reform. Indeed, in societies where socialist or revolutionary groups have come to power, health reform is often central to their political agenda. In the ordinary fabric of political debate and elections, health reforms have become central issues, as was powerfully seen in the Clinton health reform plan of 1993.

In nations around the world, health care issues and national health plans have been inextricably tied to broader social welfare programs. Importantly, those programs have not dealt solely or primarily with the poor or with certain other powerless, needy groups. Rather, social welfare reforms and accompanying health coverage are seen as universal rights of citizenship, available to all. This is a remarkably different attitude and ideology than in American society, where health services are typically seen as a commodity which reaps profit for the sellers and which is available to consumers based largely on their ability to pay.

In the United States, health politics have been manifestations of political struggle and social conflict. We see this when we examine the efforts of organized medicine to oppose Medicare and Medicaid from the Great Depression all the way until they were legislated in 1965. Community protests over cutbacks in federal health programs have been a common part of American political life over the last two

605

decades of economic recession and social spending cuts. The introduction of Maternal and Child Health Services (1963), Community Mental Health Centers (1963 and 1965), Neighborhood Health Centers (1964), and Medicare and Medicaid (1965) were part of a national reform program, and the results of those efforts should be seen in that larger social context, not just as limited health interventions.

That social context of the 1960s was one of general social protest—the largest national insurgency since the Great Depression of the 1930s. Health concerns were very important in this period. The women's movement put much energy into organizing for abortion rights, for an end to sterilization abuse, and for other reproductive rights. This was also a period of unionization of hospital workers, a movement which played a key role in the repoliticization of part of the trade union movement by linking unionism to civil rights and opposition to the Vietnam War. Related to the growth of radical sectors of the labor movement, there was an upsurge of occupational safety and health issues. Struggles over black lung in coal miners, asbestosis and mesothelioma in asbestos workers, white lung in textile mills, toxic threats in chemical plants, and shopfloor safety in factories involved union efforts as well as large social pressures to push through the Occupational Safety and Health Act (1970). The readings in the early section on Environmental and Occupational Health both deal with social movement responses to such health crises.

Political organizations often saw the establishment of their own health centers as a major focus for organizing efforts. Most notable were the Black Panther Party's community health clinics and a large number of women's clinics. The women's health movement went very far in providing alternative services, in reforming established institutions, in creating self-help groups, in pushing for the empowerment of and participation by patients, and in examining core social perceptions and ideologies held by laypeople and health professionals. In its many ramifications, the women's health movement has exerted tremendous positive influences on the field of medical sociology.

Steven Epstein, in "Democracy, Expertise, and AIDS Treatment Activism," provides a fascinating look at AIDS activism. In particular, he emphasizes how activists marshaled their own knowledge that led them to challenge traditional models of scientific discovery and clinical trials. Similarly to the earlier article on popular epidemiology organizing by victims of toxic waste, these AIDS activists transformed themselves into a new type of expert—laypeople who could credibly participate in scientific discourse with scientists and government leaders.

Byllye Y. Avery, in "Breathing Life Into Ourselves: The Evolution of the National Black Women's Health Project," talks about that women's health movement legacy in the context of black women's health activism. This edited version of a speech conveys the emotional power of activists finding new ways to organize to serve women's health needs, to counteract violence against women, and to expand their efforts by setting up self-help groups throughout the country and even in some other countries. At the same time, it shows you the personal transitions made by Avery as she moved through different stages of health activism.

In "Getting the Lead Out of the Community," Janet Phoenix returns us to earlier discussions about environmental health. As you see, it is virtually impossible to talk about environmental health without reference to social activism. Lead poisoning affects poor and minority people the most. It is especially harmful to children, though it is also a common occupational and environmental problem. The single most effective approach to this disease is to prevent it by getting rid of lead and lead exposure. Yet despite this long-established knowledge, public health efforts are paltry. Phoenix illustrates the way that community organizations have developed in order to combat this "silent epidemic."

David U. Himmelstein and Steffie Woolhandler are among the founders of the Physicians for a National Health Plan, which was an important organization starting in the late 1980s that pushed for a full-fledged health coverage system. Many doctors who previously might have frowned on such a plan changed their mind in the face of inroads against their autonomy by HMOs, insurers, and federal regulations. In "A National Health Plan for the United States: A Physicians' Proposal," Himmelstein and Woolhandler detail what such a plan would cover, how it would be financed, and what benefits it would provide. Much of this 1989 document became part of national discussions in the 1993 Clinton national health reform debates.

This discussion of social movements has taken us full circle, back to the first discussions of social epidemiology and the social context of health and illness. We have examined social constructions of disease and illness, and we have seen differences in lay and medical worldviews concerning health and illness. We have talked about the social nature of scientific knowledge, the inequalities in the overall society and in the medical encounter, and the problems of access to and quality of health care. We have developed a framework of political economy in which to study the distribution, composition, and function of the health care system. We have studied the convergence of economic factors and political forces in the relations between government and profit-making health industries and providers. We have analyzed professionalism in terms of the development of American medicine and in terms of lay-professional relations. And we have ended with a reminder of how the social nature of health and illness is once again reaffirmed in light of the importance of social movements in health care.

Throughout this process we have maintained a focus on the three major structural forces: political economy, professionalism, and institutional structure. At the same time we have seen the dialectical (interconnected and interdependent) relationships between the micro- and macro-levels of health care, and have learned that we can never fully understand one end of the macro-micro continuum unless we are taking into account the other end.

I hope the material in this book has made sense to you and leads you to pursue further study in the exciting field of medical sociology.

33
Democracy, Expertise, and AIDS Treatment Activism

Steven Epstein

In 1987, thousands of AIDS activists around the United States began confronting doctors, biomedical researchers, and federal health officials in visually arresting, angry, and provocative demonstrations. Although the targets varied, a lot of this new wave of AIDS activism focused on the organization and pace of research on AIDS treatments. The messages were not subtle. At one scientific forum, activists handed out cups of Kool-Aid as a prominent researcher came to the podium, likening the effects of his research methods upon AIDS patients to that of cult leader Jim Jones upon his followers in Jonestown, Guyana (Crowley 1991:40). When the Commissioner of the Food and Drug Administration (FDA) came to speak at a public forum in Boston in 1987, activists in the audience held wristwatches aloft ("FDA allows," 1988), implying that time was running out for people with AIDS. In October of that year, more than 1,000 demonstrators converged on FDA headquarters in Rockville, Maryland to "seize control" of what some labeled the "Federal Death Administration" (Bull 1988).

Fast-forward to 1992: A subset of these same activists now sat as regular voting members on the committees of the AIDS Clinical Trials Group (ACTG), established by the National Institutes of Health (NIH) to oversee all federally funded AIDS clinical research. Serving alongside the most prominent AIDS researchers in the country (including the one who had been compared to Jim Jones), activists now worked with scientists to determine the most profitable research directions, debate research methodologies, and allocate research funds. Activists also served on institutional review boards at research hospitals around the country, evaluating the methods and ethics of clinical trials of AIDS drugs. At conferences, where once they had shouted from the back of the room, activists now chaired sessions. And their publications, like San Francisco-based *AIDS Treatment News*, had become routine sources of information

From *Democracy, Expertise, and AIDS Treatment Activism* (ed. Daniel Kleinman), pp. 15–32. Reprinted by permission of the State University of New York Press © 2000, State University of New York. All rights reserved.

about AIDS therapies for many doctors around the world. The aptitude of AIDS treatment activists in understanding such matters as the stages of viral replication, the immunopathogenesis of HIV, and the methodology of the randomized clinical trial was widely acknowledged by prominent experts. As Dr. John Phair (1994), a former chair of the Executive Committee of the AIDS Clinical Trials Group, commented in 1994: "I would put them up against—in this limited area—many, many physicians, including physicians working in AIDS [care]. They can be very sophisticated."

The unusual social movement trajectory that I have sketched is interesting for all sorts of reasons. Here I would like to focus on the *politics of knowledge and expertise*: How did a grassroots movement produce a cadre of activist-experts? More generally, in what circumstances can patients and laypeople challenge hierarchies of expertise and participate effectively in processes of biomedical knowledge-production—or transform such processes? How do they gain entry to these privileged domains, and what are the consequences, intended or unintended, of these kinds of incursions?[1]

What I want to argue here is that activist movements, through amassing different forms of credibility, can in certain circumstances bring about changes in the epistemological practices of science—our ways of knowing the natural world. Nothing guarantees that such changes will be useful in advancing knowledge or in curing disease, but in this case, lay participation in science had some tangible benefits, though not without risks. This finding is at variance with popular notions of science as a relatively autonomous arena with high barriers to entry. And it runs counter to the view that many might normally voice—that science must be safeguarded from external pressures in order to prevent the deformation of knowledge.[2] By scientific "credibility," I refer to the capacity of claims-makers to enroll supporters behind their claims and present themselves as the sort of people who can give voice to scientific truths.[3] I understand credibility as a form of authority that combines aspects of power, legitimation, trust, and persuasion (Weber 1978:212–254). However, this case differs from other sociological studies of scientific credibility by suggesting how diverse can be the cast of characters who strive for credibility in scientific controversies, and how varied can be the routes by which credibility is made manifest. More typically in science the attestations of credibility are recognizable markers like academic degrees, research track records, and institutional affiliations. In the case of AIDS research, we find a multiplication of the successful pathways to the establishment of credibility, a diversification of the personnel beyond the formally credentialed, and hence more convoluted routes to the resolution of controversy and the construction of belief.

This study also presumes a particular historical moment in which, perhaps especially in the United States, popular attitudes toward science and medicine are highly polarized: a deep faith on the part of the public proceeds hand in hand with skepticism and disillusionment. The emergence of a new epidemic disease, in a society inclined to consider itself as having advanced beyond such mundane risks, had the effect of amplifying this ambivalence. When experts appeared unable to solve the problem of AIDS, the resulting disappointment created space for unconventional voices. Therefore, the study of credibility in AIDS research must also be a study of the public negotiation of the "credibility crisis" surrounding biomedical science—and a study of how the boundaries around scientific institutions become more porous, more open to the intervention of outsiders, precisely in such moments. Again perhaps especially in the United States, interventions by outsiders may get organized in the form of full-fledged social movements.

Origins of the AIDS Treatment Activist Movement

The U.S. AIDS treatment activist movement is best conceived as a subset of a much larger, but considerably more diffuse, "AIDS movement" that dates to the early years of the epidemic; that encompasses a wide range of grassroots activists, lobbying groups, service providers, and community-based organizations; and that now represents the diverse interests of people of various races, ethnicities, genders, sexual preferences, and HIV "risk behaviors." The AIDS movement has engaged in manifold projects directed at a variety of social institutions, including the state, the church, the mass media, and the health care sector (Altman 1994; Cohen 1993; Corea 1992; Crimp and Rolston 1990; Elbaz 1992; Emke 1993; Geltmaker 1992; Indyk & Rier 1993; Patton 1990; Quimby and Friedman 1989; Treichler 1991; Wachter 1991)—though at times it has been less concerned with achieving institutional change than with posing general challenges to cultural norms (J. Gamson 1989).

In its emergence and mobilization, the AIDS movement was a beneficiary of "social movement spillover" (Meyer and Whittier 1994): it was built on the foundation of other movements and borrowed from their particular strengths and inclinations. Most consequential was the link to the lesbian and gay movement of the 1970s and early

1980s (Adam 1987; Altman 1982, 1986). In the wake of fierce debates in the 1970s over whether homosexuality should be classified as an illness (Bayer 1981), gay men and lesbians were often inclined toward critical or skeptical views of medical authorities (Bayer 1985). It mattered that gay communities had pre-existing organizations that could mobilize to meet a new threat; these community organizations and institutions also provided the face-to-face "micro-mobilization contexts" that are particularly useful in drawing individuals into activism (Lo 1992). It mattered, too, that these communities contained (and were substantially dominated by) white, middle-class men with a degree of political clout and fundraising capacity unusual for an oppressed group. And it was crucially important that gay communities possessed relatively high degrees of "cultural capital"—cultivated dispositions for appropriating knowledge and culture (Bourdieu 1990). Within these communities are many people who are themselves doctors, scientists, educators, nurses, professionals, or other varieties of intellectuals. On one hand, this has provided the AIDS movement with an unusual capacity to contest the mainstream experts on their own ground. On the other hand, it affords important sources of intermediation and communication between "experts" and "the public." Treatment activists themselves have tended to be science novices, but ones who were unusually articulate, self-confident, and well-educated—"displaced intellectuals from other fields," as Jim Eigo, a New York City treatment activist with a background in the arts, expressed it (Antiviral Drugs Advisory Committee 1991:50).

The fact that many lesbians (and heterosexual women) who would become active in the AIDS movement were schooled in the tenets of the feminist health movement of the 1970s (Corea 1992; Winnow 1992)—with its skepticism toward medical claims-making and insistence upon the patient's decision-making autonomy (Boston Women's Health Book Collective 1973; Fee 1982; Ruzek 1978)—also had important implications for the identity and strategies of the movement. Other activists, both men and women, had prior direct experience in social movements such as the peace movement (Elbaz 1992:72).

Central to the early goals of the AIDS movement was the repudiation of helplessness or "victim" status and the insistence upon self-representation. "We condemn attempts to label us as 'victims', which implies defeat, and we are only occasionally 'patients', which implies passivity, helplessness, and dependence upon others. We are 'people with AIDS'," read a widely-reprinted manifesto of the New York-based PWA [People with AIDS] Coalition (PWA Coalition 1988). This is "self-help with a vengeance," as Indyk and Rier (1993:6) nicely characterize it—an outright rejection of medical paternalism and an insistence that neither the medical establishment, nor the government, nor any other suspect authority would speak on behalf of people with AIDS or HIV.

AIDS activism entered a new and more radical phase in the second half of the 1980s, in the face of increasing concern about the inadequacy of the federal response to the epidemic, the stigmatization of people with AIDS or HIV, and the lack of availability of effective therapies for AIDS or its associated opportunistic infections and cancers. The year 1987 marked the birth, in New York City and then elsewhere around the country, of a new organization, called the AIDS Coalition to Unleash Power, but better known by its deliberately provocative acronym, ACT UP (Anonymous 1991). A magnet for radical young gay men and women in the late 1980s, ACT UP practiced an in-your-face politics of "no business as usual." Adopting styles of political and cultural practice deriving from sources as diverse as anarchism, the peace movement, the punk subculture, and gay liberation "zaps" of the 1970s, ACT UP became famous for its imaginative street theater, its skill at attracting the news cameras, and its well-communicated sense of urgency. ACT UP groups typically had no formal leaders, and meetings in many cities operated by the consensus process.

ACT UP was only the most visible of a diverse set of groups that became interested in issues of medical treatment and research for AIDS around the United States in the mid to late 1980s—the constellation of organizations that can be called the AIDS treatment activist movement. So-called "buyers clubs," existing on the fringes of the law, supplied patients with unapproved or experimental treatments smuggled in from other countries or manufactured in basement laboratories. Project Inform, a San Francisco-based organization with a more conventional structure than ACT UP, emerged as an advocate for the use of such experimental therapies and evolved into a multi-focal treatment advocacy organization with its own lobbying campaigns, publications, and educational projects. A range of grassroots treatment publications appeared, providing their readers with a rich mix of scientific information, political commentary, and anecdotes about treatments gleaned from patient reports (Arno and Feiden 1992; Kwitny 1992). *AIDS Treatment News*, the most well-known of these alternative publications, had been advocating for some time for greater attention to be paid to issues of drug research and regulation. "So far, community-based AIDS organizations have been uninvolved in treatment issues, and have seldom followed what is going on," wrote its editor, John James, a former computer programmer, in a call to arms in May 1986. To "rely solely on official institutions for our information," James bluntly advised, "is a form of group suicide" (James 1986).

Gaining Credibility

Although treatment activists began by employing highly confrontational modes of direct action, they always assumed that effective solutions to AIDS would have to come, in large measure, from doctors and scientists. Therefore, they resisted the notion—found, for example, in the animal rights movement (Jasper and Nelkin 1992)—that the scientific establishment was "the enemy" in an absolute sense. "I wouldn't exaggerate how polite we were," Mark Harrington (1994), one of the leaders of ACT UP/New York's Treatment & Data Committee reflected:

> At the same time, I would just say that it was clear from the very beginning, as Maggie Thatcher said when she met Gorbachev, "We can do business." We wanted to make some moral points, but we didn't want to wallow in being victims, or powerless, or oppressed, or always right. We wanted to engage and find out if there was common ground.

How did this rapprochement proceed? In effect, activists (or some subset of them) accomplished an identity shift: They reconstituted themselves as a new species of expert—as laypeople who could speak credibly about science in dialogues with the scientific research community. I cannot here consider in detail the specific tactics that activists employed to construct their scientific credibility (see Epstein 1995), but I would argue that four tactics were most important. First, activists acquired cultural competence by learning the language and culture of medical science. Through a wide variety of methods—including attending scientific conferences, scrutinizing research protocols, and learning from sympathetic professionals both inside and outside the movement—the core treatment activists gained a working knowledge of the medical vocabulary. Second, activists presented themselves as the legitimate, organized voice of people with AIDS or HIV infection (the current or potential clinical trial subject population). Once activists monopolized the capacity to say "what patients wanted," researchers could be forced to deal with them in order to ensure that research subjects would both enroll in their trials in sufficient numbers and comply with the study protocols.[4] Third, activists yoked together methodological (or epistemological) arguments and moral (or political) arguments, so as to multiply their "currencies" of credibility. For example, activists insisted that the inclusion of women and people of color in clinical trials was not only morally necessary (to ensure equal access to potentially promising therapies) but was also scientifically advisable (to produce more fully generalizable data about drug safety and efficacy in different populations). Finally, activists took advantage of pre-existing lines of cleavage within the scientific establishment to form strategic alliances. For example, activists struck alliances with biostatisticians in their debates with infectious disease researchers about appropriate clinical trial methodology.

A key victory for activists, at a time when many AIDS researchers remained deeply suspicious of the activist agenda, was the support of Dr. Anthony Fauci, prominent immunologist and AIDS researcher, and director of NIH's Office of AIDS Research. "Something happened along the way," Fauci told a reporter in 1989: "People started talking to each other. . . . I started to listen and read what [activists] were saying. It became clear to me that they made sense" (Garrison 1989:A-1). Of course, Fauci and others may have deemed it strategic to incorporate activists into the process: As Fauci (1994) later commented, the assumption was that "on a practical level, it would be helpful in some of our programs, because we needed to get a feel for what would play in Peoria, as it were." Prominent academic researchers also acknowledged the gradual acquisition of scientific competence on the part of key activists. Dr. Douglas Richman (1994), an important AIDS researcher from the University of California, San Diego, described how Harrington of ACT UP/New York, in an early meeting with researchers, "got up and gave a lecture on CMV [cytomegalovirus] . . . that I would have punished a medical student for—in terms of its accuracy and everything else—and he's now become a very sophisticated, important contributor to the whole process."

As this encounter between different social worlds unfolded, activists pressed for more substantial degrees of inclusion in the NIH decision-making apparatus. Crucial decisions about clinical trials— how to fund and conduct them, as well as how to choose eligible patients and analyze data—were being made by the academic researchers who comprised the advisory committees of the ACTG. To the consternation of the researchers, activists demanded representation on these committees; when Fauci stalled, activists decided to "Storm the NIH." This demonstration, at the NIH campus in

Bethesda, Maryland on May 21, 1990, proved to be another graphic media spectacle, like the FDA protest two years earlier (Hilts 1990). Soon afterward, activists were informed that most ACTG meetings would be opened to the public, and that there would be a representative of the patient community, with full voting rights, assigned to each ACTG committee. In addition, by the early 1990s, activists acted as informal representatives to FDA advisory committees charged with evaluating new drugs, as appointed members of "community advisory boards" established by pharmaceutical companies, and as regular members of "institutional review boards" supervising clinical studies at hospitals and academic centers around the country. Activists began to have an important say in how studies were conducted, which patients were allowed into studies, how results from studies were evaluated, and which lines of research should be funded (Epstein 1996; Arno and Feiden 1992; Kwitny 1992; Jonsen and Stryker 1993).

Consequences

A defining moment was the publication in the *New England Journal of Medicine*, in November 1990, of an article by AIDS researcher Thomas Merigan (1990) of Stanford, entitled, "You *Can* Teach an Old Dog New Tricks: How AIDS Trials Are Pioneering New Strategies." Praising the new "partnership of patients, their advocates, and clinical investigators," Merigan proceeded to endorse precisely those methodological stances that activists had promoted. He argued, for example, that "all limbs [of a trial] should offer an equal potential advantage to patients, as good as the best available clinical care"; that no one in a trial should be denied treatment for their opportunistic infections; that trials should not be "relentlessly pursued as originally designed" when "data appeared outside the trial suggesting that patients would do better with a different type of management"; and that "the entry criteria for trials should be as broad as scientifically possible to make their results useful in clinical practice."

By pressing researchers to develop clinically relevant trials with designs that research subjects would find acceptable, activists helped to ensure more rapid accrual of the required numbers of subjects and to reduce the likelihood of noncompliance. And by working toward methodological solutions that satisfy, simultaneously, the procedural concerns of researchers and the ethical demands of the patient community, AIDS activists have, at least in specific instances, improved a tool for the production of scientific facts in ways that even researchers acknowledge. In this sense, AIDS activists' efforts belie the commonplace notion that only the insulation of science from "external" pressures guarantees the production of secure and trustworthy knowledge.

Those who were critical of lay participation in medical research were quick to suggest, and with some reason, that AIDS activists had muddied the waters of knowledge in their haste to see drugs approved. Yet any such assessment has to consider the larger picture. Absent the activists, what sort of knowledge strategies would have been pursued? Pristine studies addressing less-than-crucial questions? Methodologically unimpeachable trials that failed to recruit or maintain patients? Inevitably, there are risks inherent in the interruption of the status quo. But these must be weighed against all the other attendant risks, including those that may follow from letting normal science take its course while an epidemic rages.

One reason why this case is so important is because it is quite conceivable that these changes in AIDS research will have an enduring impact on biomedicine in the United States.[5] The past few years have seen a marked upsurge of health-related activism of a distinctive type: the formation of groups that construct identities around particular disease categories and assert political and scientific claims on the basis of these new identities. Just as the AIDS movement drew on the experiences of other movements that preceded it, now its own tactics and understandings have begun to serve as a model for a new series of challengers.

Most notably patients with breast cancer, but also those suffering from chronic fatigue, environmental illness, prostate cancer, mental illness, Lyme disease, Lou Gehrig's disease, and a host of other conditions, have displayed a new militancy and demanded a voice in how their conditions are conceptualized, treated, and researched (Barinaga 1992; Kingston 1991; Kroll-Smith and Floyd 1997). These groups have criticized not only the quality of their care, but also the ethics of clinical research ("Are placebo controls acceptable?") and the control over research directions ("Who decides which presentations belong on a conference program?"). While not every such group owes directly to AIDS activism, the tactics and political vocabulary of organizations like ACT UP would seem, at a minimum, to be "in the wind." (Could one imagine, before the AIDS activist repudiation of "victimhood," people with muscular dystrophy denouncing the Jerry Lewis Telethon as an "Annual Ritual of Shame" and chanting "Power, not pity" before the news cameras?) (MD Telethon, 1991). To date, none of these constituencies has engaged in epistemological interventions that approach, in their depth or extent, AIDS treatment activists' critiques of the methodology of clinical trials. But Bernadine Healy, then the director of the NIH, got it right in 1992 when she told a reporter: "The AIDS activists have led the way . . . . [They] have created a template for all activist groups looking for a cure" (Gladwell 1992).

Breast cancer activism is an intriguing instance of this new wave, because the links to AIDS activism have been so explicit and so readily acknowledged. In 1991, more than 180 U.S. advocacy groups came together to form the National Breast Cancer Coalition. "They say they've had it with politicians and physicians and scientists who 'there, there' them with studies and statistics and treatments that suggest the disease is under control," read a prominent account in the *New York Times Sunday Magazine* (Ferraro 1993:26). In its first year of operation, the coalition convinced Congress to step up funding for breast cancer research by $43 million, an increase of almost 50 percent. "The next year, armed with data from a seminar they financed, the women asked for, wheedled, negotiated and won a whopping $300 million more" (Ferraro 1993:27). The debt to AIDS activism was widely noted by activists and commentators alike. "They showed us how to get through to the Government," said a Bay Area breast cancer patient and organizer: "They took on an archaic system and turned it around while we have been quietly dying." Another activist described how she met with the staff of *AIDS Treatment News* to learn the ropes of the drug development and regulatory systems (Gross 1991).

Of course, it would be rash to assume that AIDS activism has created an automatic receptiveness on the part of scientists or doctors to such health movements, and that the next round of activists can simply step up to the counter and claim their rewards. A more likely scenario is that AIDS activism will usher in a new wave of democratization struggles in the biomedical sciences and health care—struggles that may be just as hard fought as those of the past decade. It is worth remembering, too, how difficult this sort of activism is to sustain: Organizing a social movement is arduous enough, without having to learn oncology in your spare time.

Complications

Other qualifications to this story deserve notice. Certainly it should be clear that such activism, no matter how broad ranging it becomes, is unlikely to bring about the thorough transformation of the knowledge-based hierarchies that structure the society we live in. In fact, my analysis suggests a profound tension built into AIDS treatment activists' own project of democratizing expertise. On one hand, by pursuing an educational strategy to disseminate AIDS information widely, activists have promoted the development of broad-based knowledge-empowerment at the grassroots. On the other hand, as treatment activist leaders have become quasi-experts, they have tended to replicate the expert/lay divide within the movement itself: a small core of activists became insiders who "knew their stuff"; others were left outside to man the barricades. Furthermore, as many of the treatment activists moved "inward," took their seats at the table and became sensitized to the logic of biomedical research, their conceptions of scientific methods sometimes turned in more conventional directions.

"I've seen a lot of treatment activists get seduced by the power, get seduced by the knowledge, and end up making very conservative arguments," contends Michelle Roland (1993), formerly active with ACT UP in San Francisco: "They understand . . . the methodology, they can make intelligent arguments, and it's like, 'Wait a minute . . . okay, you're smart. We accept that. But what's your role?'" Ironically, insofar as activists start thinking like scientists and not like patients, the grounding for their unique contributions to the science of clinical trials may be in jeopardy of erosion. Researcher John Phair (1994) notes that activists "have given us tremendous insight into the feasibility of certain studies," but adds that "some of the activists have gotten very sophisticated and then forget that the idea might not sell" to the community of patients.

Can one be both activist and scientist? Is the notion of a "lay expert" a contradiction in terms? I don't think there are any simple answers here. But arguably, it was not possible for the key treatment activists to become authorities on clinical trials and sit on the ACTG committees, without, in some sense, growing closer to the world-view of the researchers—and without moving a bit away from their fellow activists engaged in other pursuits. Furthermore, the new hierarchies of expertise that have emerged within the ranks of the activists have, to a certain, predictable degree, superimposed themselves upon the bedrock of other dimensions of social inequality, including racial, gender, and class differences among activists. And this has led to sharp tensions and outright splits within several activist organizations (Epstein 1996:290–294; Epstein 1997b; Vollmer 1990; DeRanleau 1990).

These questions of identity and strategy among knowledge-empowered social movements deserve extended attention. Here I intend only to suggest two implications of my analysis. First, the AIDS activist project of reconfiguring the knowledge-making practices of biomedicine has been executed in ways that are tentative, partial, and shot through with some powerful contradictions. Second, it proves to be not enough to ask what impact AIDS activists have had on the conduct of biomedical research. In addition, we need to ask the reciprocal question: What impact does the encounter with science have upon the social movement? How does the "expertification" or "scientization" of activism affect the goals and tactics of a social movement, as well as its collective identity (Epstein 1997b)? Without doubt, the reciprocal relation between AIDS activists and AIDS researchers was equally transformative in both directions.

Let me now raise a final worry about the democratization of science: the obvious risk that lay participation will interfere with the good conduct of science and indeed delay the goals that all want to see achieved. What is to prevent real harm from being done? In this regard, it is important to note that the process of activist intervention in biomedicine is not without some painful ironies. On one hand, the enterprise appears significantly driven by the dictates of expediency and dire need—"I'm dying so give me the drug now!"—yet on the other hand, the core treatment activists have increasingly become believers in science (however understood), and desperately want clinical trials to generate usable knowledge that can guide medical practice. As David Barr of the Treatment Action Group (a spinoff of ACT UP/New York) put it: "My doctors and I make decisions in the dark with every pill I put in my mouth" (Cotton 1991:1362)—and this is not an easy way to live.

Insofar as activists want clinical trials to succeed, they must wrestle with the consequences of their own interventions. Do such interventions enhance activists' capacity to push clinical research in the directions they choose? Or do activists and researchers alike become subject to the unintended effects of their actions, trapped within an evolving system whose trajectory no one really controls? Here is a sort of worst-case scenario of the spiraling consequences of community-based interventions in the construction of belief in antiviral drugs—a caricature sketch, to be sure, but one that combines elements from a number of cases in the late 1980s and early 1990s. Drug X performs well in preliminary studies, and an NIH official is quoted as saying that X is a promising drug. The grassroots treatment publications write that X is the up-and-coming thing; soon everyone in the community wants access to X, and activists are demanding large, rapid trials to study it. Everyone wants to be in the trial, because they believe that X will help them; but researchers want to conduct the trial in order to determine whether X has any efficacy. Those who cannot get into the trial demand expanded access, while others begin importing X from other countries or manufacturing it in clandestine laboratories. As X becomes more prevalent and emerges as the de facto standard of care, physicians begin to suggest that patients get hold of it however they can. Meanwhile, participants in the clinical trial of X who fear they are receiving a placebo mix and match their pills with other participants. When the trial's investigators report potential treatment benefits, activists push for accelerated approval of X, leaving the final determination of X's efficacy to post-marketing studies. But who then wants to sign up for those studies, when everyone now believes that the drug works, since, after all, the FDA has licensed it and any doctor can prescribe it?

This is a scary scenario, but it must be pointed out that, in recent years, activists themselves have sought to control this troubling escalation and to extricate themselves from what they rightly call the "hype cycle." As Mark Harrington (1993:7) wrote in late 1993: "One disturbing but inevitable result of the urgency engendered by the AIDS crisis is that both researchers and community members tend to invest preliminary trials with more significance than they can possibly bear." To the extent that activists can develop a critique of this phenomenon of expecting too much from research, and to the extent that they can communicate the *relative uncertainty* of clinical trials to the broader public of HIV-infected persons, it may be possible to imagine a clinical research process that more fully reflects the interests of those who are most in need of answers.[6]

Notes

[1] This analysis of AIDS treatment activists derives from a larger research project concerned with studying the conduct of science in the AIDS epidemic and the role of laypeople, and particularly activists, in the transformation of biomedical knowledge-making practices (see especially Epstein [1996]). Much of the text of this article has appeared previously (see Epstein 1995, 1996, 1997a, 1997b). This account is based on interviews conducted with AIDS activists, AIDS researchers, and government health officials at the National Institutes of Health and the Food and Drug Administration; as well as on analyses of the accounts, claims-making, and framing of issues presented in scientific and medical journals, the mass media, the gay and lesbian press, activist publications, activist documents, and government documents.

[2] On the politics of public participation in science and medicine, see, for example, Balogh (1991); Blume et al. (1987); Brown (1992); Cozzens and Woodhouse (1995); Di Chiro (1992); Indyk and Rier (1993); Irwin and Wynne (1996); Kleinman (1995); Martin (1980); Moore (1996); Nelkin (1975); Petersen (1984); Rycroft (1991); White (1993); and Wynne (1992).

[3] My conception of credibility borrows from scholarship in science studies that includes Barnes (1985); Barnes and Edge (1982); Cozzens (1990); Latour and Woolgar (1986); Shapin (1994); Shapin and Schaffer (1985); Star (1989); and Williams and Law (1980).

[4] To borrow Bruno Latour's (1987: 132) term, activists constructed themselves as an "obligatory passage point" standing between researchers and the trials they sought to conduct. Of course, activists also needed the researchers to conduct the trials, so the relationship is best seen as symbiotic. See also Crowley (1991).

[5] Here I mean to go beyond the argument, now routinely heard, that AIDS has forever changed conceptions of the doctor-patient relationship. That may be true, although probably the old-fashioned model of the omnipotent physician and the dependent patient was already on the way out.

[6] This perspective brings activists into alignment with sociologists of scientific knowledge who advocate that public understanding of science can be improved if the public acquires a greater appreciation of the high degree of uncertainty in science (see Collins and Pinch 1993).

References

Adam, Barry D. 1987. *The Rise of a Gay and Lesbian Movement*. Boston: Twayne Publishers.

Altman, Dennis. 1982. *The Homosexualization of America*. Boston: Beacon Press.

———. 1986. *AIDS in the Mind of America*. Garden City, NJ: Anchor Press/Doubleday.

———. 1994. *Power and Community: Organizational and Cultural Responses to AIDS*. London: Taylor & Francis.

Anonymous. 1991. *ACT UP/New York Capsule History*. New York: AIDS Coalition to Unleash Power.

Antiviral Drugs Advisory Committee of the U.S. Food and Drug Administration. 1991. Meeting transcript. Bethesda, MD: Food and Drug Administration, 13–14 February.

Arno, Peter S., and Karyn L. Feiden. 1992. *Against the Odds: The Story of AIDS Drug Development, Politics and Profits*. New York: HarperCollins.

Balogh, Brian. 1991. *Chain Reaction: Expert Debate and Public Participation in American Commercial Nuclear Power, 1945–1975*. Cambridge, England: Cambridge University Press.

Barinaga, Marcia. 1992. Furor at Lyme disease conference. *Science* 256:1384–1385.

Barnes, Barry. 1985. *About Science*. Oxford: Basil Blackwell.

Barnes, Barry, and David Edge. 1982. Science as Expertise. In *Science in Context: Readings in the Sociology of Science*, ed. Barry Barnes and David Edge, pp. 233–2149. Cambridge, MA: MIT Press.

Bayer, Ronald. 1981. *Homosexuality and American Psychiatry: The Politics of Diagnosis*. New York: Basic Books.

———. 1985. AIDS and the gay movement: Between the specter and the promise of medicine. *Social Research* 52: 581–606.

Blume, Stuart, Joske Bunders, Loet Leydesdorff and Richard Whitley (eds.). 1987. *The Social Direction of the Public Sciences*. Dordrecht, Holland: D. Reidel.

Boston Women's Health Book Collective. 1973. *Our Bodies, Ourselves: A Book by and for Women*. New York: Simon & Schuster.

Bourdieu, Pierre. 1990. *The Logic of Practice*. Stanford, CA: Stanford University Press.

Brown, Phil. 1992. Popular epidemiology and toxic waste contamination: Lay and professional ways of knowing. *Journal of Health and Social Behavior* 33:267–281.

Bull, Chris. 1988. Seizing control of the FDA. *Gay Community News*, 16–22 October, 1, 3.

Cohen, Cathy Jean. 1993. Power, Resistance and the Construction of Crisis: Marginalized Communities Respond to AIDS. Ph.D. dissertation, University of Michigan.

Collins, Harry, and Trevor Pinch. 1993. *The Golem: What Everyone Should Know about Science*. Cambridge, England: Cambridge University Press.

Corea, Gena. 1992. *The Invisible Epidemic: The Story of Women and AIDS*. New York: Harper Collins.

Cotton, Paul. 1991. HIV surrogate markers weighed. *Journal of the American Medical Association* 265 (11) (20 March):1357, 1361, 1362.

Cozzens, Susan E. 1990. Autonomy and Power in Science. In *Theories of Science in Society*, ed. Susan E. Cozzens and Thomas F. Gieryn, pp. 164–184. Bloomington: Indiana University Press.

Cozzens, Susan E., and Edward J. Woodhouse. 1995. Science, Government, and the Politics of Knowledge. In *Handbook of Science and Technology Studies*, ed. Sheila Jasanoff, Gerald Markle, James C. Petersen, and Trevor Pinch, pp. 533–553. Thousand Oaks, CA: Sage.

Crimp, Douglas, and Adam Rolston. 1990. *AIDS Demographics*. Seattle: Bay Press.

Crowley, William Francis Patrick, III. 1991. Gaining Access: The Politics of AIDS Clinical Drug Trials in Boston. Undergraduate thesis, Harvard College.

DeRanleau, Michele. 1990. How the "conscience of an epidemic" unraveled, *San Francisco Examiner*, 1 October, A-15.

Di Chiro, Giovanna. 1992. Defining environmental justice: Women's voices and grassroots politics. *Socialist Review* 22:93–130.

Elbaz, Gilbert. 1992. The Sociology of AIDS Activism, the Case of ACT UP/New York, 1987–1992. Ph.D. dissertation. City University of New York.

Emke, Ivan. 1993. Medical authority and its discontents: The case of organized noncompliance. *Critical Sociology* 19:57–80.

Epstein, Steven. 1995. The construction of lay expertise: AIDS activism and the forging of credibility in the reform of clinical trials. *Science, Technology, & Human Values* 20:408–437.

———. 1996. *Impure Science: AIDS, Activism, and the Politics of Knowledge*. Berkeley: University of California Press.

———. 1997a. Activism, drug regulation, and the politics of therapeutic evaluation in the AIDS era: A case study of ddC and the "surrogate markers" debate, *Social Studies of Science* 27: 691–726.

———. 1997b. AIDS activism and the retreat from the genocide frame, *Social Identities* 3: 415–438.

Fauci, Anthony. 1994. Interview by author. Bethesda, MD, 31 October.

FDA allows AIDS patients to import banned drugs. 1988. *Los Angeles Times*, 24 July, 18.

Fee, Elizabeth (ed.).·1982. *Women and Health: The Politics of Sex in Medicine*. Farmingdale, NY: Baywood.

Ferraro, Susan. 1993. The anguished politics of breast cancer. *New York Times Sunday Magazine*, 15 August, pp. 25–27, 58–62.

Gamson, Joshua. 1989. Silence, death, and the invisible enemy: AIDS activism and social movement "newness." *Social Problems* 36:351–365.

Garrison, Jayne. 1989. AIDS activists being heard. *San Francisco Examiner*, 5 September, A-1, A-8.

Geltmaker, Ty. 1992. The queer nation acts up: Health care, politics, and sexual diversity in the County of Angels. *Society and Space* 10:609–650.

Gladwell, Malcolm. 1992. Beyond HIV: The legacies of health activism. *Washington Post*, 15 October, A-29.

Gross, Jane. 1991. Turning disease into political cause: First AIDS, and now breast cancer. *New York Times*, 7 January, A-12.

Harrington, Mark. 1993. *The Crisis in Clinical AIDS Research*. New York: Treatment Action Group.

———. 1994. Interview by author. New York City, 29 April.

Hilts, Philip J. 1990. 82 held in protest on pace of AIDS research. *New York Times*, 22 May, C-2.

Indyk, Debbie, and David Rier. 1993. Grassroots AIDS knowledge: Implications for the boundaries of science and collective action. *Knowledge: Creation, Diffusion, Utilization* 15:3–43.

Irwin, Alan, and Brian Wynne. 1996. *Misunderstanding Science? The Public Reconstruction of Science and Technology*. Cambridge, England: Cambridge University Press.

James, John S. 1986. What's wrong with AIDS treatment research? *AIDS Treatment News*, 9 May.

Jasper, James M., and Dorothy Nelkin. 1992. *The Animal Rights Crusade: The Growth of a Moral Protest*. New York: Free Press.

Jonsen, Albert R., and Jeff Stryker (eds.). 1993. *The Social Impact of AIDS in the United States*. Washington, DC: National Academy Press.

Kingston. 1991. The "white rats" rebel: Chronic fatigue patients sue drug manufacturer for breaking contract to supply promising CFIDS drug. *San Francisco Bay Times*, 7 November, pp. 8, 44.

Kleinman, Daniel Lee. 1995. *Politics on the Endless Frontier: Postwar Research Policy in the United States*. Durham, NC: Duke University Press.

Kroll-Smith, Steve, and H. Hugh Floyd. 1997. *Bodies in Protest: Environmental Illness and the Struggle over Medical Knowledge*. New York: New York University Press.

Kwitny, Jonathan. 1992. *Acceptable Risks*. New York: Poseidon Press.

Latour, Bruno. 1987. *Science in Action: How to Follow Scientists and Engineers through Society*. Cambridge, MA: Harvard University Press.

Latour, Bruno, and Steven Woolgar. 1986. *Laboratory Life: The Construction of Scientific Facts*. Princeton, NJ: Princeton University Press.

Lo, Clarence Y. H. 1992. Communities of Challengers in Social Movement Theory. In *Frontiers in Social Movement Theory*, ed. Aldon D. Morris and Carol McClurg Mueller, pp. 224–47. New Haven: Yale University Press.

Martin, Brian. 1980. The goal of self-managed science: Implications for action. *Radical Science Journal* 10:3–16.

MD telethon boycott urged. 1991. *San Francisco Examiner*, 2 September, B-1.

Merigan, Thomas C. 1990. Sounding board: You *can* teach an old dog new tricks: How AIDS trials are pioneering new strategies. *New England Journal of Medicine* 323:1341–1343.

Meyer, David S., and Nancy Whittier. 1994. Social movement spillover. *Social Problems* 41:277–298.

Moore, Kelly. 1996. Organizing integrity: American science and the creation of public interest organizations, 1955–1975. *American Journal of Sociology* 101:1592–1627.

Nelkin, Dorothy. 1975. The political impact of technical expertise. *Social Studies of Science* 5:35–54.

Patton, Cindy. 1990. *Inventing AIDS*. New York: Routledge.

Petersen, James C. (ed.). 1984. *Citizen Participation in Science Policy*. Amherst: University of Massachusetts Press.

Phair, John. 1994. Interview by author. Chicago, 15 November.

PWA Coalition. 1988. Founding Statement of People with AIDS/ARC. In *AIDS: Cultural Analysis, Cultural Activism*, ed. Douglas Crimp, pp. 148–49. Cambridge, MA: MIT Press.

Quimby, Ernest, and Samuel R. Friedman. 1989. Dynamics of black mobilization against AIDS in New York City. *Social Problems* 36:403–415.

Richman, Douglas. 1994. Interview by author. San Diego, 1 June.

Roland, Michelle. 1993. Interview by author. Davis, CA, 18 December.

Ruzek, Sheryl Burt. 1978. *Feminist Alternatives to Medical Control*. New York: Praeger.

Rycroft, Robert W. 1991. Environmentalism and science: Politics and the pursuit of knowledge. *Knowledge: Creation, Diffusion, Utilization* 13:150–169.

Shapin, Steven. 1994. *A Social History of Truth: Civility and Science in Seventeenth-Century England*. Chicago: University of Chicago Press.

Shapin, Steven, and Simon Schaffer. 1985. *Leviathan and the Air-Pump: Hobbes, Boyle, and the Experimental Life*. Princeton, NJ: Princeton University Press.

Star, Susan Leigh. 1989. *Regions of the Mind: Brain Research and the Quest for Scientific Certainty*. Stanford, CA: Stanford University Press.

Treichler, Paula A. 1991. How to Have Theory in an Epidemic: The Evolution of AIDS Treatment Activism. In *Technoculture*, ed. Constance Penley and Andrew Ross, pp. 57–106. Minneapolis and Oxford: University of Minnesota Press.

Vollmer, Tim. 1990. ACT-UP/SF splits in two over consensus, focus. *San Francisco Sentinel*, 20 September, 1.

Wachter, Robert M. 1991. *The Fragile Coalition: Scientists, Activists, and AIDS*. New York: St. Martins.

Weber, Max. 1978. *Economy and Ssociety*, vol. 1, ed. G. Roth and C. Wittich. Berkeley: University of California Press.

White, Stuart. 1993. Scientists and the environmental movement. *Chain Reaction* 68:31–33.

Williams, Rob, and John Law. 1980. Beyond the bounds of credibility. *Fundamenta Scientiae* 1:295–315.

Winnow, Jackie. 1992. Lesbians evolving health care: Cancer and AIDS. *Feminist Review* 41:68–77.

Wynne, Brian. 1992. Misunderstood misunderstanding: Social identities and public uptake of science. *Public Understanding of Science* 1:281–304.

34
Breathing Life into Ourselves: The Evolution of the National Black Women's Health Project

Byllye Y. Avery

I got involved in women's health in the 1970s around the issue of abortion. There were three of us at the University of Florida, in Gainesville, who just seemed to get picked out by women who needed abortions. They came to us. I didn't know anything about abortions. In my life that word couldn't even be mentioned without having somebody look at you crazy. Then someone's talking to me about abortion. It seemed unreal. But as more women came (and at first they were mostly white women), we found out this New York number we could give them, and they could catch a plane and go there for their abortions. But then a black woman came and we gave her the number, and she looked at us in awe: "I can't get to New York. . . ." We realized we needed a different plan of action, so in May 1974 we opened up the Gainesville Women's Health Center.

As we learned more about abortions and gynecological care, we immediately started to look at birth, and to realize that we are women with a total reproductive cycle. We might have to make different decisions about our lives, but whatever the decision, we deserved the best services available. So, in 1978, we opened up Birthplace, an alternative birthing center. It was exhilarating work; I assisted in probably around two hundred births. I understood life, and working in birth, I understood death, too. I certainly learned what's missing in prenatal care and why so many of our babies die.

Through my work at Birthplace, I learned the importance of being involved in our own health. We have to create environments that say "yes." Birthplace was a wonderful space. It was a big, old turn-of-the-century house that we decorated with antiques. We went to people's houses and, if we liked something, we begged for it—things off their walls, furniture, rugs. We fixed the place so that when women walked in, they would say, "Byllye, I was excited when I got up today because

Reprinted by permission of the Health Policy Advisory Board from *Health-PAC Bulletin*, copyright 1989 by the Health Policy Advisory Board.

this was my day to come to Birthplace." That's how prenatal care needs to be given—so that people are excited when they come. It's about eight and a half or nine months that a woman comes on a continuous basis. That is the time to start affecting her life so that she can start making meaningful lifestyle changes. So you see, health provides us with all sorts of opportunities for empowerment.

Through Birthplace, I came to understand the importance of our attitudes about birthing. Many women don't get the exquisite care they deserve. They go to these large facilities, and they don't understand the importance of prenatal care. They ask, "Why is it so important for me to get in here and go through all this hassle?" We have to work around that.

Through the work of Birthplace, we have created a prenatal caring program that provides each woman who comes for care with a support group. She enters the group when she arrives, leaves the group to go for her physical checkup, and then returns to the group when she is finished. She doesn't sit in a waiting room for two hours. Most of these women have nobody to talk to. No one listens to them; no one helps them plan. They're asking: "Who's going to get me to the hospital if I go into labor in the middle of the night, or the middle of the day, for that matter? Who's going to help me get out of this abusive relationship? Who's going to make sure I have the food I need to eat?" Infant mortality is not a medical problem; it's a social problem.

One of the things that black women have started talking about regarding infant mortality is that many of us are like empty wells; we give a lot, but we don't get much back. We're asked to be strong. I have said, "If one more person says to me that black women are strong I'm going to scream in their face." I am so tired of that stuff. What are you going to do—just lay down and die? We have to do what's necessary to survive. It's just a part of living. But most of us are empty wells that never really get replenished. Most of us are dead inside. We are walking around dead. That's why we end up in relationships that reinforce that particular thought. So you're talking about a baby being alive inside of a dead person; it just won't work.

We need to stop letting doctors get away with piling up all this money, buying all these little machines. They can keep the tiniest little piece of protoplasm alive, and then it goes home and dies. All this foolishness with putting all this money back into their pockets on that end of the care and not on the other end has to stop. When are we going to wake up?

The National Black Women's Health Project

I left the birthing center around 1980 or 1981, mostly because we needed more midwives and I wasn't willing to go to nursing school. But an important thing had happened for me in 1979. I began looking at myself as a black woman. Before that I had been looking at myself as a woman. When I left the birthing center, I went to work in a Comprehensive Employment Training Program (CETA) job at a community college and it brought me face-to-face with my sisters and face-to-face with my self. Just by the nature of the program and the population that I worked with, I had, for the first time in my life, a chance to ask a 19-year-old why—please give me the reason why—you have four babies and you're only 19 years old. And I was able to listen, and bring these sisters together to talk about their lives. It was there that I started to understand the lives of black women and to realize that we live in a conspiracy of silence. It was hearing these women's stories that led me to start conceptualizing the National Black Women's Health Project.

First I wanted to do an hour-long presentation on black women's health issues, so I started doing research. I got all the books, and I was shocked at what I saw. I was angry—angry that the people who wrote these books didn't put it into a format that made sense to us, angry that nobody was saying anything to black women or to black men. I was so angry I threw one book across the room and it stayed there for three or four days, because I knew I had just seen the tip of the iceberg, but I also knew enough to know that I couldn't go back. I had opened my eyes, and I had to go on and look.

Instead of an hour-long presentation we had a conference. It didn't happen until 1983, but when it did, 2,000 women came. But I knew we couldn't just have a conference. From the health statistics I saw, I knew that there was a deeper problem. People needed to be able to work individually, and on a daily basis. So we got the idea of self-help groups. The first group we formed was in a rural area outside of Gainesville, with twenty-one women who were severely obese. I thought, "Oh this is a piece of cake. Obviously these sisters don't have any information. I'll go in there and talk to them about losing weight, talk to them about high blood pressure, talk to them about diabetes—it'll be easy."

Little did I know that when I got there, they would be able to tell me everything that went into a 1,200-calorie-a-day diet. They all had been to Weight Watchers at least five or six times; they all had blood-pressure-reading machines in their homes as well as medications they were on. And when we sat down to talk, they said, "We know all that information, but what we also know is that living in the world that we are in, we feel like we are absolutely nothing." One woman said to me, "I work for General Electric making batteries, and, from the stuff they suit me up in, I know it's killing me." She said, "My home life is not working. My old man is an alcoholic. My kids got babies. Things are not well with me. And the one thing I know I can do when I come home is cook me a pot of food and sit down in front of the TV and eat it. And you can't take that away from me until you're ready to give me something in its place."

So that made me start to think that there was some other piece to this health puzzle that had been missing, that it's not just about giving information; people need something else. We just spent a lot of time talking. And while we were talking, we were planning the 1983 conference, so I took the information back to the planning committee. Lillie Allen (a trainer who works with NBWHP) was there. We worked with her to understand that we are dying inside. That unless we are able to go inside of ourselves and touch and breathe fire, breathe life into ourselves, that, of course, we couldn't be healthy. Lillie started working on a workshop that we named "Black and Female: What Is the Reality?" This is a workshop that terrifies us all. And we are also terrified not to have it, because the conspiracy of silence is killing us.

Stopping Violence

As we started to talk, I looked at those health statistics in a new way. Now, I'm not saying that we are not suffering from the things we die from—that's what the statistics give us. But what causes all this sickness? Like cardiovascular disease—it's the number one killer. What causes all that heart pain? When sisters take their shoes off and start talking about what's happening, the first thing we cry about is violence. The violence in our lives. And if you look in statistics books, they mention violence in one paragraph. They don't even give numbers, because they can't count it: the violence is too pervasive.

The number one issue for most of our sisters is violence—battering, sexual abuse. Same thing for their daughters, whether they are 12 or 4. We have to look at how violence is used, how violence and sexism go hand in hand, and how it affects the sexual response of females. We have to stop it, because violence is the training ground for us.

When you talk to young people about being pregnant, you find out a lot of things. Number one is that most of these girls did not get pregnant by teenage boys; most of them got pregnant by their mother's boyfriends or their brothers or their daddies. We've been sitting on that. We can't just tell our daughter, "Just say no." What do they do about all those feelings running around their bodies? And we need to talk to our brothers. We need to tell them, the incest makes us crazy. It's something that stays on our minds all the time. We need the men to know that. And they need to know that when they hurt us, they hurt themselves. Because we are their mothers, their sisters, their wives; we are their allies on this planet. They can't just damage one part of it without damaging themselves. We need men to stop giving consent, by their silence, to rape, to sexual abuse, to violence. You need to talk to your boyfriends, your husbands, your sons, whatever males you have around you—talk to them about talking to other men. When they are sitting around womanizing, talking bad about women, make sure you have somebody stand up and be your ally and help stop this. For future generations, this has got to stop somewhere.

Mothers and Daughters

If violence is the number one thing women talk about, the next is mothers too early and too long. We've developed a documentary called "On Becoming a Woman: Mothers and Daughters Talking Together." It's 8 mothers and 8 daughters—16 ordinary people talking about extraordinary things.

The idea of the film came out of my own experience with my daughter. When Sonja turned 11, I started bemoaning that there were no rituals left; there was nothing to let a girl know that once you get your period your life can totally change, nothing to celebrate that something wonderful is happening. So I got a cake that said, "Happy Birthday! Happy Menstruation!" It had white icing with red writing. I talked about the importance of becoming a woman, and, out of that, I developed a workshop for mothers and daughters for the public schools. I did the workshops in Gainesville, and, when we came to Atlanta, I started doing them there. The film took ten years, from the first glimmer of an idea to completion.

The film is in three parts. In the first part all the mothers talk about when we got our periods. Then the daughters who have their periods talk about getting theirs, and the ones who are still waiting talk about that. The second part of the film deals with contraception, birth control, anatomy, and physiology. This part of the film is animated, so it keeps the kids' attention. It's funny. It shows all the anxiety: passing around condoms, hating it, saying, "Oh no, we don't want to do this."

The third part of the film is the hardest. We worked on communication with the mothers and daughters. We feel that the key to birth control and to controlling reproduction is the nature of the relationship between the parents and their young people. And what's happening is that everybody is willing to beat up on the young kids, asking, "Why did you get pregnant? Why did you do this?" No one is saying to the parents, "Do you need some help with learning how to talk to your young person? Do you want someone to sit with you? Do you want to see what it feels like?" We don't have all the answers. In this film, you see us struggling.

What we created, which was hard for the parents, is a safe space where everybody can say anything they need to say. And if you think about that, as parents, we have that relationship with our kids: we can ask them anything. But when we talk about sex, it's special to be in a space where the kids can ask *us,* "Mama, what do you do when you start feeling funny all in your body?" What the kids want to know is, what about lust? What do we do about it? And that's the very information that we don't want to give up. That's "our business." But they want to hear it from us, because they can trust us. And we have to struggle with how we do that: How do we share that information? How do we deal with our feelings?

Realizing the Dream

The National Black Women's Health Project has 96 self-help groups in 22 states, 6 groups in Kenya, and a group in Barbados and in Belize. In addition, we were just funded by the W. K. Kellogg Foundation to do some work in three housing projects in Atlanta. We received $1,032,000 for a three-year period to set up three community centers. Our plan is to do health screening and referral for adolescents and women, and in addition to hook them up with whatever social services they need—to help cut through the red tape. There will be computerized learning programs and individualized tutorial programs to help young women get their General Equivalency Degrees (GED), along with a panel from the community who will be working on job readiness skills. And we'll be doing our self-help groups—talking about who we are, examining, looking at ourselves.

We hope this will be a model program that can be duplicated anywhere. And we're excited about it. Folks in Atlanta thought it was a big deal for a group of black women to get a million dollars. We thought it was pretty good, too. Our time is coming.

35
Getting the Lead Out of the Community

Janet Phoenix

Lead poisoning, while completely preventable, is one of the most common environmental health diseases in the United States (Agency for Toxic Substances and Disease Registry 1988). Some of the symptoms of lead toxicity are fatigue, pallor, malaise, loss of appetite, irritability, sleep disturbance, sudden behavioral change, and developmental regression. The more serious symptoms include clumsiness, muscular irregularities, weakness, abdominal pain, persistent vomiting, constipation, and changes in consciousness. Lead exposure is particularly harmful to children. It damages their developing brains and nervous systems. Indeed, even low-level lead exposure can lead to attention disorders, learning disabilities, and emotional disturbances that can affect a child for the rest of his or her life. While once controversial, the effects of lead poisoning have now been carefully analyzed by several investigators and have gained wide acceptance within the public health field (Needleman et al. 1992; Dietrich et al. 1987; Baghurst et al. 1987; Environmental Defense Fund 1990; Alliance to End Childhood Lead Poisoning 1991).

One key source of lead poisoning has been dramatically reduced over the last two decades. A reduction in the mean blood lead level in the U.S. population occurred between 1976 and 1980 when the sale of leaded gasoline declined in this country. Yet, the problem of lead poisoning is still widespread. It has been estimated that between four to five million U.S. children are routinely exposed to lead in sufficient amounts to be considered dangerous to their health. As pointed out by the Centers for Disease Control:

> Childhood lead poisoning is one of the most common pediatric health problems in the United States today, and it is entirely preventable. Enough is now known about the sources and pathways of lead exposure and about ways of preventing this exposure

Reprinted by permission of (Boston) South End Press, from Robert Bullard (ed.), *Confronting Environmental Racism: Voices from the Grassroots*, 1993, pp. 77–88.

to begin the efforts to eradicate permanently this disease. The persistence of lead poisoning in the United States, in light of all that is known, presents a singular and direct challenge to public health authorities, clinicians, regulatory agencies, and society (Centers for Disease Control 1991).

In 1988, the Agency for Toxic Substances and Disease Registry (ATSDR) estimated the extent of childhood lead poisoning in Standard Metropolitan Statistical Areas (SMSA) and provided breakdowns by race, income, and urban status (Agency for Toxic Substances and Disease Registry 1988). The estimates of affected children are largely based on the numbers of children in these areas who live in pre-1950 housing, where lead paint is most common, though data generated by childhood lead poisoning screening programs was also incorporated for the cities where such programs exist. Given the fact that the study focused on lead paint and largely ignored other common sources of lead exposure, it is possible that this study actually underestimates the extent of the problem. The sources of continuing exposure include lead-based paint and paint dust, but also include contamination at work and neighborhood pollution by nearby industries and waste treatment facilities.

Whatever the limitations of this study, it does clearly show that lead exposure is not randomly distributed across population groups. Its distribution is directly related to both class and race. A disproportionate impact, for example, is felt in African-American communities, as are so many environmental health problems (Agency for Toxic Substances and Disease Registry 1988). Indeed, African Americans, at all class levels, have a significantly greater chance of being lead poisoned than do whites.

Given the de facto residential and occupational segregation that still affects African Americans and other minorities, such a finding should probably not come as a surprise. Yet, the figures are astounding. According to ATSDR's report to Congress, 49 percent of African-American inner-city children are exposed to dangerous levels of lead, compared to 16 percent of white inner-city children. Outside the nation's large urban areas, 36 percent of African-American children are exposed to dangerous levels, compared to 9 percent of white children. This disparity has existed for decades (Agency for Toxic Substances and Disease Registry 1988; Schwartz and Levin 1992, pp. 42–44).

What makes these statistics even more alarming is the fact that the blood lead level deemed dangerous has gone down as a result of recent research. During the 1980s, the federal Centers for Disease Control

(CDC) mandated medical intervention for children with blood lead levels of 25 μg/dl or higher. In October 1991, the CDC issued a statement, *Preventing Lead Poisoning in Young Children*, lowering the acceptable blood lead level from 25 μg/dl to 10 μg/dl. Today, the average level for all children in the United States is under 6 μg/dl (Schwartz and Levin 1992, p. 43). However, the Second National Health and Nutrition Examination Survey II (NHANES II), conducted between 1976 and 1980, found that the average blood lead level for African-American children was 21 μg/dl, and for poor African-American children in the inner city, 23 μg/dl. This average has gone down along with the decline of lead gasoline. Yet, the average blood lead level in African-American children is still well above 6 μg/dl. Indeed, many African-American children have blood levels well above the 10 μg/dl limit.

Lead poisoning has been termed the *silent epidemic*, for it most often leaves no outward sign of its arrival. Years after lead levels return to normal it becomes apparent in the difficulty a child has in school, in frank mental retardation, or in the onset of kidney disease in a previously healthy adult. Yet, health policy in the United States largely leaves prevention, screening, and treatment to individuals rather than taking a proactive, public health approach that does not penalize poor people without sufficient means to pay for screening and treatment or moving out of dangerous housing, jobs, and neighborhoods. Nor has a proactive policy been developed to break through the de facto segregation that keeps people of color trapped in contaminated houses, jobs, and communities. Activists of color thus need to ask: Where does lead come from? How does it damage the health of those who come into contact with it? What can we do to mitigate the damage? What can be done to prevent it?

Lead Paint and Dust in the Home

In 1989–1990, the U.S. Department of Housing and Urban Development conducted a national survey of lead-based paint in housing. The results were published in its *A Comprehensive and Workable Plan for the Abatement of Lead-Based Paint in Privately Owned Housing* (1990). It details the prevalence of lead-based paint in housing stock, as well as the average lead-dust levels in the researched housing units. The HUD researchers discovered that 57 million of the 100 million housing units in the United States contain lead-based paint on interior or exterior surfaces. Some seventeen million of them are in a deteriorated condition and pose an immediate hazard. Three to four million of these homes are occupied by children under six, those at greatest risk of being poisoned. Most of the homes in the worst condition are in our inner cities, and a disproportionate number of the inhabitants are people of color.

Part of the danger comes from children eating peeling lead-based paint chips, yet paint dust is perhaps an even more significant problem since dust covers a larger surface area and is more readily absorbed into the bloodstream from a child's stomach. Those who inhale the dust absorb it through their lungs, and from there it enters their bloodstream. Such exposure can cause lead poisoning even though it may take place over only a short period of time.

Lead dust is also harder to clean up. Children come into contact with it because it clings to toys, collects on flat surfaces (especially around windows), and then sticks to children's hands. So when they put their hands in their mouths, they swallow lead dust. Over time, enough can accumulate to poison a child. Studies done in Cincinnati "support the hypothesis the peeling paint is eventually ground into dust which then contaminates hands, toys, and food" (Bornschein et al., 1986).

Large amounts of lead dust are frequently generated during home renovation projects. This dust can remain airborne for up to 24 hours after work has ceased, during which time it can be inhaled, posing a hazard to workers as well as the families living in the homes. Adults as well as children are poisoned this way. The dust settling out of the air coats household surfaces (including children's toys) and can travel a long distance from where the work is being done. Because work done on the outside of a building can contaminate rooms on the inside, a thorough cleanup is necessary. Pregnant women and children should not enter a renovated home for 24 hours after the work has been completed and a thorough cleanup has been done.

A good case study of lead problems in the home is provided by Jeremy, a two-year-old living in a well-maintained, older apartment building in a large urban center in the eastern United States. His family always had trouble with the apartment's old wooden windows. The maintenance people had to come in at least twice a year to scrape and repaint them. Because it seemed to Jeremy's dad that as soon as they left the paint would start to peel again, and he was constantly complaining.

The workers never thoroughly scraped off all the old paint, and so the new layer began to blister and peel almost immediately after they left. Also, when they worked on the outside of the apartment building, they never covered the ground. Chips would fall into the yard, and lead dust blew into the urban garden plots next door, where Jeremy's family had gardened for three years.

While Jeremy's parents had not yet noticed any behavioral changes, his mother regularly took him to the neighborhood health clinic for routine checkups. She was very upset when his lead test came back positive. The clinic outreach workers who visited the house talked about cleaning up paint chips, but Jeremy's mother was always careful to sweep up the chips after the renovation workers left. Moreover, she tried to make sure that Jeremy never ate paint chips in the yard. At first everyone was puzzled by how such a high level of lead contamination could happen.

Paint chips would have been the obvious answer had Jeremy's mother not been so conscientious. The paint chip samples taken from the windows tested positive as lead-based paint. The city lead inspector had brought in an XRF (a hand-held device which aims X-rays at painted surfaces and measures how much is reflected) and used this to determine how much lead was in the paint on their walls and windows.

The main problem was the dust, however. A lot of dust was released when the workers came in to scrape and repaint the windows twice a year. Regardless of his mother's thorough cleaning, Jeremy should have stayed elsewhere until the cleanups had been completed, preferably using a high phosphate dishwasher powder which has proved useful for cleaning up lead dust.

Furthermore, before the situation was researched, no one suspected that lead dust from the maintenance work on the nearby apartment building had settled in the adjacent garden plots. Yet, soil lead levels in the garden were well above 1,000 parts per million (ppm). The U.S. Environmental Protection Agency has determined that 500–1,000 ppm and greater are toxic levels of lead in soil. Growing vegetables can concentrate this lead in vegetables thus endangering everyone who eats vegetables grown in the contaminated soil. This was a very likely source of contamination for Jeremy. His parents were active gardeners and very proud of the vegetables they grew to supplement their diet. As active gardeners, they also brought lead dust into the home on their hands and work clothes.

Jeremy's blood lead level was 16 μg/dl, high enough to do damage but not high enough to cause obvious symptoms. Other children are not so lucky. A fifteen-month-old named Vincent seemed to be progressing well; he had learned to say a few words. He liked to rise early and play vigorously. Yet, it was not long before his parents noticed a marked change in his behavior: he seemed to forget how to talk and stopped wanting to play. Instead, he would take his blanket into a corner and lie quietly. Food no longer interested him. His lead level was 45 μg/dl.

Unlike Vincent, Jeremy did not need to be hospitalized for the expensive procedure of chelation therapy which cleans the blood of lead contamination. His parents were simply told to eradicate the sources of contamination in his environment and have him tested every three months until his level fell below 10 μg/dl. Eradicating the source of contamination is a difficult proposition for poor families, however. Jeremy's family, for example, cannot afford to move out of the apartment, nor are they allowed to remove the paint themselves. They can stop growing and eating food from their garden, but this only makes their food costs more expensive. To help cover their medical and home improvement costs, Jeremy's parents hired an attorney to file a lawsuit against their landlord for not properly maintaining the building and contributing to Jeremy's poisoning. No settlement has yet been reached, however.

In spite of their financial limitations, Jeremy's family has done a good job in lowering his lead level. They covered the window sills and walls with contact paper, washed Jeremy's hands more frequently, and supplemented his diet with iron and calcium. (Such nutritional supplements have been found to help limit lead contamination.) His mother also used trisodium phosphate (TSP, a powdered detergent, usually found in hardware stores, which is good at cleaning up lead dust) to wash the floors and the toys. After a few months, Jeremy's lead level came down.

No one knows whether Jeremy will suffer any permanent damage from his early exposure to lead, or if he will suffer mental retardation. Little can be done at his age to diagnose the long-term effects of his lead exposure. His parents have been told that when his language skills are more fully developed, he can undergo developmental testing, provided they can afford it. These tests can pinpoint learning disabilities. Yet, even if problems are discovered, it would be difficult, if not impossible, to "prove" they were caused by the lead exposure. Many lead-poisoned children live in a harsh environment that lacks those elements children need to compensate for learning disabilities and realize their potential. It is not easy to separate the general effects of poverty and racism from the specific effects of lead. Yet, we do know that lead causes attention deficit disorder and other behavioral problems which interfere with school performance. Lead-poisoned children have trouble learning to speak and write. They may not have the same problem-solving ability as other children. Jeremy's mother worries that he may have trouble in school in the future, although he seems bright and alert right now.

For any individual child it is difficult to predict the effects of lead exposure. We do know that children whose lead levels rise above 50 μg/dl are much more likely to suffer profound damage, such as mental retardation. At levels of 50 μg/dl, or even below, hearing can be affected as well as Vitamin D metabolism and synthesis of the oxygen-carrying components of the blood. Also, as the blood lead level rises above 50 μg/dl, disorders such as colic (a complex of symptoms ranging from abdominal pain or cramps to constipation) may result. Effects of lower levels of exposure are much less predictable but no less real.

Contamination on the Job and in the Community

Perhaps the most common source of contamination for adults is at their workplace. Hazardous industries with well-known lead exposure problems include battery manufacturing plants, lead smelters, brass foundries, firing ranges, radiator repair shops, and construction sites. Large industries are required to inform their employees of these hazards and to test their blood lead levels regularly. Some states mandate that levels above 25 μg/dl be reported to a state occupational registry maintained by occupational health departments that monitor hazardous work sites. Also, when employees are removed from a work site because of elevated blood lead levels, the state's occupational health department is supposed to monitor their progress. (State requirements normally reflect federal regulations.) Furthermore, retesting has to take place before the employee can return to work. Unfortunately, such state efforts are often underfunded and the actual regulation is often completely inadequate. Furthermore, small businesses often escape from taking precautions because they don't employ enough people for federal or state regulations to apply. This leaves many workers unprotected.

A good case study of these problems is provided by Randall, a former worker in a battery manufacturing plant who worked with lead every day. Written warnings about lead had been handed out when he was first hired; but Randall could not read well and so hadn't understood the warnings. Also, he was afraid to question his employer closely about the dangers because he desperately needed the job.

After several months, Randall started to have stomach cramps and headaches, but they were not bad enough to stop him from working. They merely robbed him of the joy of his leisure time by making him not feel good. A colleague complained one day that although lead tests were supposed to be given periodically to workers at the plant, none had been given since the physical exams they had received when hired. Blood had been taken then, but the results had not been shared with the workers.

This comment sparked Randall's curiosity and he asked the co-worker to explain the dangers of lead to him. What he learned concerned Randall enough that he sought out a clinic in his neighborhood and asked to be tested. Because his lead level was 92 $\mu g/dl$, the clinic doctor recommended that he be hospitalized immediately for therapy. When his employer learned of the hospitalization, Randall was laid off. He thus had to be hospitalized in a charity hospital because he was no longer covered by health insurance.

Randall was treated with chelation therapy to remove the lead from his blood. Although his lead level was high enough to kill a child, as an adult he was in no danger of dying. His physicians were concerned, however, about his developing hypertension and kidney damage. As noted, lead can affect the kidneys, the reproductive system, the gastrointestinal system, and the nervous system.

Fortunately, Randall recovered almost completely and was released from the hospital. He was told, however, that he could not return to his trade or other similar work because of the risk of re-exposure, which in even small amounts could send his lead level soaring again because a significant amount of lead was now stored in his bones which would render a new round of chelation therapy much less effective.

Randall and his wife were also concerned that their children may have been exposed to the lead dust he brought home on his clothing. While people who work in lead-related industries are often unaware of the hazards they pose to their families, secondary exposure of children whose parents work with lead is quite common. If those who work with lead handle their children before removing their work clothing, they can contaminate them. If their work clothing is washed with the rest of the family's laundry, further contamination can take place. Over time, lots of lead dust can accumulate in the home through such exposure and cause the blood lead levels of family members to rise. Clothes, upholstered furniture, automobile upholstery, and carpets are common accumulation sites for lead dust.

Randall's wife took the children to the clinic, where they too were tested and found to have high blood lead levels. The local children's hospital offered outpatient treatment for the children, but the family had to scramble to find the money to pay for it. With Randall no longer employed, his wife's income was the only source of support for the family. Randall felt he should have received some consideration and benefits from his employers, but the company denied all responsibility. Randall has since applied for unemployment compensation and work-men's compensation but his case has not yet been acted on.

A small community in an eastern state provides a good case study of primary lead poisoning of poor communities through industrial pollution. This community sits in the midst of a solid waste incinerator, an oil company, and a water pollution control plant. The plant has been operating over capacity for years and spills hazardous wastes into the adjacent river. The oil company has spilled approximately 17 million gallons of petroleum into underground areas, thus contaminating the aquifer of the community. The incinerator receives solid wastes above 25 μg/dl from neighboring communities. Although scrubbers are in place in its smokestacks, these scrubbers do not yet efficiently remove heavy metal particles from the smoke. Hazardous metals such as lead, cadmium, and mercury are regularly emitted which adversely affect human health.

These heavy metals have settled into the air, soil, and water of this community and adjacent ones. Their residents, mostly people of color, are being assaulted on a number of fronts. The workers in these plants—and their families—are not only at risk from these facilities; the entire community is poisoned and becomes contaminated simply by living near these facilities. It has been estimated that three-fourths of the children in this community have elevated blood lead levels.

Waste incineration may soon rival lead-based gasoline and lead smelting as major sources of lead in the air. Researchers project that millions of pounds of lead per year will be emitted from the nation's waste incinerator facilities in the next few years. All of it is being released into the environment, despite what we know about its hazardous effects. Little has been done to improve the capacity of these facilities to clean the air they release.

Communities Fight Back

Changes need to be made to prevent this very preventable disease. Some of these changes involve educating individuals on how they can better protect themselves and their children. However, other needed changes are deeply political and require greater social and economic justice, a more responsive democracy, and a socially responsible economic system that does not make profit the sole or highest guide to economic decisionmaking. Such changes will certainly require the growth and strengthening of a grassroots social movement for environmental justice that can educate local communities and hold governments and corporations accountable to the needs and desires of oppressed communities.

Happily, this is already beginning to happen. A report on the hazardous conditions facing communities of color and low-income communities in one state was recently prepared and presented to the state legislature. The following goals were recommended in the report:

- establishment of a Task Force on Environmental Equity;
- research on the health and safety impacts of environmental conditions in at-risk communities;
- greater public notice of hazards through publications that target communities of color and their organizations;
- research and documentation of fish consumption patterns and resulting health concerns in the rivers and lakes of the state;
- training and certification of lead inspectors, abatement contractors, and others who engage in the inspection, removal, covering, or replacement of paint, plaster, or other material containing a lead hazard;
- state-funded lead poisoning prevention, inspection, education and abatement programs;
- mandatory lead screening for children at the age of six months, one year, and annually thereafter until age six;
- a "safe house" program that provides free temporary housing during the abatement and cleanup of contaminated homes; and
- research and documentation of the sources and prevalence of occupational disease and the need for occupational health services for residents in low-income communities and communities of color.

Other communities have gone even farther. Recently a state government opted to study three counties to determine if lead poisoning existed in their state and, if so, to what extent. The state had not regularly screened its citizens since the early 1980s, when federal funds earmarked for lead poisoning prevention had been cut. At that time, the funding was shifted into the Maternal and Child Health Block Grant program, which left it up to individual states to decide whether, and to what extent, to fund lead poisoning prevention. During the study, children, as well as soil and paint samples, were tested for lead. The data from the three counties were then used to make estimates for the state as a whole.

In one county, families whose children had been screened became concerned about the results, but the state refused to release the data until the final drafting of the report could take place. The data was politically explosive. It indicated that more than 20 percent of the children in the county were lead poisoned. It also showed that 67 percent of the African-American, Latino, and Asian children were found to have lead levels greater than 10 μg/dl. Many of the minority families tested came together and formed a new community organization.

In 1989, this grassroots organization undertook its own health survey, covering 1,012 households in which eight different languages were spoken (Calpotura 1991). The survey revealed that:

- 33 percent of the households had no health insurance;
- 98 percent had no lead screening for household members;
- 31 percent had received no immunizations for children in the household;
- outpatient clinics which they frequented had little or no bilingual or multilingual capacity; and
- 96 percent of people eligible for the existing free testing program were unaware of it.

The community also continued to hold public meetings, focusing on:
- the results of its own health survey and the need to obtain results of the lead screening done by the state;
- the need for lead testing of playgrounds and schools;
- the need to gain access to free testing programs; and
- the need for fully funded lead abatement programs.

The organization's initial successes included:
- obtaining the results of the state survey;

- expansion of free testing services; and
- an agreement by the city to test selected school and playground sites for lead contamination.

Later the organization campaigned for a Comprehensive Screening and Abatement Program and got the town council to pass it. The county residents and the organization they formed will continue to work for implementation of their plan. Revenue from the property tax on older housing will go into a fund to be used for the lead abatement of low-income dwellings, as well as educational programs for the county residents. Training low-income people to do lead abatement work is also an integral part of the plan.

The community organization has mobilized the county's citizens to devise and implement a successful strategy to address lead poisoning on a community-wide basis. It has thus served as an example for other communities in the country. Similar efforts have been made in other parts of the country. In 1991, for example, a coalition of civil rights, environmental, and public health advocates in Alameda County (NAACP Legal Defense and Educational Fund, ACLU, Natural Resources Defense Council, National Health Law Program, and the Legal Aid Society of Alameda County) obtained an agreement from the state of California to screen an estimated 500,000 poor children for lead poisoning at a cost of $15–20 million (Lee 1992). The agreement is part of an out-of-court settlement in a class-action lawsuit, *Matthews v. Coye*. The plaintiffs charged California with failure to routinely conduct blood lead testing of some 557,000 Medicaid-eligible children below the age of five—a violation of the federal Medicaid Act and its implementation guidelines.

References

Agency for Toxic Substances and Disease Registry, *The Nature and Extent of Lead Poisoning in Children in the United States: A Reprint to Congress*. Atlanta: U.S. Department of Health and Human Services, 1988.

Alliance to End Childhood Lead Poisoning. *Childhood Lead Poisoning Prevention: A Resource Directory*. 2nd ed. Washington, DC: National Center for Education in Maternal and Child Health, 1991.

Baghurst, P. A.; Robertson, E. F.; and McMichael, A. J. "The Port Pirie Cohort Study: Lead Effects on Pregnancy Outcome and Early Childhood Development." *Neurotoxicology* 8(1987): 395–401.

Bornschein, R. L.; Hammond, P. B.; and Dietrich, K. N. "The Cincinnati Prospective Study of Low-Level Lead Exposure and Its Effects on Child Development: Protocol and Status Report." *Environmental Research* 38(1986): 4–18.

Calpotura, Francis. "PUEBLO (People United for a Better Oakland) and Lead Poisoning." Excerpts from speech presented at the National Conference on Preventing Childhood Lead Poisoning, Washington, DC (October 7, 1991).

Dietrich, K. N.; Kraft, K. M.; and Bornschein, R. L. "Low-Level Fetal Lead Exposure Effect on Neurobehavioral Development in Early Infancy." *Pediatrics* 80 (November 1987): 721–730.

Environmental Defense Fund. *Legacy of Lead: America's Continuing Epidemic of Childhood Lead Poisoning: A Report and Proposal for Legislative Action.* March 1990.

Lee, Bill Lann. "Environmental Litigation on Behalf of Poor, Minority Children: *Matthews v. Coye:* A Case Study." Paper presented at the Annual Meeting of the American Association for the Advancement of Science, Chicago, April 1992.

Needleman, H. L; Schell, A.; Bellinger, D.; Leviton, A.; and Allred, E. N. "The long-term effects of exposure to low doses of lead in children: an 11-year follow-up report. *New England Journal of Medicine*, 322(1992): 83–88.

Schwartz, Joel and Levin, Ronnie. "Lead: An Example of the Job Ahead." *EPA Journal* 18 (March/April 1992): 42–44.

36
A National Health Program for the United States: A Physicians' Proposal

David U. Himmelstein and Steffie Woolhandler

With the Writing Committee of the Working Group on Program Design of Physicians for a National Health Program

Our health care system is failing. It denies access to many in need and is expensive, inefficient, and increasingly bureaucratic. The pressures of cost control, competition, and profit threaten the traditional tenets of medical practice. For patients, the misfortune of illness is often amplified by the fear of financial ruin. For physicians, the gratifications of healing often give way to anger and alienation. Patchwork reforms succeed only in exchanging old problems for new ones. It is time to change fundamentally the trajectory of American medicine—to develop a comprehensive national health program for the United States.

We are physicians active in the full range of medical endeavors. We are primary care doctors and surgeons, psychiatrists and public health specialists, pathologists and administrators. We work in hospitals, clinics, private practices, health maintenance organizations (HMOs), universities, corporations, and public agencies. Some of us are young, still in training; others are greatly experienced, and some have held senior positions in American medicine.

As physicians, we constantly confront the irrationality of the present health care system. In private practice, we waste countless hours on billing and bureaucracy. For uninsured patients, we avoid procedures, consultations, and costly medications. Diagnosis-related groups (DRGs) have placed us between administrators demanding early discharge and elderly patients with no one to help at home—all the while glancing over our shoulders at the peer-review organization. In HMOs we walk a tightrope between thrift and penuriousness, too often under the pressure of surveillance by bureaucrats more concerned with the bottom line than with other measures of achievement. In public health work we are frustrated in the face of plenty; the world's richest health care system is unable to ensure such basic services as prenatal care and immunizations.

Despite our disparate perspectives, we are united by dismay at the current state of medicine and by the conviction that an alternative must be developed. We hope to spark debate, to transform disaffection with what exists into a vision of what might be. To this end, we submit for public review, comment, and revision a working plan for a rational and humane health care system—a national health program.

We envisage a program that would be federally mandated and ultimately funded by the federal government but administered largely at the state and local level. The proposed system would eliminate financial barriers to care; minimize economic incentives for both excessive and insufficient care, discourage administrative interference and expense, improve the distribution of health facilities, and control costs by curtailing bureaucracy and fostering health planning. Our plan borrows many features from the Canadian national health program and adapts them to the unique circumstances of the United States. We suggest that, as in Canada's provinces, the national health program be tested initially in statewide demonstration projects. Thus, our proposal addresses both the structure of the national health program and the transition process necessary to implement the program in a single state. In each section below, we present a key feature of the proposal, followed by the rationale for our approach. Areas such as long-term care; public, occupational, environmental, and mental health; and medical education need much more development and will be addressed in detail in future proposals.

Coverage

Everyone would be included in a single public plan covering all medically necessary services, including acute, rehabilitative, long-term, and home care; mental health services; dental services; occupational health care; prescription drugs and medical supplies; and preventive and public health measures. Boards of experts and community representatives would determine which services were unnecessary or ineffective, and these would be excluded from coverage. As in Canada, alternative insurance coverage for services included under the national health program would be eliminated, as would patient copayments and deductibles.

Universal coverage would solve the gravest problem in health care by eliminating financial barriers to care. A single comprehensive program is necessary both to ensure equal access to care and to minimize the complexity and expense of billing and administration. The public administration of insurance funds would save tens of billions of dollars each year. The more than 1500 private health insurers in the United States now consume about 8 percent of revenues for overhead, whereas both the Medicare program and the Canadian national health program have overhead costs of only 2 to 3 percent. The complexity of our current insurance system, with its multiplicity of payers, forces U.S. hospitals to spend more than twice as much as Canadian hospitals on billing and administration and requires U.S. physicians to spend about 10 percent of their gross incomes on excess billing costs.[1] Eliminating insurance programs that duplicated the national health program coverage, though politically thorny, would clearly be within the prerogative of the Congress.[2] Failure to do so would require the continuation of the costly bureaucracy necessary to administer and deal with such programs.

Copayments and deductibles endanger the health of poor people who are sick,[3] decrease the use of vital inpatient medical services as much as they discourage the use of unnecessary ones,[4] discourage preventive care,[5] and are unwieldy and expensive to administer. Canada has few such charges, yet health costs are lower than in the United States and have risen slowly.[6,7] In the United States, in contrast, increasing copayments and deductibles have failed to slow the escalation of costs.

Instead of the confused and often unjust dictates of insurance companies, a greatly expanded program of technology assessment and cost-effectiveness evaluation would guide decisions about covered services, as well as about the allocation of funds for capital spending, drug formularies, and other issues.

Payment for Hospital Services

Each hospital would receive an annual lump-sum payment to cover all operating expenses—a "global" budget. The amount of this payment would be negotiated with the state national health program payment board and would be based on past expenditures, previous financial and clinical performance, projected changes in levels of services, wages and other costs, and proposed new and innovative programs. Hospitals would not bill for services covered by the national health program. No part of the operating budget could be used for hospital expansion, profit, marketing, or major capital purchases or leases.

These expenditures would also come from the national health program fund, but monies for them would be appropriated separately.

Global prospective budgeting would simplify hospital administration and virtually eliminate billing, thus freeing up substantial resources for increased clinical care. Before the nationwide implementation of the national health program, hospitals in the states with demonstration programs could bill out-of-state patients on a simple per diem basis. Prohibiting the use of operating funds for capital purchases or profit would eliminate the main financial incentive for both excessive intervention (under fee-for-service payment) and skimping on care (under DRG-type prospective-payment systems), since neither inflating revenues nor limiting care could result in gain for the institution. The separate appropriation of funds explicitly designated for capital expenditures would facilitate rational health planning. In Canada, this method of hospital payment has been successful in containing costs, minimizing bureaucracy, improving the distribution of health resources, and maintaining the quality of care.[6-9] It shifts the focus of hospital administration away from the bottom line and toward the provision of optimal clinical services.

Payment for Physicians' Services, Ambulatory Care, and Medical Home Care

To minimize the disruption of existing patterns of care, the national health program would include three payment options for physicians and other practitioners: fee-for-service payment, salaried positions in institutions receiving global budgets, and salaried positions within group practices or HMOs receiving per capita (capitation) payments.

Fee-for-Service Payment

The state national health program payment board and a representative of the fee-for-service practitioners (perhaps the state medical society) would negotiate a simplified, binding fee schedule. Physicians would submit bills to the national health program on a simple form or by computer and would receive extra payment for any bill not paid within 30 days. Payments to physicians would cover only the services provided by physicians and their support staff and would exclude reimbursement for costly capital purchases of equipment for the office, such as CT scanners. Physicians who accepted payment from the national health program could bill patients directly only for uncovered services (as is done for cosmetic surgery in Canada).

Global Budgets

Institutions such as hospitals, health centers, group practices, clinics serving migrant workers, and medical home care agencies could elect to receive a global budget for the delivery of outpatient, home care, and physicians' services, as well as for preventive health care and patient-education programs. The negotiation process and the regulations covering capital expenditures and profits would be similar to those for inpatient hospital services. Physicians employed in such institutions would be salaried.

Capitation

HMOs, group practices, and other institutions could elect to be paid fees on a per capita basis to cover all outpatient care, physicians' services, and medical home care. The regulations covering the use of such payments for capital expenditures and for profits would be similar to those that would apply to hospitals. The capitation fee would not cover inpatient services (except care provided by a physician), which would be included in hospitals' global budgets. Selective enrollment policies would be prohibited, and patients would be permitted to leave an HMO or other health plan with appropriate notice. Physicians working in HMOs would be salaried, and financial incentives to physicians based on the HMO's financial performance would be prohibited.

The diversity of existing practice arrangements, each with strong proponents, necessitates a pluralistic approach. Under all three proposed options, capital purchases and profits would be uncoupled from payments to physicians and other operating costs—a feature that is essential for minimizing entrepreneurial incentives, containing costs, and facilitating health planning.

Under the fee-for-service option, physicians' office overhead would be reduced by the simplification of billing.[1] The improved coverage would encourage preventive care.[10] In Canada, fee-for-service practice with negotiated fee schedules and mandatory assignment (acceptance of the assigned fee as total payment) has proved to be compatible with cost containment, adequate incomes for physicians, and a high level of access to and satisfaction with care on the part of patients.[6,7] The Canadian provinces have responded to the inflationary potential of fee-for-service payment in various ways: by limiting the number of physicians, by monitoring physicians for outlandish practice patterns, by setting overall limits on a province's spending for physicians' services (thus relying on the profession to police itself), and even by capping the total reimbursement of individual physicians. These regulatory options have been made possible (and have not required an extensive bureaucracy) because all payment comes from a single source. Similar measures might be needed in the United States, although our penchant for bureaucratic hypertrophy might require a concomitant cap on spending for the regulatory apparatus. For example, spending for program administration and reimbursement bureaucracy might be restricted to 3 percent of total costs.

Global budgets for institutional providers would eliminate billing, while providing a predictable and stable source of income. Such funding could also encourage the development of preventive health programs in the community, such as education programs on the acquired immunodeficiency syndrome (AIDS), whose costs are difficult to attribute and bill to individual patients.

Continuity of care would no longer be disrupted when patients' insurance coverage changed as a result of retirement or a job change. Incentives for providers receiving capitation payments to skimp on care would be minimized, since unused operating funds could not be devoted to expansion or profit.

Payment for Long-Term Care

A separate proposal for long-term care is under development, guided by three principles. First, access to care should be based on need rather than on age or ability to pay. Second, social and community-based services should be expanded and integrated with institutional care. Third, bureaucracy and entrepreneurial incentives should be minimized through global budgeting with separate funding for capital expenses.

Allocation of Capital Funds, Health Planning, and Return on Equity

Funds for the construction or renovation of health facilities and for purchases of major equipment would be appropriated from the national health program budget. The funds would be distributed by state and regional health-planning boards composed of both experts and

community representatives. Capital projects funded by private donations would require approval by the health-planning board if they
entailed an increase in future operating expenses.

The national health program would pay owners of for-profit hospitals, nursing homes, and clinics a reasonable fixed rate of return on
existing equity. Since virtually all new capital investment would be
funded by the national health program, it would not be included in
calculating the return on equity.

Current capital spending greatly affects future operating costs, as
well as the distribution of resources. Effective health planning requires
that funds go to high-quality, efficient programs in the areas of greatest
need. Under the existing reimbursement system, which combines
operating and capital payments, prosperous hospitals can expand and
modernize, whereas impoverished ones cannot, regardless of the
health needs of the population they serve or the quality of services they
provide. The national health program would replace this implicit
mechanism for distributing capital with an explicit one, which would
facilitate (though not guarantee) allocation on the basis of need and
quality. Insulating these crucial decisions from distortion by narrow
interests would require the rigorous evaluation of the technology and
assessment of needs, as well as the active involvement of providers
and patients.

For-profit providers would be compensated for existing investments. Since new for-profit investment would be barred, the proprietary sector would gradually shrink.

Public, Environmental, and Occupational Health Services

Existing arrangements for public, occupational, and environmental
health services would be retained in the short term. Funding for
preventive health care would be expanded. Additional proposals dealing with these issues are planned.

Prescription Drugs and Supplies

An expert panel would establish and regularly update a list of all
necessary and useful drugs and outpatient equipment. Suppliers
would bill the national health program directly for the wholesale cost,
plus a reasonable dispensing fee, of any item in the list that was
prescribed by a licensed practitioner. The substitution of generic for
proprietary drugs would be encouraged.

Funding

The national health program would disburse virtually all payments for health services. The total expenditure would be set at the same proportion of the gross national product as health costs represented in the year preceding the establishment of the national health program. Funds for the national health program could be raised through a variety of mechanisms. In the long run, funding based on an income tax or other progressive tax might be the fairest and most efficient solution, since tax-based funding is the least cumbersome and least expensive mechanism for collecting money. During the transition period in states with demonstration programs, the following structure would mimic existing funding patterns and minimize economic disruption.

Medicare and Medicaid

All current federal funds allocated to Medicare and Medicaid would be paid to the national health program. The contribution of each program would be based on the previous year's expenditures, adjusted for inflation. Using Medicare and Medicaid funds in this manner would require a federal waiver.

State and Local Funds

All current state and local funds for health care expenditures, adjusted for inflation, would be paid to the national health program.

Employer Contributions

A tax earmarked for the national health program would be levied on all employers. The tax rate would be set so that total collections equaled the previous year's statewide total of employers' expenditures for health benefits, adjusted for inflation. Employers obligated by preexisting contracts to provide health benefits could credit the cost of those benefits toward their national health program tax liability.

Private Insurance Revenues

Private health insurance plans duplicating the coverage of the national health program would be phased out over three years. During this transition period, all revenues from such plans would be turned over to the national health program, after the deduction of a reasonable fee to cover the costs of collecting premiums.

General Tax Revenues

Additional taxes, equivalent to the amount now spent by individual citizens for insurance premiums and out-of-pocket health costs, would be levied.

It would be critical for all funds for health care to flow through the national health program. Such single-source payment (monopsony) has been the cornerstone of cost containment and health planning in Canada. The mechanism of raising funds for the national health program would be a matter of tax policy, largely separate from the organization of the health care system itself. As in Canada, federal funding could attenuate inequalities among the states in financial and medical resources.

The transitional proposal for demonstration programs in selected states illustrates how monopsony payment could be established with limited disruption of existing patterns of health care funding. The employers' contribution would represent a decrease in costs for most firms that now provide health insurance and an increase for those that do not currently pay for benefits. Some provision might be needed to cushion the impact of the change on financially strapped small businesses. Decreased individual spending for health care would offset the additional tax burden on individual citizens. Private health insurance, with its attendant inefficiency and waste, would be largely eliminated. A program of job placement and retraining for insurance and hospital-billing employees would be an important component of the program during the transition period.

Discussion

The Patient's View

The national health program would establish a right to comprehensive health care. As in Canada, each person would receive a national health program card entitling him or her to all necessary medical care without copayments or deductibles. The card could be used with any fee-for-service practitioner and at any institution receiving a global budget. HMO members could receive nonemergency care only through their HMO, although they could readily transfer to the non-HMO option.

Thus, patients would have a free choice of providers, and the financial threat of illness would be eliminated. Taxes would increase by an amount equivalent to the current total of medical expenditures by individuals. Conversely, individuals' aggregate payments for medical care would decrease by the same amount.

The Practitioner's View

Physicians would have a free choice of practice settings. Treatment would no longer be constrained by the patient's insurance status or by bureaucratic dicta. On the basis of the Canadian experience, we anticipate that the average physician's income would change little, although differences among specialties might be attenuated.

Fee-for-service practitioners would be paid for the care of anyone not enrolled in an HMO. The entrepreneurial aspects of medicine—with the attendant problems as well as the possibilities—would be limited. Physicians could concentrate on medicine; every patient would be fully insured, but physicians could increase their incomes only by providing more care. Billing would involve imprinting the patient's national health program card on a charge slip, checking a box to indicate the complexity of the procedure or service, and sending the slip (or a computer record) to the physician-payment board. This simplification of billing would save thousands of dollars per practitioner in annual office expenses.

Bureaucratic interference in clinical decision making would sharply diminish. Costs would be contained by controlling overall spending and by limiting entrepreneurial incentives, thus obviating the need for the kind of detailed administrative oversight that is characteristic of the DRG program and similar schemes. Indeed, there is much less administrative intrusion in day-to-day clinical practice in Canada (and most other countries with national health programs) than in the United States.[11,12]

Salaried practitioners would be insulated from the financial consequences of clinical decisions. Because savings on patient care could no longer be used for institutional expansion or profits, the pressure to skimp on care would be minimized.

The Effect on Other Health Workers

Nurses and other health care personnel would enjoy a more humane and efficient clinical milieu. The burdens of paperwork associated with billing would be lightened. The jobs of many administrative and insurance employees would be eliminated, necessitating a major effort at job placement and retraining. We advocate that many of these displaced workers be deployed in expanded programs of public health, health promotion and education, and home care and as support personnel to free nurses for clinical tasks.

The Effect on Hospitals

Hospitals' revenues would become stable and predictable. More than half the current hospital bureaucracy would be eliminated,[1] and the remaining administrators could focus on facilitating clinical care and planning for future health needs.

The capital budget requests of hospitals would be weighed against other priorities for health care investment. Hospitals would neither grow because they were profitable nor fail because of unpaid bills—although regional health planning would undoubtedly mandate that some expand and others close or be put to other uses. Responsiveness to community needs, the quality of care, efficiency, and innovation would replace financial performance as the bottom line. The elimination of new for-profit investment would lead to a gradual conversion of proprietary hospitals to not-for-profit status.

The Effect on the Insurance Industry

The insurance industry would feel the greatest impact of this proposal. Private insurance firms would have no role in health care financing, since the public administration of insurance is more efficient[1,13] and single-source payment is the key to both equal access and cost control. Indeed, most of the extra funds needed to finance the expansion of care would come from eliminating the overhead and profits of insurance companies and abolishing the billing apparatus necessary to apportion costs among the various plans.

The Effect on Corporate America

Firms that now provide generous employee health benefits would realize savings, because their contribution to the national health program would be less than their current health insurance costs. For example, health care expenditures by Chrysler, currently $5,300 annually per employee,[14] would fall to about $1,600, a figure calculated by dividing the total current U.S. spending on health by private employers by the total number of full-time-equivalent, nongovernment employees. Since most firms that compete in international markets would save money, the competitiveness of U.S. products would be enhanced. However, costs would increase for companies that do not now provide health benefits. The average health care costs for employers would be unchanged in the short run. In the long run, overall health costs would rise less steeply because of improved health planning and greater efficiency. The funding mechanism ultimately adopted would determine the corporate share of those costs.

Health Benefits and Financial Costs

There is ample evidence that removing financial barriers to health care encourages timely care and improves health. After Canada instituted a national health program, visits to physicians increased among patients with serious symptoms.[15] Mortality rates, which were higher than U.S. rates through the 1950s and early 1960s, fell below those in the United States.[16] In the Rand Health Insurance Experiment, free care reduced the annual risk of dying by 10 percent among the 25 percent of U.S. adults at highest risk.[3] Conversely, cuts in California's Medicaid program led to worsening health.[17] Strong circumstantial evidence links the poor U.S. record on infant mortality with inadequate access to prenatal care.[18]

We expect that the national health program would cause little change in the total costs of ambulatory and hospital care; savings on administration and billing (about 10 percent of current health spending[1]) would approximately offset the costs of expanded services.[19,20] Indeed, current low hospital-occupancy rates suggest that the additional care could be provided at low cost. Similarly, many physicians with empty appointment slots could take on more patients without added office, secretarial, or other overhead costs. However, the expansion of long-term care (under any system) would increase costs. The experience in Canada suggests that the increased demand for acute care would be modest after an initial surge[21,22] and that improvements in health planning[8] and cost containment made possible by single-source payment[9] would slow the escalation of health care costs. Vigilance would be needed to stem the regrowth of costly and intrusive bureaucracy.

Unsolved Problems

Our brief proposal leaves many vexing problems unsolved. Much detailed planning would be needed to ease dislocations during the implementation of the program. Neither the encouragement of preventive health care and healthful life styles nor improvements in occupational and environmental health would automatically follow from the institution of a national health program. Similarly, racial, linguistic, geographic, and other nonfinancial barriers to access would persist. The need for quality assurance and continuing medical education would be no less pressing. High medical school tuitions that skew specialty choices and discourage low-income applicants, the under-representation of minorities, the role of foreign medical graduates, and other issues in medical education would remain. Some patients would still seek inappropriate emergency care, and some physicians might still succumb to the temptation to increase their incomes by encouraging unneeded services. The malpractice crisis would be only partially ameliorated. The 25 percent of judgments now awarded for future medical costs would be eliminated, but our society would remain litigious, and legal and insurance fees would still consume about two-thirds of all malpractice premiums.[23] Establishing research priorities and directing funds to high-quality investigations would be no easier. Much further work in the area of long-term care would be required. Regional health planning and capital allocation would make possible, but not ensure, the fair and efficient allocation of resources. Finally, although insurance coverage for patients with AIDS would be ensured, the need for expanded prevention and research and for new models of care would continue. Although all these problems would not be solved, a national health program would establish a framework for addressing them.

Political Prospects

Our proposal will undoubtedly encounter powerful opponents in the health insurance industry, firms that do not now provide health benefits to employees, and medical entrepreneurs. However, we also have allies. Most physicians (56 percent) support some form of national health program, although 74 percent are convinced that most other doctors oppose it.[24] Many of the largest corporations would enjoy substantial savings if our proposal were adopted. Most significant, the great majority of Americans support a universal, comprehensive, publicly administered national health program, as shown by virtually every opinion poll in the past 30 years.[25,26] Indeed, a 1986 referendum question in Massachusetts calling for a national health program was approved two to one, carrying all 39 cities and 307 of the 312 towns in the commonwealth.[27] If mobilized, such public conviction could override even the most strenuous private opposition.

Notes

[1] Himmelstein, D. U., Woolhandler, S. Cost without benefit: administrative waste in U.S. health care. *N Engl J Med* 1986; 314:441–5.

[2] Advisory opinion regarding House of Representatives Bill 85–H–7748 (No. 86-269–MP, R.I. Sup. Ct. Jan 5, 1987).

[3] Brook, R. H., Ware, J. E., Jr, Rogers, W. H., et al. Does free care improve adults' health? Results from a randomized controlled trial. *N Engl J Med* 1983; 309:1426–34.

[4] Siu, A. L., Sonnenberg, F. A., Manning, W. G., et al. Inappropriate use of hospitals in a randomized trial of health insurance plans. *N Engl J Med* 1986; 315:1259–66.

[5] Brian, E. W., Gibbens, S. F. California's Medi-Cal copayment experiment. *Med Care* 1974; 12:Suppl 12:1–303.

[6] Iglehart, J. K. Canada's health care system. *N Engl J Med* 1986; 315:202–8, 778–84.

[7] *Idem.* Canada's health care system: addressing the problem of physician supply. *N Engl J Med* 1986; 315:1623–8.

[8] Detsky, A. S., Stacey, S. R., Bombardier, C. The effectiveness of a regulatory strategy in containing hospital costs: the Ontario experience, 1967–1981. *N Engl J Med* 1983; 309:151–9.

[9] Evans, R. G. Health care in Canada: patterns of funding and regulation. In: McLachlan, G., Maynard, A., eds. The public/private mix for health: the relevance and effects of change. London: Nuffield Provincial Hospitals Trust, 1982:369–424.

[10] Woolhandler, S., Himmelstein, D. U. Reverse targeting of preventive care due to lack of health insurance. *JAMA* 1988; 259:2872–4.

[11] Reinhardt, U. E. Resource allocation in health care: the allocation of lifestyles to providers. *Milbank Q* 1987; 65:153–76.

[12] Hoffenberg, R. Clinical freedom. London: Nuffield Provincial Hospitals Trust, 1987.

[13] Horne, J. M., Beck, R. G. Further evidence on public versus private administration of health insurance. *J Public Health Policy* 1981; 2:274–90.

[14] Cronin, C. Next Congress to grapple with U.S. health policy, competitiveness abroad. *Bus Health* 1986; 4(2):55.

[15] Enterline, P. E., Salter, V., McDonald, A. D., McDonald, J. C. The distribution of medical services before and after "free" medical care—the Quebec experience. *N Engl J Med* 1973; 289:1174–8.

[16] Roemer, R., Roemer, M. I. Health manpower policy under national health insurance: the Canadian experience. Hyattsville, MD: Health Resources Administration, 1977. (DHEW publication no. (HRA) 77–37.)

[17] Lurie, N., Ward, N. B., Shapiro, M. F., et al. Termination of Medi-Cal benefits: a follow-up study one year later. *New Engl J Med* 1986; 314:1266–8.

[18] Institute of Medicine. Preventing low birthweight. Washington, DC: National Academy Press, 1985.

[19] Newhouse, J. P., Manning, W. G., Morris, C. N., et al. Some interim results from a controlled trial of cost sharing in health insurance. *N Engl J Med* 1981; 305:1501–7.

[20] Himmelstein, D. U., Woolhandler, S. Free care: a quantitative analysis of the health and cost effects of a national health program. *Int J Health Serv* 1988; 18:393–9.

[21]LeClair, M. The Canadian health care system. In: Andreopoulos, S., ed. *National health insurance: can we learn from Canada?* New York: John Wiley, 1975:11–92.

[22]Evans, R. G. Beyond the medical marketplace: expenditure, utilization and pricing of insured health care in Canada. In: Andreopoulos, S., ed. *National health insurance: can we learn from Canada?* New York: John Wiley, 1975:129–78.

[23]Danzon, P. M. *Medical malpractice: theory, evidence, and public policy.* Cambridge: Harvard University Press, 1985.

[24]Colombotas, J., Kirchner, C. *Physicians and social change.* New York: Oxford University Press, 1986.

[25]Navarro, V. Where is the popular mandate? *N Engl J Med* 1982; 307:1516–8.

[26]Pokorny, G. Report card on health care. *Health Manage Q* 1988; 10(1): 3–7.

[27]Danielsen, D. A., Mazer, A. Results of the Massachusetts Referendum on a national health program. *J Public Health Policy* 1987; 8:28–35.

APPENDIX 1

Sources of Data
Steven Jonas

Introduction

This Appendix is a guide to the principal sources of health and health-services data for the United States, as of 2000. It contains descriptions of those sources, indicates how frequently each is published as of 2000, lists the categories of data and other information they contain, and gives the address of the publisher of each and other ordering information as indicated.

There are two comprehensive guides to sources of data that are published annually. The first appears in *Health, United States* (see item 7, below; as of this writing, the most recent edition, made publicly available only on a limited basis, was for 1999, published in 1999 [DHHS Pub. No. (PHS) 99-1232]). Its Appendix I contains very useful, detailed descriptions of all the common health data sources published by the several branches of the Federal government, the United Nations, and private agencies ranging from the American Medical Association to the National League for Nursing. The second appears in the *Statistical Abstract of the United States* (see item 1, below; the most recent edition as of this writing is for 1999, published in October, 1999). Appendix I contains an extensive listing of sources for statistics, ranging from the Administrative Office of United States Courts to the Social Security Administration, from the Advisory Commission on Intergovernmental Relations to the World Health Organization, from the state of Alabama to the state of Wyoming. Appendix III of that publication presents brief descriptions and analyses of the limitations of the major sources of data, including those for health data, used in the Abstract.

Almost all Federal sources of data are available for purchase through the United Government Printing Office (USGPO, or GPO for short), Superintendent of Documents, Mail Stop SSOP, Washington, DC 20402-9328, tel. (202) 512-1800, website: http://www.access.gpo.gov/su docs/sale.html. There are local GPO publication phone-ordering centers located in major cities around the United States. They are listed in the Federal government section of the blue pages of many local telephone directories under "Government Printing Office," and in the back of the USGPO's "Health Resources Statistics" catalog.

Also, the *AHA Guide*, published annually by the American Hospital Association (see item 10, below), in its Section C lists the major national, international, U.S. government, state and local government, and private "Health Organizations, Agencies, and Providers," with addresses, phone numbers, and, in some cases, e-mail and/or website addresses. Health and health care data can be obtained from many of them.

Principal Sources of Health and Health Care Data

1. *Statistical Abstract of the United States*
Published annually by the Bureau of the Census, U.S. Department of Commerce, Washington, DC 20233, the *Statistical Abstract* contains a vast collection of tables reporting information and data collected by many different government (and in certain cases nongovernment) agencies. They are accumulated under the following headings: Population; Vital Statistics; Health and Nutrition; Education; Law Enforcement, Courts, and Prisons; Geography and Environment; Parks, Recreation, and Travel; Elections; State and Local Government Finances and Employment; Federal Government Finances and Employment; National Defense and Veterans' Affairs; Social Insurance and Human Services; Social Insurance and Human Services; Labor Force, Employment, and Earnings; Income, Expenditures, and Wealth; Prices; Banking, Finance, and Insurance; Business Enterprise; Communications and Information Technology; Energy; Science and Technology; Transportation—Land; Transportation—Air and Water; Agriculture; Natural Resources; Construction and Housing; Manufactures; Domestic Trade and Services; Foreign Commerce and Aid; Outlying Areas [under the Jurisdiction of the United States]; Comparative International Statistics; and, for the first time, "20th Century Statistics." There are health and health-services data of varying kinds reported in many of these categories.

2. *U.S. Census of Population*

As noted above, the Bureau of the Census is part of the U.S. Department of Commerce. The U.S. Constitution requires that a census be taken every ten years, at the beginning of each decade. The original purpose of the census was to apportion among the states the seats in the House of Representatives, thus also distributing the seats in the Electoral College that chooses the president. In modern times, in addition to the simple counts required to meet this Constitutional requirement, a great deal of demographic data is collected by the Census Bureau.

Many reports on the decennial censuses as well as interim special counts are published by the Census Bureau (see item #3, below), but a good place to begin looking at these data is in Section 1, "Population," of the *Statistical Abstract*. Hardcover compendia of decennial national census data are published periodically. Also available are special analyses for a wide variety of geographical subdivisions of the country. Census Bureau publications may be ordered from the GPO, which offers for sale a comprehensive *Census Catalog and Guide*. Many Census Bureau products and data are also available through their website, www.census.gov.

3. *Current Population Reports*

In addition to reports from the decennial censuses, on a continuing basis the Census Bureau publishes seven series of reports, called the "Current Population Reports." These include estimates, projections, sample counts, and special studies of selected segments of the population. The seven series each have a "P" number. They are: P-20, Population Characteristics; P-23, Special Studies; P-25, Population Estimates and Projections; P-26, Local Population Estimates; P-28, Special Censuses; P-60, Consumer Income and Poverty; P-70, Household Economic Studies. Catalogs and information on the content of each series are available directly from the Census Bureau. Publications may be ordered through the GPO.

4. *National Vital Statistics Reports (NVSR)*

Formerly *Monthly Vital Statistics Report*, the *National Vital Statistics Reports* is published by the National Center for Health Statistics (NCHS), Centers for Disease Control and Prevention (CDCP), Public Health Service (PHS), U.S. Department of Health and Human Services (USDHHS), 6525 Belcrest Road, Hyattsville, MD 20782-2003, website www.gov/nchs/. (The NCHS periodically publishes catalogs of its various publications and electronic data products, available free.) The *NVSR*, combining several different sections of the old *MVSR*, provides the most recent data for the traditional "vital statistics"—births, marriages, divorces, and deaths—and also special reports on subsets of the vital statistics such as pregnancy trends and twin and triplet births, both over time.

There are also reports entitled "Advance Data." They present regularly collected statistics on the health care delivery system from, for example, the "Hospice Care Survey," the "National Hospital Ambulatory Medical Care Survey," and the "National Hospital Discharge Survey," as well as the results of special studies and technical information on methodology. All *NVSR* reports may be obtained by annual subscription, through the USGPO.

5. *Vital Statistics of the United States*
These are the full, highly detailed annual reports on vital statistics from the NCHS, the summary versions of which are published in the *NVSR*.

6. *Vital and Health Statistics*
These publications of the NCHS, distinct from the "Vital Statistics" reports described in items 4 and 5 above, appear at irregular intervals. As of 2000, there were 15 series (not numbered consecutively). Most of them report data from ongoing studies and surveys that the NCHS has carried out. The place of publication of some data shifts periodically between *Vital and Health Statistics* and *Monthly Vital Statistics Report*. The 15 series of *Vital and Health Statistics* are as follows: Series 1, Programs and Collection Procedures; Series 2, Data Evaluation and Methods Research; Series 3, Analytical and Epidemiological Studies; Series 4, Documents and Committee Reports; Series 5, International Vital and Health Statistics Reports; Series 6, Cognition and Survey Measurement; Series 10, Data from the Health Interview Survey; Series 11, Data from the National Health Examination Survey, the National Health and Nutrition Examination Surveys, and the Hispanic Health and Nutrition Examination Survey; Series 13, Data from the National Health Care Survey; Series 15, Data from Special Surveys; Series 16, Compilations of Advance Data from Vital and Health Statistics; Series 20, Data on Mortality; Series 21, Data on Natality, Marriage, and Divorce; Series 23, Data from the National Survey of Family Growth; Series 24, Compilations of Data on Natality, Mortality, Marriage, Divorce, and Induced Terminations of Pregnancy.

7. Health, United States

Health, United States is published annually by the NCHS/CDCP and is ordinarily available for purchase from the GPO (although for unknown reason the sale of the 1999 edition was "frozen" shortly after its release). A wide variety of health and health care delivery-system data are presented in such categories as: infant mortality, life expectancy, low birth-weight babies, heart disease mortality, dental care, cigarette smoking, physician contacts, avoidable hospitalization, health personnel, national health expenditures, and Medicare/Medicaid. It also contains a useful appendix, "Sources and Limitations of Data" (briefly described above) as well as a Glossary. It is a boon to students and researchers in health care delivery because it provides one-stop shopping for most important health and health care data.

8. Morbidity and Mortality Weekly Report (MMWR)

This is a regular publication of the Centers for Disease Control and Prevention of the PHS, USDHHS. It is available on an annual subscription basis from the GPO. However, following a large subscription price increase in 1982, *MMWR*, in the public domain, has been photocopied and circulated at cost by several organizations, including the Massachusetts Medical Society, P.O. Box 549120, Waltham, MA 02254-9120. In the past, *MMWR* has been concerned primarily with communicable disease reporting. These reports are still included, as of 2000 for AIDS, chlamydia, cryptosporiodosis, E. coli infections, gonorrhea, hepatitis types A, B, C, non-A, non-B, H. influenzae, legionellosis, Lyme disease, malaria, measles, meningococcal disease, mumps, pertussis, rabies (animal), rubella, salmonellosis, shigellosis, syphilis (primary and secondary), and tuberculosis. *MMWR* also reports deaths in 122 U.S. cities on a weekly basis. Equally or perhaps more important, each week *MMWR* presents brief reports on special studies of such diverse health topics as: human exposure to rabies in a bear cub, progress towards poliomyelitis eradication, measles control and regional elimination, firearm-related injuries, the Great American Smoke-out, diabetes preventive-care practices in managed care organizations, a vaccination campaign for Kosovar refugee children, pedestrian fatalities, and progress in fluoridation. *MMWR* also periodically publishes "Recommendations and Reports" of various governmental and non-governmental health agencies and organizations, on such topics as the prevention of hepatitis A through immunization and "Guidelines for the Prevention of Opportunistic Infections in Persons Infected with HIV," and the results of "CDC Surveillance Summaries" on such topics as "Youth Risk Behavior" and "Trends in Self-Reported Use of Mammograms."

9. *Health Care Financing Review*
The *Health Care Financing Review* is a quarterly publication of the Health Care Financing Administration (HCFA), USDHHS, Office of Strategic Panning, 7500 Security Boulevard, C3-24-07, Baltimore, MD 21244-1850. It is available on subscription through the GPO. It annually publishes the official reports, "National Health Expenditures" and the results of the "Medicare Beneficiary Survey." It also publishes an extensive and wide-ranging series of academic articles, reports, and studies, specifically on Medicare/Medicaid (for which HCFA is directly responsible), as well as on "a broad range of health care financing and delivery issues."

10. *American Hospital Association Guide to the Health Care Field*
This is a two-part publication of the American Hospital Association (One North Franklin, Chicago, Illinois 60606, tel. [800] 821-2039), available for purchase from the AHA. The first part, the *AHA Guide*, is published annually. It contains a listing of almost every hospital in the United States by location and gives basic data on size, type, ownership, and facilities, a listing and brief description of the multi-hospital Health Care Systems, and information on the AHA itself, as well as the comprehensive lists of health and health care organizations referred to in the introductory section of the Appendix, above. The second part, *AHA Hospital Statistics*, as of the turn of the new century is published biennially. It contains a great deal of summary descriptive, utilization, and financial data on U.S. hospitals, presented in many different cross-tabulations. Some of the data are presented historically as well. The two parts together contain the most detailed data available on hospitals in the United States.

11. *Center for Health Policy Research of the American Medical Association*
The Center, located in AMA National Headquarters, 515 North State Street, Chicago, Illinois 60610, produces a variety of useful data on the physician work force and related subjects. As of 2000, titles appearing on a regular basis included: "Physician Socioeconomic Statistics," "State Medical Licensure Requirements and Statistics," "Physician Characteristics and Distribution in the U.S.," "Medical Group Practices in the U.S.," and the "Graduate Medical Education Directory."

APPENDIX 2

Annotated Bibliography of Journals in Medical Sociology and Related Areas

This bibliography includes some journals from which selections in this book were taken, and others as well. It is very informative to browse and scan journals in the library. You can get a good idea of the major issues, debates, and methods in medical sociology and in related areas. The categories in this list are in some case overlapping.

The Major Medical Sociology Journals

You can get a good overview of issues and debates in the field by regularly scanning these few journals.

Journal of Health and Social Behavior (American Sociological Association; quarterly)

This journal is published by the American Sociological Association, and for many sociologists it is the most respected journal in the field. For some, this journal has not always represented the whole spectrum of research in medical sociology. Articles are largely quantitative, though qualitative material has increased in recent years. This journal is widely looked to as a major source of research. It covers a wide range of topics, including a large amount on the sociology of mental health and illness.

Social Science & Medicine (Pergamon Press, 24 issues per year)

This widely respected journal, published in England, has a very international flavor. It is broadly multidisciplinary, with sections on medical sociology, medical geography, medical anthropology, medical psychology, health economics, medical ethics, and health policy. The journal sponsors an annual international Conference on the Social Sciences and Medicine.

Sociology of Health and Illness (Blackwell Publishers, 6 times per year, plus one edited special issue)

Reflecting the nature of British medical sociology, this journal is largely qualitative. It covers a broad range of topics, with strength in doctor-patient interaction, experience of illness, and theory. It features interesting special issues that are later released as books, the most recent being on sociological perspectives on the new genetics.

Health (Sage Publications, quarterly)

This is the newest of the medical sociology journals, edited in England but with Australian and U.S. coeditors. It covers a broad range of topics, with strength in the place of health and medicine in social and cultural theory, health maintenance and promotion, and the relationship of health and social issues. It is similar in overall tone to *Sociology of Health and Illness* but includes some quantitative articles.

Journals Covering a Broad Range of Areas in Social Science And Health

International Journal of Health Services (Baywood Publishing, quarterly)

This journal is multidisciplinary, covering health policy, political economy, medical history, and medical ethics. It is quite international in context and includes diverse perspectives, but it is particularly known for it strengths in political economy, Marxism, and radical analyses of the health care system.

Milbank Quarterly (Milbank Memorial Fund, quarterly)

Previously known as the *Milbank Memorial Fund Quarterly/Health and Society*, this journal is published by a foundation that sponsors medical research and education. The journal covers a broad range of areas, especially health policy, history, and medical ethics. Articles are often longer than in other journals, and some are analytical and interpretive essays.

Journal of Health Politics, Policy and Law (Duke University, Department of Health Administration, quarterly)

This journal has a strong constituency among political scientists who study health. It covers a broad range of topics, with special emphasis on health policy, analysis of government health programs, government regulation, hospitals, ethics, and legal issues. It features interesting special issues, the most recent on the backlash against managed care.

Qualitative Health Research (Sage Publications, quarterly)

This is an interdisciplinary journal for the enhancement of health care through using qualitative research methods. Particular areas of interest: the description and analysis of the illness experience, health and health-seeking behaviors, the experiences of caregivers, the sociocultural organization of health care, and health care policy.

Health Policy

Journal of Public Health Policy (National Association For Public Health Policy, quarterly)

This journal covers a wide range of policy issues, health planning, and public health interventions, with emphasis on social structural factors. It features interesting editorials on health politics, such as national health insurance and national health plans, and is aimed at an educated lay audience as well as health specialists.

Health Affairs (Project Hope, quarterly)

This journal covers lots of useful and up-to-date articles on issues in health services and health policy, with frequent special issues on major topics. It includes commentaries, brief notes on health statistics, and resources on health data and grants. The journal is very useful for keeping up-to-date on major developments.

Women's Health

Women and Health (Haworth Press, quarterly)

This is the major source of journal-style research on women and health, although there are other sources, such as newletters published by advocacy groups. The journal covers a wide range of issues, such as sex differences in health, sexism in the health care system, and reproductive rights.

The Network News (National Women's Health Network, bimonthly)

This newsletter is the central information clearinghouse for the women's health movement. It contains news briefs and analyses of developments in pregnancy and childbirth reproductive rights, health hazards affecting women, special health conditions affecting women, women health workers, pharmaceutical and surgical dangers, and health policy.

Women's Health Issues (Elsevier, 6 times a year)

This is the official publication of the Jacobs Institute of Women's Health. *WHI* is devoted to women's health issues at the medical/social interface. It is a journal for health professionals, social scientists, policy makers, and others concerned with the complex and diverse facets of health care delivery to women.

Disability Studies

Disability Studies Quarterly (University of Illinois at Chicago, Department of Disability and Human Development, quarterly)

This is the leading source of current information on all aspects of disability. Its main emphasis is on physical disability, although there is ample coverage of mental illness and mental retardation. It covers a wide range of topics in independent living, self-help, the disability rights movement, chronic illness, legislation, and policy.

Disability and Society (Carfax Publishing, 7 issues per year)

This journal provides a focus for debate about such issues as human rights, discrimination, definitions, policy and practices. While publishing articles that represent all the professional perspectives, it also provides an opportunity for consumers of services to speak for themselves.

Medical Ethics

Hastings Center Reports (The Hastings Center, bimonthly)

Ethics are covered in a number of other journals mentioned already, but this publication is the most central source of developments in the area of health ethics. It incorporates the work of medical professionals, social scientists, and philosophers, some of who are resident scholars and visiting lecturers at the Hastings Center. It also includes coverage of ethical issues of health policies.

Journal of Medicine and Philosophy (Society for Health and Human Values, quarterly)

This journal features articles on ethical issues, theoretical and philosophical concerns, the nature of medical knowledge, and client-provider relationships.

Medical Anthropology

Culture, Medicine, and Psychiatry (D. Reidel Publishing, quarterly)
Although this journal includes research from a variety of disciplines, it is primarily a source for work in medical anthropology. The journal has a very international flavor, with special attention to cultural beliefs and health practices in third world countries.

Medical Anthropology Quarterly (American Anthropological Association, and Society for Medical Anthropology, quarterly)

This publication is a major source for research in medical anthropology. While it does cover international topics, it contains more American material than the above journal.

Medical Anthropology (Redgrave, published quarterly)

This journal explores the relationships among health, disease, illness, treatment and human social life. Emphasis is placed on the cross-cultural similarities and differences in the way people cope with health problems.

Anthropology & Medicine (Carfax, 3 times a year)

This publication covers issues on the border of culture and medicine, such as the globalization and politics of biomedicine, narrative approaches to illness, new reproductive technologies, indigenous medicine, and modern and post-modern identities of individual states and their impact on sickness.

Health Services Research and Program Evaluation

Medical Care (Medical Care Section of the American Public Health Association, monthly)

This is a major public health journal featuring scholarship in research, planning, organization, financing, service provision, and evaluation of health services. It includes research from other countries as well.

Public Health Reports (Journal of the U.S. Public Health Service, published in collaboration with the Association of Schools of Public Health by Oxford University Press, bimonthly)

This journal covers a wide range of research on health status and mortality, with many brief articles. It contains editorials, letters, news and notes, original research articles, and international reports.

Health Services Research (Association for Health Services Research, bimonthly)

This journal features studies of financing, access, utilization, medical practice, and planning issues in the provision of health services. It includes many studies of large data sets, including national surveys.

Inquiry (Blue Cross and Blue Shield Association, quarterly)

This publication covers health care organization, service provision, and financing. It features lots of attention to Medicare, Medicaid, and private health insurers.

Health Care Financing Review (United States Department of Health and Human Services, Health Care Financing Administration, quarterly)

This publication emphasizes studies of the costs of medical services, forecasts for future needs and costs, and the impact of costs on federal programs. It often analyzes large national data sets, especially those involving federal programs.

Medicine and Public Health

New England Journal of Medicine (Massachusetts Medical Society, weekly)

This is widely considered to be the most important general medical journal in the United States. It features occasional articles on health policy, medical ethics, professional behavior, and client-provider relations. Since such articles reach a large medical and public audience, they are frequently widely cited.

The Lancet (Lancet, Ltd., weekly)

This is one of the two major medical journals in England. More than the *New England Journal of Medicine*, it features articles on public health concerns and health policy.

American Journal of Public Health (American Public Health Association, monthly)

This journal contains many clinical, epidemiological, and public health studies. Articles cover risk factors in health, preventive programs, large-scale surveys of disease, evaluations of treatment programs, and health outcomes of government health programs.

Critical Public Health (Carfax, published quarterly)

This publication goes beyond narrower public health, with a political-economic analysis of the relation between health and society, including the interaction of health with various forms of social stratification. Many articles deal with intersectoral social policy.

Medical History

Medical History (Wellcome Institute for the History of Medicine, quarterly)

This is the major English source for medical history. It gives special attention to the evolution of scientific and social concepts in medicine. Articles deal with the history of medical practice, disease concepts, hospitals, and epidemics.

Bulletin of the History of Medicine (American Association for the History of Medicine/Johns Hopkins Institute of the History of Medicine, quarterly)

This is the major U.S. publication on medical history. The journal covers much of the same as the above. It also includes some work on the history of biological sciences.

Journal of the History of Medicine and Allied Sciences (University of Connecticut School of Medicine, quarterly)

This publication is similar in coverage to the above two journals, with perhaps more coverage of the history of science.

Social History of Medicine (Oxford University Press, three time a year)

This journal covers social history of medicine from a variety of disciplines. It includes critical assessments of archives and sources, conference reports, and up-to-date information on research in progress.